Louisiana Soldiers

in

the War of 1812

compiled by
Marion John Bennett Pierson

CLEARFIELD

Copyright © 1963
by Louisiana Genealogical and Historical Society
All Rights Reserved.

Originally published
Baton Rouge, Louisiana, 1963

Reprinted with permission of
Louisiana Genealogical and Historical Society
Baton Rouge, Louisiana

Reprinted for
Clearfield Company, Inc. by
Genealogical Publishing Co., Inc.
Baltimore, Maryland
1999, 2003

International Standard Book Number: 0-8063-4912-3

Made in the United States of America

FOREWORD

Publication of this alphabetical listing of soldiers who served in Louisiana units during the War of 1812 fills an obvious need. Although similar lists have been published for a number of other states, the search for data on Louisiana soldiers has heretofore had to be conducted by directing inquiries to one or several Washington agencies, or by the tedious process of scanning copies of the original listings reproduced on microfilm.

This is, in fact, an index to the compiled service records of the 1812 soldiers from Louisiana. Copies of the records themselves may be obtained from the National Archives for a fee. The considerable task of copying these entries from the cards in the office of the Adjutant General in Washington was undertaken by the late Marion John Bennett Pierson. It took Mr. Pierson, a retired building contractor and independent family researcher, about a year to complete the work. He had planned to publish an index himself. However, death intervened. Mr. Pierson died suddenly in Washington on January 27, 1960.

The story of how the Louisiana Genealogical and Historical Society came into possession of his papers is an interesting one. In June of 1961, Mr. Pierson's sister, Mrs. Thomas M. McDaniel of South Pasadena, California, visited Louisiana in the process of settling her brother's estate. Conner Davis, well known Amite teacher and local historian, learned of Mr. Pierson's work and suggested that Mrs. McDaniel get in touch with Mrs. J. P. Morris, Jr., of Kentwood, then president of the state society.

The result was a happy one. Mrs. McDaniel agreed to turn over the fruits of her brother's work to the society, with the provision that his compilation of 1812 soldiers appear in a publication such as he had planned himself. The original transcripts, and other of the Pierson Papers, are now housed in the Louisiana Genealogical and Historical Society Collection in the Louisiana State Library in Baton Rouge.

The efforts of Mr. Pierson cannot be praised enough, or Mrs. McDaniel's foresight and generosity in making her brother's work available to hundreds and indeed thousands of others engaged in Louisiana research. But neither would this work have been possible without the labors of Irene Morris, who committed the society to a worthwhile course and then willingly undertook much of the work of seeing the index into print. Mary Elizabeth Sanders took time out from her duties as editor of the Genealogical Register to lend a helping hand, E. S. Diman of the LSU Press staff gave of his time and talents in matters of design, and Ed Olexy, Farris and Theo Bryan, as always, served above and beyond the call of duty. To all these, the society is grateful.

Charles East

Baton Rouge, Louisiana
January 8, 1963

NAME	RANK	COMPANY	NAME	RANK	COMPANY
Abadie, J.	Private	2 Reg't (Cavelier's) La. Mil.	Adams, Samuel	Private	17, 18 and 19 Consolidated Regiment, La. Mil.
Abare, Antoine	Private	16 Reg't (Thompson's) La. Mil.			
Abat, Antoine	Private	2 Reg't (Cavelier's) La. Mil.	Adams, Shared	Private	12 and 13 Consolidated Regiment, La. Mil.
Abat, Merrit	Private	Capt. Colsson's Co., Art'y., La. Vols. (Original filed under Abat, Morriss)	Adams, William	Sergeant	De Clouet's Regiment, La. Mil.
			Adams, William	Private	Capt. Odgen's Co., Dragoons, La. Mil.
Abat, Morriss	Private	Capt. Colsson's Co., Art'y., La. Vols. (Original filed under Abat, Morriss)	Adams, William	Private	10 and 20 Consolidated Regiment, La. Mil.
			Adams, William E.	Corporal	Capt. Griffith's Mounted Riflemen, La. Vols.
Abbett, Benjamin	Private	12 and 13 Consolidated Regiment, La. Mil.	Adde, Jeanty	Sergeant	2 Batt'n (Peire's) La. Volunteers
Abbey, Dennis	Private	4 Reg't (Morgan's) La. Mil.	Adderson, Britten	1 Lieutenant	12 and 13 Consolidated Regiment, La. Mil.
Abbott, Benjamin	Private	12 and 13 Consolidated Reg. La. Mil. (Original filed under Abbett, Benjamin)	Adderson, John	Private	12 and 13 Consolidated Regiment, La. Mil.
Abel, Michel	Private	DeClouet's Regiment La. Mil.	Adderson, Thomas	Private	12 and 13 Consolidated Regiment, La. Mil.
Able, Wilson	Sergeant	Capt. Ramsey's Co., Mounted Riflemen, La. Mil.	Addison, John	Private	12 and 13 Consolidated Regiment, La. Mil. (Original filed under Adderson, John)
Absher, Abraham	Private	Baker's Regiment, La. Mil.			
Absher, Benjamin	Private	Baker's Regiment, La. Mil.	Addonson, James	Private	De Clouet's Regiment, La. Mil. (Original filed under Anderson, James)
Abshire, John	Private	DeClouet's Regiment, La. Mil.			
Acantara, Joseph	Private	2 Battalion (Peire's) La. Vols. (Original filed under Alcantara, Joseph)	Adelle, N.	Private	6 Reg't (Landry's) La. Mil. (Original filed under Aydelle, Nicholas)
Acart, P.	Private	Plauche's Battalion La. Mil.			
Ache, Elvix,	1 Lieut.	3 Reg't (de la Ronde's) La. Mil.	Ade', Jeanty	Private	Captain Songy's Company, Marines, La. Volunteers
Achand, --	Private	1 Reg't (Dejan's) La. Mil. (Orig. filed under Achand)	Adison, John	Private	12 and 13 Consolidated Reg. La. Mil. (Original - Adderson, John)
Achart, --	Private	1 Reg't (Dejan's) La. Mil. (Orig. filed under Achart)	Adison, Thomas	Private	12 and 13 Consolidated Reg. La. Mil. (Original - Adderson, Thomas)
Achi, Joseph	Private	6 Reg't (Landry's) La. Mil.			
Acorn, George	Corporal	Captain Sprigg's Company, Boatmen, La. Vols. (Orig. - Alcorn, George)	Adkinson, Jesse	Private	12 and 13 Consolidated Reg. La. Mil.
			Adle, Antoine	Private	17, 18 and 19 Consolidated Reg. La. Mil. (Orig. - Adli, Antoine)
Acosta, Antoine	Private	Captain Hubbard's Mounted Company La. Mil.	Adli, Antoine	Private	17, 18 and 19 Consolidated Reg. La. Mil. (Orig. - Adli, Antoine)
Acosta, Baptiste	Private	3 Reg't (de la Ronde's) La. Mil.			
Acosta, Christopher	Private	8 Reg't (Meriam's) La. Vol.	Adlin, Louis	Private	Captain Songy's Company, Marines, La. Volunteers
Acosta, Ignacio	Private	17, 18 and 19 Consolidated Regiment, La. Mil.			
Acosta, Jn. Isadras	Private	17, 18 and 19 Consolidated Regiment, La. Mil.	Admiralty, Pierre	Private	6 Reg't (Landry's) La. Mil.
			Adolfe, George	Private	7 Reg't (Le Beuf's) La. Mil.
Acosta, Jose	Private	17, 18 and 19 Consolidated Regiment, La. Mil.	Adolphe, --	Servant	2 Batt'n (D'Aquin's) La. Mil.
			Adrien, Ive	Private	Plauche's Battalion La. Mil.
Acosta, Juan	Private	17, 18 and 19 Consolidated Regiment, La. Mil.	Agard, Elienne Bastiste	Private	Capt. Lagan's Co., La. Volunteers
Acosta, Lorenzo	Private	Captain Hubbard's Mounted Company, La. Mil.	Agmon, Syphorin	Private	16 Reg't (Thompson's) La. Mil. (Orig. filed under Aymon, Syphorian)
Acosta, Lorenzo	Corporal	3 Reg't (de la Ronde's) La. Mil.			
Acosta, Roco	Private	3 Reg't (de la Ronde's) La. Mil.	Aguera, Anthony	Private	2 Batt'n (Peire's) La. Volunteers
Acosta, John	Private	8 Reg't (Meriam's) La. Mil.	Aguerra, Antonio	Private	2 Batt'n (Peire's) La. Volunteers (Orig. under Aguera, Anthony)
Acoste, Lorrance	Private	8 Reg't (Meriam's) La. Mil.			
Acqueduc, --	Private	4 Reg't (Morgan's) La. Mil.	Aguerre, Anthony	Private	2 Batt'n (Peire's) La. Volunteers (Orig. under Aguera, Anthony)
Acquera, Anthony	Private	2 Batt'n (Peire's) La. Vols. (Orig. under Aquera, Anthony)			
			Aguilera, Torribio	Private	2 Batt'n (Peire's) La. Volunteers
Acres, John	Private	16 Reg't (Thompson's) La. Mil.	Aguillard, Fcois	Private	2 Reg't (Cavelier's) La. Mil.
Adam, Alexandrie	Private	7 Reg't (Le Beuf's) La. Mil.	Aguillard, Jn.	Private	2 Reg't (Cavelier's) La. Mil.
Adam, Andre	Private	7 Reg't (Le Beuf's) La. Mil.	Aiken, David	Private	Captain Allen's Company, Artillerists, La. Volunteers
Adam, Claude	Fusilier-Private	5 Reg't (La Branche's) La. Mil.			
Adam, Hilaire	Private	4 Reg't (Morgan's) La. Mil.	Aime, Michel	Private	Captain Trudeau's Troop of Horse, La. Mil.
Adam, Jn Bte	Private	4 Reg't (Morgan's) La. Mil.			
Adam, Louis	Private	1 Reg't (Dejan's) La. Mil.	Aime, Valcome	Private	Captain Trudeau's Troop of Horse, La. Mil.
Adam, Louis	Fusilier-Private	5 Reg't (La Branche's) La. Mil.			
Adam, Lucien	Private	1 Reg't (Dejan's) La. Mil.	Aisne, Michel	Private	Captain Trudeau's Troop of Horse, La. Mil. (Orig. filed under Aime, Michel)
Adam, Marcellin	Private	7 Reg't (LeBeuf's) La. Mil.			
Adams, Aaron	Private	12 and 13 Consolidated Regiment, La. Mil.	Akers, George	Private	16 Reg't (Thompson's) La. Mil.
Adams, Christopher	Private	Capt. Odgen's Co., Dragoons, La. Mil.	Aladonisse, --	Private	2 Batt'n (D'Aquin's) La. Mil. (Orig. filed under Aleidonisse)
Adams, Elijah	Captain	10 and 20 Consolidated Regiment, La. Mil.	Alamas, Jn. Jose	Private	17, 18 and 19 Consolidated Regiment, La. Mil.
Adams, Holden	Private	12 and 13 Consolidated Regiment, La. Mil.	Alamia, Lancia	Private	17, 18 and 19 Consolidated Regiment, La. Mil.
Adams, Isaac	Private	10 and 20 Consolidated Regiment, La. Mil.	Alamias, J. Jose	Private	17, 18 and 19 Consolidated Regiment, La. Mil. (Orig. filed under Alamas Jn Jose)
Adams, James	Private	17, 18 and 19 Consolidated Regiment, La. Mil.			
Adams, John	Private	Capt. Thomas' Co., La. Mil.	Alamilla, Hilario	Private	17, 18 and 19 Consolidated Regiment, La. Mil.
Adams, John	Private	8 Reg't (Meriam's) La. Mil.			
Adams, John	Private	12 and 13 Consolidated Regiment, La. Mil.	Alan, Jacque	Private	Plauche's Battalion La. Mil.
			Alard, Aramin	Private	3 Reg't (de la Ronde's) La. Mil.
Adams, Joseph	Private	De Clouet's Regiment, La. Mil.	Albarades, Balthazer	Private	7 Reg't (Le Beuf's) La. Mil.
Adams, Samuel	Private	De Clouet's Regiment, La. Mil.	Albarado, Francisco	3 Lieutenant	17, 18 and 19 Consolidated Reg. La. Mil.

Albaras, Antoine	Private	6 Reg't (Landry's) La. Mil.
Albaras, John	Private	6 Reg't (Landry's) La. Mil.
Albaraz, John	Private	6 Reg't (Landry's) La. Mil. (Orig. filed under Albaras, John)
Albares, Francisco	Private	2 Batt'n (Peire's) La. Vols.
Albarez, Francisco	Private	2 Batt'n (Peire's) La. Vols. (Orig. filed under Albares, Francisco)
Albarodo, Fs.	3 Lieutenant	17, 18 and 19 Consolidated Regiment, La. Mil. (Albarado, Francisco)
Alber, Bernard	Private	2 Batt'n (Peire's) La. Vols. (Orig. - Albert, Bernard)
Albert, Bernard	Private	2 Batt'n (Peire's) La. Vols. (Orig. - Albert, Bernard)
Albert, Jean	Sergeant	2 Reg't (Cavelier's) La. Mil.
Alberten, Richard	Private	12 and 13 Consolidated Regiment, La. Mil. (Albritton, Richard)
Alberton, John	Private	De Clouet's Regiment, La. Mil.
Albertons, --	Private	4 Reg't (Morgan's) La. Mil.
Albin, Alexander	Private	2 Reg't (Cavelier's), La. Militia
Alborado, Manuel	Private	De Clouet's Regiment, La. Mil.
Albretan, John	Private	De Clouet's Regiment, La. Mil. (Orig. filed under Alberton, John)
Albreton, Richard	Private	12 and 13 Consolidated Regt., La. Mil. (Orig. filed under Albritton, Richard)
Albritton, James	Private	10 and 20 Consolidated Regt. La. Mil.
Albritton, John	Private	De Clouet's Regiment, La. (Orig. filed under Alberton, John)
Albritton, Richard	Private	12 and 13 Consolidated Regiment, La. Mil.
Alby, Dennis	Private	4 Reg't (Morgan's) La. Mil. (Orig. filed under Abbey, Dennis)
Alcaerdet, Jean P.	Private	2 Batt'n (Peire's) La. Vol. (Orig. under Alcaudet, Jean Pierre)
Alcantara, Joseph	Private	2 Batt'n (Peire's) La. Vol.
Alcaudet, Jean Pierre	Private	2 Batt'n (Peire's) La. Vol.
Alcebdo, Peter	Private	2 Batt'n (Peire's) La. Vol. (See also 7 Reg't.)
Alcindor, --	Servant	De Clouet's Regiment, La. Mil.
Alcindor, --	Waiter	2 Reg't. (Cavelier's), La. Mil.
Alcorn, George	Corporal	Captain Sprigg's Co., Boatmen, La. Vols.
Alcorn, James	Private	Captain Sprigg's Co., Boatmen, La. Vols.
Alde, Inacio	Private	17, 18 and 19 Consolidated Regiment, La. Mil.
Aldea, Ignacio	Private	17, 18 and 19 Consolidated Regiment, La. Mil.
Alden, Samuel	Private	1 Reg't (DeJan's), La. Mil.
Aldrich, Jesse	Private	10 and 20 Consolidated Regiment, La. Mil.
Aldricks, John	Private	2 Reg't. (Cavelier's), La. Mil.
Aldridy, Jesse	Private	10 and 20 Cons. Reg't., La. Mil. (Orig. under Aldrich, Jesse)
Ale'gre, Thomas	Private	2 Reg't. (Cavelier's), La. Mil.
Alridonisse, --	Private	2 Batt'n. (D'Aquin's), La. Mil.
Aleman, Jean	Private	7 Reg't. (Le Beuf's), La. Mil.
Aleman, Manuel	Private	Louisiana (War of 1812)
Alexander, A.	Private	Capt. Hughes' Co., Mounted Riflemen, La. Mil.
Alexander, Alex	Private	19 Regiment, La. Militia
Alexander, Benjamin	Private	Louisiana (War of 1812) See also 1 Batt'n. (Henry's), US Vols.
Alexander, James	Trumpeter	Capt. Hughes' Co. Mounted Riflemen, La. Militia
Alexander, John P.	Private	Capt. Hughes' Co. Mounted Riflemen, La. Militia
Alexander, Joshua	Corporal	Capt. Thomas' Co., La. Mil.
Alexander, Josiah	Corporal	16 Reg't. (Thompson's), La. Mil.
Alexander, Robert	Private	12 and 13 Consolidated Regiment, La. Mil.
Alexander, William	Private	10 and 20 Consolidated Regiment, La. Mil.
Alexandre, --	Sergeant	Plauche's Battalion, La. Militia (Orig. filed under Bonneval Alexandre)
Alexandre, --	Sergeant	2 Batt'n. (D'Aquin's), La. Mil.
Alexandre, --	Servant	Detachment Field and Staff Officers, 4 Brigade, La. Mil.
Alexandre, fils	Private	5 Reg't. (La Branche's) La. Mil.
Alexandre, Charles	Private	2 Batt'n. (D'Aquin's), La. Mil.
Alexandre, Vzaine	Private	1 Batt'n. (Fortier's), La. Mil. De Clouet's Regiment, La. Mil.
Alexis, --	Servant	2 Batt'n. (D'Aquin's), La. Mil.
Alexis, Richard	Private	Captain Hubbard's Mounted Company, La. Militia
Alfonce, Jean	Private	3 Reg't. (de la Ronde's) La. Mil. (Orig. under Alphonse Jean)
Alford, Edwin	Private	12 and 13 Consolidated Regiment, La. Mil.
Algire, Theodore	Private	2 Reg't. (Cavelier's), La. Mil.
Alin, Jn	Private	Plauche's Battalion, La. Mil.
Alito, Simon	Private	2 Reg't. (Cavelier's), La. Mil.
Allain, Bernard	Private	8 Reg't. (Meriam's), La. Mil.
Allain, John Bte	Private	8 Reg't. (Meriam's), La. Mil.
Allain, L.	Private	8 Reg't. (Meriam's), La. Mil.
Allain, Pierre	Private	8 Reg't. (Meriam's), La. Mil.
Allain, Pierre	Private	8 Reg't. (Meriam's), La. Mil.
Allain, V.	Private	8 Reg't. (Meriam's), La. Mil.
Allain, Z.	Captain	8 Reg't. (Meriam's), La. Mil.
Alle', Louis	Private	8 Reg't. (Meriam's), La. Mil.
Allegre, Charles	Private	1 Batt'n. (Fortier's), La. Mil. (Orig. under Legre, Charles A.)
Allerman, Jean	Private	7 Reg't. (Le Beuf's), La. Militia (Orig. under Aleman, Jean)
Allemand, Antoine	Private	Captain Hubbard's Mounted Company, La. Mil.
Allemand, Jean	Private	7 Reg't. (Le Beuf's), La. Mil.
Allemand, Manuel	Private	Captain Hubbard's Mounted Company, La. Mil.
Allen, Daniel	Private	De Clouet's Regiment, La. Mil.
Allen, David	Private	De Clouet's Regiment, La. Mil.
Allen, Gideon	Private	10 and 20 Consolidated Regiment, La. Mil.
Allen, James	Private	Captain Colsson's Company, Artillery, La. Vols.
Allen, James	Sergeant	De Clouet's Regiment, La. Mil.
Allen, Janorer	Sergeant	8 Reg't. (Meriam's), La. Mil.
Allen, John	Private	De Clouet's Regiment, La. Mil.
Allen, John	Private	17, 18 and 19 Consolidated Regiment, La. Mil.
Allen, John S.	Private	12 and 13 Consolidated Regiment, La. Mil.
Allen, Nathaniel	Private	12 and 13 Consolidated Regiment, La. Mil.
Allen, Peter	Private	Capt. Thomas' Co., La. Militia
Allen, William	Private	10 and 20 Consolidated Regiment, La. Militia
Allen, William	Private	De Clouet's Regiment, La. Mil.
Allen, William	Captain	Captain Allen's Company, Artillerists, La. Volunteers
Alleque, Narcisse	Sergeant	1 Batt'n. (Fortier's), La. Mil.
Allimo, Bartholomy	Private	Capt. Thomas' Co., La. Mil.
Allimo, Nicholas	Private	Capt. Thomas' Co., La. Mil.
Almajor, Joseph	2 Lieut.	1 Batt'n. (Fortier's), La. Mil.
Alnet, Jean	Private	Captain Songy's Company, Marines, La. Vols.
Alom, Benite	Private	1 Batt'n. (Fortier's), La. Mil.
Alphonse, Francois	Private	3 Reg't. (de la Ronde's), La. Mil.
Alphonse, Jean	Private	3 Reg't. (de la Ronde's), La.Mil.
Alphuente, Joseph	Private	2 Reg't. (Cavelier's), La. Militia (Orig. under Alpuente, Joseph
Alpuente, Edouard	Private	3 Reg't. (de la Ronde's), La. Mil.
Alpuente, Francis	Captain	Capt. Alpuente's Co., La. Mil.
Alpuente, Jeans St.	Private	Capt. Alpuente's Co., La. Mil.
Alpuente, Joseph	Private	2 Reg't. (Cavelier's), La. Mil.
Alston, Solomon	Private	10 Reg't., Louisiana Militia
Alston, Soloman	Private	10 and 20 Consolidated Regiment, La. Mil.
Alva, Narcisse	Sergeant	3 Reg't. (de la Ronde's), La.Mil.
Alvarado, Francisco	Private	17, 18 and 19 Consolidated Regiment, La. Mil.
Alvarez, P.	Corporal	Plauche's Battalion, La. Mil.
Amador, Thomas	Private	17, 18 and 19 Consolidated Regiment, La. Mil.
Amador, Thomas	Private	17, 18 and 19 Consolidated Regiment, La. Mil.
Amelin, Julien	Private	1 Batt'n. (Fortier's), La. Mil.
Amelun, Ferdinand H.	1 Lt.-Capt.	2 Batt'n. (Peire's), La. Vols. (Orig. filed under Ameling, Ferdinand L.)

Ameling, Ferdinand L.	1 Lt.-Capt.	2 Batt'n. (Peire's), La. Vols.
Amiot, Cherubin	Artificer	Capt. Chaudurier's Co., Artificers, Art'y., La. Vols. (Orig. filed under Arnot, Cherubin)
Amon, Michael	Private	17, 18 and 19 Consolidated Regiment, La. Mil.
Amon, Peter	Private	17, 18 and 19 Consolidated Regiment, La. Mil.
Amon, Stephenson	Private	17, 18 and 19 Consolidated Regiment, La. Mil.
Amonds, Joshua	Sergeant	11 Reg't. (Hickey's), La. Mil.
Amot, Cherubin	Artificer	Capt. Chaudurier's Co., Artificers, Art'y., La. Militia
Amoth, Cherubin	Artificer	Capt. Chaudurier's Co., Artificers, Art'y. La. Mil. (Orig. filed under Amot, Cherubin)
Amotte, Cheruben	Private	2 Batt'n. (D'Aquin's), La. Mil.
Amotte, Zami	Private	2 Batt'n. (D'Aquin's), La. Mil.
Amslimg, Ferdinand	1 Lt.-Capt.	2 Batt'n. (Peire's) La. Vols (Orig. under Amelimg, Ferdinand L.)
Ancoin, Antoine	Private	7 Reg't. (Le Beuf's), La. Mil.
Ancoin, Eli	Private	10 and 20 Consolidated Reg't. La. Mil. (Orig. under Aucoin, Eli)
Ancoin, Elie	Corporal	7 Reg't. (Le Beuf's), La. Mil.
Ancoin, Francois	Private	7 Reg't. (Le Beuf's), La. Mil.
Ancoin, Fs	Private	7 Reg't. (Le Beuf's), La. Mil.
Ancoin, Iysaint	Private	7 Reg't. (Le Beuf's), La. Mil.
Ancoin, Michel	Sergeant	7 Reg't. (Le Beuf's), La. Mil.
Ancoin, Paul	Corporal	7 Reg't. (Le Beuf's), La. Mil.
Anderson, Abraham	Private	12 and 13 Consolidated Regiment La. Militia
Anderson, Arthur	Private	Captain Allen's Company, Artillerists, La. Vols.
Anderson, Isaac	Private	12 and 13 Consolidated Regiment La. Mil.
Anderson, James	Private	De Clouet's Regiment, La. Mil.
Anderson, James	1 Lieut.	16 Reg't. (Thompson's), La. Mil.
Anderson, John	Private	De Clouet's Regiment, La. Mil.
Anderson, John	Corporal	Capt. Hughes' Co., Mounted Riflemen, La. Mil.
Anderson, John B.	Corporal	Capt. Hughes' Co., Mounted Riflemen, La. Mil.
Anderson, Samuel W.	1 Sgt.-Sgt.	12 and 13 Consolidated Reg't. La. Mil.
Anderson, Valentine	Private	De Clouet's Reg't., La. Militia
Anderson, William R.	Cpl.-Sgt.	De Clouet's Reg't., La. Militia
Andra, Anni	Private	6 Reg't. (Landry's), La. Mil.
Andre, --	Servant	Gov. Claiborne and Staff, La. Mil.
Andre, --	Waiter	1 Division (Villere's) La. Militia
André, Jacques	Private	7 Reg't. (LeBeuf's), La. Mil.
Andre, Jean	Private	Capt. Lagan's Co., La. Vols.
Andres, Joseph	Private	Baker's Regiment, La. Militia
Andrew, William	Private	Capt. Dodge's Co., Mounted Riflemen, La. Mil.
Andrew, William	Private	Capt. Henry's Co., Mounted Riflemen, La. Mil.
Andrews, Adam	Private	10 and 20 Consolidated Regiment, La. Mil.
Andrews, Benjamin	Private	16 Reg't. (Thompson's) La. Mil.
Andrews, Coonrod	Private	10 and 20 Consolidated Regiment, La. Mil.
Andrews, Dotrief	Private	16 Reg't. (Thompson's) La. Mil. (Original filed under Andrus, Dotrief)
Andrews, James	Private	De Clouet's Regiment, La. Mil.
Andrews, James	Private	16 Reg't. (Thompson's) La. Mil. (Orig. under Andrus, James)
Andrews, John	Private	10 and 20 Consolidated Regiment, La. Mil.
Andrews, John	Private	16 Reg't. (Thompson's) La. Mil. (Orig. under Andrus, John)
Andrews, Joseph	Private	Baker's Regiment, La. Militia (Orig. under Andres, Joseph)
Andrews, Joseph	Sergeant	Captain Rankin's Co., Mounted Riflemen, La. Militia
Andrews, Joseph	Private	16 Reg't. (Thompson's) La. Mil. Orig. under Andrus, Joseph)
Andrews, Robert	Depy. Q. M. Gen.	General and Staff (Morgan), La. Mil.
Andri, Baptiste	Private	17, 18 and 19 Consolidated Regiment, La. Mil.
Andrie, Biscinte	Private	1 Batt'n. (Fortier's), La. Mil.
Andro, A.	Private	6 Reg't. (Landry's), La. Militia (Orig. under Andra, Anni)
Andrus, Benjamin	Sergeant	16 Reg't. (Thompson's) La. Mil.
Andrus, Benjamin	Private	16 Reg't. (Thompson's) La. Mil. (Orig. under Andrews, Benjamin)
Andrus, Dotrief	Private	16 Reg't. (Thompson's) La. Mil.
Andrus, James	Private	De Clouet's Regiment, La. Mil. (Orig. under Andrews, James)
Andrus, James	Private	16 Reg't. (Thompson's) La. Mil.
Andrus, Jesse	Private	16 Reg't. (Thompson's) La. Mil.
Andrus, John	Private	16 Reg't. (Thompson's) La. Mil.
Andrus, Joseph	Private	16 Reg't. (Thompson's) La. Mil.
Andrus, Joseph	Private	16 Reg't. (Thompson's) La. Mil.
Andrus, Joseph Elah	Private	16 Reg't. (Thompson's) La. Mil.
Andrus, Narsus	Private	16 Reg't. (Thompson's) La. Mil.
Andry, Alexcis	Private	1 Batt'n. (Fortier's), La. Mil.
Andry, Hortaire	2 Lieut.	3 Reg't. (de la Ronde's) La. Mil. (Orig. under Andry, Orthur)
Andry, Michel	Captain	3 Reg't. (de la Ronde's) La. Mil.
Andry, Orthur	2 Lieut.	3 Reg't. (de la Ronde's) La. Mil.
Angel, Joseph	Private	16 Reg't. (Thompson's) La. Mil.
Angle, John	Private	Capt. Ashley's Co., Mounted Riflemen, La. Mil.
Antoine, --	--	Captain Songy's Company, Marines, La. Volunteers
Antoine, --	Waiter	1 Division (Villeres), La. Mil.
Antoine, --	Waiter	1 Division (Villeres), La. Mil.
Antoine, --	Servant	4 Reg't. (Morgan's), La. Mil.
Antoine, Dominique	Private	2 Batt'n. (Peire's) La. Volunteers
Antoine, Francisque	Private	2 Batt'n. (Cavelier's) La. Militia
Antoine, Jh.	Private	4 Reg't. (Morgan's), La. Mil.
Antoine, Joseph	Private	De Clouet's Regiment, La. Mil.
Antonio, Jose	Private	2 Batt'n. (Peire's) La. Volunteers
Antonio, Joseph	Private	2 Batt'n. (Peire's) La. Volunteers (Orig. filed under Antonio, Jose)
Antonio, Pre.	Private	4 Reg't. (Morgan's), La. Mil.
Anty, Sylvester	Private	17, 18 and 19 Consolidated La. Mil.
Aplegate, Jeremiah	Private	17, 18 and 19 Consolidated, La. Mil.
Appe', Charles	Private	2 Reg't. (Cavelier's), La. Mil.
Aquera, Antonio	Private	2 Batt'n (Peire's) La. Vols. (Orig. under Aguera, Anthony)
Arabele, Santo	Private	17, 18 and 19 Consolidated Regiment La. Mil. (Orig. filed under Arebaleo, Santo)
Arabie, Antoine	Private	Capt. Hubbard's Mounted Co. La. Mil.
Araby, Joseph	Private	De Clouet's Regiment, La. Mil.
Aranago, Jose M.	Private	17, 18 and 19 Consolidated Reg't. La. Mil.
Araouz, Joseph	Private	1 Batt'n. (Fortier's), La. Mil.
Aravieux, Joseph	Private	1 Batt'n. (Fortier's), La. Militia (Orig. under Araouz, Joseph)
Arban, Pierre	Sergeant	2 Batt'n. (Peire's), La. Vols. Orig. under Arband, Pierre)
Arbana, Pierre	Sergeant	2 Batt'n. (Peire's), La. Vols. (Orig. under Arband, Pierre)
Arband, Pierre	Sergeant	2 Batt'n. (Peire's), La. Vols. (Orig. under Arband, Pierre)
Arbeaud, Pierre	Sergeant	2 Batt'n. (Peire's), La. Vols. (Orig. under Arband, Pierre)
Arband, Pierre	Sergeant	2 Batt'n. (Peire's), La. Vols.
Arband, Pierre	Sergeant	2 Batt'n. (Peire's), La. Vols.
Arbeaud, Pierre	Sergeant	2 Batt'n. (Peire's), La. Vols.
Arbell, Angel	Private	De Clouet's Regiment, La. Mil.
Arbour, Fr.	Private	8 Reg't. (Meriam's), La. Mil.
Arboy, Pierre	Sergeant	2 Batt'n. (Peire's), La. Vols. (Orig. under Arband, Pierre)
Arcanaux, I	Sergeant	6 Reg't. (Landry's), La. Mil. (Orig. under Arcenaux, I.)
Arcby, Joseph	Private	De Clouet's Regiment, La. Mil. (Orig. under Araby, Joseph)
Arcenau, Surville	Private	De Clouet's Regiment, La. Mil. (Orig. under Arseneau, Surville)
Arcenaux, Abraham	Captain	6 Reg't. (Landry's), La. Militia
Arcenaux, Auguste	Private	6 Reg't. (Landry's), La. Militia
Arcenaux, Cyprien	Private	De Clouet's Regiment, La. Mil.
Arcenaux, Frs.	Private	De Clouet's Regiment, La. Mil.
Arcenaux, Gabriel	Private	6 Reg't. (Landry's) La. Mil. (Orig. under Arceneau, Gabriel)

Arcenaux, I	Sergeant	6 Reg't. (Landry's) La. Mil.
Arcenaux, Jh.	Private	6 Reg't. (Landry's) La. Mil.
Arcenaux, Joicin	Private	De Clouet's Regiment, La. Mil.
Arcenaux, Pierre	Private	7 Reg't. (Le Beuf's), La. Mil.
Arcenaux, Simon	2 Lieut.	6 Reg't. (Landry's), La. Militia
Arcenaux, Surville	Private	De Clouet's Reg't., La. Mil. (Orig. under Arseneau Surville)
Arcenaux, Zenon	Corporal	6 Reg't. (Landry's), La. Mil.
Arcenau, Alexis	Private	6 Reg't. (Landry's), La. Mil.
Arceneau, Cyprien	Fusilier-Pvt.	5 Reg't. (LaBranche's) La. Mil. (Orig. under Arsenaux, Cyprien)
Arceneau, Francois	Corporal	6 Reg't. (Landry's), La. Mil.
Arceneau, Gariel	Private	6 Reg't. (Landry's), La. Mil.
Arceneau, Guillaurn	Private	7 Reg't. (LeBeuf's), La. Mil.
Arceneaux, Jn.	Private	6 Reg't. (Landry's) La. Mil. (Orig. under Arcenaux, Jh.)
Arceneaux, Louis	Private	6 Reg't. (Landry's) La. Mil.
Arche, Eloi	1 Lieut.	3 Reg't. (de la Ronde's) La. Mil. (Orig. filed under Ache, Elvix)
Archer, Singleton	Private	10 and 20 Consolidated Regiment, La. Mil.
Archy, --	--	10 and 20 Consolidated Regiment, La. Mil.
Arcineau, Cyprien	Private	De Clouet's Reg't., La. Militia (Orig. under Arcenaux, Cyprien)
Arconaux, Franc S.	Private	De Clouet's Reg't., La. Militia (Orig. under Arcenaux, Frs.)
Arconaux, Jocin	Private	De Clouet's Reg't., La. Militia (Orig. under Arcenaux, Joicin)
Ard, William	Private	12 and 13 Consolidated Regiment, La. Militia
Ardenne Jr., Baptiste	Private	2 Batt'n. (D'Aquin's), La. Mil.
Arden, John	Corporal	16 Reg't. (Thompson's) La. Mil.
Arden, Thomas	Private	17, 18 and 19 Consolidated Regiment, La. Mil.
Ardy, Jacque	Private	1 Batt'n. (Fortier's), La. Mil.
Arebaleo, Santo	Private	17, 18 and 19 Consolidated Regiment, La. Mil.
Arelle, Joseph	Private	Louisiana War of 1812 (see also 2 Batt'n. (Peire's), La. Vols Ref. Card)
Arelle, Joseph	Pvt-Cpl.	2 Batt'n (Peire's) La. Vols. (see also 44 Reg't.
Argote, Ed	2 Lieut.	2 Reg't. (Cavelier's), La. Mil.
Arial, Manna	Private	De Clouet's Regiment, La. Mil.
Ariel, Manna	Private	De Clouet's Regiment, La. Mil. (Orig. under Arial, Manna)
Arington, Charles	Private	Baker's Regiment, La. Mil.
Arlasin, Bte.	Private	8 Reg't. (Meriam's), La. Mil.
Armand, --	Waiter	2 Reg't. (Cavelier's), La. Mil.
Armand, Antoine	Private	De Clouet's Regiment, La. Mil.
Armand, Jn Bte	Private	6 Reg't. (Landry's), La. Mil.
Armand, Valery	Private	6 Reg't. (Landry's), La. Mil.
Armanda, --	Private	1 Reg't. (Dejan's), La. Mil.
Armandes, Joseph	Private	8 Reg't. (Meriam's), La. Mil.
Armas, Autunas	Private	17, 18 and 19 Consolidated Regiment, La. Mil.
Armas, Bertolo	Private	3 Reg't. (de la Ronde's), La. Mil.
Armas, C. D.	Private	1 Reg't. (Dejan's), La. Mil.
Armas, Md. D.	Private	1 Reg't. (Dejan's), La. Mil.
Armires, Etienne	Sergeant	1 Batt'n. (Fortier's), La. Mil.
Armitage, --	Private	Plauche's Battalion, La. Mil.
Armstrong, --	Private	Plauche's Battalion, La. Mil.
Armstrong, Abraham	Private	Captain Hubbard's Mounted Company, La. Mil.
Armstrong, C.	Private	4 Reg't. (Morgan's), La. Mil.
Armstrong, Daniel D.	Private	17, 18 and 19 Consolidated Regiment, La. Mil.
Armstrong, John	Private	Baker's Regiment, La. Mil.
Armstrong, John	Private	Baker's Regiment, La. Mil.
Armstrong, Samuel	Private	Captain Wallace's Company, Boatmen, La. Vols.
Armstrong, William	Private	Baker's Regiment, La. Mil.
Armstrong, William	Private	De Clouet's Regiment, La. Mil.
Armstrong, William	Corporal	1 Reg't. (DeJan's), La. Mil.
Armurier Jn., Lis. Nicolas	Fusilier-Private	5 Reg't. (LaBranche's), La. Mil.
Arnandes, I. Bte.	Private	8 Reg't. (Meriam's), La. Mil. (Orig. under Arnandez, J. Bte.)
Arnandes, Jacques	Private	8 Reg't. (Meriam's), La. Mil.
Arnandes, Joseph Armand	Private	8 Reg't. (Meriam's), La. Mil.
Arnandes, Oliver	Private	8 Reg't. (Meriam's), La. Mil.
Arnandez, Ilbert	Private	8 Reg't. (Meriam's), La. Mil. (Orig. under Arnandez, Jilbert)
Arnandez, J. Bte.	Private	8 Reg't. (Meriam's), La. Mil.
Arnandez, Jilbert	Private	8 Reg't. (Meriam's), La. Mil.
Arnandez, Joseph	1 Lieut.	8 Reg't. (Meriam's), La. Mil. (Orig. under Hernandez, Joseph)
Arnaud, Jacques	Private	De Clouet's Regiment, La. Mil.
Arnaud, Michel	Private	Capt. Lagan's Co., La. Vols.
Arnaud, Paul	Brig.-Major	2 Brigade (Hopkins'), La. Mil.
Arnaud, Rene'	Sgt.-Major	6 Reg't. (Landry's), La. Mil.
Arnaux, Jean	Private	Captain Lagan's Co., La. Vols. (Orig. under Arnoux, Jean)
Arnaux, Louis	Private	Captain Lagan's Co., La. Vols. (Orig. under Arnoux, Louis)
Arneau, Jaques	Private	De Clouet's Regiment, La. Mil. (Orig. under Arnaud, Jacques)
Arneau, Louis	Private	Capt. Lagan's Co., La. Vols. (Orig. under Arnoux, Louis)
Arnell, Henry	Private	12 and 13 Cons. Reg't., La. Mil. (Orig. under Arnold, Henry)
Arno, Bartholomew	Private	Captain Sprigg's Co., Boatmen, La. Vols.
Arnold, Henry	Private	12 and 13 Cons. Reg't., La. Mil.
Arnold, John	Private	19 Regiment, La. Mil.
Arnold, William	Private	19 Regiment, La. Mil.
Arnolds, John	Private	19 Regiment, La. Mil. (Orig. under Arnold, John)
Arnoul, Ceril	Private	De Clouet's Regiment, La. Mil.
Arnoul, Cirille	Corporal	4 Reg't. (Morgan's), La. Mil. (Orig. under Arnould, Cirille)
Arnould, Cirille	Corporal	4 Reg't. (Morgan's), La. Mil.
Arnould, Gervais	Private	Captain Chauveau's Company, Cavalry, La. Militia
Arnoux, Jean	Private	Capt. Lagan's Co., La. Vols.
Arnoux, Louis	Private	Capt. Lagan's Co., La. Vols.
Arrelle, Joseph	Private	2 Batt'n. (Peire's), La. Vol. (Orig. under Arelle, Joseph)
Arroyo, Francois	1 Lieut.	5 Reg't. (La Branche's), La. Mil.
Arroyo, Patris	Fusilier-Pvt.	5 Reg't. (La Branche's), La. Mil.
Arsenaux, Ciprien	Fusilier-Pvt.	5 Reg't. (La Branche's), La. Mil.
Arseneau, Alexandre	Private	Captain Hubbard's Mounted Company, La. Mil.
Arseneau, Pierre	Private	Captain Hubbard's Mounted Company, La. Mil.
Arseneau, Surville	Private	De Clouet's Regiment, La. Mil.
Arseneau, Urbain	Private	Captain Hubbard's Mounted Co., La. Mil.
Artache, Antoine	Private	De Clouet's Regiment, La. Mil.
Arthur, George	Private	4 Reg't. (Morgan's), La. Mil.
Arthurs, John	Private	4 Reg't. (Morgan's), La. Mil.
Artice, Antonio	Private	3 Reg't. (de la Ronde's), La. Mil.
Arvil, Paul	Private	Capt. Lagan's Co., La. Vols.
Ashcraft, John	Private	6 Reg't. (Landry's), La. Mil.
Ashley, William H.	Captain	Captain Ashley's Co., Mounted Riflemen, La. Mil.
Asmar, Baptiste	Private	1 Batt'n. (Fortier's), La. Mil.
Asmard, Anthony	Private	De Clouet's Reg., La. Mil. (Orig. under Armand, Antoine)
Asmard, Joisim	Sergeant	1 Batt'n. (Fortier's), La. Mil.
Asner, Jean Louis	Corporal	1 Batt'n. (Fortier's), La. Mil. (Orig. under Astier Jean Louis)
Assclaire, Jacob	Private	8 Reg't. (Meriam's), La. Mil. (Orig. under Assclare, Jacob)
Assclare, Jacob	Private	8 Reg't. (Meriam's), La. Mil.
Asselaire, Jacob	Private	8 Reg't. (Meriam's), La. Mil. (Orig. under Assclare, Jacob)
Astier, Jean Louis	Corporal	1 Batt'n. (Fortier's), La. Mil.
Aswell, George	Private	De Clouet's Reg't., La. Mil.
Atherton, Cornelius	Private	Captain Rankin's Co., Mounted Riflemen, La. Militia
Atindor, --	Servant	De Clouet's Reg't., La. Militia (Orig. under Alcindor)
Atkins, James	Private	Captain Griffith's Co., Mounted Riflemen, La. Vols.
Atkinson, David	Private	16 Reg't. (Thompson's), La. Mil.
Atkison, David	Private	16 Reg't. (Thompson's), La. Mil. (Orig. under Atkinson, David)
Attentis, J.	Private	De Clouet's Reg't., La. Mil.
Aubert, Batiste	Corporal	11 Reg't. (Hickey's), La. Mil.
Aubre, Martin	1 Lieut.	Baker's Regiment, La. Mil. (Orig. under Aubrie Martin)

Aubrie, Martin	1 Lieut.	Baker's Regiment, La. Mil.
Aubry, Marcelin	Private	1 Batt'n. (Fortier's), La. Mil.
Aubry, Martin	1 Lieut.	Baker's Reg't., La. Mil. (Orig. under Aubrie, Martin)
Aubry, Pierre	Private	1 Batt'n. (Fortier's), La. Mil.
Aucoin, Antoine	Private	Captain Hubbard's Mounted Co., La. Mil.
Aucoin, Celestin	Corp.-Sgt.	De Clouet's Reg't., La. Mil.
Aucoin, Eli	Private	10 and 20 Cons. Reg't., La. Mil.
Aucoin, Firmin	Private	Captain Hubbard's Mounted Co., La. Mil.
Aucoin, Pierre	Private	16 Reg't. (Thompson's), La. Mil.
Audebert, William	1 Lieut.	2 Reg't. (Cavelier's), La. Mil.
Audige, --	Private	Plauche's Battalion, La. Mil.
Auger, Pierre	Private	5 Reg't. (La Branche's), La. Mil.
August, --	Servant	Captain Dubuclet's Troop; Hussars, La. Vols. (Orig. under Auguste)
August, Renale	Private	5 Reg't. (La Branche's), La. Mil. (Orig. under Auguste, Renale)
August, Virgile	Private	5 Reg't. (La Branche's), La. Mil. (Orig. under Auguste, Virgile)
Auguste, --	Servant	Captain Dubuclet's Troop, Hussars, La. Vols.
Auguste, --	Sergeant	2 Batt'n. (D'Aquin's), La. Mil.
Auguste, Chavane	Sergeant	5 Reg't. (La Branche's), La. Mil.
Auguste, Jn. Baptiste	Private	2 Batt'n. (D'Aquin's), La. Mil.
Auguste, Moliere	Private	1 Batt'n. (Fortier's), La. Mil.
Auguste, Renale	Private	5 Reg't. (La Branche's), La. Mil.
Auguste, Virgile	Private	5 Reg't. (La Branche's), La. Mil.
Auguste, Voltaire	Private	1 Batt'n. (Fortier's), La. Mil.
Auguste, Voltaire	Private	1 Batt'n. (Fortier's), La. Mil.
Augustin, --	Servant	Plauche's Battalion, La. Mil.
Augustin, --	Servant	1 Reg't. (DeJan's), La. Mil.
Augustin, Joseph	Private	1 Batt'n. (Fortier's), La. Mil.
Augustin, Pierre	Fusilier-Pvt.	2 Batt'n. (D'Aquin's), La. Mil.
Augustine, Patricio	Private	Capt. Thomas' Co., La. Mil.
Aurely, --	Private	8 Reg't. (Meriam's), La. Mil. (Orig. under Auriley, --)
Auriley, --	Private	8 Reg't. (Meriam's), La. Mil.
Ausser, --	Private	2 Reg't. (Cavelier's), La. Mil.
Austin, --	Private	Plauche's Battalion, La. Mil. (Orig. under Ostin, --)
Austin, Charles A.	Sergeant	Captain Rankin's Co., Mounted Riflemen, La. Mil.
Austin, Jean	Private	8 Reg't. (Meriam's), La. Mil.
Austin, John	1 Lt. & Adjt.	10 Reg't., Louisiana Militia
Autin, Paul	Private	6 Reg't. (Landry's), La. Mil.
Auving, Jn. C.	Private	2 Reg't. (Cavelier's), La. Mil. (Orig. under Cauvin, Jn.)
Auzalle, Louis	Private	2 Battn. (Peire's), La. Vols. (Orig. under Auzole, Louis)
Auzole, Louis	Private	2 Battn. (Peire's), La. Vols.
Avare, Jean	Private	Capt. Lagan's Co., La. Vols.
Avarie, Jean	Private	Capt. Lagan's Co., La. Vols. (Orig. under Avare, Jean)
Avart, Celestin	Private	4 Reg't. (Morgan's), La. Mil.
Avart, E.	Private	Plauche's Batt'n., La. Mil.
Avart, J. R.	1 Lieut.	2 Reg't. (Cavelier's), La. Mil.
Avart, Robert	Private	4 Reg't. (Morgan's), La. Mil.
Avila, Anthony	Private	2 Batt'n (Peire's), La. Vols.
Avilla, Anthony	Private	2 Batt'n (Peire's), La. Vols. (Orig. under Avila, Anthony)
Avril, --	Fusilier-Pvt.	2 Batt'n. (D'Aquin's), La. Mil.
Awzole, Louis	Private	2 Batt'n (Peire's), La. Vols. (Orig. under Auzole, Louis)
Ayaux, Joseph	Corporal	7 Reg't. (Le Beuf's), La. Mil.
Ayaux, Maturin	Private	7 Reg't. (Le Beuf's), La. Mil.
Aycock, Burrell	Captain	7 Reg't. (Le Beuf's), La. Mil.
Aydelle, Nicholas	Private	6 Reg't. (Landry's), La. Mil.
Ayez, L.	Private	8 Reg't. (Meriam's), La. Mil.
Ayez, Ths.	Private	8 Reg't. (Meriam's), La. Mil.
Aymon, Lavo	Private	16 Reg't. (Thompson's), La. Mil.
Aymon, Syphorian	Private	16 Reg't. (Thompson's), La. Mil.
Ayot, Etienne	Private	Plauche's Batt'n., La. Mil.
Ayuera, Antonio	Private	2 Batt'n (Peire's), La. Vols. (Orig. under Aquere, Anthony)
Azar, --	Private	De Clouet's Reg't., La. Militia (Orig. under Ozor, --)
Azarrette, B.	Private	Plauche's Batt'n., La. Militia
Azole, Louis	Private	2 Batt'n (Peire's), La. Vols. (Orig. under Auzole, Louis)
Azor, --	Servant	1 Batt'n. (Fortier's), La. Mil.
Azor, --	Waiter	2 Reg't. (Cavelier's), La. Mil.
Azore, --	Servant	2 Brigade (Hopkins's), La. Mil.
Babban, Alexander	Private	De Clouet's, La. Mil. (Orig. under Babin, Alexander)
Babbino, David	Private	De Clouet's, La. Mil. (Orig. under Babinau, David)
Babbino, Joseph	Private	De Clouet's, La. Mil. (Orig. under Babinau, Joseph)
Babin, Alexander	Private	De Clouet's, La. Mil.
Babin, Ate.	Private	8 Reg't. (Meriam's), La. Mil.
Babin, Auguste	Private	De Clouet's Reg't., La. Militia
Babin, Auguste	Private	8 Reg't. (Meriam's), La. Mil.
Babin, Charles	Sergeant	8 Reg't. (Meriam's), La. Mil.
Babin, Dartoise	Private	6 Reg't. (Landry's), La. Mil.
Babin, Eugene	Private	6 Reg't. (Landry's), La. Mil.
Babin, Frans	Private	8 Reg't. (Meriam's), La. Mil.
Babin, Henry	Private	8 Reg't. (Meriam's), La. Mil.
Babin, Hubert	Corporal	8 Reg't. (Meriam's), La. Mil.
Babin, Jh.	2 Lieut.	8 Reg't. (Meriam's), La. Mil.
Babin, Isaac	Corporal	8 Reg't. (Meriam's), La. Mil.
Babin, John	Private	8 Reg't. (Meriam's), La. Mil.
Babin, Joseph	Private	Bakers' Regiment, La. Militia
Babin, Joseph	Private	6 Reg't. (Landry's), La. Militia
Babin, Joseph	Private	8 Reg't. (Meriam's), La. Militia
Babin, Lessier	Private	6 Reg't. (Landry's), La. Militia (Orig. under Babin, Lifrin)
Babin, Lifrin	Private	6 Reg't. (Landry's), La. Militia
Babin, Ls.	Private	8 Reg't. (Meriam's), La. Militia
Babin, Narcisse	Private	6 Reg't. (Landry's), La. Militia
Babin, P.	Private	8 Reg't. (Meriam's), La. Militia
Babin, Paul	Private	8 Reg't. (Meriam's), La. Militia
Babin, Pet	Private	8 Reg't. (Meriam's), La. Militia
Babin, R.	Private	6 Reg't. (Landry's), La. Militia
Babin, S.	Private	6 Reg't. (Landry's), La. Militia
Babin, Senator	Private	8 Reg't. (Meriam's), La. Militia
Babin, Simon	Private	6 Reg't. (Landry's), La. Militia
Babin, Simon	Private	8 Reg't. (Meriam's), La. Militia
Babin, Simon	1 Lieut.	8 Reg't. (Meriam's), La. Militia
Babin, V.	Private	6 Reg't. (Landry's), La. Militia
Babinau, Alexander	Private	De Clouet's Reg't., La. Militia
Babinau, David	Private	De Clouet's Reg't., La. Militia
Babinau, Francois	Private	De Clouet's Reg't., La. Militia
Babinau, Joseph	Private	De Clouet's Reg't., La. Militia
Babino, Alexander	Private	De Clouet's Reg't., La. Militia (Orig. under Babinau, Alexander)
Babinot, Fran	Private	De Clouet's Reg't., La. Militia (Orig. under Babinau, Francois)
Babtiste, Michel	Private	2 Batt'n (Peire's), La. Vols. (Orig. under Bautiste, Miguel)
Baca, Leon	1 Lieut.	5 Reg't. (La Branche's), La. Mil.
Bacas, B.	Private	Plauche's Battalion, La. Militia
Bacca, Leon	1 Lieut.	5 Reg't. (La Branche's), La. Mil. (Orig. under Baca, Leon)
Baccar, B.	Private	Plauche's Batt'n. La. Militia (Orig. under Bacas, B.)
Bachalier, Cadet	Private	2 Batt'n (D'Aquin's), La. Militia
Bachelot, Pierre	1 Sgt.	5 Reg't. (La Branche's), La. Mil.
Bachemin, fils	Private	3 Reg't. (de la Ronde's), La. Mil.
Bacher, Honore	Private	De Clouet's Reg't., La. Militia
Backer, Jacob	Private	17, 18 and 19 Consolidated Reg't. La. Militia
Backus, Augustus	2 Lieut.	Captain Wallace's Co., Boatmen, La. Vols.
Bacon, Ludwell	Private	Captain McNair's Co., Mounted Riflemen, La. Mil.
Bacon, Nathaniel	Private	Captain McNair's Co., Mounted Riflemen, La. Mil.
Bacon, William	Private	Captain McNair's Co., Mounted Riflemen, La. Mil.
Bacors, --	Sergeant	3 Reg't. (de la Ronde's) La. Mil. (Orig. under Bucois, --)
Bacquet, Baptiste	Private	De Clouet's Reg't., La. Militia (Orig. under Paquet, Batiste)
Bacrenaith, John Wm.	Private	2 Batt'n (Peire's), La. Vols.
Bacrnaith, J. W.	Private	2 Batt'n (Peire's), La. Vols. (Orig. under Bacrenaith, John Wm.)
Bactave, Belas	Private	2 Batt'n (D'Aquin's), La. Militia
Bactave, Bienaime	Private	2 Batt'n (D'Aquin's), La. Militia

Baddo, Augustus	Private	12 and 13 Cons. Reg't., La. Mil. (Orig. under Bade, Augustus)
Bade, Augustus	Private	12 and 13 Cons. Reg't., La. Mil.
Badeau, Hermogene	Fusilier-Pvt.	5 Reg't. (La Branche's), La. Mil.
Badeau, Pierre	Private	6 Reg't. (Landry's), La. Militia
Badell, Pierre	Private	1 Batt'n (Fortier's), La. Militia
Badia, Jose	Private	2 Reg't. (Cavelier's), La. Mil.
Badie, Jacques	Artificer-Corp.	Capt. Chaudurier's Co., Artificers, Art'y., La. Vols.
Badille, Jacques	Sergeant	1 Batt'n. (Fortier's), La. Militia
Badille, Pierre	Private	1 Batt'n. (Fortier's), La. Militia
Bagby, Abner	Private	Capt. Sprigg's Co., Boatmen, La. Vols.
Bagby, Abner	Private	Capt. Wallace's Co., Boatmen, La. Vols.
Bagby, Absar	Private	Capt. Sprigg's Co., Boatmen, La. Vols. (Orig. under Bagby, Abner)
Baggot, Jesse	Private	12 and 13 Consolidated Regiment, La. Militia
Bagley, Abner	Private	Capt. Wallace's Co., Boatmen, La. Vols. (Orig. under Bagby, Abner)
Bagneris, Lainy	Private	3 Reg't. (de la Ronde's), La. Mil.
Bahno, Andre	Private	Capt. Lagan's, La. Vols.
Bahon, Andre	Private	Capt. Lagan's Co., La. Vols. (Orig. under Bahno, Andre)
Baile, James	Private	De Clouet's Regiment, Louisiana Militia (Orig. under Bailey, James)
Bailey, James	Private	De Clouet's Regiment, Louisiana Militia
Bailey, Peter	Private	De Clouet's Regiment, Louisiana Militia
Baillieux, Francois	Private	2 Batt'n (Peire's), La. Vols.
Bailly, B.	Musician-Drummer	2 Batt'n (Peire's), La. Vols. (Orig. under Bailly, Eugene)
Bailly, B. Eugene	Mus.-Drummer	2 Batt'n (Peire's), La. Vols. (Orig. under Bailly, Eugene)
Bailly, Eugene	Mus.-Drummer	2 Batt'n (Peire's), La. Vols.
Bailly, Eugine	Mus.-Drummer	4 Reg't. (Morgan's), La. Mil.
Bailly, Pierre	Private	1 Batt'n (Fortier's), La. Militia
Baily, Pierre Fils	Private	1 Batt'n (Fortier's), La. Militia
Baily, Peter	Private	De Clouet's Reg't., La. Militia (Orig. under Bailey, Peter)
Baily, Samuel	Private	Capt. Collard's Co., La. Militia
Baird, Hiram	Private	6 Reg't. (Landry's), La. Militia
Baird, William	Corporal	De Clouet's Reg't., La. Militia
Bairfield, Hugh	Captain	11 Reg't. (Hickey's), La. Militia
Baker, Isaac	Private	12 and 13 Cons. Reg't., La. Mil.
Baker, Jacob	Private	17, 18 and 19 Cons. Reg't., La. Mil. (Orig. under Backer, Jacob)
Baker, John	Private	Capt. Dodge's Co. Mounted Riflemen, La. Militia
Baker, John	Private	Capt. Henry's Co., Mounted Riflemen, La. Militia
Baker, Joshua	Colonel	Detachment Field and Staff Officers, 4 Brigade, La. Militia
Balahon, Jean	Private	7 Reg't. (Le Beuf's), La. Mil.
Baldridge, Robert	Private	Capt. Van Bibber's Co., La. Mil. (Orig. under Baldrige, Robert)
Baldrige, Robert	Private	Capt. Van Bibber's Co., La. Mil.
Baldwin, Isaac	Sergeant	16 Reg't. (Thompson's), La. Mil.
Baldwin, Mordicai	Sgt.-Ensign	10 and 20 Cons. Reg't., La. Mil.
Baligny, --	Private	1 Reg't. (Dejan's), La. Militia (Orig. under Batigny)
Balin, Joseph	Private	Baker's Regiment, La. Militia (Orig. under Babin, Joseph)
Bakkanora, Francisco	Private	17, 18 and 19 Cons. Reg't., La. Mil. (Orig. under Ballanoro, Francisco)
Ballanoro, Francisco	Private	17, 18 and 19 Cons. Reg't., La. Militia
Ballard, Lewis F.	Private	10 and 20 Consolidated Regiment, La. Militia
Ballard, Lewis T.	Private	10 and 20 Consolidated Regiment, La. Militia (Orig. under Ballard, Lewis F.)
Ballew, Charles	Corporal	10 and 20 Consolidated Regiment, La. Militia
Ballieux, Francois	Private	2 Batt'n (Peire's), La. Vols. (Orig. under Baillieux, Francois)
Ballin, Joseph	Private	2 Batt'n (Peire's), La. Vols. (Orig. under Bastin, Joseph)
Ballio, John	Private	17, 18 and 19 Cons. Reg't., La. Militia
Ballix, --	Private	Plauche's Battalion, La. Militia
Ballou, I. T.	Sergeant	Captain Chauveau's Co. Cavalry, La. Militia
Baltiena, Vicent	Private	17, 18 and 19 Con. Reg't., La. Mil. (Orig. under Bastrina, Vicente)
Baltiera, Bezte	Private	17, 18 and 19 Cons. Reg't., La. Mil. (Orig. under Baltieria, Bezte)
Baltieria Bezte	Private	17, 18 and 19 Cons. Reg't., La.
Bandreau, M.	Private	6 Reg't. (Landry's), La. Militia
Bandreou, M.	Private	6 Reg't. (Landry's), La. Militia (Orig. under Bandreau, M.)
Bandro, G. G.	Private	7 Reg't. (Le Beuf's), La. Militia (Orig. under Bandro I. I.)
Banks, Thomas	Private	Captain Beale's Co., Riflemen, La. Militia
Bankston, Henry	Private	12 and 13 Cons. Reg't., La. Mil.
Bankston, Howell	Private	12 and 13 Cons. Reg't., La. Mil.
Bankston, John	Private	12 and 13 Cons. Reg't., La. Mil.
Bankston, Levi	Private	12 and 13 Cons. Reg't., La. Mil.
Banson, James	Private	Louisiana (War of 1812)
Bantiste, Miguel	Private	2 Batt'n. (Peire's), La. Vols. (Orig. under Bautiste, Miguel)
Baoul, --	Sergeant	2 Batt'n (D'Aquin's), La. Militia
Baour, Andre	Private	Capt. Lagan's Co., La. Vols. (Orig. under Bakno, Andre)
Baptisse, Jean	Musician	1 Batt'n (Fortier's), La. Militia
Baptist, --	Servant	16 Reg't. (Thompson's), La. Mil.
Baptiste, --	Servant	1 Batt'n (Fortier's), La. Militia
Baptiste, --	Waiter	2 Reg't. (Cavelier's), La. Mil.
Baptiste, --	Private	4 Reg't. (Morgan's), La. Militia
Baptiste, --	Servant	5 Reg't. (LaBranche's), La. Mil.
Baptiste, Jean	Musician	1 Batt'n. (Fortier's), Louisiana Militia (Orig. under Baptisse, Jean)
Baptiste, Jean	Private	2 Batt'n (D'Aquin's), La. Militia
Baptiste, Jn.	Waiter	2 Reg't. (Cavelier's), La. Mil.
Baptiste, Jn.	Waiter	2 Reg't. (Cavelier's), La. Mil.
Baptiste, Jn.	Servant	2 Batt'n (D'Aquin's), La. Militia
Baptiste, Jn.	Sergeant	2 Batt'n (D'Aquin's), La. Militia
Baptiste, John	Servant	Gov. Claiborne and Staff, La. Mil.
Baptiste, John	Servant	General and Staff (Labatut), La. Mil.
Baptiste, John	Waiter	2 Reg't. (Cavelier's), La. Mil.
Baptiste, John	Private	2 Reg't. (Cavelier's), La. Mil.
Baptiste, John	Tambour, Drummer	2 Batt'n (D'Aquin's), La. Militia
Baptiste, Peter	Private	De Clouet's Reg't., La. Militia
Baque, Frederique	Corporal	2 Batt'n (D'Aquin's), La. Militia
Baqueste, --	Private	5 Reg't. (La Branche's), La. Militia
Baquette, --	Private	5 Reg't. (La Branche's), La. Militia, (Orig. under Baqueste)
Barabino, Steffino	Tr. Master	Detachment Field and Staff Officers, 4 Brigade, La. Militia
Barar, Antoine	Sergeant	Captain Hubbard's Mounted Co., La. Militia
Barar, Lufroi	Corporal	Captain Hubbard's Mounted Co., La. Militia
Barba, Joseph	Private	10 and 20 Consolidated Reg't., La. Mil. (Orig. under Barbee, Joseph)
Barbara, --	Private	4 Reg't. (Morgan's), La. Militia
Barbarin, --	Private	Plauche's Battalion, La. Militia
Barbarin, Aine	Private	Plauche's Battalion, La. Militia
Barbarouse, Etienne	Private	De Clouet's Reg't., La. Militia (Orig. under Barbarousse, Etienne)
Barbarousse, Etienne	Private	De Clouet's Reg't., La. Mil.
Barbe, Mathiew	Private	1 Batt'n. (Fortier's), La. Mil.
Barbee, Joseph	Private	10 and 20 Cons. Reg't., La. Mil.
Barber, Samuel	Private	16 Reg't. (Thompson's), La. Mil.
Barbero, Joseph	Private	8 Reg't. (Meriam's), La. Mil.
Barbet, Henry	2 Lieut.	2 Reg't. (Cavelier's), La. Mil.
Barbier, Charles	Sgt.-Major	6 Reg't. (Landry's), La. Militia (See also 7 Reg't. Reference Card)

Barbier, Charles	Sgt.-Major	7 Reg't. (LeBeuf's), La. Militia (See also 6 Regiment)
Barbier, Jacques	Fusilier-Pvt.	5 Reg't. (La Branche's), La. Mil.
Barbier, Pierre	Private	3 Reg't. (de la Ronde's), La. Mil.
Barbin, Abraham	Private	16 Reg't. (Thompson's) La. Mil. (Orig. under Barrier, Abram)
Barbin, Samuel	Private	16 Reg't. (Thompson's) La. Mil. (Orig. under Barber, Samuel)
Baarceno, Simon	Private	17, 18 and 19 Cons. Reg't. La. Mil. (Orig. under Barceno, Simon)
Barefield, Jesse	Private	10 and 20 Cons. Reg't., La. Mil.
Barefield, Miles	Private	10 and 20 Cons. Reg't., La. Mil. (Orig. under Barfield, Miles)
Barfield, Jesse	Private	10 and 20 Cons. Reg't., La. Mil. (Orig. under Barefield, Jesse)
Barfield, Miles	Private	10 and 20 Cons. Reg't., La. Mil.
Barget, Louis	Private	2 Batt'n (D'Aquin's), La. Militia
Bargo, W. L.	Private	De Clouet's Reg't., La. Militia (Orig. under Labarge, William)
Bariaux, Francois	Private	7 Regt. (Le Beuf's), La. Militia
Barie, Francois	Private	7 Reg't. (Le Beuf's), La. Militia (Orig. under Bariaux, Francois)
Barie, J. B.	Private	7 Reg't. (Le Beuf's), La. Militia
Barillo, Jacques fil	--	Captain Hubbard's Mounted Company, La. Militia
Barillo, Pierre	Private	Captain Hubbard's Mounted Company, La. Militia
Bario, Jean Bte	Private	7 Reg't. (Le Beuf's), La. Militia
Barjouis, Francis	Private	Capt. Price's Co., La. Militia
Barker, Eli	Private	10 Reg't., La. Militia
Barlen, Joseph	Private	2 Batt'n (Peire's), La. Vols. (Orig. under Bastin, Joseph)
Barler, Francois	Private	2 Batt'n (Peire's), La. Vols. (Orig. under Barlet, Francois)
Barlet, Francois	Private	2 Batt'n (Peire's), La. Vols.
Barlow, Miles	Private	10 and 20 Cons. Reg't., La. Mil.
Barlow, Thomas	Private	12 and 13 Cons. Reg't. La. Mil.
Barnabe', Jean Baptiste	Private	1 Batt'n. (Fortier's), La. Mil.
Barnes, Adam	Private	10 and 20 Consolidated Regiment, La. Militia
Barnes, Allen	Private	De Clouet's Reg't., La. Militia (Orig. under Barns, Allen)
Barnes, John	Private	Captain Allen's Company, Artillerists, La. Volunteers
Barnes, Samuel	Sergeant	10 and 20 Cons. Reg't., La. Mil.
Barnet, Jonathan	Private	Louisiana (War of 1812) (See 2 Batt'n. Peire's), La. Vols.
Barnett --	Private	Plauche's Battalion, La. Militia
Barnett, James	Sergeant	De Clouet's, Reg't., La. Militia
Barnett, Jonathan	Private	2 Batt'n. (Peire's), La. Vols.
Barnett, Joseph	Private	17, 18 and 19 Cons. Reg't., La. Militia
Barnhill, Henry	Private	De Clouet's Reg't., La. Militia
Barns, Allen	Private	De Clouet's Reg't., La. Militia
Barnteau, --	Private	Plauche's Batt'n., La. Militia
Barnz, Allen	Private	De Clouet's Reg't., La. Militia (Orig. under Barns, Allen)
Baro, Iyasente	Artificer	Capt. Chaudurier's Co., Artificers, Art'y., La. Vols. (Orig. under Caro, Yacint)
Baro, Maxim	Private	2 Reg't. (Cavelier's), La. Mil.
Baron, Etienne	Private	1 Batt'n (Fortier's), La. Militia (Orig. under Barons, Etienne)
Baron, Eugenio	Private	17, 18 and 19 Cons. Reg't., La. Mil.
Baron, N. A., Jr.	Cornet	Captain Chauveau's Co., Cavalry, La. Militia
Barone, Imio	Private	17, 18 and 19 Cons. Reg't., La. Mil. (Orig. under Barono, Iinio)
Barono, Iinio	Private	17, 18 and 19 Cons. Reg't., La. Mil.
Barons, Etienne	Private	1 Batt'n (Fortier's), La. Militia
Barque, D.	Private	8 Reg't. (Meriam's), La. Militia
Barra, Vallery	Private	De Clouet's, Reg't., La. Militia
Barraud, Julian	Private	De Clouet's Reg't., La. Militia (Orig. under Braud, Julien)
Barre', Eugene	Fusilier-Pvt.	5 Reg't. (La Branche's), La. Mil.
Barre', Zephirin	Fusilier-Pvt.	5 Reg't. (La Branche's), La. Mil.
Barres, John D.	Private	Capt. Allen's Co., Artillerists, La. Vols. (Orig. under Barrs, John D.)
Barrett, James	Private	De Clouet's, Reg't., La. Militia
Barrett, Michael	Private	12 and 13 Cons. Reg't., La. Mil.
Barri, Joseph	Private	Louisiana (War of 1812)
Barrier, Abram	Private	16 Reg't. (Thompson's), La. Mil.
Barrio, John Maria	Private	De Clouet's Reg't., La. Militia
Barrios, John	Private	7 Reg't. (Le Beuf's), La. Militia
Barrlow, Thomas	Private	12 and 13 Cons. Reg't. La. Mil. (Orig. under Barlow, Thomas)
Barrois, Francois	Private	3 Reg't. (de la Ronde's), La. Mil.
Barrois, Jean	Private	3 Reg't. (de la Ronde's), La. Mil.
Barrois, Jean Pierre	Private	3 Reg't. (de la Ronde's), La. Mil.
Barron, Gabriel	Private	Capt. Ashley's Co., Mounted Riflemen, La. Mil.
Barron, Matthew	Private	De Clouet's Reg't., La. Militia
Barrow, Levi	Corporal	16 Reg't. (Thompson's), La. Mil.
Barrow, Richard	Private	16 Reg't. (Thompson's), La. Mil.
Barrow, Richard	Private	17, 18 and 19 Cons. Reg't., La. Mil.
Barrow, Zadock	Private	12 and 13 Cons. Reg't., La. Mil.
Barrs, Joh D.	Private	Captain Allen's Co. Artillerists, La. Vols.
Barry, Andrew	Private	De Clouet's Reg't., La. Militia (Orig. under Berry, Andrew)
Bart, Jean	Private	Plauche's Batt'n., La. Militia
Barte, Pierre	Private	1 Batt'n. (Fortier's), La. Mil.
Barten, James	Private	19 Regiment La. Volunteers (Orig. under Barton, James)
Barth, Jean	Private	1 Batt'n (Fortier's), La. Mil.
Barthe, Jn	Private	1 Batt'n (Fortier's), La. Mil. (Orig. under Barth, Jean)
Barthelemi, Francois	Private	De Clouet's Reg't., La. Militia
Barthelemi, Jaques	Private	De Clouet's Reg't., La. Militia
Barthelemy, --	Private	Plauche's Batt'n., La. Mil.
Barthelemy, Francois	Private	De Clouet's Reg't., La. Militia (Orig. under Barthelemi, Francois)
Barthelemy, Jaques	Private	De Clouet's Reg't., La. Militia (Orig. under Barthelemi, Jaques)
Barthelemy, Jean	Private	De Clouet's Reg't., La. Militia
Bartholocour, Andre'	Private	Capt. Songy's Co., Marines, La. Vols. (Orig. under Bartholocur, Andre)
Bartholocur, Andre'	Private	Capt. Songy's Co., Marines, La. Vols.
Bartle, Jean	Private	1 Batt'n. (Fortier's), La. Mil. (Orig. under Barth, Jean)
Bartley, Hugh	Private	Captain McNair's Co., Mounted Riflemen, La. Mil.
Bartly, Hugh	Private	Captain McNair's Co., Mounted Riflemen, La. Mil. (Orig. under Bartley, Hugh)
Barton, James	Private	16 Reg't. (Thompson's), La. Mil.
Barton, James	Private	16 Reg't. (Thompson's), La. Mil.
Barton, James	Private	19 Regiment, La. Militia
Barton, William	Private	De Clouet's Reg't., La. Militia
Bartte, Jacob	Private	12 and 13 Cons. Reg't., La. Mil.
Baruno, Simon	Private	17, 18 and 19 Cons Reg't., La. Mil. (Orig. under Barceno, Simon)
Basinet, John B.	Private	19 Reg't., La. Vols. (Orig. under Bassinet, John B.)
Basque, Sacramenta	Sergeant	17, 18 and 19 Cons. Reg't., La. Militia
Basques, St. Yago	Private	2 Batt'n (Peire's), La. Vols.
Basquez, Sacremento	Sergeant	17, 18 and 19 Cons. Reg't. La. Militia
Bass, Elijah	2 Lieut.	10 and 20 Cons. Reg't. La. Mil.
Bass, Isaac	Private	17, 18 and 19 Cons. Reg't., La. Militia
Basset, Ralph	Private	Captain Beale's Co., Riflemen, La. Militia
Basset, Thomas	Private	1 Reg't. (Dejan's), La. Militia
Bassin, Joseph	Private	2 Batt'n (Peire's), La. Vols. (Orig. under Bastin, Joseph)
Bassinet, --	Private	Plauche's Batt'n., La. Militia
Bassinet, John B.	Private	19 Reg't., La. Militia
Bastien, J.	Private	4 Reg't. (Morgan's), La. Mil.
Bastien, Nicholas	Private	4 Reg't. (Morgan's), La. Mil.
Bastien, T.	Private	4 Reg't. (Morgan's), La. Mil.
Bastien, Valerien	Private	4 Reg't. (Morgan's), La. Mil.
Bastin, Joseph	Private	2 Batt'n. (Peire's), La. Vols.
Bastrina, Vicente	Private	17, 18 and 19 Cons. Reg't., La. Mil.
Batancourt, Patris	Fusilier-Pvt.	5 Reg't. (La Branche's), La. Mil.

Bateave, --	Private	2 Reg't. (Cavelier's), La. Mil.
Bateman, Carlton	Private	Baker's Regiment, La. Militia
Bateman, John M.	Private	Baker's Regiment, La. Militia
Bateman, Noah	Private	De Clouet's Reg't., La. Militia
Bates, John	Private	12 and 13 Cons. Reg't., La. Mil.
Bates, Joseph	Private	12 and 13 Cons. Reg't., La. Mil.
Bates, William	Private	Capt. Dodge's Co., Mounted Riflemen, La. Militia
Bates, William	Private	Capt. Henry's Co., Mounted Riflemen, La. Militia
Batesto, I.	Private	6 Reg't. (Landry's), La. Militia
Batigny, --	Private	1 Reg't. (Dejan's), La. Militia
Batista, Miguel	Private	2 Batt'n (Peire's), La. Vols. (Orig. Under Bautiste, Miguel)
Batiste, --	Waiter	11 Reg't. (Hickey's), La. Mil.
Batley, Ed	Private	10 Regiment, La. Militia
Bauche, Jean	Artificer	Capt. Chaudurier's Co., Artificers, Artillery, La. Vols. (Orig. under Bouche, Jean)
Baudier, Jean	Servant	Captain Hubbard's Mounted Co., La. Militia
Baudin, Silvin	Sergeant	6 Reg't. (Landry's), La. Militia
Baudoin, Henry	Private	5 Reg't. (LaBranche's), La. Mil.
Baudoin, Honore	Fusilier-Pvt.	5 Reg't. (LaBranche's), La. Mil.
Baudoin, Jan. Bte.	Fusilier-Pvt.	5 Reg't (LeBranche's), La. Mil.
Baudoin, Pierre	Corporal	5 Reg't. (LeBranche's), La. Mil.
Baudoin, Sylvain	Fusilier-Pvt.	5 Reg't. (LeBranche's), La. Mil.
Baudoin, Thelesphore	Fus.-Pvt.	5 Reg't. (LeBranche's), La. Mil.
Baudoins, Henry	Private	5 Reg't. (LeBranche's), La. Mi. (Orig. under Baudoin, Henry)
Baudrea, Paul Marie	Sergeant	7 Reg't. (Le Beuf's), La. Mil.
Baudreau, Florentine	Private	Captain Hubbard's Mounted Co., Louisiana Militia
Baudreau, Joseph	Private	7 Reg't. (LeBeuf's), La. Mil.
Baudreau, Jye	Private	7 Reg't. (LeBeuf's), La. Mil.
Baudreau, Narcisse	Private	Capt. Hubbard's Mounted Co., La. Mil.
Baudreau, Pierre	Private	Captain Hubbard's Mounted Co., La. Militia
Baudro, Baptiste	Private	7 Reg't. (LeBeuf's), La. Mil.
Baudro, Charles M.	Private	7 Reg't. (Le Beuf's), La. Mil.
Baudro, Felix	Private	7 Reg't. (LeBeuf's), La. Mil.
Baudro, Guillome	Private	7 Reg't. (LeBeuf's), La. Mil.
Baudro, I.	Private	7 Reg't. (LeBeuf's), La. Mil.
Baudro, I Bte	Private	7 Reg't. (Le Beuf's), La. Militia
Baudro, I. I.	Private	7 Reg't. (Le Beuf's), La. Militia
Baudro, Jean (dit meto)	Private	7 Reg't. (Le Beuf's), La. Militia
Baudro, Jesse	Private	7 Reg't. (Le Beuf's), La. Militia (Orig. under Baudreau, Jye)
Baudro, Laurent	Private	7 Reg't. (Le Beuf's), La. Mil.
Baudro, Valentin	Corporal	7 Reg't. (Le Beuf's), La. Militia
Baudry, Jn. Bte	1 Sergeant	5 Reg't. (La Branche's), La. Mil.
Baugnon, Louis	Fusilier-Pvt.	5 Reg't. (La Branche's), La. Mil.
Bauillon, Bte	Private	8 Reg't. (Meriam's), La. Militia
Bauldage, Daniel	Private	Capt. Collard's Co., La. Militia
Bauldage, James	Private	Capt. Collard's Co., La Militia
Baulieu, Louis	Private	De Clouet's Reg't., La. Militia
Baulieux, Charles	Private	Capt. Alpuente's Co., La. Mil. (Orig. under Beaulieux, Charles)
Bauliste, Michl	Private	2 Batt'n (Peire's), La. Vols. (Orig. under Bautiste, Miguel)
Bauliste, Miguel	Private	2 Batt'n (Peire's), La. Vols. (Orig. under Bautiste Miguel)
Baulvac, Francois	Sergeant	2 Batt'n (Peire's), La. Vols. (Orig. under Boulvaque, Francois)
Baum, Alexander	Private	10 and 20 Cons. Regiment, La. Militia
Baumond, L.	Sergeant	4 Reg't. (Morgan's), La. Militia (Orig. under Baumont, Livandais)
Baumont, Livandais	Sergeant	4 Reg't. (Morgan's), La. Militia
Baurck, B.	Corporal	8 Reg't. (Meriam's), La. Militia (Orig. under Baurk, B.)
Baurgais, Jean Bte	Private	6 Reg't. (Landry's), La. Militia
Baurgeais, Edward	Sergeant	6 Reg't. (Landry's), La. Militia
Baurgeais, J. Ls	Private	6 Reg't. (Landry's), La. Militia
Baurgeais, Joseph	Private	6 Reg't. (Landry's), La. Militia
Baurgeais, Pierre	Corporal	6 Reg't. (Landry's), La. Militia
Baurgeais, Paul	Private	6 Reg't. (Landry's), La. Militia
Baurgeais, Timon	Private	6 Reg't. (Landry's), La. Militia
Baurgeois, Jean Restival	Private	6 Reg't. (Landry's), La. Militia
Baurgeois, Joseph	Private	7 Reg't. (Le Beuf's), La. Militia
Baurgeois, M.	Private	6 Reg't. (Landry's), La. Militia
Baurgeois, Olivier	Private	6 Reg't. (Landry's), La. Militia
Baurgeois, Paul A.	Private	6 Reg't. (Landry's), La. Militia
Baurgeois, St. Arnand	Private	6 Reg't. (Landry's), La. Militia
Baurgue, Alexis	Private	6 Reg't. (Landry's), La. Militia
Baurk, B.	Corporal	8 Reg't. (Meriam's), La. Militia
Baurque, Alexis	Private	6 Reg't. (Landry's), La. Militia (Orig. under Baurgue, Alexis)
Baurque, Maurice	Private	6 Reg't. (Landry's), La. Militia
Bautiste, Miguel	Private	2 Batt'n (Peire's), La. Vols.
Bauvais, Guillaume	Sergeant	5 Reg't. (Le Branche's) La. Mil. (Orig. under Beauvais, Guillaume)
Bauvais, St. Gemme	Private	De Clouet's Reg't., La. Militia
Bauvier, Andre	Fusilier-Pvt.	5 Reg't. (LeBranche's), La. Mil.
Bauvier, Georges	Fusilier-Pvt.	5 Reg't. (LeBranche's), La. Mil.
Bauvier, Victor	Corp.-Pvt.	5 Reg't. (LeBranche's), La. Mil.
Bauzan, B.	Private	Plauche's Battalion, La. Militia
Bauzan, I	Private	Plauche's Battalion, La. Militia
Bayanoba, Francisco	Private	17, 18 and 19 Cons. Reg't., La. Militia
Bayard, C.	Private	4 Reg't. (Morgan's), La. Militia
Bayard, Julien	Private	Plauche's Batt'n, La. Militia
Bayeux, Colas	Private	DeClouet's Reg't., La. Militia (Orig. under Cayeux, Colas)
Bayhi, Bonre	Corporal	3 Reg't. (de la Ronde's), La. Mil.
Bayhi, Pierre	1 Lieut.	3 Reg't. (de la Ronde's), La. Mil.
Bayoone, Jacque	Private	2 Batt'n (D'Aquin's), La. Militia
Bayou, Antoine	1 Lt. & Adjt.	6 Reg't. (Landry's), La. Militia
Baysset, --	Private	2 Reg't. (Cavelier's), La. Mil.
Bazanac, --	Private	2 Reg't. (Cavelier's), La. Mil.
Bazile, --	Servant	1 Batt'n (Fortier's), La. Mil.
Bazile, --	Private-Serv.	Brigade, (Flanjae's), La. Mil. (Private Servant 4 Brigade)
Bazile, --	Servant	5 Reg't. (La Branche's), La. Mil.
Bazillier, Math	Private	2 Reg't. (Cavelier's), La. Mil.
Beale, Thomas	Captain	Captain Beale's Co., Rifleman, La. Militia
Bean, E.	Private	Plauche's Batt'n., La. Militia
Beard, Syby	Private	17, 18 and 19 Cons. Reg't., La. Militia
Beasley, William	Private	17, 18 and 19 Cons. Reg't., La. Militia
Beasly, Martin	Private	17, 18 and 19 Cons. Reg't., La. Militia
Beason, Uriah	Private	12 and 13 Cons. Reg't., La. Mil.
Beatie, Andrew	Corporal	De Clouet's Reg't., La. Militia
Beattie, Andrew	Corporal	De Clouet's Reg't., La. Militia (Orig. under Beatie, Andrew)
Beau, --	Private	Plauche's Batt'n., La. Mil.
Beauderelle, E.	Private	8 Reg't. (Meriam's), La. Militia
Beaudoin, Honore	Fusilier-Pvt.	5 Regiment (La Branche's), La. Mil. (Orig. Baudoin, Honore)
Beaudoin, Jn Bte	Fusilier-Pvt.	5 Regiment (La Branche's), La. (Orig. under Baudoin, Jn Bte)
Beaudoin, Sylvain	Fusilier-Pvt.	5 Regiment (La Branche's), La. (Orig. under Baudoin, Sylvain)
Beaudoin, Thelesphore	Fus.-Pvt.	5 Regiment (La Branche's), La. (Orig. under Baudoin, Thelesphore)
Beauduit, Seraphin	Private	1 Batt'n (Fortier's), La. Militia
Beaugard, I. P.	Private	7 Reg't. (Le Beuf's), La. Militia
Beauheu, Philippe	Private	1 Batt'n (Fortier's), La. Militia (Orig. under Bollieu, Phillippe)
Beaulier, Pierre	Private	De Clouet's Reg't., La. Militia
Beaulieau, Sterlin	Private	1 Batt'n (Fortier's), La. Militia (Orig. under Beaulieu, Hurbin)
Beaulieau, Urbarn	Private	1 Batt'n (Fortier's), La. Militia (Orig. under Beaulieu, Hurbin)
Beaulieu, Etienne	Private	1 Batt'n (Fortier's), La. Militia
Beaulieu, Gilbert	Private	1 Batt'n (Fortier's), La. Militia (Orig. under Bollieu, Gilbert)
Beaulieu, Hurbin	Private	1 Batt'n (Fortier's), La. Militia
Beaulieu, Jean Baptiste	Private	1 Batt'n (Fortier's), La. Militia (Orig. under Bolliett, Jean Baptisse)
Beaulieu, Lindor	Private	1 Batt'n (Fortier's), La. Militia (Orig. under Bollieu, Lindore)
Beaulieu, Maurice	Private	1 Batt'n (Fortier's), La. Militia (Orig. under Bollieu, Maurice)
Beaulieux, Charles	Private	Capt. Alpuente's Co., La. Mil.
Beaupre, Jean	Private	De Clouet's Reg't., La. Militia

Beaurais, Andre	Private	Capt. Colsson's Co., Artillery, La. Vols.
Beauregard, B.	Private	2 Reg't. (Cavelier's), La. Mil.
Beauregard, Manuel	Private	4 Reg't. (Morgan's), La. Militia
Beauregard, Toutant	Sergeant	3 Reg't. (de la Ronde's), La. Mil.
Beauvais, Guillaume	Sergeant	5 Reg't. (La Branche's), La. Mil.
Bebee, Henry	Private	4 Reg't. (Morgan's), La. Militia
Bechner, Jean	Fusilier-Pvt.	5 Reg't. (La Branche's), La. Mil.
Beck, George	Private	16 Reg't., (Thompson's) La. Mil.
Becnel, Benjamin	1 Lieutenant	5 Reg't. (La Branche's), La. Mil.
Becnel, Pre	Private	5 Reg't. (La Branche's), La. Mil.
Bedeman, Henry	1 Lieutenant	16 Reg't. (Thompson's), La. Mil.
Bedwell, William	Serg.-Pvt.	12 and 13 Cons. Reg't., La. Mil.
Beebe, John	Private	Plauche's Battalion, La. Militia
Beecham, Stephen	Private	10 and 20 Cons. Reg't., La. Mil.
Beenel, Pre	Private	5 Reg't. (La Branche's), La. Mil. (Orig. under Becnel, Pre)
Beferano, Jean	Private	3 Reg't. (de la Ronde's), La. Mil.
Beferans, Jean	Private	3 Reg't. (de la Ronde's), La. Mil. (Orig. under Beferano, Jean)
Bega, Miguel	Private	2 Batt'n (Peire's), La. Vols.
Begnaud, Jean	Private	De Clouet's Reg't, La. Militia
Begnaud, Narcisse	Private	De Clouet's Reg't, La. Militia
Begnaut, Narcise	Private	De Clouet's Reg't, La. Militia (Orig. under Begnaud, Narcisse)
Belair, Jean	Corporal	1 Batt'n (Fortier's), La. Militia (Orig. under Belaire, Jean)
Belaire, Jean	Corporal	1 Batt'n (Fortier's), La. Militia
Belange', Juan	Private	17, 18 and 19 Cons. Reg't., La. Mil.
Belasse, Joseph	Private	2 Batt'n (D'Aquin's), La. Militia
Belaume, Jacque	Corporal	Plauche's Batt'n, La. Mil. (Orig. under Ballaume, Jacque)
Belbedert, Celestin	Fusilier-Pvt.	2 Batt'n (D'Aquin's), La. Militia
Belbidert, Celestin	Fusilier-Pvt.	2 Batt'n (D'Aquin's), La. Militia (Orig. under Belbedert, Celestin)
Belew, Solomon	Private	Capt. Rankin's Co., Mounted Riflemen, La. Mil.
Belew, William	Private	12 and 13 Cons. Reg't., La. Mil. (Orig. under Belue, William)
Belezince, --	Servant	2 Batt'n (D'Aquin's), La. Militia
Belhomme, --	Servant	1 Batt'n (Fortier's), La. Militia
Belhumert, Godfroe	Servant	17, 18 and 19 Cons. Reg't., La. Mil.
Belhumeur, Godefroi	Servant	17, 18 and 19 Cons. Reg't., La. Mil. (Orig. under Belhumert, Godfroe)
Belizer, --	Sergeant	2 Batt'n (D'Aquin's), La. Militia (Orig. under Bellizaire)
Bell, David	Private	10 and 20 Cons. Reg't., La. Mil.
Bell, David	Private	10 and 20 Cons. Reg't., La. Mil.
Bell, Guy H.	Captain	16 Reg't. (Thompson's), La. Mil.
Bell, George W.	Corporal	De Clouet's Reg't., La. Militia
Bell, John	Private	De Clouet's Reg't., La. Militia
Bell, John	Private	12 and 13 Cons. Reg't., La.Mil.
Bell, John	Private	12 and 13 Cons. Reg't., La. Mil.
Bell, Joseph	Private	10 and 20 Cons. Reg't., La. Mil.
Bell, Josiah H.	Private	Capt. Hughes' Co., Mounted Riflemen, La. Militia
Bell, Nicholas	Private	17, 18 and 19 Const. Regt., La. Mil.
Bell, Robert	Corporal	De Clouet's Reg't., La. Militia
Bell, Robert	Private	8 Reg't. (Meriam's), La. Militia
Bell, William	Private	12 and 13 Cons. Reg't., La. Mil.
Bellair, Michel	Corporal	16 Reg't. (Thompson's), La. Mil. (Orig. under Bellard, Michel)
Bellair, W.	Private	4 Reg't. (Morgan's), La. Militia
Bellange, Hubert	Private	De Clouet's Reg't., La. Militia (Orig. under Bellanger, Hubert)
Bellanger, Hubert	Private	De Clouet's (Reg't., La. Militia
Bellard, Louis	Private	16 Reg't. (Thompson's), La. Mil.
Bellard, Michel	Corporal	16 Reg't. (Thompson's), La. Mil.
Bellaume, --	Private	Plauche's Battalion, La. Militia
Bellaume, Jacque	Corporal	Plauche's Battalion, La. Militia
Belle, Jean	Private	Capt. Songy's Co., Marines, La. Vols.
Bellegas, Joseph	Private	2 Batt'n. (Peire's), La. Vols. (Orig. Under Billegas, Joseph)
Bellevier, --	Corporal	De Clouet's Reg't., La. Militia (Orig. under Bellevieu, Tisappin)
Bellevieu, Tisappin	Corporal	De Clouet's Reg't., La. Militia
Bellevue, Pierre	Private	16 Reg't. (Thompson's), La. Mil.
Bellile, Auguste	Private	Capt. Hubbard's Mounted Co., La. Militia
Bellile, John	Sergeant	7 Reg't. (Le Beuf's), La. Militia
Bellizaire, --	Sergeant	2 Batt'n. (D'Aquin's), La. Mil.
Belloe, --	Sergeant	Plauche's Batt'n., La. Mil.
Bellot --	Private	2 Reg't. (Cavelier's), La. Mil.
Belleview, Pierre	Private	16 Reg't. (Thompson's), La. Mil. (Orig. under Bellevue, Pierre)
Belly, --	Private	3 Reg't. (de la Ronde's), La. Mil.
Belly, Ned	Private	8 Reg't. (Meriam's), La. Mil.
Belme, Michael	Private	16 Reg't. (Thompson's), La. Mil.
Belnaut, Francis	Private	Plauche's Batt'n., La. Militia
Belome, George	Private	16 Reg't. (Thompson's), La. Mil. (Orig. under Belome, Gregoire)
Belome, Gregoire	Corporal	2 Batt'n. (Peire's), La. Vols.
Belome, Gregoire	Private	16 Reg't. (Thompson's), La. Mil.
Belomme, Gregoire	Corporal	2 Batt'n. (Peire's), La. Vols. (Orig. under Belome, Gregoire)
Belon, William	Private	5 Reg't. (La Branche's), La. Mil.
Belony, --	Private	1 Reg't. (Dejan's), La. Mil.
Belsom, Andre	Fusilier-Pvt.	5 Reg't. (Le Branche's), La. Mil.
Belsom, Henri	Fusilier-Pvt.	5 Reg't. (Le Branche's), La. Mil.
Belsom, Henri, Son	Fusilier-Pvt.	5 Reg't. (Le Branche's), La. Mil.
Belsome, --	Private	4 Reg't. (Morgan's), La. Mil.
Belsomes, --	Private	4 Reg't. (Morgan's), La. Mil. (Orig. under Belsome)
Beluche, --	Lieutenant	Plauche's Batt'n., La. Militia
Belue, William	Private	12 and 13 Cons. Reg't., La. Mil.
Ben, --	Servant	Plauche's Batt'n., La. Militia
Ben, --	Servant	2 Brigade (Hopkins'), La. Mil.
Ben, --	Servant	17, 18 and 19 Cons. Reg't., La. Mil.
Bendick, George	Private	10 Reg't., La. Militia
Bendor, Lott	Private	17, 18 and 19 Cons. Reg't., La. Mil.
Benedick, John C.	Corporal	Capt. Rankin's Co. Mounted Riflemen, La. Militia
Benetanud, --	2 Lieutenant	Plauche's Battalion, La. Militia (Orig. under Benetand)
Benetaud, --	2 Lieutenant	Plauche's Battalion, La. Militia (Orig. under Benetand)
Benetaul, --	2 Lieutenant	Plauche's Battalion, La. Militia (Orig. under Benetand)
Benetaut, --	2 Lieutenant	Plauche's Battalion, La. Militia (Orig. under Benetand)
Benevice, Zenon	Private	16 Reg't. (Thompson's), La. Mil. (Orig. under Bennarice, Zenon)
Benit, Joseph	2 Lieutenant	De Clouet's Reg't., La. Militia
Benite, Jean Baptiste	Captain	2 Reg't. (Cavelier's), La. Mil.
Benite, Me	Sergeant	2 Reg't. (Cavelier's), La. Mil.
Benejamain, --	Private	2 Batt'n. (D'Aquin's), La. Mil.
Benejamin, --	Private	2 Batt'n. (D'Aquin's), La. Mil. (Orig. under Benjamain, --)
Benejamin, --	Servant	5 Reg't. (La Branche's), La. Mil.
Benejamin, fils	Private	5 Reg't. (La Branche's), La. Mil.
Benejamin, Pierre	Private	6 Reg't. (Landry's), La. Militia
Bennarice, Zenon	Private	16 Reg't. (Thompson's), La. Mil.
Benne, Joseph	Private	Baker's Reg't., La. Militia (Orig. under Reyne, Joseph)
Bennet, Henry	Private	10 and 20 Consolidated Reg't., La. Mil.
Bennet, William	Private	Capt. Callaway's Co., Mounted Riflemen, La. Militia
Bennett, Isaac	Private	Captain Sprigg's Co., Boatmen, La. Vols.
Bennett, Reuben	Corp.-Sgt.	De Clouet's Regiment, Louisiana Militia
Bennett, Samuel B.	Sergeant	4 Reg't. (Morgan's), La. Mil. (1 Sergeant, Sergeant)
Bennette, Isaac	Private	Captain Sprigg's Co., Boatmen, La. Vols. (Orig. under Bennett, Isaac)
Bennington, Jonathan	Private	Capt. Price's Co., La. Militia
Bennoit, Charles	Private	De Clouet's Reg't., La. Militia
Benoist, Jean Bte	Private	16 Reg't. (Thompson's), La. Mil.
Benoist, Jean M.	Private	7 Reg't. (Le Beuf's), La. Mil.
Benoist, Olevier	Private	De Clouet's Reg't., La. Militia
Benoist, Pierre	Private	2 Batt'n. (Peire's), La. Vols.
Benoiste, Bastien	Private	7 Reg't. (Le Beuf's), La. Mil.
Benoiste, Pierre	Private	7 Reg't. (Le Beuf's), La. Militia
Benoit, Andre	Private	3 Reg't. (de la Ronde's), La. Mil.
Benoit, Augustin	Corporal	De Clouet's Reg't., La. Militia

Benoit, Baptiste	Private	1 Batt'n (Fortier's), La. Militia
Benoit, Bastien	Private	7 Reg't. (Le Beuf's), La. Militia (Orig. under Benoiste, Bastien)
Benoit, Elroy	Corporal	Baker's Reg't., La. Militia
Benoit, Fs.	Private	2 Reg't. (Cavelier's), La. Mil.
Benoit, Jean M.	Private	7 Reg't. (Le Beuf's), La. Militia (Orig. under Benoist, Jean M.)
Benoit, Joseph	Private	De Clouet's Reg't., La. Mil.
Benoit, Joseph	Corporal	7 Reg't. (LeBeuf's), La. Militia
Benoit, Pierre	Private	2 Batt'n (Peire's), La. Vols. (Orig. under Benoist, Pierre)
Benoit, Pierre	Private	7 Reg't. (Le Beuf's), La. Militia (Orig. under Benoiste, Pierre)
Benoit, Zarvier	Private	De Clouet's Reg't., La. Militia
Bensan, James	Private	2 Reg't. (Peire's), La. Vols.
Benson, I.	Corporal	Captain Beale's Co., Riflemen, La. Militia
Benson, James	Private	2 Batt'n. (Peire's), La. Vols. (Orig. under Bensan, James)
Benson, William	Private	10 Regiment Louisiana Militia
Benson, William	Private	Capt. Price's Co., La. Militia
Benton, John	Private	10 and 20 Cons. Reg't., La. Mil.
Beny, Joseph	Private	11 Reg't. (Hickey's), La. Militia
Beoist, Olevier	Private	De Clouet's Reg't., La. Militia (Orig. under Benoist, Olevier)
Beranard, Sanon	Private	1 Batt'n. (Fortier's), La. Mil.
Berard, Achille	Private	Captain Dubuclet's Troop, Hussars, La. Vols.
Berassor, Lewis	Private	De Clouet's Reg't., La. Militia
Berbin, Auguste	Private	De Clouet's Reg't., La. Militia (Orig. under Babin, Auguste)
Beret, Joseph	Private	8 Reg't. (Meriam's), La. Militia
Bergan, Jeremiah	Corporal	De Clouet's Reg't., La. Militia (Orig. under Briant, Jeremiah)
Bergeron, Baptiste	Private	De Clouet's Reg't., La. Militia
Bergeron, Guillaume	Private	De Clouet's Reg't., La. Militia
Bergeron, Joseph	Private	16 Reg't. (Thompson's), La. Mil.
Bergeron, Pierre	Private	Captain Callaway's Co., Cavalry, La. Militia
Bergeron, Pierre	Private	De Clouet's Regiment, Louisiana Militia
Bergerou, Auguste	Private	Captain Hubbard's Mounted Company, Louisiana Militia
Bergeson, Jean Bte	Private	8 Reg't. (Meriam's), La. Militia
Berio, John Maria	Private	De Clouet's Reg't., La. Militia (Orig. under Barrio, John Maria)
Berise, Jacques	Private	4 Reg't. (Morgan's), La. Mil.
Berjeran, Pirre	Private	6 Reg't. (Landry's), La. Mil.
Berjero, Jean	Private	6 Reg't. (Landry's), La. Mil.
Berjeron, Germain	Private	7 Reg't. (LeBeuf's), La. Militia (Orig. under Berjeron, Jermain)
Berjeron, Jean	Private	6 Reg't. (Landry's), La. Militia (Orig. under Berjero, Jean)
Berjeron, Jermain	Private	7 Reg't. (Le Beuf's), La. Militia
Berjeron, V.	Private	8 Reg't. (Meriam's), La. Militia
Berjeson, Pierre	Private	6 Reg't. (Landry's), La. Militia (Orig. under Berjeran, Pierre)
Berlangey, Hubert	Private	De Clouet's Reg't., La. Militia (Orig. under Bellanger, Hubert)
Berlin, Francois	Private	8 Reg't. (Meriam's), La. Mil.
Berluchan, A.	Private	Plauche's Batt'n., La. Militia
Berluchand, Pierre	Sergeant	Capt. Chaudurier's Co., Artificers, Art'y., La. Vols. (Orig. under Berluchaux, Pierre)
Berluchand, Pierre	Private	4 Reg't. (Morgan's), La. Mil.
Berluchau, A.	Private	Plauche's Batt'n., La. Mil. (Orig. under Berluchan, A.)
Berluchau, Pierre	Sergeant	Capt. Chaudurier's Co., Artificers, Arty., La. Vols. (Orig. under Berluchauz, Pierre)
Berluchaux, Pierre	Sergeant	Capt. Chaudurier's Co., Artificers, Arty., La. Vols.
Berlucheau, --	Private	Plauche's Batt'n., La. Militia
Bermero, Raymond	Sergeant	6 Reg't. (Landry's), La. Militia
Bermondy, Clairville	Private	Capt. Trudeau's Troop of Horse, La. Mil. (Orig. under Bernoudy, Clairville)
Bermude, Joseph	Private	2 Reg't. (Cavelier's), La. Mil. (Orig. under Bermudez, Joseph)
Bermudez, Joseph	Private	2 Reg't. (Cavelier's), La. Mil.
Bernard, --	Private	7 Reg't. (Le Beuf's), La. Militia
Bernard, Antoine	Private	2 Batt'n. (Peire's), La. Vols.
Bernard, Auguste	Private	2 Reg't. (Cavelier's), La. Mil.
Bernard, E. L.	Corp.	Capt. Chauveau's Co., Cavalry, La. Mil.
Bernard, Felix	Private	8 Reg't. (Meriam's), La. Militia
Bernard, Francois	Private	De Clouet's Reg't., La. Mil.
Bernard, J. B.	Private	7 Reg't. (Le Beuf's), La. Militia
Bernard, Jean B.	Private	7 Reg't. (Le Beuf's), La. Militia
Bernard, Jn.	Private	2 Batt'n. (D'Aquin's), La. Mil.
Bernard, Jn. Bte	Fusilier-Pvt.	5 Reg't. (Le Branche's), La. Mil.
Bernard, John L.	Private	De Clouet's Reg't., La. Militia
Bernard, Joseph	Private	Captain Beale's Co., Riflemen, La. Mil.
Bernard, Joseph	Private	De Clouet's Reg't., La. Militia
Bernard, Joseph	Private	6 Reg't. (Landry's), La. Militia
Bernard, Joseph	Private	16 Reg't. (Thompson's), La. Militia
Bernard, L.	Private	8 Reg't. (Meriam's), La. Militia
Bernard, O.	Private	8 Reg't. (Meriam's), La. Militia
Bernard, Restival	Private	7 Reg't. (Le Beuf's), La. Militia
Bernard, Sanon	Private	1 Batt'n. (Fortier's), La. Mil. (Orig. under Beranard, Sanon)
Bernard, Simon	Private	De Clouet's Reg't., La. Mil.
Bernard, Ursin	Private	De Clouet's Reg't., La. Mil.
Bernavice, Ancisco	Private	16 Reg't. (Thompson's), La. Mil.
Berne, G.	Private	8 Reg't. (Meriam's), La. Militia
Berne, Henry	Private	Capt. Songy's Co., Marines, La. Vols.
Bernodie, --	Private	4 Reg't. (Morgan's), La. Militia (Orig. under Bernondy, --)
Bernondy, --	Private	4 Reg't. (Morgan's), La. Militia
Bernoudy, Bernard	Private	Capt. Trudeau's Troop of Horse, La. Mil.
Bernoudy, Clairvill	Private	Capt. Trudeau's Troop of Horse, La. Mil.
Bernoudy, Louis	Private	Capt. Trudeau's Troop of Horse, La. Mil.
Bernuchot, Gilbert	Private	Capt. Hubbard's Monted Co., La. Militia
Bercche', Elie	Musician	1 Batt'n. (Fortier's), La. Militia
Berque, Augustine	Private	16 Reg't. (Thompson's), La. Mil.
Berque, Eloi	Private	16 Reg't. (Thompson's), La. Mil.
Berque, Valve	Private	16 Reg't. (Thompson's), La. Mil.
Berque, Verglan	Private	16 Reg't. (Thompson's), La. Mil.
Berrard, John fils	Private	De Clouet's Regiment, Louisiana Militia
Berrey, Abraham	Private	De Clouet's Regiment, Louisiana Mil. (Orig. under Berry, Abraham)
Berry, Abraham	Private	De Clouet's Regiment, Louisiana Militia
Berry, Andrew	Private	De Clouet's Regiment, Louisiana Militia (See also 44 U.S. Reg't.)
Berry, George C.	Surg.-Mate	10 and 20 Cons. Reg't., La. Mil.
Berry, I.	Private	4 Reg't. (Morgan's), La. Militia (Orig. under Berry, T.)
Berry, Peter	Private	Louisiana War of 1812 (See 1 Batt'n. (Henry's), U. S. Vols. Ref. Card)
Berry, T.	Private	4 Reg't. (Morgan's), La. Militia
Berry, William	Private	Capt. McNair's Co., Mounted Riflemen, La. Militia
Berteaux, Agle	Private	6 Reg't. (Landry's), La. Militia
Berteaux, Jerome	Private	6 Reg't. (Landry's), La. Militia
Berteaux, Joseph	Private	6 Reg't. (Landry's), La. Militia
Berteaux, Jerome	Private	6 Reg't. (Landry's), La. Militia (Orig. under Berteaux, Jerome)
Bertel, Etienne	2 Lieut.	Plauche's Batt'n., La. Militia
Bertelot, Romain	Private	5 Reg't. (La Branche's), La. Mil.
Bertelot, I. P.	Private	7 Reg't. (Le Beuf's), La. Militia
Berteloth, Pre	Private	5 Reg't. (Le Branche's), La. Mil.
Berthelot, Jean Louis	Private	6 Reg't. (Landry's), La. Militia
Bertin, Francois	Private	8 Reg't. (Meriam's), La. Militia (Orig. under Berlin, Francois)
Bertin, Pierre	Private	17, 18 and 19 Cons. Reg't., La. Militia
Bertion, Francois	Private	Capt. Ramsey's Co. Mounted Riflemen, La. Mil.
Bertoaux, Auguste	Private	6 Reg't. (Landry's), La. Militia (Orig. under Berteaux, Agte)
Bertonniere, --	Private	1 Reg't. (Dejan's), La. Mil.
Bertrain, Joseph	Private	6 Reg't. (Landry's), La. Militia (Orig. under Bertaux, Joseph)
Bertram, Francis	Private	Capt. Ramsey's Co., Mounted Riflemen, La. Mil. (Orig. under Bertiom, Francois)

Bertram, R.	Private	2 Reg't. (Cavelier's), La. Mil. (Orig. under Bertran, R.)
Bertran, Antoine	2 Lieut.	2 Reg't. (Cavelier's), La. Mil.
Bertran, Me	Private	2 Reg't. (Cavelier's), La. Mil.
Bertran, R.	Private	2 Reg't. (Cavelier's), La. Mil.
Bertrand, --	Private	Plauche's Batt'n., La. Mil.
Bertrand, Alexander	Private	De Clouet's Reg't., La. Militia
Bertrand, Christoph	Sergeant	De Clouet's Reg't., La. Militia
Bertrand, Christopher	Sergeant	16 Reg't. (Thompson's), La. Mil.
Bertrand, Jaques	Private	De Clouet's Reg't., La. Militia
Bertrand, Jean	Private	De Clouet's Reg't., La. Militia
Bertrand, Joseph	Private	De Clouet's Reg't., La. Militia
Bertrand, Joseph	Fusilier-Pvt.	5 Reg't. (Le Branche's), La. Mil.
Bertus, --	Sgt.-Major	1 Reg't. (DeJan's), La. Mil.
Berwick, Joseph	Sergeant	Baker's Reg't., La. Militia
Berwick, Thomas, Jr.	Private	16 Reg't. (Thompson's), La. Mil.
Berwick, Thomas, Sr.	1 Sergeant	16 Reg't. (Thompson's), La. Mil.
Berwick, William	Private	16 Reg't. (Thompson's), La. Mil.
Berza, August	Private	16 Reg't. (Thompson's), La. Mil.
Besan, James	Private	2 Batt'n. (Peire's), La. Vols. (Orig. under Bensan, James)
Besionet, Jean	Private	8 Reg't. (Meriam's), La. Militia
Besse, Francois	Private	2 Batt'n. (Peire's), La. Vols.
Betsoms, Henry	Private	5 Reg't. (La Branche's), La. Mil.
Betz, William	Private	Capt. Henry's Co. Mounted Riflemen, La. Militia (Orig. under Bates, William)
Bibart, Pierre	Private	Plauche's Batt'n., La. Militia
Bibas, Jn.	Private	1 Reg't. (Dejan's), La. Militia
Bibbs, Edward	Private	10 and 20 Cons. Reg't., La. Mil.
Bichme, Michael	Private	16 Reg't. (Thompson's), La. Mil. (Orig. under Belme, Michael)
Bickel, Tobias	Private	Captain Beale's Co., Riflemen, La. Militia
Bickham, Abner	3 Lieut.	De Clouet's Reg't., La. Militia
Bickham, Benjamin	Private	12 and 13 Cons. Reg't., La. Mil.
Bickham, Francis	Private	12 and 13 Cons. Reg't., La. Mil.
Bickham, James	Private	12 and 13 Cons. Reg't., La. Mil.
Bickham, Thomas	Captain	12 and 13 Cons. Reg't., La. Mil.
Bickham, William	Private	12 and 13 Cons. Reg't., La. Mil.
Bickham, William	Captain	12 and 13 Cons. Reg't., La. Mil.
Bickim, Alexander	3 Lieutenant	De Clouet's Reg't., La. Militia (Orig. under Bickham, Abner)
Bickrum, Lewis	Private	17, 18 and 19 Cons. Reg't., La. Militia (Orig. under Buckram, Lewis)
Biddel, John	Private	De Clouet's Reg't., La. Militia (Orig. under Biddle, John)
Biddle, John	Private	De Clouet's Reg't., La. Militia
Biderman, Henry	1 Lieutenant	16 Reg't. (Thompson's), La. Mil. (Orig. under Bedeman, Henry)
Bidington, Henry	Private	16 Reg't. (Thompson's), La. Mil.
Biemont, Jacob	Artificer	Capt. Chaudurier's Co., Artificers, Ar'ty., La. Vols. (Orig. under Biemont, Jacque)
Biemont, Jacque	Artificer	Capt. Chaudurier's Co., Artificers, Ar'ty., La. Vols.
Biemont, Laurent	Artificer	Capt. Chaudurier's Co., Artificers, Ar'ty., La. Vols. (Orig. under Bremont, Laurent)
Biemont, Pierre	Artificer	Capt. Chaudurier's Co., Artificers, Ar'ty., La. Vols. (Orig. under Biemont, Jacque)
Bienel, Benjamin	1 Lieutenant	5 Reg't. (La Branche) La. Mil. (Orig. under Becnel, Benjamin)
Bienveaw, Michael	Private	1 Batt'n. (Fortier's), La. Mil. (Orig. under Bienvenue, Michelle)
Bienvenn, Celestin	Private	1 Batt'n. (Fortier's), La. Mil. (Orig. under Bienvenue, Celestin)
Bienvenu, A. Devino	Private	4 Reg't. (Morgan's), La. Militia
Bienvenue, --aine	1 Lieutenant	3 Reg't. (de la Ronde's), La. Mil.
Bienvenu, Berthelenne	Private	1 Batt'n. (Fortier's), La. Mil.
Bienvenu, Celestin	Private	1 Batt'n. (Fortier's), La. Mil. (Orig. under Bienvenue, Celestin)
Bienvenu, Firnville	Private	3 Reg't. (de la Ronde's), La. Mil.
Bienvenu, Marcelle	Private	3 Reg't. (de la Ronde's), La. Mil.
Bienvenu, Michel	Private	1 Batt'n. (Fortier's), La. Mil. (Orig. under Bienvenue, Michelle)
Bienvenu, Vileor	2 Lieutenant	3 Reg't. (de la Ronde's), La. Mil.
Bienvenue, Celestin	Private	1 Batt'n. (Fortier's), La. Mil.
Bienvenue, Michelle	Private	1 Batt'n. (Fortier's), La. Mil.
Bienville, Julien	Private	8 Reg't. (Meriam's), La. Mil.
Bigande, Pascal	Private	2 Batt'n. (Peire's), La. Vols. (Orig. under Bignardy, Pascal)
Bigarier, Louis	Private	4 Reg't. (Morgan's), La. Militia
Bige, Joseph C.	Lt.-1 Lt.	2 Batt'n. (Peire's), La. Vols.
Biggs, Eli	Private	Baker's Reg't., La. Mil. (Orig. under Riggs, Eli)
Biggs, William	Captain	Baker's Reg't., La. Mil.
Bigier, John Michael	Private	2 Batt'n. (Peire's), La. Vols. (Orig. under Biziere, Jean Michel)
Bignardy, Pascal	Private	2 Batt'n. (Peire's), La. Vols.
Bigot, Francois	Fusilier-Pvt.	2 Batt'n. (D'Aquin's), La. Mil.
Bihm, Jacob	Private	16 Reg't. (Thompson's), La. Mil.
Bijos, Orsin	Corp.-Pvt.	2 Batt'n. (Peire's), La. Vols. (Orig. under Bijos, Ursin)
Bijos, Ursin	Corp.-Pvt.	2 Batt'n. (Peire's), La. Vols.
Bilk, Hamilton	Private	5 Reg't. (Le Branche's), La. Mil.
Bill, --	Servant	Plauche's Batt'n., La. Militia
Bill, --	Waiter	1 Division (Villere's), La. Mil.
Bill, --	Servant	8 Reg't. (Meriam's), La. Mil.
Bill, Hamilton	Private	5 Reg't. (La Branche's), La. Mil. (Orig. under Bilk, Hamilton)
Bill, Samuel	Private	10 and 20 Cons. Reg't., La. Mil.
Billegas, Joseph	Private	2 Batt'n. (Peire's), La. Vols.
Billenne, T.	1 Sgt.-Sgt.	8 Reg't. (Meriam's), La. Militia
Billey, Jeanpierre	Corporal	Plauche's Batt'n., La. Mil.
Billiau, Salvador	Private	2 Reg't. (Cavelier's), La. Mil. (Orig. under Billiaux, Salvador)
Billiaux, Salvador	Private	2 Reg't. (Cavelier's), La. Mil.
Billigos, Joseph	Private	2 Batt'n. (Peire's), La. Vols. (Orig. under Billegas, Joseph)
Billingas, Joseph	Private	2 Batt'n. (Peire's), La. Vols. (Orig. under Billegas, Joseph)
Billings, William	Private	8 Reg't. (Meriam's), La. Mil.
Billot, --	Private	2 Reg't. (Cavelier's), La. Mil. (Orig. under Bellot, --)
Billot, John	Private	5 Reg't. (La Branche's), La. Mil.
Billot, Pierre	Fusilier-Pvt.	5 Reg't. (La Branche's), La. Mil.
Bills, Abraham	Private	10 and 20 Cons. Reg't., La. Mil.
Bills, Abram	Private	10 and 20 Cons. Reg't., La. Mil. (Orig. under Bills, Abraham)
Bills, John	Captain	10 and 20 Cons. Reg't., La. Mil.
Billy, William	Private	Plauche's Batt'n., La. Mil.
Binitle, Me	Sergeant	2 Reg't. (Cavelier's), La. Mil. (Orig. under Benite, Me)
Bioge, Pierre	Private	3 Reg't. (de la Ronde's), La. Mil.
Birchfield, Frederick	Private	Captain Sprigg's Co., Boatmen, La. Vols.
Bird, Abraham	Private	17, 18 and 19 Const. Reg't., La. Mil.
Bird, Mounce	Private	17, 18 and 19 Consolidated Reg't. La. Mil.
Bird, Stephen	Private	Capt. Young's Co., Mounted Riflemen, La. Mil.
Bird, Thomas	Private	Captain Sprigg's Co., Boatmen, La. Vols.
Biscarre, Pedro Jose	Private	2 Batt'n. (Peire's), La. Vols.
Bise', --	Private	4 Reg't. (Morgan's), La. Mil.
Bisere, Jean Michel	Private	2 Batt'n. (Peire's), La. Vols. (Orig. under Biziere, Jean Michel)
Biset, Francis	Private	17, 18 and 19 Cons. Reg't., La. Mil.
Bishop, Squire	Private	10 and 20 Cons. Reg't., La. Mil.
Bisiere, Jean Michel	Private	2 Batt'n. (Peire's), La. Vols. (Orig. under Biziere, Jean Michel)
Bisoro, Martin	1 Lieut.	2 Reg't. (Cavelier's), La. Mil. (Orig. under Visoro, Martin)
Bisscarrie, Pedro Jose	Private	2 Batt'n. (Peire's), La. Vols. (Orig. under Biscarre, Pedro Jose)
Bister, Francis	Private	De Clouet's Reg't., La. Militia
Bister, Francis, Jr.	Private	De Clouet's Reg't., La. Militia
Bizier, Jean Michel	Private	2 Batt'n. (Peire's), La. Vols. (Orig. under Biziere, Jean Michel)
Biziere, Jean Michel	Private	2 Batt'n. (Peire's), La. Vols.
Bizierre, Jean M.	Private	2 Batt'n. (Peire's), La. Vols. (Orig. under Biziere, Jean Michel)

Name	Rank	Unit
Bizot, Celestin	Musician	1 Batt'n. (Fortier's), La. Mil.
Black, Benjamin	Private	Baker's Reg't., La. Militia
Black, Charles	Private	12 and 13 Cons. Reg't., La. Mil.
Black, John	Private	Capt. Dodge's Co., Mounted Riflemen, La. Militia
Black, John	Private	Capt. Henry's Co., Mounted Riflemen, La. Militia
Black, Joseph	Corporal	17, 18 and 19 Cons. Reg't., La. Mil.
Black, Samuel	Sergeant	17, 18 and 19 Cons. Reg't., La. Mil.
Black, William	Private	Capt. Thomas' Co., La. Militia
Black, William, Sr.	Private	10 and 20 Cons. Reg't., La. Mil.
Black, William, Jr.	Private	10 and 20 Cons. Reg't., La. Mil.
Blackburn, Alexander S.	Private	Capt. Griffith's Co., Mounted Riflemen, La. Vols.
Blackburn, Gabriel	1 Sgt.-Pvt.	Capt. Griffith's Co., Mounted Riflemen, La. Vols.
Blackburn, I.	Private	1 Reg't. (De jan's), La. Militia
Blackburne, Alexander S.	Private	Capt. Griffith's Co. Mounted Riflemen, La. Vols. (Orig. under Blackburn, Alexander S.)
Blackwell, Jesse	Sergeant	Capt. Ashley's Co., Mounted Riflemen, La. Mil. (Blanckwell, Jesse)
Blackwell, Nathan	Private	12 and 13 Cons. Reg't., La. Mil.
Blackwell, W.	Private	4 Reg't. (Morgan's), La. Mil.
Blactot, John	Sergeant	2 Batt'n. (D'Aquin's), La. Mil.
Blai, Henri	Private	11 Reg't. (Hickey's), La. Mil.
Blaise, --	Servant	Gov. Claiborne and Staff, La. Militia
Blaise, --	Private	2 Batt'n. (D'Aquin's), La. Mil.
Blaise, Julian	Private	16 Reg't. (Thompson's), La. Mil.
Blaisse, Julien	Private	16 Reg't. (Thompson's), La. Mil. (Orig. under Blaise, Julian)
Blake, William	Private	8 Reg't. (Meriam's), La. Mil.
Blakeley, William	Private	10 and 20 Cons. Reg't., La. Mil.
Blakely, William	Private	10 and 20 Cons. Reg't., La. Mil. (Orig. under Blakeley, William)
Blanc, F. A.	Captain	Aid de Camp, General and Staff (Labatut), Louisiana Militia
Blanc, Louis	Private	10 and 20 Cons. Reg't., La. Mil.
Blanc, P.	Private	Baker's Reg't., La. Mil. (Orig. under Le Blanc, Peer)
Blanc, Savinin	Private	Capt. Alpuente's, La. Militia
Blanca, Joseph	Private	2 Batt'n. (Peire's), La. Vols. (Orig. under Blanco, Joseph)
Blancard, --	Private	2 Reg't. (Cavelier's), La. Mil.
Blanchard, --	Private	Plauche's Batt'n., La. Militia
Blanchard, B.	Private	Plauche's Batt'n., La. Militia (Orig. under Blanchard, --)
Blanchard, Edward	Private	8 Reg't. (Meriam's), La. Militia
Blanchard, Elie	Private	7 Reg't. (Le Beuf's), La. Militia
Blanchard, Elie D.	Private	7 Reg't. (Le Beuf's), La. Militia
Blanchard, Etienne	Private	7 Reg't. (Le Beuf's), La. Militia
Blanchard, Firmin	Private	Captain Hubbard's Mounted Co., La. Militia
Blanchard, Firmin	Private	7 Reg't. (Le Beuf's), La. Militia
Blanchard, Fred	Private	De Clouet's Reg't. La. Militia
Blanchard, I.	Major	6 Reg't. (Landry's), La. Mil.
Blanchard, I. C.	Private	7 Reg't. (Le Beuf's), La. Militia
Blanchard, J. pere	Private	8 Reg't. (Meriam's), La. Militia
Blanchard, Jean	Private	1 Batt'n. (Fortier's), La. Militia
Blanchard, Jean	Private	7 Reg't. (Le Beuf's), La. Militia
Blanchard, Jean C.	Private	7 Reg't. (Le Beuf's), La. Militia
Blanchard, Jerome	Private	8 Reg't. (Meriam's), La. Militia
Blanchard, Joseph	Private	6 Reg't. (Landry's), La. Militia
Blanchard, Joseph	Private	6 Reg't. (Landry's), La. Militia
Blanchard, Joseph	Private	8 Reg't. (Meriam's), La. Militia
Blanchard, Jque	Private	8 Reg't. (Meriam's), La. Militia
Blanchard, Louis	Corporal	7 Reg't. (Le Beuf's), La. Militia
Blanchard, M.	Private	8 Reg't. (Meriam's), La. Militia
Blanchard, P.	Private	8 Reg't. (Meriam's), La. Militia
Blanchard, Peter pere	Private	8 Reg't. (Meriam's), La. Militia
Blanchard, Pierre	Private	6 Reg't. (Landry's), La. Militia
Blanchard, Victor	Private	8 Reg't. (Meriam's), La. Militia
Blanchard, William	1 Lieut.	Captain Sprigg's Co., Boatmen, Vols.
Blanchard, Z.	Private	8 Reg't. (Meriam's), La. Militia
Blanchet, A.	Private	1 Reg't. (DeJan's), La. Mil.
Blanchette, Oliver	Private	Baker's Reg't., La. Militia
Blanckwell, Jesse	Sergeant	Captain Ashley's Co., Mounted Riflemen, La. Militia
Blanco, Fs.	Private	2 Reg't. (Cavelier's), La. Mil.
Blanco, Joseph	Private	2 Batt'n. (Peire's), La. Vols.
Blancon, Louis	Private	10 and 20 Cons. Reg't., La. Mil. (Orig. under Blanc, Louis)
Blancq, Pre	Private	1 Reg't. (Dejan), La. Militia
Bland, John B.	Private	Captain McNair's Co., Mounted Riflemen, La. Mil.
Bland, Peyton	Sergeant	Baker's Reg't., La. Militia
Blandin, Jean	Private	Baker's Reg't., La. Militia
Blane, Louis	Private	10 and 20 Cons. Reg't., La. Mil. (Orig. under Blanc, Louis)
Blangard, --	Private	2 Reg't. (Cavelier's), La. Mil. (Orig. under Blancard, --)
Blanigan, Peter	Private	2 Batt'n. (Peire's), La. Vols.
Blaudine, Maurice	Private	De Clouet's Reg't., La. Militia
Blaunt, I. W.	Corporal	8 Reg't. (Meriam's), La. Militia
Blevings, William	Private	Captain Ogden's Co., Dragoons, La. Militia
Bleze, Lorenzo	Private	2 Batt'n. (Peire's), La. Vols. (Orig. under Blezo, Lorenzo)
Blezo, Lorenzo	Private	2 Batt'n. (Peire's), La. Vols.
Blizo, Laurzo	Private	2 Batt'n. (Peire's), La. Vols. (Orig. under Blezo, Lorenzo)
Block, John	Private	10 and 20 Cons. Reg't., La. Mil.
Blacker, Michael	Private	10 and 20 Cons. Reg't., La. Mil.
Blondin, Valiere	Private	1 Batt'n. (Fortier's), La. Militia
Bloodsworth, Franklin I.	Major	17, 18 and 19 Cons. Reg't., La. Militia
Bloodsworth, James	Colonel	17, 18 and 19 Cons. Reg't., La. Militia
Bloodworth, F. I.	Major	17, 18 and 19 Cons. Reg't., La. Mil. (Orig. under Bloodsworth, Franklin I.)
Bloodworth, James	Colonel	17, 18 and 19 Cons. Reg't., La. Mil. (Orig. under Bloodsworth, James)
Blouin, Augustin	2 Lieut.	De Clouet's Reg't., La. Militia
Blouin, Charles	Private	De Clouet's Reg't., La. Militia
Blouin, Daniel	Private	6 Reg't. (Landry's), La. Militia
Blouin, Evariste	Private	6 Reg't. (Landry's), La. Militia
Blouin, Hyacinthe	Private	De Clouet's Reg't., La. Militia
Blouin, Zenon	Private	6 Reg't. (Landry's), La. Militia
Blount, Elias	Private	10 and 20 Cons. Reg't., La. Mil. (Orig. under Blunt, Elias)
Blount, William	Sergeant	10 and 20 Cons. Reg't., La. Mil.
Bludsworth, Milton	2 Lieut.	17, 18 and 19 Cons. Reg't., La. Mil.
Bludworth, Franklin I.	Major	17, 18 and 19 Cons. Reg't., La. Mil. (Orig. under Bloodsworth, Franklin I.)
Bludworth, James	Colonel	17, 18 and 19 Cons. Reg't., La. Mil. (Orig. under Bloodsworth, James)
Blumpee, William	Private	De Clouet's Reg't., La. Militia
Blundle, William	Private	17, 18 and 19 Cons. Reg't., La. Mil.
Blunt, Elias	Private	10 and 20 Cons. Reg't., La. Mil.
Blunt, William	Sergeant	10 and 20 Cons. Reg't., La. Mil. (Orig. under Blount, William)
Blutaud, Peter	Private	2 Batt'n. (Peire's), La. Vols. (Orig. under Bluteaud, Pierre)
Bluteau, Pierre	Private	2 Batt'n. (Peire's), La. Vols. (Orig. under Bluteaud, Pierre)
Bluteaud, Pierre	Private	2 Batt'n. (Peire's), La. Vols.
Blutrand, Pierre	Private	2 Batt'n. (Peire's), La. Vols. (Orig. under Bluteand, Pierre)
Bob, --	Servant	Baker's Reg't., La. Militia
Bob, --	Officer's Serv.	De Clouet's Reg't., La. Militia
Bob, --	Servant	De Clouet's Reg't., La. Militia
Bocfrun, Julien	Private	De Clouet's Reg't., La. Militia (Orig. under Boucquin, Julian)
Bode, Henry	Private	5 Reg't. (La Branche's), La. Mil.
Bodoin, Alfonce	Private	Baker's Reg't., La. Militia
Bodoin, Gregoir	Private	De Clouet's Reg't., La. Militia
Bodoin, Salvadore	Private	De Clouet's Reg't., La. Militia
Bodreau, Joseph	Private	De Clouet's Reg't., La. Militia
Bodro, Semmonet	Private	16 Reg't. (Thompson's), La. Mil.
Bodry, Francis	Private	Capt. Dodge's Co., Mounted Riflemen, La. Militia

Name	Rank	Unit
Bodry, Francis	Private	Capt. Henry's Co., Mounted Riflemen, La. Militia
Bodwine, Salvadore	Private	De Clouet's Reg't., La. Militia (Orig. under Bedoin, Salvadore)
Bogan, John	Private	Capt. Thomas' Co., La. Militia
Bogan, Samuel	Private	10 and 20 Cons. Reg't., La. Mil.
Bogar, Samuel	Private	10 and 20 Cons. Reg't., La. Mil. (Orig. under Bogan, Samuel)
Bogard, Samuel	Private	17, 18 and 19 Cons. Reg't., La. Militia (Orig. under Boggard, Samuel)
Boges, Joseph	Private	Capt. Dodge's Co., Mounted Riflemen, La. Mil. (Orig. under Boyes, Joseph)
Boggard, Samuel	Private	17, 18 and 19 Cons. Reg't., La. Militia
Bohannon, George	Corporal	De Clouet's Reg't., La. Militia (Orig. under Bohanon, George)
Bohanon, George	Corporal	De Clouet's Reg't., La. Militia
Boidore, Antoine	Private	1 Batt'n. (Fortier's), La. Militia
Boidorer, Francois	Private	1 Batt'n. (Fortier's), La. Militia
Boidorer, Regisse	Private	1 Batt'n. (Fortier's), La. Militia
Boie, Gregoria, Jolie	Private	7 Reg't., (Le Beuf's), La. Mil.
Boifontaine, Baron	Private	Capt. Chauveau's Co., Cavalry, La. Militia
Boiris,	Corporal	2 Reg't. (Cavelier's), La. Mil.
Bois, Alexandre	Private	De Clouet's Reg't., La. Militia
Boisblanc, --	Private	1 Reg't. (Dejan's), La. Mil.
Boisdore, Francois	Private	1 Batt'n. (Fortier's), La. Militia (Orig. under Boidorer, Francois)
Boisdore, Regisse	Private	1 Batt'n. (Fortier's), La. Militia (Orig. under Boidorer, Regisse)
Boisdore', Valery	Sergeant	4 Reg't. (Morgan's), La. Militia
Boissie, Jean, Bte	Private	8 Reg't. (Meriam's), La. Militia
Boistelanc, --	Private	1 Reg't. (De jan's), La. Militia (Orig. under Boisblanc, --)
Boivin, Pierre	Private	1 Batt'n. (Fortier's), La. Militia
Bolan, Eli	Private	De Clouet's Reg't., La. Militia
Boland, Eli	Private	De Clouet's Reg't., La. Militia (Orig. under Bolan, Eli)
Bolduc, Pierre	Private	Capt. Dodge's Co., Mounted Riflemen, La. Militia
Bolduc, Pierre	Private	Capt. Henry's Co., Mounted Riflemen, La. Militia
Boldue, Pierre	Private	Capt. Dodge's Co., Mounted Riflemen, La. Mil. (Orig. under Bolduc, Pierre)
Boler, Peter	Sergeant	Captain Musick's Co., Mounted Riflemen, La. Militia
Boler, Peter	Sergeant	Capt. Musick's Co., La. Militia
Bolew, Charles	Corporal	10 and 20 Cons. Reg't., La. Mil. (Orig. under Ballew, Charles)
Bolian, Charles	Private	16 Reg't. (Thompson's), La. Mil.
Bolin, Elin	Private	De Clouet's Reg't., La. Militia (Orig. under Bolan, Eli)
Boling, Christian	Private	10 and 20 Cons. Reg't., La. Mil. (Orig. under Boling, Christopher)
Boling, Christopher	Private	10 and 20 Cons. Reg't., La. Mil.
Boling, William	Private	10 Reg't., Louisiana Militia
Bollen, Eli	Private	De Clouet's Reg't., La. Militia (Orig. under Bolan, Eli)
Bollieu, Gilbert	Private	1 Batt'n. (Fortier's), La. Militia
Bollieu, Jean Baptiste	Private	1 Batt'n. (Fortier's), La. Militia
Bollieu, Lindore	Private	1 Batt'n. (Fortier's), La. Militia
Bollieu, Maurice	Private	1 Batt'n. (Fortier's), La. Militia
Bollieu, Phillippe	Private	1 Batt'n. (Fortier's), La. Militia
Bollon, --	Private	4 Reg't. (Morgan's), La. Militia
Bomgor, Hippolite	Private	2 Batt'n. (Peire's), La. Militia (Orig. under Bourgor, Hipolite)
Bona, Bertelme	Private	Baker's Regiment, Louisiana Mil.
Bonabel, J.	Corporal	2 Reg't. (Cavelier's), La. Mil. (Orig. under Branabel, John)
Bonain, Baptiste	2 Lieut.	De Clouet's Regiment, La. Mil.
Bonain, John Bte	Private	Baker's Reg't., La. Militia
Bonamente, Andre'	Private	Capt. Songy's Co., Marines, La. Vols.
Bonaventure, Michl	Private	Plauche's Batt'n., La. Militia (Orig. under Bonnaventure, Michel)
Bond, Solomon	Private	10 and 20 Cons. Reg't., La. Mil.
Bonds, Solomon	Private	10 and 20 Cons. Reg't., La. Mil. (Orig. under Bond, Solomon)
Bonicar, Isidar	Fusilier-Pvt.	5 Reg't. (La Branche's), La. Mil. (Orig. under Bonnicarre, Isidor)
Bonicard, Jn.	1 Sgt.-Sgt.	5 Reg't. (La Branche's), La. Mil.
		Capt. Dubuclet's Troop, Hussars, La. Vols.
Bonjean, --	Sergeant	2 Reg't. (Cavelier's), La. Mil.
Bonnain, Baptist	2 Lieut.	De Clouet's Reg't., La. Militia (Orig. under Bonain, Baptiste)
Bonnant, B.	Private	4 Reg't. (Morgan's), La. Militia
Bonnant, Pierre	Private	4 Reg't. (Morgan's), La. Militia
Bonnaus, Pre	Private	2 Batt'n. (D'Aquin's), La. Militia
Bonnaventure, Michel	Private	Plauche's Batt'n., La. Militia
Bonne, Baptiste	Private	1 Batt'n. (Fortier's), La. Militia
Bonne, Charles	Private	1 Batt'n. (Fortier's), La. Militia
Bonne, Jacques	Private	1 Batt'n. (Fortier's), La. Militia
Bonne, Maison	Private	Plauche's Batt'n., La. Militia
Bonner, William	Private	17, 18 and 19 Cons. Reg't., La. Militia
Bonner, Henry	Private	17, 18 and 19 Cons. Reg't., La. Militia
Bonnes, Charles	Private	1 Batt'n. (Fortier's), La. Militia (Orig. under Bonne, Charles)
Bonnet, Louis	Fusilier-Pvt.	2 Batt'n. (D'Aquin's), La. Mil.
Bonneval, Alexandre	Sergeant	Plauche's Batt'n., La. Mil.
Bonnicarre, Isidor	Fusilier-Pvt.	5 Reg't. (LaBlanche's), La. Mil.
Bonnier, Bellone	Private	De Clouet's Reg't., La. Militia (Orig. under Bonnin, Belloni)
Bonnignese, Alsender	Artificer	Capt. Chaudurier's Co., Artificers, Art'y., La. Vols. (Orig. under Bonseigneur, Alsendor)
Bonnin, Battice	Private	Baker's Reg't., La. Militia
Bonnin, Belloni	Private	De Clouet's Reg't., La. Militia
Bonnin, Cyrus	Private	Baker's Reg't., La. Militia
Bonnin, Joseph	Private	Baker's Regt., La. Militia
Bonrepos, Charles	Private	Baker's Reg't., La. Militia
Bonrjioit, Francois	Private	Capt. Lagan's Co., La. Vols.
Bonseigneur, Alandor	Private	2 Batt'n. (D'Aquin's), La. Militia
Bonseigneur, Alsendor	Pvt.-Arti.	Capt. Chaudurier's Co., Artificers, Art'y., La. Vols.
Bonseigneur, Detervil	Private	2 Batt'n. (D'Aquin's), La. Mil.
Bonseigneur, Paulin	Private	2 Batt'n. (D'Aquin's), La. Mil.
Bonseigneur, Seser	Private	2 Batt'n. (D'Aquin's), La. Mil.
Bonsigneur, Alsendor	Artificer	Capt. Chaudurier's Co., Artificers, Art'y., La. Vols. (Orig. under Bonseigneur, Alsendor)
Bonvilian, Leufroi	Private	De Clouet's Reg't., La. Militia (Orig. under Bonvillain, Leufroi)
Bonvillain, Jn Bte	Private	Baker's Reg't., La. Mil.
Bonvillain, Leufroi	Private	De Clouet's Reg't., La. Militia
Bood, Henri	Fusilier-Pvt.	5 Reg't. (La Branche's), La. Mil.
Booker, John	Private	10 and 20 Cons. Reg't., La. Mil.
Boon, Needham	Private	19 Reg't., La. Militia
Booulie, Peer	Private	De Clouet's Reg't., La. Militia (Orig. under Beaulier, Pierre)
Boranmier, --	Private	6 Reg't. (Landry's), La. Militia
Borclin, Andre	Artificer	Capt. Chaudurier's Co., Artificers, Art'y., La. Vols. (Orig. under Bordin, Andre)
Bordalon, Louis	Private	17, 18 and 19 Cons. Reg't., La. Mil. (Orig. under Bordelon, Lewis)
Bordela, Valery	1 Lieut.	17, 18 and 19 Cons. Reg't., La. Mil.
Bordelan, Francis	Private	17, 18 and 19 Cons. Reg't., La. Mil. (Orig. under Bordelon, Frasy)
Bordeloin, Francis	Corporal	17, 18 and 19 Cons. Reg't., La. Mil.
Bordelon, Auguste	Private	16 Reg't. (Thompson's), La. Mil.
Bordelon, Celestin	Private	17, 18 and 19 Cons. Reg't., La. Mil.
Bordelon, Frasy	Private	17, 18 and 19 Cons. Reg't., La. Mil.
Bordelon, Hilaire	Private	16 Reg't. (Thompson's), La. Mil.
Bordelon, Joseph	Private	16 Reg't. (Thompson's), La. Mil. (Orig. under Bordelong, Joseph)
Bordelon, Lewis	Private	17, 18 and 19 Cons. Reg't., La. Mil.
Bordelon, Zenon	Private	16 Reg't. (Thompson's), La. Mil. (Orig. under Bordelong, Zenon)
Bordelong, Joseph	Private	16 Reg't. (Thompson's), La. Mil.

Name	Rank	Unit
Bordelong, Michel	Private	16 Reg't. (Thompson's), La. Mil.
Bordelong, Zenon	Private	16 Reg't. (Thompson's), La. Mil.
Bordeugh, David	Private	See also U. S. Artillery, De Clouet's Reg't., La. Mil.
Bordevielle, --	Surgeon	5 Reg't. (La Branche's), La. Mil.
Bordin, Andre	Artificer	Capt. Chaudurier's Co., Artificers, Art'y., La. Vols.
Bordin, Antoine	Artificer	Capt. Chaudurier's Co., Artificers, Art'y., La. Vols. (Orig. under Bordin, Andre)
Bordore, Antoine	Private	1 Batt'n. (Fortier's), La. Militia (Orig. under Boidore, Antoine)
Bordro, Hypolyte	Private	De Clouet's Reg't., La. Militia (Orig. under Boudreau, Hypolite)
Borel, Benjamin	Private	De Clouet's Reg't., La. Militia
Borel, Eugene, Jr.	Private	Baker's Regiment, La. Militia (Orig. under Barrel, Eugene, Jr.)
Borgard, Honore	Private	5 Reg't. (La Branche's), La. Mil.
Borgues, Juan	Private	17, 18 and 19 Cons. Reg't., La. Mil.
Borie, Auguste	Private	8 Reg't. (Meriam's), La. Militia
Borie, H. F.	Private	Captain Beale's Co., Riflemen, La. Militia
Borie, H. T.	Private	Captain Beale's Co., Riflemen, La. Militia (Orig. under Borie, H. F.)
Borie, P. Sully	Private	Capt. Chauveau's Co., Cavalry, La. Militia
Borne, Antoine	Fusilier-Pvt.	5 Reg't. (La Branche's), La. Mil.
Borne, Chrisostome	Fus.-Pvt.	5 Reg't. (La Branche's), La. Mil.
Borne, Drauzin	Fus.-Pvt.	5 Reg't. (La Branche's), La. Mil.
Borne, Jean	Fus.-Pvt.	5 Reg't. (La Branche's), La. Mil.
Borne, Jean father	Fus.-Pvt.	5 Reg't. (La Branche's), La. Mil.
Borne, Siforien	Sergeant	5 Reg't. (La Branche's), La. Mil.
Boroninier, --	Private	6 Reg't. (Landry's), La. Militia (Orig. under Boranmier, --)
Borrel, Eugen	Private	Baker's Regiment, La. Militia
Borrel, Eugene, Jr.	Private	Baker's Regiment, La. Militia
Borrel, Helier	Private	Baker's Regiment, La. Militia
Borrel, Louis	Private	Baker's Regiment, La. Militia
Borrel, Louis	Private	Baker's Regiment, La. Militia
Borrel, Louis	Private	Capt. Colsson's Co., Artillery, La. Vols. (Orig. Borel, Louis)
Borrel, Pierre	Sergeant	Baker's Reg't., La. Mil. (Orig. under Borel, Pierre)
Borrel, Pierre	Sergeant	Baker's Reg't., La. Mil.
Borsenas, Simon	Private	17, 18 and 19 Cons. Reg't., La. Mil.
Borsenes, Simon	Private	17, 18 and 19 Cons. Reg't., La. Mil. (Orig. under Borsenas, Simon)
Bosan, James	Private	2 Batt'n. (Peire's), La. Vols. (Orig. under Bensan, James)
Bosse, Jaimes	Private	Capt. Lagan's, La. Vols. (Orig. under Cosse, Jaime)
Bossie, Antoine	Fusilier-Pvt.	5 Reg't. (La Branche's), La. Mil.
Bossie, Edouard	Fusilier-Pvt.	5 Reg't. (La Branche's), La. Mil.
Bossie, George, fils	Sergeant	5 Reg't. (La Branche's), La. Mil.
Bossie, Justin	Fusilier-Sgt.	5 Reg't. (La Branche's), La. Mil.
Bossie, Maximilion	Fusilier-Pvt.	5 Reg't. (La Branche's), La. Mil.
Bossier, Ceasar	Private	16 Reg't. (Thompson's), La. Mil.
Bossier, Cezair	Private	17, 18 and 19 Cons. Reg't., La. Mil.
Bossier, Dassille	Private	17, 18 and 19 Cons. Reg't., La. Mil.
Bossier, Evariste	Private	17, 18 and 19 Cons. Reg't., La. Mil.
Bossier, Francois	Private	3 Reg't. (de la Ronde's), La. Mil.
Bottlier, Cezair	Private	17, 18 and 19 Cons. Reg't., La. Mil. (Orig. under Bossier, Cezair)
Bottier, Evaristo	Private	17, 18 and 19 Cons. Reg't., La. Mil. (Orig. under Bossier, Evariste)
Boube', --	Private	2 Reg't. (Cavelier's), La. Mil.
Boubortris, F.	Private	2 Reg't. (Cavelier's), La. Mil.
Bouche, Jean	Artificer	Capt. Chaudurier's Co., Artificers, Art'y., La. Vols.
Boucherau, Justin	Fusilier-Pvt.	2 Batt'n. (D'Aquin's), La. Mil.
Boucquin, Julian	Pvt.-Corporal	De Clouet's Reg't., La. Militia
Boudeye, Jean	1 Sgt.-Sgt.	2 Batt'n. (D'Aquin's), La. Mil.
Boudom, Charles	Private	De Clouet's Reg't., La. Militia
Boudousquer, Godefray	Private	Capt. Trudeau's Troop of Horse, La. Mil. (Orig. under Bondousquier, Godefroy)
Boudousquie, N.	Qr. Ms.	5 Reg't. (Le Branche's), La. Mil.
Boudousquie, Zenon	1 Lt.-Capt.	5 Reg't. (Le Branche's), La. Mil.
Boudousquier, Godefroy	Private	Capt. Trudeau's Troop of Horse, La. Mil.
Boudrau, Jerome	Private	8 Reg't. (Meriam's), La. Militia
Bondre, Valenten	Corporal	7 Reg't. (Meriam's), La. Militia (Orig. under Bandro, Valentin)
Bondreau, Blaize	Private	7 Reg't. (Meriam's), La. Militia
Bodreau, Etienne	1 Lieut.	7 Reg't. (Meriam's), La. Militia
Bodreau, Hypolite	Private	De Clouet's Reg't., La. Militia
Boudreau, Jean	Sergeant	De Clouet's Reg't., La. Militia
Boudrean, Jean	Private	7 Reg't. (Le Beuf's), La. Militia
Boudreau, Joseph	Private	De Clouet's Reg't., La. Militia
Boudreau, Lefroy	Private	16 Reg't. (Thompson's), La. Mil.
Boudreau, Lufroy	Private	De Clouet's Reg't., La. Militia
Boudreau, Magloire	Private	7 Reg't. (Le Beuf's), La. Militia
Boudreau, Oliver	Private	De Clouet's Reg't., La. Militia
Boudreau, Paul Marie	Sergeant	7 Reg't. (Le Beuf's), La. Militia (Orig. under Baudrea, Paul Marie)
Boudreau, Philemon	Private	De Clouet's Reg't., La. Militia
Boudro, Auguste	Private	7 Reg't. (Le Beuf's), La. Militia
Boudro, Charles	Private	7 Reg't. (Le Beuf's), La. Militia
Boudro, Felix	Private	7 Reg't. (Le Beuf's), La. Militia (Orig. under Baudro, Felix)
Boudro, Guillom	Private	7 Reg't. (Le Beuf's), La. Militia (Orig. under Baudro, Guillome)
Boudro, I. B.		7 Reg't. (Le Beuf's), La. Militia (Orig. under Baudro, I. B.
Boudro, Jean	Private	7 Reg't. (Le Beuf's), La. Militia
Boudro, Jean	Private	7 Reg't. (Le Beuf's), La. Militia (Orig. under Baudro, Jean)
Boudro, Laurent	Private	7 Reg't. (Le Beuf's), La. Militia (Orig. under Baudro, Laurent)
Boudrou, Loufroi	Private	De Clouet's Reg't., La. Militia (Orig. under Boudreau, Lufroy)
Boudrow, Simeon	Private	De Clouet's Reg't., La. Militia (Orig. under Boudrow, Simon)
Boudrow, Simon	Private	De Clouet's Reg't., La. Militia
Bouffar, Laurent	Private	Plauche's Batt'n., La. Mil.
Bouffard, Laurent	Private	Plauche's Batt'n., La. Mil. (Orig. under Bouffar, Laurent)
Bouffard, Laurent	Private	4 Reg't. (Morgan's), La. Mil.
Bouffart, Laurent	Private	Plauche's Batt'n., La. Mil. (Orig. under Bouffar, Laurent)
Bouffao, Laurent	Private	Plauche's Batt'n., La. Mil. (Orig. under Bouffar, Laurent)
Bougart, Antoine	Private	2 Batt'n. (Peire's), La. Vols. (Orig. under Bouguart, Antoine)
Bougham, Hector	Corporal	12 and 13 Cons. Reg't., La. Mil.
Boughman, Antinie	Private	Capt. Thomas', La. Mil. (Orig. under Brougham, Antonio)
Bougnoi, --	Private	1 Reg't. (De jan's), La. Militia
Bougor, Hippolite	Private	2 Batt'n. (Peire's), La. Vols. (Orig. under Bourgor, Hipolite)
Bouguart, Antoine	Private	2 Batt'n. (Peire's), La. Vols.
Bouie, Archy	Private	De Clouet's, La. Militia
Bouillet, --	Private	Plauche's Batt'n., La. Militia
Bouis, Jean Jacques	Private	3 Reg't. (de la Ronde's), La. Mil.
Bouis, Joseph	Private	3 Reg't. (de la Ronde's), La. Mil.
Bouis, Pierre	Private	3 Reg't. (de la Ronde's), La. Mil.
Boulanger, Antoine	Private	2 Reg't. (Cavelier's), La. Mil.
Boules, James	Private	Capt. Price's Co., La. Militia
Boulet, --	Private	1 Reg't. (De jan's), La. Militia
Boulet, Louis	Private	De Clouet's Reg't., La. Militia
Boulet, Michel	Private	De Clouet's Reg't., La. Militia
Boulevatre, J.	Private	2 Reg't. (Cavelier's), La. Mil.
Bouligny, Louis	Private	3 Reg't. (de la Ronde's), La. Mil.
Bouligny, Ursin	Private	3 Reg't. (de la Ronde's), La. Mil.
Boullemet, Rd	Corporal	Plauche's Batt'n., La. Militia
Boullemet, Rolland	Corporal	Plauche's Batt'n., La. Mil. (Orig. under Boullemet, Rd)
Boulvague, Francois	Sergeant	2 Batt'n. (Peire's), La. Vols. (Orig. under Boulvaque, Francois)
Boulvagues, Francois	Sergeant	2 Batt'n. (Peire's), La. Vols. (Orig. under Boulvaque, Francois)

Name	Rank	Unit
Boulvaque, Francois	Sergeant	2 Batt'n. (Peire's), La. Vols.
Bounard, Pierre	Private	3 Reg't.(de la Ronde's), La. Mil.
Bounis, Pierre	Private	3 Reg't. (de la Ronde's), La. Mil.
Bountea, Isidro	Private	17, 18 and 19 Cons. Reg't., La. Mil.
Bouny, --	Corporal	Plauche's Batt'n., La. Mil.
Bouquart, Antoine	Private	2 Batt'n. (Peire's), La. Vols. (Orig. under Bouguart, Antoine)
Bouquin, J.	Private	De Clouet's Reg't., La. Mil.(Orig. under Boucquin, Julian)
Bourassard, Pierre	Private	2 Batt'n. (Peire's), La. Vols. (Orig. under Bourassare, Pierre)
Bourassare, Pierre	Private	2 Batt'n. (Peire's), La. Vols.
Bourassarre, Pierre	Private	2 Batt'n. (Peire's), La. Vols. (Orig. under Bourassare, Pierre)
Bourbon, Joseph	Private	Capt. Songy's Co., Marines, La. Vols.
Bourch, Hypolite	Private	7 Reg't. (Le Beuf's), La. Militia (Orig. under Bourke, Hypolite)
Bourdalon, -- fils	Private	17, 18 and 19 Cons. Reg't., La. Militia
Bourdelon, -- fils	Private	17, 18 and 19 Cons. Reg't., La. Mil. (Orig. under Bourdalon, -- fils)
Bourdier, Louis	Sergeant	6 Reg't. (Landry's), La. Militia
Bourg, --	Private	Plauche's Batt'n., La. Militia
Bourg, Amant	Private	7 Reg't. (Le Beuf's), La. Militia
Bourg, Auguste	Private	Captain Hubbard's Mounted Company, La. Militia
Bourg, Baptiste fabien	Private	Captain Hubbard's Mounted Company, La. Militia
Bourg, Francois	Private	Captain Hubbard's Mounted Company, La. Militia
Bourg, Hypolite	Private	Captain Hubbard's Mounted Company, La. Militia
Bourg, I.	Private	8 Reg't. (Meriam's), La. Militia
Bourg, I. P.	Private	7 Reg't. (Le Beuf's), La. Militia
Bourg, Jean	Corporal	3 Reg't. (de la Ronde's), La. Mil.
Bourg, John Babtist	Private	De Clouet's Reg't., La. Militia
Bourg, Joseph F.	Private	Captain Hubbard's Mounted Co., La. Militia
Bourg, Louis	Private	Captain Hubbard's Mounted Co., La. Mil.
Bourg, Made'	Private	6 Reg't. (Landry's), La. Militia
Bourg, Madue	Private	6 Reg't. (Landry's), La. Militia (Orig. under Bourg, Made')
Bourg, Marin	Private	7 Reg't. (Le Beuf's), La. Militia
Bourg, Olivier	Private	16 Reg't. (Thompson's), La. Mil.
Bourg, Pierre Marin	Private	Captain Hubbard's Mounted Co., La. Militia
Bourg, Theodore	Private	7 Reg't. (Le Beuf's), La. Militia
Bourgeau, Antoine	1 Lieut.	2 Reg't. (Cavelier's), La. Mil.
Bourgeaux, Valery	Private	7 Reg't. (Le Beuf's), La. Militia
Bourgeois, --	Private	Plauche's Batt'n., La. Militia
Bourgeois, --	Private	4 Reg't. (Morgan's), La. Militia
Bourgeois, --	Surg. Mate	4 Reg't. (Morgan's), La. Militia
Bourgeois, Abraham	Fusilier-Sgt.	5 Reg't. (La Branche's), La. Mil.
Bourgeois, Abraham Nephew	Fusilier-Pvt.	5 Reg't. (La Branche's), La. Mil.
Bourgeois, Andre' fils	Private	8 Reg't. (Meriam's), La. Militia
Bourgeois, Francois	Private	1 Batt'n. (Fortier's), La. Militia
Bourgeois, Joseph	Private	Plauche's Batt'n., La. Militia
Bourgeois, Joseph	Private	7 Reg't. (Le Beuf's), La. Militia (Orig. under Baurgeois, Joseph)
Bourgeois, Valery	Private	7 Reg't. (Le Beuf's), La. Militia (Orig. under Bourgeaux, Valery)
Bourgeois, V. B. P.	Private	7 Reg't. (Le Beuf's), La. Militia
Bourgeoiz, Francois	Private	1 Batt'n. (Fortier's), La. Militia (Orig. under Bourgeois, Francois)
Bourgeous, Edward	Sergeant	6 Reg't. (Landry's), La. Militia (Orig. under Baurgeais, Edward)
Bourgeous, Jean Bte.	Private	6 Reg't. (Landry's), La. Militia (Orig. under Baurgais, Jean Bte)
Bourgeous, Joseph	Private	6 Reg't. (Landry's), La. Militia (Orig. under Baurgeais, Joseph)
Bourgeous, J. R.	Private	6 Reg't. (Landry's), La. Militia (Orig. under Baurgeois, Jean Restival)
Bourgeous, L.	Private	6 Reg't. (Landry's), La. Militia (Orig. under Baurgeois, J. Ls)
Bourgeous, M.	Private	6 Reg't. (Landry's), La. Militia (Orig. under Baurgeois, M.)
Bourgeous, Paul	Private	6 Reg't. (Landry's), La. Militia (Orig. under Baurfeais, Paul)
Bourgeous, Paul A.	Private	6 Reg't. (Landry's), La. Militia (Orig. under Baurgeous,Paul A.)
Bourgeous, Pierre	Corporal	6 Reg't. (Landry's), La. Militia (Orig. under Bauregeais, Pierre)
Bourgeous, S. A.	Private	6 Reg't. (Landry's), La. Militia (Orig. under Baurgeois, St. Armand)
Bourgeous, Timon	Private	6 Reg't. (Landry's), La. Militia (Orig. under Baurgeais, Timon)
Bourgeuis, Olivier	Private	6 Reg't. (Landry's), La. Militia (Orig. under Baurgeois, Olivier)
Bourglois, Abrahm	Fusilier-Pvt.	5 Reg't. (La Branche's), La. Mil. (Orig. under Bourgeous, Abraham Nephew)
Bourgne, Charles	Private	7 Reg't. (Le Beuf's), La. Militia
Bourgne, Joseph	Corporal	7 Reg't. (Le Beuf's), La. Militia
Bourgne, Pierre	Private	7 Reg't. (Le Beuf's), La. Militia
Bourgogne, --	Servant	1 Batt'n. (Fortier's), La. Militia
Bourgois, Abraham	Fusilier-Sgt.	5 Reg't. (La Branche's), La. Mil. (Orig. under Bourgeois, Abraham)
Bourgois, Etienne	Private	De Clouet's Reg't., La. Militia (Orig. under Burgois, Etienne)
Bourgor, Hipolite	Private	2 Batt'n. (Peire's), La. Vols.
Bourgue, Paul	Private	Louisiana, War of 1812
Bouria, F co	Private	2 Reg't. (Cavelier's), La. Mil.
Bourjeau, A.	1 Lieut.	2 Reg't. (Cavelier's), La. Mil. (Orig. under Bourgeau, Antoine)
Bourk, Charles	Private	Baker's Regiment, Louisiana Mil.
Bourke, Charles	Private	Baker's Regiment, Louisiana Mil. (Orig. under Bourk, Charles)
Bourke, Charles	Private	De Clouet's Reg't., La. Militia
Bourke, Francois	Private	De Clouet's Reg't., La. Militia
Bourke, Hypolite	Private	7 Reg't. (Le Beuf's), La. Militia
Bourke, John	Private	De Clouet's Reg't., La. Mil.
Bourke, Louis	Private	7 Reg't. (Le Beuf's), La. Militia
Bournos, -- Jr.	Private	Plauche's Batt'n., La. Militia
Bournos, -- Sr.	Private	Plauche's Batt'n., La. Militia
Bourque, Auguste	Private	16 Reg't. (Thompson's), La. Mil.
Bourque, Maurice	Private	6 Reg't. (Landry's), La. Militia (Orig. under Baurque, Maurice)
Bourrassard, Pierre	Private	2 Batt'n. (Peire's), La. Vols. (Orig. under Bourassare, Pierre)
Bourrie, Francois	Pvt.-Cpl.	2 Batt'n. (Peire's), La. Vols. (Orig. under Bourrier, Francois)
Bourriee, Francois	Pvt.-Cpl.	2 Batt'n. (Peire's), La. Vols. (Orig. under Bourrier, Francois)
Bourrier, Francois	Pvt.-Cpl.	2 Batt'n. (Peire's), La. Vols.
Bourtrell, I.	Private	1 Reg't. (De jan's), La. Mil.
Bouis, Francis	Private	Captain Dodge's Co., Mounted Riflemen, La. Mil.
Bouis, Francis	Private	Captain Henry's Co., Mounted Riflemen, La. Mil.
Bouseigneur, Alexander	Private	Capt. Chaudurier's Co., Artificers, Art'y., La. Vols. (Orig. under Bonseigneur, Alsendor)
Bousquet, Nichs	Corporal	2 Reg't. (Cavelier's), La. Mil.
Boussard, Pierre	Private	3 Reg't. (de la Ronde's), La. Mil. (Orig. under Bounard, Pierre)
Boussevang, Alexandre	Private	7 Reg't. (Le Beuf's), La. Mil.
Boute', Antoine	Private	4 Reg't. (Morgan's), La. Mil.
Boute, Charles	Private	Baker's Reg't., La. Mil.
Boute, Francois	Private	Capt. Dubuclet's Troop, Hussars, La. Vols. (Orig. under Boutte, Francois)
Boute, Godefroy	Private	4 Reg't. (Morgan's), La. Militia
Boute, Philip	1 Lieut.	4 Reg't. (Morgan's), La. Militia
Boute, Pierre	Private	Baker's Reg't., La. Mil.
Boute, Zenon	Corporal	Capt. Dubuclet's Troop, Hussars, La. Vols. (Orig. under Boutee, Zenon)
Boureillier, --	Private	Sergt. Hog's Detachment, La. Vols.
Bouten, Joseph	Private	16 Reg't. (Thompson's), La. Mil. (Orig. under Boutin, Joseph)
Bouterllier, --	Private	Sergt. Hog's Det., La. Vols. (Orig. under Bouteiillier, --)
Boutet, Francois	Private	Capt. Dubuclet's Troop, Hussars, La. Vols. (Orig. under Boutte, Francois)

Name	Rank	Unit
Boutet, Zenon	Corporal	Capt. Dubuclet's Troop, Hussars, La. Vols. (Orig. under Boutte, Zenon)
Boutin, Baptiste	Private	16 Reg't. (Thompson's), La. Mil.
Boutin, Bat	Private	16 Reg't. (Thompson's), La. Mil.
Boutin, Jean	Private	16 Reg't. (Thompson's), La. Mil.
Boutin, Joseph	Private	Plauche's Batt'n., La. Mil.
Boutin, Joseph	Private	16 Reg't. (Thompson's), La. Mil.
Boutte, Antoine	Private	De Clouet's Regiment, La. Mil.
Boutte, Baptiste	Sergeant	De Clouet's Regiment, La. Mil.
Boutte', Francois	Private	Capt. Dubuclet's Troop, Hussars, La. Vols.
Boutte, Godefroid	Private	De Clouet's Reg't., La. Militia
Boutte, Philip	1 Lieut.	4 Reg't. (Morgan's), La. Militia (Orig. under Boute, Philip)
Boutte, Tisaphin	Private	De Clouet's Reg't., La. Militia
Boutte, Valcourt	Private	De Clouet's Reg't., La. Militia
Boutte', Zenon	Corporal	Capt. Dubuclet's Troop, Hussars, La. Vols.
Bouvier, Andre	Fusilier-Pvt.	5 Reg't. (La Branche's), La. Mil. (Orig. under Bauvier, Andre)
Bowie, James	Private	17, 18 and 19 Cons. Reg't., La. Mil. (Orig. under Bouyee, James)
Bouvier, Francois	Sergeant	De Clouet's Reg't., La. Militia
Bouvier, Victor	Cpl.-Pvt.	5 Reg't. (La Branche's), La. Mil. (Orig. under Bauvier, Victor)
Bowin, John H.	Private	Captain Sprigg's Co., Boatmen, La. Vols.
Bowique, Leander	Private	16 Reg't. (Thompson's), La. Mil.
Bowles, Evan	Private	Baker's Reg't., La. Mil.
Bowles, John	Private	Captain Sprigg's Co., Boatmen, La. Vols.
Bowles, Robert	Private	17, 18 and 19 Cons. Reg't., La. Militia
Bowles, Thomas	Private	17, 18 and 19 Cons. Reg't., La. Militia
Bowman, Richardson	Private	12 and 13 Consolidated Regiment, Louisiana Militia
Bown, B.	Private	3 Reg't. (de la Ronde's), La. Mil.
Bouyee, James	Private	17, 18 and 19 Cons. Reg't., La. Mil.
Bouyee, Reason	Private	17, 18 and 19 Cons. Reg't., La. Mil.
Bouzan, --	Sergeant	1 Reg't. (Dejan's), La. Militia (Orig. under Rosan, Me)
Boy, Samuel	Private	Capt. Musick's Co., La. Militia
Boyas, Juan	Private	17, 18 and 19 Cons. Reg't., La. Mil.
Boyd, Robert	Private	8 Reg't. (Meriam's), La. Militia
Boyd, Roland	Private	Captain Lodge's Co., Mounted Riflemen, La. Mil.
Boyd, Roland	Private	Captain Henry's Co., Mounted Riflemen, La. Mil.
Boye', --	Private	2 Reg't. (Cavelier's), La. Mil.
Boyea, Joseph	Private	17, 18 and 19 Cons. Reg't., La. Mil.
Boyer, Desiret	Private	7 Reg't. (Le Beuf's), La. Militia
Boyer, Mathiew	Corporal	Captain Lagan's Co., La. Vols.
Boyers, --	Private	2 Batt'n. (D'Aquin's), La. Mil.
Boyes, Joseph	Private	Captain Dodge's Co., Mounted Riflemen, La. Militia
Boyes, Joseph	Private	Captain Henry's Co., Mounted Riflemen, La. Militia
Boyle, James	Private	2 Batt'n. (Peire's), La. Vols.
Boyles, John	Corporal	Captain Rankin's Co., Mounted Riflemen, La. Militia
Boyois, Andre'	Private	8 Reg't. (Meriam's), La. Militia
Boys, Joseph	Private	Captain Henry's Co., Mounted Riflemen, La. Mil. (Orig. under Boyes, Joseph)
Braban, Laville	Fusilier-Pvt.	2 Batt'n. (D'Aquin's), La. Mil.
Brabin, Henry	Private	8 Reg't. (Meriam's), La. Militia (Orig. under Babin, Henry)
Brabo, Hipolito	Private	17, 18 and 19 Cons. Reg't., La. Militia
Bradburn, John D.	3 Lieut.	17, 18 and 19 Cons. Reg't., La. Militia
Bradburn, Richard D.	Private	17, 18 and 19 Cons. Reg't., La. Militia
Bradford, Edmd	1 Lieut.	10 Reg't., Louisiana Militia
Bradford, Nathan	Private	10 and 20 Cons. Reg't., La. Mil.
Bradley, Benjamin	Private	17, 18 and 19 Cons. Reg't., La. Militia
Bradley, Francis	Private	17, 18 and 19 Cons. Reg't., La. Militia
Bradley, James	Private	17, 18 and 19 Cons. Reg't., La. Militia
Bradley, John A.	Private	16 Reg't. (Thompson's), La. Mil.
Bradly, James	Private	12 and 13 Cons. Reg't., La. Mil.
Bradner, Andrew	Private	2 Batt'n. (Peire's), La. Vols.
Bradock, John	Private	12 and 13 Cons. Reg't., La. Mil.
Brady, Coonrod	Private	Capt. Thomas' Co., La. Militia
Brady, James	Corporal	Capt. Price's Co., La. Militia
Braken, Hugh	Private	8 Reg't. (Meriam's), La. Militia
Brakins, Hugh	Private	8 Reg't. (Meriam's), La. Militia (Orig. under Braken, Hugh)
Brampin, Bennette	Private	2 Batt'n. (Peire's), La. Vols.
Brampin, Benite	Private	De Clouet's Reg't., La. Militia (See also 44 U. S. Infantry)
Branabel, John	Corporal	2 Reg't. (Cavelier's), La. Mil.
Brand, Alexander	Private	6 Reg't. (Landry's), La. Militia
Brand, Alexander	Private	8 Reg't. (Meriam's), La. Militia
Brand, Baptiste	Private	De Clouet's Reg't., La. Militia
Brand, Casimire	Private	6 Reg't. (Landry's), La. Militia
Brand, Charles	Private	De Clouet's Reg't., La. Militia
Brand, Edward	Private	6 Reg't. (Landry's), La. Militia
Brand, Emelien	Private	6 Reg't. (Landry's), La. Militia
Brand, Etienne	Private	6 Reg't. (Landry's), La. Militia
Brand, Hyler	Private	7 Reg't. (Le Beuf's), La. Militia
Brand, Hypolite	Sergeant	De Clouet's Reg't., La. Militia
Brand, Hypolite	Private	6 Reg't. (Landry's), La. Militia
Brand, I. Louis	Private	8 Reg't. (Meriam's), La. Militia (Orig. under Parent, I. Ls.)
Brand, Jean Bte	Private	6 Reg't. (Landry's), La. Militia
Brand, Joseph	Private	De Clouet's Reg't., La. Militia
Brand, Joseph	Private	8 Reg't. (Meriam's), La. Militia
Brand, Julien	Private	De Clouet's Reg't., La. Militia
Brand, Lefroy	Private	6 Reg't. (Landry's), La. Militia
Brand, Marcellin	Private	Louisiana, War of 1812
Brand, Michael	Private	6 Reg't. (Landry's), La. Militia
Brand, Olivere	Private	8 Reg't. (Meriam's), La. Militia
Brand, Pierre	Private	6 Reg't. (Landry's), La. Militia
Brand, R.	Corporal	6 Reg't. (Landry's), La. Militia
Brand, Urbain	Private	6 Reg't. (Landry's), La. Militia
Brand, Urcellen	Corporal	De Clouet's Reg't., La. Militia (Orig. under Bruce, Urcelin)
Brand, Valery	Private	8 Reg't. (Meriam's), La. Militia
Brandegee, Jacob	Private	Capt. Beale's Co., Riflemen, La. Militia
Brandegee, John	Corporal	1 Reg't. (Dejan's), La. Militia
Brandon, William	Private	De Clouet's Reg't., La. Militia
Branet, Andre	Private	2 Reg't. (Cavelier's), La. Mil. (Orig. under Brunet, Andre)
Brangier, Donradon	Private	Capt. Chauveau's Co., Cavalry, La. Militia
Braning, Michael	Private	11 Reg't. (Hickey's), La. Mil.
Brannan, George	Private	10 and 20 Cons. Reg't., La. Mil.
Brannan, Thomas	Private	10 and 20 Cons. Reg't., La. Mil.
Branpin, Benette	Private	2 Batt'n. (Peire's), La. Vols. (Orig. under Brampin, Benette)
Brant, Jeremiah	Corporal	De Clouet's Reg't., La. Militia (Orig. under Briant, Jeremiah)
Brant, William	Private	10 and 20 Cons. Reg't., La. Mil. (Orig. under Brent, William)
Brashear, Thomas B.	3 Lieut.	De Clouet's Reg't., La. Militia
Brashears, James	Private	10 and 20 Cons. Reg't., La. Mil.
Brashears, John	Private	Captain Griffith's Co., Mounted Riflemen, La. Vols.
Brashear, Thomas B.	Adjutant	Detachment Field and Staff Officers, 4 Brigade, La. Militia
Brasseux, Alexandre	Private	16 Reg't. (Thompson's), La. Mil.
Bratton, Robert	1 Sgt.-Sgt.	12 and 13 Cons. Reg't., La. Mil.
Braud, A.	Private	8 Reg't. (Meriam's), La. Militia (Orig. under Braud, Alexander)
Braud, Aurelien	Private	De Clouet's Reg't., La. Militia
Braud, C.	Private	8 Reg't. (Meriam's), La. Militia
Braud, Casimire	Private	6 Reg't. (Landry's), La. Militia (Orig. under Brand, Casimire)
Braus, Chs	Sergeant	8 Reg't. (Meriam's), La. Militia
Braud, Eduard	Private	6 Reg't. (Landry's), La. Militia (Orig. under Brand, Eduard)
Braud, Etienne	Private	6 Reg't. (Landry's), La. Militia (Orig. under Brand, Etienne)
Braud, F.	Private	8 Reg't. (Meriam's), La. Militia
Braud, I.	Corporal	8 Reg't. (Meriam's), La. Militia

Name	Rank	Unit
Braud, Joseph	Private	8 Reg't. (Meriam's), La. Militia (Orig. under Brand, Joseph)
Braud, Nabord	Corporal	6 Reg't. (Landry's), La. Militia
Braud, Or	Private	8 Reg't. (Meriam's), La. Militia (Orig. under Brand, Olivere)
Braud, P.	Private	8 Reg't. (Meriam's), La. Militia
Braud, Pierre	Private	8 Reg't. (Meriam's), La. Militia
Braud, R.	Corporal	6 Reg't. (Landry's), La. Militia (Orig. under Brand, R.)
Braud, Raymond	Private	6 Reg't. (Landry's), La. Militia
Braud, Rosd	Private	6 Reg't. (Landry's), La. Militia
Braud, Tlle	Corporal	8 Reg't. (Meriam's), La. Militia
Braud, Urbain	Private	6 Reg't. (Landry's), La. Militia (Orig. under Brand, Urbain)
Braud, Vy.	Private	8 Reg't. (Meriam's), La. Militia (Orig. under Brand, Valery)
Braugier, Louis	Private	Capt. Chauveau's Co., Cavalry, La. Mil.
Brauner, Thomas	Private	17, 18 and 19 Cons. Reg'v., La. Militia
Braux, Allain	Corporal	8 Reg't. (Meriam's), La. Militia (Orig. under Breau, Allain)
Braux, Asene	Private	9 Reg't. (Meriam's), La. Militia (Orig. under Breau, Asese)
Braux, Francois	Private	Capt. Songy's Co., Marines, La. Vols. (Orig. under Breau, Francois)
Braux, Pierre	Private	7 Reg't. (Le Beuf's), La. Militia
Bravat, --	Musician	Plauche's Batt'n., La. Militia
Bravate, --	Musician	Plauche's Batt'n., La. Militia (Orig. under Bravat, --)
Bravo, Ipolito	Private	17, 18 and 19 Cons. Reg't., La. Militia
Brawen, Thomas	Corporal	Captain Collard's Co., La. Mil. (Orig. under Brown, Thomas)
Brazier, Louis	Private	Louisiana, War of 1812
Breading, William	Private	Captain Price's Co., La. Militia
Bready, James	Corporal	Captain Price's Co., La. Militia (Orig. under Brady, James)
Breau, Allain	Corporal	8 Reg't. (Meriam's), La. Militia
Breau, Asene	Private	8 Reg't. (Meriam's), La. Militia
Breau, Charles	Private	7 Reg't. (Le Beuf's), La. Militia
Breau, Felix	Private	8 Reg't. (Meriam's), La. Militia
Breau, Froncois	Private	Capt. Songy's Co., Marines, La. Volunteers
Breau, Henry	Private	8 Reg't. (Meriam's), La. Militia
Breau, I. E.	Private	De Clouet's Reg't., La. Militia (Orig. under Breau, Jos)
Breau, Jos.	Private	De Clouet's Reg't., La. Militia
Breau, Joseph	Private	8 Reg't. (Meriam's), La. Militia
Breau, Joseph	Corporal	8 Reg't. (Meriam's), La. Militia
Breau, Laurent	Private	8 Reg't. (Meriam's), La. Militia
Breau, Louis	Private	8 Reg't. (Meriam's), La. Militia
Breau, Marin	Fusilier-Pvt.	2 Batt'n. (D'Aquin's), La. Mil.
Breau, Michel	Private	8 Reg't. (Meriam's), La. Militia
Breau, Olisernce	Private	8 Reg't. (Meriam's), La. Militia
Breau, Pierre	Private	8 Reg't. (Meriam's), La. Militia
Breau, Pierre	Private	16 Reg't. (Thompson's), La. Mil.
Breau, Urban	Private	8 Reg't. (Meriam's), La. Militia
Breden, Paul	Private	12 and 13 Cons. Reg't., La. Mil. (Orig. under Breden, Paul)
Bredy, Philip	Fusilier-Pvt.	5 Reg't. (La Branche's), La. Mil.
Breed, Avery	Private	12 and 13 Cons. Reg't., La. Mil.
Breeland, John	Private	De Clouet's Reg't., La. Militia (Orig. under Breland, John)
Breedlove, Spencer	Private	19 Regiment, Louisiana Militia
Breland, John	Private	De Clouet's Reg't., La. Militia
Bremont, Laurens Cs	Artificer	Capt. Chaudurier's Co., Artificers, Art'y., La. Vols. (Orig. under Bremont, Laurent)
Bremont, Laurent	Artificer	Capt. Chaudurier's Co., Artificers, Art'y., La. Vols.
Breniack, Simon	Private	12 and 13 Cons. Reg't., La. Mil. (Orig. under Brennack, Simon)
Brennack, Simon	Private	12 and 13 Cons. Reg't., La. Mil.
Brent, William	Private	10 and 20 Cons. Reg't., La. Mil.
Breshears, James	Private	10 and 20 Cons. Reg't., La. Mil. (Orig. under Brashears, James)
Brelet, T.	Corporal	Plauche's Batt'n., La. Militia
Bretel, --	Corporal	Plauche's Batt'n., La. Militia (Orig. under Brelet, T.)
Bretoniere, Rosemond	Private	2 Reg't. (Cavelier's), La. Mil.
Brew, Urclin	Corporal	De Clouet's Reg't., La. Militia (Orig. under Brue, Urcelin)
Brewer, Balaam	Private	De Clouet's Reg't., La. Militia
Brewer, John	Private	Capt. Hughes' Co., Mounted Riflemen, La. Militia
Brewer, Joseph	Private	De Clouet's Reg't., La. Militia
Brewer, Joseph	Private	Captain Ashley's Co., Mounted Riflemen, La. Militia
Brewin, Edmund	Private	De Clouet's Reg't., La. Militia (Orig. under Bruin, Edmund)
Brewster, Smith	Corporal	De Clouet's Reg't., La. Militia
Breyard, Bernard	Private	De Clouet's Reg't., La. Militia
Breze, --	Private	Plauche's Batt'n., La. Militia
Briam, Hardy Sr.	Private	10 and 20 Cons. Reg't., La. Mil. (Orig. under Bryan, Hardy Sr.)
Briant, George	Private	Baker's Reg't., La. Militia
Briant, Jeremiah	Corporal	De Clouet's Reg't., La. Militia
Briant, Jerry	Private	De Clouet's Reg't., La. Militia (Orig. under Brient, Jerry)
Brias, Tousant	Private	1 Reg't. (Dejan's), La. Militia
Brien, Louis	Private	2 Reg't. (Cavelier's), La. Mil.
Brient, Jeramia	Corporal	De Clouet's Reg't., La. Militia (Orig. under Briant, Jeremiah)
Brient, Jerry	Private	De Clouet's Reg't., La. Militia
Briere, --	Private	2 Reg't. (Cavelier's), La. Mil.
Brierre, --	Private	2 Reg't. (Cavelier's), La. Mil. (Orig. under Briere, --)
Brige, --	Private	Plauche's Batt'n., La. Mil. (Orig. under Brese, --)
Briggs, S.	Private	8 Reg't. (Meriam's), La. Militia
Brignack, Francois	Private	16 Reg't. (Thompson's), La. Mil.
Brignoc, Matthew	Private	6 Reg't. (Landry's), La. Mil.
Brignoe, Mathurin	Private	6 Reg't. (Landry's), La. Militia (Orig. under Brignoc, Matthew)
Brimberry, William	Private	17, 18 and 19 Cons. Reg't., La. Militia
Briniac, Alexander	Private	Capt. Thomas' Co., La. Militia
Briniac, Semo	Private	Capt. Thomas' Co., La. Militia
Brinkley, John	Private	12 and 13 Cons. Reg't., La. Mil.
Brinock, Simon	Private	12 and 13 Cons. Reg't., La. Mil. (Orig. under Brennack, Simon)
Brion, Basile	Sergeant	1 Batt'n. (Fortier's), La. Militia (Orig. under Brions, Basile)
Brions, Basile	Sergeant	1 Batt'n. (Fortier's), La. Militia
Brisson, --	Private	2 Reg't. (Cavelier's), La. Mil.
Brisson, Joseph	Private	De Clouet's Reg't., La. Militia
Brize, --	Private	Plauche's Batt'n., La. Mil. (Orig. under Breze, --)
Brocar, Cheris	Artificer	Capt. Chaudurier's Co., Artificers, Art'y., La. Vols. (Orig. under Brocard, Cheris)
Brocard, Cheris	Artificer	Capt. Chaudurier's Co., Artificers, Art'y., La. Vols.
Brocard, Chery	Private	2 Batt'n. (D'Aquin's), La. Mil.
Broccard, Cheris	Artificer	Capt. Chaudurier's Co., Artificers, Art'y., La. Vols. (Orig. under Brocard, Cheris)
Brodrick, Adam	Private	De Clouet's Reg't., La. Militia
Brodry, Francis	Private	Capt. Henry's Co., Mounted Riflemen, La. Mil. (Orig. under Bodry, Francis)
Bromfield, Charles	Private	12 and 13 Cons. Reg't., La. Mil. (Orig. under Brumfield, Charles)
Bromfield, Davis	Private	12 and 13 Cons. Reg't., La. Mil. (Orig. under Brumfield, Davis)
Bromfield, Willis	Corporal	12 and 13 Cons. Reg't., La. Mil. (Orig. under Brumfield, Willis)
Bron, --	Corporal	2 Reg't. (Cavelier's), La. Mil.
Brook, Henry Rose	Private	7 Reg't. (Le Beuf's), La. Militia
Brooker, Hardy	Private	10 Reg't., Louisiana Militia
Brooks, Dolphus	Sergeant	Captain Thomas' Co., La. Militia
Brooks, Joseph	Private	12 and 13 Cons. Reg't., La. Mil.
Broshears, James	Private	10 and 20 Cons. Reg't., La. Mil. (Orig. under Brashears, James)
Brossand, Peter	Private	2 Batt'n. (Peire's), La. Vols.
Brossand, Peter	Private	2 Batt'n. (Peire's), La. Vols. (Orig. under Bourassare, Pierre)
Brosset, Athanas	Corporal	17, 18 and 19 Cons. Reg't., La. Militia
Brosset, John B.	Private	17, 18 and 19 Cons. Reg't., La. Militia
Brosset, Philippe	Private	17, 18 and 19 Cons. Reg't., La. Militia

Name	Rank	Unit
Brosset, Pierre	Private	17, 18 and 19 Cons. Reg't., La. Militia
Brou, Jacques	Fusilier-Pvt.	5 Reg't. (La Branche's), La. Mil. (Orig. under Brous, Jacques)
Brouart, Antaine	Private	2 Batt'n. (Peire's), La. Vols. (Orig. under Bouguart, Antoine)
Broudrau, Jerome	Private	8 Reg't. (Meriam's), La. Militia (Orig. under Boudrau, Jerome)
Brouet, --	Private	Plauche's Batt'n., La. Militia
Brougham, Antonio	Private	Captain Thomas' Co., La. Mil.
Brousard, Alexander	Private	Baker's Regiment, La. Militia
Brousard, Armand	Private	Baker's Regiment, La. Militia
Brousard, Edward	Private	Baker's Regiment, La. Militia
Brousard, Edward Jr.	Private	Baker's Regiment, La. Militia
Brousard, Eloy	Corporal	Baker's Reg't., La. Mil. (Orig. under Broussard, Elroy)
Brousard, Eusant	Corporal	De Clouet's Reg't., La. Militia (Orig. under Broussard, Ursin)
Brousard, I.	Private	De Clouet's Reg't., La. Militia (Orig. under Broussard, Isidore)
Brousard, Joseph	Private	De Clouet's Reg't., La. Militia (Orig. under Broussard, Joseph)
Brousard, Louis	Private	Baker's Regiment, La. Militia
Brousard, Raphial	Private	Baker's Regiment, La. Militia
Broussard, Alexander	Private	Baker's Regiment, La. Militia (Orig. under Brousard, Alexander)
Broussard, Armand	Private	Baker's Regiment, La. Militia (Orig. under Brousard, Armand)
Broussard, Collin	Private	16 Reg't. (Thompson's), La. Mil.
Brossard, Collin	Private	16 Reg't. (Thompson's), La. Mil. (Orig. under Broussard, Collin)
Broussard, Dominique	Private	7 Reg't. (Le Beuf's), La. Militia
Broussard, Edward	Corporal	Baker's Regiment, La. Militia
Broussard, Edward	Private	Baker's Reg't., La. Mil. (Orig. under Brousard, Edward)
Broussard, Edward Jr.	Private	Baker's Reg't., La. Mil. (Orig. under Brosard, Edward Jr.)
Broussard, Edward	Private	De Clouet's Reg't., La. Militia
Broussard, Eloi	Private	De Clouet's Reg't., La. Militia
Broussard, Eloi	Corporal	De Clouet's Reg't., La. Militia
Broussard, Eloi	Private	16 Reg't. (Thompson's), La. Mil.
Broussard, Elroy	Corporal	Baker's Regiment, La. Militia
Broussard, Firmin	Private	8 Reg't. (Meriam's), La. Militia
Broussard, Francois	Private	De Clouet's Reg't., La. Militia
Broussard, Isadore	Private	De Clouet's Reg't., La. Militia
Broussard, Isidore	Private	De Clouet's Reg't., La. Militia
Broussard, Jean Olidon	Private	De Clouet's Reg't., La. Militia
Broussard, John	Corporal	De Clouet's Reg't., La. Militia
Broussard, John	Private	De Clouet's Reg't., La. Militia
Broussard, J. Oliver	Private	De Clouet's Reg't., La. Militia (Orig. under Broussard, Jean Olidon)
Broussard, Eloi Joseph	Private	Baker's Regiment, La. Militia
Broussard, Joseph	Private	De Clouet's Reg't., La. Militia
Broussard, L.	Private	8 Reg't. (Meriam's), La. Militia
Broussard, Louis	Private	Baker's Regiment, La. Militia
Broussard, Louis	Private	Baker's Regiment, La. Militia (Orig. under Brousard, Louis)
Broussard, Louis	Private	De Clouet's Reg't., La. Militia
Broussard, Pierre	Private	8 Reg't. (Meriam's), La. Militia
Broussard, Pierro	Private	De Clouet's Reg't., La. Militia
Broussard, Pirre	Private	Baker's Regiment, La. Militia
Broussard, Raphiell	Private	Baker's Regiment, La. Militia (Orig. under Broussard, Raphial)
Broussard, Simon	Private	8 Reg't. (Meriam's), La. Militia
Broussard, Sloi I.	Private	Baker's Regiment, La. Militia (Orig. under Broussard, Eloi Joseph)
Broussard, Ursin	Corporal	De Clouet's Regiment, La. Mil.
Broussard, Vallery	Private	De Clouet's Regiment, La. Mil.
Brousse, John	Private	1 Reg't. (De jan's), La. Militia
Broussean, --	Private	Plauche's Batt'n., La. Militia
Brousseau, Peter	Corporal	2 Reg't. (Cavelier's), La. Mil.
Broutin, Norbert	Private	2 Reg't. (Cavelier's), La. Mil.
Broux, Ambroise	Corporal	5 Reg't. (Le Branche's), La. Mil.
Broux, Jacques	Fusilier-Pvt.	5 Reg't. (Le Branche's), La. Mil.
Broux, Joseph	Fusilier-Pvt.	5 Reg't. (Le Branche's), La. Mil.
Browin, Thomas	Private	8 Reg't. (Meriam's), La. Militia
Brown, --	Private	1 Reg't. (De jan's), La. Militia
Brown, Absalum	Private	17, 18 & 18 Cons. Reg't., La. Mil.
Brown, Benjamin H.	1 Lieut.	De Clouet's Reg't., La. Militia
Brown, Burr	Sergeant	Captain Ashley's Co., Mounted Riflemen, La. Militia
Brown, Gregory	Private	Captain Thomas' Co., La. Militia
Brown, Gregory	Private	12 and 13 Cons. Reg't., La. Mil.
Brown, Henry	Private	Captain Musick's Co., Mounted Riflemen, La. Militia
Brown, Hiram	Private	Captain Beale's Co., Riflemen, La. Militia
Brown, Isaac	Private	De Clouet's Reg't., La. Militia
Brown, James	Drummer	De Clouet's Reg't., La. Militia
Brown, James	Private	10 and 20 Cons. Reg't., La. Mil.
Brown, James	Private	10 and 20 Cons. Reg't., La. Mil.
Brown, James	Private	17, 18 and 19 Cons. Reg't., La. Militia
Brown, John	Private	10 and 20 Cons. Reg't., La. Mil.
Brown, Joseph	Private	Captain Wallace's Co., Boatmen, La. Vols.
Brown, Joseph	Private	10 and 20 Cons. Reg't., La. Mil.
Brown, Joseph	Private	17, 18 and 19 Cons. Reg't., La. Militia
Brown, Josiah	Private	De Clouet's Reg't., La. Militia
Brown, Martin R.	Sergeant	12 and 13 Cons. Reg't., La. Mil.
Brown, Moses	Private	De Clouet's Reg't., La. Militia
Brown, Nathaniel	Private	4 Reg't. (Morgan's), La. Militia
Brown, N. B.	2 Lieut.	De Clouet's Reg't., La. Militia
Brown, Reddin	2 Lieut.	10 and 20 Cons. Reg't., La. Mil.
Brown, Shepherd	Captain	2 Brigade (McCausland's), La. Militia
Brown, Thomas	Corporal	Captain Collard's Co., La. Militia
Brown, Thomas	Private	De Clouet's Reg't., La. Militia
Brown, Ths.	Private	8 Reg't. (Meriam's), La. Militia
Brown, Thomas	Private	10 and 20 Cons. Reg't., La. Mil.
Brown, Thomas	Private	10 and 20 Cons. Reg't., La. Mil.
Brown, Thomas	Corporal	17, 18 and 19 Cons. Reg't., La. Militia
Brown, William	Private	Captain McNair's Co., Mounted Riflemen, La. Militia
Brown, William	Private	Captain Musick's Co., Mounted Riflemen, La. Militia
Brown, William	Private	Capt. Musick's Co., La. Militia
Brown, William	Sergeant	5 Reg't. (La Branche's), La. Mil.
Brown, William	Private	10 and 20 Cons. Reg't., La. Mil.
Brown, William	Private	17, 18 and 19 Cons. Reg't., La. Militia
Brown, William	2 Lieut.	17, 18 and 19 Cons. Reg't., La. Militia
Brown, William	2 Lieut.	17, 18 and 19 Cons. Reg't., La. Militia
Brown, William	Corporal	17, 18 and 19 Cons. Reg't., La. Militia
Browne, N. B.	2 Lieut.	De Clouet's Reg't., La. Militia (Orig. under Brown, N. B.)
Browne, N. B.	2 Lieut. & Aide de Camp	General and Staff (Morgan), La. Militia
Browning, Isaac	Private	Captain Griffith's Co., Mounted Riflemen, La. Vols.
Browning, John	Private	De Clouet's Reg't., La. Militia
Brownson, Alexander	Private	Plauche's Batt'n., La. Militia
Broyard, Henry	Private	4 Reg't. (Morgan's), La. Militia
Broyard, Gilbert	Private	4 Reg't. (Morgan's), La. Militia
Bru, Fs	Private	1 Reg't. (De jan's), La. Militia
Bruce, James	Sergeant	De Clouet's Reg't., La. Militia
Bruden, Paul	Private	12 and 13 Cons. Reg't., La. Mil.
Brue, Urcelin	Corporal	De Clouet's Reg't., La. Militia
Bruez, --	Private	4 Reg't. (Morgan's), La. Militia
Bruin, Edmund	Private	De Clouet's Reg't., La. Militia
Brule, Camile	Private	1 Reg't. (De jan's), La. Militia (Orig. under Brusle, Camile)
Brulé, Camille	Lieut.	2 Batt'n. (D'A'quin's), La. Mil. (Orig. under Bruslé, Camille)
Brulé, Maximilion	Ensign	1 Batt'n. (Fortier's), La. Mil.
Brulean, P.	Private	Plauche's Batt'n., La. Militia
Bruleau, Prre	Private	Capt. Colsson's Co., Artillery, La. Vols.
Brumfiel, Charles	Private	12 and 13 Cons. Reg't., La. Mil.
Brumfield, Davis	Private	12 and 13 Cons. Reg't., La. Mil.
Brumfield, Ezekiel	Corporal	De Clouet's Reg't., La. Militia
Brumfield, Flemming	Private	12 and 13 Cons. Reg't., La. Mil.
Brumfield, Ridley	Corporal	12 and 13 Cons. Reg't., La. Mil.
Brumfield, Solomon	Sergeant	4 Reg't. (Morgan's), La. Militia
Brumfield, William	Sergeant	12 and 13 Cons. Reg't., La. Mil.
Brumfield, Willis	Corporal	12 and 13 Cons. Reg't., La. Mil.

Name	Rank	Unit
Brumfield, Ezwkiel	Cp.-Pvt.	De Clouet's Reg't., La. Militia (Orig. under Brumfield, Ezekiel)
Brun, --	Private	2 Reg't. (Cavelier's), La. Militia
Brun, Charles	Sergeant	De Clouet's Reg't., La. Militia
Brun, Charles	Private	Capt. Songy's Co., Marines, La. Vols.
Bruna, F. A.	Private	16 Reg't. (Thompson's), La. Mil.
Brunate, Auguste	Private	17, 18 and 19 Cons. Reg't., La. Militia
Brunce, Pierre	Private	2 Batt'n. (Peire's), La. Vols. (Orig. under Brunel, Pierre)
Brune, Charles	Sergeant	De Clouet's Reg't., La. Militia (Orig. under Brun, Charles)
Bruneaux, Joseph	Private	8 Reg't. (Meriam's), La. Militia
Brunel, --	Private	Plauche's Batt'n., La. Militia (Orig. under Brunet, --)
Brunel, Pierre	Private	2 Batt'n. (Peire's), La. Vols.
Bruner, William	Pvt.-Cpl.	4 Reg't. (Morgan's), La. Militia
Brunet, --	Private	Plauche's Batt'n., La. Militia
Brunet, Andre	Private	2 Reg't. (Cavelier's), La. Mil.
Brunet, Auguste	Private	17, 18 and 19 Cons. Reg't., La. Mil. (Orig. under Brunate, Auguste)
Brunet, F.	Private	8 Reg't. (Meriam's), La. Militia
Brunet, Francois	Private	7 Reg't. (Le Beuf's), La. Militia
Brunet, Michel	Private	2 Batt'n. (Peire's), La. Vols.
Brunier, Germain	Private	De Clouet's Reg't., La. Militia
Brunier, Germain L.	Corporal	2 Batt'n. (Peire's), La. Vols.
Bruniez, Germain	Pvt.-Cpl.	2 Batt'n. (Peire's), La. Vols. (Orig. under Brunier, Germain L.)
Brunt, Bienvene	Private	17, 18 and 19 Cons. Reg't., La. Militia
Brunto, Peter	Private	4 Reg't. (Morgan's), La. Militia
Brush, John	Private	Captain Price's Co., La. Militia
Brush, Philippe	Private	De Clouet's Reg't., La. Militia
Brusle, Camile	Private	1 Reg't. (De jan's), La. Militia
Brusle, Camille	Lieut.-3 Lieut.	2 Batt'n. (D'Aquin's), La. Mil.
Brusle, Victor	Fusilier-Pvt.	5 Reg't. (La Branche's), La. Mil.
Brussard, Cola	Private	Baker's Regiment, La. Militia
Brussard, Joseph	Private	16 Reg't. (Thompson's), La. Mil.
Brussard, Ursin	Corporal	De Clouet's Reg't., La. Militia (Orig. under Broussard, Ursin)
Brulteaud, Pierre	Private	2 Batt'n. (Peire's), La. Vols. (Orig. under Bluteaud, Pierre)
Bryan, Christopher	1 Lieut.	Baker's Regiment, La. Militia
Bryan, Hardy, Jr.	Private	10 and 20 Cons. Reg't., La. Mil.
Bryan, Hardy Sr.	Private	10 and 20 Cons. Reg't., La. Mil.
Bryan, Morgan	2 Lieut.	11 Reg't. (Hickey's), La. Militia
Bryan, William	Private	De Clouet's Reg't., La. Militia See also 44 U. S. Infy.
Bryan, William	Private	10 and 20 Cons. Reg't., La. Mil.
Bryant, I.	Corporal	De Clouet's Reg't., La. Militia (Orig. under Briant, Jeremiah)
Bryol, Edmond	Private	6 Reg't. (Landry's), La. Militia
Bryon, Benjamin	Sergeant	8 Reg't. (Meriam's), La. Militia
Buard, John L.	Captain	17, 18 and 19 Cons. Reg't., La. Militia
Buard, Joseph	Corporal	17, 18 and 19 Cons. Reg't., La. Militia
Buard, Onezime	1 Lieut.	17, 18 and 19 Cons. Reg't., La. Militia
Bucker, William	2 Lieut & Paymaster	10 Reg't., Louisiana Militia
Buckram, Lewis	Private	17, 18 and 19 Cons. Reg't., La. Militia
Bucois, --	Sergeant	3 Reg't. (de la Ronde's), La. Mil.
Budreau, Antoine	Private	16 Reg't. (Thompson's), La. Mil.
Buckheart, Joshus H.	2 Lieut.	Captain Mc Nair's Co., Mounted Riflemen, La. Mil. (Orig. under Burkhart, Joshus H.)
Budroe, Antoine	Private	16 Reg't. (Thompson's), La. Mil. (Orig. under Budreau, Antoine)
Budwell, Ezekiel	Private	10 and 20 Cons. Reg't., La. Mil.
Buford, James	Private	Baker's Regiment, La. Militia
Bugnoi, --	Private	1 Reg't. (De jan's), La. Militia (Orig. under Bougnoi, --)
Bugole, I.	Corporal	6 Reg't. (Landry's), La. Militia
Buguoi, Honnore	Corporal	2 Batt'n. (Peire's), La. Vols. (Orig. under Buquoi, Honore)
Buie, Archy	Private	De Clouet's Reg't., La. Militia (Orig. under Bouie, Archy)
Bujac, M.	Private	Plauche's Batt'n., La. Militia
Bujeau, Ursin	Private	16 Reg't. (Thompson's), La. Mil.
Bujo, Ursin	Cpl.-Pvt.	2 Batt'n. (Peire's), La. Vols. (Orig. under Bijos, Ursin)
Bujole, I.	Corporal	6 Reg't. (Landry's), La. Militia (Orig. under Bugole, I.)
Bullet, George	1 Lieut.	Capt. Dodge's Co., Mounted Riflemen, La. Militia
Bullet, George	1 Lieut.	Capt. Henry's Co., Mounted Riflemen, La. Militia
Bullitt, George	1 Lieut.	Capt. Henry's Co., Mounted Riflemen, La. Mil. (Orig. under Bullet, George)
Bullock, James	Private	12 and 13 Cons. Reg't., La. Mil.
Bumstead, Thomas	Private	Capt. Price's Co., La. Mil. (Orig. under Bunstead, Thomas)
Bunch, William	Private	17, 18 and 19 Cons. Reg't., La. Militia
Bundick, Charles	Sergeant	16 Reg't. (Thompson's), La. Mil.
Bundick, Robert	Private	16 Reg't. (Thompson's), La. Mil.
Bungh, John	Private	17, 18 and 19 Cons. Reg't., La. Militia
Bunstead, Thomas	Private	Capt. Price's Co., La. Mil.
Buquet, Louis	Corporal	2 Batt'n. (D'Aquin's), La. Mil.
Buquoi, Honore'	Corporal	2 Batt'n. (Peire's), La. Vols.
Buquoy, Honnore	Corporal	2 Batt'n. (Peire's), La. Vols. (Orig. under Buquoi, Honore)
Bura, Francois Narcisse	Private	3 Reg't. (de la Ronde's), La. Mil.
Bura, Jean Pierre	Private	3 Reg't. (de la Ronde's), La. Mil.
Bura, Joseph fils	Private	3 Reg't. (de la Ronde's), La. Mil.
Bura, Pierre	Private	3 Reg't. (de la Ronde's), La. Mil.
Bura, Pierre Bastien	Private	3 Reg't. (de la Ronde's), La. Mil.
Burat, Jn. Bte.	Private	3 Reg't. (de la Ronde's), La. Mil.
Burbanks, Moois	Private	Captain Collard's Co., La. Mil. (Orig. under Burbanks, Moses)
Burbanks, Moses	Private	Captain Collard's Co., La. Mil.
Burcard, Francois	Private	5 Reg't. (La Branche's), La. Mil.
Burchamps, Stephen	Private	10 and 20 Cons. Reg't., La. Mil. (Orig. under Beecham, Stephen)
Burck, --	Private	4 Reg't. (Morgan's), La. Militia
Burck, Richard	Private	12 and 13 Cons. Reg't., La. Mil.
Burd, Thomas	Private	Captain Sprigg's Co., Boatman, La. Vols. (Orig. under Bird, Thomas)
Burde, John	Private	Capt. Musick's Co., La. Militia
Burel, Valcour	Private	1 Batt'n. (Fortier's), La. Mil.
Burgess, Bazile	Private	10 and 20 Cons. Reg't., La. Mil.
Burgess, William	Corporal	10 and 20 Cons. Reg't., La. Mil.
Burgin, Robert	Private	17, 18 and 19 Cons. Reg't., La. Militia
Burgois, Etienne	Private	De Clouet's Reg't., La. Militia
Burgois, Jean Pierre	Private	De Clouet's Reg't., La. Militia
Burgois, Louis	Private	De Clouet's Reg't., La. Militia
Burir, Jean	Private	Captain Lagan's Co., La. Vols. (Orig. under Rieux, Jean)
Burk, David	Sergeant	Captain Musick's Co., La. Mil.
Burke, Benjamin	Private	De Clouet's Reg't., La. Militia
Burke, Charles	Private	De Clouet's Reg't., La. Militia (Orig. under Bourke, Charles)
Burke, John	Private	De Clouet's Reg't., La. Militia (Orig. under Bourke, John)
Burkhart, Jonathan H.	2 Lieut.	Captain McNair's Co., Mounted Riflemen, La. Mil. (Orig. under Burkhart, Joshua H.)
Burkhart, Joshua H.	2 Lieut.	Captain McNair's Co., Mounted Riflemen, La. Militia
Burkhart, Nicholas S.	Private	Captain McNair's Co., Mounted Riflemen, La. Militia
Burleigh, Robert	Private	16 Reg't. (Thompson's), La. Mil.
Burlson, Aaron	Private	12 and 13 Cons. Reg't., La. Mil.
Burlston, Aaron	Private	12 and 13 Cons. Reg't., La. Mil. (Orig. under Burlson, Aaron)
Burnard, Antoine	Private	2 Batt'n. (Peire's), La. Vols. (Orig. under Bernard, Antoine)
Burnes, George	Private	Capt. Collard's Co., La. Militia (Orig. under Burns, Georges)
Burnes, James	Private	Capt. Dodge's Co., Mounted Riflemen, La. Militia
Burnes, James	Private	Capt. Henry's Co., Mounted Riflemen, La. Militia
Burnes, Robert	Private	Capt. Callaway's Co., Mounted Riflemen, La. Mil. (Orig. under Burns, Robert)

Name	Rank	Unit
Burnet, Dabney	Private	Capt. Collard's Co., La. Militia
Burnet, Richard H.	Private	8 Reg't. (Meriam's), La. Militia
Burnet, Thomas	Cpl.-Sgt.	De Clouet's Reg't., La. Militia
Burney, Abraham	Private	De Clouet's Reg't., La. Militia (Orig. under Berry, Abraham)
Burney, N. N.	Sergeant	17, 18 and 19 Cons. Reg't., La. Militia
Burney, Robert	Private	17, 18 and 19 Cons. Reg't., La. Militia
Burney, Simon	Private	12 and 13 Cons. Reg't., La. Mil.
Burney, William	Private	De Clouet's Reg't., La. Militia
Burnos, --	Corporal	1 Reg't. (Dejan's), La. Militia
Burns, Andrew	Ensign	Capt. Young's Co., Mounted Riflemen, La. Militia (Orig. under Byrnes, Andrew)
Burns, Dennis	Private	16 Reg't. (Thompson's), La. Mil.
Burns, Georges	Private	Capt. Collard's Co., La. Militia
Burns, Robert	Private	Capt. Callaway's Co., Mounted Riflemen, La. Militia
Burnside, R.	Private	1 Reg't. (Dejan's), La. Militia
Buron, Antoine	Private	2 Batt'n. (D'Aquin's), La. Mil.
Burord, Antoine	Private	2 Batt'n. (D'Aquin's), La. Mil. (Orig. under Buron, Antoine)
Burot, Francois	Private	2 Batt'n. (D'Aquin's), La. Mil.
Burquoi, Honore	Corporal	2 Batt'n. (Peire's), La. Vols. (Orig. under Buquoi, Honore)
Burrass, Samuel	Lieut.	Capt. Price's Co., La. Militia
Burrel, Egan	Private	Baker's Reg't., La. Mil. (Orig. under Borrel, Eugen)
Burrel, Hilair	Private	Baker's Reg't., La. Mil. (Orig. under Borrel, Helier)
Burriss, Thomas	Private	De Clouet's Reg't., La. Militia
Burrows, Samuel	Lieut.	Capt. Price's Co., La. Militia (Orig. under Burrass, Samuel)
Burruss, Thomas	Private	De Clouet's Reg't., La. Militia (Orig. under Burriss, Thomas)
Burton, John B.	Private	Bakers Regiment, La. Militia
Burtrelle, I.	Private	1 Reg't. (Dejan's), La. Militia (Orig. under Bourtrell, I.)
Burwell, Benjamin	Private	De Clouet's Reg't., La. Militia (Orig. under Borel, Benjamin)
Bush, Reuben	Private	8 Reg't. (Meriam's), La. Militia
Bushel, James	Private	17, 18 and 19 Cons. Reg't., La. Mil. (Orig. under Bushil, James)
Bushil, James	Private	17, 18 and 19 Cons. Reg't., La. Militia
Butler, Jonathan	Private	10 and 20 Cons. Reg't., La. Mil.
Butler, Joseph	Sergeant	6 Reg't. (Landry's), La. Militia
Butler, Noble	Private	12 and 13 Cons. Reg't., La. Mil.
Butler, Ripton	Private	Captain Sprigg's Co., Boatmen, La. Vols. (Orig. under Butler, Upton)
Butler, Thomas	Private	17, 18 and 18 Cons. Reg't., La. Militia
Butler, Upton	Private	Captain Sprigg's Co., Boatmen, La. Vols.
Buvette, Jean	Private	Captain Lagan's Co., La. Vols. (Orig. under Cuvette, Jean)
Buxton, Alesander	Private	De Clouet's Reg't., La. Militia
Byers, James	Private	10 and 20 Cons. Reg't., La. Mil.
Bynum, Francis	Private	10 and 20 Cons. Reg't., La. Mil.
Bynes, James	Private	10 and 20 Cons. Reg't., La. Mil. (Orig. under Byers, James)
Byrd, Mourice	Private	17, 18 and 19 Cons. Reg't., La. Mil. (Orig. under Bird, Mounce)
Byres, James	Private	10 and 20 Cons. Reg't., La. Mil. (Orig. under Byers, James)
Byrnes, Andrew	Ensign	Capt. Young's Co., Mounted Riflemen, La. Militia
Byrnes, James	Private	Capt. Young's Co., Mounted Riflemen, La. Mil.
Cabaret, Alexandre	1 Lieut.	Capt. Trudeau's Troop of Horse, La. Militia
Cabaret, Jd	Quartermaster	1 Batt'n. (Fortier's), La. Militia
Caberret, Alexa	1 Lieut.	Capt. Trudeau's Troop of Horse, La. Mil. (Orig. under Cabaret, Alexandre)
Cabette, Julien	Private	2 Batt'n. (D'Aquin's), La. Militia
Cable, Jean	Private	6 Reg't. (Landry's), La. Militia
Cabrera, Francisco	Private	2 Batt'n. (Peire's), La. Vols.
Cabrille, I. B.	Private	Capt. Sprigg's Co., Boatmen, La. Vols.
Cachelier, Cadet	Private	2 Batt'n. (D'Aquin's), La. Mil. (Orig. under Bachelier, Cadet)
Cadenas, Manuel	Private	17, 18 and 19 Cons. Reg't., La. Militia
Cadet, --	Corporal	2 Reg't. (Cavelier's), La. Mil.
Cadet, --	Servant	2 Batt'n. (D'Aquin's), La. Mil.
Cadet, Dominique Bado	Private	7 Reg't. (LeBeuf's), La. Militia
Cadey, --	Drummer-Pvt.	7 Reg't. (LeBeuf's), La. Militia (Orig. under Cady, --)
Cadet, Pierre	Private	Louisiana War of 1812
Cadey, Francois	Private	7 Reg't. (Le Beuf's), La. Militia
Cadillan, --	Corporal	1 Reg't. (Dejan's), La. Militia
Cadina, Manuel	Private	17, 18 and 19 Cons. Reg't., La. Militia
Cady, --	Private	6 Reg't. (Landry's), La. Militia
Cady, --	Drummer-Pvt.	7 Reg't. (Le Beuf's), La. Militia
Caeler, Francos	Private	6 Reg't. (Landry's), La. Militia
Caffery, Donnaldson	Private	Baker's Regiment, La. Militia
Cage, Francis	Private	Capt. Thomas' Co., La. Militia
Cagle, Coonrod	Private	10 and 20 Cons. Reg't., La. Mil.
Cahier, I.	Private	8 Reg't. (Meriam's), La. Militia
Caillau, P.	Private	4 Reg't. (Morgan's), La. Militia
Caillaute, Jean Bte.	1 Sgt.-Sgt.	6 Reg't. (Landry's), La. Militia
Caille, Pierre	Private	4 Reg't. (Morgan's), La. Militia
Caillet, Martin	Corporal	De Clouet's Reg't., La. Militia
Caillou, Olivier	Private	Capt. Hubbard's Mounted Co., La. Militia
Caillou, Pierre	Private	Capt. Chauveau's Co. Cav., La. Mil. (Orig. under Cailloux, Pierre)
Caillout, Jean Bte.	1 Sgt.-Sgt.	6 Reg't. (Landry's), La. Militia (Orig. under Caillaute, Jean Bte)
Caillout, Joseph	Private	6 Reg't. (Landry's), La. Militia
Cailloute, Jacque	Private	6 Reg't. (Landry's), La. Militia
Cailloute, Joseph	Private	6 Reg't (Landry's), La. Militia (Orig. under Caillout, Joseph)
Cailloux, Pierre	Private	Capt. Chauveau's Co., Cavalry, La. Militia
Cain, William	Private	10 and 20 Cons. Reg't., La. Mil.
Cainy, Daniel	Private	10 Reg't., Louisiana Militia
Calaham, Joseph	Private	16 Reg't. (Thompson's), La. Mil.
Calahan, James	Private	16 Reg't. (Thompson's), La. Mil. (Orig. under Callagham, James)
Calais, Baptiste	Private	De Clouet's Reg't., La. Militia
Caldwell, John	Sergeant	Capt. Young's Co., Mounted Riflemen, La. Mil.
Caldwell, Patrick	Private	De Clouet's Reg't., La. Militia
Caldwell, Philip	Lt. Colonel	De Clouet's Reg't., La. Militia
Caldwell, Robert	Private	Capt. Dodge's Co., Mounted Riflemen, La. Militia
Caldwell, Robert	Private	Capt. Henry's Co., Mounted Riflemen, La. Militia
Caldwell, Robert	Private	17, 18 and 19 Cons. Reg't., La. Mil.
Calelnay, Thomas	Private	2 Batt'n. (Peire's), La. Vols. (Orig. under Catelnay, Thomas)
Calender, Alexander	Private	10 and 20 Cons. Reg't., La. Mil.
Calender, Stephen	Private	10 and 20 Cons. Reg't., La. Mil. (Orig. under Callender, Stephen)
Call, James	Private	10 and 20 Cons. Reg't., La. Mil.
Callagham, James	Private	16 Reg't. (Thompson's), La. Mil.
Callaghan, Joseph	Private	16 Reg't. (Thompson's), La. Mil. (Orig. under Calaham, Joseph)
Callaway, George	Sergeant	Capt. Callaway's Co., Mounted Riflemen, La. Militia
Callaway, James	Captain	Capt. Callaway's Co., Mounted Riflemen, La. Militia
Callaway, John	Captain	Capt. Callaway's Co., Mounted Riflemen, La. Militia
Callaway, Larkin S.	Sergeant	Capt. Callaway's Co., Mounted Riflemen, La. Militia
Callaway, Peter	Private	Capt. Callaway's Co., Mounted Riflemen, La. Militia
Callender, Alexander	Private	10 and 20 Cons. Reg't., La. Mil. (Orig. under Calender, Alexander)
Callender, Stephen	Private	10 and 20 Cons. Reg't., La. Mil.
Callico, Asa	Private	Capt. Musick's Co., La. Militia
Callin, James	Private	1 Reg't. (Dejan's), La. Militia
Calliway, George	Sergeant	Capt. Callaway's Co., Mounted Riflemen, La. Mil. (Orig. under Callaway, George)

Name	Rank	Unit
Calliway, Peter	Private	Capt. Callaway's Co., Mounted Riflemen, La. Mil. (Orig. under Callaway, Peter)
Calliways, --	Captain	Capt. Callaway's Co., Mounted Riflemen, La. Mil. (Orig. under Callaway, John)
Calloote, John B.	Private	Capt. Van Bibber's Co., La. Mil.
Calloway, Larken	Private	Capt. Collard's Co., La. Militia
Calloway, W.	Private	Captain Sprigg's Co., Boatmen, La. Vols.
Calotate, Pierre	Corporal	3 Reg't. (de la Ronde's), La. Mil.
Caloze, --	Private	2 Batt'n. (D'Aquin's), La. Mil.
Calvin, --	Private	6 Reg't. (Landry's), La. Militia
Camarsac, Martin	Private	16 Reg't. (Thompson's), La. Mil.
Camas, Hubert	Fusilier-Pvt.	5 Reg't. (La Branche's), La. Mil. (Orig. under Camus, Hubert)
Cambelle, N.	Private	8 Reg't. (Meriam's), La. Militia
Cambre, Adam	Fusilier-Pvt.	5 Reg't. (La Branche's), La. Mil.
Cambre, Alexander	Private	5 Reg't. (La Branche's), La. Mil.
Cambre, Antoine	Fusilier-Pvt.	5 Reg't. (La Branche's), La. Mil.
Cambre, Etienne	Fusilier-Pvt.	5 Reg't. (La Branche's), La. Mil.
Cambre, George	Fusilier-Pvt.	5 Reg't. (La Branche's), La. Mil.
Cambre, Leonard	Private	5 Reg't. (La Branche's), La. Mil.
Cambre, Mathieu	Private	5 Reg't. (La Branche's), La. Mil.
Cambre, Matthias	Fusilier-Pvt.	5 Reg't. (La Branche's), La. Mil.
Cambre, Michel	Fusilier-Pvt.	5 Reg't. (La Branche's), La. Mil.
Cameron, John		Capt. Wallace's Co., Boatmen, La. Vols.
Cameron, John	1 Lieut.	10 and 20 Cons. Reg't., La. Mil.
Camille, --	Sergeant	2 Reg't. (Cavelier's), La. Militia
Cammack, Yelverton	Pvt.-Cpl.	10 and 20 Cons. Reg't., La. Mil.
Cammel, Thomas	Private	10 and 20 Cons. Reg't., La. Mil. (Orig. under Campbell, Thomas)
Camonruo, Francoil	2 Lieut.	Captain Lagan's Co., La. Vols. (Original under Lamoureux, Francois)
Camorind, John	Private	Captain Sprigg's Co., Boatmen, La. Vols.
Camp, Caleb	Private	12 and 13 Cons. Reg't., La. Mil.
Camp, Charles	Private	12 and 13 Cons. Reg't., La. Mil.
Camp, Dempsey	Private	12 and 13 Cons. Reg't., La. Mil.
Campain, --	Private	De Clouet's Reg't., La. Militia (Orig. under Champain, --)
Campanell, Bartmy	Sen Musician	1 Batt'n. (Fortier's), La. Militia
Campanella, --	Private	1 Reg't. (Dejan's), La. Mil.
Campbell, Beasley	Private	12 and 13 Cons. Reg't., La. Mil.
Campbell, Allen	Private	Baker's Regiment, La. Militia
Campbell, Benajah	Private	Baker's Regiment, La. Militia
Campbell, Farquar	Private	Baker's Regiment, La. Militia
Campbell, James	Private	12 and 13 Cons. Reg't., La. Mil.
Campbell, James	Corporal	16 Reg't. (Thompson's), La. Mil.
Campbell, James	Private	17, 18 and 19 Cons. Reg't., La. Militia
Campbell, John	Sergeant	De Clouet's Reg't., La. Militia
Campbell, John	Private	10 and 20 Cons. Reg't., La. Mil.
Campbell, John	Private	16 Reg't. (Thompson's), La. Mil.
Campbell, Johnson	Private	Captain Callaway's Co., Mounted Riflemen, La. Militia
Campbell, Martin	Private	Baker's Regiment, La. Militia
Campbell, Nathaniel	Private	16 Reg't. (Thompson's), La. Mil.
Campbell, P.	Private	Baker's Regiment, La. Militia
Campbell, Samuel	Private	10 and 20 Cons. Reg't., La. Mil.
Campbell, Thomas	Private	10 and 20 Cons. Reg't., La. Mil.
Campbell, William	Private	De Clouet's Reg't., La. Militia
Campbell, William	Private	Captain Musick's Co., Mounted Riflemen, La. Militia
Campbell, William	Private	Capt. Musick's Co., La. Militia
Campean, Auguste	Private	7 Reg't. (Le Beuf's), La. Militia (Orig. under Compean, August)
Campean, Joseph	Sergeant	7 Reg't. (Le Beuf's), La. Militia
Campianno, Juan	Private	Captain Lagen's Co., La. Vols.
Campo, Joseph	Private	Louisiana War of 1812
Campos, Jose Maria	Private	2 Batt'n. (Peire's), La. Vols. (See also Barthelemy, Perez)
Campos, Joseph Marie	Private	De Clouet's Reg't., La. Militia
Camps, Joseph	Sergeant	1 Batt'n. (Fortier's), La. Militia
Camre, --	Private	4 Reg't. (Morgan's), La. Militia
Camus, --	Private	Plauche's Batt'n., La. Militia
Camus, Fs.	Sergeant	2 Reg't. (Cavelier's), La. Mil.
Camus, Hubert	Fusilier-Pvt.	5 Reg't. (La Branche's), La. Mil.
Camus, Zenon	Fusilier-Pvt.	5 Reg't. (La Branche's), La. Mil.
Camvens, Chery	Drummer	2 Reg't. (Cavelier's), La. Militia
Can, Richard	Private	10 Regiment, La. Militia
Can, Vincent	Private	10 and 20 Cons. Reg't., La. Mil. (Orig. under Carr, Vincent)
Candole, Andre	Cornet	Captain Hubbard's Mounted Co., La. Militia
Canelas, Fs	Private	1 Reg't. (Dejan's), La. Mil.
Canelle, Esci	Private	8 Reg't. (Meriam's), La. Militia
Canelle, Pierre	Private	De Clouet's Reg't., La. Militia
Canelle, Pierre	Private	1 Batt'n. (Fortier's), La. Militia
Caniler, Constance	Private	Baker's Regiment, La. Militia
Cannelle, Pierre	Private	1 Batt'n. (Fortier's), La. Mil. (Orig. under Canelle, Pierre)
Cannely, William	Private	De Clouet's Reg't., La. Militia (Orig. under Connelly, William)
Canner, Lemuel	1 Lieut.	7 Reg't. (Le Beuf's), La. Militia (Orig. under Tanner, Lemuel)
Cannes, --	Private	Plauche's Batt'n., La. Militia (Orig. under Camus, --)
Cannon, John	Private	17, 18 and 19 Cons. Reg't., La. Militia
Cannon, John M.	Private	17, 18 and 19 Cons. Reg't., La. Mil. (Orig. under Cannon, John)
Canon, --	Private	Plauche's Batt'n., La. Militia
Canteloup, Bernard	Private	2 Batt'n. (Peire's), La. Vols. (Orig. under Canteloupe, Bernard)
Canteloupe, Bernard	Private	2 Batt'n. (Peire's), La. Vols.
Cantero, --	Private	4 Reg't. (Morgan's), La. Militia
Cantrell, Armogene	Private	6 Reg't. (Landry's), La. Militia
Cantrille, A.	Private	6 Reg't. (Landry's), La. Militia (Orig. under Cantrell, Armogene)
Cantrelle, Jacques	Private	6 Reg't. (Landry's), La. Militia
Cantrelle, M. B.	Pvt.-Sgt.	6 Reg't. (Landry's), La. Militia
Cantrelle, Silver	2 Lieut.	6 Reg't. (Landry's), La. Militia
Cantren, Thomas	Private	17, 18 and 19 Cons. Reg't., La.
Canty, Thomas	Private	12 and 13 Cons. Reg't., La. Mil.
Cany, --	Musician	Plauche's Batt'n., La. Militia
Capaho, Juan	Private	2 Batt'n. (Peire's), La. Vols.
Capao, Juan	Private	2 Batt'n. (Peire's), La. Vols. (Orig. under Capaho, Juan)
Capaz, Juan	Private	2 Batt'n. (Peire's), La. Vols. (Orig. under Capaho, Juan)
Capdefert, Ane	Captain	1 Reg't. (Dejan's), La. Militia
Capdeveau, Joseph	Private	2 Reg't. (Cavelier's), La. Mil.
Capdeveille, Ferdinand	Private	8 Reg't. (Meriam's), La. Militia
Capdevielle, --fils	Private	8 Reg't. (Meriam's), La. Militia
Capdeville, Edmond	Private	8 Reg't. (Meriam's), La. Militia
Capdivielle, Joseph	Private	8 Reg't. (Meriam's), La. Militia
Capela, Jose Maria	Private	17, 18 and 19 Cons. Reg't., La. Militia
Capman, Joseph	Private	De Clouet's Reg't., La. Militia (Orig. under Chapman, Joseph)
Caponi, --	Musician	Plauche's Batt'n., La. Militia
Capony, --	Musician	Plauche's Batt'n., La. Militia (Orig. under Caponi, --)
Capor, T. M.	Private	2 Batt'n. (Peire's), La. Vols. (Orig. under Campos, Jose Maria)
Cappel, Charles	1 Lieut.	17, 18 and 19 Cons. Reg't., La. Militia
Cappel, Charles	2 Lieut.	17, 18 and 19 Cons. Reg't., La. Militia
Capucin, Augustin	Private	1 Batt'n. (Fortier's), La. Mil. (Orig. under Calisom, Augustin)
Capusin, Augustin	Private	1 Batt'n. (Fortier's), La. Mil.
Car, C.	Sergeant	1 Reg't. (Dejan's), La. Militia
Car, Laurent	Private	2 Reg't. (Cavelier's), La. Mil. (Orig. under Caro, Laurand)
Carabone, Joseph	Private	Capt. Colsson Co., Art'y., La. Vols. (Orig. under Tarabone, Joseph)
Caraby, Antoine	Private	4 Reg't. (Morgan's), La. Militia
Caraby, Arneaud	Sergeant	4 Reg't. (Morgan's), La. Militia
Caragan, James	Private	De Clouet's Reg't., La. Militia (Orig. under Carragan, James)
Caraghan, James	Private	De Clouet's Reg't., La. Militia (Orig. under Carragan, James)
Caramouse, Hte	Private	6 Reg't. (Landry's), La. Militia
Carantin, Michel	Captain	5 Reg't. (La Branche's), La. Mil.
Carantin, Pierre	Fusilier-Pvt.	5 Reg't. (La Branche's), La. Mil.
Cararail, Antoine	Private	De Clouet's Reg't., La. Militia (Orig. under Charravel, Anthony)
Caravail, Antoine	Private	De Clouet's Reg't., La. Militia (Orig. under Charravel, Anthony)

Name	Rank	Unit
Cardenab, Ignacio	Private	2 Batt'n. (Peire's), La. Vols. (Orig. under Cardenas, Ignacio)
Cardenas, Ignacio	Private	2 Batt'n. (Peire's), La. Vols.
Cardenaz, Ignacio	Private	2 Batt'n. (Peire's), La. Vols. (Orig. under Cardenas, Ignacio)
Cardinas, Ignacio	Private	2 Batt'n. (Peire's), La. Vols. (Orig. under Cardenas, Ignacio)
Cardinaz, Ignacio	Private	2 Batt'n. (Peire's), La. Vols. (Orig. under Cardenas, Ignacio)
Carel, Charles	Captain	3 Reg't. (de la Ronde's), La. Mil.
Carian, --	2 Lieut.	2 Batt'n. (D'Aquin's), La. Militia (Orig. under Casimir, --)
Carian, A.	2 Lieut.	2 Batt'n. (D'Aguin's), La. Militia (Orig. under Carian, --)
Carico, Asa	Private	Captain Musick's Co., Mounted Riflemen, La. Mil.
Cariere, Batiste	Private	17, 18 and 19 Const. Reg't., La. Militia
Carimire, --	Servant	Plauche's Batt'n., La. Militia (Orig. under Casimir, --)
Cario, Gregorio	Private	2 Reg't. (Cavelier's), La. Mil. (Orig. under Caro, Gregorio)
Carles, P.	Private	4 Reg't. (Morgan's), La. Militia
Carlin, Alexis	Private	Baker's Regiment, La. Militia
Carlin, Cadet	Private	Baker's Regiment, La. Militia
Carlin, Celestine	Private	Baker's Regiment, La. Militia
Carlin, Dennis	Private	Baker's Regiment, La. Militia
Carlin, Eugene	Private	4 Reg't. (Morgan's), La. Militia
Carlin, Francois	Private	2 Batt'n. (D'Aquin's), La. Mil. (Orig. under Carlon, Francois)
Carlin, James C.	Private	De Clouet's Reg't., La. Militia
Carlin, John	Private	Capt. Hughes' Co., Mounted Riflemen, La. Militia
Carlin, Lefroy	Private	De Clouet's Reg't., La. Militia
Carlin, Terrance	Private	Baker's Regiment, La. Militia
Carlin, Ursin	Private	Baker's Regiment, La. Militia (Orig. under Carline, Urien)
Carline, Alexis	Private	Baker's Regiment, La. Militia (Orig. under Carlin, Alexis)
Carline, Celestin	Private	Baker's Regiment, La. Militia (Orig. under Carlin, Celestine)
Carline, Dennis	Private	Baker's Regiment, La. Militia (Orig. under Carlin, Dennis)
Carline, Hilair	Private	Baker's Regiment, La. Militia
Carline, Honori	Private	Baker's Regiment, La. Militia
Carline, Terrance	Private	Baker's Regiment, La. Militia (Orig. under Carlin, Terrance)
Carline, Urien	Private	Baker's Regiment, La. Militia
Carlon, Etienne	Private	2 Batt'n. (D'Aquin's), La. Mil.
Carlon, Francois	Private	2 Batt'n. (D'Aquin's), La. Mil.
Carlton, Henry	2 Lieut.	1 Reg't. (Dejan's), La. Militia
Carmona, Jose	Private	17, 18 and 19 Cons. Reg't., La. Mil.
Carmona, Jose	Private	17, 18 and 19 Cons. Reg't., La. Mil.
Carmono, Jose	Private	17, 18 and 19 Cons. Reg't., La. Mil. (Orig. under Carmona, Jose)
Carmouch, Amalien	Private	De Clouet's Reg't., La. Militia (Orig. under Carmouche, Amalien)
Carmouch, Francis	Captain	De Clouet's Reg't., La. Militia (Orig. under Carmouche, Francis)
Carmouche, Amelien	Private	De Clouet's Reg't., La. Militia
Carmouche, Francois	Captain	De Clouet's Reg't., La. Militia
Carnaham, John	Private	17, 18 and 19 Cons. Reg't., La. Mil.
Carnale, Charles	Private	Capt. Van Bibber's Co., La. Mil. (Orig. under Carnole, Charles)
Carnaro, Francis	Private	De Clouet's Reg't., La. Militia
Carnaro, Hiram	Private	De Clouet's Reg't., La. Militia
Carnes, John	Cpl.-Pvt.	Captain Griffith's Co., Mounted Riflemen, La. Vols.
Carney, Hosea	Private	De Clouet's Reg't., La. Militia
Carney, Hugh	Private	De Clouet's Reg't., La. Militia
Carney, John	Private	Captain Griffith's Co., Mounted Riflemen, La. Vols.
Carney, John G.	Private	Captain Griffith's Co., Mounted Riflemen, La. Vols.
Carnole, Charles	Private	Capt. Van Bibber's Co., La. Mil.
Carny, Hosea	Private	De Clouet's Reg't., La. Militia (Orig. under Carney, Hosea)
Caro, Gregorio	Private	2 Reg't. (Cavelier's), La. Militia
Caro, Hyacinth	Artificer	Capt. Chaudurier's Co., Artificers, Art'y. La. Vols. (Orig. under Caro, Yacint)
Caro, Iyasente	Artificer	Capt. Chaudurier's Co., Artificers, Art'y. La. Vols. (Orig. under Caro, Yacint)
Caro, Joichem	Private	2 Reg't. (Cavelier's), La. Mil.
Caro, Laurand	Private	2 Reg't. (Cavelier's), La. Mil.
Caro, Yacint	Artificer	Capt. Chaudurier's Co., Artificers, Art'y. La. Vols.
Caron, Joseph	Private	16 Reg't. (Thompson's), La. Mil. (Orig. under Carron, Joseph)
Carpela, Jose Maria	Private	17, 18 and 19 Cons. Reg't., La. Mil.
Carpelo, Jose Maria	Private	17, 18 and 19 Cons. Reg't., La. Mil. (Orig. under Carpela, Jose Maria)
Carpenter, Lawrence	Private	De Clouet's Reg't., La. Militia
Carpenter, Michail	Private	Baker's Regiment, La. Militia
Carpenter, Samuel	Private	De Clouet's Reg't., La. Militia
Carpentere, Joseph	Private	2 Batt'n. (Peire's), La. Vols. (Orig. under Carpintero, Joseph)
Carpentero, Joseph	Private	2 Batt'n. (Peire's), La. Vols. (Orig. under Carpintero, Joseph)
Carpinter, Joseph	Private	2 Batt'n. (Peire's), La. Vols. (Orig. under Carpintero, Joseph)
Carpintero, Joseph	Private	2 Batt'n. (Peire's), La. Vols.
Carr, Cornelius	Private	10 and 20 Cons. Reg't., La. Mil.
Carr, George	Private	Captain Sprigg's Co., Boatmen, La. Vols. (Orig. under Kerr, George)
Carr, H.	Private	4 Reg't. (Morgan's), La. Militia
Carr, Richard	Private	10 and 20 Cons. Reg't., La. Mil.
Carr, Vincent	Private	10 and 20 Cons. Reg't., La. Mil.
Carrabey, Ene	Private	1 Reg't. (Dejan's), La. Militia (Orig. under Carraby, Etienne)
Carraby, --	Private	Plauche's Batt'n., La. Militia
Carraby, Etienne	Private	1 Reg't. (Dejan's), La. Militia
Carraby, Lufroy	Private	2 Batt'n. (Peire's), La. Vols. (See also Jean B. Deschamps - 44 Reg't.
Carragan, James	Private	Capt. Allen's Co., Artillerists, La. Vols.
Carragan, James	Private	De Clouet's Reg't., La. Militia
Carrall, William	Corporal	10 and 20 Cons. Reg't., La. Mil. (Orig. under Carroll, William)
Carranza, Joseph	Private	2 Batt'n. (Peire's), La. Vols.
Carrar, Domingo	Private	2 Batt'n. (Peire's), La. Vols. (Orig. under Carrera, Domingo)
Carrara, Domingo	Private	2 Batt'n. (Peire's), La. Vols. (Orig. under Carrera, Domingo)
Carrava, Antoine	Private	De Clouet's Reg't., La. Militia (Orig. under Charravel, Anthony)
Carrell, William	Corporal	10 and 20 Cons. Reg't., La. Mil. (Orig. under Carroll, William)
Carrera, Domingo	Private	2 Batt'n. (Peire's), La. Vols.
Carrico, Asa	Private	Captain Musick's Co., Mounted Riflemen, La. Mil. (Orig. under Carico, Asa)
Carriere, Fcs	Private	Capt. Colsson's Co., Artillery, La. Vols.
Carriere, Joseph	Private	16 Reg't. (Thompson's), La. Mil.
Carriere, Joseph	1 Lieut.	17, 18 and 19 Cons. Reg't., La. Militia
Carriere, Louis	Private	16 Reg't. (Thompson's), La. Mil.
Carriere, Michel, fils	Private	16 Reg't. (Thompson's), La. Mil.
Carriere, Noel	1 Lieut.	1 Batt'n. (Fortier's), La. Militia
Carriere, Zeno	Private	16 Reg't. (Thompson's), La. Mil.
Carriler, Constance	Private	Baker's Regiment, La. Militia (Orig. under Caniler, Constance)
Carro, Hyacinth	Artificer	Capt. Chaudurier's Co., Artificers, Art'y. La. Vols. (Orig. under Caro, Yacint)
Carrol, John	Private	De Clouet's Reg't., La. Militia
Carroll, William	Corporal	10 and 20 Cons. Reg't., La. Mil.
Carron, Francois	Private	16 Reg't. (Thompson's), La. Mil.
Carron, Joseph	Private	16 Reg't. (Thompson's), La. Mil.
Carruth, William C.	Corp.-Pvt.	12 and 13 Cons. Reg't., La. Mil.
Carsey, Melzar	Private	Capt. Ashley's Co., Mounted Rifleman, La. Militia

Name	Rank	Unit
Carsey, Metzer	Private	Capt. Ashley's Co., Mounted Rifleman, La. Mil. (Orig. under Carsey, Melzar)
Carson, Thomas	Corporal	4 Reg't. (Morgan's), La. Militia
Carsner, George	Private	Captain McNair's Co., Mounted Riflemen, La. Mil. (Orig. under Corsnor, George)
Cart, Louis	Private	16 Reg't. (Thompson's), La. Mil.
Cartagene, --	Private	4 Reg't. (Morgan's), La. Militia
Carter, James	Private	10 and 20 Cons. Reg't., La. Mil.
Carter, John	Sergeant	12 and 13 Cons. Reg't., La. Mil.
Carter, Redman	Private	12 and 13 Cons. Reg't., La. Mil.
Carterau, John	Artificer	Capt. Chaudurier's Co., Artificers, Art'y. La. Vols. (Orig. under Tartereau, Jean)
Cartereau, John	Artificer	Capt. Chaudurier's Co., Artificers, Art'y. La. Vols. (Orig. under Tartereau, Jean)
Carthy, James	Private	17, 18 and 19 Cons. Reg't., La. Militia
Cartras, Vicente	Private	17, 18 and 19 Cons. Reg't., La. Militia
Cartrat, Vincent	Private	17, 18 and 19 Cons. Reg't., La. Mil. (Orig. under Cartras, Vicente)
Cartwright, John	Private	4 Reg't. (Morgan's), La. Militia
Caruthers, James	Private	De Clouet's Reg't., La. Militia
Caruthers, John	Private	16 Reg't. (Thompson's), La. Mil. (Orig. under Cruthers, John)
Caruthers, Julien	Private	De Clouet's Reg't., La. Militia
Caruthers, Samuel	Private	De Clouet's Reg't., La. Militia
Caruthers, William	Private	De Clouet's Reg't., La. Militia
Cary, Pierre	Artificer	Capt. Chaudurier's Co., Artificers, Art'y. La. Vols. (Orig. under Clarick, Pierre)
Casanora, Manuel	Sergeant	17, 18 and 19 Cons. Reg't., La. Mil. (Orig. under (Casanore, Manuel)
Casanore, Manuel	Sergeant	17, 18 and 19 Cons. Reg't., La. Mil.
Casanova, Graviel	Private	3 Reg't. (de la Ronde's), La. Mil.
Casanova, Jean	Private	3 Reg't. (de la Ronde's), La. Mil.
Casban, Bte	Corporal	6 Reg't. (Landry's), La. Militia (Orig. under Casbon, Bte)
Casbere, Antoine	Private	4 Reg't. (Morgan's), La. Militia
Casbere, Francis	Private	4 Reg't. (Morgan's), La. Militia
Casbergue, In Ls	Corporal	2 Reg't. (Cavelier's), La. Mil.
Casbon, Bte	Corporal	6 Reg't. (Landry's), La. Militia
Cascognol, Joseph	Private	8 Reg't. (Meriam's), La. Militia
Cascy, Thomas	Sgt.-Pvt.	4 Reg't. (Morgan's), La. Militia (Orig. under Casey, Thomas)
Caselar, Pierre	Private	3 Reg't. (de la Ronde's), La. Mil.
Casellas, Maximo	Private	17, 18 and 19 Cons. Reg't., La. Militia
Casemire, --	Private	2 Batt'n. (D'Aquin's), La. Militia
Casenavo, Chery	Private	2 Batt'n. (D'Aquin's), La. Militia
Casenare, Francois	Private	2 Batt'n. (D'Aquin's), La. Militia
Casetney, Thomas	Private	2 Batt'n. (Peire's), La. Vols. (Orig. under Catelnay, Thomas)
Casey, Thomas	Sgt.-Pvt.	4 Reg't. (Morgan's), La. Militia
Cash, B.	Private	Captain Sprigg's Co., Boatmen, La. Vols.
Cash, Burrel	Private	Capt. Wallace's Co., Boatmen, La. Vols.
Casimir, --	Servant	Plauche's Batt'n., La. Militia
Casimer, --	Private	2 Batt'n. (D'Aquin's), La. Militia (Orig. under Casemire, --)
Casimire, --	Private	2 Reg't. (Cavelier's), La. Militia
Cason, John	Private	Captain Griffith's Co., Mounted Riflemen, La. Vols.
Cason, Robert	Private	17, 18 and 19 Cons. Reg't., La. Militia
Cassanave, John	Private	Baker's Regiment, La. Militia
Casseneuve, Vincent	Private	De Clouet's Reg't., La. Militia
Cassenuve, Vincent	Private	De Clouet's Reg't., La. Militia (Orig. under Casseneuve,Vincent)
Casson, --	Private	Plauche's Batt'n., La. Militia (Orig. under Cassou, --)
Casson, Jn	Private	Plauche's Batt'n., La. Militia
Cassou, --	Private	Plauche's Batt'n., La. Militia
Castain, Louis	1 Lieut.	Capt. Colsson's Co., Artillery, La. Vols.
Castanedo, Barnardo	Private	17, 18 and 19 Cons. Reg't., La. Militia
Castanedo, I.	Private	2 Reg't. (Cavelier's), La. Militia
Castanida, Fernando	Private	17, 18 and 19 Cons. Reg't., La. Militia
Castanido, Bernardo	Private	17, 18 and 19 Cons. Reg't., La. Mil. (Orig. under Castenado, Bernardo)
Castaret, Jean Matin	Private	3 Reg't. (de la Ronde's), La. Mil.
Castel, Francois	Private	Capt. Songy's Co., Marines, La. Vols.
Castelin, Andre'	Private	De Clouet's Reg't., La. Militia
Castelin, Bernard	Private	De Clouet's Reg't., La. Militia
Castelin, Jean	Private	De Clouet's Reg't., La. Militia
Castelney, Thomas	Private	2 Batt'n. (Peire's), La. Vols. (Orig. under Catelnay, Thomas)
Castenado, Fernando	Private	17, 18 and 19 Cons. Reg't., La. Mil. (Orig. under Castanida, Fernando)
Castens, Louis	1 Lieut.	Capt. Colsson's Co., Artillery, La. Vols. (Orig. under Castain, Louis)
Castilin, Andre	Private	De Clouet's Reg't., La. Militia (Orig. under Castelin, Andre)
Castilin, Bernard	Private	De Clouet's Reg't., La. Militia (Orig. under Castelin, Bernard)
Castille, Jean Bte	Private	16 Reg't. (Thompson's), La. Mil.
Castille, Joseph	Corporal	De Clouet's Reg't., La. Militia
Castillen, Antonio	Private	2 Batt'n. (Peire's), La. Vols. (Orig. under Castillon, Antonio)
Castillera, Manuel	Private	2 Batt'n. (Peire's), La. Vols.
Castillian, Antonea	Private	2 Batt'n. (Peire's), La. Vols. (Orig. under Castillon, Antonio)
Castillion, Antoine	Private	2 Batt'n. (Peire's), La. Vols. (Orig. under Castillon, Antonio)
Castillon, Andrew	Private	Sergt. Hog's Detachment, La. Vols.
Castillon, Antonio	Private	2 Batt'n. (Peire's), La. Vols.
Castincan, John	Private	Capt. Chauveau's Co., Cavalry, La. Militia
Castineau, John	Private	Capt. Chauveau's Co., Cavalry, (Orig. under Castincan, John)
Castozan, --	Private	2 Reg't. (Cavelier's), La. Militia
Castras, Juan	Private	17, 18 and 19 Cons. Reg't., La. Militia
Castras, Migl	Private	17, 18 and 19 Cons. Reg't., La. Mil.
Castre', --	Private	2 Reg't. (Cavelier's), La. Militia
Castres, J. M.	Private	De Clouet's Reg't., La. Militia
Castro, Antonio	1 Lieut.	17, 18 and 19 Cons. Reg't., La. Militia
Castro, Juan	Private	17, 18 and 19 Cons. Reg't., La. Mil.
Castro, Miguel	Private	17, 18 and 19 Cons. Reg't., La. Mil.
Castro, Vicente	Private	17, 18 and 19 Cons. Reg't., La. Militia
Castrot, Juan	Private	17, 18 and 19 Cons. Reg't., La. Mil. (Orig. under Castras, Juan)
Caswell, John	Private	2 Batt'n. (Peire's), La. Vols.
Casydey, Andre	Private	8 Reg't. (Meriam's), La. Militia
Catalan, Jn. Antoine	Private	4 Reg't. (Morgan's), La. Militia
Catelnay, Thomas	Private	2 Batt'n. (Peire's), La. Vols.
Catelney, Thomas	Private	2 Batt'n. (Peire's), La. Vols. (Orig. under Catelnay, Thomas)
Catelny, Thomas	Private	2 Batt'n. (Peire's), La. Vols. (Orig. under Catelnay, Thomas)
Cathe, George	Private	17, 18 and 19 Cons. Reg't. La. Militia (Orig. under Cather, George)
Cathe, John	Private	17, 18 and 19 Cons. Reg't., La. Mil. (Orig. under Cather, Hohn)
Cathelinay, Thomas	Private	2 Battn. (Peire's), La. Vols. (Orig. under Catelnay, Thomas)
Cather, George	Private	17, 18 and 19 Cons. Reg't., La. Militia
Cather, John	Private	17, 18 and 19 Cons. Reg't., La. Militia
Catilnay, Thomas	Private	2 Batt'n. (Peire's), La. Vols. (Orig. under Catelnay, Thomas)
Cato, Cullen	Private	Capt. Allen's Co., Artillerists, La. Vols.
Cato, Cullen	Private	2 Batt'n. (Peire's), La. Vols.
Catoir, Cadet	Private	5 Reg't. (La Branche's), La. Mil.

Name	Rank	Unit
Catoir, Jean	Private-Cpl.	2 Batt'n. (Peire's), La. Vols.
Catoir, John Peter	Private-Cpl.	2 Batt'n. (Peire's), La. Vols. (Orig. under Catoir, Jean)
Catoire, P.	Private	2 Reg't. (Cavelier's), La. Mil.
Caton, John Peter	Corporal	2 Batt'n. (Peire's), La. Vols. (Orig. under Catoir, Jean)
Catorie, --	Private	4 Reg't. (Morgan's), La. Militia
Catrieux, --	Corporal	2 Reg't. (Cavelier's), La. Militia
Cauagan, James	Private	De Clouet's Reg't., La. Militia (Orig. under Carragan, James)
Caucotte, Phillip	Sergeant	6 Reg't. (Landry's), La. Militia
Caucoutle, Phillip	Sergeant	6 Reg't. (Landry's), La. Militia (Orig. under Caucotte, Phillip)
Cauffield, James	Private	Capt. Allen's Co., Artillerists, La. Vols.
Caulk, Richard	Private	Captain Mc Nair's Co., Mounted Riflemen, La. Militia
Caumean, Auguste	Private	7 Reg't. (Le Beuf's), La. Militia (Orig. under Coumean, Auguste)
Caumeau, Joseph	Private	7 Reg't. (Le Beuf's), La. Militia (Orig. under Coumeau, Joseph)
Caurat, Jques	Fusilier-Pvt.	5 Reg't. (La Branche's), La. Mil. (Orig. under Conrat, Jacques)
Cauvin, In	Private	2 Reg't. (Cavelier's), La. Militia
Cava, François	Private	16 Reg't. (Thompson's), La. Mil. (Orig. under Cave, Francois)
Cavalero, --	Private	4 Reg't. (Morgan's), La. Militia
Cavalerro, I.	Private	6 Reg't. (Landry's), La. Militia
Cavalier, --	Corporal	Plauche's Batt'n., La. Militia
Cavalier, Charles	Private	De Clouet's Reg't., La. Militia
Cavalier, Jean Baptiste	Corporal	3 Reg't. (de la Ronde's), La. Mil.
Cavalier, Joseph	Private	De Clouet's Reg't., La. Militia
Cavalier, Remi	Private	3 Reg't. (de la Ronde's), La. Mil.
Cavaller, Prre	Fusilier-Pvt.	5 Reg't. (La Branche's), La. Mil. (Orig. under Cuvillier, Pierre)
Cavanah, Charles	Private	12 and 13 Cons. Reg't., La. Mil.
Cavannah, Charles	Private	12 and 13 Cons. Reg't., La. Mil. (Orig. under Cavanah, Charles)
Cave, Francois	Private	16 Reg't. (Thompson's), La. Mil.
Cavelier, Anthony	2 Lieut.-Q.M.	2 Reg't. (Cavelier's), La. Militia
Cavelier, I.	Private	4 Reg't. (Morgan's), La. Militia
Cavelier, I. L.	Private	4 Reg't. (Morgan's), La. Militia
Cavelier, Zenon	Colonel	2 Reg't. (Cavelier's), La. Mil.
Cavens, William	Private	1 Reg't. (Dejan's), La. Militia
Cavey, Joseph	Private	19 Reg't., La. Militia
Cavey, Peer	Private	19 Reg't., La. Militia
Cavey, Pierre	Private	19 Reg't., La. Vols.(Orig. under Cavey, Peer)
Cavillier, Antoine	Fusilier-Pvt.	5 Reg't. (La Branche's), La. Mil.
Cavur, Andre	Private	Captain Lugan's Co., La. Vols. (Orig. under Bahno, Andre)
Cayemares, Domingo	Private	2 Reg't. (Cavelier's), La. Militia
Cayeux, Colas	Private	De Clouet's Reg't., La. Militia
Caymares, Domingo	Private	2 Reg't. (Cavelier's), La. Militia (Orig. filed under Cayemares, Domingo)
Cayonne, Jacques	Private	2 Batt'n. (D'Aquin's), La. Militia (Orig. under Bayonne, Jacque)
Cazeau, Pre	Sergeant	2 Reg't. (Cavelier's), La. Militia
Cazelar, Pierre	Private	3 Reg't. (de la Ronde's), La. Mil. (Orig. under Caselar, Pierre)
Cazille, --	Servant	Capt. Trudeau's Troop of Horse, La. Militia
Cazur, --	Servant	4 Reg't. (Morgan's), La. Militia
Cc all, Jn	Private	1 Reg't. (Dejan's), La. Militia (Orig. under McCall, Jn)
Cotte, Thomas	Captain	De Clouet's Reg't., La. Militia (Orig. under Scott, Thomas W.)
Ceasar, --	Private-Servant	4 Brigade (Flanjae's), La. Mil.
Celestin, --	Waiter	2 Reg't. (Cavelier's), La. Militia
Celestin, --	Servant	16 Reg't. (Thompson's), La. Mil.
Celezince, --	Servant	2 Batt'n. (D'Aquin's), La. Militia (Orig. under Belezince, --)
Celecour, --	Sergeant	2 Batt'n. (D'Aquin's), La. Militia
Cemer, Joachim	Private	17, 18 and 19 Cons. Reg't., La. Mil. (Orig.under Xemer, Joachin)
Cemor, --	Private	2 Batt'n. (D'Aquin's), La. Militia (Orig. under Cemore, --)
Cemore, --	Private	2 Batt'n. (D'Aquin's), La. Militia
Cerbera, Urer	Private	17, 18 and 19 Cons. Reg't., La. Mil.
Ceresol, Andre	Private	Plauche's Batt'n., La. Militia
Ceresole, Andre	Private	Capt. Colsson's Co., Artillery, La. Vols.
Ceressol, --	Private	Plauche's Batt'n., La. Militia
Ceressol, Francis	Sergeant	2 Reg't. (Cavelier's), La. Militia
Cernin, Antoinnee	Private	Captain Lagan's Co., La. Vols. (Orig. under Servin, Antoine)
Certellemy, Jacques	Private	De Clouet's Reg't., La. Militia
Certellemy, Jean	Private	De Clouet's Reg't., La. Militia
Certellimy, Francois	Private	De Clouet's Reg't., La. Militia
Cesaine, Louis	Private	17, 18 and 19 Cons. Reg't., La. Mil. Orig. under Cezaire, Louis)
Cesar, --	Private	2 Batt'n. (D'Aquin's), La. Militia
Cesar, --	Servant	3 Reg't. (de la Ronde's), La. Mil.
Cesard, --	Private	7 Reg't. (Le Beuf's), La. Militia
Cesse, George	Private	3 Reg't. (de la Ronde's), La. Mil.
Cesserol, --	Private	Plauche's Batt'n., La. Militia (Orig. under Ceressol, --)
Cevalles, Nepomeceno	Private	17, 18 and 19 Cons. Reg't., La. Militia
Cevallos, Domingo	Private	Capt. Hubbard's Mounted Co., La. Militia
Cevallos, Joseph	Private	Capt. Hubbard's Mounted Co., La. Militia
Cevallos, Juan	Private	Capt. Hubbard's Mounted Co., La. Militia
Cevine, Antoine	Private	Captain Lagan's Co., La. Vols. (Orig. under Servin, Antoine)
Cezaire, Louis	Private	17, 18 and 19 Cons. Reg't., La. Militia
Cezar, --	Servant	Gov. Claiborne and Staff, La.Mil.
Cezar, --	Private	2 Batt'n. (D'Aquin's), La. Militia (Orig. under Cezar, --)
Chabert, Peter	Private	2 Batt'n. (Peire's), La. Vols.
Chabert, Pierre	Private	2 Batt'n. (Peire's), La. Vols. (Orig. under Chabert, Peter)
Chabot, Joseph	Private	16 Reg't. (Thompson's), La. Mil.
Chachera, Delelle	Private	16 Reg't. (Thompson's), La. Mil.
Chacherie, Louis	Sergeant	16 Reg't. (Thompson's), La. Mil.
Chachrie, Delille	Private	16 Reg't. (Thompson's), La. Mil. (Orig. under Chachera, Delelle)
Chadue, Po	Private	2 Reg't. (Cavelier's), La. Militia (Orig. under Chapdue, Pre)
Chagneaux, --	Private	1 Reg't. (Dejan's), La. Militia
Chaies, --	Servant	De Clouet's Reg't., La. Militia
Chaigneau, Pre	Private	Capt. Colsson's Co., Artillery, La. Vols.
Chain, Hugh	Private	1 Reg't. (Dejan's), La. Militia
Chain, William	Private	12 and 13 Cons. Reg't., La. Mil.
Chaire, Christophe	Sergeant	Plauche's Batt'n., La. Militia
Chaise, Anderson	Private	Capt. Van Bibber's Co., La. Mil.
Chaison, Jean Bte	Private	6 Reg't. (Landry's), La. Militia
Chaisson, Etienne	Private	8 Reg't. (Meriam's), La. Militia (Orig. under Chiasson, Etienne)
Chaisson, Louis	Private	De Clouet's Reg't., La. Militia (Orig. under Chiasson, Louis)
Chaland, Bibi	Private	5 Reg't. (La Branche), La.Militia
Chalarte, Francis	Private	8 Reg't. (Meriam's), La. Militia
Chalere, Ursin	Private	Capt. Trudeau's Troop of Horse, La. Militia
Chalire, Ursin	Private	Capt. Trudeau's Troop of Horse, La. Mil. (Orig. under Chalere, Ursin)
Challon, Joseph	Corporal	Capt. Alpuente's Co., La. Mil.
Chalmbers, Alexander	Pvt.-Cpl.	Captain McNair's Co., Mounted Riflemen, La. Mil. (Orig. under Chambers, Alexander)
Chalumet, --	Private	2 Reg't. (Cavelier's), La. Mil. (Orig. under Chalumette, --)
Chalumette, --	Private	2 Reg't. (Cavelier's), La. Mil.
Chamar, Rosamon	Private	De Clouet's Reg't., La. Militia (Orig. under Chamard, Rosamond)
Chamard, Rosamond	Private	De Clouet's Reg't., La. Militia
Chambers, Alexander	Private	Captain McNair's Co., Mounted Riflemen, La. Militia
Chambers, John	Private	10 and 20 Cons. Reg't., La. Mil.
Chambers, Wesley	1 Lieut.	10 and 20 Cons. Reg't., La. Mil.
Chambion, --	Private	1 Reg't. (Dejan's), La. Militia
Champagne, Antoine	Private	De Clouet's Reg't., La. Militia
Champagne, Baptiste	Private	De Clouet's Reg't., La. Militia
Champagne, Elie	Corporal	5 Reg't. (La Branche's), La. Mil.
Champagne, Eugene	Fusilier-Pvt.	5 Reg't. (La Branche's), La. Mil.
Champagne, Evariste	Fus.-Pvt.	5 Reg't. (La Branche's), La. Mil.

Name	Rank	Unit
Champagne, Francois	Fus.-Pvt.	5 Reg't. (La Branche's), La. Mil.
Champagne, Honore'	Fus.-Pvt.	5 Reg't. (La Branche's), La. Mil.
Champagne, Paul	Fus.-Pvt.	5 Reg't. (La Branche's), La. Mil.
Champagne, Vt	Private	4 Reg't. (Morgan's), La. Militia
Champagny, Louis	Private	2 Batt'n. (Peire's), La. Vols. (Orig. under Champigny, Louis)
Champaigne, Antoine	Private	De Clouet's Reg't., La. Militia (Orig. under Champagne, Antoine)
Champaigne, Jean Ss	Private	De Clouet's Reg't., La. Militia
Champain, --	Private	De Clouet's Reg't., La. Militia
Champain, J. Louis	Private	De Clouet's Reg't., La. Militia (Orig. under Champaigne, Jean Ss)
Champain, Vincent	Private	De Clouet's Reg't., La. Militia
Champigne, John Bte	Private	8 Reg't. (Meriam's), La. Militia
Champigni, Ls	Sergeant	2 Reg't. (Cavelier's), La. Militia (Orig. under Champigny, Lenus)
Champigny, Lenus	Sergeant	2 Reg't. (Cavelier's), La. Militia
Champigny, Louis	Private	2 Batt'n. (Peire's), La. Vols.
Champlain, John B.	Private	Capt. Price's Co., La. Militia
Chamutte, --	Private	Plauche's Batt'n., La. Militia
Chance, Benjamin	Private	10 and 20 Cons. Reg't., La. Mil.
Chance, Eli Jr.	Sergeant	10 and 20 Cons. Reg't., La. Mil.
Chance, Eli Sr.	Sergeant	10 and 20 Cons. Reg't., La. Mil.
Chance, James	Private	De Clouet's Reg't., La. Militia
Chance, John	Private	10 and 20 Cons. Reg't., La. Mil.
Chance, Samuel	Private	12 and 13 Cons. Reg't., La. Mil.
Chance, Stephen	Private	10 and 20 Cons. Reg't., La. Mil.
Chance, Vincent	Private	De Clouet's La. Mil. (See also Melsor Crier & Luke Powers)
Chance, William	Captain	11 Reg't. (Hickey's), La. Militia
Chancey, George	Private	Captain Griffith's Co., Mounted Riflemen, La. Vols.(Orig. under Chancy, George)
Chancey, James B.	Private	Captain Griffith's Co., Mounted Riflemen, La. Vols.(Orig. under Chancy, James B.)
Chancey, James I.	Private	Captain Griffith's Co., Mounted Riflemen, La. Vols. (Orig. under Chancy, James I.)
Chancey, John	Private	Captain Griffith's Co., Mounted Riflemen, La. Vols. (Orig. under Chancy, John)
Chancey, William I.	Private	Captain Griffith's Co., Mounted Riflemen, La. Vols. (Orig. under Chancy, William I.)
Chancy, Baley	Private	Captain Griffith's Co., Mounted Riflemen, La. Vols.
Chancy, George	Private	Captain Griffith's Co., Mounted Riflemen, La. Vols.
Chancy, James	Private	11 Reg't. (Hickey's), La. Militia
Chancy, James B.	Private	Captain Griffith's Co., Mounted Riflemen, La. Mil.
Chancy, James I.	Private	Captain Griffith's Co., Mounted Riflemen, La. Militia
Chancy, John	Private	Captain Griffith's Co., Mounted Riflemen, La. Militia
Chancy, William I.	Private	Captain Griffith's Co., Mounted Riflemen, La. Militia
Chandler, John	Sergeant-Pvt.	Captain McNair's Co., Mounted Riflemen, La. Militia
Chandler, Jonathan	Private	Captain Young's Co., Mounted Riflemen, La. Militia
Chapautier, -- fils	Private	7 Reg't. (Le Beuf's), La. Militia
Chapaton, N.	Private	8 Reg't. (Meriam's), La. Militia
Chapdue, Pre	Private	2 Reg't. (Cavelier's), La. Militia
Chapelle, Jean Baptiste	Private	1 Batt'n. (Fortier's), La. Militia
Chaperon, --	Private	3 Reg't. (de la Ronde's), La. Mil.
Chapman, James	Private	11 Reg't. (Hickey's), La. Militia
Chapman, John	Private	10 and 20 Cons. Reg't. La. Mil.
Chapman, John	Private	12 and 13 Cons. Reg't., La. Mil.
Chapman, John Junr.	Private	16 Reg't. (Thompson's), La. Mil.
Chapman, John Sent.	Private	16 Reg't. (Thompson's), La. Mil.
Chapman, Joseph	Private	De Clouet's Reg't., La. Militia
Chapman, Robert	Private	De Clouet's Reg't., La. Militia
Chapman, Thomas	Sergeant	11 Reg't. (Hickey's), La. Militia
Chapman, Wiley	Private	12 and 13 Cons. Reg't., La. Mil.
Chapron, Charles	Private	1 Batt'n. (Fortier's), La. Militia
Charaux, Arnd	Private	2 Reg't. (Cavelier's), La. Militia (Orig. under Charreaux, Ard)
Carbonier, --	Private	1 Reg't. (Dejan's), La. Militia
Charbonnet, --	Private	4 Reg't. (Morgan's), La. Militia
Charbonnet, A. B.	1 Sergeant	4 Reg't. (Morgan's), La. Militia
Charbonnet, Jacques	Private	Capt. Trudeau's Troop of Horse, La. Militia
Charbonnier, --	Private	1 Reg't. (Dejan's), La. Militia (Orig. under Charbonier, --)
Chardavoine, --	1 Lieut.	2 Batt'n. (D'Aquin's), La. Militia
Chardonnet, Michel	Private	Captain Lagan's Co., La. Vols.
Charet, Phillippe	Private	2 Batt'n. (Peire's), La. Vols. (Orig. under Chavez, Philipps)
Charles, --	Servant	Baker's Regiment, La. Militia
Charles, --	Servant	Gov. Claiborne and Staff, La. Mil.
Charles, --	Servant	Gov. Claiborne and Staff, La. Mil.
Charles, --	Servant	1 Reg't. (Dejan's), La. Militia
Charles, --	Private	1 Batt'n. (Fortier's), La. Militia
Charles, --	Servant	1 Batt'n. (Fortier's), La. Militia
Charles, --	Servant	1 Batt'n. (Fortier's), La. Militia
Charles, --	Servant	1 Batt'n. (Fortier's), La. Militia
Charles, --	Servant	16 Reg't. (Thompson's), La. Mil.
Charles, I	Private	7 Reg't. (Le Beuf's), La. Militia
Charles, Jean	Private	2 Batt'n. (D'Aquin's), La. Militia
Charles, Jean	Private	7 Reg't. (Le Beuf's), La. Militia
Charles, Marselin	Private	1 Batt'n. (Fortier's), La. Militia
Charleville, --	Private	Plauche's Batt'n., La. Militia
Charlot, Ls	Musician	1 Batt'n. (Fortier's), La. Militia
Charlote, Ls	Musician	1 Batt'n. (Fortier's), La. Militia (Orig. under Charlot, Ls.)
Charne, John	Private	10 and 20 Cons. Reg't., La. Mil. (Orig. under Chance, John)
Charpantier, Maraux	Private	6 Reg't. (Landry's), La. Militia
Charpantier, Michael	Private	Baker's Regiment, La. Militia (Orig. under Carpenter, Michail)
Charpentier, Jean B.	Private	Captain Hubbard's Mounted Co., La. Militia
Charpie, Antoine	Private	2 Batt'n. (Peire's), La. Vols.
Charraval, Anthony	Private	De Clouet's Reg't., La. Militia
Charre, Piere	Private	17, 18 and 19 Cons. Reg't., La. Militia
Charreaux, Ard	Private	2 Reg't. (Cavelier's), La. Militia
Charrie, Antoine	Private	17, 18 and 19 Cons. Reg't., La. Militia
Chasagne, Amant	Artificer	Capt. Chaudurier's Co., Artificers, Art'y., La. Vols. (Orig. under Chassagne, Amant)
Chase, Anderson	Private	Capt. Van Bibber's Co., La. Mil. (Orig. under Chaise, Anderson)
Chaspaulier, --	Private	7 Reg't. (Le Beuf's), La. Militia (Orig. under Chapautier, -- fils)
Chassagne, --	Private	Plauche's Batt'n., La. Militia
Chassagne, Amant	Artificer	Capt. Chaudurier's Co., Artificers, Art'y., La. Vols.
Chassaigne, Aman	Artificer	Capt. Chaudurier's Co., Artificers, Art'y., La. Vols. (Orig. under Chassagne, Amant)
Chastan, I. B.	Private	Plauche's Batt'n., La. Militia
Chastant, --	Private	Plauche's Batt'n., La. Militia
Chateau, --	Corporal	2 Batt'n. (D'Aquin's), La. Militia
Chateaugai, Joseph	Private	Capt. Van Bibber's Co., La. Mil.
Chatheben, Belloin	Private	17, 18 and 19 Cons. Reg't., La. Mil. (Orig. under Chathelen, Belloin)
Chathelen, Belloin	Private	17, 18 and 19 Cons. Reg't., La. Militia
Chatry, Francois	Adjutant	1 Batt'n. (Fortier's), La. Militia
Chatry, I. L. F.	Adjutant	1 Batt'n. (Fortier's), La. Militia (Orig. under Chatry, Francois)
Chaudurier, Antoine	Captain	Capt. Chaudurier's Co., Artificers, Art'y., La. Vols. (Orig. under Chatry, Francois)
Chauguinot, Rene	Private	De Clouet's Reg't., La. Militia (Orig. under Chauguinot, Rene)
Chauquinot, Rene	Private	De Clouet's Reg't., La. Militia (Orig. under Chauguinot, Rene)
Chausse, George	Private	5 Reg't. (La Branche's), La. Mil.
Chauveau, John	Captain	Capt. Chauveau's Co., Cavalry, La. Militia
Chauvin, Jacque	Private	6 Reg't. (Landry's), La. Militia
Chauvin, Louis	Private	7 Reg't. (Le Beuf's), La. Militia
Chauvin, Zeno	Private	7 Reg't. (Le Beuf's), La. Militia
Chavalier, Pierre	Private	De Clouet's Reg't., La. Militia (Orig. under Chevalier, Pierre)
Chavanne, Auguste,	Sergeant	2 Batt'n. (Peire's), La. Vols.
Chaven, Shadrach	Private	10 and 20 Cons. Reg't., La. Mil.

Name	Rank	Unit
Chaves, Samuel	Private	10 and 20 Cons. Reg't., La. Mil. (Orig. under Schaves, Samuel)
Chavets, Phillip	Private	2 Batt'n. (Peire's), La. Vols. (Orig. under Chavez, Philippe)
Chavez, Philippe	Private	2 Batt'n. (Peire's), La. Vols.
Chavis, Gideon	Private	12 and 13 Cons. Reg't., La. Mil.
Chavis, Joseph	Private	12 and 13 Cons. Reg't., La. Mil.
Chevert, Marolun	Corporal	17, 18 and 19 Cons. Reg't., La. Militia
Chayo, --	Servant	Capt. Trudeau's Troop of Horse, La. Militia
Chazal, --	Private	Plauche's Batt'n., La. Militia
Chedoteau, Auguste	Private	7 Reg't. (Le Beuf's), La. Militia
Chedoteau, Bte	Private	7 Reg't. (Le Beuf's), La. Militia
Chedoteau, Pierre	Private	7 Reg't. (Le Beuf's), La. Militia
Chegnier, Louis	Private	De Clouet's Reg't., La. Militia (Orig. under Chevnier, Louis)
Cheminard, --	Private	Plauche's Batt'n., La. Militia
Chenaue, --	Private	1 Reg't. (Dejan's), La. Militia
Chene, Auguste	Fusilier-Pvt.	5 Reg't. (La Branche's), La. Mil.
Chenet, Alexandre	Captain	5 Reg't. (La Branche's), La. Mil.
Chenet, Eugene	2 Lieut.	5 Reg't. (La Branche's), La. Mil.
Chenet, Pierre	Corporal	6 Reg't. (Landry's), La. Militia
Cheney, David	3 Lieut.	17, 18 and 19 Cons. Reg't., La. Militia
Cheney, Hampton I.	Sgt.-Pvt.	17, 18 and 19 Cons. Reg't., La. Militia
Cheney, Thomas G.	Lieutenant	17, 18 and 19 Cons. Reg't., La. Militia
Chenier, F. H.	Drummer	De Clouet's Reg't., La. Militia (Orig. under Chenier, J. F.)
Chenier, Francois	Fusilier-Pvt.	5 Reg't. (La Branche's), La. Mil. (Orig. under Cheynier, Francois)
Chenier, Francois	Private	16 Reg't. (Thompson's), La. Mil.
Chenier, J. Bte	Private	6 Reg't. (Landry's), La. Militia
Chenier, J. F.	Drummer	De Clouet's Reg't., La. Militia
Chenier, Pierre	Fusilier-Pvt.	5 Reg't. (La Branche's), La. Mil. (Orig. under Cheynier, Pierre)
Chenow, --	Private	1 Reg't. (Dejan's), La. Militia (Orig. under Chenaue, --)
Chenvert, Marolin	Corporal	17, 18 and 19 Cons. Reg't., La. Militia (Orig. under Chevert, Marolum)
Cheny, Thomas G.	Lieutenant	17, 18 and 19 Cons. Reg't., La. Mil. (Orig. under Cheney,Thomas Y.)
Chepan, Francois	Private	7 Reg't. (Le Beuf's), La. Militia
Chepan, Pierre	Private	7 Reg't. (Le Beuf's), La. Militia
Cherie, Benjamin	Private	Capt. Songy's Co., Marines, La. Vols.
Cherino, Anto	Private	17, 18 and 19 Cons. Reg't., La. Militia
Cheron, Phillip	Drum Major	6 Reg't. (Landry's), La. Militia
Cheron, Phillippe	Cpl.-Artificer	Capt. Chaudurier's Co., Artificers, Art'y., La. Vols.
Cherpentier, Lazarre	Private	2 Batt'n. (D'Aguin's), La. Militia
Cherrior, Phillip	Private	Capt. Chaudurier's Co., Artificers, Art'y., La. Vols. (Orig. under Cheron, Phillipe)
Cherton, L.	Private	16 Reg't. (Thompson's), La. Mil. (Orig. under Chertron, L.)
Chertron, L.	Private	16 Reg't. (Thompson's), La. Mil.
Cherubin, Amot	Artificer	Capt. Chaudurier's Co., Artificers, Art'y., La. Vols. (Orig. under Cherubin, Amot)
Chervin, Jean	Private	Captain Lagan's Co., La. Vols.
Chery, --	Servant	Capt. Chauveau's Co., Cavalry, 4 Reg't. (Morgan's), La. Militia
Chery, --	Private	2 Batt'n. (D'Aguin's), La. Militia
Chery, Pierre	Private	17, 18 and 19 Cons. Reg't., La. Militia
Chesette, -- fils	Private	Capt. Le Doux's Co., Cav., La. Vols.
Chesse, Jr.	Private	7 Reg't. (Le Beuf's), La. Militia (Orig. under Chedoteau, Auguste)
Chetodeau, August	Private	1 Batt'n. (Fortier), La. Militia
Cheval, Celestin	Private	2 Batt'n. (Peire's), La. Vols.
Chevalier, Peter	Sergeant	De Clouet's Reg't., La. Militia
Chevalier, Pierre	Private	2 Batt'n. (Cavelier's), La. Militia
Chevalier, Pierre	Private	1 Batt'n. (Fortier's), La. Militia Orig. under Cheval, Celestin)
Chevalle, Celestin	Private	2 Batt'n. (Peire's), La. Vols. (Orig. under Chevalier, Peter)
Chevalliur, Pierre	Sergeant	2 Batt'n. (Peire's), La. Vols. (Orig. under Chevallier, Peter)
Chevallur, --	Sergeant	Plauche's Batt'n., La. Militia
Chevalon, Charles	Sgt.-Major	2 Batt'n. (Peire's), La. Vols. (Orig. under Chavanne, Auguste)
Chevanne, Auguste	Sergeant	2 Batt'n. (Peire's), La. Vols. (Orig. under Creve, Valentin)
Chever, Valentin	Sergeant	Captain Beale's Co., Riflemen, La. Militia
Chew, Beverly	Sergeant	5 Reg't. (La Branche's), La. Mil.
Chexnaidre, Albert	Fus.-Pvt.	5 Reg't. (La Branche's), La. Mil.
Chexnaidre, Andre son	Fus.-Pvt.	5 Reg't. (La Branche's), La. Mil.
Chexnaidre, Henri	Fus.-Pvt.	5 Reg't. (La Branche's), La. Mil.
Chexnaidre, Jean	Fus.-Pvt.	5 Reg't. (La Branche's), La. Mil.
Chexnaidre, Joseph	Fus.-Pvt.	5 Reg't. (La Branche's), La. Mil.
Chexnaidre, Tipham	Private	5 Reg't. (La Branche's), La. Mil.
Chexnayte, Ubin	Private	Baker's Regiment, La. Militia
Chexneyte, Urbin	Private	Baker's Regiment, La. Militia (Orig. under Chexnayte, Urbin)
Cheynier, Francois	Fus.-Pvt.	5 Reg't. (La Branche's), La. Mil.
Cheynier, Louis	Private	De Clouet's Reg't., La. Militia
Cheynier, Pierre	Fus.-Pvt.	5 Reg't. (La Branche's), La. Mil.
Cheyron, Phillippe	Cor.-Artificier	Capt. Chaudurier's Co., Artificers, Ar'y., La. Vols. (Orig. under Cheron, Phillippe)
Chiasson, Charles	Private	16 Reg't. (Thompson's), La. Mil.
Chiasson, Etienne	Private	8 Reg't. (Meriam's), La. Militia
Chiasson, Louis	Private	De Clouet's Reg't., La. Militia
Chiasson, Pierre	Private	16 Reg't. (Thompson's), La. Mil.
Chiasson, Victor	Private	8 Reg't. (Meriam's), La. Militia
Chichester, William	Private	8 Reg't. (Meriam's), La. Militia
Chichieter, William	Private	8 Reg't. (Meriam's), La. Militia (Orig. under Chichester, William)
Chico, Emanuel	Private	10 and 20 Cons. Reg't., La. Mil.
Chicque, Gregoire	Private	De Clouet's Reg't., La. Militia (Orig. under Chique, Gregoire)
Chide., Doine	Private	8 Reg't. (Meriam's), La. Militia
Chierpie, Antoine	Private	Louisiana War of 1812
Chietz, Laurent	Pri.-Cpl.	De Clouet's Reg't., La. Militia (Orig. under Chitz, Laurent)
Childs, Joshua	Private	17, 18 and 19 Cons. Reg't., La. Militia
Chiles, Garland	Private	Capt. Thomas' Co., La. Militia
Chique, Gregoire	Private	De Clouet's Reg't., La. Militia
Chirina, Julian	Private	17, 18 and 19 Cons. Reg't., La. Militia
Chirino, Juan	Private	17, 18 and 19 Cons. Reg't., La. Militia
Chirnoir, Jean	Private	Captain Lagan's Co., La. Vols. (Orig. under Chervin, Jean)
Chiron, F. M.	Private	5 Reg't. (La Branche's), La. Mil. (Orig. under Chiron, L. M.)
Chiron, L. M.	Private	5 Reg't. (La Branche's), La. Mil.
Chiron, Pre M.	Fusilier	5 Reg't. (La Branche's), La. Mil.
Chisholm, Cockburn	Private	10 and 20 Cons. Reg't., La. Mil.
Chism, Cockburn	Private	10 and 20 Cons. Reg't., La. Mil. (Orig. under Chisholm,Cockburn)
Chitz, Laurant	Pri.-Cpl.	De Clouet's Reg't., La. Militia
Chlatre, Francois	Private	8 Reg't. (Meriam's), La. Militia
Chlatre, John	Private	8 Reg't. (Meriam's), La. Militia
Choate, Jean	Private	Baker's Regiment, La. Militia
Choate, Thomas	Private	16 Reg't. (Thompson's), La. Mil.
Choff, Charles	Fusilier-Pvt.	5 Reg't. (La Branche's), La. Mil.
Choff, Georges	Fusilier-Pvt.	5 Reg't. (La Branche's), La. Mil.
Choffe, John L.	Private	De Clouet's Reg't., La. Militia
Chomat, --	Private	1 Reg't. (Dejan's), La. Militia (Orig. under Choumat, --)
Chonce, Vinson	Private	De Clouet's Reg't., La. Militia (Orig. under Chance, Vincent)
Chonestre, Francois	Corporal	7 Reg't. (Le Beuf's), La. Militia
Choppin, A.	Sergeant	Plauche's Batt'n., La. Militia
Choumat, --	Private	1 Reg't. (Dejan's), La. Militia
Chreswell, Robert	Private	10 and 20 Cons. Reg't., La. Mil. (Orig. under Creswell, Robert)
Chretien, Francois	Private	De Clouet's Reg't., La. Militia (Orig. under Chritien, Francois)
Chretien, Gerard	Captain	16 Reg't. (Thompson's), La. Mil.
Chretien, Hypolite	Private	16 Reg't. (Thompson's), La. Mil.
Chretien, Pierre	Private	16 Reg't. (Thompson's), La. Mil.
Chrion, Phillippe	Corp.-Artificer	Capt. Chaudurier's Co., Artificers, Art'y., La. Vols. (Orig. under Cheron, Phillippe)

Name	Rank	Unit
Chrisholm, Cockburn	Private	10 and 20 Cons. Reg't., La. Mil. (Orig. under Chisholm, Cockburn)
Christie, --	Private	2 Reg't. (Cavelier's), La. Militia
Christmas, Henry	Corporal	De Clouet's Reg't., La. Militia
Christmas, John	Sergeant	De Clouet's Reg't., La. Militia
Christoph, Sinforien	Private	1 Batt'n. (Fortier's), La. Militia
Christophe, Firmins	Private	1 Batt'n. (Fortier's), La. Militia
Christophe, Sinfarien	Private	1 Batt'n. (Fortier's), La. Militia (Orig. under Christoph, Sinforien)
Christoval, --	Private	2 Reg't. (Cavelier's), La. Militia
Christwell, R.	Private	5 Reg't. (La Branche's), La. Mil.
Christy, --	Private	2 Reg't. (Cavelier's), La. Militia (Orig. under Christie, --)
Christy, William	Qr.Mr.-Gen'l.	B. Q. Master, Field and Staff Officers, La. Militia
Chriswell, John	Private	Capt. Price's Co., La. Militia
Chritien, Francois	Private	De Clouet's Reg't., La. Militia
Chrochet, Amant	Private	7 Reg't. (Le Beuf's), La. Militia
Chumb, I.	Private	4 Reg't. (Morgan's), La. Militia (Orig. under Clumb, I.)
Church, --	Private	4 Reg't. (Morgan's), La. Militia
Cibilot, Jr.	Private	Plauche's Batt'n., La. Militia
Cibilot, aine	Private	Plauche's Batt'n., La. Militia
Cibilot, F.	Private	Plauche's Batt'n., La. Militia (Orig. under Cybillatte, --)
Cicer, Thomas	Private	10 and 20 Cons. Reg't., La. Mil. (Orig. under Ticer, Thomas)
Cidot, Pierre	1 Lieut.	Capt. Chaudurier's Co., Artificers, Art'y., La. Vols.
Cilcreast, Guil	Private	16 Reg't. (Thompson's), La. Mil.
Ciprien, --	Servant	1 Batt'n. (Fortier's), La. Militia
Cire, Pierre	Private	8 Reg't. (Meriam's), La. Militia
Ciro, Felix	Private	Capt. Songy's Co., Marines, La. Vols. (Orig. under Curos, Felix)
Clabion, Duminy	Private	Plauche's Batt'n., La. Militia
Clagord, James	Private	Capt. Price's Co., La. Militia
Clagore, James	Private	Capt. Price's Co., La. Militia (Orig. under Clagord, James)
Claiborne, W.C.C.	Cond in Chief	Gov. Claiborne and Staff, La. Mil.
Claire, A. Jr.	Private	6 Reg't. (Landry's), La. Militia
Claire, Antoine Sr.	Private	6 Reg't. (Landry's), La. Militia
Claire, Francais	Private	6 Reg't. (Landry's), La. Militia
Clairo, Antoine, Jr.	Private	6 Reg't. (Landry's), La. Militia (Orig. under Claire, A. Jr.)
Clairo, Antoine Sr.	Private	6 Reg't. (Landry's), La. Militia (Orig. under Claire, Antoine Sr.)
Clairo, Francois	Private	6 Reg't. (Landry's), La. Militia (Orig. under Claire, Francais)
Clamcy, --	Waiter	2 Reg't. (Cavelier's), La. Militia
Clanque, Raymond	Private	Captain Legan's Co., La. Vols.
Claond, William	Private	Aspt Alpuente's Co., La. Militia
Clarck, Jesse	Private	De Clouet's Reg't., La. Militia (Orig. under Clark, Jesse)
Clarck, John	Private	17, 18 and 19 Cons. Reg't., La. Mil. (Orig. under Clark, Joseph)
Claric, Pierre	Artificer	Capt. Chaudurier's Co., Artificers, Art'y., La. Vols. (Orig. under Clarick, Pierre)
Clarick, Pierre	Artificer	Capt. Chaudurier's Co., Artificers, Art'y., La. Vols.
Clarisse, Pierre	Private	2 Batt'n. (D'Aquin's), La. Militia
Clarit, Pierre	Artificer	Capt. Chaudurier's Co., Artificers, Art'y., La. Vols. (Orig. under Clarick, Pierre)
Clark, Daniel	Private	17, 18 and 19 Cons. Reg't., La. Militia
Clark, James	1 Sgt.-Sgt.	Capt. Collard's Co., La. Militia
Clark, James	Private	Captain Musick's Co., Mounted Riflemen, La. Militia
Clark, Jesse	Private	De Clouet's Reg't., La. Militia
Clark, John	Private	Capt. Musick's Co., La. Militia
Clark, John Jr.	Sergeant	16 Reg't. (Thompson's), La. Mil.
Clark, Joseph	Sergeant	16 Reg't. (Thompson's), La. Mil.
Clark, Joseph	Private	17, 18 and 19 Cons. Reg't., La. Militia
Clark, Patrick	Private	17, 18 and 19 Cons. Reg't., La. Militia
Clark, Richard	Private	Captain Price's Co., La. Militia
Clark, Stephen	Private	Capt. Allen's Co., Artillerists, La. Vols. (Orig. under Clarke, Stephen)
Clark, Terrance	Private	17, 18 and 19 Cons. Reg't., La. Militia
Clark, William	Private	16 Reg't. (Thompson's), La. Mil.
Clark, William	Corporal	16 Reg't. (Thompson's), La. Mil.
Clarke, Daniel	Private	17, 18 and 19 Cons. Reg't., La. Mil. (Orig. under Clark, Daniel)
Clarke, James	Private	De Clouet's Reg't., La. Militia
Clarke, John Jr.	Sergeant	16 Reg't. (Thompson's), La. Mil. (Orig. under Clark, John Jr.)
Clarke, Samuel	Private	Captain Griffith's Co., Mounted Riflemen, La. Vols.
Clarke, Stephen	Private	Capt. Allen's Co., Artillerists, La. Vols.
Clartaux, Andre	Fusilier-Private	5 Reg't. (La Branche's), La. Mil.
Clary, Pierre	Artificer	Capt. Chaudurier's Co., Artificers, Art'y., La. Vols. (Orig. under Clarick, Pierre)
Clauatre, Michel	Private	6 Reg't. (Landry's), La. Militia
Claude, --	Private	7 Reg't. (Le Beuf's), La. Militia
Claude, P.	Private	4 Reg't. (Morgan's), La. Militia
Clause, Pierre	Sergeant	3 Reg't. (de la Ronde's), La. Mil.
Clauson, Richard	Private	Capt. Allen's Co., Artillerists, La. Vols.
Clautre, Joseph	Private	8 Reg't. (Meriam's), La. Militia
Claver, Valentin	Private	1 Batt'n. (Fortier's), La. Mil.
Clay, John	1 Lieut.-Q.M.	6 Reg't. (Landry's), La. Militia
Clay, John	Private	8 Reg't. (Meriam's), La. Militia
Clayburn, Thomas	Private	Capt. Rankin's Co., Mounted Riflemen, La. Militia
Clayton, James	Private	17, 18 and 19 Cons. Reg't., La. Militia
Clayton, John	Private	10 and 20 Cons. Reg't., La. Mil.
Clayton, Thomas	Private	12 and 13 Cons. Reg't., La. Mil.
Cleaver, James	Private	Capt. Callaway's Co., Cavalry, La. Militia
Clemancaux, --	Private	5 Reg't. (La Branche's), La. Mil.
Clemencaux, --	Private	5 Reg't. (La Branche's), La. Mil. (Orig. under Clemancaux, --)
Clemens, James	Private	1 Batt'n. (Henry's), U. S. Vols. (La. War 1812) See Reference Card U. S.
Clement, Andrew	Private	Captain Ramsey's Co., Mounted Riflemen, La. Militia
Clement, Francis	Private	16 Reg't. (Thompson's), La. Mil.
Clement, Francois	Private	16 Reg't. (Thompson's), La. Mil.
Clement, Francs	Private	5 Reg't. (La Branche's), La. Mil.
Clement, Henry	Private	Captain Beale's Co., Riflemen, La. Militia
Clement, Jacques	Private	5 Reg't. (La Branche's), La. Mil.
Clement, Joseph	Private	Captain Lagan's Co., La. Vols.
Clement, Louis	Private	De Clouet's Reg't., La. Militia
Clement, Mannan	Corporal	Captain Ramsey's Co., Mounted Riflemen, La. Militia
Clement, Nicholas	Private	5 Reg't. (La Branche's), La. Mil.
Clement, P.	Private	8 Reg't. (Meriam's), La. Militia
Clement, William	Private	Captain Wallace's Co., Boatmen, La. Vols.
Clemmens, Edward	Private	10 and 20 Cons. Reg't., La. Mil. (Orig. under Clemmons, Edward)
Clemment, Louis	Private	De Clouet's Reg't., La. Militia (Orig. under Clement, Louis)
Clemmons, Edward	Private	10 and 20 Cons. Reg't., La. Mil.
Clemmons, John	Private	De Clouet's Reg't., La. Militia
Clemont, Francois	Private	16 Reg't. (Thompson's), La. Mil. (Orig. under Clement, Francois)
Clemont, I. P.	Private	7 Reg't. (Le Beuf's), La. Militia
Clermont, --	Private	Plauche's Batt'n., La. Militia
Cleveland, Daniel	Private	10 Reg't., Louisiana Militia
Cline, Barnard D.	Private	Capt. Wallace's Co., Boatmen, La. Vols.
Clinton, Thomas	Private	2 Batt'n. (Peire's), La. Vols. (Orig. under Clinton, Thomas H.)
Clinton, Thomas H.	Private	2 Batt'n. (Peire's), La. Vols.
C'omm, Christoff	Private	De Clouet's Reg't., La. Militia
Close, John	1 Lieutenant	16 Reg't. (Thompson's), La. Mil.
Cloud, Jeremiah	Private	19 Reg't., La. Militia
Cloux, Pierre	Private	4 Reg't. (Morgan's), La. Militia
Cluatre, M.	Private	6 Reg't. (Landry's), La. Militia (Orig. under Clauatre, Michel)
Clumb, I.	Private	4 Reg't. (Morgan's), La. Militia
Cluseau, Jn Bte	Private	Baker's Reg't., La. Militia

Name	Rank	Unit
Coatney, Alexander	Private	12 and 30 Cons. Reg't., La. Mil. (Orig. under Courtney, Alexander)
Cobb, Daniel	Private	Capt. Thomas' Co., La. Militia
Cobb, Ezekiel	Private	10 and 20 Cons. Reg't., La. Mil.
Cobb, Nathaniel	Private	De Clouet's Reg't., La. Militia
Cobb, Nathaniel	Private	10 and 20 Cons. Reg't., La. Mil.
Cobb, Samuel	Sergeant	De Clouet's Reg't., La. Militia
Cobbs, Samuel	Sergeant	De Clouet's Reg't., La. Militia (Orig. under Cobb, Samuel)
Cobern, Ebenezer	Private	12 and 13 Cons. Reg't., La. Mil.
Cobette, Julien	Private	2 Batt'n. (D'Aquin's), La. Militia (Orig. under Cabette, Julien)
Cochram, Thomas	Private	De Clouet's Reg't., La. Militia
Cochran, George W.	1 Sgt.-Sgt.	Captain Young's Co., Mounted Riflemen, La. Militia (Orig. under Cohran, George W.)
Cochran, Josiah	Private	10 and 20 Cons. Reg't., La. Mil.
Cockram, Thomas	Private	De Clouet's Reg't., La. Militia (Orig. under Cochram, Thomas)
Cochran, Nathaniel	Priv-Sgt.	De Clouet's Reg't., La. Militia
Cochran, William	Surgeon	4 Reg't. (Morgan's), La. Militia
Cockran, John	Sergeant	17, 18 and 19 Cons. Reg't., La. Militia
Cockran, Nathaniel	Pvt.-Sgt.	De Clouet's Reg't., La. Militia (Orig. under Cochran, Nathaniel)
Cockrane, William E.	Private	Captain Beale's Co., Riflemen, La. Militia
Coe, James	Private	16 Reg't. (Thompson's), La. Mil.
Coeler, Francois	Private	6 Reg't. (Landry's), La. Militia (Orig. under Caeler, Francos)
Coeur, de Roy C.	1 Lieutenant	Plauche's Batt'n., La. Militia
Coglin, Honore'	Private	1 Batt'n. (Fortier's), La. Militia
Coffie, Jean Baptiste	Private	1 Batt'n. (Fortier's), La. Militia
Cohanon, Paul	Private	2 Batt'n. (Peire's), La. Vols.
Cohen, --	Sergeant	Plauche's Batt'n., La. Militia
Cohran, George W.	1 Sgt.-Sgt.	Captain Young's Co., Mounted Riflemen, La. Militia
Coignard, --	Private	Plauche's Batt'n., La. Militia
Coin, Charles	Private	De Clouet's Reg't., La. Militia
Colas, --	Servant	3 Reg't. (de la Ronde's), La. Mil.
Cole, Jacob	Private	Capt. Thomas' Co., La. Militia
Cole, James	Private	10 and 20 Cons. Reg't., La. Mil.
Cole, James	Private	16 Reg't. (Thompson's), La. Mil.
Cole, Solomon	Private	12 and 13 Cons. Reg't., La. Mil.
Cole, Solomon	Private	16 Reg't. (Thompson's), La. Mil.
Colein, Mathurine	Private	17, 18 and 19 Cons. Reg't., La. Militia
Coleman, Daniel	Private	Capt. Allen's Co., Artillerists, La. Vols.
Coleman, Daniel	Private	2 Batt'n. (Peire's), La. Vols.
Coleman, Daniel	Private	12 and 13 Cons. Reg't., La. Mil.
Coleman, John	Private	De Clouet's Reg't., La. Militia
Colette, Pierre	Private	3 Reg't. (de la Ronde's), La. Mil.
Colimau, Francois	Private	De Clouet's Reg't., La. Militia
Colin, Henry	Private	8 Reg't. (Meriam's), La. Militia (Orig. under Collin, Henry)
Colins, Jacob	Private	10 and 20 Cons. Reg't., La. Mil. (Orig. under Collins, Jacob)
Collard, Elijah	Captain	Capt. Collard's Co., La. Militia
Colleins, William	Private	10 and 20 Cons. Reg't., La. Mil. (Orig. under Collins, William)
Collens, Hiram	Private	Captain Beale's Co., Riflemen, La. Militia
Collian, --	Private	Plauche's Batt'n., La. Militia (Orig. under Collins, --)
Collier, Gray W.	Private	8 Reg't. (Meriam's), La. Militia
Collin, --	Private	Plauche's Batt'n., La. Militia (Orig. under Collins, --)
Collin, Henry	Private	8 Reg't. (Meriam's), La. Militia
Colline, --	Private	De Clouet's Reg't., La. Militia (Orig. under Collins, --)
Collins, --	Private	De Clouet's Reg't., La. Militia
Collins, --	Private	Plauche's Batt'n., La. Militia
Collins, Allen,	Corporal	19 Regiment, La. Militia
Collins, Fielding	Private	10 and 20 Cons. Reg't., La. Mil.
Collins, Jacob	Private	10 and 20 Cons. Reg't., La. Mil.
Collins, John	Private	10 and 20 Cons. Reg't., La. Mil.
Collins, John W.	Captain	4 Reg't. (Morgan's), La. Militia
Collins, Luke W.	Private	16 Reg't. (Thompson's), La. Mil.
Collins, Murlock	Private	16 Reg't. (Thompson's), La. Mil.
Collins, William	Private	10 and 20 Cons. Reg't., La. Mil.
Colmini, Fraise	Sergeant	2 Batt'n. (D'Aquin's), La. Militia
Colombe, Joseph	Private	De Clouet's Reg't., La. Militia
Colombe, Joseph	Private	2 Reg't. (Cavelier's), La. Militia
Colombi, J.	Private	De Clouet's Reg't., La. Militia (Orig. under Colombe, Joseph)
Colome', Celestin	Private	2 Batt'n. (D'Aquin's), La. Militia
Colsson, Jn. Bte	Captain	Capt. Colsson's Co., Artillery, La. Vols.
Colun, Mathurine	Private	17, 18 and 19 Cons. Reg't., La. Mil. (Orig. under Colein, Mathurine)
Coma, Cadet	Private	De Clouet's Reg't., La. Militia (Orig. under Comau, Cadet)
Comau, Bernard	Private	8 Reg't. (Meriam's), La. Militia
Comau, Cadet	Private	De Clouet's Reg't., La. Militia
Comau, Etienne	Private	8 Reg't. (Meriam's), La. Militia
Comau, Gilbert	Private	8 Reg't. (Meriam's), La. Militia
Comau, Hypolite	Private	De Clouet's Reg't., La. Militia
Comau, John Louis	Private	8 Reg't. (Meriam's), La. Militia
Comau, Julian	Corporal	8 Reg't. (Meriam's), La. Militia
Comau, Julien	Sergeant	De Clouet's Reg't., La. Militia
Combel, --	Private	Plauche's Batt'n., La. Militia
Combell, --	Private	1 Reg't. (Dejan's), La. Militia (Orig. under Combelle, --)
Combelle, --	Private	1 Reg't. (Dejan's), La. Militia
Come, Polite	Private	10 and 20 Cons. Reg't., La. Mil. (Orig. under Commo, Politte)
Comeau, Alexandre	Private	Capt. Hubbard's Mounted Company, La. Militia
Comeau, Simon	Private	8 Reg't. (Meriam's), La. Militia
Comes, Marcellin	1 Sergeant	6 Reg't. (Landry's), La. Militia
Comman, Benjamin	Private	10 Regiment, La. Militia
Commeau, Cs	Private	8 Reg't. (Meriam's), La. Militia
Commens, George	Private	Captain Beale's Co., Riflemen, La. Militia
Commestock, John	Corporal	6 Reg't. (Landry's), La. Militia
Commo, Cellestin	Private	6 Reg't. (Landry's), La. Militia
Commo, Charles	Private	6 Reg't. (Landry's), La. Militia
Commo, Ellistin	Private	6 Reg't. (Landry's), La. Militia (Orig. under Commo, Cellestin)
Commo, Politte	Private	10 and 20 Cons. Reg't., La. Mil.
Commo, Valery	Private	Baker's Regiment, La. Militia (Orig. under Como, Vallery)
Como, Julien	Sergeant	De Clouet's Reg't., La. Militia (Orig. under Comau, Julien)
Como, Polite	Private	10 and 20 Cons. Reg't., La. Mil. (Orig. under Commo, Politte)
Como, Vallery	Private	Baker's Reg't., La. Militia
Compeau, August	Private	7 Reg't. (Le Beuf's), La. Militia
Compianno, Juan	Private	Captain Lagan's Co., La. Vols.
Compton, Charles	Bugler	Captain Beale's Co., Riflemen, La. Militia
Compton, John	Ensign	17, 18 and 19 Cons. Reg't., La. Militia
Comus, Valery	Private	Baker's Regiment, La. Militia (Orig. under Como, Vallery)
Con, John M.	Sergeant	12 and 13 Cons. Reg't., La. Mil.
Conaway, Joseph	Private	Captain McNair's Co., Mounted Riflemen, La. Militia
Conaway, Walter	Private	Captain McNair's Co., Mounted Riflemen, La. Militia (Orig. under Connaway, Walter)
Conciliam, Michell	Artificer	Capt. Chaudurier's Co., Artificers, Art'y., La. Vols.
Concilliam, Michell	Artificer	Capt. Chaudurier's Co., Artificers, Art'y., La. Vols. (Orig. under Conciliam, Michell)
Concinne, Olivier	Private	7 Reg't. (Le Beuf's), La. Militia
Cone, Davis	Private	2 Batt'n. (Peire's), La. Vols. (Orig. under Conr, Dewis)
Coner, Davis	Private	2 Batt'n. (Peire's), La. Vols. (Orig. under Conr, Dewis)
Coney, William	Private	Baker's Regiment, La. Militia (Orig. under Coxey, William)
Congourdan, Caliste	Private	4 Reg't. (Morgan's), La. Militia (Orig. under Corgourdan, Caliste)
Conir, Dewis	Private	2 Batt'n. (Peire's), La. Vols. (Orig. under Conr, Dewis)
Conley, William	Private	De Clouet's Reg't., La. Militia (Orig. under Connelly, William)
Connally, Price	3 Lieut.	12 and 13 Cons. Reg't., La. Mil. (Orig. under Connely, Price)

Name	Rank	Unit
Connaway, Joseph	Private	Captain McNair's Co., Mounted Riflemen, La. Militia (Orig. under Connaway, Joseph)
Connaway, Walter	Private	Captain McNair's Co., Mounted Riflemen, La. Militia
Connellier, A.	Private	4 Reg't. (Morgan's), La. Militia
Connelly, William	Private	De Clouet's Reg't., La. Militia
Connely, Price	3 Lieutenant	12 and 13 Cons. Reg't., La. Mil.
Conner, Evans	Private	16 Reg't. (Thompson's), La. Mil.
Conner, John	Private	17, 18 and 19 Cons. Reg't., La. Militia
Connor, Jeremiah	Private	Captain McNair's Co., Mounted Riflemen, La. Militia
Conny, --	Private	2 Reg't. (Cavelier's), La. Militia
Conr, Dewis	Private	2 Batt'n. (Peire's), La. Vols.
Conrat, Andre	Fusilier-Private	5 Reg't. (La Branche's), La. Mil.
Conrat, Georges	Sergeant	5 Reg't. (La Branche's), La. Mil.
Conrat, Henry	Fusilier-Private	5 Reg't. (La Branche's), La. Mil.
Conrat, Jacques	Fusilier-Private	5 Reg't. (La Branche's), La. Mil.
Conrat, Michel	Fusilier-Private	5 Reg't. (La Branche's), La. Mil.
Conrat, Philip	Corporal	5 Reg't. (La Branche's), La. Mil.
Conrat, Pierre	Fusilier-Private	5 Reg't. (La Branche's), La. Mil.
Conrjear, Francois	Private	Captain Lagan's Co., La. Vols.
Consolat, Joseph	Private	4 Reg't. (Morgan's), La. Militia
Constant, Michel	Private	2 Reg't. (Cavelier's), La. Militia
Constatine, Jean	Musician	16 Reg't. (Thompson's), La. Mil.
Cantaloupe, Bernard	Private	2 Batt'n. (Peire's), La. Vols. (Orig. under Canteloupe, Bernard)
Contan, Thomas	Private	17, 18 and 19 Cons. Reg't., La. Militia (Orig. under Cantren, Thomas)
Contrelle, Ique	Private	6 Reg't. (Landry's), La. Militia (Orig. under Cantrelle, Jacques)
Conty, John B.	Private	17, 18 and 19 Cons. Reg't., La. Militia
Converse, Theodore	Private	4 Reg't. (Morgan's), La. Militia
Converse, Wright	Private	Capt. Thomas' Co., La. Militia
Cook, Absalom	Private	De Clouet's Reg't., La. Militia
Cook, Levi	Private	De Clouet's Reg't., La. Militia
Cook, Robert	Private	De Clouet's Reg't., La. Militia
Cooney, John	Private	Captain Griffith's Co., Mounted Riflemen, La. Vols.
Coons, James	Private	De Clouet's Reg't., La. Militia
Coons, John A.	Private	16 Reg't. (Thompson's), La. Mil.
Cooper, Carlton	Private	12 and 13 Cons. Reg't., La. Mil.
Cooper, Harrison	Corporal	12 and 13 Cons. Reg't., La. Mil.
Cooper, James C.	Private	19 Regiment, La. Militia
Cooper, John	Private	Capt. Musick's Co., La. Militia
Cooper, Warren	Private	De Clouet's Reg't., La. Militia
Cooper, William	Private	10 and 20 Cons. Reg't., La. Mil.
Cooper, William	Private	12 and 13 Cons. Reg't., La. Mil.
Copao, Juan	Private	2 Batt'n. (Peire's), La. Vols. (Orig. under Capaho, Juan)
Copel, John B.	Private	Baker's Regiment, La. Militia
Coper, James C.	Private	19 Reg't., La. Vols. (Orig. under Cooper, James C.)
Coquell, C. J.	Private	De Clouet's Reg't., La. Militia (Orig. under Coquell, Casimir)
Coquell, Casimir	Private	De Clouet's Reg't., La. Militia
Corbe', Jh.	Private	2 Batt'n. (D'Aquin's), La. Militia
Corbeau, I	Private	6 Reg't. (Landry's), La. Militia
Cordeale, Arthur	Private	Captain Callaway's Co., Cavalry, La. Militia
Cordell, Hiram	Corporal	Captain McNair's Co., Mounted Riflemen, La. Militia
Corder, John	Private	10 and 20 Cons. Reg't., La. Mil.
Cordier, I.	Private	8 Reg't. (Meriam's), La. Mil.
Cordon, --	Private	4 Reg't. (Morgan's), La. Militia
Corelle, Manuel	Private	Sergeant Hog's Detachment, La. Vols. (Orig. under Courille, Manuel)
Coreny, William	Private	Capt. Dodge's Co., Mounted Riflemen, La. Militia
Coreny, William	Private	Capt. Henry's Co., Mounted Riflemen, La. Militia
Corgourdan, Caliste	Private	4 Reg't. (Morgan's), La. Militia
Corkan, Anthony	Private	16 Reg't. (Thompson's), La. Mil. (Orig. under Corkran, Anthony)
Corker, James	Private	12 and 13 Cons. Reg't., La. Mil.
Corkins, John	Private	16 Reg't. (Thompson's), La. Mil.
Corkran, Anthony	Private	16 Reg't. (Thompson's), La. Mil.
Corliss, John	Private	Capt. Hughes' Co., Mounted Riflemen, La. Militia
Cormeer, Narcisse	Sergeant	De Clouet's Reg't., La. Militia
Cormier, Narcis	Sergeant	De Clouet's Reg't., La. Militia (Orig. under Cormeer, Narcisse)
Cormier, Nlas	Private	2 Reg't. (Cavelier's), La. Militia
Cormier, Piere	Private	De Clouet's Reg't., La. Militia
Cormier, Raphial	Private	De Clouet's Reg't., La. Militia
Cornier, Becoud	Fusilier-Private	2 Batt'n. (D'Aquin's), La. Militia
Cornier, Louis	Lieut.-2 Lieut.	2 Batt'n. (D'Aquin's), La. Militia
Corniere, Nicholas	Private	Captain Lagan's Co., La. Vols.
Cornillier, M.	Private	8 Reg't. (Meriam's), La. Militia
Corpecon, Jean Bte	Artificer	Capt. Chaudurier's Co., Artificers, Art'y., La. Vols. (Orig. under Corpron, Jean Bats)
Corpion, I. B.	Artificer	Capt. Chaudurier's Co., Artificers, Art'y., La. Vols. (Orig. under Corpron, Jean Bats)
Corpron, Jean Bats	Artificer	Capt. Chaudurier's Co., Artificers, Art'y., La. Vols.
Corre, John	Private	Capt. Alpuente's Co., La. Mil.
Correau, Etienne	Private	Capt. Colsson's Co., Artillery, La. Vols. (Orig. under Torreau, Etienne)
Corrowette, Jean V.	Private	Capt. Alpuente's Co., La. Militia (Orig. under Norrowette, Jean)
Corsnor, George	Private	Captain McNair's Co., Mounted Riflemen, La. Militia
Cortes, Jose	Private	17, 18 and 19 Cons. Reg't., La. Militia
Cortina, Is Maria	Corporal	17, 18 and 19 Cons. Reg't., La. Mil. (Orig. under Cortinos, Jose Maria)
Cortines, Jose Maria	Corporal	17, 18 and 19 Cons. Reg't., La. Mil. (Orig. under Cortinos, Jose Maria)
Cortinos, Jose Maria	Corporal	17, 18 and 19 Cons. Reg't., La. Militia
Cortis, Nathaniel	Private	10 and 20 Cons. Reg't., La. Mil. (Orig. under Curtis, Nathaniel)
Corwaisier, Jacques	Private	Captain Hubbard's Mounted Co., La. Militia
Cosse, Andre	Private	3 Reg't. (de la Ronde's), La. Mil.
Cosse, George	Private	3 Reg't. (de la Ronde's), La. Mil. (Orig. under Cesse', George)
Cosse, Honore	Private	3 Reg't. (de la Ronde's), La. Mil.
Cosse, Jaime	Private	Captain Lagan's Co., La. Vols.
Coste, J.	Private	8 Reg't. (Meriam's), La. Militia
Cotner, Jacob	Private	Capt. Young's Co., Mounted Riflemen, La. Militia
Cotner, John	Private	Capt. Young's Co., Mounted Riflemen, La. Militia
Cotoret, --	Private	3 Reg't. (de la Ronde's), La. Mil. (Orig. under Cotteret, --)
Cotten, G. B.	Corporal-Sgt.	4 Reg't. (Morgan's), La. Militia (Orig. under Cotton, Godwin B.)
Cotter, William	Private	Captain Sprigg's Co., Boatmen, La. Vols.
Cotterell, Rowland	Private	Capt. Allen's Co., Artillerists, La. Vols.
Cotteret, --	Private	3 Reg't. (de la Ronde's), La. Mil.
Cotterill, Rowland	Private	Capt. Allen's Co., Artillerists, La. Vols. (Orig. under Cotterell, Rowland)
Cottle, Almond	Sergeant	Capt. Collard's Co., La. Militia
Cottle, Andrew	Private	Capt. Van Bibber's Co., La. Mil.
Cottle, Edward	Private	Capt. Van Bibber's Co., La. Mil.
Cottle, Isaac	Private	Capt. Collard's Co., La. Militia
Cottle, James	1 Sgt.-Sgt.	Capt. Collard's Co., La. Militia (Orig. under Clark, James)
Cottle, Lee L.	Private	Capt. Collard's Co., La. Militia
Cottle, Oliver	1 Sgt.-Sgt.	Capt. Van Bibber's Co., La. Mil.
Cottle, Silvanus	Private	Capt. Collard's Co., La. Militia
Cottle, Warren	Sergeant	Capt. Collard's Co., La. Militia
Cottman, Auguste	Private	6 Reg't. (Landry's), La. Militia
Cotton, Godwin B.	Corporal-Sgt.	4 Reg't. (Morgan's), La. Militia
Cotton, J.	Private	4 Reg't. (Morgan's), La. Militia
Cotton, James	Private	12 and 13 Cons. Reg't., La. Mil.
Cotty, Joseph	Private	Capt. Van Bibber's Co., La. Mil.
Coucinne, Pierre	Private	7 Reg't. (Le Beuf's), La. Militia
Coudrin, --	Private	1 Reg't. (Dejan's), La. Militia

Name	Rank	Unit
Cougeard, Jean	Artificer	Capt. Chaudurier's Co., Artificers, Art'y., La. Vols. (Orig. under Coupard, Jean)
Couli, Charles	Private	4 Reg't. (Morgan's), La. Militia
Coulon, --	Fusilier-Private	5 Reg't. (La Branche's), La. Mil.
Coumeau, Auguste	Private	7 Reg't. (Le Beuf's), La. Militia
Coumeau, Joseph	Private	7 Reg't. (Le Beuf's), La. Militia
Coummont, I	Private	8 Reg't. (Meriam's), La. Militia
Counseller, John	Sergeant	16 Reg't. (Thompson's), La. Mil.
Counselor, John	Sergeant	16 Reg't. (Thompson's), La. Mil. (Orig. under Counseller, John)
Coupard, Francois	Private	De Clouet's Reg't., La. Militia
Coupard, Jean	Artificer	Capt. Chaudurier's Co., Artificers, Art'y., La. Vols.
Coupel, Augustin	Private	Captain Hubbard's Mounted Co., La. Militia
Coupelle, Joseph	2 Lieutenant	1 Batt'n. (Fortier's), La. Militia
Couple, John B.	Private	Baker's Regiment, La. Militia (Orig. under Copel, John B.)
Coupless, George	Private	De Clouet's Reg't., La. Militia
Courajo, --	Private	2 Reg't. (Cavelier's), La. Militia
Courat, Philip	Corporal	5 Reg't. (La Branche's), La. Mil. (Orig. under Ceurat, Philip)
Courcell, Joncin	Private	Capt. Chauveau's Co., Cavalry, La. Militia
Courcello, Leon	Private	4 Reg't. (Morgan's), La. Militia
Courderoy, C.	1 Lieutenant	Plauche's Batt'n., La. Militia (Orig. under Coeur, de Roy C.)
Courejeole, Jr.	Private	Plauche's Batt'n., La. Militia (Orig. under Courjeole, Jr.)
Courejeole, aine	Private	Plauche's Batt'n., La. Militia (Orig. under Courjeolle, aine)
Courille, Manuel	Private	Sergeant Hog's Detachment, La. Vols.
Courejeolle, aine	Private	Plauche's Batt'n., La. Militia
Courjeolle, Jr.	Private	Plauche's Batt'n., La. Militia
Cournesey, Joseph	Private	Capt. Songy's Co., Marines, La. Vols. (Orig. under Fournesy, Jh)
Couron, J.	2 Lieut.	2 Reg't. (Cavelier's), La. Militia (Orig. under Touron, Julien)
Coursey, Braxton	Private	10 and 20 Cons. Reg't., La. Mil.
Coursey, Louis	Private	De Clouet's Reg't., La. Militia
Coursier, Gullamne	Private	Captain Lagan's Co., La. Vols. (Orig. under Coussier, Gullamne)
Courtier, F.	Private	8 Reg't. (Meriam's), La. Militia
Courtier, Pre	Private	8 Reg't. (Meriam's), La. Militia
Courtney, Alexander	Private	12 and 13 Cons. Reg't., La. Mil.
Courtney, Benjamin	Private	De Clouet's Reg't., La. Militia
Courtney, Benjamin	Private	De Clouet's Reg't., La. Militia (Orig. under Courtney, Benjamin)
Courtny, Alexander	Private	12 and 13 Cons. Reg't., La. Mil. (Orig. under Courtney, Alexander)
Courtois, Severe	Sgt.-Major	2 Batt'n. (D'Aquin's), La. Militia
Cousinne, P.	Private	7 Reg't. (Le Beuf's), La. Militia (Orig. under Concinne, Oliver)
Cousinne, Pierre	Private	7 Reg't. (Le Beuf's), La. Militia (Orig. under Coucinne, Pierre)
Cousot, Charles	Private	4 Reg't. (Morgan's), La. Militia
Coussier, Gullamne	Private	Capt. Lagan's Co., La. Vols.
Coussol, Francisco	Sergeant	2 Reg't. (Cavelier's), La. Militia (Orig. under Ceressol, Francis)
Coute, Fars	Private	2 Batt'n. (D'Aquin's), La. Militia
Couti, Frans	Private	2 Batt'n. (D'Aquin's), La. Militia (Orig. under Coute, Fars)
Coutin, --	Private	1 Reg't. (Dejan's), La. Militia
Couvellon, Pierre	Private	17, 18 and 19 Cons. Reg't., La. Mil. (Orig. under Couvillon, Prince)
Couvertier, Jr.	Sergeant	Plauche's Batt'n., La. Militia
Couvertier, Sr.	Sergeant	Plauche's Batt'n., La. Militia
Couvillon, Adnen	Private	17, 18 and 19 Cons. Reg't., La. Militia
Couvillon, Prince	Private	17, 18 and 19 Cons. Reg't., La. Militia
Couvreur, Tervallon	Fusilier-Pvt.	2 Batt'n. (D'Aquin's), La. Militia
Covington, Strother	Lieutenant	Capt. Ashley's Co., Mounted Riflemen, La. Militia
Cowan, Josee	Corporal	Captain Beale's Co., Riflemen, La. Militia
Cox, --	Private	1 Reg't. (Dejan's), La. Militia
Cox, Caleb	Captain	1 Reg't. (Dejan's), La. Militia
Cox, Charles	Private	8 Reg't. (Meriam's), La. Militia
Cox, Francis S.	Private	Captain Beale's Co., Riflemen, La. Militia
Cox, John	Private	Captain Sprigg's Co., Boatmen, La. Vols.
Cox, Nathaniel	Private	Captain Beale's Co., Riflemen, La. Militia
Coxey, William	Private	Baker's Regiment, La. Militia
Coyle, William	Private	10 and 20 Cons. Reg't., La. Mil.
Cozard, --	--	De Clouet's Reg't., La. Militia
Cracrop, William	Private	Captain Ramsey's Co., Mounted Riflemen, La. Militia
Craig, Charles	Sergeant	De Clouet's Reg't., La. Militia
Craig, I. P.	Corporal	4 Reg't. (Morgan's), La. Militia
Craig, Peter	Burser	Captain Ramsey's Co., Mounted Riflemen, La. Militia
Craig, William	Private	Captain McNair's Co., Mounted Riflemen, La. Militia
Craker, Cornelius	Private	12 and 13 Cons. Reg't., La. Mil.
Craker, Isaac	Private	12 and 13 Cons. Reg't., La. Mil.
Crane, Dennis	Private	12 and 13 Cons. Reg't., La. Mil.
Crapper, John	Private	10 and 20 Cons. Reg't., La. Mil. (Orig. under Cropper, John)
Crapper, Nathaniel	1 Lieut.	8 Reg't. (Meriam's), La. Militia
Crapper, Thomas	Private	8 Reg't. (Meriam's), La. Militia
Crauford, William	Sgt.-Private	De Clouet's Reg't., La. Militia (Orig. under Crawford, William)
Cravan, --	Private	1 Reg't. (Dejan's), La. Militia (Orig. under Craven, --)
Craven, --	Private	1 Reg't. (Dejan's), La. Militia
Craven, William S.	Private	Captain Beale's Co., Riflemen, La. Mil.
Crawfor, Thompson	Private	Captain Callaway's Co., Mounted Riflemen, La. Mil. (Orig. under Crawford, Thompson)
Crawfor, William	Private	Captain Callaway's Co., Mounted Riflemen, La. Mil. (Orig. under Crawford, William)
Crawford, George	Private	Capt. Ashley's Co., Mounted Riflemen, La. Mil. (Orig. under Crofford, George)
Crawford, George	Private	12 and 13 Cons. Reg't., La. Mil.
Crawford, John	Private	10 and 20 Cons. Reg't., La. Mil.
Crawford, Joseph	Private	6 Reg't. (Landry's), La. Militia
Crawford, Robert	Private	De Clouet's Reg't., La. Militia
Crawford, Thompson	Private	Captain Callaway's Co., Mounted Riflemen, La. Militia
Crawford, William	Private	Captain Callaway's Co., Mounted Riflemen, La. Militia
Crawford, William	Sgt.-Private	De Clouet's Reg't., La. Militia
Crawley, John	Private	De Clouet's Reg't., La. Militia
Craycraft, --	Private	2 Reg't. (Cavelier's), La. Militia
Crebe, Valentin	Sergeant	2 Batt'n. (Peire's), La. Vols. (Orig. under Creve, Valentin)
Creber, Valentine	Sergeant	2 Batt'n. (Peire's), La. Vols. (Orig. under Creve, Valentin)
Crefre, Philippe	Private	3 Reg't. (de la Ronde's), La. Mil. (Orig. under Crespo, Phillippe)
Cremona, --	Musician	Plauche's Batt'n., La. Militia
Crepin, Francois	Musician	1 Batt'n. (Fortier's), La. Militia
Crespo, Joseph	Corporal	3 Reg't. (de la Ronde's), La. Mil.
Crespo, Phillippe	Private	3 Reg't. (de la Ronde's), La. Mil.
Creswell, Robert	Private	10 and 20 Cons. Reg't., La. Mil.
Creusel, --	Musician	Plauche's Batt'n., La. Militia (Orig. under Creuzel, B.)
Creuzel, --	Private	Plauche's Batt'n., La. Militia
Creuzel, B.	Musician	Plauche's Batt'n., La. Militia
Creve, Valentin	Sergeant	2 Batt'n. (Peire's), La. Vols.
Crever, Valentin	Sergeant	2 Batt'n. (Peire's), La. Vols. (Orig. under Creve, Valentin)
Crevignau, L.	Private	4 Reg't. (Morgan's), La. Militia
Crevre, Valentin	Sergeant	2 Batt'n. (Peire's), La. Vols. (Orig. under Creve, Valentin)
Criar, William	Corporal	17, 18 and 19 Cons. Reg't., La. Militia
Crier, Melsor	Private	De Clouet's Reg't., La. Militia See also Luke Powers & Vincent Chance
Crinecher, Pierre	Private	1 Batt'n. (Fortier's), La. Militia (Orig. under Crinicher, Pierre)
Criniche, Pierre	Private	1 Batt'n. (Fortier's), La. Militia (Orig. under Crinicher, Pierre)
Crinicher, Pierre	Private	1 Batt'n. (Fortier's), La. Militia

Name	Rank	Unit
Crismias, In Cs	Private	Capt. Songy's Co., Marines, La. Vols. (Orig. under Crismias, Jean C.)
Crismias, Jean C.	Private	Capt. Songy's Co., Marines, La. Vols.
Crispain, --	Servant	Capt. Colsson's Co., Artillery, La. Vols.
Criss, Aron	Private	Captain Price's Co., La. Militia
Crissimias, In Cs	Private	Capt. Songy's Co., Marines, La. Vols. (Orig. under Crismias, Jean C.)
Cristofle, Charles	Private	5 Reg't. (La Branche's), La. Mil.
Cristophe, Charles	Private	5 Reg't. (La Branche's), La. Mil. (Orig. under Cristofle, Charles)
Cristwell, Robert	Private	10 and 20 Cons. Reg't., La. Mil. (Orig. under Creswell, Robert)
Criswell, Mathw	Private	10 Regiment, La. Militia
Criswell, Robert	Private	10 and 20 Cons. Reg't., La. Mil. (Orig. under Crewwell, Robert)
Critington, Jeremiah	Private	12 and 13 Cons. Reg't., La. Mil. (Orig. under Crittenton, Jeremiah)
Crittenton, Bartlet	Private	12 and 13 Cons. Reg't., La. Mil.
Crittenton, Jeremiah	Private	12 and 13 Cons. Reg't., La. Mil.
Crodret, A.	Private	7 Reg't. (Le Beuf's), La. Militia (Orig. under Chrochet, Amant)
Crochet, Francois	Private	7 Reg't. (Le Beuf's), La. Militia
Croese, J. B.	Private	De Clouet's Reg't., La. Militia (Orig. under Croise, J. B.)
Crofford, George	Private	Capt. Ashley's Co., Mounted Riflemen, La. Militia
Crofford, George	Private	12 and 13 Cons. Reg't., La. Mil. (Orig. under Crawford, George)
Crofford, James	Private	12 and 13 Cons. Reg't., La. Mil.
Croise, J. B. (I. B.)	Private	De Clouet's Reg't., La. Militia
Croisiere, --	Corporal	2 Batt'n. (D'Aquin's), La. Militia
Croix, Jean	Private	8 Reg't. (Meriam's), La. Militia
Cropper, John	Private	10 and 20 Cons. Reg't., La. Mil.
Crosby, John	Private	De Clouet's Reg't., La. Militia (Orig. under Crawley, John)
Crouch, Winder	Sergeant	De Clouet's Reg't., La. Militia
Crouche, Winder	Sergeant	De Clouet's Reg't., La. Militia (Orig. under Crouch, Winder)
Croudson, Samuel	Private	Capt. Ogden's Co., Dragoons, La. Militia (Orig. under Crowdson, Samuel)
Crow, Bazil	Private	Baker's Regiment, La. Militia
Crow, Lewis	Private	Capt. Collard's Co., La. Militia
Crow, Michael	Private	Capt. Collard's Co., La. Militia
Crowdson, Samuel	Private	Capt. Ogden's Co., Dragoons, La. Militia
Crownover, Abraham	Private	10 and 20 Cons. Reg't., La. Mil.
Cruan, --	Private	2 Reg't. (Cavelier's), La. Militia
Crudeau, Senior	Private	4 Reg't. (Morgan's), La. Militia
Crudeau, Zenon	Private	4 Reg't. (Morgan's), La. Militia
Crumb, Henry	Private	Capt. Wallace's Co., Boatmen, La. Vols.
Crumpton, Isaiah	Private	12 and 13 Cons. Reg't., La. Mil. (Orig. under Cumpton, Isaiah)
Crusas, fils	Private	3 Reg't. (de la Ronde's), La. Mil.
Crutcher, William	Corporal	17, 18 and 19 Cons. Reg't., La. Militia
Crutcher, William C.	Corporal	17, 18 and 19 Cons. Reg't., La. Militia (Orig. under Crutcher, William)
Cruthers, John	Private	16 Reg't. (Thompson's), La. Mil.
Crutzher, William C.	Corporal	17, 18 and 19 Cons. Reg't., La. Militia
Cryer, Daniel	Private	12 and 13 Cons. Reg't., La. Mil.
Cryer, Honor	Private	12 and 13 Cons. Reg't., La. Mil.
Cryer, Melsor	Private	De Clouet's Reg't., La. Militia (Orig. under Crier, Melsor)
Cryer, Thomas	Private	12 and 13 Cons. Reg't., La. Mil.
Cubbage, George	Private	Captain Sprigg's Co., Boatmen, La. Vols.
Cubidon, Vincent	Private	1 Batt'n. (Fortier's), La. Militia
Cuelland, Manuel	Private	2 Batt'n. (Peire's), La. Vols. (Orig. under Cuellard, Manuel)
Cuellar, Manuel	Private	2 Batt'n. (Peire's), La. Vols. (Orig. under Cuellard, Manuel)
Cuellard, Manuel	Private	2 Batt'n. (Peire's), La. Vols.
Cuellare, Manuel	Private	2 Batt'n. (Peire's), La. Vols. (Orig. under Cuellard, Manuel)
Cuerail, Louis	Private	1 Batt'n. (Fortier's), La. Militia (Orig. under Curail, Louis)
Culbertson, Robert	Private	10 and 20 Cons. Reg't., La. Mil.
Cumegan, Thomas	Private	Capt. Callaway's Co., Cavalry, La. Militia
Cummings, John	Private-Cpl.	De Clouet's Reg't., La. Militia
Cummings, William	Private	1 Reg't. (Dejan's), La. Militia
Cummins, John	Private-Cpl.	De Clouet's Reg't., La. Militia (Orig. under Cummings, John)
Cummins, John	Private-Cpl.	17, 18 and 19 Cons. Reg't., La. Militia
Cummins, Wilson	Private-Cpl.	10 and 20 Cons. Reg't., La. Mil.
Cumo, Henry	Private	8 Reg't. (Meriam's), La. Militia
Cumpton, Isaiah	Private-Cpl.	12 and 13 Cons. Reg't., La. Mil.
Cuney, Cesar	Private-Cpl.	17, 18 and 19 Cons. Reg't., La. Militia
Cunning, Edward	Private-Cpl.	10 and 20 Cons. Reg't., La. Mil. (Orig. under Clemmons, Edward)
Cunning, Willson	Private-Cpl.	10 and 20 Cons. Reg't., La. Mil. (Orig. under Cummins, Wilson)
Cunningham, George	Private	16 Reg't. (Thompson's), La. Mil.
Cunningham, George H.	Private	16 Reg't. (Thompson's), La. Mil. (Orig. under Cunningham, George)
Cunningham, Joseph	Private	Captain McNair's Co., Mounted Riflemen, La. Militia
Cupidon, --	Servant	Gov. Claiborne & Staff, La. Militia
Cupidon, Vincent	Private	1 Batt'n. (Fortier's), La. Militia (Orig. under Cubidon, Vincent)
Cur, Martin	Private	2 Batt'n. (Peire's), La. Vols.
Curail, Louis	Private	1 Batt'n. (Fortier's), La. Militia
Cure, Martin	Private	2 Reg't. (Cavelier's), La. Militia
Cure, Martin	Private	3 Reg't. (de la Ronde's), La. Mil.
Cureau, Jean Louis	Private	6 Reg't. (Landry's), La. Militia
Cureau, Joseph	Fusilier-Private	5 Reg't. (La Branche's), La. Mil.
Cureuil, Louis	Private	1 Batt'n. (Fortier's), La. Militia (Orig. under Curail, Louis)
Curion, Terence	Private	De Clouet's Reg't., La. Militia
Curos, Felix	Private	Capt. Songy's Co., Marines, La. Vols.
Currier, Joseph	Private	16 Reg't. (Thompson's), La. Mil. (Orig. under Carriere, Joseph)
Curtis, Benjamin	Private	10 and 20 Cons. Reg't., La. Mil.
Curtis, Levi	Private	10 and 20 Cons. Reg't., La. Mil.
Curtis, Nathaniel	Private	10 and 20 Cons. Reg't., La. Mil.
Cusbere, Francis	Private	4 Reg't. (Morgan's), La. Militia (Orig. under Casbere, Francis)
Cushman, Conrad	Private	Captain Price's Co., La. Militia
Custard, George	Private	17, 18 and 19 Cons. Reg't., La. Militia
Custard, William	Private	17, 18 and 19 Cons. Reg't., La. Militia
Cutrer, Henry	Private	12 and 13 Cons. Reg't., La. Mil.
Cuvette, Jean	Private	Captain Lagan's Co., La. Vols.
Cuviller, Ant	Fusilier-Private	5 Reg't. (La Branche's), La. Mil. (Orig. under Cuvillier, Antoine)
Cuvillier, Henry	Private	7 Reg't. (Le Beuf's), La. Militia
Cuvillier, Joseph	Fusilier-Private	5 Reg't. (La Branche's), La. Mil.
Cuvillier, P. A.	Private	4 Reg't. (Morgan's), La. Militia
Cuvillier, Pierre	Fusilier-Private	5 Reg't. (La Branche's), La. Mil.
Cybillatte, --	Private	Plauche's Batt'n., La. Militia
Cybillot, --	Private	Plauche's Batt'n., La. Militia (Orig. under Cybillatte, --)
Cyer, Charles	Private	Baker's Regiment, La. Militia (Orig. under Oyer, Charles)
Cyrus, --	Servant	Captain Griffith's Co., Mounted Riflemen, La. Vols.
Dabenouo, Hipolite	Private	Plauche's Batt'n., La. Militia (Orig. under Dabenour, Hipolite)
Dabenour, Hipolite	Private	Plauche's Batt'n., La. Militia
Dablon, Honore'	Private	1 Batt'n. (Fortier's), La. Militia
Dablon, Honoree	Private	1 Batt'n. (Fortier's), La. Militia
Dablong, Honere	Private	1 Batt'n. (Fortier's), La. Militia (Orig. under Dablon, Honoree)
Dabnour, Hipolite	Private	Plauche's Batt'n., La. Militia (Orig. under Dabenour, Hipolite)
Dagle, L.	Private	8 Reg't. (Meriam's), La. Militia
Dagra, Etienne Batiste	Private	Captain Lagan's Co., La. Vols.
Dagusan, --	Private	4 Reg't. (Morgan's), La. Militia
Dahmer, --	Private	1 Reg't. (Dejan's), La. Militia
Daigle, Alexandre	Corporal	De Clouet's Reg't., La. Militia
Daigle, Alexandre	Private	8 Reg't. (Meriam's), La. Militia
Daigle, B.	Private	8 Reg't. (Meriam's), La. Militia

Name	Rank	Unit
Daigle, Baptiste	Private	Captain Hubbard's Mounted Co., La. Militia
Daigle, Cadet	Private	8 Reg't. (Meriam's), La. Militia
Daigle, Daniel	Private	8 Reg't. (Meriam's), La. Militia
Daigle, Etienne	Sergeant	7 Reg't. (Le Beuf's), La. Militia
Daigle, Etienne	Private	16 Reg't. (Thompson's), La. Mil.
Daigle, Honore	Private	8 Reg't. (Meriam's), La. Militia
Daigle, Ianot	1 Lieutenant	7 Reg't. (Le Beuf's), La. Militia
Daigle, Joh	Private	8 Reg't. (Meriam's), La. Militia
Daigle, John	Private	16 Reg't. (Thompson's), La. Mil.
Daigle, John Pierre	Private	De Clouet's Reg't., La. Militia
Daigle, Joseph	Private	De Clouet's Reg't., La. Militia
Daigle, Joseph	Private	6 Reg't. (Landry's), La. Militia
Daigle, Joseph	Private	7 Reg't. (Le Beuf's), La. Militia
Daigle, Joseph	Private	7 Reg't. (Le Beuf's), La. Militia
Daigle, Joseph	Private	7 Reg't. (Le Beuf's), La. Militia
Daigle, Joseph	Private	8 Reg't. (Meriam's), La. Militia
D'aigle, Joseph	Private	16 Reg't. (Thompson's), La. Mil.
Daigre, Bovier	Private	10 and 20 Cons. Reg't., La. Mil.
Daigle, Z.	Private	8 Reg't. (Meriam's), La. Militia
Daigre, David	Private	10 and 20 Cons. Reg't., La. Mil.
Daigre, Lawrence	Private	10 and 20 Cons. Reg't., La. Mil.
Daigre, Oliver	Private	10 and 20 Cons. Reg't., La. Mil.
Dail, Aron	Private	Baker's Regiment, La. Militia (Orig. under Dial, Aaron)
Dainee, H.	Private	Captain Sprigg's Co., Boatmen, La. Vols.
Dairne, Joseph	Private	2 Batt'n. (Peire's), La. Vols. (Orig. under Darne, Joseph)
Dairon, Isaac	Private	8 Reg't. (Meriam's), La. Militia
Dairon, M.	Private	8 Reg't. (Meriam's), La. Militia
Daison, August	Private	7 Reg't. (Le Beuf's), La. Militia
Daison, I.	Private	8 Reg't. (Meriam's), La. Militia (Orig. under Doison, I.)
Dalberge, Louis	1 Sgt.-Sergeant	Capt. Songy's Co., Marines, La. Vols.
Dalbiere, Jean	Private	2 Batt'n. (Peire's), La. Vols.
Dalbierre, Jean	Private	2 Batt'n. (Peire's), La. Vols. (Orig. under Dalbiere, Jean)
Dalcour, Valcour	Private	1 Batt'n. (Fortier's), La. Militia
Dalcourt, Valcour	Private	1 Batt'n. (Fortier's), La. Militia (Orig. under Dalcour, Valcour)
Daley, William	Private	4 Reg't. (Morgan's), La. Militia (Orig. under Daly, William)
Dalley, Benjamin	Private	10 and 20 Cons. Reg't., La. Mil.
Dalley, William	Private	De Clouet's Reg't., La. Militia
Dally, William	Private	De Clouet's Reg't., La. Militia (Orig. under Dalley, Willam)
Dalmont, Lewis	Private	Baker's Regiment, La. Militia (Orig. under Dalmont, Louis)
Dalmont, Louis	Private	Baker's Regiment, La. Militia
Dalton, Ewel	Capt.-Aid de Camp	3 Brigade (Mc Causland's), La. Militia
Dalton, Lasy	Private	2 Batt'n. (Peire's), La. Vols. (Orig. under Dolten, Lasy)
Dalton, Valentine	Sergeant	10 and 20 Cons. Reg't., La. Mil.
Daly, William	Private	4 Reg't. (Morgan's), La. Militia
Dameron, Christian	Private	Plauche's Batt'n., La. Militia
Dames, --	Private	2 Batt'n. (D'Aquin's), La. Militia (Orig. under Damis, --)
Damis, --	Private	2 Batt'n. (D'Aquin's), La. Militia
Damor, --	Private	2 Batt'n. (D'Aquin's), La. Militia (Orig. under Zamor, --)
Danaley, Amos	Private	De Clouet's Reg't., La. Militia (Orig. under Daniley, Amos)
Danbry, Talmage	Private	Baker's Regiment, La. Militia
Dancome, Jeaqus	Private	Captain Lagan's Co., La. Vols. (Orig. under Dancone, Jeaques)
Dancone, Jeaques	Private	Captain Lagan's Co., La. Vols.
Dangluse, Monplaisire	Private	2 Batt'n. (D'Aquin's), La. Militia
Danham, John	Private	10 and 20 Cons. Reg't., La. Mil. (Orig. under Dunham, John)
Danial, Nicholas	Private	2 Batt'n. (Peire's), La. Vols. (Orig. under Daniel, Nicholas)
Daniel, --	Waiter	3 Reg't. (de la Ronde's), La. Mil.
Daniel, --	Servant	3 Brigage (Mc Causland's), La. Militia
Daniel, --	Servant	Detachment Field and Staff Officers, 4 Brigade, La. Militia
Daniel, Jacques	Private	De Clouet's Reg't., La. Militia
Daniel, Jean	Private	Captain Lagan's Co., La. Vols.
Daniel, Nicholas	Private	2 Batt'n. (Peire's), La. Vols. (La. War of 1812 Ref. Card)
Daniel, Nicholas	Private	2 Batt'n. (Peire's), La. Vols. (La. War of 1812 Ref. Card)
Daniele, Louis	Artificer	Capt. Chaudurier's Co., Artificers, Art'y., La. Vols. (Orig. under Daniell, Louis)
Daniell, Louis	Artificer	Capt. Chaudurier's Co., Artificers, Art'y., La. Vols.
Danielle, Louis	Artificer	Capt. Chaudurier's Co., Artificers, Art'y., La. Vols. (Orig. under Daniell, Louis)
Daniells, Louis	Artificer	Capt. Chaudurier's Co., Artificers, Art'u., La. Vols. (Orig. under Daniell, Louis)
Daniels, Jabish	Private	17, 18 and 19 Cons. Reg't., La. Militia
Daniels, Louis	Artificer	Capt. Chaudurier'r Co., Artificers, Art'y., La. Vols. (Orig. under Daniell, Louis)
Daniley, Amos	Private	De Clouet's Reg't., La. Militia
Danillon, Ant	Private	2 Reg't. (Cavelier's), La. Militia (Orig. under Denillon, Ant)
Danio, Marcel	Private	7 Reg't. (Le Beuf's), La. Militia
Danion, Vicent	Private	7 Reg't. (Le Beuf's), La. Militia
Dannelly, Amos	Private	De Clouet's Reg't., La. Militia (Orig. under Daniley, Amos)
Dannels, Elisha	Private	17, 18 and 19 Cons. Reg't., La. Militia
Dannely, Amous	Private	De Clouet's Reg't., La. Militia (Orig. under Daniley, Amos)
Danos, Jean	Private	8 Reg't. (Meriam's), La. Militia
Dantilly, --	Private	3 Reg't. (de la Ronde's), La. Mil.
Dantin, Baptiste	Private	De Clouet's Reg't., La. Militia
Dantin, Charles	Private	De Clouet's Reg't., La. Militia
Dantin, Fabian	Corporal	De Clouet's Reg't., La. Militia
Dantreu, Lewis	Sergeant	Baker's Reg't., La. Mil. (Orig. under Dautreul, Louis)
D'Apremond, --	Private	Plauche's Batt'n., La. Militia (Orig. under D'Apremont, --)
D'Apremont, --	Private	Plauche's Batt'n., La. Militia
Dapremont, Chevalier	Private	4 Reg't. (Morgan's), La. Militia
Daquin, Louis	Major	1 Reg't. (Dejan's), La. Militia
Daquin, Louis	Major	2 Batt'n. (D'Aquin's), La. Militia
Daquin, Silvin	2 Lieutenant	2 Batt'n. (D'Aquin's), La. Militia
Darbois, --	Chief of Drummers Chief Musician	Plauche's Batt'n., La. Militia
Darby, Celestin	Private	Baker's Regiment, La. Militia
Darby, Charles	Sergeant	Baker's Regiment, La. Militia
Darby, John	1 Lieutenant	Capt. Dubuclet's Troop, Hussars, La. Vols.
Darby, Pierre	Private	Baker's Regiment, La. Militia
Darby, St. Marc	Corporal	Capt. Dubuclet's Troop, Hussars, La. Vols.
Darby, Ursin	Sergeant	Capt. Dubuclet's Troop, Hussars, La. Vols.
Darden, Jean Bte	Private	8 Reg't. (Meriam's), La. Militia (Orig. under Dardenne, Jean Bte)
Dardenil, Poupon	Private	2 Batt'n. (D'Aquin's), La. Militia
Dardenne, Alexis	Private	8 Reg't.(Meriam's), La. Militia
Dardenne, F.	Sergeant	8 Reg't.(Meriam's), La. Militia
Dardenne, Jean Bte	Private	8 Reg't. (Meriam's), La. Militia
Dardenne, Joseph	Corporal	8 Reg't.(Meriam's), La. Militia
Dardenne, T. L.	Corporal	8 Reg't. (Meriam's), La. Militia
Dare, Major O.	Private	De Clouet's Reg't., La. Militia (Orig. under O'Dare, Major)
Darensbourg, Adolphe	Corporal	5 Reg't. (La Branche's), La. Mil.
Darensbourg, Ch-aime	Fusilier-Pvt.	5 Reg't. (La Branche's), La. Mil.
Darensbourg, Charles	Fusilier-Pvt.	5 Reg't. (La Branche's), La. Mil.
Darensbourg, Edoire	Private	5 Reg't. (La Branche's), La. Mil.
Darensbourg, Zenon	Fusilier-Pvt.	5 Reg't. (La Branche's), La. Mil.
Darigol, Jean	Private	Captain Lagan's Co., La. Vols.
Darjous, Dominique	Corporal	Capt. Songy's Co., Marines, La.
Darle, Joseph	Private	De Clouet's Reg't., La. Militia
D'Armas, C.	Private	Plauche's Batt'n., La. Militia
D'Armas, Me	Private	Plauche's Batt'n., La. Militia
Darne, Joseph	Private	2 Batt'n. (Peire's), La. Vols.
Daronsbour, --	Fusilier-Private	5 Reg't. (La Branche's), La. Mil. (Orig. under Darensbourg, Zenon)
Darsina, (Negro)	Servant-Private	17, 18 and 19 Cons. Reg't., La. Militia

Name	Rank	Unit
Darst, Jacob C.	Private	Capt. Callaway's Co., Cavalry, La. Militia
Dart, John	Private	Capt. Dodge's Co., Mounted Rifleman, La. Militia
Dart, John	Private	Capt. Henry's Co., Mounted Riflemen, La. Militia
Dartch, Thomas	Private	Captain Griffith's Co., Mounted Riflemen, La. Vols.
Dartes, Darty	Private	De Clouet's Regiment, La. Mil.
Dartes, Pirre	Private	Baker's Regiment, La. Militia
Dasprement, Emmanuel	Sergeant	Capt. Dubuclet's Troop, Hussars, La. Vols. (Orig. under D'Aspremont, Emmaneul)
D'Aspremont, Emmanuel	Sergeant	Capt. Dubuclet's Troop, Hussars, La. Vols.
Dassena, (Negro)	Servant-Pvt.	17, 18 and 19 Cons. Reg't., La. Mil. (Orig. under Darsina, Negro)
Dast, Jacob	Private	Capt. Collard's Co., La. Militia
Dastorgues, In Bte	Private	2 Reg't. (Cavelier's), La. Militia (Orig. under Dastugues, In Bte)
Dastugue, --	Private	Plauche's Batt'n., La. Militia
Dastugues, In Bte	Private	2 Reg't. (Cavelier's), La. Militia
Datara, Francois	Artificer	Capt. Chaudurier's Co., Artificers, Art'y., La. Vols. (Orig. under Dutara, Francois)
Daubard, Charles	Private	3 Reg't. (de la Ronde's), La. Mil.
Daubard, Louis	Private	3 Reg't. (de la Ronde's), La. Mil.
Daubard, Pierre	Private	3 Reg't. (de la Ronde's), La. Mil.
Daudard, Valmond	Private	1 Batt'n. (Fortier's), La. Militia
Daugherty, James	1 Lieutenant	12 and 13 Cons. Reg't., La. Mil.
Daughty, Robert	Ensign	17, 18 and 19 Cons. Reg't., La. Mil. (Orig. under Dorighty, Robert)
Daugleese, Monplesire	Private	2 Batt'n. (D'Aquin's), La. Militia (Orig. under Dangluse, Monplaisire)
Dauly, James	Private	Captain Callaway's Co., Mounted Riflemen, La. Militia
Daunois, Favre (father)	Private	2 Reg't. (Cavelier's), La. Militia
Daunois, Favre (son)	Private	2 Reg't. (Cavelier's), La. Militia
Daunoy, --	Private	Plauche's Batt'n., La. Militia
Daunoy, Louis	Private	1 Batt'n. (Fortier's), La. Militia
Daunoy, Pre	Private	8 Reg't. (Meriam's), La. Militia
Dauphin, Chs.	Sergeant	2 Reg't. (Cavelier's), La. Militia
Dauphin, Francis	Sergeant	De Clouet's Reg't., La. Militia
Dauphin, J. B.	1 Lieutenant	De Clouet's Reg't., La. Militia
Dauphin, Joseph	Private	De Clouet's Reg't., La. Militia
Dauphine, Francis	Sergeant	De Clouet's Reg't., La. Militia (Orig. under Dauphin, Francis)
Dauphine, J. B.	1 Lieutenant	De Clouet's Reg't., La. Militia (Orig. under Dauphin, J. B.)
Dautreul, Louis	Sergeant	Baker's Regiment, La. Militia
Dauterive, Marigny	Private	4 Reg't. (Morgan's), La. Militia
Dautrive, Marignie	Private	4 Reg't. (Morgan's), La. Militia (Orig. under Daurerive, Marigny)
Davenport, Charles	Private	10 and 20 Cons. Reg't., La. Mil.
Davenport, John	2 Lieutenant	De Clouet's Reg't., La. Militia (Orig. under Devenport, John)
Davias, John	Sergeant	2 Batt'n. (D'Aquin's), La. Militia
Davican, Pierre	Private	Captain Lagan's Co., La. Vols.
Davicon, Pierre	Private	Captain Lagan's Co., La. Vols. (Orig. under Davican, Pierre)
David, --	Private	Plauche's Batt'n., La. Militia
David, --	Private	4 Reg't. (Morgan's), La. Militia
David, Baptiste	Sergeant	16 Reg't. (Thompson's), La. Mil.
David, Desir	Fusilier-Private	2 Batt'n. (D'Aquin's), La. Militia
David, John	Private	Capt. Chauveau's Co., Cavalry, La. Militia
David, Michael	Private	De Clouet's Reg't., La. Militia
David, Patrick	Private	De Clouet's Reg't., La. Militia
David, Peter	Private	De Clouet's Reg't., La. Militia
Davide, Jean	Private	6 Reg't. (Landry's), La. Militia
Davidson, Ephram	3 Lieutenant	10 and 20 Cons. Reg't., La. Mil.
Davidson, Richard	Private	12 and 13 Cons. Reg't., La. Mil.
Davidson, Samuel	Private	17, 18 and 19 Cons. Reg't., La. Militia
Davidson, William D.	Private	12 and 13 Cons. Reg't., La. Mil.
Davieau, Pierre	Private	Captain Lagan's Co., La. Vols. (Orig. under Davican, Pierre)
Davine, Jacob	Private	17, 18 and 19 Cons. Reg't., La. Mil.
Davine, Joseph	Private	Discharged Volunteers, Louisiana (See La. Vols Ref. Card, also 2 Batt'n. Peire's)
Davinport, Charles	Private	10 and 20 Cons. Reg't., La. Mil. (Orig. under Davenport, Charles)
Davis, --	Private	Plauche's Batt'n., La. Militia
Davis, Daniel	Private	10 and 20 Cons. Reg't., La. Mil.
Davis, David	Private	11 Reg't. (Hickey's), La. Militia
Davis, David	Private	2 Batt'n. (Peire's), La. Vols.
Davis, Ebenezer	Private	Captain Callaway's Co., Cavalry, La. Militia
Davis, Edward	Private	10 and 20 Cons. Reg't., La. Mil.
Davis, Elijah	Private	Captain Callaway's Co., Cavalry, La. Militia
Davis, John	Private	Capt. Allen's Co., Artillerists, La. Vols.
Davis, Jonathan	Private	Captain Wallace's Co., Boatmen, La. Vols.
Davis, Lindsey	Private	10 and 20 Cons. Reg't., La. Mil.
Davis, Louis	Captain	10 Reg't., Louisiana Militia
Davis, Raphel	Private	12 and 13 Cons. Reg't., La. Mil.
Davis, Robert	Major	10 Reg't., Louisiana Militia
Davis, Samuel	Private	Capt. Dodge's Co., Mounted Riflemen, La. Militia
Davis, Samuel	Private	Capt. Henry's Co., Mounted Riflemen, La. Militia
Davis, Samuel	Corporal	Capt. Thomas' Co., La. Militia
Davis, Thomas	Private	De Clouet's Reg't., La. Militia
Davis, William	Corporal	12 and 13 Cons. Reg't., La. Mil.
Davis, William	Private	16 Reg't. (Thompson's), La. Mil.
Davison, Ephram	Lieutenant	10 and 20 Cons. Reg't., La. Mil. (Orig. under Davidson, Ephram)
Davoine, Jesse	Private	17, 18 and 19 Cons. Reg't., La. Militia
Daws, Isaac	Private	12 and 13 Cons. Reg't., La. Mil.
Dawson, James	Drummer	De Clouet's Reg't., La. Militia
Dawson, William	Sergeant	10 and 20 Cons. Reg't., La. Mil.
Day, Asa	Private	12 and 13 Cons. Reg't., La. Mil.
Day, Henry	Private	12 and 13 Cons. Reg't., La. Mil.
Day, Jesse	Private	12 and 13 Cons. Reg't., La. Mil.
Day, John	Private	12 and 13 Cons. Reg't., La. Mil.
Day, Orlton	Private	12 and 13 Cons. Reg't., La. Mil.
Day, Samuel	Sergeant	12 and 13 Cons. Reg't., La. Mil.
Day, Thomas	Private	12 and 13 Cons. Reg't., La. Mil.
Day, William	Private	12 and 13 Cons. Reg't., La. Mil.
Dayer, --	Private	4 Reg't. (Morgan's), La. Militia
Dayle, Joseph	Private	De Clouet's Reg't., La. Militia (Orig. under Daigle, Joseph)
Dayson, William	Sergeant	19 Reg't., La. Vols. (Orig. under Deeson, William)
Dayton, Ebenezer	Corporal	10 and 20 Cons. Reg't., La. Mil. (Orig. under Dayton, James E.)
Dayton, James E.	Corporal	10 and 20 Cons. Reg't., La. Mil.
Deague, Pierre	Private	2 Batt'n. (Peire's), La. Vols. (Orig. under Drague, Pierre)
Deal, Ephraim	Sergeant	De Clouet's Reg't., La. Militia
De Alba, Jean	Private	3 Reg't. (de la Ronde's), La. Mil.
Deare, Samuel S.	Private	1 Reg't. (Dejan's), La. Militia
De Armas C.	Private	1 Reg't. (Dejan's), La. Militia (Orig. under Armas, C. D.)
De Armas, Carlos	Private	8 Reg't. (Meriam's), La. Militia
De Armas, M.	Private	1 Reg't. (Dejan's), La. Militia (Orig. under Armas, Md D)
Dearmond, David F.	Private	Captain Grittith's Co., Mounted Riflemen, La. Vols.
Dearmond, David F.	Captain	10 and 20 Cons. Reg't., La. Mil.
Dearmond, Samuel	Private	10 and 20 Cons. Reg't., La. Mil.
Dearmond, Thomas F.	Private	Captain Griffith's Co., Mounted Riflemen, La. Vols.
Dearmond, William	Private	Captain Griffith's Co., Mounted Riflemen, La. Vols.
Deas, Jesse	Private	12 and 13 Cons. Reg't., La. Mil.
Deas, John	Private	Capt. Thomas' Co., La. Militia
Deas, Joseph Sr.	Private	Capt. Thomas' Co., La. Militia
Deas, Joseph Jr.	Private	Capt. Thomas' Co., La. Militia
Deaunoy, Louis	Private	1 Batt'n. (Fortier's), La. Militia (Orig. under Daunoy, Louis)
Deauphin, Joseph	Private	De Clouet's Reg't., La. Militia (Orig. under Dauphin, Joseph)
Deban, --	Private	Plauche's Batt'n., La. Militia
Debar, Verbin	Private	Captain Lagan's Co., La. Vols. (Orig. under Dibart, Verbin)

Name	Rank	Unit
Debergue, Me	Musician	1 Batt'n. (Fortier's), La. Militia
Deblanc, Cesair	Private	4 Reg't. (Morgan's), La. Militia (Orig. under LeBlanc, Cesair)
De Blanc, Despanay	Corporal	4 Reg't. (Morgan's), La. Militia
De Blanc, Dorsino	Private	Capt. Dubuclet's Troop, Hussars, La. Vols.
Deblanc, Dorsinos	Private	4 Reg't. (Morgan's), La. Militia
Deblanc, Joseph	Captain	Baker's Regiment, La. Militia
Deblanc, Louis	Private	Baker's Regiment, La. Militia
De Blanc, Ls Chr	Corporal	Capt. Dubuclet's Troop, Hussars, La. Vols.
Deblieux, A. L.	Ensign	17, 18 and 19 Cons. Reg't., La. Militia
Debon, --	Private	Plauche's Batt'n., La. Militia
Debrock, Joseph	Private	De Clouet's Reg't., La. Militia
Debrock, Martin	Private	De Clouet's Reg't., La. Militia
Debuys, P.	Private	Plauche's Batt'n., La. Militia
Debuys, William	Private	Plauche's Batt'n., La. Militia
Decadie, Paul	Private	2 Batt'n. (Peire's), La. Vols. (Orig. under Dequary, Paul)
Decampe, Jean	Private	Captain Lagan's Co., La. Vols.
Decary, Paul	Private	2 Batt'n. (Peire's), La. Vols. (Orig. under Dequary, Paul)
Decken, Christian	Private	De Clouet's Reg't., La. Militia (Orig. under Decker, Christian)
Decker, Abraham	Private	10 and 20 Cons. Reg't., La. Mil.
Decker, Christian	Private	De Clouet's Reg't., La. Militia
Declouet, Alber	Private	Baker's Regiment, La. Militia
De Clouet, Alexander	Colonel	De Clouet's Reg't. La. Militia
Declouet, Charles	Private	Baker's Regiment, La. Militia
Declouet, Frs	Private	Baker's Regiment, La. Militia (Orig. under Declouette, Franc)
Declouet, Simon	Corporal	Baker's Regiment, La. Militia
Declouette, Franc	Private	Baker's Regiment, La. Militia
Decou, Charles	Private	1 Batt'n. (Fortier's), La. Mil.
Decoup, L.	Private	2 Reg't. (Cavelier's), La. Militia
Decource, --	Private	2 Batt'n. (D'Aquin's), La. Militia (Orig. under Desourse, --)
DeCoux, Heppolithe	2 Lieutenant	Capt. Le Doux's Co., Cav., La. Vols.
Decuir, Baptiste	Private	Capt. Le Doux's Co., Cav., La. Vols.
Decuir, Godefroy	Private	Capt. Dubuclet's Troop, Hussars, La. Vols.
De Dias, Perez Juan	Private	17, 18 and 19 Cons. Reg't., La. Militia
De Dias, Porez Juan	Private	17, 18 and 19 Cons. Reg't., La. (Orig. under DeDias, Perez Juan)
Dedios, Juan	Private	Capt. Colsson's Co., Artillery, La. Vols.
Dedune, In Bte (Jn)	Private	2 Reg't. (Cavelier's), La. Militia
Deece, Jesse	Private	12 and 13 Cons. Reg't., La. Mil. (Orig. under Deas, Jesse)
Deekammel, John	Surgeon	Detachment Field and Staff Officers, 4 Brigade, La. Militia
De Ende, Henry	Private	Plauche's Batt'n., La. Militia
De Ende, Henry	1 Sergeant-Sgt.	1 Reg't. (Dejan's), La. Militia
De Endes, --	Private	Plauche's Batt'n., La. Militia (Orig. under De Ende, Henry)
Dees, James	Private	10 and 20 Cons. Reg't., La. Mil.
Deeson, William	Sergeant	19 Regiment, La. Militia
Defage, --	Private	4 Reg't. (Morgan's), La. Militia
Defarge, Demomai	Private	De Clouet's Reg't., La. Militia
Defarge, Louis	2 Lieutenant	De Coulet's Reg't., La. Militia
Defarge, Sevesex	Private	De Clouet's Reg't., La. Militia
De Favrot, L.	Major	6 Reg't. (Landry's), La. Militia
De Favrot, L.	Major	8 Reg't. (Meriam's), La. Militia
De Feriet, Louis	Private	4 Reg't. (Morgan's), La. Militia
Defile, Lewis	Private	Baker's Regiment, La. Militia (Orig. under Defils, Louis)
Defils, Louis	Private	Baker's Regiment, La. Militia
Deford, James	Private	10 and 20 Cons. Reg't., La. Mil.
Degre, Francois	Private	2 Reg't. (Cavelier's), La. Militia
Defuentes, Joseph	Private	2 Reg't. (Cavelier's), La. Militia
Degar, Jean Bt	Private	1 Batt'n. (Fortier's), La. Militia
Degre, Jno Bt	Private	1 Batt'n. (Fortier's), La. Militia (Orig. under Degae, Jean Bt)
Degrenier, Ene	Private	2 Reg't. (Cavelier's), La. Militia
Degruis, --	Private	4 Reg't. (Morgan's), La. Militia
Degruise, --	Private	4 Reg't. (Morgan's), La. Militia (Orig. under Degruis, --)
Degruy, Dufochar	Private	Plauche's Batt'n., La. Militia
Degruys, Peter	Corporal	4 Reg't. (Morgan's), La. Militia
De Hart, Robinson	Private	Captain Beale's Co., Riflemen, La. Militia
Dehery, Felix	Private	4 Reg't. (Morgan's), La. Militia (Orig. under Delery, Felix)
Dehon, Joseph	Private	8 Reg't. (Meriam's), La. Militia
Deison, William	Sergeant	19 Reg't., La. Vols. (Orig. under Deeson, William)
Dejan, J. B.	Colonel	1 Reg't. (Dejan's), La. Militia
Dejan, Ursin	Private	3 Reg't. (de la Ronde's), La. Mil.
Dejan, Zenon	Private	3 Reg't. (de la Ronde's), La. Mil.
Dejean, fils	Private	16 Reg't. (Thompson's), La. Mil.
Dejonge, --	Sergeant of Musicians, Chief Musician	Plauche's Batt'n., La. Militia
Delabostrie, Fcis	Captain	2 Reg't. (Cavelier's), La. Militia
Delachaise, P. A.	Private	16 Reg't. (Thompson's), La. Mil.
De La Croix, --	Musician	Plauche's Batt'n., La. Militia (Orig. under La Croix, --)
De La Croix, Dusuan	Private	3 Reg't. (de la Ronde's), La. Mil.
De la Garca, Anto	Private	17, 18 and 19 Cons. Reg't., La. Militia
De la Garca, Antonio	Private	17, 18 and 19 Cons. Reg't., La. Militia
De la Garca, Caetano	Private	17, 18 and 19 Cons. Reg't., La. Militia
Delages, Jean	Private	2 Reg't. (Cavelier's), La. Militia (Orig. under Delayer, Jean)
Delahoussaye, Balth	2 Lieutenant	Capt. Dubuclet's Troop, Hussars, La. Vols.
Dela Houssaye, Frs Cherr	Cornet	Capt. Dubuclet's Troop, Hussars, La. Vols.
Dela Houssaye, Gustave	Private	Capt. Dubuclet's Troop, Hussars, La. Vols.
Dela Houssaye, Louis	Private	Capt. Dubuclet's Troop, Hussars, La. Vols.
Dela Houssaye, Octave	Private	Capt. Dubuclet's Troop, Hussars, La. Vols.
Dela Houssaye, Pelletier	Private	Capt. Dubuclet's Troop, Hussars, La. Vols.
Dela Houssaye, S.	Cornet	Capt. Dubuclet's Troop, Hussars, La. Vols. (Orig. under Dela Houssaye, Frs Chevt)
Dela Houssaye, Terence	Private	Capt. Dubuclet's Troop, Hussars, La. Vols.
De la luz, Cortes Jose	Private	17, 18 and 19 Cons. Reg't., La. Militia
Delamothe, F.	Private	Plauche's Batt'n., La. Militia
Deland, Louis	2 Lieutenant	1 Batt'n. (Fortier's), La. Militia
De'land, Zenon	Private	1 Batt'n. (Fortier's), La. Militia
Delangny, Augustin	Private	2 Batt'n. (Peire's), La. Vols.
Delanney, David	Adjt. & Insp. Genl.	Field and Staff Officers, La. Mil.
Delanney, Jean Batis	Artificer	Capt. Chaudurier's Co., Artificers, Art'y., La. Vols. (Orig. under Delauney, Jean Batis)
Delanny, Jean Batis	Artificer	Capt. Chaudurier's Co., Artificers, Art'y., La. Vols. (Orig. under Delauney, Jean Batis)
Dela, Pona Jose	Private	17, 18 and 19 Cons. Reg't., La. Militia
Delaroche, --	Private	4 Reg't. (Morgan's), La. Militia
De Laroude, P. Denis	Colonel	3 Reg't. (de la Ronde's), La. Mil.
Delarue, --	Private	Plauche's Batt'n., La. Militia
De la Serda Feliciano	Corporal	17, 18 and 19 Cons. Reg't., La. Militia
Delassaz, Duhant	Private	4 Reg't. (Morgan's), La. Militia
Delassus, Duhant	Private	4 Reg't. (Morgan's), La. Militia (Orig. under Delassaz, Duhaut)
Delatee, Noel	Fusilier-Private	5 Reg't. (La Branche's), La. Mil.
Delatte, Noel	Fusilier-Private	5 Reg't. (La Branche's), La. Mil. (Orig. under Delatee, Noel)
Delaud, Moliere	2 Lieutenant	1 Batt'n. (Fortier's), La. Militia (Orig. under Delaud, Louis)
Delaunay, Jean Batis	Artificer	Capt. Chaudurier's Co., Artificers, Art'y., La. Vols. (Orig. under Delauney, Jean Batis)
Delaunay, Louis	Private	2 Batt'n. (Peire's), La. Vols.
Delaune, Alexandre	Private	7 Reg't. (Le Beuf's), La. Militia
Delaune, I. B. (J.B.?)	Private	7 Reg't. (Le Beuf's), La. Militia
Delauney, Jean Batis	Artificer	Capt. Chaudurier's Co., Artificers, Art'y., La. Vols.

Name	Rank	Unit
Delaunuy, David	Adjt. & Insp. Genl.	Field and Staff Officers, La. Mil. (Orig. under Delanney, David)
Delaure, I. B. (J. B. ?)	Private	7 Reg't. (Le Beuf's), La. Militia (Orig. under Delaune, I. B. (J. B. ?)
Delayer, Jean	Private	2 Reg't. (Cavelier's), La. Militia
Delemos, Louis	Private	Capt. Colsson's Co., Artillery, La. Vols.
Delemos, Markos	Private	Capt. Colsson's Co., Artillery, La. Vols.
Delery, --	Private	3 Reg't. (de la Ronde's), La. Mil.
Delery, Bmy Chauvin	Fusilier-Pvt.	5 Reg't. (La Branche's), La. Mil.
Delery, Felix	Private	4 Reg't. (Morgan's), La. Militia
Delery, Jacques	Private	3 Reg't. (de la Ronde's), La. Mil.
Delery, Louis	1 Lieutenant	5 Reg't. (La Branche's), La. Mil.
Delery, Melchauvin	Fusilier-Pvt.	5 Reg't. (La Branche's), La. Mil.
Delery, Nlas Chauvin	Captain	5 Reg't. (La Branche's), La. Mil.
Delferiere, Jne Bte	Private	Capt. Alpuente's Co., La. Militia (Orig. under Delferierre, Jean Bte)
Delferierre, Jean Bte	Private	Capt. Alpuente's Co., La. Militia
Delgad, Juan	Private	Sergeant Hog's Detachment, La. Vols. (Orig. under Delgado, Juan)
Delgado, Francisco	Private	Capt. Lagan's Co., La. Vols.(Orig. under Delgardo, Francisco)
Delgado, Juan	Private	Capt. Colsson's Co., Artillery, La. Vols.
Delgado, Juan	Private	Sergeant Hog's Detachment, La. Vols.
Delgardo, Francisco	Private	Captain Lagan's Co., La. Vols.
Delhate, Antoine	Corporal	Capt. Alpuente's Co., La. Militia
Delhome, Charles	Sergeant	De Clouet's Reg't., La. Militia (Orig. under Delhomme, Charles)
Delhomme, Alexandre	Private	Capt. Trudeau's Troop of Horse, La. Militia
Delhomme, Charles	Sergeant	De Clouet's Reg't., La. Militia
Delhomme, Octave	Fusilier-Pvt.	5 Reg't. (La Branche's), La. Mil.
Delhonnere, Alex.	Private	Capt. Trudeau's Troop of Horse, La. Mil.(Orig. under Delhomme, Alexandre)
Delile, Felix	Private	1 Batt'n. (Fortier's), La. Militia
Delille, Bazil	Private	Captain Sprigg's Co., Boatmen, La. Vols.
Delille, Felix	Private	1 Batt'n. (Fortier's), La. Militia (Orig. under Delile, Felix)
Delille, O.	Private	Captain Sprigg's Co., Boatmen, La. Vols.
Delino, Peter	Private	Capt. Dubuclet's Troop, Hussars, La. Vols.
Delino, Tierre	Private	Capt. Dubuclet's Troop, Hussars, La. Vols. (Orig. under Delino, Peter)
Delmare, J. Bte.	Private	6 Reg't. (Landry's), La. Militia
Delmere, Jn. Bte.	Private	6 Reg't. (Landry's), La. Militia (Orig. under Delmare, J. Bte)
De Lmetrie, Andre	Private	2 Reg't. (Cavelier's), La. Militia (Orig. under Dimitry, Andre)
Delogny, Edward R.	Private	Capt. Trudeau's Troop of Horse, La. Militia
Delogny, Evard R.	Private	Capt. Trudeau's Troop of Horse, La. Mil. (Orig. under Delogny, Edward R.)
Delonde, George	Private	5 Reg't. (La Branche's), La. Mil.
Delone, Gn Bte	Artificer	Capt. Chaudurier's Co., Artificers, Art'y., La. Vols. (Orig. under Delauney, Jean Batis)
Delone, Jean Bte	Artificer	Capt. Chaudurier's Co., Artificers, Art'y., La. Vols. (Orig. under Delauney, Jean Batis)
Delonne, Jean Batis	Artificer	Capt. Chaudurier's Co., Artificers, Art'y., La. Vols. (Orig. under Delauney, Jean Batis)
De Lorme, Auguste	Private	8 Reg't. (Meriam's), La. Militia
Delouche, John L.	Corporal	17, 18 and 19 Cons. Reg't., La. Militia
Delouche, Julien	Sergeant	17, 18 and 19 Cons. Reg't., La. Militia
Delouche, Michael	Private	17, 18 and 19 Cons. Reg't., La. Militia
Delouche, Pierre	Private	17, 18 and 19 Cons. Reg't., La. Militia
Delphin, --	Servant	1 Batt'n. (Fortier's), La. Militia
Delpit, --	Corporal	2 Reg't. (Cavelier's), La. Militia
Delpit, Peter Andre	2 Lieutenant	2 Batt'n. (Peire's), La. Vols.
Deltera, Juan Jose	Sergeant	17, 18 and 19 Cons. Reg't., La. Mil. (Orig. under Destera, Juan Jose)
Del Terriblo, Juan	Private	1 Batt'n. (Fortier's), La. Militia
Del Toro, Jose	Sergeant	17, 18 and 19 Cons. Reg't., La. Militia
Delvalet, --	Private	2 Reg't. (Cavelier's), La. Militia
De Maran, Louis	Captain	2 Batt'n. (Peire's), La. Vols. (Orig. under De Marance, Louis)
De Marance, Louis	Captain	2 Batt'n. (Peire's), La. Vols.
De Marans, Louis	Captain	2 Batt'n. (Peire's), La. Vols. (Orig. under Demarance, Louis)
Demare, Usant	Private	Baker's Regiment, La. Militia
Demaret, Adelard	Private	De Clouet's Reg't., La. Militia
Demarit, Adelard	Private	De Clouet's Reg't., La. Militia (Orig. under Demaret, Adelard)
Demarra, Adelard	Private	De Clouet's Reg't., La. Militia (Orig. under Demaret, Adelard)
De Marrans, Louis	Captain	2 Batt'n. (Peire's), La. Vols. (Orig. under Demarance, Louis)
Demart, Martin	Private	Baker's Regiment, La. Militia
Demazelliere, Basile	Captain	1 Batt'n. (Fortier's), La. Militia
Demeret, Adelard	Private	De Clouet's Reg't., La. Militia (Orig. under Demaret, Adelard)
De Mirepoix, Esquin	Captain	2 Batt'n. (Peire's), La. Vols.
Demolette, F.	Private	8 Reg't. (Meriam's), La. Militia
Demollite, I.	Private	8 Reg't. (Meriam's), La. Militia (Orig. under Demolette, F.)
Demouille, Yacinte	Private	1 Batt'n. (Fortier's), La. Militia
Demozellier, Baltazar	1 Lieutenant	1 Batt'n. (Fortier's), La. Militia
Demsey, Solomon	Private	10 and 20 Cons. Reg't., La. Mil.
Denesse, --	Private	Plauche's Batt'n., La. Militia
Denesse, Hubert	Sergeant	3 Reg't. (de la Ronde's), La. Mil.
Denesse, Joseph	Sergeant	3 Reg't. (de la Ronde's), La. Mil.
Denesse, Pierre	Private	Capt. Colsson's Co., Artillery, La. Vols.
Denillon, Ant.	Private	2 Reg't. (Cavelier's), La. Militia
Denis, Athanas	Private	17, 18 and 19 Cons. Reg't., La. Militia
Denis, William	Private	De Clouet's Reg't., La. Militia
Denize, --	Private	Plauche's Batt'n., La. Militia
Denizier, --	Fusilier-Private	2 Batt'n. (D'Aquin's), La. Militia
Denizier, --	Fusilier-Private	2 Batt'n. (D'Aquin's), La. Militia (Orig. under Denizie, --)
Denneville, Celestin	Private	1 Batt'n. (Fortier's), La. Militia
Denning, Patrick	Private	De Clouet's Reg't., La. Militia (Orig. under Dunning, Patrick)
Dennis, --	Musician	Plauche's Batt'n., La. Militia
Dennis, B.	Private	1 Reg't. (Dejan's), La. Militia
Dennis, John	Private	10 and 20 Cons. Reg't., La. Mil.
Dennis, William	Private	De Clouet's Reg't., La. Militia (Orig. under Denis, William)
Denny, Charles	Private	Capt. Van Bibber's Co., La. Mil.
Dent, Wilfort	Private	17, 18 and 19 Cons. Reg't., La. Militia
Dentin, Baptiste	Private	De Clouet's Reg't., La. Militia (Orig. under Dantin, Baptiste)
Dentin, Charles	Private	De Clouet's Reg't., La. Militia (Orig. under Dantin, Charles)
Dentin, Fabien	Corporal	De Clouet's Reg't., La. Militia (Orig. under Dantin, Fabian)
Deny, James	Private	17, 18 and 19 Cons. Reg't., La. Militia
De Oca, Manuel	Private	17, 18 and 19 Cons. Reg't., La. Militia
Depanto, Jn.	Private	2 Reg't. (Cavelier's), La. Militia
Depayster, William A.	3 Lieutenant	Captain Beale's Co., Riflemen, La. Mil.(Orig. under Depeyster, William A.)
Deperville, Pierre	Corporal	2 Batt'n. (Peire's), La. Vols.
Depeyster, William A.	3 Lieutenant	Captain Beale's Co., Riflemen, La. Militia
Deplassard, Charles	Corporal	De Clouet's Reg't., La. Militia
Deporte, --	Corporal	2 Reg't. (Cavelier's), La. Militia
Depree, James	Private	10 and 20 Cons. Reg't., La. Mil. (Orig. under Dupree, James)
Depuis, Michel	Private	De Clouet's Reg't., La. Militia (Orig. under Dupuis, Michel)
Depuivalle, Pierre	Corporal	2 Batt'n. (Peire's), La. Vols. (Orig. under Deperville, Pierre)

Name	Rank	Unit
Dequary, Paul	Private	2 Batt'n. (Peire's), La. Vols.
Derashett, Louis	Private	De Clouet's Reg't., La. Militia (See also U.S. Artillery)
Derbanne, Placide	Private	17, 18 and 19 Cons. Reg't., La. Militia
Derbaue, Larly	Private	17, 18 and 19 Cons. Reg't., La. Mil. (Orig. under Derbaune, Larty)
Derbaune, Baptiste	Private	17, 18 and 19 Cons. Reg't., La. Militia
Derbaune, Francois	Private	17, 18 and 19 Cons. Reg't., La. Militia
Derbaune, John Baptist	Private	17, 18 and 19 Cons. Reg't., La. Militia
Derbaune, Larty	Private	17, 18 and 19 Cons. Reg't., La. Militia
Derbaune, Michael	Private	17, 18 and 19 Cons. Reg't., La. Militia
Derbaune, Pierre	Private	17, 18 and 19 Cons. Reg't., La. Militia
Derbaune, Placide	Private	17, 18 and 19 Cons. Reg't., La. Militia (Orig. under Derbanne, Placide)
Derbigney, Peter	Private	Capt. Chauveau's Co., Cavalry, La. Mil. (Orig. under Derbigny, Peter)
Derbigny, Peter	Private	Capt. Chauveau's Co., Cavalry, La. Militia
Derenoir, --	Private	2 Reg't. (Cavelier's), La. Militia (Orig. under Durenoir, --)
Deres, David	Private	2 Batt'n. (Peire's), La. Vols. (Orig. under Davis, David)
Derige, Francois	Private	2 Batt'n. (Peire's), La. Vols.
Derinsbourg, Edouard	Private	5 Reg't. (La Branche's), La. Mil. (Orig. under Darensbourg, Edoire)
Derioche, J.	Private	2 Reg't. (Cavelier's), La. Militia (Orig. under Drioche, J.)
Deris, David	Private	2 Batt'n. (Peire's), La. Vols. (Orig. under Davis, David)
Derneville, Theophile	Private	1 Batt'n. (Fortier's), La. Militia
Deroche, Louis	Fusilier-Private	5 Reg't. (La Branche's), La. Mil. (Orig. under Desroche, Louis)
Deroche, Pierre	Fusilier-Private	5 Reg't. (La Branche's), La. Mil.
Deronce, --	Private	2 Batt'n. (D'Aquin's), La. Militia
Derosia, Francis	Private	16 Reg't. (Thompson's), La. Mil.
Derosie, Francis	Private	16 Reg't. (Thompson's), La. Mil. (Orig. under Derosia, Francis)
Derris, David	Private	2 Batt'n. (Peire's), La. Vols. (Orig. under Davis, David)
Derry, (Negro)	Servant-Waiter	De Clouet's Reg't., La. Militia
Dertas, Derto	Private	16 Reg't. (Thompson's), La. Mil.
Dertrehan, --	Private	Capt. Trudeau's Troop of Horse, La. Militia
Dertrehan, Nicolas	Corporal	Capt. Trudeau's Troop of Horse, La. Militia
De Russ, Baptiste	Private	16 Reg't. (Thompson's), La. Mil.
De Russel, Colas	Private	16 Reg't. (Thompson's), La. Mil. (Orig. under Russel, Cola)
Derwaw, Joseph	Private	Baker's Regiment, La. Militia
Derwin, James	Private	16 Reg't. (Thompson's), La. Mil.
Desarmeaux, Pierre	Private	De Clouet's Reg't., La. Militia (Orig. under Desormeaux, Pierre)
Desban, --	Private	Plauche's Batt'n., La. Militia (Orig. under Deban, --)
Descampe, Jean	Private	Captain Lagan's Co., La. Vols. (Orig. under Decampe, Jean)
Deschamps, Jean Baptiste	Sergeant	2 Batt'n. (Peire's), La. Vols. (See also Lufroy, Carraby)
Deschapeller, Le Breton	Lieutenant	4 Reg't. (Morgan's), La. Militia (Orig. under Deschapelles, LeBreton)
Deschapelles, Le Breton	1 Lieut.-Lt.	4 Reg't. (Morgan's), La. Militia
Descoteau, Frans	Private	8 Reg't. (Meriam's), La. Militia
Descuire, Piere	Sergeant	1 Batt'n. (Fortier's), La. Militia
Deserman, Ievassirue	Private	De Clouet's Reg't., La. Militia
Desertel, Hilver	Private	17, 18 and 19 Cons. Reg't., La. Mil. (Orig. under Disortel, Hilver)
Deseuirs, Pierre	Sergeant	1 Batt'n. (Fortier's), La. Militia (Orig. under Descuire, Piere)
Desex, Louis	Private	De Clouet's Reg't., La. Militia (Orig. under Dessaix, Louis)
Desforges, --	Private	Plauche's Batt'n., La. Militia
Deshon, Daniel	Private	Captain Beale's Co., Riflemen, La. Militia
Deshon, James	Corporal-Sergeant	4 Reg't. (Morgan's), La. Militia
Deshotel, fils	Private	16 Reg't. (Thompson's), La. Mil.
Deshotel, Antoine	Private	16 Reg't. (Thompson's), La. Mil.
Deshotel, Nicolas, fils	Private	16 Reg't. (Thompson's), La. Mil.
Deshotel, Similien	Private	16 Reg't. (Thompson's), La. Mil.
Deshotel, Valerien	Private	16 Reg't. (Thompson's), La. Mil.
Deshotel, Zenon	Private	16 Reg't. (Thompson's), La. Mil.
Deshotell, Lorance	Private	De Clouet's Reg't., La. Militia
Deshroo, Levin	Private	Baker's Regiment, La. Militia (Orig. under Dishroo, Levin)
Deslate, J. L.	Private	De Clouet's Reg't., La. Militia (Orig. under Detale, John Lewis)
Deslattes, J. L.	Private	De Clouet's Reg't., La. Militia (Orig. under Detale, John Lewis)
Deslonde, Andre	Captain	5 Reg't. (La Branche's), La. Mil.
Desmarates, --	Private	Plauche's Batt'n., La. Militia
Desmorchy, --	Private	1 Reg't. (Dejan's), La. Militia
Desnoyer, Jean	Corporal	5 Reg't. (La Branche's), La. Mil.
Desobry, --	Private	1 Reg't. (Dejan's), La. Militia
Deson, James	Private	Capt. Callaway's Co., Cavalry, La. Militia
Deson, John	Private	Capt. Callaway's Co., Cavalry, La. Militia
Deson, Wilfred	Private	Capt. Callaway's Co., Cavalry, La. Militia
Desormeaux, Pierre	Private	De Clouet's Reg't., La. Militia
Desougel, --	Private	Plauche's Batt'n., La. Militia (Orig. under De Souges, --)
De Souges, --	Private	Plauche's Batt'n., La. Militia
Desource, --	Private	2 Batt'n. (D'Aquin's), La. Militia (Orig. under Desourse, --)
Desourse, --	Private	2 Batt'n. (D'Aquin's), La. Militia
Desportel, --	Private	Plauche's Batt'n., La. Militia (Orig. under Desportes, --)
Desportes, --	Private	Plauche's Batt'n., La. Militia
Desroche, In Bte (Jn?)	Fusilier-Pvt.	5 Reg't. (La Branche's), La. Mil.
Desroche, Louis	Fusilier-Private	5 Reg't. (La Branche's), La. Mil.
Desroche, Pierre	Fusilier-Private	5 Reg't. (La Branche's), La. Mil. (Orig. under Deroche, Pierre)
Dessaix, Louis	Private	De Clouet's Reg't., La. Militia
Dessales, Jaques	Sergeant	De Clouet's Reg't., La. Militia
Dessales, Louis	Private	De Clouet's Reg't., La. Militia
Dessalles, Jaques	Sergeant	De Clouet's Reg't., La. Militia (Orig. under Dessales, Jaques)
Dessalles, Louis	Private	De Clouet's Reg't., La. Militia (Orig. under Dessales, Louis)
Dessanto, Jn.	Private	2 Reg't. (Cavelier's), La. Militia (Orig. under Depanto, Jn)
Desselle, Lambert	Private	17, 18 and 19 Cons. Reg't., La. Militia
Dessex, Louis	Private	De Clouet's Reg't., La. Militia (Orig. under Dessaix, Louis)
Desteham, --	Private	Capt. Trudeau's Troop of Horse, La. Mil. (Orig. under Dertrehan, --)
Destenval, Prosper	Private	De Clouet's Reg't., La. Militia
Destera, Juan Jose	Sergeant	17, 18 and 19 Cons. Reg't., La. Militia
Destinval, P.	Private	De Clouet's Reg't., La. Militia (Orig. under Destenval, Prosper)
Destinval, Prosper	Private-Musician	2 Batt'n. (Peire's), La. Vols.
Destouches, Marin	Private	Plauche's Batt'n., La. Militia
De St Romes, Charles	1 Lieutenant	Plauche's Batt'n., La. Militia
Desvignen, Jn.	Sergeant	Plauche's Batt'n., La. Militia (Orig. under Desvignes, J.)
Desvignes, J.	Sergeant	Plauche's Batt'n., La. Militia
Detale, John Lewis	Private	De Clouet's Reg't., La. Militia
Deterville, Theodore	Sergeant	17, 18 and 19 Cons. Reg't., La. Militia
De Toledo, I. A.	Engineer	Gov. Claiborne and Staff, La. Mil. (Could be J. A.)
De Torre, F.	Private	Plauche's Batt'n., La. Militia (Orig. under De Torres, --)
De Torres, --	Private	Plauche's Batt'n., La. Militia
De Toulilien, St. Julian	Private	De Clouet's Reg't., La. Militia (Orig. under De Tournilion, St. Julian)
De Tournilion, St. Julian	Private	De Clouet's Reg't., La. Militia
Detreham, Nicolas	Corporal	Capt. Trudeau's Troop of Horse, La. Mil. (Orig. under Dertrehan, Nicolas)

Name	Rank	Unit
Detreval, Michelle	Private	6 Reg't. (Landry's), La. Militia
Detreval, Pierre	Private	6 Reg't. (Landry's), La. Militia
Deurror, Jn. Marie	Sergeant	2 Batt'n. (D'Aquin's), La. Militia
Deurus, Baptiste	Private	16 Reg't. (Thompson's), La. Mil. (Orig. under De Russ, Baptisre)
Deval, V.	1 Sergeant	2 Reg't. (Cavelier's), La. Militia (Orig. under Durel, U.)
Deveze, Jean	1 Lieutenant	Captain Lagan's Co., La. Vols. (Orig. under Devize, Jean)
Deveze, John	1 Lieutenant	Captain Lagan's Co., La. Vols. (Orig. under Devize, Jean)
Devezin, J. C.	Private	4 Reg't. (Morgan's), La. Militia
Devince, Terence	Private	Capt. Dubuclet's Troop, Hussars, La. Vols.
Devince, Terville	Private	Capt. Dubuclet's Troop, Hussars, La. Vols.
Devince, Thimecourt	Private	Capt. Dubuclet's Troop, Hussars, La. Vols.
Devince, Timoleon	Private	Capt. Dubuclet's Troop, Hussars, La. Vols.
Devize, Jean	1 Lieutenant	Captain Lagan's Co., La. Vols.
Devore, David	Private	10 and 20 Cons. Reg't., La. Mil.
Devaut, --	Musician	Plauche's Batt'n., La. Militia
De've', Pre	Private	8 Reg't. (Meriam's), La. Militia
Devenport, John	2 Lieutenant	De Clouet's Reg't., La. Militia
DeVerbois, D.	Private	8 Reg't. (Meriam's), La. Militia
De Verbois, Francois	Private	8 Reg't. (Meriam's), La. Militia
Deverney, Pierre	Private	De Clouet's Reg't., La. Militia (Orig. under Duverney, Pierre)
Devers, Philip P.	Private-Cpl.	16 Reg't. (Thompson's), La. Mil.
Deves, Adrian	Private	8 Reg't. (Meriam's), La. Militia
Devilier, Louis	Private	16 Reg't. (Thompson's), La. Mil. (Orig. under Devillier, Louis)
Devillier, Francois C.	Captain	16 Reg't. (Thompson's), La. Mil.
Devillier, Louis	Private	16 Reg't. (Thompson's), La. Mil.
De Villiere, Antoine	2 Lieutenant	8 Reg't. (Meriam's), La. Militia (Orig. under De Villiers, Antoine)
De Villiere, Jacques	Captain	8 Reg't. (Meriam's), La. Militia (Orig. under Devilliers, Jacques)
De Villiers, Antoine	2 Lieutenant	8 Reg't. (Meriam's), La. Militia
De Villiers, Jacques	Captain	8 Reg't. (Meriam's), La. Militia
De Villiers, Ricard	Private	8 Reg't. (Meriam's), La. Militia
Devine, John	Private-Sergeant	De Clouet's Reg't., La. Militia (Orig. under Divire, John)
Devis, Adrian	Private	8 Reg't. (Meriam's), La. Militia (Orig. under Deves, Adrian)
DeWan, Joseph	Private	Baker's Regiment, La. Militia (Orig. under Derwaw, Joseph)
Dewit, Green	Sergeant	Capt. Ashley's Co., Mounted Riflemen, La. Militia
Dhebicourt, Fran	Private	2 Reg't. (Cavelier's), La. Militia
Dhebierert, Fran	Private	2 Reg't. (Cavelier's), La. Militia (Orig. under Dhebicourt, Fran)
Dial, Aaron	Private	Baker's Regiment, La. Militia
Diard, --	Private	4 Reg't. (Morgan's), La. Militia
Dias, Antoine	Private	2 Reg't. (Cavelier's), La. Militia
Dias, Louis	Private	Sergeant Hog's Detachment, La. Vols.
Dibart, Verbin	Private	Captain Lagan's Co., La. Vols.
Dick, --	Servant	De Clouet's Reg't., La. Militia
Dick, --	Servant	Plauche's Batt'n., La. Militia
Dick, --	Servant	Detachment Field and Staff Officers, 4 Brigade, La. Militia
Dick, --	Servant	8 Reg't. (Meriam's), La. Militia
Dick, --	Servant	16 Reg't. (Thompson's), La. Mil.
Dick, John	Private	Capt. Ogden's Co., Dragoons, La. Militia
Dicker, Abraham	Private	10 and 20 Cons. Reg't., La. Mil. (Orig. under Decker, Abraham)
Dicker, Christian	Private	De Clouet's Reg't., La. Militia (Orig. under Decker, Christian)
Dickison, Michael	Private	Capt. Thomas' Co., La. Militia
Dickison, Willis	Private	Capt. Thomas' Co., La. Militia
Dicks, John	Private	12 and 13 Cons. Reg't., La. Mil.
Dickson, C.	Private	10 Regiment, La. Militia
Dickson, Church	Private	De Clouet's Reg't., La. Militia (Orig. under Dixon, Church)
Dickson, Elisha	Private	10 and 20 Cons. Reg't., La. Mil.
Dickson, Martin	Private	10 and 20 Cons. Reg't., La. Mil.
Dickson, William G.	Private	10 and 20 Cons. Reg't., La. Mil.
Dicson, Martin	Private	10 and 20 Cons. Reg't., La. Mil. (Orig. under Dickson, Martin)
Diesse, Antoine	Captain	1 Batt'n. (Fortier's), La. Militia
Diere, Francois	Private	Captain Lagan's Co., La. Vols.
Dieudonne, --	Q. M. Sergeant	5 Reg't. (La Branche's), La. Mil.
Diez, Antoine	Captain	1 Batt'n. (Fortier's), La. Militia (Orig. under Diesse, Antoine)
Diez, Francois	Sergeant	1 Batt'n. (Fortier's), La. Militia (Orig. under Dieze, Francois)
Dieze, Francois	Sergeant	1 Batt'n. (Fortier's), La. Militia
Diggs, James	Private	Captain Griffith's Co., Mounted Riflemen, La. Vols.
Dillard, Henry B.	Private	17, 18 and 19 Cons. Reg't., La. Militia
Dimitry, Andre	Private	2 Reg't. (Cavelier's), La. Militia
Dinsmore, John	Private	16 Reg't. (Thompson's), La. Mil.
Dioca, Manuel	Private	17, 18 and 19 Cons. Reg't., La. Militia
Dishotell, Lorance	Private	De Clouet's Reg't., La. Militia (Orig. under Deshotell, Lorance)
Dishroo, Leven	Private	Baker's Regiment, La. Militia
Disortel, Hilver	Private	17, 18 and 19 Cons. Reg't., La. Militia
Dissard, Francis	Sergeant	2 Reg't. (Cavelier's), La. Militia
Ditch, John	Private	De Clouet's Reg't., La. Militia
Diveze, Jean	1 Lieut.	Captain Lagan's Co., La. Vols. (Orig. under Devize, Jean)
Divize, John	1 Lieut.	Captain Lagan's Co., La. Vols. (Orig. under Devize, Jean)
Dixon, Church	Private	De Clouet's Reg't., La. Militia
Dize, Francis	Sergeant	1 Batt'n. (Fortier's), La. Militia (Orig. under Dieze, Francois)
Dobbin, Peter	Private	Capt. Wallace's Co., Boatmen, La. Vols.
Dobbs, Senr.	Private	4 Reg't. (Morgan's), La. Militia
Dobbs, Hector	Corporal	Plauche's Batt'n., La. Militia
Dod, Michael	Private	Capt. Hughes's Co., Mounted Riflemen, La. Militia
Dodard, Valmont	Private	1 Batt'n. (Fortier's), La. Militia (Orig. under Daudard, Valmond)
Dodart, Valmont	Private	2 Batt'n. (D'Aquin's), La. Militia
Dodge, Henry	Major	Field and Staff Officers, La. Mil. (Orig. under Dodges, Henry)
Dodge, Henry	Captain	Captain Dodge's Co., Mounted Riflemen, La. Militia
Dodge, Israel, Sr.	Private	Captain Henry's Co., Mounted Riflemen, La. Militia
Dodge, Israel, Jr.	Private	Captain Dodge's Co., Mounted Riflemen, La. Militia
Dodge, Israel, Sr.	Private	Captain Dodge's Co., Mounted Riflemen, La. Militia
Dodge, Israel, Jr.	Private	Captain Henry's Co., Mounted Riflemen, La. Militia
Dodge, John	Private	Captain Dodge's Co., Mounted Riflemen, La. Militia
Dodge, John	Private	Captain Henry's Co., Mounted Riflemen, La. Militia
Dodge, Josiah	Private	Captain Dodge's Co., Mounted Riflemen, La. Militia
Dodge, Josiah	Private	Captain Henry's Co., Mounted Riflemen, La. Militia
Dodges, Henry	Major	Field and Staff Officers, La. Mil.
Dodson, John	Private	Captain Callaway's Co., Mounted Riflemen, La. Militia
Doesar, Antoine	Private	17, 18 and 19 Cons. Reg't., La. Mil. (Orig. under Doisar, Antoine)
Doeyty, Edouard	Private	19 Reg't., La. Vols. (Orig. under Doughty, Edward)
Doge, Joseph	Private	Capt. Songy's Co., Marines, La. Vols.
Doggett, Asa	Private	Captain McNair's Co., Mounted Riflemen, La. Militia
Doggett, John	Private-Sgt.	Captain McNair's Co., Mounted Riflemen, La. Militia
Dogi, --	Corporal	2 Batt'n. (D'Aquin's), La. Militia
Doherty, Daniel	Sergeant	10 and 20 Cons. Reg't., La. Mil. (Orig. under Dougherty, Daniel)
Doiere, Francois	Private	De Clouet's Reg't., La. Militia (Orig. under Dore, Francois)
Doiron, B.	Private	8 Reg't. (Meriam's), La. Militia
Doiron, C.	Corporal	De Clouet's Reg't., La. Militia
Doiron, I.	Private	8 Reg't. (Meriam's), La. Militia
Doisar, Antoine	Private	17, 18 and 19 Cons. Reg't., La. Militia

Name	Rank	Unit
Doison, I.	Private	8 Reg't. (Meriam's), La. Militia
Doison, Remy	Private	8 Reg't. (Meriam's), La. Militia
Doison, Willis	Private	10 Regiment, La. Militia
Dolhonde, Louis	1 Sergeant-Sgt.	5 Reg't. (La Branche's), La. Mil.
Dolhonde, Pierre	Lieutenant	5 Reg't. (La Branche's), La. Mil.
Doliole, Jn Ls.	Private	1 Batt'n. (Fortier's), La. Militia
Dolisle, Jean Louis	Private	1 Batt'n. (Fortier's), La. Militia (Orig. under Dolliole, Jean Louis)
Dolliole, Jean Louis	Private	1 Batt'n. (Fortier's), La. Militia
Dolliole, Jph.	Order Sergeant	1 Batt'n. (Fortier's), La. Militia
Dolliole, Pierre	Private	1 Batt'n. (Fortier's), La. Militia
Dologni, Augustin	Private	2 Batt'n. (Peire's), La. Vols. (Orig. under Delangny, Augustin)
Dolten, Lasy	Private	2 Batt'n. (Peire's), La. Vols.
Dombar, William	Private	10 and 20 Cons. Reg't., La. Mil.
Dominge, Dominique	Private	8 Reg't. (Meriam's), La. Militia
Domingo, Joseph	Private	Baker's Regiment, La. Militia
Domingo, Santo	Sergeant	2 Batt'n. (Peire's), La. Vols. (War of 1812) Reference Card
Domingo, Santo	Sergeant-Major	2 Batt'n. (Peire's), La. Vols. (War of 1812) Reference Card
Domingue, Francisque	Private	7 Reg't. (Le Beuf's), La. Militia
Domingue, Joseph	Private	De Clouet's Reg't., La. Militia
Domingue, Joseph	Private	Baker's Regiment, La. Militia (Orig. under Domingo, Joseph)
Domingue, Manuel	Private	Plauche's Batt'n., La. Militia
Domingue, Manuel	Private	7 Reg't. (Le Beuf's), La. Militia
Dominguez, Brune	Private	17, 18 and 19 Cons. Reg't., La. Militia
Dominico, Pierre	Private	11 Reg't. (Hickey's), La. Militia
Dominique, --	Captain	Plauche's Batt'n., La. Militia
Dominique, Jean	Private	7 Reg't. (Le Beuf's), La. Militia
Dominique, Manuel	Private	Capt. Colsson's Co., Artillery, La. Vols.
Dominique, Zenon	Private	1 Batt'n. (Fortier's), La. Militia
Domo, Francis	Private	De Clouet's Reg't., La. Militia
Donaldson, William	Private	Captain Sprigg's Co., Boatmen, La. Vols.
Donas, Guillaume	Private	8 Reg't. (Meriam's), La. Militia
Doncan, --	Private	2 Reg't. (Cavelier's), La. Militia (Orig. under Doneau, --)
Doneau, --	Private	2 Reg't. (Cavelier's), La. Militia
Donegan, Michael O.	Private	De Clouet's Reg't., La. Militia (Orig. under O'Donegan, Michael)
Donerly, James	Private	Baker's Regiment, La. Militia (Orig. under Donnely, James)
Donis, Marcel	Private	7 Reg't. (Le Beuf's), La. Militia (Orig. under Danio, Marcel)
Donnely, James	Private	Baker's Regiment, La. Militia
Donnohoe, Harvay	Private	Capt. Ogden's Co. Dragoons, La. Militia
Donnoley, Anmos	Private	De Clouet's Reg't., La. Militia (Orig. under Daniley, Amos)
Donoho, Isaac	Sergeant	De Clouet's Reg't., La. Militia
Donohoe, Isaac	Sergeant	De Clouet's Reg't., La. Militia (Orig. under Donoho, Isaac)
Donoldson, William	Private	Captain Sprigg's Co., Boatmen, La. Vols.(Orig. under Donaldson, William)
Donsonville, Louis	Private	Captain Lagan's Co., La. Vols. (Orig. under Dorsonville, Louis)
Dooly, William	Private	Baker's Regiment, La. Militia
Dophon, Alexander	Private	Captain Price's Co., La. Militia
Dore', Francois	Private	De Clouet's Reg't., La. Militia
Dore, In	Private	5 Reg't. (La Branche's), La. Mil.
Dorell, John	Private	2 Batt'n. (Peire's), La. Vols. (Orig. under Dorrell, John)
Dorello, John	Private	2 Batt'n. (Peire's), La. Vols. (Orig. under Dorrell, John)
Dorfeuil, --	Private	1 Reg't. (Dejan's), La. Militia
Dorherty, Daniel	Sergeant	10 and 20 Cons. Reg't., La. Mil. (Orig. under Dougherty, Daniel)
Doricourt, Valcourt	Private	4 Reg't. (Morgan's), La. Militia (Orig. under Doriocourt, Valcourt)
Dorighty, Robert	Ensign	17, 18 and 19 Cons. Reg't., La. Militia
Dorin, Joseph	Private	2 Reg't. (Cavelier's), La. Militia
Doriocourt, Anthony	Captain	4 Reg't. (Morgan's), La. Militia
Doriocourt, Anthony, Jr.	2 Lieut.	4 Reg't. (Morgan's), La. Militia
Doriocourt, Valcourt	Private	4 Reg't. (Morgan's), La. Militia
Dorman, James	Adjutant	Detachment Field and Staff Officers, 4 Brigade, La. Militia
Dorman, John G.	1 Lieutenant	16 Reg't. (Thompson's), La. Mil.
Dormoy, Jean	Private	Captain Hubbard's Mounted Co., La. Militia
Dorrell, John	Private	2 Batt'n. (Peire's), La. Vols.
Dorsey, Samuel	Corporal	10 and 20 Cons. Reg't., La. Mil.
Dorsonville, Louis	Private	Captain Lagan's Co., La. Vols.
Dorville, Jr.	Corporal	4 Reg't. (Morgan's), La. Militia
Dorville, F. F.	Private	4 Reg't. (Morgan's), La. Militia
Dorville, J. O.	Private	4 Reg't. (Morgan's), La. Militia
Dorville, Narcisse	Private	De Clouet's Reg't., La. Militia
Dorville, Narcisse	Private	1 Batt'n. (Fortier's), La. Militia
Dorville, Theodore	Private	Louisiana (War of 1812)
Dorville, Theodore	Private	1 Batt'n. (Fortier's), La. Militia
Dorvin, Andre	Fusilier-Private	5 Reg't. (La Branche's), La. Mil.
Dorway, Michael	Private	Capt. Van Bibber's Co., La. Mil.
Dosar, Celestin	Private	17, 18 and 19 Cons. Reg't., La. Militia
Dosar, John Baptiste	Private	17, 18 and 19 Cons. Reg't., La. Militia
Dosar, Rafael	Private	17, 18 and 19 Cons. Reg't., La. Militia
Dosgros, Pierre Michel	Private	6 Reg't. (Landry's), La. Militia
Doss, Joel	Q. M. Sergeant	12 and 13 Cons. Reg't., La. Mil.
Doss, Parker	Private	Captain Wallace's Co., Boatmen, La. Vols.
Doublet, --	Sergeant	2 Reg't. (Cavelier's), La. Militia
Doubrere, Felix	Sergeant	2 Reg't. (Cavelier's), La. Militia
Doubure, Felix	Sergeant	2 Reg't. (Cavelier's), La. Militia (Orig. under Doubrere, Felix)
Douce, A.	Private	Plauche's Batt'n., La. Militia
Doucet, Hebert	Private	16 Reg't. (Thompson's), La. Mil.
Doucet, Maurie	Private	8 Reg't. (Meriam's), La. Militia
Doucet, Pierre	Private	16 Reg't. (Thompson's), La. Mil.
Doucett, Ursin	Private	De Clouet's Reg't., La. Militia
Doucette, Pierre	Private	16 Reg't. (Thompson's), La. Mil.
Doucette, Ursin	Private	16 Reg't. (Thompson's), La. Mil.
Dougherty, Daniel	Sergeant	10 and 20 Cons. Reg't., La. Mil.
Dougherty, Hugh	Private	2 Batt'n. (Peire's), La. Vols.
Dougherty, James	1 Lieutenant	12 and 13 Cons. Reg't., La. Mil. (Orig. under Daugherty, James)
Doughty, Edward	Private	19 Regiment, La. Militia
Douglas, Jepther	Private	De Clouet's Reg't., La. Militia
Douglass, James S.	Private	Captain Musick's Co., La. Mil.
Douglass, Martin	Private	Captain Musick's Co., La. Mil.
Douglass, William	Private	Captain Musick's Co., La. Mil.
Dougless, James S.	Private	Captain Musick's Co., La. Mil. (Orig. under Douglass, James S.)
Dougless, Martin	Private	Captain Musick's Co., La. Mil. (Orig. under Douglass, Martin)
Dougless, Wam	Private	Captain Musick's Co., La. Mil. (Orig. under Douglass, William)
Douriocourt, Anthony	Captain	4 Reg't. (Morgan's), La. Militia (Orig. under Doriocourt, Anthony)
Dourville, --	Ord. Sgt.-Sgt.	2 Batt'n. (D'Aquin's), La. Militia
Doutal, Joseph	Private	7 Reg't. (Le Beuf's), La. Militia
Dowell, John	Private	19 Regiment, La. Militia
Downey, Samuel	Private	Capt. Ogden's Co.,Dragoons, La. Militia
Downing, Patrick	Private	De Clouet's Reg't., La. Militia (Orig. under Dunning, Patrick)
Downs, Jeremiah	Brig. Major	3 Brigade (McCausland's), La. Militia
Doyal, Martin	Corporal	10 and 20 Cons. Reg't., La. Mil. Orig. under Doyle, Martin)
Doyle, Isaac	Private	17, 18 and 19 Cons. Reg't., La. Militia
Doyle, John	Private	Captain Ramsey's Co., Mounted Riflemen, La. Militia
Doyle, John	Private	17, 18 and 19 Cons. Reg't., La. Militia
Doyle, Martin	Corporal	10 and 20 Cons. Reg't., La. Mil.
Doyle, Richard	Private	17, 18 and 19 Cons. Reg't., La. Militia
Dozar, Celestin	Private	17, 18 and 19 Cons. Reg't., La. Militia (Orig. under Dosar, Celestin)
Dozer, James I.	Private	Captain McNair's Co., Mounted Riflemen, La. Militia

Name	Rank	Unit
Dozier, James I.	Private	Captain McNair's Co., Mounted Riflemen, La. Militia (Orig. under Dozer, James I.)
Drago, Etienne	Private	1 Reg't. (Dejan's), La. Militia
Drago, Pierre	Private	2 Batt'n. (Peire's), La. Vols. (Orig. under Drague, Pierre)
Drague, Pierre	Private	De Clouet's Reg't., La. Militia
Drague, Pierre	Private	2 Batt'n. (Peire's), La. Vols.
Draughon, Robert	2 Lieutenant	10 and 20 Cons. Reg't., La. Mil.
Draughon, William	Private	10 and 20 Cons. Reg't., La. Mil.
Draque, Pierre	Private	De Clouet's Reg't., La. Militia (Orig. under Drague, Pierre)
Drauquet, Benjamin	Private	17, 18 and 19 Cons. Reg't., La. Militia
Drawhan, Jeremiah	Private	10 and 20 Cons. Reg't., La. Mil.
Drayden, --	Fusilier-Private	5 Reg't. (La Branche's), La. Mil. (Orig. under Dryden, Jesse)
Drenen, William	Private	10 and 20 Cons. Reg't., La. Mil. (Orig. under Drennan, William)
Drennan, William	Private	10 and 20 Cons. Reg't., La. Mil.
Dreux, Gentilly	Private	3 Reg't. (de la Ronde's), La. Mil.
Dreux, Guy	Private	2 Reg't. (Cavelier's), La. Militia
Dreux, Severin	Servant	1 Batt'n. (Fortier's), La. Militia
Drioche, J.	Private	2 Reg't. (Cavelier's), La. Militia
Dromgool, John	Private	10 and 20 Cons. Reg't., La. Mil.
Dronet, Antoin	Private	Baker's Reg't., La. Mil. (Orig. under Drouet, Antoine)
Drouet, Antoine	Private	Baker's Regiment, La. Militia
Drouet, Cadet	Corporal	1 Reg't. (Dejan's), La. Militia
Drouet, Cadet	Private	4 Reg't. (Morgan's), La. Militia
Drouet, E.	Private	4 Reg't. (Morgan's), La. Militia
Drouette, N.	Private	7 Reg't. (Le Beuf's), La. Militia
Droughen, Jeremiah	Private	10 and 20 Cons. Reg't., La. Mil. (Orig. under Drawhan, Jeremiah)
Drouillard, Pre	Sergeant	Capt. Songy's Co., Marines, La. Vols.
Drouvandre, Desire	Musician	2 Batt'n. (Peire's), La. Vols.
Druet, Senior	Private	4 Reg't. (Morgan's), La. Militia
Drum, John	Private	Capt. Callaway's Co., Mounted Riflemen, La. Militia
Drumgold, John	Private	10 and 20 Cons. Reg't., La. Mil. (Orig. under Dromgool, John)
Druneau, Pre	Private	8 Reg't. (Meriam's), La. Militia
Dryden, Jesse	Fusilier-Private	5 Reg't. (La Branche's), La. Mil.
Du Beson, Juan	Private	12 and 13 Cons. Reg't., La. Mil.
Dubeure, Francois	Private	Captain Lagan's Co., La. Vols. (Orig. under Dubur, Francois)
Dubier, John R.	Private	7 Reg't. (Le Beuf's), La. Militia (Orig. under Dubieu, Johm R.)
Dubieu, John R.	Private	7 Reg't. (Le Beuf's), La. Militia
Dubignon, --	Corporal	Plauche's Batt'n., La. Militia
Dubois, --	Private	Plauche's Batt'n., La. Militia
Dubois, Antoine	Private	7 Reg't. (Le Beuf's), La. Militia
Dubois, Baptiste, fils	Private	17, 18 and 19 Cons. Reg't., La. Militia
Dubois, Joseph	Private	7 Reg't. (Le Beuf's), La. Militia
Dubois, Louis	Private	7 Reg't. (Le Beuf's), La. Militia
Dubois, Pierre	Fusilier-Private	5 Reg't. (La Branche's), La. Mil.
Dubois, Oliver	Private	17, 18 and 19 Cons. Reg't., La. Militia
Duboug, --	Private	2 Reg't. (Cavelier's), La. Militia (Orig. under Dubourg, --)
Dubourg, --	Private	2 Reg't. (Cavelier's), La. Militia
Dubourg, --	Sergeant	4 Reg't. (Morgan's), La. Militia
Du Bourg, P. F.	Adj. & Insp. Genl.	Gov. Claiborne and Staff, La. Mil.
Dubreuil, Louis	Sergeant	11 Reg't. (Hickey's), La. Militia
Dubrocard, Bernard	Private	8 Reg't. (Meriam's), La. Militia
Dubrocard, Ls	Private	8 Reg't. (Meriam's), La. Militia
Dubrock, Joseph	Private	De Clouet's Reg't., La. Militia (Orig. under Debrock, Joseph)
Dubrock, Martin	Private	De Clouet's Reg't., La. Militia (Orig. under Debrock, Martin)
Dubuclet, Joseph	Captain	Capt. Dubuclet's Troop, Hussars, La. Vols.
Dubue, --	Private	Plauche's Batt'n., La. Militia
Dubuelet, Antoine	Private	8 Reg't. (Meriam's), La. Militia
Dubur, Francois	Private	Captain Lagan's Co., La. Vols.
Ducass, Pierre	Private	2 Batt'n. (Peire's), La. Vols.
Ducasse, Pierre	Private	2 Batt'n. (Peire's), La. Vols. (Orig. under Ducass, Pierre)
Ducayet, --	Corporal	Plauche's Batt'n., La. Militia
Ducayet, --	Private	Plauche's Batt'n., La. Militia
Ducet, Elohi	Private	16 Reg't. (Thompson's), La. Mil.
Ducet, John	Private	16 Reg't. (Thompson's), La. Mil.
Ducett, Ursin	Private	De Clouet's Reg't., La. Militia (Orig. under Doucett, Ursin)
Ducette, Elohi	Private	16 Reg't. (Thompson's), La. Mil. (Orig. under Ducet, Elohi)
Ducette, John	Private	16 Reg't. (Thompson's), La. Mil. (Orig. under Ducet, John)
Ducette, Ursin	Private	16 Reg't. (Thompson's), La. Mil. (Orig. under Doucette, Ursin)
Ducey, Francois	Private	7 Reg't. (Le Beuf's), La. Militia
Ducey, Francois	Private	7 Reg't. (Le Beuf's), La. Militia
Duchamp, --	Private	1 Reg't. (Dejan's), La. Militia
Duchamp, Bernard	Private	Plauche's Batt'n., La. Militia
Duchamp, Charles	Private	Plauche's Batt'n., La. Militia
Duchane, Pierre	Corporal	De Clouet's Reg't., La. Militia
Duclairac, Emil	Private	2 Reg't. (Cavelier's), La. Militia
Duclaisae, Emil	Private	2 Reg't. (Cavelier's), La. Militia (Orig. under Duclairac, Emil)
Duclos, --	Drummer	2 Batt'n. (D'Aquin's), La. Militia
Du Closet, Oliver	Private	Capt. Dubuclet's Troop, Hussars, La. Vols. (Orig. under Duclozel, Oliver)
Duclozel, Oliver	Private	Capt. Dubuclet's Troop, Hussars, La. Vols.
Duconge', Cherubin	Sergeant	2 Batt'n. (D'Aquin's), La. Militia
Duconge, Frederick	Private	2 Batt'n. (D'Aquin's), La. Militia
Duconge', Pierre	Private	2 Batt'n. (D'Aquin's), La. Militia
Ducos, Jean	Private	2 Reg't. (Cavelier's), La. Militia
Ducote, John Pierre	Private	17, 18 and 19 Cons. Reg't., La. Militia
Ducrea, Leander	Private	12 and 13 Cons. Reg't., La. Mil.
Ducros, fils	Private	3 Reg't. (de la Ronde's), La. Mil.
Ducros, Antonio	2 Lieutenant	4 Reg't. (Morgan's), La. Militia
Ducros, Edouard	Captain	3 Reg't. (de la Ronde's), La. Mil.
Ducros, Joseph	Private	4 Reg't. (Morgan's), La. Militia
Ducy, Louis	Private	7 Reg't. (Le Beuf's), La. Militia
Dudley, Richard	Private	Capt. Alpuente's Co., La. Mil.
Dudly, Richard	Private	Capt. Alpuente's Co., La. Mil. (Orig. under Dudley, Richard)
Due, Urbin	Sergeant	5 Reg't. (La Branche's), La. Mil.
Duee, Louis	Private	Captain Hubbard's Mounted Co., La. Militia
Dueouin, --	Private	Plauche's Batt'n., La. Militia
Dufan, --	Private	1 Reg't. (Dejan's), La. Militia
Dufau, A.	Private	8 Reg't. (Meriam's), La. Militia
Dufau, John Louis	Private	De Clouet's Reg't., La. Militia
Duff, John M.	Private	Captain Callaway's Co., Cavalry, La. Militia
Duffeau, Jean	Corporal	Captain Lagan's Co., La. Vols. (Orig. under Dusteau, Jean)
Duffee, Charles	Private	De Clouet's Reg't., La. Militia
Duffour, Jean	Corporal	Captain Lagan's, Co., La. Vols.
Dufilho, --	Musician	Plauche's Batt'n., La. Militia
Dufilho, Louis	Private	(La Branche's), La. Militia
Duforest, B.	2 Lieutenant	4 Reg't. (Morgan's), La. Militia
Dufossar, Cyprien	Private	1 Batt'n. (Fortier's), La. Militia
Dufossat, Jn. Bte	Private	4 Reg't. (Morgan's), La. Militia
Dufossat, Joh Soniat	Private	4 Reg't. (Morgan's), La. Militia (Check census for name)
Dufossat, P. J.	Sergeant	4 Reg't. (Morgan's), La. Militia
Dufossat, Soniat, Sr.	Private	4 Reg't. (Morgan's), La. Militia
Dufour, Charles	Private	Capt. Le Doux's Co., Cavalry, La. Vols.
Dufour, Joseph	Sergeant	2 Batt'n. (Peire's), La. Vols.
Dufour, Louis	Sergeant	2 Batt'n. (Peire's), La. Vols. (Orig. under Dufour, Joseph)
Dufour, Pierre	Private	Captain Hubbard's Mounted Co., La. Militia
Dufresne, Louis	Private	2 Batt'n. (D'Aquin's), La. Militia
Duga, Charlite	Private	De Clouet's Reg't., La. Militia
Dugan, Joseph	Private	2 Batt'n. (Peire's), La. Vols.
Dugar, Paul	Sergeant	De Clouet's Reg't., La. Militia
Dugas, Ambroise	Private	La. War of 1812
Dugas, Bte	2 Lieutenant	7 Reg't. (Le Beuf's), La. Militia
Dugas, Gregoire	Private	6 Reg't. (Landry's), La. Militia
Dugas, I.	Private	6 Reg't. (Landry's), La. Militia
Dugas, Olliver	Private	La. War of 1812
Dugas, Paul	Private	6 Reg't. (Landry's), La. Militia
Dugat, Augustin	Corporal	De Clouet's Reg't., La. Militia
Dugat, Isidore	Private	6 Reg't. (Landry's), La. Militia
Dugat, Jerome	Private	6 Reg't. (Landry's), La. Militia

Name	Rank	Unit
Dugat, Jerome	Private	6 Reg't. (Landry's), La. Militia
Dugat, Joseph	1 Lieutenant	De Clouet's Reg't., La. Militia
Dugat, Maximilian	Private	De Clouet's Reg't., La. Militia
Dugat, Olivier	Private	De Clouet's Reg't., La. Militia
Dugat, Olivier	Private	16 Reg't. (Thompson's), La. Mil.
Dugee, Francis	Private	De Clouet's Reg't., La. Militia
Duggett, William	Private	17, 18 and 19 Cons. Reg't., La. Militia
Duggins, John	Private	17, 18 and 19 Cons. Reg't., La. Militia
Dugne, Pierre	Private	2 Batt'n. (D'Aquin's), La. Militia
Dugruise, Celestin	Private	8 Reg't. (Meriam's), La. Militia
Dugruise, Joseph	Private	8 Reg't. (Meriam's), La. Militia
Dugue, Junr.	Private	4 Reg't. (Morgan's), La. Militia
Dugue, Js.	Private	De Clouet's Reg't., La. Militia
Dugue, Livandais	Private	4 Reg't. (Morgan's), La. Militia
Duhe, Elie	Fusilier-Private	5 Reg't. (La Branche's), La. Mil.
Duhe, Enoc	Fusilier-Private	5 Reg't. (La Branche's), La. Mil.
Duhon, Charles	Private	De Clouet's Reg't., La. Militia
Duhon, Francois, Jr.	Private	6 Reg't. (Landry's), La. Militia (Orig. under Duon, Francois, Jr.)
Duhon, Francois, Sr.	Private	6 Reg't. (Landry's), La. Militia (Orig. under Duon, Francois, Sr.)
Duhon, Joseph	Private	De Clouet's Reg't., La. Militia
Duhon, Joseph	Private	6 Reg't. (Landry's), La. Militia
Duhon, Phirmin	Private	De Clouet's Reg't., La. Militia
Duhon, Placide	Private	De Clouet's Reg't., La. Militia
Duhulquod, --	3 Lieutenant	Plauche's Batt'n., La. Militia
Duhy, --	Private	Plauche's Batt'n., La. Militia
Duke, Joseph	Private	Capt. Allen's Co., Artillerists, La. Vols.
Dulate, J. L.	Private	De Clouet's Reg't., La. Militia (Orig. under Detale, John Lewis)
Dulie, J. C.	Private	Plauche's Batt'n., La. Militia (Orig. under Dullie, Jh. C.)
Duliut, Neville	Major	Detachment Field and Staff Officers, 4 Brigade, La. Militia
Dullie, Jh. C.	Private	Plauche's Batt'n., La. Militia
Dulong, Antoine	Sergeant	3 Reg't. (de la Ronde's), La. Mil.
Dumaine, --	Private	Capt. Trudeau's Troop of Horse, La. Militia
Dumaine, Cadet	Private	6 Reg't. (Landry's), La. Militia
Dumaine, Michael	Corporal	6 Reg't. (Landry's), La. Militia
Dumaine, Pie	Captain	5 Reg't. (La Branche's), La. Mil.
Dumalar, Cheri	Private	2 Batt'n. (D'Aquin's), La. Militia
Dumarest, Jean Bte	Private	16 Reg't. (Thompson's), La. Mil.
Dumartrait, Adrien	1 Sergeant	Capt. Dubuclet's Troop, Hussars, La. Vols.
Dumas, --	Sergeant	2 Reg't. (Cavelier's), La. Militia
Dumas, Andrew	Private	17, 18 and 19 Cons. Reg't., La. Militia
Dumouille, Honore	Private	8 Reg't. (Meriam's), La. Militia
Dumouille, Terrence	Private	8 Reg't. (Meriam's), La. Militia
Dumouille, Valerie	Private	8 Reg't. (Meriam's), La. Militia
Dumoulle, Bernard	Sergeant	1 Batt'n. (Fortier's), La. Militia
Dunaine, Cadet	Private	6 Reg't. (Landry's), La. Militia (Orig. under Dumaine, Cadet)
Dunavan, Amos	Private	17, 18 and 19 Cons. Reg't., La. Militia
Dunbar, Thomas	Private	De Clouet's Reg't., La. Militia (See also 44 U.S. Reg't.)
Dunbar, William	Private	10 Regiment, La. Militia
Dunbry, Talmage	Private	Baker's Regiment, La. Militia (Orig. under Danbry, Talmage)
Duncan, George	Private	Captain Wallace's Co., Boatmen, La. Vols.
Duncan, Lewis	Private	10 and 20 Cons. Reg't., La. Mil.
Duncan, Samuel, R.	Private	De Clouet's Reg't., La. Militia
Dunfield, David	Corporal	Captain Sprigg's Co., Boatmen, La. Vols.
Dunford, John	Private	12 and 13 Cons. Reg't., La. Mil.
Dungeon, Jordan	Musician-Pvt.	4 Reg't. (Morgan's), La. Militia
Dunham, John	Private	10 and 20 Cons. Reg't., La. Mil.
Duning, Patrick	Private	De Clouet's Reg't., La. Militia (Orig. under Dunning, Patrick)
Duning, William	Private	10 and 20 Cons. Reg't., La. Mil.
Dunington, Francis	Sergeant	1 Reg't. (Dejan's), La. Militia
Dunkan, William	Private	17, 18 and 19 Cons. Reg't., La. Militia
Dunkin, William	Private	17, 18 and 19 Cons. Reg't., La. Militia (Orig. under Dunkan, William)
Dunks, Andrew	Private	16 Reg't. (Thompson's), La. Mil.
Dunks, Andrew	Private	16 Reg't. (Thompson's), La. Mil.
Dunkum, John	Private	11 Reg't. (Hickey's), La. Militia
Dunman, Joseph	Private	De Clouet's Reg't., La. Militia
Dunn, Beverly	Sergeant	10 and 20 Cons. Reg't., La. Mil.
Dunn, Gray	Private-Sergeant	De Clouet's Reg't., La. Militia
Dunn, Isom	Private	10 and 20 Cons. Reg't., La. Mil.
Dunning, Patrick	Private	De Clouet's Reg't., La. Militia (See also Artillery)
Dunoho, Harvey	Private	16 Reg't. (Thompson's), La. Mil.
Dunot, Don Louis	Private	16 Reg't. (Thompson's), La. Mil.
Dunwoodie, John	Private	17, 18 and 19 Cons. Reg't., La. Militia
Duoete, John Pierre	Private	17, 18 and 19 Cons. Reg't., La. Mil. (Orig. under Ducote, Joh Pierre)
Duon, Firman	Private	16 Reg't. (Thompson's), La. Mil.
Duon, Francois, Jr.	Private	6 Reg't. (Landry's), La. Militia
Duon, Francois, Sr.	Private	6 Reg't. (Landry's), La. Militia
Duon, Michel	Private	Captain Hubbard's Mounted Co., La. Militia
Duon, Pierre	Private	16 Reg't. (Thompson's), La. Mil.
Dupa, Mitchell	Private	De Clouet's Reg't., La. Militia
Dupard, August	Private	1 Batt'n. (Fortier's), La. Militia (Orig. under Dupart, August)
Dupard, Celestin	Sergeant	1 Batt'n. (Fortier's), La. Militia
Dupard, Charles	Sergeant	1 Batt'n. (Fortier's), La. Militia
Dupard, Hilaire	Sergeant	1 Batt'n. (Fortier's), La. Militia
Dupard, Zenon	Private	7 Reg't. (Le Beuf's), La. Militia
Dupare, Hilaire	Sergeant	1 Batt'n. (Fortier's), La. Militia (Orig. under Dupard, Hilaire)
Dupare, S. D. (L. ?)	Private	6 Reg't. (Landry's), La. Militia
Dupare, P. D.	Private	6 Reg't. (Landry's), La. Militia
Dupart, August	Private	1 Batt'n. (Fortier's), La. Militia
Dupart, Joseph fils	Private	De Clouet's Reg't., La. Militia
Dupart, Martial	1 Lieutenant	De Clouet's Reg't., La. Militia
Dupart, Pierre	Sergeant	1 Batt'n. (Fortier's), La. Militia
Dupas, John Bte	Captain	De Clouet's Reg't., La. Militia
Dupas, Mitchell	Private	De Clouet's Reg't., La. Militia (Orig. under Dupa, Mitchell)
Duperon, --	Private	Plauche's Batt'n., La. Militia
Duperon, Louis	Private	De Clouet's Reg't., La. Militia (Orig. under Duperron, Louis)
Duperron, Louis	Private	De Clouet's Reg't., La. Militia
Dupey, Edmond	Private	De Clouet's Reg't., La. Militia (Orig. under Dupuy, Edmond)
Dupey, Noel Gaspard	1 Lieutenant	2 Batt'n. (Peire's), La. Vols. (Orig. under Dupuy, Noel Gaspard)
Dupheking, Honore	Corporal	De Clouet's Reg't., La. Militia (Orig. under Duplechin, Honore)
Duplaissy, Jph	Sergeant	1 Batt'n. (Fortier's), La. Militia
Duplantier, --	Private	Plauche's Batt'n., La. Militia
Duplantier, Senr.	Private	4 Reg't. (Morgan's), La. Militia
Duplantier, Armand	Private	6 Reg't. (Landry's), La. Militia
Duplantier, Fergus	Corporal	4 Reg't. (Morgan's), La. Militia
Duplantier, Jacques	--	4 Reg't. (Morgan's), La. Militia
Duplechin, Honore	Corporal	De Clouet's Reg't., La. Militia
Duplessie, Charles	Private	De Clouet's Reg't., La. Militia (Orig. under Duplessis, Charles)
Duplessie, Cyprien	Private	De Clouet's Reg't., La. Militia (Orig. under Duplessis, Ciprien)
Duplessie, Honore	Private	De Clouet's Reg't., La. Militia (Orig. under Duplessis, Honore)
Duplessie, Molliere	Private	De Clouet's Reg't., La. Militia (Orig. under Duplessis, Molliere)
Duplessis, A.	Private	Plauche's Batt'n., La. Militia
Duplessis, Charles	Private	De Clouet's Reg't., La. Militia
Duplessis, Ciprien	Private	De Clouet's Reg't., La. Militia
Duplessis, F.	Private	1 Reg't. (Dejan's), La. Militia (Orig. under Duplissis, F.)
Duplessis, Honore'	Private	De Clouet's Reg't., La. Militia
Duplessis, Molliere	Private	De Clouet's Reg't., La. Militia
Duplessis, P.	Private	2 Reg't. (Cavelier's), La. Militia
Duplex, Thomas	Private	De Clouet's Reg't., La. Militia
Duplichon, Jean	Corporal	De Clouet's Reg't., La. Militia
Duplissis, F.	Private	1 Reg't. (Dejan's), La. Militia
Dupont, Francois	Fusilier-Private	5 Reg't. (La Branche's), La. Mil.
Dupont, John	Private	2 Batt'n. (Peire's), La. Vols. (Orig. under Dupont, Julien)
Dupont, Julien	Private	2 Batt'n. (Peire's), La. Vols.
Dupont, Pierre	Servant	1 Batt'n. (Fortier's), La. Militia

Name	Rank	Unit
Dupont, Severin	Fusilier-Private	5 Reg't. (La Branche's), La. Mil.
Dupre, --	Corporal	3 Reg't. (de la Ronde's), La. Mil.
Dupre', Francois	Private	16 Reg't. (Thompson's), La. Mil.
Dupre, Laurent	Private	16 Reg't. (Thompson's), La. Mil.
Dupre, Ls	Private	1 Batt'n. (Fortier's), La. Militia
Dupre, Onizeme	Sergeant	16 Reg't. (Thompson's), La. Mil.
Dupre', Solart	A.D.C.	4 Brigade (Flanjae's), La. Mil.
Dupree, James	Private	10 and 20 Cons. Reg't., La. Mil.
Dupres, Jacques	Private	1 Batt'n. (Fortier's), La. Militia
Dupres, Louis	Private	5 Reg't. (La Branche's), La. Mil.
Dupres, Pierre	Private	2 Batt'n. (D'Aquin's), La. Militia
Dupries, Noel	Private	6 Reg't. (Landry's), La. Militia (Orig. under Dupuis, Noel)
Dupries, Simon	Private	6 Reg't. (Landry's), La. Militia (Orig. under Dupuis, Simon)
Duprey, Jaques	Major	Detachment Field and Staff Officers, 4 Brigade, La. Militia
Duprey, Noel Gaspard	1 Lieutenant	2 Batt'n. (Peire's), La. Vols. (Orig. under Dupuy, Noel Gaspard)
Dupui, Peter	Private	10 and 20 Cons. Reg't., La. Mil.
Dupuis, A.	Sergeant	8 Reg't. (Meriam's), La. Militia
Dupuis, Alexander	Private	6 Reg't. (Landry's), La. Militia
Dupuis, Alexis	Private	17, 18 and 19 Cons. Reg't., La. Militia
Dupuis, Ante Son	Corporal	5 Reg't. (La Branche's), La. Mil.
Dupuis, Antoine	Fusilier-Private	5 Reg't. (La Branche's), La. Mil.
Dupuis, Cadet	Private	7 Reg't. (Le Beuf's), La. Militia
Dupuis, Charles	Corporal	7 Reg't. (Le Beuf's), La. Militia
Dupuis, Charles	Private	8 Reg't. (Meriam's), La. Militia
Dupuis, Edmond	Corporal	1 Batt'n. (Fortier's), La. Militia
Dupuis, Eloi	Corporal	8 Reg't. (Meriam's), La. Militia (Orig. under Dupuy, Elois)
Dupuis, Etienne	Private	7 Reg't. (Le Beuf's), La. Militia
Dupuis, Gideon	Sergeant	8 Reg't. (Meriam's), La. Militia
Dupuis, Hypolite	Private	De Clouet's Reg't., La. Militia
Dupuis, Jean	Private	7 Reg't. (Le Beuf's), La. Militia
Dupuis, Jno Bte	Private	8 Reg't. (Meriam's), La. Militia
Dupuis, John Bte	Private	8 Reg't. (Meriam's), La. Militia
Dupuis, Joseph	Corporal	6 Reg't. (Landry's), La. Militia
Dupuis, Joseph	Private	7 Reg't. (Le Beuf's), La. Militia
Dupuis, Marcel	2 Lieutenant	8 Reg't. (Meriam's), La. Militia
Dupuis, Maxamillun	Private	17, 18 and 19 Cons. Reg't., La. Militia
Dupuis, Michel	Private	De Clouet's Reg't., La. Militia
Dupuis, Noel	Private	6 Reg't. (Landry's), La. Militia
Dupuis, Paul	Private	8 Reg't. (Meriam's), La. Militia
Dupuis, Pierre	Private	7 Reg't. (Le Beuf's), La. Militia
Dupuis, Pierre	Private	8 Reg't. (Meriam's), La. Militia
Dupuis, Pierre	Private	17, 18 and 19 Cons. Reg't., La. Militia
Dupuis, Simon	Private	6 Reg't. (Landry's), La. Militia
Dupuy, --	Private	Plauche's Batt'n., La. Militia
Dupuy, Aubry	Major	6 Reg't. (Landry's), La. Militia
Dupuy, Aubry	Major	8 Reg't. (Meriam's), La. Militia
Dupuy, B.	Lt. Adjutant	6 Reg't. (Landry's), La. Militia
Dupuy, B.	Lt. Adjutant	8 Reg't. (Meriam's), La. Militia
Dupuy, Edmond	Private	De Clouet's Reg't., La. Militia
Dupuy, Edward	Private	De Clouet's Reg't., La. Militia (Orig. under Dupuy, Edmund)
Dupuy, Elois	Corporal	8 Reg't. (Meriam's), La. Militia
Dupuy, F.	Private	Capt. Cahuveau's Co., Cavalry, La. Militia
Dupuy, Mag.	Private	8 Reg't. (Meriam's), La. Militia
Dupuy, Mercel	2 Lieutenant	8 Reg't. (Meriam's), La. Militia (Orig. under Dupuis, Marcel)
Dupuy, Noel Gaspard	1 Lieutenant	2 Batt'n. (Peire's), La. Vols.
Dupuy, Peter	Private	10 and 20 Cons. Reg't., La. Mil.
Duque, Joseph	Private	3 Reg't. (de la Ronde's), La. Mil.
Durald, --	Private	1 Reg't. (Dejan's), La. Militia
Duralde, V.	Private	8 Reg't. (Meriam's), La. Militia
Duraled, --	Private	1 Reg't. (Dejan's), La. Militia (Orig. under Durald, --)
Durand, --	Private	Plauche's Batt'n., La. Militia
Durand, --	Lieutenant	2 Batt'n. (D'Aquin's), La. Militia (Orig. under Durant, --)
Durand, Anthy	Private	2 Reg't. (Cavelier's), La. Militia
Durand, Charles	Private	1 Batt'n. (Fortier's), La. Militia
Durand, M.	Private	Plauche's Batt'n., La. Militia
Durand, M.	Private	1 Reg't. (Dejan's), La. Militia
Durand, P.	Private	8 Reg't. (Meriam's), La. Militia
Durand, Pre	Private	2 Batt'n. (D'Aquin's), La. Militia
Durant, --	Lieutenant, 3 Lieut.	2 Batt'n. (D'Aquin's), La. Militia
Duranto, Firmin	Private	2 Reg't. (Cavelier's), La. Militia
Durantot, Firmin	Private	2 Reg't. (Cavelier's), La. Militia (Orig. under Duranto, Firmin)
Durbaune, Michael	Private	17, 18 and 19 Cons. Reg't., La. Militia (Orig. under Derbaune, Michael)
Durben, Ignashus	Private	De Clouet's Reg't., La. Militia
Durben, James	Private	12 and 13 Cons. Reg't., La. Mil. (Orig. under Durbin, James)
Durbin, James	Private	12 and 13 Cons. Reg't., La. Mil.
Durbin, Jeremiah	Private	12 and 13 Cons. Reg't., La. Mil.
Durcy, F.	Private	De Clouet's Reg't., La. Militia (Orig. under Dursey, F.)
Durcy, Francois	Captain	17, 18 and 19 Cons. Reg't., La. Militia
Durel, aine	Private	Plauche's Batt'n., La. Militia
Durel, In Frent	Captain	2 Reg't. (Cavelier's), La. Militia (Orig. under Durel, Fs)
Durel, Michel	Private	2 Reg't. (Cavelier's), La. Militia
Durel, N.	Private	Plauche's Batt'n., La. Militia
Durel, U.	1 Sergeant	2 Reg't. (Cavelier's), La. Militia
Durenoir, --	Private	2 Reg't. (Cavelier's), La. Militia
Duret, Joseph	Private	Plauche's Batt'n., La. Militia
Durham, John	Private	10 and 20 Cons. Reg't., La. Mil. (Orig. under Durham, John)
Durhu, --	Private	Plauche's Batt'n., La. Militia
Duriaux, Pierre	Private	1 Batt'n. (Fortier's), La. Militia
Durillas, --	Private	Plauche's Batt'n., La. Militia (Orig. under Duvillas, --)
Durillas, Pierre	Private	2 Batt'n. (Peire's), La. Vols. (Orig. under Duvillasse, Pierre)
Durillas, Pierre	Private	2 Batt'n. (Peire's), La. Vols. (Orig. under Duvillasse, Pierre)
Durivage, Victor	Private	2 Reg't. (Cavelier's), La. Militia
Durlack, Baptiste	Private	Capt. Van Bibber's Co., La. Mil.
Duro, Joseph	Private	Captain Lagan's Co., La. Vols.
Duroche, Barthelemy	Private	De Clouet's Reg't., La. Militia (Orig. under Durocher, Barthelamy)
Duroche, Bernard	Private	De Clouet's Reg't., La. Militia (Orig. under Durocher, Bernard)
Durochee, Joseph	Private	7 Reg't. (Le Beuf's), La. Militia
Durocher, Barthelemy	Private	De Clouet's Reg't., La. Militia
Durocher, Bernard	Private	De Clouet's Reg't., La. Militia
Durone, Jacob	Private	6 Reg't. (Landry's), La. Militia
Duronseau, Felix	Sergeant	2 Reg't. (Cavelier's), La. Militia (Orig. under Durouseau, Felix)
Durouseau, Felix	Sergeant	2 Reg't. (Cavelier's), La. Militia
Dursey, F.	Private	De Clouet's Reg't., La. Militia
Durst, John	Private	17, 18 and 19 Cons. Reg't., La. Mil. (Orig. under Dust, John)
Durbon, Philip	Private	Capt. Callaway's Co., Cavalry, La. Militia
Dusfeau, Jean	Corporal	Captain Lagan's Co., La. Vols. (Orig. under Dusteau, Jean)
Dusseau, Francis	Sergeant	De Clouet's Reg't., La. Militia
Dussiore, Francis	Sergeant	De Clouet's Reg't., La. Militia
Dussnau, B.	Sergeant	5 Reg't. (La Branche's), La. Mil.
Dusson, Pre	Corporal	2 Batt'n. (D'Aquin's), La. Militia
Dussnan, Jr.	Private	4 Reg't. (Morgan's), La. Militia (Orig. under Dersuan, Jr.)
Dussuan, B.	2 Lieutenant	4 Reg't. (Morgan's), La. Militia (Orig. under Dusuan, B.)
Dussnau, Francis	Sergeant	De Clouet's Reg't., La. Militia (Orig. under Dusseau, Francis)
Dussuau, St. Ford	Corporal	1 Batt'n. (Fortier's), La. Militia (Orig. under Dusuar, St. Ford)
Dust, John	Private	17, 18 and 19 Cons. Reg't., La. Militia
Dusteau, Jean	Corporal	Captain Lagan's Co., La. Vols.
Dusto, Certrand	Private	Captain Lagan's Co., La. Vols.
Dusuan, Jr.	Private	4 Reg't. (Morgan's), La. Militia
Dusuan, Auguste	Private	5 Reg't. (La Branche's), La. Mil.
Dusuan, B.	2 Lieut.	4 Reg't. (Morgan's), La. Militia
Dusuan, St. Alban	Private	5 Reg't. (La Branche's), La. Mil.
Dusuan, St. Ford	Corporal	1 Batt'n. (Fortier's), La. Militia (Orig. under Dusuar, St. Ford)
Dusuan, St. Louis	Private	5 Reg't. (La Branche's), La. Mil.
Dusuar, St. Ford	Corporal	1 Batt'n. (Fortier's), La. Militia
Dusuare, St. Ford	Corporal	1 Batt'n. (Fortier's), La. Militia (Orig. under Dusuar, St. Ford)
Dutara, Francois	Artificer	Capt. Chaudurier's Co., Artificers, Art'y., La. Vols.

Name	Rank	Unit
Dutaua, F.	Private	De Clouet's Reg't., La. Militia (Orig. under Dutava, F.)
Dutarra, Francois	Artificer	Capt. Chaudurier's Co., Artificers, Art'y., La. Vols. (Orig. under Dutara, Francois)
Dutarrd, F.	Private	De Clouet's Reg't., La. Militia (Orig. under Dutava, F.)
Dutava, F.	Private	De Clouet's Reg't., La. Militia
Duterrat, F.	Private	De Clouet's Reg't., La. Militia (Orig. under Dutava, F.)
Duval, --	Private	1 Reg't. (Dejan's), La. Militia
Duval, --	Private	4 Reg't. (Morgan's), La. Militia
Duval, Ardien F.	Sergeant, Adj.	2 Batt'n. (Peire's), La. Vols.
Duval, Billy	Private	8 Reg't. (Meriam's), La. Militia
Duval, Francois	Private	1 Batt'n. (Fortier's), La. Militia
Duval, Francois	Private	1 Batt'n. (Fortier's), La. Militia
Duval, Julien	Private	Capt. Dubuclet's Troop, Hussars, La. Vols.
Duvall, Charles	Private	Captain Sprigg's Co., Boatmen, La. Vols.
Duvall, Francis	Private	19 Reg't., La. Militia
Duverge, Pierre	Qr. Master	3 Reg't. (de la Ronde's), La. Mil.
Duvevje, --	Private	3 Reg't. (de la Ronde's), La. Mil.
Duvernais, --	Private	4 Reg't. (Morgan's), La. Militia
Duvernay, Fs	1 Lieutenant	3 Reg't. (de la Ronde's), La. Mil.
Duvernay, Fs fils	Private	3 Reg't. (de la Ronde's), La. Mil.
Duvernay, Francois	1 Lieutenant	1 Batt'n. (Fortier's), La. Militia (Orig. under Duverne, Francois)
Duvernay, Jh	Private	3 Reg't. (de la Ronde's), La. Mil.
Duvernay, Joseph	Private	De Clouet's Reg't., La. Militia (Orig. under Duverney, Joseph)
Duvernay, Pierre	Private	De Clouet's Reg't., La. Militia (Orig. under Duverney, Pierre)
Duverne, Francois	1 Lieutenant	1 Batt'n. (Fortier's), La. Militia
Duverne, Joseph	Private	De Clouet's Reg't., La. Militia (Orig. under Duverney, Joseph)
Duverney, Joseph	Private	De Clouet's Reg't., La. Militia
Duverney, Pierre	Private	De Clouet's Reg't., La. Militia
Duvilasse, Pierre	Private	2 Batt'n. (Peire's), La. Vols. (Orig. under Duvillasse, Pierre)
Duvillas, --	Private	Plauche's Batt'n., La. Militia
Duvillas, Pierre	Private	2 Batt'n. (Peire's), La. Vols. (Orig. under Duvillasse, Pierre)
Duvillasse, Pierre	Private	2 Batt'n. (Peire's), La. Vols.
Dwire, John	Private-Sergeant	De Clouet's Reg't., La. Militia
Dwyre, John	Private-Sergeant	De Clouet's Reg't., La. Militia (Orig. under Dwire, John)
Dychas, William	Private	De Clouet's Reg't., La. Militia (Orig. under Dykes, William)
Dyches, Barden	Private	Du Clouet's Reg't., La. Militia (Orig. under Dykes, Barden)
Dyches, William	Private	De Clouet's Reg't., La. Militia (Orig. under Dykes, William)
Dychex, Isaac	Corporal	12 and 13 Cons. Reg't., La. Mil.
Dyer, Robert	Private	10 and 20 Cons. Reg't., La. Mil. (Orig. under Dyre, Robert)
Dyhes, Barden	Private	De Clouet's Reg't., La. Militia (Orig. under Dykes, Barden)
Dykes, Barden	Private	De Clouet's Reg't., La. Militia
Dykes, Dennis	Private	12 and 13 Cons. Reg't., La. Mil.
Dykes, William	Private	De Clouet's Reg't., La. Militia
Dyre, Robert	Private	10 and 20 Cons. Reg't., La. Mil.
Dyson, Clement	Private	16 Reg't. (Thompson's), La. Mil.
Dyson, Thomas	Private	16 Reg't. (Thompson's), La. Mil.
Eady, John	Private	12 and 13 Cons. Reg't., La. Mil. (Orig. under Eddey, John)
Earley, William	Private	Capt. Thomas' Co., La. Militia (Orig. under Early, William)
Early, William	Private	Capt. Thomas' Co., La. Militia
East, Isaac	Private	10 and 20 Cons. Reg't., La. Mil.
East, John	Private	De Clouet's Reg't., La. Militia
East, Thomas	Private	10 and 20 Cons. Reg't., La. Mil.
Eastep, Joseph	Private	12 and 13 Cons. Reg't., La. Mil. (Orig. under Estep, Joseph)
Eastice, Ransom	Pay Master	Detachment Field and Staff Officers, 4 Brigade, La. Militia
Eastin, Herbert	1 Lieutenant	De Clouet's Reg't., La. Militia (Orig. under Easton, Herbert)
Eastin, Ransom	3 Lieutenant	De Clouet's Reg't., La. Militia
Easton, Herbert	1 Lieutenant	De Clouet's Reg't., La. Militia
Eaton, James	Private	Louisiana War of 1812
Eavanes, James	Private	Captain Ramsey's Co., Mounted Riflemen, La. Militia
Eavans, John	Private	De Clouet's Reg't., La. Militia (Orig. under Evans, John)
Ebar, Francis	Private	17, 18 and 19 Cons. Reg't., La. Militia
Ebar, John Lacroy	Private	Baker's Regiment, La. Militia
Ebare, John Lefroi	Private	Baker's Regiment, La. Militia (Orig. under Ebar, John Lacroy)
Ebert, Jean	Private	7 Reg't. (Le Beuf's), La. Militia
Ebert, Louis	Private	7 Reg't. (Le Beuf's), La. Militia
Ebert, Maturin	Private	7 Reg't. (Le Beuf's), La. Militia
Ebert, Michael	Private	8 Reg't. (Meriam's), La. Militia
Ebert, Pierre	Private	7 Reg't. (Le Beuf's), La. Militia
Ebert, Siril	Private	7 Reg't. (Le Beuf's), La. Militia
Ebert, Ths. (fils)	Private	8 Reg't. (Meriam's), La. Militia (Orig. under Hebert, Thomas fils)
Ebert, Zacharie	Private	8 Reg't. (Meriam's), La. Militia
Echo, Jean Baptiste	Private	1 Batt'n. (Fortier's), La. Militia
Eddardo, Evangelist	Sergeant	10 and 20 Cons. Reg't., La. Mil.
Eddey, John	Private	12 and 13 Cons. Reg't., La. Mil.
Eddy, Hezekiah	Private	1 Reg't. (Dejan's), La. Militia
Edelmer, Henry	Private	8 Reg't. (Meriam's), La. Militia
Edgar, Nicholas	Sergeant	Baker's Regiment, La. Militia
Edington, Thomas	Corporal-Sgt.	2 Batt'n. (Peire's), La. Vols. (Orig. under Edrington, Thomas)
Edler, Andrew	Private	De Clouet's Reg't., La. Militia
Edoire, --	Private	2 Batt'n. (D'Aquin's), La. Militia
Edonary, Baptiste	Corporal	2 Batt'n. (D'Aquin's), La. Militia
Edouard, --	Private	De Clouet's Reg't., La. Militia
Edouard, --	Private	2 Batt'n. (D'Aquin's), La. Militia (Orig. under Edoire, --)
Edouard, --	Servant	3 Reg't. (de la Ronde's), La. Mil.
Edrington, Thomas	Corporal-Sgt.	2 Batt'n. (Peire's), La. Vols.
Edvard, Nathaniel	Private	De Clouet's Reg't., La. Militia (Orig. under Edwards, Mathew)
Edward, --	Servant	2 Batt'n. (D'Aquin's), La. Militia
Edwards, C.	Private	Captain Sprigg's Co., Boatmen, La. Vols.
Edwards, D.	Private	10 Regiment, La. Militia
Edwards, H.	Private	4 Reg't. (Morgan's), La. Militia
Edwards, James	Private	Capt. Wallace's Co., Boatmen, La. Vols.
Edwards, James	Private	16 Reg't. (Thompson's), La. Mil.
Edwards, John	Private	12 and 13 Cons. Reg't., La. Mil.
Edwards, Joshua	Private	Captain Callaway's Co., Mounted Riflemen, La. Militia
Edwards, Mathew	Private	De Clouet's Reg't., La. Militia
Edwards, Robert	Private	12 and 13 Cons. Reg't., La. Mil.
Edy, Caleb	Private	Baker's Regiment, La. Militia
Egiste, --	Drummer	2 Reg't. (Cavelier's), La. Militia
Egle', Jacques	Private	4 Reg't. (Morgan's), La. Militia
Egudy, Charles	Corporal	5 Reg't. (La Branche's), La. Mil.
Elair, Moese	Private	16 Reg't. (Thompson's), La. Mil.
Elam, William W.	Private	Capt. Wallace's Co., Boatmen, La. Vols.
Elborado, Manuel	Private	De Clouet's Reg't., La. Militia (Orig. under Alborado, Manuel)
Elene, Frs	Private	Baker's Regiment, La. Militia
Elfer, Christophe	Fusilier-Private	5 Reg't. (La Branche's), La. Mil.
Elinder, Michael	Private	De Clouet's Reg't., La. Militia
Elli, Josiah S.	4th Burser	Captain Dodge's Co., Mounted Riflemen, La. Militia (Orig. under Ellis, Josiah S.)
Elliot, Cadet	Private	2 Reg't. (Cavelier's), La. Militia
Elliot, Ellias, A.	2 Lieutenant	Captain Henry's Co., Mounted Riflemen, La. Militia
Elliott, Elias A.	2 Lieutenant	Captain Dodge's Co., Mounted Riflemen, La. Militia
Elliott, Leroy	Private	Captain Price's Co., La. Militia
Elliott, William	Qr. Ms. Sergeant	10 and 20 Cons. Reg't., La. Mil.
Elliott, Willis	Private	10 and 20 Cons. Reg't., La. Mil.
Elliotte, Cadet	Private	2 Reg't. (Cavelier's), La. Militia (Orig. under Elliot, Cadet)
Ellis, Abraham	Private	Captain Musick's Co., La. Mil.
Ellis, Charles	Private	Captain Dodge's Co., Mounted Riflemen, La. Militia
Ellis, Charles	Private	Captain Henry's Co., Mounted Riflemen, La. Militia
Ellis, Ellis	Sergeant	17, 18 and 19 Cons. Reg't., La. Militia
Ellis, Josiah S.	4th Burser	Captain Dodge's Co., Mounted Riflemen, La. Militia

Name	Rank	Unit
Ellis, Josiah S.	Sergeant	Captain Henry's Co., Mounted Riflemen, La. Militia
Ellybrant, Christian	Private	De Clouet's Reg't., La. Militia
Elsoneth, John	Private	2 Batt'n. (Peire's), La. Vols.
Elsouth, John	Private	2 Batt'n. (Peire's), La. Vols. (Orig. under Elsoneth, John)
Elsworth, John	Private	2 Batt'n. (Peire's), La. Vols.
Elsworth, John	Private	2 Batt'n. (Peire's), La. Vols. (Orig. under Elsoneth, John)
Elte, Georges	Fusilier-Private	5 Reg't. (La Branche's), La. Mil.
Elte, Jn Pre	Fusilier-Private	5 Reg't. (La Branche's), La. Mil.
Elwell, Uriah	Private	12 and 13 Cons. Reg't., La. Mil.
Embeau, Martin	Private	De Clouet's Reg't., La. Militia
Emblare, --	Sergeant	2 Batt'n. (D'Aquin's), La. Militia
Emery, --	Private	1 Reg't. (Dejan's), La. Militia
Emery, Francois	Private	2 Batt'n. (Peire's), La. Vols. (Orig. under Emmery, Francois)
Emery, John	Private	4 Reg't. (Morgan's), La. Militia
Emmerson, W.	Private	1 Reg't. (Dejan's), La. Militia
Emmery, Francois	Private	2 Batt'n. (Peire's), La. Vols.
Emmons, Julien	Private	Capt. Ashley's Co., Mounted Riflemen, La. Militia
Enaid, David	Private	6 Reg't. (Landry's), La. Militia
Encare, Charles	Private	De Clouet's Reg't., La. Militia
Enette, L.	1 Sgt.-Sergeant	Capt. Le Doux's Co., Cav., La. Vols.
Englehard, Guillaime	Fus.-Private	5 Reg't. (La Branche's), La. Mil.
Engles, Thomas	Private	1 Reg't. (Dejan's), La. Militia
English, Chester	Private	De Clouet's Reg't., La. Militia
Enoul, --	Private	3 Reg't. (de la Ronde's), La. Mil.
Enoul, Balthazar	Private	3 Reg't. (de la Ronde's), La. Mil.
Enoul, Livandais	Private	3 Reg't. (de la Ronde's), La. Mil.
Erera, Jean	Private	3 Reg't. (de la Ronde's), La. Mil. (Orig. under Herrera, Jean)
Ernandez, A.	Private	7 Reg't. (Le Beuf's), La. Militia
Ernest, --	Private	Capt. Chauveau's Co., Cavalry, La. Militia
Ernoul, Balthazar	Private	3 Reg't. (de la Ronde's), La. Mil. (Orig. under Enoul, Balthazar)
Erou, --	Private	3 Reg't. (de la Ronde's), La. Mil. (Orig. under Enoul, --)
Errieux, --	Fusilier-Private	2 Batt'n. (D'Aquin's), La. Militia
Ertouflet, Joseph	Private	Capt. Hubbard's Co., Mounted Co., La. Militia
Erver, Michelle	Private	2 Batt'n. (D'Aquin's), La. Militia
Erwin, Joseph	Private	8 Reg't. (Meriam's), La. Militia
Escague, Bernard	Private	6 Reg't. (Landry's), La. Militia
Escala, Gabriel	Private	3 Reg't. (de la Ronde's), La. Mil.
Escalern, Decloset	Private	17, 18 and 19 Cons. Reg't., La. Militia
Esclavon, Andore	Private	1 Batt'n. (Fortier's), La. Militia
Escola, Gabriel	Private	3 Reg't. (de la Ronde's), La. Mil. (Orig. under Escale, Gabriel)
Escopia, C.	Private	17, 18 and 19 Cons. Reg't., La. Militia
Escopia, Casimir	Private	17, 18 and 19 Cons. Reg't., La. Militia (Orig. under Escopia, C.)
Escot, Antoine	Corporal	1 Batt'n. (Fortier's), La. Militia
Escot, Louis	Private	1 Batt'n. (Fortier's), La. Militia
Esnard, A.	Sergeant	8 Reg't. (Meriam's), La. Militia
Esnault, Jean	Fusilier-Private	5 Reg't. (La Branche's), La. Mil.
Espenosa, Joseph	Private	2 Batt'n. (Peire's), La. Vols. (Orig. under Espinosa, Joseph)
Espinos, M.	Private	17, 18 and 19 Cons. Reg't., La. Mil. (Orig. under Espenosa, Ml)
Espinosa, Joseph	Private	2 Batt'n. (Peire's), La. Vols.
Espinose, Jose Manuel	Private	17, 18 and 19 Cons. Reg't., La. Militia
Espinoza, Joseph	Private	2 Batt'n. (Peire's), La. Vols. (Orig. under Espinosa, Joseph)
Esponosa, Ml	Private	17, 18 and 19 Cons. Reg't., La. Militia
Essex, John R.	Sgt.-Private	Capt. Allen's Co., Artillerists, La. Vols.
Estell, James	Private	10 and 20 Cons. Reg't., La. Mil.
Estep, Joseph	Private	12 and 13 Cons. Reg't., La. Mil.
Estere, Fernandez	Private	3 Reg't. (de la Ronde's), La. Mil.
Esteve, Jean	Private	3 Reg't. (de la Ronde's), La. Mil.
Esteve, Pierre	Corporal	3 Reg't. (de la Ronde's), La. Mil.
Esty, E.	Private	6 Reg't. (Landry's), La. Militia
Etienne, Hiacinth	Private	1 Batt'n. (Fortier's), La. Militia
Eugene, Joseph	Private	De Clouet's Reg't., La. Militia (Orig. under Ugene, Joseph)
Eugene, --	Fusilier-Private	2 Batt'n. (D'Aquin's), La. Militia
Evanes, James	Private	Captain Ramsey's Co., Mounted Riflemen, La. Militia (Orig. under Eavanes, James)
Evanes, Zopher	Private	Captain Dodge's Co., Mounted Riflemen, La. Militia (Orig. under Evans, Zopher)
Evanes, Zopher	Private	Captain Henry's Co., Mounted Riflemen, La. Militia (Orig. under Evans, Zopher)
Evans, David	Private	Captain Young's Co., Mounted Riflemen, La. Militia
Evans, Henry	Private	De Clouet's Reg't., La. Militia
Evans, Jesse	Private	12 and 13 Cons. Reg't., La. Mil.
Evans, Jess J.	Q.M.-Sergeant	12 and 13 Cons. Reg't., La. Mil.
Evans, John	Private	De Clouet's Reg't., La. Militia
Evans, Joseph	Servant	De Clouet's Reg't., La. Militia
Evans, Joseph	Private	Captain Ramsey's Co., Mounted Riflemen, La. Militia
Evans, Stephen	Private	Captain Sprigg's Co., Boatmen, La. Vols.
Evans, Zopher	Private	Captain Dodge's Co., Mounted Riflemen, La. Militia
Evans, Zopher	Private	Captain Henry's Co., Mounted Riflemen, La. Militia
Evanson, Jessee	Private	Louisiana War of 1812
Evar, Francis	Private	17, 18 and 19 Cons. Reg't., La. Mil. (Orig. under Ebar, Francis)
Everalls, William	Sergeant	Capt. Van Bibber's Co., La. Mil. (Orig. under Overalls, William)
Everard, Charles	1 Sergeant	De Clouet's Reg't., La. Militia
Everett, Charles	Private	Captain Griffith's Co., Mounted Riflemen, La. Vols.
Everson, George	Corporal	17, 18 and 19 Cons. Reg't., La. Militia
Evines, David	Private	Capt. Young's Co., Mounted Riflemen, La. Mil. (Orig. under Evans, David)
Evins, Joseph	Private	Captain Ramsey's Co., Mounted Riflemen, La. Mil. (Orig. under Evans, Joseph)
Ewing, William	Private	Capt. Collard's Co., La. Militia
Fabean, John	Private	16 Reg't. (Thompson's), La. Mil.
Fabien, John	Private	16 Reg't. (Thompson's), La. Mil. (Orig. under Fabean, John)
Fabre, Faustin	Private	8 Reg't. (Meriam's), La. Militia (Orig. under Favre, Faustin)
Fabre, Jean Batiste	Private	Capt. Songy's Co., Marines, La. Vols.
Fache, Joseph	Private	2 Reg't. (Cavelier's), La. Militia
Faget, I. B. (J?)	Musician	Plauche's Batt'n., La. Militia
Fagot, --	Private	Plauche's Batt'n., La. Militia
Fagot, Charles	Sergeant	3 Reg't. (de la Ronde's), La. Mil.
Fair, Charles	Corporal	Captain Price's Co., La. Militia (Orig. under Fair, Chesley)
Fair, Chesley	Corporal	Captain Price's Co., La. Militia
Fairair, Phillip	Private	De Clouet's Reg't., La. Militia
Fairchilds, Abraham	Private	10 and 20 Cons. Reg't., La. Mil.
Falcon, E.	Private	6 Reg't. (Landry's), La. Militia
Falcon, Jean	Private	3 Reg't. (de la Ronde's), La. Mil.
Falcon, Jesus	Private	17, 18 and 19 Cons. Reg't., La. Militia
Falcon, Joseph	Private	2 Batt'n. (Peire's), La. Vols.
Falcon, Louis fils	Private	6 Reg't. (Landry's), La. Militia
Falcon, M.	Private	6 Reg't. (Landry's), La. Militia
Falcon, Michel	Private	7 Reg't. (Le Beuf's), La. Militia
Falcon, P.	Private	6 Reg't. (Landry's), La. Militia
Falcona, J.	Private	De Clouet's Reg't., La. Militia (Orig. under Falcone, Jose)
Falcone, Jose	Private	De Clouet's Reg't., La. Militia
Falconne, Jose	Private	De Clouet's Reg't., La. Militia (Orig. under Falcone, Jose)
Falconny, --	Private	2 Reg't. (Cavelier's), La. Militia (Orig. under Falcony, --)
Falcony, --	Private	2 Reg't. (Cavelier's), La. Militia
Falgau, Leonce	Private	De Clouet's Reg't., La. Militia (Orig. under Falgon, Leonce)
Falgaus, A.	Private	6 Reg't. (Landry's), La. Militia
Falgaus, A.	Private	6 Reg't. (Landry's), La. Militia

Name	Rank	Unit
Falgaus, Michell	Corporal	6 Reg't. (Landry's), La. Militia (Orig. under Falgous, Michelle)
Falgou, Leonce	Private	De Clouet's Reg't., La. Militia
Falgou, Marcellin	Private	De Clouet's Reg't., La. Militia
Falgous, Michelle	Corporal	6 Reg't. (Landry's), La. Militia
Fandino, --	Private-Sgt.	Hog's Detachment, La. Vols.
Fangu, Edmond	Private	De Clouet's Reg't., La. Militia (Orig. under Fangui, Edmond)
Fangue, Edmond	Private	De Clouet's Reg't., La. Militia (Orig. under Fangui, Edmond)
Fangui, Edmond	Private	De Clouet's Reg't., La. Militia
Farges, M.	Private	Plauche's Batt'n., La. Militia
Faris, James	Private	17, 18 and 19 Cons. Reg't., La. Militia
Faris, Thomas	Private	Captain Sprigg's Co., Boatmen, La. Vols. (Orig. under Farris, Thomas)
Farland, Louis	Private	De Clouet's Reg't., La. Militia (Orig. under Ferland, Louis)
Farman, Isaac	Private-Sergeant	De Clouet's Reg't., La. Militia (Orig. under Turman, Isaac)
Fame', --	Fusilier-Private	2 Batt'n. (D'Aquin's), La. Militia
Farmer, Millis	Sergeant	19 Regiment, La. Militia
Farnell, Anton	Private	Capt. Wallace's Co., Boatmen, La. Vols.
Farone, Antoine	Private	Capt. Songy's Co., Marines, La. Vols.
Farpy, Colar	Private	De Clouet's Reg't., La. Militia
Farral, Michael	Private	Captain Dodge's Co., Mounted Riflemen, La. Militia
Farrall, Michael	Private	Captain Henry's Co., Mounted Riflemen, La. Militia
Farrar, Bernard G.	Surgeon	Field and Staff Officers, La. Mil.
Farris, Thomas	Private	Captain Sprigg's Co., Boatmen, La. Vols.
Fasnell, Anthony	Private	Capt. Wallace's Co., Boatmen, La. Vols. (Orig. under Farnell, Anton)
Fatcon, Jesus	Private	17, 18 and 19 Cons. Reg't., La. Mil. (Orig. under Falcon, Jesus)
Fauche, Jean	Private	2 Reg't. (Cavelier's), La. Militia
Fauche', Prre	Private	Capt. Songy's Co., Marines, La. Vols.
Faucheu, Celestin	Fusilier-Private	5 Reg't. (La Branche's), La. Mil. (Orig. under Foucheux, Celestin)
Faucheux, Celestin	Fusilier-Private	5 Reg't. (La Branche's), La. Mil. (Orig. under Foucheux, Celestin)
Faucheux, Farncois	Fusilier-Pvt.	5 Reg't. (La Branche's), La. Mil. (Orig. under Foucheux, Francois)
Fauchet, --	Musician	Plauche's Batt'n., La. Militia
Fauchet, Jr.	Musician	Plauche's Batt'n., La. Militia
Fauchez, Cadet	Fusilier-Private	2 Batt'n. (D'Aquin's), La. Militia
Faucinet, C. M.	Private	De Clouet's Reg't., La. Militia (Orig. under Fauconnet, C. M.)
Fauconet, C. M.	Private	De Clouet's Reg't., La. Militia (Orig. under Fauconnet, C. M.)
Fauconet, Gaspard Ml	Private	2 Batt'n. (Peire's), La. Vols.
Fauconnet, C. M.	Private	De Clouet's Reg't., La. Militia
Fauconnet, Gaspard Ml	Private	2 Batt'n. (Peire's), La. Vols. (Orig. under Fauconet, Gaspard Ml)
Faufin, Joachim	Private	De Clouet's Reg't., La. Militia
Faul, John T.	Private	De Clouet's Reg't., La. Militia (Orig. under Faulk, John T.)
Faulk, George	Private	Baker's Reg't., La. Militia
Faulk, John T.	Private	De Clouet's Reg't., La. Militia
Faulse, Louis	2 Lieut.	5 Reg't. (La Branche's), La. Mil.
Faulse, Zepren	Private	5 Reg't. (La Branche's), La. Militia
Fauillane, E.	Sergeant	De Clouet's Reg't., La. Militia (Orig. under Fouiane, Etienne)
Faure, --	Private	Plauche's Batt'n., La. Militia
Faure, John	Private	De Clouet's Reg't., La. Militia (Orig. under Foure, John)
Faurian, Jean	Private	2 Batt'n. (Peire's), La. Vols.
Faurin, Jean	Private	2 Batt'n. (Peire's), La. Vols. (Orig. under Faurian, Jean)
Faurion, John	Private	2 Batt'n. (Peire's), La. Vols. (Orig. under Faurian, Jean)
Fausse, --	Corporal	2 Reg't. (Cavelier's), La. Militia
Faussier, George	Private	6 Reg't. (Landry's), La. Militia (Orig. under Fossier, George)
Fautin, Brunet	Private	17, 18 and 19 Cons. Reg't., La. Mil. (Orig. under Tautin, Brunet)
Fauver, Nathaniel	Private	10 and 20 Cons. Reg't., La. Mil.
Fauvre, Nathaniel	Private	10 and 20 Cons. Reg't., La. Mil. (Orig. under Fauver, Nathaniel)
Faveron, August	Private	16 Reg't. (Thompson's), La. Mil.
Favre, Andre	Private	2 Reg't. (Cavelier's), La. Militia
Favre, Barthelemy	Captain	2 Reg't. (Cavelier's), La. Militia
Favre, Faustin	Private	8 Reg't. (Meriam's), La. Militia
Favre, George F.	1 Lieutenant	2 Reg't. (Cavelier's), La. Militia
Favre, Joseph	Private	De Clouet's Reg't., La. Militia
Favre, Lindor	Private	1 Batt'n. (Fortier's), La. Militia (Orig. under Favres, Lindor)
Favre, Nathaniel	Private	10 and 20 Cons. Reg't., La. Mil. (Orig. under Fauver, Nathaniel)
Favres, Lindore	Private	1 Batt'n. (Fortier's), La. Militia
Favrot, Bouvier	Private	8 Reg't. (Meriam's), La. Militia
Favrote, Edoire	Private	5 Reg't. (La Branche's), La. Mil.
Fazende, --	Private	4 Reg't. (Morgan's), La. Militia
Fazende, Moriere	Corporal	De Clouet's Reg't., La. Militia
Fazende, Moriere	Captain & Aid	1 Division (Villere's), La. Mil.
Fedric, Charles	Private	Baker's Regiment, La. Militia
Fedrick, Charles	Private	Baker's Regiment, La. Militia (Orig. under Fedric, Charles)
Fee, Charles	Private	Plauche's Batt'n., La. Militia
Fee, James	Private	17, 18 and 19 Cons. Reg't., La. Militia
Feireira, Louis	Private	Sergeant Hog's Detachment, La. Vols.
Felix, --	1 Lieutenant	2 Batt'n. (D'Aquin's), La. Militia
Felix, Baptiste	Private	16 Reg't. (Thompson's), La. Mil.
Felps, James	Private	10 and 20 Cons. Reg't., La. Mil.
Felps, Joseph	Corporal	10 and 20 Cons. Reg't., La. Mil.
Felps, Thomas	Private	10 and 20 Cons. Reg't., La. Mil.
Fenian, Joseph	Private	De Clouet's Reg't., La. Militia
Fente, Christian	Private	Captain Dodge's Co., Mounted Riflemen, La. Mil. (Orig. under Fenter, Christian)
Fenter, Christian	Private	Captain Dodge's Co., Mounted Riflemen, La. Militia
Fenter, Christian	Private	Captain Henry's Co., Mounted Riflemen, La. Militia
Fenter, David	Private	Captain Dodge's Co., Mounted Riflemen, La. Militia
Fenter, David	Private	Captain Henry's Co., Mounted Riflemen, La. Militia
Fenter, John	Private	Captain Dodge's Co., Mounted Riflemen, La. Militia
Fenter, John	Private	Captain Henry's Co., Mounted Riflemen, La. Militia
Fenetre, Louis	Private	De Clouet's Reg't., La. Militia
Fenwick, Ezekiel	Private	Captain Dodge's Co., Mounted Riflemen, La. Militia
Fenwick, Ezekiel	Private	Captain Henry's Co., Mounted Riflemen, La. Militia
Ferchaud, B.	Private	8 Reg't. (Meriam's), La. Militia
Fereehaud, B.	Private	8 Reg't. (Meriam's), La. Militia (Orig. under Ferchaud, B.)
Feren, Celestin	1 Lieutenant	5 Reg't. (La Branche's), La. Mil.
Fergersom, Robert	Private	Captain Henry's Co., Mounted Riflemen, La. Mil. (Orig. under Ferguson, Robert)
Fergerson, Robert	Private	Captain Dodge's Co., Mounted Riflemen, La. Militia
Fergerson, Robert	Private	Captain Henry's Co., Mounted Riflemen, La. Mil. (Orig. under Ferguson, Robert)
Fergurson, James	Private	12 and 13 Cons. Reg't., La. Mil.
Ferguson, James	Q.M.-Sergeant	Detachment Field and Staff Officers, 4 Brigade, La. Militia
Ferguson, Joseph	Private-Corporal	10 and 20 Cons. Reg't., La. Mil.
Ferguson, Robert	Private	Captain Dodge's Co., Mounted Riflemen, La. Mil. (Orig. under Fergerson, Robert)
Ferguson, Robert	Private	Captain Henry's Co., Mounted Riflemen, La. Militia
Ferguson, Robert	Private	2 Batt'n. (Peire's), La. Vols.
Fergusson, Robert	Private	2 Batt'n. (Peire's), La. Vols. (Orig. under Ferguson, Robert)
Ferianne, Valentin	Private	7 Reg't. (Le Beuf's), La. Militia
Ferion, Valentin	Private	7 Reg't. (Le Beuf's), La. Militia (Orig. under Ferianne, Valentin)
Ferland, L.	Private	8 Reg't. (Meriam's), La. Militia
Ferland, Louis	Private	De Clouet's Reg't., La. Militia

Name	Rank	Unit
Fermier, Etienne	2 Lieutenant	7 Reg't. (Le Beuf's), La. Militia
Fermier, Narcisse	Private	7 Reg't. (Le Beuf's), La. Militia
Fernand, Antonio	Private	2 Reg't. (Cavelier's), La. Militia (Orig. under Fernandez, Antonio)
Fernandes, Jacques	Private	2 Reg't. (Cavelier's), La. Militia
Fernandez, Joseph	Private	De Clouet's Reg't., La. Militia (Orig. under Fernandez, Joseph)
Fernandez, --	Private	1 Reg't. (Dejan's), La. Militia
Fernandez, A.	Musician	Plauche's Batt'n., La. Militia
Fernandez, Antonio	Private	2 Reg't. (Cavelier's), La. Militia
Fernandez, Bieint	Private	7 Reg't. (Le Beuf's), La. Militia (May be Breint)
Fernandez, Joseph	Private	De Clouet's Reg't., La. Militia
Fernsworth, William	Private	Capt. Van Bibber's Co., La. Mil.
Ferran, Antoine	Private	2 Batt'n. (Peire's), La. Vols.
Ferran, Dominique	Private	2 Batt'n. (Peire's), La. Vols.
Ferrand, --	Private	Plauche's Batt'n., La. Militia
Ferrand, --	Private	1 Reg't. (Dejan's), La. Militia
Ferrand, --	Private	4 Reg't. (Morgan's), La. Militia
Ferrand, Dominique	Private	2 Batt'n. (Peire's), La. Vols. (Orig. under Ferran, Dominique)
Ferrand, Louis, fils	Sgt.-Major	2 Batt'n. (D'Aquin's), La. Militia
Ferrand, Pierre	Private	Plauche's Batt'n., La. Militia
Ferrant, Celestin	1 Lieutenant	5 Reg't. (La Branche's), La. Mil. (Orig. under Feren, Celestin)
Ferrara, Louis	Private	Sergeant Hog's Detachment, La. Vols. (Orig. under Feireira, Louis)
Ferrer, I.	Ensign	2 Batt'n. (Peire's), La. Vols.
Ferrer, --	Private	Plauche's Batt'n., La. Militia
Ferrere, --	Private	Plauche's Batt'n., La. Militia
Ferrere, --	Private	Plauche's Batt'n., La. Militia (Orig. under Ferrer, --)
Ferrere, I.	Ensign	2 Batt'n. (Peire's), La. Vols. (Orig. under Ferrer, I.)
Ferret, Louis	Private	Capt. Colsson's Co., Artillery, La. Vols.
Ferrey, Robert	Private	De Clouet's Reg't., La. Militia (Orig. under Terry, Robert)
Ferrier, --	Private	Plauche's Batt'n., La. Militia
Ferry, -- Son	Private	2 Reg't. (Cavelier's), La. Militia
Ferry, John	Private	De Clouet's Reg't., La. Militia
Fessiden, Charles	Private	6 Reg't. (Landry's), La. Militia
Fetter, J. B.	Private	4 Reg't. (Morgan's), La. Militia
Fhraham, Joseph	Private	10 and 20 Cons. Reg't., La. Mil. (Orig. under Thraham, Joseph)
Fhraham, Joseph	Private	10 and 20 Cons. Reg't., La. Mil. (Orig. under Thraham, Joseph)
Fiche, Chars	Private	5 Reg't. (La Branche's), La. Mil. (Orig. under Friche, Cs)
Fiche, Daniel	Private	8 Reg't. (Meriam's), La. Militia
Fiche, Joseph	Private	De Clouet's Reg't., La. Militia
Fiche, Joshua	Sergeant	8 Reg't. (Meriam's), La. Militia
Ficher, Amos	Private	19 Reg't., La. Vols. (Orig. under Fisher, Amos)
Ficher, Joseph	Private	2 Batt'n. (Peire's), La. Vols.
Fick, Joseph	Private	De Clouet's Reg't., La. Militia (Orig. under Fiche, Joseph)
Ficker, John	Private	2 Batt'n. (Peire's), La. Vols.
Fielding, John	Private	De Clouet's Reg't., La. Militia
Fielding, Joseph	Private	De Clouet's Reg't., La. Militia (Orig. under Fielding, John)
Figaro, --	Servant	1 Batt'n. (Fortier's), La. Militia
Figaro, --	Sergant	3 Reg't. (de la Ronde's), La. Mil.
Figurant, Jean Bte	Private	16 Reg't. (Thompson's), La. Mil.
Fils, Forret	Private	8 Reg't. (Meriam's), La. Militia
Filson, Joseph	Private	Captain Sprigg's Co., Boatmen, La. Vols.
Filton, Archibald	Private	Captain Sprigg's Co., Boatmen, La. Vols. (Orig. under Tilton, Archibald)
Finch, Francis	Private	12 and 13 Cons. Reg't., La. Mil.
Fine, David	Private	Captain McNair's Co., Mounted Riflemen, La. Militia
Fine, Philip	Private	Captain McNair's Co., Mounted Riflemen, La. Militia
Finimont, William	Private	1 Reg't. (Dejan's), La. Militia
Finimount, William	Private	1 Reg't. (Dejan's), La. Militia (Orig. under Finimont, William)
Finis, Mc	Private	8 Reg't. (Meriam's), La. Militia
Finley, Alexander	Private	Louisiana War of 1812. See also 1 Batt'n. (Henry's), U. S. Vols. Ref. Card
Fiot, --	Private	Plauche's Batt'n., La. Militia
Firaille, --	Private	2 Reg't. (Cavelier's), La. Militia
Firmier, Narcisse	Private	7 Reg't. (Le Beuf's), La. Militia (Orig. under Fermier, Narcisse)
Fischer, John	Private	De Clouet's Reg't., La. Militia (Orig. under Fisher, John)
Fischer, John	Private	2 Batt'n. (Peire's), La. Vols. (Orig. under Fisher, John)
Fish, A.	1 Sergeant-Sergeant	1 Reg't. (Dejan's), La. Militia (Orig. under Fisk, A.)
Fish, Joshua	Private	8 Reg't. (Meriam's), La. Militia
Fisher, Amos	Private	19 Regiment, La. Militia
Fisher, John	Corporal	De Clouet's Reg't., La. Militia
Fisher, John	Private	De Clouet's Reg't., La. Militia
Fisher, John	Private	2 Batt'n. (Peire's), La. Vols.
Fisher, Joseph	Private	De Clouet's Reg't., La. Militia (Orig. under Fisher, Joshua)
Fisher, Joshua	Private	De Clouet's Reg't., La. Militia
Fisher, Samuel	Sergeant	16 Reg't. (Thompson's), La. Mil.
Fisher, Spencer	Private	10 and 20 Cons. Reg't., La. Mil.
Fisk, A.	1 Sergeant-Sergeant	1 Reg't. (Dejan's), La. Militia
Fisker, Stephen	Private	10 and 20 Cons. Reg't., La. Mil. (Orig. under Fisher, Spencer)
Fitz, Gideon	Private	16 Reg't. (Thompson's), La. Mil.
Fitz, Jean	Private	3 Reg't. (de la Ronde's), La. Mil.
Fitz, Renaud	Private	3 Reg't. (de la Ronde's), La. Mil.
Flamant, Ceprien	Private	16 Reg't. (Thompson's), La. Mil.
Flaming, E.	Sergeant	4 Reg't. (Morgan's), La. Militia (Orig. under Fleming, E.)
Flanagen, John	Private	De Clouet's Reg't., La. Militia
Flanagin, John	Private	De Clouet's Reg't., La. Militia (Orig. under Flanagen, John)
Flanigon, John	Private	De Clouet's Reg't., La. Militia (Orig. under Flanagen, John)
Flanjae, Garrigues	Brig. General	4 Brigade (Flanjae's), La. Mil.
Flanment, Glaude	Private	Baker's Regiment, La. Militia
Flannagen, John	Private	De Clouet's Reg't., La. Militia (Orig. under Flanagen, John)
Flannegan, John	Private	De Clouet's Reg't., La. Militia (Orig. under Flanagan, John)
Flatcher, Jahua	Private	De Clouet's Reg't., La. Militia (Orig. under Fletcher, Jehu)
Flatcher, John	Private	De Clouet's Reg't., La. Militia (Orig. under Fletcher, John)
Fleitas, Paulen	Private	3 Reg't. (de la Ronde's), La. Mil. (Orig. under Fleytas, Paulin)
Fleret, Antoine	Private	2 Batt'n. (Peire's), La. Vols. (Orig. under Flenret, Antoine)
Flemeen, John	Private	5 Reg't. (La Branche's), La. Mil. (Orig. under Flenret, Antoine)
Flemen, John	Private	5 Reg't. (La Branche's), La. Mil.
Fleming, E.	Sergeant	4 Reg't. (Morgan's), La. Militia
Fleming, William	Private	Capt. Allen's Co., Artillerists, La. Vols. (Orig. under Flemmong, William)
Flemmant, Glaud	Private	Baker's Reg't., La. Mil. (Orig. under Flanment, Glaude)
Flemming, William	Private	Capt. Allen's Co., Artillerists, La. Vols.
Fletcher, Henry	Corporal	1 Batt'n. (Fortier's), La. Militia
Fletcher, James H.	Private	Captain Beale's Co., Riflemen, La. Militia
Fletcher, Jehu	Private	De Clouet's Reg't., La. Militia
Fletcher, John	Private	De Clouet's Reg't., La. Militia
Fletcher, Joseph	Private	10 and 20 Cons. Reg't., La. Mil.
Fletcher, Samuel	Private	12 and 13 Cons. Reg't., La. Mil.
Fletcher, Thomas	Private	12 and 13 Cons. Reg't., La. Mil.
Fleure, Antoine	Private	2 Batt'n. (Peire's), La. Vols. (Orig. under Fleuret, Antoine)
Fleuret, Antoine	Private	2 Batt'n. (Peire's), La. Vols.
Fleurie, Michelle	Private	Capt. Chaudurier's Co., Artificers, Art'y., La. Vols.
Fleury, --	Private	Plauche's Batt'n., La. Militia
Fleury, --	Sergeant	2 Reg't. (Cavelier's), La. Militia
Fleury, Michelle	Private	Capt. Chaudurier's Co., Artificers, Art'y., La. Vols. (Orig. under Fleurie, Michelle)
Fleytas, Celestin	Private	2 Reg't. (Cavelier's), La. Militia
Fleytas, Paulin	Private	3 Reg't. (de la Ronde's), La. Mil.
Flinn, William	Private	Captain Henry's Co., Mounted Riflemen, La. Militia

Name	Rank	Unit
Flinn, William	Private	Captain Dodge's Co., Mounted Riflemen, La. Militia
Floras, Anthony	Private	De Clouet's Reg't, La. Militia (See also 44 Regiment)
Flore, Antoine	Private	De Clouet's Reg't, La. Militia
Flores, Antoine	Private	De Clouet's Reg't, La. Militia (Orig. under Flore, Antoine)
Flores, Leonardo	Private	17, 18 and 19 Cons. Reg't., La. Militia
Flower, William	Private	Captain Beale's Co., Riflemen, La. Militia
Floyd, James	Private	De Clouet's Reg't, La. Militia (See also U. S. Army)
Fluallen, Thomas	Private	12 and 13 Cons. Reg't., La. Mil.
Fluker, David	Major	10 and 20 Cons. Reg't., La. Mil.
Fluker, Robert	Private	12 and 13 Cons. Reg't., La. Mil.
Fluret, Antoine	Private	2 Batt'n. (Peire's), La. Vols. (Orig. under Fleuret, Antoine)
Fluret, Antonio	Private	2 Batt'n. (Peire's), La. Vols. (Orig. under Fleuret, Antoine)
Flynn, John C.	Private	10 and 20 Cons. Reg't., La. Mil.
Foelkill, L. V.	1 Lieut. & Paymaster	DeClouet's Reg't., La. Mil.
Fogleman, George	Private	16 Reg't. (Thompson's), La. Mil.
Fogleman, John	Private	16 Reg't. (Thompson's), La. Mil.
Foix, R. Prosper	1 Lt. Adj. & Major	Plauche's Batt'n., La. Militia
Folk, John	Private	De Clouet's Reg't., La. Militia
Folk, Joseph	Private	De Clouet's Reg't., La. Militia
Follin, Joseph	Drummer-Private	2 Batt'n. (Peire's), La. Vols.
Follis, Thomas	Private	Captain Price's Co., La. Militia
Fols, John Bte	Private	5 Reg't. (La Branche's), La. Mil.
Fols, John Pre	Private	5 Reg't. (La Branche's), La. Mil.
Folse, Alexander	Private	5 Reg't. (La Branche's), La. Mil.
Folse, Alexis	Fusilier-Private	5 Reg't. (La Branche's), La. Mil.
Folse, Benjamin	Fusilier-Private	5 Reg't. (La Branche's), La. Mil.
Folse, Jean Pre	Fusilier-Private	5 Reg't. (La Branche's), La. Mil.
Folse, Louis	2 Lieutenant	5 Reg't. (La Branche's), La. Mil. (Orig. under Faulse, Louis)
Fondal, Jh	Private	1 Batt'n. (Fortier's), La. Militia
Fonde, Violle	Private	Plauche's Batt'n., La. Militia
Fonds, Manuel	Private	2 Reg't. (Cavelier's), La. Militia
Fontain, Jques	Private	1 Reg't. (Dejan's), La. Militia
Fontenau, John	Private	De Clouet's Reg't., La. Militia (Orig. under Fontino, John)
Fontenau, Stanislaus	Private	De Clouet's Reg't., La. Militia
Fonteneau, Alexander	Private	16 Reg't. (Thompson's), La. Mil.
Foteneau, Alexis	Fusilier-Private	5 Reg't. (La Branche's), La. Mil.
Fonteneau, Cezair	Private	17, 18 and 19 Cons. Reg't., La. Mil. (Orig. under Fontineau, Cesar)
Fonteneau, Henry	2 Lieutenant	5 Reg't. (La Branche's), La. Mil.
Fonteneau, John B.	Corporal	17, 18 and 19 Cons. Reg't., La. Mil. (orig. under Fonteneau, John D.)
Fonteneau, John D.	Corporal	17, 18 and 19 Cons. Reg't., La. Militia
Fonteneau, Leandre	Private	16 Reg't. (Thompson's), La. Mil. (Orig. under Fontemot, Leander)
Fontenelle, Barthilemy	Private	3 Reg't. (de la Ronde's), La. Mil.
Fontenett, Andre	Corporal	Baker's Regiment, La. Militia
Fontenette, Andre	Corporal	Baker's Regiment, La. Militia (Orig. under Fontenett, Andre)
Fontenette, Charles	Private	Baker's Regiment, La. Militia
Fontenette, Pierre	Private	Baker's Regiment, La. Militia
Fontinette, Pierre	Private	Baker's Regiment, La. Militia (Orig. under Fontenette, Pierre)
Fontenette, Zeno	Private	Baker's Regiment, La. Militia
Fonteno, J. Bte	Private	6 Reg't. (Landry's), La. Militia
Fontenot, Alexis	Fusilier-Private	5 Reg't. (La Branche's), La. Mil. (Orig. under Fonteneau, Alexis)
Fontenot, Alexis	Private	16 Reg't. (Thompson's), La. Mil.
Fontenot, Alexander	Private	16 Reg't. (Thompson's), La. Mil. (Orig. under Fonteneau, Alexander)
Fontenot, Antoine	Private	16 Reg't. (Thompson's), La. Mil.
Fontenot, August	Private	16 Reg't. (Thompson's), La. Mil.
Fontenot, Baptiste S.	Private	16 Reg't. (Thompson's), La. Mil.
Fontenot, Ceasar	Private	16 Reg't. (Thompson's), La. Mil.
Fontenot, Celestin	Private	16 Reg't. (Thompson's), La. Mil.
Fontenot, Charles	Private	16 Reg't. (Thompson's), La. Mil.
Fontenot, Cyprien P.	Private	16 Reg't. (Thompson's), La. Mil.
Fontenot, Dondiego L.	Private	16 Reg't. (Thompson's), La. Mil.
Fontenot, Etienne	Private	16 Reg't. (Thompson's), La. Mil.
Fontenot, Fostin	Private	16 Reg't. (Thompson's), La. Mil.
Fontenot, Francois	Private	16 Reg't. (Thompson's), La. Mil.
Fontenot, Henry	Private	16 Reg't. (Thompson's), La. Mil.
Fontenot, Jean Sse	Private	16 Reg't. (Thompson's), La. Mil.
Fontenot, Jean Pierre	1 Sergeant	5 Reg't. (La Branche's), La. Mil.
Fontenot, Joachim	Fusilier-Private	5 Reg't. (La Branche's), La. Mil.
Fontenot, Joseph	Private	16 Reg't. (Thompson's), La. Mil.
Fontenot, Julien	Private	16 Reg't. (Thompson's), La. Mil.
Fontenot, Laurent	Private	16 Reg't. (Thompson's), La. Mil.
Fontenot, Leandre	Private	16 Reg't. (Thompson's), La. Mil.
Fontenot, Lefroi	Private	16 Reg't. (Thompson's), La. Mil.
Fontenot, Louis	Private	16 Reg't. (Thompson's), La. Mil.
Fontenot, Louis fils	Corporal	16 Reg't. (Thompson's), La. Mil.
Fontenot, Louis I. (J?)	Private	16 Reg't. (Thompson's), La. Mil.
Fontenot, Paul	Private	16 Reg't. (Thompson's), La. Mil.
Fontenot, Pauline	Private	16 Reg't. (Thompson's), La. Mil.
Fontenot, Philip, J. L.	Private	16 Reg't. (Thompson's), La. Mil.
Fontenot, Philip Lse	Private	16 Reg't. (Thompson's), La. Mil.
Fontenot, Pierre B.	Private	16 Reg't. (Thompson's), La. Mil.
Fontenott, John	Private	De Clouet's Reg't., La. Militia (Orig. under Fontino, John)
Fontin, Jean	Private	2 Batt'n. (D'Aquin's), La. Militia (Orig. under Frontin, Jean)
Fontineau, Cesar	Private	17, 18 and 19 Cons. Reg't., La. Militia
Fontino, John	Private	De Clouet's Reg't., La. Militia
Foot, Henry	Private	Baker's Regiment, La. Militia
Forbes, James	Private	10 and 20 Cons. Reg't., La. Mil. (Orig. under Forbis, James)
Forbes, John	Corporal	11 Reg't. (Hickey's), La. Militia
Forbes, Leonard	Private	10 and 20 Cons. Reg't., La. Mil. (Orig. under Forbis, Leonard)
Forbis, James	Private	10 and 20 Cons. Reg't., La. Mil.
Forbis, Leonard	Private	10 and 20 Cons. Reg't., La. Mil.
Forbs, James	Private	10 and 20 Cons. Reg't., La. Mil. (Orig. under Forbis, James)
Forbs, Leonard	Private	10 and 20 Cons. Reg't., La. Mil. (Orig. under Forbis, Leonard)
Force, John	Private	De Clouet's Reg't., La. Militia (Orig. under Foure, John)
Forcelle, Olivier, Son	Ensign	5 Reg't. (La Branche's), La. Mil.
Ford, Elijah	Private	10 and 20 Cons. Reg't., La. Mil.
Ford, Francois	Private	1 Batt'n. (Fortier's), La. Militia
Ford, Isaac	Private	10 and 20 Cons. Reg't., La. Mil.
Ford, Jacob D.	Corporal-Sergeant	2 Batt'n. (Peire's), La. Vols.
Ford, Joseph	Private	7 Reg't. (Le Beuf's), La. Militia
Fore, Michel	Private	16 Reg't. (Thompson's), La. Mil.
Foree, John	Private	De Clouet's Reg't., La. Militia (Orig. under Foure, John)
Foreman, Elisha	Private	De Clouet's Reg't., La. Militia
Forest, Etienne	Private	16 Reg't. (Thompson's), La. Mil.
Forest, Michel	Private	16 Reg't. (Thompson's), La. Mil.
Forest, Pierre P.	Private	7 Reg't. (Le Beuf's), La. Militia
Forest, Stephen	Private	16 Reg't. (Thompson's), La. Mil.
Forestal, E.	Corporal	Plauche's Batt'n., La. Militia (Orig. under Forstall, E.)
Forestal, Louis	Private	De Clouet's Reg't., La. Militia
Forestalle, Louis	Private	1 Batt'n. (Fortier's), La. Militia
Foret, Charles fils	Private	Captain Hubbard's Mounted Co., La. Militia
Foret, Mc	Private	8 Reg't. (Meriam's), La. Militia
Forget, --	Private	De Clouet's Reg't., La. Militia
Forgison, William	Private	16 Reg't. (Thompson's), La. Mil. (Orig. under Furguson, William)
Forguson, William	Private	16 Reg't. (Thompson's), La. Mil. (Orig. under Furguson, William)
Forman, Elisha	Private	De Clouet's Reg't., La. Militia (Orig. under Foreman, Elisha)
Forman, William	Private	16 Reg't. (Thompson's), La. Mil.
Fornandez, A.	Musician	Plauche's Batt'n., La. Militia (Orig. under Fernandez, A.)
Forneret, Charles	Captain	De Clouet's Reg't., La. Militia
Fornet, Antoine P.	Sergeant	De Clouet's Reg't., La. Militia (Orig. under Fournet, Antoine P.)
Forront, Jean Bte	Private	8 Reg't. (Meriam's), La. Militia
Forsyth, John	Private	2 Batt'n. (Peire's), La. Vols.
Forstall, E.	Corporal	Plauche's Batt'n., La. Militia
Forstall, Felix	Captain & Aid	1 Division (Villere's), La. Mil.
Forstall, Louis	Private	1 Batt'n. (Fortier's), La. Militia (Orig. under Forestalle, Louis)
Forsyth, John	Private	2 Batt'n. (Peire's), La. Vols.
Fort, Andrew	Private	Capt. Collard's Co., La. Militia

Name	Rank	Unit
Fort, Deny	Private	17, 18 and 19 Cons. Reg't., La. Militia
Fort, John	Private	Captain Beale's Co., Riflemen, La. Militia
Fort, John A.	1 Lieutenant	Capt. Ogden's Co., Dragoons, La. Militia
Forteneau, Stanislaus	Private	De Clouet's Reg't., La. Militia (Orig. under Fontenau, Stanislaus)
Fortier, Jr.	Col. Aid De Camp	Gov. Claiborne and Staff, La. Mil. (Orig. under Fortier, Michael)
Fortier, A.	Major	5 Reg't. (La Branche's), La. Mil.
Fortier, Edmond	Captain	5 Reg't. (La Branche's), La. Mil.
Fortier, Eugene	Private	4 Reg't. (Morgan's), La. Militia
Fortier, Fostein	Private	4 Reg't. (Morgan's), La. Militia
Fortier, Honore	Private	1 Battn. (Fortier's), La. Militia
Fortier, Honore	Corporal	1 Battn. (Fortier's), La. Militia
Fortier, Honore'	Private	4 Reg't. (Morgan's), La. Militia
Fortier, In Bte	Private	5 Reg't. (La Branche's), La. Mil.
Fortier, Ludger	Private	4 Reg't. (Morgan's), La. Militia
Fortier, Michael	Col. Aid De Camp	Gov. Claiborne and Staff, La. Mil.
Fortier, Michael	Lt. Colonel	1 Batt'n. (Fortier's), La. Militia
Fortier, Michel	Private	Capt. Trudeau's Troop of Horse, La. Militia
Fortier, Norbert	Private	Capt. Trudeau's Troop of Horse, La. Militia
Fortier, Norbert	Private	1 Batt'n. (Fortier's), La. Militia
Fortier, Norbert	Major	4 Reg't. (Morgan's), La. Militia
Fortier, Omer	Sergeant	Capt. Trudeau's Troop of Horse, La. Militia
Fortin, Fortune'	Private	2 Batt'n. (D'Aquin's), La. Militia
Fortin, Jules	Sergeant	2 Reg't. (Cavelier's), La. Militia
Fortune, Michael	Private	Capt. Van Bibber's Co., La. Mil.
Fosef, Fernandes	Private	2 Batt'n. (Peire's), La. Vols. (Orig. under Joseph, Fernandez)
Fosett, Timothy	Private	17, 18 and 19 Cons. Reg't., La. Militia
Fosse, Peter	2 Lieut.	Capt. Songy's Co., Marines, La. Vols.
Fossier, Alphonse	Fusilier-Private	5 Reg't. (La Branche's), La. Mil.
Fossier, George	Private	6 Reg't. (Landry's), La. Militia
Fossier, I.	Private	4 Reg't. (Morgan's), La. Militia
Foster, Isaac	Private	Captain Griffith's Co., Mounted Riflemen, La. Vols.
Foster, Jacob	Corporal	Captain Ramsey's Co., Mounted Riflemen, La. Militia
Foster, Levi	Captain	Baker's Regiment, La. Militia
Foster, Norris	Private	10 and 20 Cons. Reg't., La. Mil.
Foster, R.	Private	Captain Sprigg's Co., Boatmen, La. Vols.
Foster, Thomas	Private	Captain Ramsey's Co., Mounted Riflemen, La. Militia
Foucade, Etienne	Private	Capt. Songy's Co., Marines, La. Vols. (Orig. under Fourcade, Etienne)
Foucaud, Pre	Private	Capt. Songy's Co., Marines, La. Vols. (Orig. under Fourcaud, Pierre)
Fouche, Zenon	Private	Capt. Trudeau's Troop of Horse, La. Militia
Foucheau, Pierre	Fusilier-Private	5 Reg't. (La Branche's), La. Mil.
Foucher, A. Jr.	Adj. & Lieutenant	4 Reg't. (Morgan's), La. Militia
Foucher, E.	Private	Plauche's Batt'n., La. Militia
Foucher, Guillaume	Private-Fifer	2 Batt'n. (Peire's), La. Vols.
Foucher, Jean	Private	1 Batt'n. (Fortier's), La. Militia
Foucher, Joseph	1 Lieutenant	1 Batt'n. (Fortier's), La. Militia
Foucher, Patrice	Private	1 Batt'n. (Fortier's), La. Militia
Foucher, Valcour	Private	1 Batt'n. (Fortier's), La. Militia
Foucheux, Clestin	Fusilier-Private	5 Reg't. (La Branche's), La. Mil.
Foucheux, Eugene	Fusilier-Private	5 Reg't. (La Branche's), La. Mil.
Foucheux, Francois	Fusilier-Corp.	5 Reg't. (La Branche's), La. Mil.
Foucheux, Louis	Fusilier-Private	5 Reg't. (La Branche's), La. Mil.
Fouiane, Etienne	Sergeant	De Clouet's Reg't., La. Militia
Fouillane, E.	Sergeant	De Clouet's Reg't., La. Militia (Orig. under Fouiane, Etienne)
Fouilliane, E.	Sergeant	De Clouet's Reg't., La. Militia (Orig. under Fouiane, Etienne)
Fouler, John	Private	De Clouet's Reg't., La. Militia (Orig. under Fowler, John)
Faunteneau, Stanislaus	Private	De Clouet's Reg't., La. Militia (Orig. under Fontenau, Stanislaus)
Fourcade, Etienne	Private	Capt. Songy's Co., Marines, La. Vols.
Fourcan, Pierre	Private	Captain Lagan's Co., La. Vols.
Fourcaud, Pierre	Private	Capt. Songy's Co., Marines, La. Vols.
Foure, John	Private	De Clouet's Reg't., La. Militia
Fournes, --	Private	2 Reg't. (Cavelier's), La. Militia
Fournesy, Ih	Private	Capt. Songy's Co., Marines, La. Vols.
Fournet, Antoine P.	Sergeant	De Clouet's Reg't., La. Militia
Fournier, N.	Private	Plauche's Batt'n., La. Militia
Fourteau, --	Private	2 Reg't. (Cavelier's), La. Militia
Fouser, Joseph	Private	12 and 13 Cons. Reg't., La. Mil.
Foutenau, Henry	2 Lieut.-1 Lieut.	5 Reg't. (La Branche's), La. Mil. (Orig. under Foutenau, Henry)
Foutenot, --	Private	4 Reg't. (Morgan's), La. Militia
Foutenot, Henry	2 Lieutenant	5 Reg't. (La Branche's), La. Mil. (Orig. under Foutenau, Henry)
Fouto, Simon	Servant	Captain Hubbard's Mounted Co. La. Militia
Fowler, Alexander	Private	4 Reg't. (Morgan's), La. Militia
Fowler, Daniel	Private	Captain Sprigg's Co., Boatmen, La. Vols.
Fowler, John	Private	De Clouet's Reg't., La. Militia
Fox, --	Servant	Gov. Claiborne and Staff, La. Mil.
Fox, Benjamin	Private	4 Reg't. (Morgan's), La. Militia
Fox, Isham	2 Lieutenant	16 Reg't. (Thompson's), La. Mil.
Fox, Isham P.	2 Lieutenant	16 Reg't. (Thompson's), La. Mil. (Orig. under Foc, Isham)
Fox, Robert	Private	4 Reg't. (Morgan's), La. Militia
Frahan, Francois	Private	7 Reg't. (Le Beuf's), La. Militia
Fraiyer, Anthony	Private	De Clouet's Reg't., La. Militia (Orig. under Traigre, Anthony)
Franc, Francisco	Private	De Clouet's Reg't., La. Militia
France, Andre	Private	5 Reg't. (La Branche's), La. Mil.
Franchard, John	Private	De Clouet's Reg't., La. Militia (Orig. under Tranchard, John)
Franche, Stephen	Fusilier-Private	5 Reg't. (La Branche's), La. Mil.
Francis, --	Servant	3 Reg't. (de la Ronde's), La. Mil.
Francis, Brodry	Private	Captain Henry's Co., Mounted Riflemen, La. Mil. (Orig. under Bodry, Francis)
Francis, Francisk	Private	2 Batt'n. (Peire's), La. Vols.
Francis, Francois	Private	2 Batt'n. (Peire's), La. Vols. (Orig. under Francas, Francois)
Francis, Roger	Private	Captain Hubbard's Mounted Co., La. Militia
Francisco, Antoine	Private	De Clouet's Reg't., La. Militia
Francisco, Antonio	Musician-Pvt.	2 Batt'n. (Peire's), La. Vols.
Francisque, Iean	Private	Capt. Songy's Co., Marines, La. Vols.
Franck, --	Drummer	Plauche's Batt'n., La. Militia
Franck, Henry	Private	2 Batt'n. (Peire's), La. Vols.
Francklin, Thomas	Private	1 Reg't. (Dejan's), La. Militia (Orig. under Franklin, Thomas)
Francks, Joseph	Private	10 and 20 Cons. Reg't., La. Mil. (Orig. under Frankes, Joseph)
Franco, Louis	Private	De Clouet's Reg't., La. Militia
Francois, --	Sergant	Gov. Claiborne and Staff, La. Mil.
Francois, --	Private	Plauche's Batt'n., La. Militia
Francois, --	Servant	Capt. Trudeau's Troop of Horse, La. Militia
Francois, Jn	Servant	1 Batt'n. (Fortier's), La. Militia
Francois, Noel	Private	1 Batt'n. (Fortier's), La. Militia
Francois, Ulsaire	Private	1 Batt'n. (Fortier's), La. Militia
Francolin, Louis R.	2 Lt.-Qr.Mr.	8 Reg't. (Meriam's), La. Mil.
Frank, --	Drummer	Plauche's Batt'n., La. Militia
Frank, --	Servant	16 Reg't. (Thompson's), La. Mil.
Frank, --	Servant	16 Reg't. (Thompson's), La. Mil.
Frank, Henry	Private	2 Batt'n. (Peire's), La. Vols. (Orig. under Franck, Henry)
Frankes, Joseph	Private	10 and 20 Cons. Reg't., La. Mil.
Franklin, John	Private	Capt. Alpuente's Co., La. Mil.
Franklin, Ralph	Private	12 and 13 Cons. Reg't., La. Mil.
Franklin, Thomas	Private	1 Reg't. (Dejan's), La. Militia
Franklin, William	Private	12 and 13 Cons. Reg't., La. Mil.
Franks, Joseph	Private	10 and 20 Cons. Reg't., La. Mil. (Orig. under Frankes, Joseph)
Franton, William	Private	17, 18 and 19 Cons. Reg't., La. Militia
Fraser, Angus O.	Private	4 Reg't. (Morgan's), La. Militia
Frayd, --	Private	1 Reg't. (Dejan's), La. Militia
Frayer, George	Private	Captain Musick's Co., La. Mil.
Frayet, --	Private	1 Reg't. (Dejan's), La. Militia (Orig. under Frayd, --)

Name	Rank	Unit
Frazer, James	Private	17, 18 and 19 Cons. Reg't., La. Militia
Frazer, John	Private	6 Reg't. (Landry's), La. Militia
Frazer, William	Private	17, 18 and 19 Cons. Reg't., La. Militia
Frazier, George	Private	Captain Musick's Co., La. Mil. (Orig. under Frayer, George)
Frazier, John	Private	6 Reg't. (Landry's), La. Militia (Orig. under Frazer, John)
Frechinette, Honore	Private	1 Batt'n. (Fortier's), La. Militia
Frederic, --	Private	4 Reg't. (Morgan's), La. Militia
Frederic, Alphonse	Private	5 Reg't. (La Branche's), La. Mil.
Frederic, Andre	Private	Captain Lagan's Co., La. Vols.
Frederic, Bastien	Private	Plauche's Batt'n., La. Militia (Orig. under Frederick, Bastien)
Frederic, Bazile	Private	Plauche's Batt'n., La. Militia (Orig. under Frederick, Bazile)
Frederic, Jean	Fusilier-Private	5 Reg't. (La Branche's), La. Mil.
Frederic, Laurent	Private	2 Reg't. (Cavelier's), La. Militia
Frederic, Noel	2 Lieutenant	3 Reg't. (de la Ronde's), La. Mil. (Orig. under Frederique, Noel)
Frederic, Paul	Private	8 Reg't. (Meriam's), La. Militia
Frederic, Veu	Private	Capt. LeDoux's Co., Cav., La. Vols.
Frederick, --	Private	Plauche's Batt'n., La. Militia
Frederick, --	Servant	Detachment Field and Staff Officers, 4 Brigade, La. Militia
Frederick, fils	Private	17, 18, and 19 Cons. Reg't., La. Militia
Frederick, A.	Private	6 Reg't. (Landry's), La. Militia
Frederick, Bastien	Private	Plauche's Batt'n., La. Militia
Frederick, Bazile	Private	Plauche's Batt'n., La. Militia
Frederick, Francois	Private	De Clouet's Reg't., La. Militia
Frederick, Francois	Private	6 Reg't. (Landry's), La. Militia
Frederick, J. B.	Private	6 Reg't. (Landry's), La. Militia (Orig. under Frederick, J. P.)
Frederick, Ieefe	Private	10 Regiment, La. Militia
Frederick, John	Private	17, 18 and 19 Cons. Reg't., La. Militia
Frederick, J. P.	Private	6 Reg't. (Landry's), La. Militia
Frederick, Joseph	Private	10 and 20 Cons. Reg't., La. Mil.
Frederick, Mathias	Private	6 Reg't. (Landry's), La. Militia
Frederick, Philippe	Private	17, 18 and 19 Cons. Reg't., La. Militia
Frederick, Sylvain	Private	De Clouet's Reg't., La. Militia
Frederick, Sylvain	Private	De Clouet's Reg't., La. Militia (Orig. under Frederick, Silvan)
Frederick, Ursin	Private	Plauche's Batt'n., La. Militia
Frederick, Francois	Private	6 Reg't. (Landry's), La. Militia (Orig. under Frederick, Francois)
Fredericke, Mathias	Private	6 Reg't. (Landry's), La. Militia (Orig. under Frederock, Mathias)
Fredrick, Joseph	Private	10 and 20 Cons. Reg't., La. Mil. (Orig. under Frederick, Joseph)
Fredrick, Urrin	Private	De Clouet's Reg't., La. Militia (Orig. under Fredrick, Urren)
Frederique, --	Private	2 Batt'n. (D'Aquin's), La. Militia
Frederique, Noel	2 Lieutenant	3 Reg't. (de la Ronde's), La. Mil.
Freeland, George	Private	Captain Griffith's Co., Mounted Riflemen, La. Vols.
Freeland, Isaac	Private	Captain Griffith's Co., Mounted Riflemen, La. Vols.
Freeland, James	Private	Captain Griffith's Co., Mounted Riflemen, La. Vols.
Freeland, John	Private	12 and 13 Cons. Reg't., La. Mil.
Freeland, John	Private	12 and 13 Cons. Reg't., La. Mil.
Freeman, Harris	Sergeant	10 and 20 Cons. Reg't., La. Mil.
Freeman, Nathan	Private	10 and 20 Cons. Reg't., La. Mil.
Frelot, Lewis	Private	Baker's Reg't., La. Militia (Orig. under Frilot, Louis)
Frem, Hiler	Private	Baker's Regiment, La. Militia
Frem, Helier	Private	Baker's Regiment, La. Militia (Orig. under Frem, Hiler)
Freman, Harris	Sergeant	10 and 20 Cons. Reg't., La. Mil. (Orig. under Freeman, Harris)
Freman, John Baptiste	Private	De Clouet's Reg't., La. Militia
Fremont, Eustache	1 Lieutenant	Plauche's Batt'n., La. Militia
French, Josiah	Private	17, 18 and 19 Cons. Reg't., La. Militia
French, Stephen	Fusilier-Private	5 Reg't. (La Branche's), La. Mil. (Orig. under Franche, Stephen)
Frere, Elouis	Private	2 Batt'n. (Peire's), La. Vols.
Frere, Eloy	Private	2 Batt'n. (Peire's), La. Vols.
Frerre, Elouis	Private	2 Batt'n. (Peire's), La. Vols. (Orig. under Frere, Elouis)
Frerre, Eloy	Private	2 Batt'n. (Peire's), La. Vols. (Orig. under Frere, Eloy)
Freyer, Robert	Private	Baker's Regiment, La. Militia
Freyr, Robert	Private	Baker's Regiment, La. Militia (Orig. under Freyer, Robert)
Friche, Andre	Private	5 Reg't. (La Branche's), La. Mil.
Friche, Balasard	Private	5 Reg't. (La Branche's), La. Mil.
Friche, Cs	Private	5 Reg't. (La Branche's), La. Mil.
Friche, Nicholas	Private	5 Reg't. (La Branche's), La. Mil.
Frick, Celestin	Private	2 Batt'n. (Peire's), La. Vols.
Frick, Jh	Private	1 Batt'n. (Fortier's), La. Militia
Fridge, A.	Private	11 Reg't. (Hickey's), La. Militia
Fridien, Cesar	Private	17, 18 and 19 Cons. Reg't., La. Militia
Friedrick, Urren	Private	De Clouet's Reg't., La. Militia (See also John I. Faldevos)
Friland, John	Private	12 and 13 Cons. Reg't., La. Mil. (Orig. under Freeland, John)
Frillou, Filbert	Private	Captain Hubbard's Mounted Co., La. Militia
Frillou, Francois	Private	Captain Hubbard's Mounted Co., La. Militia
Frilot, Louis	Private	Baker's Regiment, La. Militia
Friloux, Endjer	Fusilier-Private	5 Reg't. (La Branche's), La. Mil. (Orig. under Frilouc, Ludger)
Friloux, Louis	Fusilier-Private	5 Reg't. (La Branche's), La. Mil.
Friloux, Ludger	Fusilier-Private	5 Reg't. (La Branche's), La. Mil.
Friloux, Paul	Sergeant	5 Reg't. (La Branche's), La. Mil.
Friloux, Pierre	Fusilier-Private	5 Reg't. (La Branche's), La. Mil.
Frique, Celestin	Private-Corporal	2 Batt'n. (Peire's), La. Vols. (Orig. under Frick, Celestin)
Froisy, Jourd	Private	5 Reg't. (La Branche's), La. Mil.
Froisy, Jourdan	Fusilier-Private	5 Reg't. (La Branche's), La. Mil.
Froisy, Pierre	Fusilier-Private	5 Reg't. (La Branche's), La. Mil.
Fromentin, --	Private	1 Reg't. (Dejan's), La. Militia
Frond, Frcis	Private	2 Reg't. (Cavelier's), La. Militia
Frontin, Jean	Private	2 Batt'n. (D'Aquin's), La. Militia
Fruze, Joseph	Private	De Clouet's Reg't., La. Militia
Frozard, Vergl	Private	16 Reg't. (Thompson's), La. Mil.
Fryon, Joseph Eli	Private	De Clouet's Reg't., La. Militia
Fuget, Victor	Private	Captain Lagan's Co., La. Vols.
Fulcher, Benjamin	Private	6 Reg't. (Landry's), La. Militia
Fulcher, William	Private	12 and 13 Cons. Reg't., La. Mil.
Fuller, Robert	Private	12 and 13 Cons. Reg't., La. Mil.
Fuller, Simeon	Private	De Clouet's Reg't., La. Militia
Fullington, Alexander	Private	Capt. Allen's Co., Artillerists, La. Vols.
Fulton, Archibald	Private	Capt. Wallace's Co., Boatmen, La. Vols.
Fulton, S.	Private	8 Reg't. (Meriam's), La. Militia
Futton, S.	Private	8 Reg't. (Meriam's), La. Militia (Orig. under Fulton, S.)
Funel, --	Private	Plauche's Batt'n., La. Militia
Funston, I.	Private	4 Reg't. (Morgan's), La. Militia
Furgerson, James	Private	12 and 13 Cons. Reg't., La. Mil. (Orig. under Ferguson, James)
Furguson, James	Private	16 Reg't. (Thompson's), La. Mil.
Furguson, T.	Corporal	1 Reg't. (Dejan's), La. Militia
Furguson, William	Private	16 Reg't. (Thompson's), La. Mil.
Furgusson, James	Private	16 Reg't. (Thompson's), La. Mil.
Furgusson, Robert	Private	2 Batt'n. (Peire's), La. Vols. (Orig. under Ferguson, Robert)
Furmain, James	Private	Captain Price's Co., La. Militia
Furmain, Thomas	Private	Captain Price's Co., La. Militia
Fusell, William	Private	12 and 13 Cons. Reg't., La. Mil. (Orig. under Fuzzell, William)
Fusilice, Agricole	Major	Detachment Field and Staff Officers, 4 Brigade, La. Militia
Fusilier, Laclaire	2 Lieutenant	16 Reg't. (Thompson's), La. Mil.
Fussel, John	Private	De Clouet's Reg't., La. Militia
Fussell, Edwin	2 Lieutenant	12 and 13 Cons. Reg't., La. Mil. (Orig. under Fuzzell, Edwin)
Futell, William	Private	10 and 20 Cons. Reg't., La. Mil.
Fuzzell, Edwin	2 Lieutenant	12 and 13 Cons. Reg't., La. Mil.
Fuzzell, William	Private	12 and 13 Cons. Reg't., La. Mil.
Gabaille, --	Lieutenant	2 Batt'n. (D'Aquin's), La. Militia (Orig. under Gabaye, --)

Name	Rank	Unit
Gabaye, --	3 Lieutenant	2 Batt'n. (D'Aquin's), La. Militia
Gablerher, David	Sergeant	Captain Hughes' Co., Mounted Riflemen, La. Militia
Gabriel, Charles	Private	1 Batt'n. (Fortier's), La. Militia
Gabriel, Charles	Private	1 Batt'n. (Fortier's), La. Militia (Orig. under Gabrielle, Charles)
Gabrielle, Charles	Private	1 Batt'n. (Fortier's), La. Militia
Gache, Alexander	Private	16 Reg't. (Thompson's), La. Mil.
Gache, Jacques	Private	7 Reg't. (Le Beuf's), La. Militia
Gachet, Jacques	Private	Captain Hubbard's Mounted Co., La. Militia
Gachi, Jaques	Private	7 Reg't. (Le Beuf's), La. Militia (Orig. under Gache, Jaques)
Gacia, Manuel	Private	7 Reg't. (Le Beuf's), La. Militia
Gacie, Manuel	Private	7 Reg't. (Le Beuf's), La. Militia
Gade, Christophe	Private	De Clouet's Reg't., La. Militia
Gadon, --	Private	2 Reg't. (Cavelier's), La. Militia
Gahuzes, Iacques	Private	Capt. Songy's Co., Marines, La. Vols.
Gaideon, Pierre	Private	2 Batt'n. (D'Aquin's), La. Militia (Orig. under Jaideon, Pierre)
Gaigne, Jr.	Private	Capt. Chauveau's Co., Cavalry, La. Militia
Gaignee, Urbin	Corporal	Capt. Chauveau's Co., Calvalry, La. Militia
Gaignie, Francis	1 Lieut.-Lieut.	4 Reg't. (Morgan's), La. Militia (Orig. under Gainnie, Francis)
Gaignie, U.	Corporal	Capt. Chauveau's Co., Cavalry, La. Militia (Orig. under Gaignee, Urbin)
Gaignier, Jr.	Private	Capt. Chauveau's Co., Cavalry, La. Militia (Orig. under Gaigne, Jr.)
Gaillard, Raymond	Musician	1 Batt'n. (Fortier's), La. Militia
Gaillot, --	Private	Plauche's Batt'n., La. Militia (Orig. under Gallicot, --)
Gaimnie, Francis	1 Lieut.-Lieut.	4 Reg't. (Morgan's), La. Militia (Orig. under Gainnie, Francis)
Gainard, Bernard	Private	17, 18 and 19 Cons. Reg't., La. Mil. (Orig. under Gaynard, Bernard)
Gainie, Joseph	Private-Mason	Capt. Chaudurier's Co., Artificers, Art'y., La. Vols.
Gainne, Gervais	Private	6 Reg't. (Landry's), La. Militia (Orig. under Gainnie, Joseph)
Gainnie, Francis	1 Lieut.-Lieut.	4 Reg't. (Morgan's), La. Militia
Gainnie, Gerrais	Private	6 Reg't. (Landry's), La. Militia (Orig. under Gainne, Gervais)
Gainnie, Joseph	Private-Mason	Capt. Chaudurier's Co., Artificers, Art'y., La. Vols.
Gairoird, V.	Sergeant-Major	Plauche's Batt'n. La. Militia
Gairoire, V.	Sergeant-Major	Plauche's Batt'n., La. Militia (Orig. under Gairoird, V.)
Galaud, Pre In	Private	Capt. Songy's Co., Marines, La. Vols.
Galban, M.	Private	1 Reg't. (Dejan's), La. Militia
Gale, Caleb	Private	10 and 20 Cons. Reg't., La. Mil.
Gale, Caleb	Private	10 and 20 Cons. Reg't., La. Mil.
Galene, --	Private	6 Reg't. (Landry's), La. Militia
Galer, Fcis	Private	2 Reg't. (Cavelier's), La. Militia
Gales, Caleb	Private	10 and 20 Cons. Reg't., La. Mil. (Orig. under Gale, Caleb)
Gales, Fcis	Private	2 Reg't. (Cavelier's), La. Militia (Orig. under Galer, Fcis)
Gallagham, Frans	Private	6 Reg't. (Meriam's), La. Militia (Orig. under Gallaghan, Frans)
Gallaghan, Frans	Private	6 Reg't. (Meriam's), La. Militia
Gallaud, Louis	1 Lieutenant	1 Batt'n. (Fortier's), La. Militia
Galland, Maximilion	Private	1 Batt'n. (Fortier's), La. Militia
Gallaud, Noel	Private	1 Batt'n. (Fortier's), La. Militia
Galland, Pre I.	Private	Capt. Songy's Co., Marines, La. Vols. (Orig. under Galaud, Prre In)
Gallate, Isidor	Private	Capt. Colsson's Co., Artillery, La. Vols.
Gallate, Jean	Private	Capt. Colsson's Co., Artillery, La. Vols.
Gallate, John	Private	Capt. Colsson's Co., Artillery, La. Vols. (Orig. under Gallate, Jean)
Gallaway, Charles	Private	12 and 13 Cons. Reg't., La. Mil.
Gallaway, Frederick	Private	17, 18 and 19 Cons. Reg't., La. Mil. (Orig. under Galloway, Frederick)
Gallaway, John	Private	12 and 13 Cons. Reg't., La. Mil.
Gallaway, Peter	Private	12 and 13 Cons. Reg't., La. Mil.
Gallaway, William	Private	12 and 13 Cons. Reg't., La. Mil.
Galle, --	Fusilier-Private	5 Reg't. (La Branche's), La. Mil.
Gallea, Joseph	Private	De Clouet's Reg't., La. Militia (Orig. under Galliam, Joseph)
Galleand, Maximillian	Private	1 Batt'n. (Fortier's), La. Militia (Orig. under Galland, Maximilion)
Galles, --	Private	4 Reg't. (Morgan's), La. Militia
Galliam, Joseph	Private	De Clouet's Reg't., La. Militia
Gallien, Noel	Private	17, 18 and 19 Cons. Reg't., La. Militia
Galliot, --	Private	Plauche's Batt'n., La. Militia
Gallis, Prudent	Private	2 Batt'n. (Peire's), La. Vols. (Orig. under Gally, Prudent)
Galloway, Frederick	Private	17, 18 and 19 Cons. Reg't., La. Militia
Gally, Prudent	Private	2 Batt'n. (Peire's), La. Vols.
Gals, Caleb	Private	10 and 20 Cons. Reg't., La. Mil. (Orig. under Gale, Caleb)
Galt, Abraham	Pvt.-Q.M.-Sgt.	17, 18 and 19 Cons. Reg't., La. Militia
Galy, Prudent	Private	2 Batt'n. (Peire's), La. Vols. (Orig. under Gally, Prudent)
Gamache, --	Private	2 Reg't. (Cavelier's), La. Militia
Gambaba, Jose	Private	17, 18 and 19 Cons. Reg't., La. Militia
Gambala, Jose	Private	17, 18 and 19 Cons. Reg't., La. Mil. (Orig. under Gambaba, Jose)
Gamboa, J.	Private	17, 18 and 19 Cons. Reg't., La. Militia
Gamby, Vincent	Private	Plauche's Batt'n., La. Militia
Gamia, I. Inacio	Private	17, 18 and 19 Cons. Reg't., La. Mil. (Orig. under Gania, I.Inacio)
Gangey, Aron	Private	Captain Musick's Co., La. Mil. (Orig. under Gauzey, Aaron)
Gania, I. Inacio	Private	17, 18 and 19 Cons. Reg't., La. Militia
Gansey, Aaron	Sergeant	Captain Musick's Co., Mounted Riflemen, La. Militia
Ganthrir, Hipolite	Private	17, 18 and 19 Cons. Reg't., La. Mil. (Orig. under Gauthrer, Hypolite)
Ganzey, Aaron	Private	Captain Musick's Co., La. Mil.
Garas, Estiben	Private	17, 18 and 19 Cons. Reg't., La. Militia (Orig. under Garras, Estiben)
Garau, Pierre	Private	1 Batt'n. (Fortier's), La. Militia
Garcelle, Thomas	Private	1 Batt'n. (Fortier's), La. Militia (Orig. under Garsille, Thomas)
Garci, Manuel	Private	11 Reg't. (Hickey's), La. Militia
Garcia, A.	Private	1 Reg't. (Dejan's), La. Militia
Garcia, Clemente	Private	1 Reg't. (Dejan's), La. Militia
Garcia, Cs	Private	1 Reg't. (Dejan's), La. Militia
Garcia, Jean	Private	2 Batt'n. (Peire's), La. Vols.
Garcia, John	Private	De Clouet's Reg't., La. Militia
Garcia, Joseph	Private	1 Reg't. (Dejan's), La. Militia
Garcia, Joseph	Private	2 Batt'n. (Peire's), La. Vols.
Garcia, Manuel	Surgeon	2 Batt'n. (D'Aquin's), La. Militia (Orig. under Garcie, Manuel)
Garcia, Manuel	Fusilier-Private	5 Reg't. (La Branche's), La. Mil.
Garcia, Raphael	Private	2 Batt'n. (Peire's), La. Vols.
Garcie, --	Private	1 Reg't. (Dejan's), La. Militia (Orig. under Garnier, --)
Garcie, John	Private	De Clouet's Reg't., La. Militia (Orig. under Garcia, John)
Garcie, Joseph	Private	2 Batt'n. (D'Aquin's), La. Militia
Garcie, Manuel	Surgeon	2 Batt'n. (D'Aquin's), La. Militia
Garcier, John	Private	De Clouet's Reg't., La. Militia (Orig. under Garcia, John)
Garcille, Baptiste	Private	1 Batt'n. (Fortier's), La. Militia
Garcille, Thomas	Private	1 Batt'n. (Fortier's), La. Militia (Orig. under Garsille, Thomas)
Garcis, Pierre	Private	1 Batt'n. (Fortier's), La. Militia
Gardner, John	Private	17, 18 and 19 Cons. Reg't., La. Militia
Gardner, Thomas	Private	16 Reg't. (Thompson's), La. Mil.
Gardner, William	Private	16 Reg't. (Thompson's), La. Mil.
Garecile, Bb	Private	1 Batt'n. (Fortier's), La. Militia (Orig. under Garcille, Baptiste)

Name	Rank	Unit
Garge, J.	Private	Plauche's Batt'n., La. Militia
Garic, Antoine	Artificer	Capt. Chaudurier's Co., Artificers, Art'y., La. Vols. (Orig. under Garrick, Antonio)
Garick, Antoine	Artificer	Capt. Chaudurier's Co., Artificers, Art'y., La. Vols. (Orig. under Garrick, Antonio)
Garidel, A.	Private	Plauche's Batt'n., La. Militia
Garique, Antoine	Private	1 Batt'n. (Fortier's), La. Militia
Garneau, Francois	Private	7 Reg't. (Le Beuf's), La. Militia
Garneaux, --	Private	6 Reg't. (Landry's), La. Militia
Garner, Bradley	Private	17, 18 and 19 Cons. Reg't., La. Militia
Garnhart, Jacob	Private	Captain Griffith's Co., Mounted Riflemen, La. Vols.
Garnier, --	Private	1 Reg't. (Dejan's), La. Militia
Garrard, William	Private	16 Reg't. (Thompson's), La. Mil.
Garras, Estiben	Private	17, 18 and 19 Cons. Reg't., La. Militia
Garret, William	Private	Baker's Regiment, La. Militia
Garret, William	Private	Baker's Regiment, La. Militia
Garrett, Jonathan	Private	12 and 13 Cons. Reg't., La. Mil.
Garrett, Stephen	Private	De Clouet's Reg't., La. Militia
Garrette, --	Private	8 Reg't. (Meriam's), La. Militia
Garrick, Antonio	Artificer	Capt. Chaudurier's Co., Artificers, Art'y., La. Vols.
Garrick, Antoine	Private	1 Batt'n. (Fortier's), La. Militia (Orig. under Garique, Antoine)
Garrick, Jh	Private	1 Batt'n. (Fortier's), La. Militia
Garridel, A.	Private	Plauche's Batt'n., La. Militia (Orig. under Garidel, A.)
Garrigues, Francois	Private	3 Reg't. (de la Ronde's), La. Mil.
Garrique, Antoine	Private	1 Batt'n. (Fortier's), La. Militia (Orig. under Garique, Antoine)
Garrison, Samuel	Private	Captain Sprigg's Co., Boatmen, La. Vols.
Garrot, Joshua	Private	Baker's Regiment, La. Militia
Garrott, Joshuway	Private	Baker's Regiment, La. Militia (Orig. under Garrot, Joshua)
Garrus, --	Sergeant	1 Reg't. (Dejan's), La. Militia
Garry, Jean	Private	De Clouet's Reg't., La. Militia (Orig. under Gary, Joseph)
Garry, Jean fils	Private	De Clouet's Reg't., La. Militia (Orig. under Gary, Jean fils)
Garsille, Baptiste	Private	1 Batt'n. (Fortier's), La. Militia (Orig. under Garcille, Baptiste)
Garsille, Thomas	Private	1 Batt'n. (Fortier's), La. Militia
Gartlay, John	Sergeant	10 and 20 Cons. Reg't., La. Mil. (Orig. under Gartly, John)
Gartly, John	Sergeant	10 and 20 Cons. Reg't., La. Mil.
Gary, I.	Private	Captain Sprigg's Co., Boatmen, La. Vols.
Gary, Jean fils	Private	De Clouet's Reg't., La. Militia
Gary, Joseph	Private	De Clouet's Reg't., La. Militia
Gasltine, Bernard	Private	5 Reg't. (La Branche's), La. Mil.
Gaspard, Charles	Private	Baker's Regiment, La. Militia
Gaspard, Jacques	Fusilier-Private	5 Reg't. (La Branche's), La. Mil.
Gaspard, Jean	Fusilier-Private	5 Reg't. (La Branche's), La. Mil.
Gaspard, Joseph	Corporal	5 Reg't. (La Branche's), La. Mil.
Gaspard, Laurent	Fusilier-Private	5 Reg't. (La Branche's), La. Mil.
Gaspard, Pierre	Fusilier-Private	5 Reg't. (La Branche's), La. Mil.
Gaspard, Simon	Private	16 Reg't. (Thompson's), La. Mil.
Gaspart, Jques	Fusilier-Private	5 Reg't. (La Branche's), La. Mil.
Gaspart, Pierre	Fusilier-Private	5 Reg't. (La Branche's), La. Mil. (Orig. under Gaspard, Pierre)
Gassell, Joel	Private	12 and 13 Cons. Reg't., La. Mil.
Gasson, Zachariah	Private	Capt. Wallace's Co., Boatmen, La. Vols.
Gaster, Benjamin	1 Lieutenant	10 and 20 Cons. Reg't., La. Mil. (Orig. under Gastor, Benjamin)
Gaster, James	Private	10 and 20 Cons. Reg't., La. Mil. (Orig. under Gastor, James)
Gaston, James	Private	10 and 20 Cons. Reg't., La. Mil. (Orig. under Gastor, James)
Gastor, Benjamin	1 Lieutenant	10 and 20 Cons. Reg't., La. Mil.
Gastor, James	Private	10 and 20 Cons. Reg't., La. Mil.
Gastugne, Celicour	Private	2 Batt'n. (D'Aquin's), La. Militia
Gatel, --	Private	2 Reg't. (Cavelier's), La. Militia
Gates, John	Sergeant	Captain Price's Co., La. Militia
Gatreau, Edouard	Private	2 Batt'n. (D'Aquin's), La. Militia
Gauban, Agustin	Private	2 Batt'n. (D'Aquin's), La. Militia
Gauche, Francois	Private	De Clouet's Reg't., La. Militia (Orig. under Gautier, Francois)
Gauche, Zeno	Private	De Clouet's Reg't., La. Militia (Orig. under Gautier, Zeno)
Gaudait, Joseph	Captain	6 Reg't. (Landry's), La. Militia (Orig. under Gaudet, Joseph)
Gaudeau, I.	Private	8 Reg't. (Meriam's), La. Militia
Gaudet, August	Private	6 Reg't. (Landry's), La. Militia
Gaudet, Eugene	2 Lieutenant	6 Reg't. (Landry's), La. Militia
Gaudet, Joseph	Captain	6 Reg't. (Landry's), La. Militia
Gaudet, Pierre	Private	6 Reg't. (Landry's), La. Militia
Gaudet, Valey	Private	6 Reg't. (Landry's), La. Militia
Gaudier, Diego	Private	1 Reg't. (Dejan's), La. Militia (Orig. under Gaudiz, Diego)
Gaudin, Eduard	2 Lieutenant	6 Reg't. (Landry's), La. Militia
Gaudin, Jr.	Private	4 Reg't. (Morgan's), La. Militia
Gaudin, Luc	Sergeant	6 Reg't. (Landry's), La. Militia
Gaudin, Michael	Private	6 Reg't. (Landry's), La. Militia
Gaudin, Senior	Private	4 Reg't. (Morgan's), La. Militia
Gaudin, Simon	Private	2 Reg't. (Cavelier's), La. Militia
Gaudin, Valantin	Private	6 Reg't. (Landry's), La. Militia
Gaudrit, Alexandre	Private	6 Reg't. (Landry's), La. Militia
Gault, Abner	Pvt.-Q.M.-Sgt.	17, 18 and 19 Cons. Reg't., La. Mil. (Orig. under Galt, Abraham)
Gaupon, Jacque	Artificer	Capt. Chaudurier's Co., Artificers, Art'y., La. Vols.
Gaurinot, Pierre	Private	6 Reg't. (Landry's), La. Militia
Gauson, Jacob	Artificer	Capt. Chaudurier's Co., Artificers, Art'y., La. Vols. (Orig. under Gausson, Jacque)
Gaussin, A.	Private	2 Reg't. (Cavelier's), La. Militia (Orig. under Gausson, A.)
Gausson, A.	Private	2 Reg't. (Cavelier's), La. Militia
Gausson, J.	Private	2 Reg't. (Cavelier's), La. Militia
Gausson, Jacque	Artificer	Capt. Chaudurier's Co., Artificers, Art'y., La. Vols.
Gauter, Francois	Private	De Clouet's Reg't., La. Militia (Orig. under Gautier, Francois)
Gautera, P.	Private	7 Reg't. (Le Beuf's), La. Militia (Orig. under Gautreau, Pierre)
Gautan, Augustin	Private	2 Batt'n. (D'Aquin's), La. Militia (Orig. under Gauban, Augustin)
Gausson, Gargue	Artificer	Capt. Chaudurier's Co., Artificers, Art'y., La. Vols. (Orig. under Gausson, Jacque)
Gaussor, Jacque	Artificer	Capt. Chaudurier's Co., Artificers, Art'y., La. Vols. (Orig. under Gausson, Jacque)
Gauthier, --	Corporal	Plauche's Batt'n., La. Militia
Gauthier, Jh	Private	Plauche's Batt'n., La. Militia
Gauthier, Zeno	Private	De Clouet's Reg't., La. Militia (Orig. under Gautier, Zeno)
Gauthrer, Hypolite	Private	17, 18 and 19 Cons. Reg't., La. Militia
Gautier, Charles	Private	De Clouet's Reg't., La. Militia
Gautier, Francois	Private	De Clouet's Reg't., La. Militia
Gautier, Guillaume	Private	Capt. La Doux's Co., Cav., La. Vols.
Gautier, Pierre	Sergeant	De Clouet's Reg't., La. Militia
Gautier, Pierre	Private	3 Reg't. (de la Ronde's), La. Mil.
Gautier, Richard	Fusilier-Private	2 Batt'n. (D'Aquin's), La. Militia
Gautier, Zeno	Private	De Clouet's Reg't., La. Militia
Gautrat, Altrain	Corporal	6 Reg't. (Landry's), La. Militia (Orig. under Gautrot, Allain)
Gautrat, Michel	Private	6 Reg't. (Landry's), La. Militia
Gautrau, Harbin	Private	6 Reg't. (Landry's), La. Militia
Gautrau, Simon	Private	6 Reg't. (Landry's), La. Militia
Gautreau, Charles	Private	6 Reg't. (Landry's), La. Militia
Gautreau, Etienne	Private	De Clouet's Reg't., La. Militia
Gautreau, Guilfry	Private	Captain Hubbard's Mounted Co., La. Militia
Gautreau, I.	Private	7 Reg't. (Le Beuf's), La. Militia (Orig. under Gautro, Joseph)
Gautreau, Jean Bte	Private	6 Reg't. (Landry's), La. Militia
Gautreau, Joseph	Private	Captain Hubbard's Mounted Co., La. Militia
Gautreau, Joseph	Private	6 Reg't. (Landry's), La. Militia
Gautreau, Marin	Private	Captain Hubbard's Mounted Co., La. Militia
Gautreau, Pierre	Private	7 Reg't. (Le Beuf's), La. Militia
Gautreau, Simon	Private	6 Reg't. (Landry's), La. Militia (Orig. under Gautrau, Simon)
Gautro, Joseph	Private	7 Reg't. (Le Beuf's), La. Militia
Gautrol, Raphael	Private	8 Reg't. (Meriam's), La. Militia

Name	Rank	Unit
Gautrot, Allain	Corporal	6 Reg't. (Landry's), La. Militia
Gautrot, Jean L.	Private	6 Reg't. (Landry's), La. Militia (Orig. under Gotrot, Jean Lois)
Gautu, Francois	Private	De Clouet's Reg't., La. Militia (Orig. under Gautier, Francois)
Gautu, Zeno	Private	De Clouet's Reg't., La. Militia (Orig. under Gautier, Zeno)
Gavard, Manuel	Private	La. War of 1812. See also 2 Batt'n. (Peire's), La. Vols. Ref Card
Gavard, Manuel	Private	2 Batt'n. (Peire's), La. Vols. (Orig. under Guibard, Manuel)
Gaver, Emanuel	Private	De Clouet's Reg't., La. Militia
Gayard, Juan	Private	Captain Lagan's Co., La. Vols.
Gayle, John	Corporal	De Clouet's Reg't., La. Militia
Gayle, Josiah	Corporal	De Clouet's Reg't., La. Militia
Gayle, William R.	2 Lieutenant	Captain Griffith's Co., Mounted Riflemen, La. Vols.
Gaynard, Bernard	Private	17, 18 and 19 Cons. Reg't., La. Militia
Gayosa, Fernando	Private	16 Reg't. (Thompson's), La. Mil. (Orig. under Guioso, Ferdinand)
Geddrei', Jean	Private	Baker's Regiment, La. Militia (Orig. under Guidry, Jean)
Gedery, Joseph	Private	Baker's Regiment, La. Militia
Genard, Joseph	Private	17, 18 and 19 Cons. Reg't., La. Militia
Genell, Batties	Private	12 and 13 Cons. Reg't., La. Mil. (Orig. under Jennell, Baptist)
Generally, Henery	Private	Capt. Chauveau's Co., Cavalry, La. Militia
Geneste, Jean	Private	2 Reg't. (Cavelier's), La. Militia
Gennage, John W.	Private	12 and 13 Cons. Reg't., La. Mil.
Genois, aine	Private	Plauche's Batt'n., La. Militia
Genois, B.	Private	Plauche's Batt'n., La. Militia
Genois, Bernard	Corporal	4 Reg't. (Morgan's), La. Militia
Genois, Charles	2 Lieutenant	4 Reg't. (Morgan's), La. Militia (Orig. under Ginois, Charles)
Genois, Joseph	Corporal	4 Reg't. (Morgan's), La. Militia
Gentilly, Sifroix	Private	1 Batt'n. (Fortier's), La. Militia (Orig. under Jeantilly, Sifrois)
Gentilly, Silvino	Sergeant	De Clouet's Reg't., La. Militia
George, --	Servant	Capt. Colsson's Co., Artillery, La. Vols.
George (Negro)	Servant	De Clouet's Reg't., La. Militia
George, --	Waiter	Captain Ogden's Co., Dragoons, La. Militia
George, --	Servant	2 Brigade (Hopkins'), La. Militia
George, --	Servant	16 Reg't. (Thompson's), La. Mil.
George, --	Servant	17, 18 and 19 Cons. Reg't., La. Militia
George, fils	Corporal	5 Reg't. (La Branche's), La. Mil.
George, John	Private	12 and 13 Cons. Reg't., La. Mil.
George, Joseph	Private	12 and 13 Cons. Reg't., La. Mil.
George, Michel	Private	5 Reg't. (La Branche's), La. Mil.
George, Nicholas	Private	12 and 13 Cons. Reg't., La. Mil.
George, Peter	Sergeant	Captain Beale's Co., Riflemen, La. Militia
George, Ruben	Private	Capt. Callaway's Co., Mounted Riflemen, La. Militia
George, Tinque	Private	Captain Lagan's Co., La. Vols.
George, William	Captain	12 and 13 Cons. Reg't., La. Mil.
Geraud, Jean Bte	Private	De Clouet's Reg't., La. Militia
Gerault, Frs.	1 Lieutenant	Plauche's Batt'n., La. Militia (Orig. under Girault, Francis S.)
Gerbeau, Pierre	Sergeant	7 Reg't. (Le Beuf's), La. Militia (Orig. under Jerbeau, Pierre)
Gercer, --	Private	2 Batt'n. (D'Aquin's), La. Militia (Orig. under Jercer, --)
Gerdy, Benjamin	Private	Baker's Regiment, La. Militia
Germain, --	Private	2 Batt'n. (D'Aquin's), La. Militia (Orig. under Jermaine, --)
Germain, Gr.	Private	8 Reg't. (Meriam's), La. Militia
Germain, Nance	Private	16 Reg't. (Thompson's), La. Mil.
Germain, St.	Private	Plauche's Batt'n., La. Militia
Germeuil, A.	Captain	17, 18 and 19 Cons. Reg't., La. Militia
Germont, Auguste	Sergeant	2 Batt'n. (Peire's), La. Vols.
Germont, Peter	Artificer	Capt. Chaudurier's Co., Artificers, Art'y., La. Vols. (Orig. under Jermont, Pierre)
Germeuil, A.	Captain	17, 18 and 19 Cons. Reg't., La. Mil. (Orig. under Germeuil, A.)
Gernae, Frs	Private	17, 18 and 19 Cons. Reg't., La. Militia
Gerrnau, Frs	Private	17, 18 and 19 Cons. Reg't., La. Militia (Orig. under Gernai, Frs)
Gervais, --	Corporal	Plauche's Batt'n., La. Militia
Gethart, John	Private	La. War of 1812
Getor, James	Private	10 and 20 Cons. Reg't., La. Mil. (Orig. under Ictor, James)
Getor, John	Private	10 and 20 Cons. Reg't., La. Mil. (Orig. under Ictor, John)
Getor, William	Private	10 and 20 Cons. Reg't., La. Mil. (Orig. under Ictor, William)
Getraud, Paul	Private	Capt. Thomas' Co., La. Militia (Orig. under Getreaud, Paul)
Getreaud, Paul	Private	Capt. Thomas' Co., La. Militia
Geudrit, Jean Bte	Private	6 Reg't. (Landry's), La. Militia (Orig. under Guedrit, Jean Bte)
Geudry, Narcisse	Private	6 Reg't. (Landry's), La. Militia
Giage, Joseph	Private	Baker's Regiment, La. Militia
Giard, I. B.	Private	2 Reg't. (Cavelier's), La. Militia
Gibbins, Samuel	Private	Captain Hughes' Co., Mounted Riflemen, La. Militia
Gibbon, John	Private	Capt. Ashley's Co., Mounted Riflemen, La. Militia
Gibbons, Samuel	Private	Captain Hughes' Co., Mounted Riflemen, La. Militia (Orig. under Gibbins, Samuel)
Gibson, Abraham	Private	Captain Rankin's Co., Mounted Riflemen, La. Militia
Gibson, Eli	Private	10 and 20 Cons. Reg't., La. Mil.
Gibson, Garric	Private	Baker's Regiment, La. Militia (Orig. under Gibson, Gaure)
Gibson, Gaure	Private	Baker's Regiment, La. Militia
Gibson, Guion	Private	Capt. Callaway's Co., Cavalry, La. Militia
Gibson, Jesse	Private	Captain Rankin's Co., Mounted Riflemen, La. Militia
Gibson, John	Private	Capt. Callaway's Co., Cavalry, La. Militia
Gibson, Joseph	Private	Capt. C llaway's Co., Cavalry, La. Militia
Gibson, William	Cornet	Captain Rankin's Co., Mounted Riflemen, La. Militia
Gidrey, Hypolite	Private	De Clouet's Reg't., La. Militia (Orig. under Guedry, Hypolite)
Gidry, Pierre	Private	De Clouet's Reg't., La. Militia (Orig. under Guidry, Pierre)
Gifford, David	Private	17, 18 and 19 Cons. Reg't., La. Militia
Gil, Joseph	Private	11 Reg't. (Hickey's), La. Militia
Gilard, Pierre	Corporal	1 Batt'n. (Fortier's), La. Militia
Gilbaud, Alexander	Private	De Clouet's Reg't., La. Militia
Gilbaud, Alexander	Private	De Clouet's Reg't., La. Militia (Orig. under Gilbeau, Alexander)
Gilbaud, Jean Charles	Private	De Clouet's Reg't., La. Militia
Gilbaud, Placid	Private	De Clouet's Reg't., La. Militia (Orig. under Gilbeau, Placide)
Gilbeau, Alexander	Private	De Clouet's Reg't., La. Militia
Gilbeau, Joseph	Private	Baker's Regiment, La. Militia
Gilbeau, Placide	Private	De Clouet's Reg't., La. Militia
Gilbeaud, Jean	Sergeant	De Clouet's Reg't., La. Militia
Gilbert, --	Sergeant	2 Reg't. (Cavelier's), La. Militia
Gilbert, Thomas	Private	Captain Sprigg's Co., Boatmen, La. Vols.
Gilbo, Joseph	Private	Baker's Regiment, La. Militia (Orig. under Gilbeau, Joseph)
Gilbreath, James	Private	17, 18 and 19 Cons. Reg't., La. Militia
Gilchreast, David	Private	16 Reg't. (Thompson's), La. Mil. (Orig. under Gilchrist, David)
Gilchrist, David	Private	De Clouet's Reg't., La. Militia
Gilchrist, David	Private	16 Reg't. (Thompson's), La. Mil.
Gilchrist, Julius	Private	16 Reg't. (Thompson's), La. Mil.
Giles, John	Private	Captain Ramsey's Co., Mounted Riflemen, La. Militia
Gill, Charles	Private	De Clouet's Reg't., La. Militia
Gillard, John B.	Private	17, 18 and 19 Cons. Reg't., La. Militia
Gille, Louis	Private	2 Reg't. (Cavelier's), La. Militia
Gilles, Archibald	Private	Capt. Allen's Co., Artillerists, La. Vols. (Orig. under Gillis, Archibald)

Name	Rank	Unit
Gilles, Etienne	Private	2 Batt'n. (Peire's), La. Vols.
Gilliame, Celestin	Private	Baker's Regiment, La. Militia
Gilliame, Etienne	Private	Baker's Regiment, La. Militia
Gillian, Joseph	Private	De Clouet's Reg't., La. Militia (Orig. under Galliam, Joseph)
Gillin, Joseph	Private	De Clouet's Reg't., La. Militia (Orig. under Gilliam, Joseph)
Gillis, Archibald	Private	Capt. Allen's Co., Artillerists, La. Vols.
Gillon, Boisbelle	Captain-Adjt.	2 Batt'n. (D'Aquin's), La. Militia
Gillory, Frank	Private	16 Reg't. (Thompson's), La. Mil.
Gillory, John L.	Private	16 Reg't. (Thompson's), La. Mil.
Gillory, Joseph	Private	16 Reg't. (Thompson's), La. Mil.
Gillory, Joseph P.	Private	16 Reg't. (Thompson's), La. Mil.
Gillot, Marcellin	Captain	2 Batt'n. (D'Aquin's), La. Militia (Orig. under Gilot, Marcelin)
Gilly, --	Private	Plauche's Batt'n., La. Militia
Gilmore, John	Private	Captain Rankin's Co., Mounted Riflemen, La. Militia
Gilmore, John	Private	7 Reg't. (Le Beuf's), La. Militia
Gilot, Marcelin	Captain	2 Batt'n. (D'Aquin's), La. Militia
Gilvery, William A.	Private	Captain Beale's Co., Riflemen, La. Mil. (Orig. under McGilvery, William)
Gingues, Louis	Artificer	Capt. Chaudurier's Co., Artificers, Art'v., La. Vols. (Orig. under Guiges, Louis)
Ginois, Charles	2 Lieutenant	4 Reg't. (Morgan's), La. Militia
Girard, Auguste	Captain	4 Reg't. (Morgan's), La. Militia
Girard, Jean	Private	1 Batt'n. (Fortier's), La. Militia (Orig. under Girard, John)
Girard, John	Private	1 Batt'n. (Fortier's), La. Militia
Girardin, John Louis	Private	5 Reg't. (La Branche's), La. Mil.
Giraud, --	Private	2 Reg't. (Cavelier's), La. Militia
Giraud, John B.	Private	De Clouet's Reg't., La. Militia (Orig. under Geraud, Jean Bte)
Giraudau, Louis	Private	1 Batt'n. (Fortier's), La. Militia
Girault, Francis S.	1 Lieutenant	Plauche's Batt'n., La. Militia
Giro, Jean	Sergeant	3 Reg't. (de la Ronde's), La. Mil.
Giro, Simon	Sergeant	3 Reg't. (de la Ronde's), La. Mil.
Girodau, Etienne	Sergeant	Plauche's Batt'n., La. Militia (Orig. under Girodeau, Etienne)
Girodeau, Etienne	Sergeant	Plauche's Batt'n., La. Militia
Girty, James	Private	Captain Sprigg's Co., Boatmen, La. Vols.
Gisclare, J. P.	Private	6 Reg't. (Landry's), La. Militia
Givaud, --	Private	2 Reg't. (Cavelier's), La. Militia (Orig. under Giraud, --)
Givaunne, Jean	Private	Captain Lagan's Co., La. Vols.
Glais, Jean	Private	2 Batt'n. (Peire's), La. Vols. (Orig. under Glaisse, Jean)
Glaise, In	1 Lieutenant	2 Reg't. (Cavelier's), La. Militia
Glaises, Jean	Private	2 Batt'n. (Peire's), La. Vols. (Orig. under Glaisse, Jean)
Glaisse, Jean	Private	2 Batt'n. (Peire's), La. Vols.
Glaize, John	Private	De Clouet's Reg't., La. Militia
Glapion, --	Private	2 Reg't. (Cavelier's), La. Militia
Glascock, John	Private	12 and 13 Cons. Reg't., La. Mil.
Glaze, John	Private	De Clouet's Reg't., La. Militia (Orig. under Glaize, John)
Gleason, James	Private	De Clouet's Reg't., La. Militia (Orig. under Gleeson, James)
Gleeson, James	Private	De Clouet's Reg't., La. Militia
Glenn, James	Private	Captain Price's Co., La. Militia
Glover, David	Private	12 and 13 Cons. Reg't., La. Mil.
Glover, William	Private	12 and 13 Cons. Reg't., La. Mil.
Gnesnon, Ursin	Private	1 Batt'n. (Fortier's), La. Militia (Orig. under Guenon, Urcins)
Goaster, Erasine	Private	1 Batt'n. (Fortier's), La. Militia (Orig. under Goastere, Erasme)
Goastere, Erasme	Private	1 Batt'n. (Fortier's), La. Militia
Godah, M.	Private	Captain Sprigg's Co., Boatmen, La. Vols.
Godeau, Antoine	Private	16 Reg't. (Thompson's), La. Mil.
Godfrey, Jacob	Private	Captain Price's Co., La. Militia
Godfroy, I. P.	Private	2 Reg't. (Cavelier's), La. Militia
Godfroy, Jacob	Private	Captain Price's Co., La. Militia (Orig. under Godfrey, Jacob)
Godin, Pierre	Private	16 Reg't. (Thompson's), La. Mil.
Godin, Seraphim	Private	6 Reg't. (Landry's), La. Militia
Godrau, Joseph	Private	De Clouet's Reg't., La. Militia
Godreau, Joseph	Private	De Clouet's Reg't., La. Militia (Orig. under Godrau, Joseph)
Gody, Benjamin	Private	16 Reg't. (Thompson's), La. Mil.
Gody, Michel	Corporal	16 Reg't. (Thompson's), La. Mil.
Gody, Peter	Private	16 Reg't. (Thompson's), La. Mil.
Goeans, Emes	Private	12 and 13 Cons. Reg't., La. Mil. (Orig. under Goins, Amos)
Goen, Charles F.	Private	Captain Dodge's Co., Mounted Riflemen, La. Militia
Goen, Charles F.	Private	Captain Henry's Co., Mounted Riflemen, La. Militia
Goff, John K.	Captain	De Clouet's Reg't., La. Militia
Goff, Lewis	Private	10 and 20 Cons. Reg't., La. Mil.
Goforth, William	Surgeon	De Clouet's Reg't., La. Militia
Goforth, William	Corporal	Plauche's Batt'n., La. Militia
Goins, Amos	Private	12 and 13 Cons. Reg't., La. Mil.
Goldenbow, --	Private	1 Reg't. (Dejan's), La. Militia
Goldrich, Michael	Private	De Clouet's Reg't., La. Militia
Gollis, N.	Private	Plauche's Batt'n., La. Militia
Gomas, Francis	Private	8 Reg't. (Meriam's), La. Militia (Orig. under Gonas, Francis)
Gomes, D.	Private	6 Reg't. (Landry's), La. Militia
Gomes, Juan	Sergeant	2 Batt'n. (Peire's), La. Vols. (Orig. under Gomez, Juan)
Gomez, Juan	Sergeant	2 Batt'n. (Peire's), La. Vols. (See also U.S.A. 7 Reg't.)
Gomez, Joseph	Sergeant	2 Batt'n. (Peire's), La. Vols.
Gomez, Manuel	Private	17, 18 and 19 Cons. Reg't., La. Militia
Gomme, Raphael	Private	De Clouet's Reg't., La. Militia
Gommes, Raphael	Private	De Clouet's Reg't., La. Militia (Orig. under Gomme, Raphael)
Gonas, Francis	Private	8 Reg't. (Meriam's), La. Militia
Gongara, Ignacio	2 Lieutenant	17, 18 and 19 Cons. Reg't., La. Militia
Gonor, Simon	Private	16 Reg't. (Thompson's), La. Mil.
Gonsac, Dedole	Private	17, 18 and 19 Cons. Reg't., La. Militia
Gonsales, Joachine	Private	17, 18 and 19 Cons. Reg't., La. Mil. (Orig. under Gonzales, Joaquin)
Gonsales, Manuel	Private	2 Batt'n. (Peire's), La. Vols.
Gonsalve, Joseph	Private	16 Reg't. (Thompson's), La. Mil.
Gonsolin, Bomil	Private	Baker's Regiment, La. Militia (Orig. under Gonsoulin, Bomel)
Gonsolve, Joseph	Private	16 Reg't. (Thompson's), La. Mil. (Orig. under Gonsalve, Joseph)
Gonsoulin, Bomel	Private	Baker's Regiment, La. Militia
Gonsoulin, St. Clair	Private	Baker's Regiment, La. Militia
Gonsulin, St. Clair	Private	Baker's Regiment, La. Militia (Orig. under Gonsoulin, St Clair)
Gontaud, Joseph	Private	Capt. Alpuente's Co., La. Mil.
Gonzal, Joasin	Private	17, 18 and 19 Cons. Reg't., La. Mil. (Orig. under Gonzales, Joaquin)
Gonzal, Philip	Private	17, 18 and 19 Cons. Reg't., La. Mil. (Orig. under Gonzales, Philip)
Gonzale, Felip	Private	17, 18 and 19 Cons. Reg't., La. Mil. (Orig. under Gonzales, Philip)
Gonzale, Joaquin	Private	17, 18 and 19 Cons. Reg't., La. Mil. (Orig. under Gonzales, Joaquin)
Gonzaler, Salvador	Private	Captain Lagan's Co., La. Vols.
Gonzales, Antonio	Private	3 Reg't. (de la Ronde's), La. Mil.
Gonzales, F.	Private	2 Reg't. (Cavelier's), La. Militia
Gonzales, Felix	Private	3 Reg't. (de la Ronde's), La. Mil.
Gonzales, Joaquin	Private	17, 18 and 19 Cons. Reg't., La. Militia
Gonzales, John	Private	2 Reg't. (Cavelier's), La. Militia
Gonzales, Joseph	Private	Baker's Regiment, La. Militia
Gonzales, Joseph	Private	8 Reg't. (Meriam's), La. Militia
Gonzales, Mariel	Private	8 Reg't. (Meriam's), La. Militia
Gonzales, Philip	Private	17, 18 and 19 Cons. Reg't., La. Militia
Gonzales, Pierre	Private	De Clouet's Reg't., La. Militia
Gonzales, Sebastien	Private	3 Reg't. (de la Ronde's), La. Mil.
Gonzales, Thomas	Private	8 Reg't. (Meriam's), La. Militia
Gonzalez, Pierre	Private	De Clouet's Reg't., La. Militia (Orig. under Gonzales, Pierre)

Name	Rank	Unit
Gonzalles, Diego	Private	6 Reg't. (Landry's), La. Militia
Gonzalles, Jose	Private	De Clouet's Reg't., La. Militia
Gonzalles, Manuel	Private	De Clouet's Reg't., La. Militia
Gonzalves, Pedro	Private	2 Reg't. (Cavelier's), La. Militia
Gonzeles, Pierre	Private	De Clouet's Reg't., La. Militia (Orig. under Gonzales, Pierre)
Goodale, Peter	Private	Captain Rankin's Co., Mounted Riflemen, La. Militia
Goodbee, John	Private	De Clouet's Reg't., La. Militia
Goodbee, Joseph	Private	8 Reg't. (Meriam's), La. Militia
Goodby, John	Private	De Clouet's Reg't., La. Militia (Orig. under Goodbee, John)
Goode, Delanson	Private	De Clouet's Reg't., La. Militia
Goodwin, Jesse	Private	Capt. Ashley's Co., Mounted Riflemen, La. Militia
Gorden, A. W.	Private	Captain Beale's Co., Riflemen, La. Militia
Gorden, John	Private	Captain Griffith's Co., Mounted Riflemen, La. Vols.
Gordin, L.	Private	Captain Spriggs Co., Boatmen, La. Vols.
Gordon, A. W.	Private	Captain Beale's Co., Riflemen, La. Mil. (Orig. under Gorden, A. W.)
Gordon, Charles	Private	Capt. Allen's Co., Artillerists, La. Vols.
Gordon, James H.	Captain	17, 18 and 19 Reg't. Cons., La. Militia
Gordon, James H.	Capt. & Brig. Maj.	General and Staff (Morgan), La. Militia
Gordon, John	Private	Captain Griffith's Co., Mounted Riflemen, La. Vols. (Orig. under Gorden, John)
Gordon, William	Private	12 and 13 Cons. Reg't., La. Mil.
Gordy, Peter	Private	Baker's Regiment, La. Militia
Gordy, Michael	Private	Baker's Regiment, La. Militia
Gorham, William	Sergeant	Plauche's Batt'n., La. Militia
Gorman, David	Private	De Clouet's Reg't., La. Militia
Gormby, William	Q. M.-Sergeant	De Clouet's Reg't., La. Militia (Orig. under Gormly, William)
Gormley, John	Sergeant-Major	17, 18 and 19 Cons. Reg't., La. Militia
Gormly, William	Q. M.-Sergeant	De Clouet's Reg't., La. Militia
Gorrott, Joshuway	Private	Baker's Regiment, La. Militia (Orig. under Garrot, Joshua)
Goslin, Nathaniel	Private	Capt. Wallace's Co., Boatmen, La. Vols.
Goslin, Thomas	Private	16 Reg't. (Thompson's), La. Mil.
Gosliot, Jacque	Private	Captain Lagan's Co., La. Vols.
Goson, Jack	Artificer	Capt. Chaudurier's Co., Artificers, Art'y., La. Vols. (Orig. under Gausson, Jacque)
Gossiot, Jeaqus	Private	Captain Lagan's Co., La. Vols. (Orig. under Gosliot, Jacque)
Gothrow, Etienne	Private	De Clouet's Reg't., La. Militia (Orig. under Gautreau, Etienne)
Gotrot, Jean Louis	Private	6 Reg't. (Landry's), La. Militia
Gottorthun, John	Private	Capt. Thomas' Co., La. Militia
Gottorthurns, John	Private	Capt. Thomas' Co., La. Militia (Orig. under Gottorthun, John)
Gouerier, Laurent	Private	De Clouet's Reg't., La. Militia (Orig. under Gouerrir, Laurent)
Gouerrir, Laurent	Private	De Clouet's Reg't., La. Militia
Gouman, --	Waiter	1 Divison (Villere's), La. Militia
Goumouille, --	Private	1 Reg't. (Dejan's), La. Militia
Gourjon, --	Private	Plauche's Batt'n., La. Militia
Goutieres, Bernarde	Private	3 Reg't. (de la Ronde's), La. Mil. (Orig. under Gutierez, Bernardo)
Goutieres, Jean	Sergeant	3 Reg't. (de la Ronde's), La. Mil.
Goutierez, Jean	Private	3 Reg't. (de la Ronde's), La. Mil. (Orig. under Gutierez, Jean)
Gouzales, Salvador	Private	Capt. Songy's Co., Marines, La. Vols.
Gowan, --	Servant	Gov. Claiborne and Staff, La. Mil.
Goyer, Alexander	Private	Baker's Regiment, La. Militia
Goyle, Christ	Private	11 Reg't. (Hickey's), La. Militia
Goyon, Peter	Private	17, 18 and 19 Cons. Reg't., La. Militia
Gozales, Felix	Private	3 Reg't. (de la Ronde's), La. Mil. (Orig. under Gonzales, Felix)
Graber, Jacques	Private	6 Reg't. (Landry's), La. Militia
Grabes, Jacques	Private	6 Reg't. (Landry's), La. Militia (Orig. under Graber, Jacques)
Grabier, Hambrose	Private	6 Reg't. (Landry's), La. Militia
Grace, Francis	Private	De Clouet's Reg't., La. Militia (Orig. under Grasse, Francis)
Gracia, Nicholas	Private	17, 18 and 19 Cons. Reg't., La. Militia
Gracie, Joseph	Private	10 and 20 Cons. Reg't., La. Mil.
Gradenigo, Augustine	Private	16 Reg't. (Thompson's), La. Mil. (Orig. under Gradinego, Augustine)
Gradenigo, Joseph	Private	16 Reg't. (Thompson's), La. Mil. (Orig. under Gradinego, Joseph)
Gradinego, Augustine	Private	16 Reg't. (Thompson's), La. Mil.
Gradinego, Ely	Private	16 Reg't. (Thompson's), La. Mil.
Gradinego, Joseph	Private	16 Reg't. (Thompson's), La. Mil.
Grady, Joseph	Private	10 and 20 Cons. Reg't., La. Mil. (Orig. under Gracie, Joseph)
Grage, William	Private	De Clouet's Reg't., La. Militia (Orig. under Greig, William)
Grague, Pierre	Private	2 Batt'n. (Peire's), La. Vols. (Orig. under Drague, Pierre)
Graham, David	Private	10 and 20 Cons. Reg't., La. Mil.
Graham, G. E.	Private	La. War of 1812
Graham, James	Private	12 and 13 Cons. Reg't., La. Mil.
Graham, Thomas	Sergeant	17, 18 and 19 Cons. Reg't., La. Militia
Graissant, --	Lieutenant	2 Batt'n. (D'Aquin's), La. Militia
Gramond, Cadet	Fusilier-Private	2 Batt'n. (D'Aquin's), La. Militia
Gramond, Etienne	Fusilier-Private	2 Batt'n. (D'Aquin's), La. Militia
Gramont, --	Fusilier-Private	2 Batt'n. (D'Aquin's), La. Militia (Orig. under Gramond, Etienne)
Grande, Emanuel	Private	De Clouet's Reg't., La. Militia
Grandchamps, Fcis	Surgs. Mate	1 Reg't. (Dejan's), La. Militia
Grandy, Emanuel	Private	De Clouet's Reg't., La. Militia (Orig. under Grande, Emanuel)
Grange, Joseph	Private	8 Reg't. (Meriam's), La. Militia
Grange, P.	Private	8 Reg't. (Meriam's), La. Militia
Grangee, Pierre	Private	De Clouet's Reg't., La. Militia (Orig. under Granger, Pierre)
Granger, Cyprien	Private	Baker's Regiment, La. Militia
Granger, Joseph	Private	De Clouet's Reg't., La. Militia
Granger, Lorah	Private	Baker's Regiment, La. Militia
Granger, Louis	Private	De Clouet's Reg't., La. Militia
Granger, Peter	Corporal	De Clouet's Reg't., La. Militia
Granger, Pierre	Private	De Clouet's Reg't., La. Militia
Granger, Raphiel	Private	Baker's Reg't., La. Militia
Granger, Simon	Private	De Clouet's Reg't., La. Militia
Grangree, Piere	Private	De Clouet's Reg't., La. Militia (Orig. under Granger, Pierre)
Grannier, --	Private	Plauche's Batt'n., La. Militia
Grants, John	Private	17, 18 and 19 Cons. Reg't., La. Mil. (Orig. under Grantz, John)
Grantz, John	Private	17, 18 and 19 Cons. Reg't., La. Militia
Grarde, Claude	Private	6 Reg't. (Landry's), La. Militia
Gras, Antoine	Sergeant	11 Reg't. (Hickey's), La. Militia
Gras, Joseph	Private	11 Reg't. (Hickey's), La. Militia
Grass, Anthy	Sergeant	Detachment of Supernumerary Officers, La. Mil. (See also 11 Reg't.)
Grass, John	Private	Captain Beale's Co., Riflemen, La. Militia
Grasse, Francis	Private	De Clouet's Reg't., La. Militia
Grasset, --	Private	Plauche's Batt'n., La. Militia
Gravart, Bertrand	Private	De Clouet's Reg't., La. Militia (Orig. under Gravats, Bertrand)
Gravats, Bertrand	Private	De Clouet's Reg't., La. Militia
Gravatt, Bertrand	Private	De Clouet's Reg't., La. Militia (Orig. under Gravats, Bertrand)
Gravenberg, Celestin	Sergeant	Baker's Regiment, La. Militia
Graves, Humphrey	Private	10 and 20 Cons. Reg't., La. Mil.
Gravois, Armand	Fusilier-Private	5 Reg't. (La Branche's), La. Mil.
Gravois, John	Private	6 Reg't. (Landry's), La. Militia
Gravois, Valery	Private	6 Reg't. (Landry's), La. Militia
Gravolet, Joseph	Private	2 Batt'n. (Peire's), La. Vols.
Gray, Absalom	Private	Baker's Regiment, La. Militia
Gray, James	Sergeant-Private	12 and 13 Cons. Reg't., La. Mil.
Green, Aaron	Private	10 and 20 Cons. Reg't., La. Mil.
Green, Greenbery	Private	De Clouet's Reg't., La. Militia (Orig. under Green, Greenberry)
Green, John	Private	Capt. Wallace's Co., Boatmen, La. Vols.

Name	Rank	Unit
Green, John	Private	1 Reg't. (Dejan's), La. Militia
Green, John	Private	17, 18 and 19 Cons. Reg't., La. Militia
Green, Joshua	Corporal	17, 18 and 19 Cons. Reg't., La. Militia
Green, Solomon	Private	De Clouet's Reg't., La. Militia
Greene, John	Private	Capt. Wallace's Co., Boatmen, La. Vols. (Orig. under Green, John)
Greenwell, Charles	Private	17, 18 and 19 Cons. Reg't., La. Militia
Greenwell, James	Private	16 Reg't. (Thompson's), La. Mil.
Greer, Greenberry	Private	De Clouet's Reg't., La. Militia
Greer, William M.	Private	De Clouet's Reg't., La. Militia (Orig. under McGrew, William)
Gregg, Antoine	Private	De Clouet's Reg't., La. Militia (Orig. under Greggs, Antoine)
Greggs, Antoine	Private	De Clouet's Reg't., La. Militia
Gregoire, Andre	Private	Plauche's Batt'n., La. Militia
Gregoire, Francois	Private	7 Reg't. (Le Beuf's), La. Militia
Gregoire, Jacques	Private	6 Reg't. (Landry's), La. Militia
Gregoire, Laurent	Private	7 Reg't. (Le Beuf's), La. Militia
Gregoire, Zenon	Private	6 Reg't. (Landry's), La. Militia
Gregory, Charles	Private	19 Regiment, La. Militia
Greig, John	Private	De Clouet's Reg't., La. Militia
Greig, William	Private	De Clouet's Reg't., La. Militia
Grenier, John Pre	Private	8 Reg't. (Meriam's), La. Militia
Grenier, Julien	Private	8 Reg't. (Meriam's), La. Militia
Gresham, James	Private	19 Reg't., La. Militia
Gresham, John	Private	19 Reg't., La. Mil. (Orig. under Grisham, John)
Gresnard, Louis	Sergeant	2 Reg't. (Cavelier's), La. Militia
Gressant, --	Lieutenant	2 Batt'n. (D'Aquin's), La. Militia (Orig. under Graissant, --)
Gressaut, --	Lieutenant	2 Batt'n. (D'Aquin's), La. Militia (Orig. under Graissant, --)
Gresseaut, --	Lieutenant	2 Batt'n.)D'Aquin's), La. Militia (Orig. under Graissant, --)
Gressy, Manuel	Private	Captain Lagan's Co., La. Vols. (Orig. under Gussy, Manuel)
Gridley, --	Private	1 Reg't. (Dejan's), La. Militia
Grieg, John	Private	De Clouet's Reg't., La. Militia (Orig. under Greig, John)
Griffath, Isaac	Private	16 Reg't. (Thompson's), La. Mil. (Orig. under Griffith, Isaac)
Griffin, C.	Corporal	4 Reg't. (Morgan's), La. Militia
Griffith, Assa	Private	Captain Price's Co., La. Militia
Griffith, Isaac	Private	16 Reg't. (Thompson's), La. Mil.
Griffith, James		Capt. Allen's Co., Artillerists, La. Vols.
Griffith, Llewellyn C.	Captain	Captain Griffith's Co., Mounted Riflemen, La. Vols.
Griffom, Gaspard	Private	La. War of 1812
Griffon, Jean	Corporal	2 Reg't. (Cavelier's), La. Militia
Grigg, Ryall	Private	8 Reg't. (Meriam's), La. Militia
Grigoire, Zenon	Private	6 Reg't. (Landry's), La. Militia (Orig. under Gregoire, Zenon)
Grima, By	2 Lieutenant	Plauche's Batt'n., La. Militia
Grimby, Robert	Private	Capt. Wallace's Co., Boatmen, La. Vols. (Orig. under Quimby, Robert)
Grimes, George	Private	2 Batt'n. (Peire's), La. Vols.
Grims, --	Private	5 Reg't. (La Branche's), La. Mil.
Grims, George	Private	2 Batt'n. (Peire's), La. Vols. (Orig. under Grimes, George)
Grinage, John W.	Private	12 and 13 Cons. Reg't., La. Mil. (Orig. under Grennage, John W.)
Grisham, James	Private	19 Reg't., La. Vols. (Orig. under Gresham, James)
Grisham, John	Private	19 Regiment, La. Militia
Grishann, James	Private	19 Reg't., La. Vols. (Orig. under Gresham, James)
Grisley, John	Private	12 and 13 Cons. Reg't., La. Mil.
Grivot, William	Sergeant	8 Reg't. (Meriam's), La. Militia
Groff, Henry	Private	Captain McNair's Co., Mounted Riflemen, La. Militia
Gros, Andre	Corporal	5 Reg't. (La Branche's), La. Mil.
Gros, Ceprien	Surgeon	1 Reg't. (Dejan's), La. Militia
Gros, I.	Private	8 Reg't. (Meriam's), La. Militia
Gros, Jean Louis	Fusilier-Private	5 Reg't. (La Branche's), La. Mil.
Gros, Pierre	Private	7 Reg't. (Le Beuf's), La. Militia
Grosse, --	Private	4 Reg't. (Morgan's), La. Militia
Groussole, --	Corporal	2 Reg't. (Cavelier's), La. Militia
Groves, Humphrey	Private	10 and 20 Cons. Reg't., La. Mil. (Orig. under Graves, Humphrey)
Groves, James	Private	De Clouet's Reg't., La. Militia
Groyer, --	Private	Plauche's Batt'n., La. Militia
Grubbs, Benjamin	Private	16 Reg't. (Thompson's), La. Mil.
Grubbs, Francis	Private	10 and 20 Cons. Reg't., La. Mil. (Orig. under Grubs, Francis)
Grubbs, James	Private	10 Regiment, La. Militia
Grubs, Francis	Private	10 and 20 Cons. Reg't., La. Mil.
Gruyer, Aaron	Private	10 and 20 Cons. Reg't., La. Mil. (Orig. under Green, Aaron)
Guadiz, Diego	Private	1 Reg't. (Dejan's), La. Militia
Guadiz, Jn	Sergeant	Plauche's Batt'n., La. Militia
Guard, Pierre	Private	2 Batt'n. (Peire's), La. Vols.
Guatac, M.	Private	8 Reg't. (Meriam's), La. Militia
Gucho, Alyis	Private	17, 18 and 19 Cons. Reg't., La. Militia
Guedez, Joseph	Private	3 Reg't. (de la Ronde's), La. Mil.
Guedez, Joseph	Private	3 Reg't. (de la Ronde's), La. Mil.
Guedret, Emon	Private	6 Reg't. (Landry's), La. Militia
Guedrit, Francois	Corporal	6 Reg't. (Landry's), La. Militia
Guedrit, Jean Bte	Private	6 Reg't. (Landry's), La. Militia
Guedry, Edward	Private	8 Reg't. (Meriam's), La. Militia
Guedry, Firmin	Private	11 Reg't. (Hickey's), La. Militia
Guedry, Hypolite	Private	De Clouet's Reg't., La. Militia
Guedry, John Charles	Private	De Clouet's Reg't., La. Militia (Orig. under Guidry, John Charles)
Guedry, Pierre	Sergeant	De Clouet's Reg't., La. Militia
Guedry, Pierre	Private	De Clouet's Reg't., La. Militia (Orig. under Guidry, Pierre)
Guedry, Sebastian	Corporal	8 Reg't. (Meriam's), La. Militia
Gueho, Celestin	Private	17, 18 and 19 Cons. Reg't., La. Militia
Gueho, George	Private	17, 18 and 19 Cons. Reg't., La. Militia
Gueho, Joseph	Private	17, 18 and 19 Cons. Reg't., La. Militia
Gueho, Prerret George	Private	17, 18 and 19 Cons. Reg't., La. Militia
Guelline, Bernard	Private	5 Reg't. (La Branche's), La. Mil. (Orig. under Gasltine, Bernard)
Guenard, Millien	Private	De Clouet's Reg't., La. Militia
Guennin, Peter	Corporal	2 Reg't. (Cavelier's), La. Militia (Orig. under Guerrin, Peter)
Guenno, Frederick	Corporal	4 Reg't. (Morgan's), La. Militia
Guenon, Delmas	Private	2 Reg't. (Cavelier's), La. Militia
Guenon, E.	Corporal	Plauche's Batt'n., La. Militia (Orig. under Guesnon, E.)
Guenon, Joseph	Corporal	2 Reg't. (Cavelier's), La. Militia
Guenon, Joseph	Private	4 Reg't. (Morgan's), La. Militia
Guenon, Urcins	Private	1 Batt'n. (Fortier's), La. Militia
Guerin, --	Private	Plauche's Batt'n., La. Militia
Guerin, Dominique	Artificer	Capt. Chaudurier's Co., Artificers, Art'y., La. Vols.
Guerin, Edward	Sergeant	6 Reg't. (Landry's), La. Militia
Guerin, Francois	1 Lieutenant	6 Reg't. (Landry's), La. Militia
Guerin, Jean	Corporal	Plauche's Batt'n., La. Militia
Guerin, Pierre	Artificer	Capt. Chaudurier's Co., Artificers, Art'y., La. Vols.
Guern, Ap	Private	7 Reg't. (Le Beuf's), La. Militia
Guerra, Estoran	Private	17, 18 and 19 Cons. Reg't., La. Militia
Guernsey, Aaron	Sergeant	Captain Musick's Co., Mounted Riflemen, La. Mil. (Orig. under Gansey, Aaron)
Guerre, Ignatio	Private	17, 18 and 19 Cons. Reg't., La. Militia
Guerrin, Jean	Corporal	Plauche's Batt'n., La. Militia (Orig. under Guerin, Jean)
Guerrin, Peter	Corporal	2 Reg't. (Cavelier's), La. Militia
Guesnard, Louis	Sergeant	2 Reg't. (Cavelier's), La. Militia (Orig. under Gresnard, Louis)
Guesnon, E.	Corporal	Plauche's Batt'n., La. Militia
Guesnon, Jacques	Private	11 Reg't. (Hickey's), La. Militia
Gurtraut, Cherubin	Private	2 Batt'n. (D'Aquin's), La. Militia
Guiar, John Baptiste	Private	2 Batt'n. (Peire's), La. Vols. (Orig. under Guiare, John Baptiste)
Guiare, John Baptiste	Private	2 Batt'n. (Peire's), La. Vols.

Name	Rank	Unit
Guiarre, John Baptiste	Private	2 Batt'n. (Peire's), La. Vols. (Orig. under Guiare, John Baptiste)
Guibard, Manuel	Private	2 Batt'n. (Peire's), La. Vols.
Guibare, Manuel	Private	2 Batt'n. (Peire's), La. Vols. (Orig. under Guibard, Manuel)
Guibart, Manuel	Private	2 Batt'n. (Peire's), La. Vols. (Orig. under Guibard, Manuel)
Guibarrd, Ozene	Private	De Clouet's Reg't., La. Militia (Orig. under Guilbarrd, Osaine)
Guibert, Augustus	Captain	Plauche's Batt'n., La. Militia
Guichard, --	Private	Plauche's Batt'n., La. Militia
Guide, Benite	Private	3 Reg't. (de la Ronde's), La. Mil.
Guide, Jean	Private	3 Reg't. (de la Ronde's), La. Mil.
Guidraux, Cyprian	Private	7 Reg't. (Le Beuf's), La. Militia
Guidreau, Cyprian	Private	7 Reg't. (Le Beuf's), La. Militia (Orig. under Guisraux, Cyprian)
Guidree, Jean	Private	Baker's Regiment, La. Militia (Orig. under Guidry, Jean)
Guidrey, Louis	Private	16 Reg't. (Thompson's), La. Mil.
Guidrey, Philemon	Private	De Clouet's Reg't., La. Militia (Orig. under Guidry, Philemon)
Guidrey, Piere	Private	De Clouet's Reg't., La. Militia (Orig. under Guidry, Pierre)
Guidrit, Emon	Private	6 Reg't. (Landry's), La. Militia (Orig. under Guedret, Emon)
Guidrit, Francois	Corporal	6 Reg't. (Landry's), La. Militia (Orig. under Guedrit, Francois)
Guidrit, Jn Bte	Private	6 Reg't. (Landry's), La. Militia (Orig. under Guedrit, Jean Bte)
Guidry, Antoine	1 Lieutenant	De Clouet's Reg't., La. Militia
Guidry, Batiste	Private	De Clouet's Reg't., La. Militia
Guidry, Firmin	Private	11 Reg't. (Hickey's), La. Militia (Orig. under Guedry, Firmin)
Guidry, Hypolite	Private	De Clouet's Reg't., La. Militia
Guidry, Jean	Private	Baker's Regiment, La. Militia
Guidry, Jean fils	Private	De Clouet's Reg't., La. Militia
Guidry, John Charles	Private	De Clouet's Reg't., La. Militia
Guidry, Joseph	Private	Baker's Regiment, La. Militia (Orig. under Gedery, Joseph)
Guidry, Joseph	Private	De Clouet's Reg't., La. Militia
Guidry, Julien	Private	De Clouet's Reg't., La. Militia
Guidry, Louis	Private	16 Reg't. (Thompson's), La. Mil. (Orig. under Guidrey, Louis)
Guidry, Oliver	Private	De Clouet's Reg't., La. Militia
Guidry, Onizeme	1 Lieutenant	16 Reg't. (Thompson's), La. Mil.
Guidry, Philemon	Private	De Clouet's Reg't., La. Militia
Guidry, Pierre	Private	De Clouet's Reg't., La. Militia
Guidry, Pierre	Private	De Clouet's Reg't., La. Militia
Guidry, Pierre	Private	De Clouet's Reg't., La. Militia
Guidry, Treville	Private	16 Reg't. (Thompson's), La. Mil.
Guidry, Sebastian	Corporal	8 Reg't. (Meriam's), La. Militia (Orig. under Guedry, Sebastian)
Guiedrit, Alexander	Private	6 Reg't. (Landry's), La. Militia (Orig. under Gaudrit, Alexandre)
Guieu, M.	Private	1 Reg't. (Dejan's), La. Militia
Guienee, Cadet	Fusilier-Private	2 Batt'n. (D'Aquin's), La. Militia
Guienette, Etienne	Fusilier-Private	2 Batt'n. (D'Aquin's), La. Militia
Guiere, John Baptiste	Private	2 Batt'n. (Peire's), La. Vols. (Orig. under Guiare, John Baptiste)
Guifford, Thomas	Private	4 Reg't. (Morgan's), La. Militia
Guiger, John	1 Sergeant-Sgt.	Captain Rankin's Co., Mounted Riflemen, La. Militia
Guiges, Louis	Artificer	Capt. Chaudurier's Co., Artificers, Art'y., La. Vols.
Guigime, W.	Private	7 Reg't. (Le Beuf's), La. Militia (Orig. under Guigine, W.)
Guiguine, W.	Private	7 Reg't. (Le Beuf's), La. Militia
Guignan, E.	Private	4 Reg't. (Morgan's), La. Militia
Guignan, Roman	Sergeant	6 Reg't. (Landry's), La. Militia
Guignand, --	Private	Plauche's Batt'n., La. Militia
Guignaud, Julien	Private	2 Batt'n. (Peire's), La. Vols.
Guignard, Julien	Private	2 Batt'n. (Peire's), La. Vols. (Orig. under Guignaud, Julien)
Guigues, Louis	Artificer	Capt. Chaudurier's Co., Artificers, Art'y., La. Vols. (Orig. under Guiges, Louis)
Guiguis, Louis	Artificer	Capt. Chaudurier's Co., Artificers, Art'y., La. Vols. (Orig. under Guiges, Louis)
Guiho, Celestin	Private	17, 18 and 19 Cons. Reg't., La. Mil. (Orig. under Gueho, Celestin)
Guiho, Joseph	Private	17, 18 and 19 Cons. Reg't., La. Mil. (Orig. under Gueho, Joseph)
Guiho, Perret George	Private	17, 18 and 19 Cons. Reg't., La. Mil. (Orig. under Gueho, Peerret George)
Guilban, Alexander	Private	De Clouet's Reg't., La. Militia (Orig. under Gilbaud, (Alexander)
Guilbaud, J. Charles	Private	De Clouet's Reg't., La. Militia (Orig. under Gilbaud, Jean Charles)
Guilbaud, Julien	Private	De Clouet's Reg't., La. Militia
Guilbaud, Orsaime	Private	De Clouet's Reg't., La. Militia
Guilborg, John	Private	17, 18 and 19 Cons. Reg't., La. Militia
Guilbrait, James	Private	17, 18 and 19 Cons. Reg't., La. Mil. (Orig. under Gilbreath, James)
Guilfaut, Antoine	Private	Captain Hubbard's Mounted Co., La. Militia
Guilfaut, Gaspar	Private	Captain Hubbard's Mounted Co., La. Militia
Guillan, B.	Private	2 Reg't. (Cavelier's), La. Militia
Guillau, A.	Private	8 Reg't. (Meriam's), La. Militia (Orig. under Guillot, A.)
Guillau, Ls	Private	8 Reg't. (Meriam's), La. Militia (Orig. under Guillot, Ls)
Guillaume, Carter	Private	Captain Lagan's Co., La. Vols.
Guillaume, Jean	Private	3 Reg't. (de la Ronde's), La. Mil.
Guillaume, Louis	Private	3 Reg't. (de la Ronde's), La. Mil.
Guillaumett, Jn.	Fusilier-Private	2 Batt'n. (D'Aquin's), La. Militia
Guillen, Domingo	Private	17, 18 and 19 Cons. Reg't., La. Militia
Guillerman, Antoine	Private	Plauche's Batt'n., La. Militia
Guillermaint, Antoine	Private	2 Batt'n. (Peire's), La. Vols.
Guillette, I.	Private	4 Reg't. (Morgan's), La. Militia
Guilliermain, Antoine	Private	2 Batt'n. (Peire's), La. Vols. (Orig.under Guillernaint,Antoine)
Guilliermaint, Antoine	Private	2 Batt'n. (Peire's), La. Vols. (Orig.under Guillermaint,Antoine)
Guillion, Boibal	Captain-Adjt.	2 Batt'n. (D'Aquin's), La. Militia (Orig. under Gillon, Boisbelle)
Guillon, Boisbel	Captain-Adjt.	2 Batt'n. (D'Aquin's), La. Militia (Orig. under Gillon, Boisbelle)
Guillons, Cyprien	Private	17, 18 and 19 Cons. Reg't., La. Militia
Guillorey, M.	Private	8 Reg't. (Meriam's), La. Militia
Guilloroy, M.	Private	8 Reg't. (Meriam's), La. Militia (Orig. under Guillorey, M.)
Guillory, Augustine	Private	16 Reg't. (Thompson's), La. Mil.
Guillory, Charles	Private	16 Reg't. (Thompson's), La. Mil.
Guillory, Donate	Private	16 Reg't. (Thompson's), La. Mil.
Guillory, Louis fils	Private	16 Reg't. (Thompson's), La. Mil.
Guillory, M.	Private	8 Reg't. (Meriam's), La. Militia (Orig. under Guillorey, M.)
Guillory, Pierre P.	Private	16 Reg't. (Thompson's), La. Mil.
Guillory, Valery	Private	16 Reg't. (Thompson's), La. Mil.
Guillot, A.	Private	8 Reg't. (Meriam's), La. Militia
Guillot, Bte	Private	7 Reg't. (Le Beuf's), La. Militia
Guillot, Isidore	Private	7 Reg't. (Le Beuf's), La. Militia
Guillot, Jean	Captain	7 Reg't. (Le Beuf's), La. Militia
Guillot, Jean C.	Private	7 Reg't. (Le Beuf's), La. Militia
Guillot, Jean P.	Corporal	7 Reg't. (Le Beuf's), La. Militia
Guillot, Jean Pierre	Private	7 Reg't. (Le Beuf's), La. Militia
Guillot, Joseph	Private	7 Reg't. (Le Beuf's), La. Militia
Guillot, Louis	Private	7 Reg't. (Le Beuf's), La. Militia
Guillot, Ls	Private	8 Reg't. (Meriam's), La. Militia
Guillot, Marcelin	Captain	2 Batt'n. (D'Aquin's), La. Militia (Orig. under Gilot, Marcelin)
Guillot, Olivier	Private	7 Reg't. (Le Beuf's), La. Militia
Guillot, Simon	2 Lieutenant	7 Reg't. (Le Beuf's), La. Militia
Guillot, Vabien	Private	7 Reg't. (Le Beuf's), La. Militia
Guillotte, P. A.	Sergeant	Capt. Chauveau's Co., Cavalry, La. Militia
Guims, Bill	Private	3 Reg't. (de la Ronde's), La. Mil.
Guims, Thomas	Private	3 Reg't. (de la Ronde's), La. Mil.
Guin, William	Private	De Clouet's Reg't., La. Militia
Guinard, Nicolas	Private	3 Reg't. (de la Ronde's), La. Mil.
Guindon, Auguste	Private	Plauche's Batt'n., La. Militia

Name	Rank	Unit
Guines, Thomas	Private	3 Reg't. (de la Ronde's), La. Mil. (Orig. under Guims, Thomas)
Guiosa, Ferdinand	Private	16 Reg't. (Thompson's), La. Mil.
Guipson, Isaac	Private	6 Reg't. (Meriam's), La. Militia
Guire, John B.	Private	2 Batt'n. (Peire's), La. Vols. (Orig. under Guiare, John Baptiste)
Guiroye, Pierre	Private	Captain Lagan's Co., La. Vols.
Guispon, William	Private	8 Reg't. (Meriam's), La. Militia
Guiter, Charles	Private	De Clouet's Reg't., La. Militia (Orig. under Guitier, Charles)
Guitros, Ciprian	Private	Captain Hubbard's Mounted Co., La. Militia
Guitros, Etienne	Private	Captain Hubbard's Mounted Co., La. Militia
Gullaumes, Joseph	Private	1 Batt'n. (Fortier's), La. Militia (Orig. under Gullaurre, Joseph)
Gullaurre, Joseph	Private	1 Batt'n. (Fortier's), La. Militia
Gurdry, Pierre	Sergeant	De Clouet's Reg't., La. Militia (Orig. under Guedry, Pierre)
Gurin, Francois	1 Lieutenant	6 Reg't. (Landry's), La. Militia (Orig. under Guerin, Francois)
Gusliot, Jeaques	Private	Captain Lagan's Co., La. Vols. (Orig. under Gosliot, Jacque)
Gussy, Manuel	Private	Captain Lagan's Co., La. Vols.
Gustave, --	Corporal	2 Batt'n. (D'Aquin's), La. Militia
Gustave, Barthlemi	Servant	2 Batt'n. (D'Aquin's), La. Militia
Guthrin, Joseph	Private	17, 18 and 19 Cons. Reg't., La. Militia
Guthrir, Joseph	Private	17, 18 and 19 Cons. Reg't., La. Mil. (Orig. under Guthrin, Joseph)
Gutierez, Bernardo	Private	3 Reg't. (de la Ronde's), La. Mil.
Gutierez, Jean	Private	3 Reg't. (de la Ronde's), La. Mil.
Gutierres, Mara	Private	17, 18 and 19 Cons. Reg't., La. Militia
Gutney, Henry	Private	17, 18 and 19 Cons. Reg't., La. Militia
Guydrey, Philemon	Private	De Clouet's Reg't., La. Militia (Orig. under Guidry, Philemon)
Guydrey, Piere	Private	De Clouet's Reg't., La. Militia (Orig. under Guidry, Pierre)
Gwin, James	Corporal	12 and 13 Cons. Reg't., La. Mil.
Hace, John	Private	Captain Ramsey's Co., Mounted Riflemen, La. Militia
Hacha, John Bte	Private	De Clouet's Reg't., La. Militia
Hacker, --	Corporal	Plauche's Batt'n., La. Militia (Orig. under Haker, --)
Haden, Allen	Private	12 and 13 Cons. Reg't., La. Mil.
Haden, Elisha	Private	12 and 13 Cons. Reg't., La. Mil.
Hadlock, James	Corporal	Capt. Callaway's Co., Mounted Riflemen, La. Militia
Hagan, John	Private	Plauche's Batt'n., La. Militia
Hagewood, Josiah	Private	La. War of 1812 - See also 1 Batt'n. (Henry's), U.S. Vols. - Ref. Card
Haggerty, John	Corporal	10 and 20 Cons. Reg't., La. Mil.
Haggetty, John	Corporal	10 and 20 Cons. Reg't., La. Mil. (Orig. under Haggerty, John)
Haidel, Joseph	Corporal	5 Reg't. (La Branche's), La. Mil.
Haiflegh, Jacob	1 Lieutenant	De Clouet's Reg't., La. Militia (Orig. under Haifleigh, Jacob)
Haifleigh, Jacob	1 Lieutenant	De Clouet's Reg't., La. Militia
Haifley, Jacob	1 Lieutenant	De Clouet's Reg't., La. Militia (Orig. under Haifleigh, Jacob)
Hail, Thomas	Private	Captain Young's Co., Mounted Riflemen, La. Militia
Haimel, George	Fusilier-Private	5 Reg't. (La Branche's), La. Mil.
Haimel, Pierre father	Fus.-Pri.	5 Reg't. (La Branche's), La. Mil.
Haines, John	Private	4 Reg't. (Morgan's), La. Militia
Haines, Henry	Private	17, 18 and 19 Cons. Reg't., La. Militia
Haise, James	Private	De Clouet's Reg't., La. Militia
Haker, --	Corporal	Plauche's Batt'n., La. Militia
Hale, Joel	Private	De Clouet's Reg't., La. Militia
Hale, Joel W.	Private	16 Reg't. (Thompson's), La. Mil.
Hall, Braxton	Private	17, 18 and 19 Cons. Reg't., La. Militia
Hall, Britton	Private	De Clouet's Reg't., La. Militia
Hall, Hiram	Private	Capt. Ashley's Co., Mounted Riflemen, La. Militia
Hall, Instant	Sergeant	10 and 20 Cons. Reg't., La. Mil.
Hall, James	Private	De Clouet's Reg't., La. Militia
Hall, James	Private	12 and 13 Cons. Reg't., La. Mil.
Hall, Jeremiah	Private	8 Reg't. (Meriam's), La. Militia
Hall, Joel	Private	De Clouet's Reg't., La. Militia (Orig. under Hale, Joel)
Hall, John	Private	De Clouet's Reg't., La. Militia
Hall, John	Private	10 and 20 Cons. Reg't., La. Mil.
Hall, John W.	Private	17, 18 and 19 Cons. Reg't., La. Militia
Hall, Joseph	Private	De Clouet's Reg't., La. Militia
Hall, Warren D. C.	Corporal	17, 18 and 19 Cons. Reg't., La. Militia
Hall, William S.	Private	17, 18 and 19 Cons. Reg't., La. Militia
Hall, Willis	Private	10 and 20 Cons. Reg't., La. Mil.
Halleo, Jean	Private	Plauche's Batt'n., La. Militia (Orig. under Haller, Jean)
Haller, Jean	Private	Plauche's Batt'n., La. Militia
Hallom, James	Private	10 and 20 Cons. Reg't., La. Mil.
Halphen, --	Surg. Mate	1 Batt'n. (Fortier's), La. Militia
Hambleton, Arthur	Private	12 and 13 Cons. Reg't., La. Mil.
Hamelton, John	Private	10 and 20 Cons. Reg't., La. Mil.
Hamilton, Bmy	Private	8 Reg't. (Meriam's), La. Militia
Hamilton, David	Private	La. War of 1812 - See also 1 Batt'n. (Henry's), U.S. Vols. - Ref. Card
Hamilton, Henry	Private	12 and 13 Cons. Reg't., La. Mil.
Hamilton, James	Private	De Clouet's Reg't., La. Militia
Hamilton, J. D.	Private	8 Reg't. (Meriam's), La. Militia
Hamilton, John	Private	10 and 20 Cons. Reg't., La. Mil. (Orig. under Hamelton, John)
Hamilton, Samuel	Private	16 Reg't. (Thompson's), La. Mil.
Hammelton, John	Private	Captain Beale's Co., Riflemen, La. Militia
Hammer, Thomas	Private	Captain Griffith's Co., Mounted Riflemen, La. Vols.
Hammonds, Joshua	Private-Cpl.	De Clouet's Reg't., La. Militia (Orig. under Hammons, Joshua)
Hammond, Joshua	Private-Cpl.	De Clouet's Reg't., La. Militia (Orig. under Hammons, Joshua)
Hammons, Joshua	Private-Cpl.	De Clouet's Reg't., La. Militia
Hampsher, Jacob	Private	Baker's Regiment, La. Militia
Hanbey, John	Private	Capt. Allen's Co., Artillerists, La. Vols. (Orig. under Hanby, John)
Hanby, John	Private	Capt. Allen's Co., Artillerists, La. Vols.
Hanchet, Joseph L.	Private	16 Reg't. (Thompson's), La. Mil.
Hanchett, Seth	Private	16 Reg't. (Thompson's), La. Mil.
Hanchette, Cesar	2 Lieutenant	16 Reg't. (Thompson's), La. Mil.
Hancock, Moses	Private	De Clouet's Reg't., La. Militia (Orig. under Hancox, Moses)
Hancocks, Moses	Private	De Clouet's Reg't., La. Militia (Orig. under Hancox, Moses)
Hancox, Moses	Private	De Clouet's Reg't., La. Militia
Handry, Alexcis	Private	1 Batt'n. (Fortier's), La. Militia (Orig. under Andry, Alexcis)
Haner, Andre	Private	2 Batt'n. (Peire's), La. Vols. (Orig. under Hanner, Andre)
Hanley, John	Private	Capt. Allen's Co., Artillerists, La. Vols. (Orig. under Hanby, John)
Hanlon, John	Private	1 Reg't. (Dejan's), La. Militia
Hanna, William T.	Private	10 and 20 Cons. Reg't., La. Mil. (Orig. under Hannah, William T)
Hannah, William T.	Private	10 and 20 Cons. Reg't., La. Mil.
Hanner, Andre	Private	2 Batt'n. (Peire's), La. Vols.
Haquet, Jacques	Private	8 Reg't. (Meriam's), La. Militia
Harand, --	Captain	4 Reg't. (Morgan's), La. Militia (Orig. under Harang, A. L.)
Harang, Jr.	Private	4 Reg't. (Morgan's), La. Militia
Harang, A. L.	Captain	4 Reg't. (Morgan's), La. Militia
Harbaur, Pleasant	Corporal	10 and 20 Cons. Reg't., La. Mil.
Harbeau, Pierre	Sergeant	2 Batt'n. (Peire's), La. Vols.
Harbour, John	Private	10 and 20 Cons. Reg't., La. Mil.
Harbour, Pleasant	Corporal	10 and 20 Cons. Reg't., La. Mil. (Orig. under Harbaur, Pleasant)
Harbourg, John	Private	10 and 20 Cons. Reg't., La. Mil. (Orig. under Harbour, John)
Harbourg, Pleasant	Corporal	10 and 20 Cons. Reg't., La. Mil. (Orig. under Harbour, Pleasant)
Hardey, Thomas S.	2 Lieutenant	16 Reg't. (Thompson's), La. Mil. (Orig. under Hardy, Sybert)

Name	Rank	Unit
Hardie, George	Private	16 Reg't. (Thompson's), La. Mil.
Hardin, Joseph	Private	Captain Hughes' Co., Mounted Riflemen, La. Militia
Harding, I.	Private	4 Reg't. (Morgan's), La. Militia
Harding, Jeremiah	Private	Capt. Wallace's Co., Boatmen, La. Vols.
Hardy, Clarke	Private	Baker's Regiment, La. Militia
Hardy, Francs	Private	2 Batt'n. (D'Aquin's), La. Militia
Hardy, Jacques	Private	1 Batt'n. (Fortier's), La. Militia (Orig. under Ardy, Jacques)
Hardy, Sybert	2 Lieutenant	16 Reg't. (Thompson's), La. Mil.
Hargrove, Darias	Private	De Clouet's Reg't., La. Militia
Hargrove, Darius	Private	16 Reg't. (Thompson's), La. Mil.
Hargrove, James	Private	Baker's Regiment, La. Militia
Hargrove, William	Private	Baker's Regiment, La. Militia
Hargrove, William	Private	17, 18 and 19 Cons. Reg't., La. Militia
Harington, Thomas	Private	Baker's Regiment, La. Militia (Orig. under Harrington, Thomas)
Harison, Lewis	Sergeant	De Clouet's Reg't., La. Militia (Orig. under Harrison, Lewis)
Harison, William	Private	De Clouet's Reg't., La. Militia (Orig. under Harrison, William)
Harkrider, Henry	Private	Baker's Regiment, La. Militia
Harkrider, Michael	Private	Baker's Regiment, La. Militia
Harkrider, William	Private	16 Reg't. (Thompson's), La. Mil.
Harman, Abraham	Private	16 Reg't. (Thompson's), La. Mil. (Orig. under Harman, Abram)
Harman, Abram	Private	16 Reg't. (Thompson's), La. Mil.
Harman, John	Private	Baker's Regiment, La. Militia
Harnandez, Joseph	1 Lieutenant	8 Reg't. (Meriam's), La. Militia (Orig. under Hernandez, Joseph)
Harness, Jacob	Private	Captain Rankin's Co., Mounted Riflemen, La. Militia
Harns, John	Private	De Clouet's Reg't., La. Militia (Orig. under Horner, John)
Harper, William	Private	8 Reg't. (Meriam's), La. Militia
Harque, Emille	Private	2 Reg't. (Cavelier's), La. Militia (Orig. under Kergue, Emille)
Harrel, Elisha	1 Lieutenant	12 and 13 Cons. Reg't., La. Mil.
Harrell, Hezekiah	Private	Captain Griffith's Co., Mounted Riflemen, La. Vols.
Harrell, Levi	Private	Captain Griffith's Co., Mounted Riflemen, La. Vols.
Harrell, Jacob	Private	Captain Griffith's Co., Mounted Riflemen, La. Vols.
Harrell, James	Private	Captain Griffith's Co., Mounted Riflemen, La. Vols.
Harrell, Lewis	Private	Captain Griffith's Co., Mounted Riflemen, La. Vols.
Harrell, Moses	Private	12 and 13 Cons. Reg't., La. Mil. (Orig. under Harroll, Moses)
Harrell, Samuel	Private	Captain Griffith's Co., Mounted Riflemen, La. Vols.
Harrington, Thomas	Private	Baker's Regiment, La. Militia
Harrington, William	Private	Baker's Regiment, La. Militia
Harris, --	Private	3 Reg't. (de la Ronde's), La. Mil.
Harris, Barnebes	1 Lieutenant	Captain Musick's Co., La. Mil.
Harris, Edmund	Corporal	Captain Riffith's Co., Mounted Riflemen, La. Vols.
Harris, Edoward	Private	Capt. Alpuente's Co., La. Mil.
Harris, Enoch	Private	16 Reg't. (Thompson's), La. Mil.
Harris, Garrot	Private	10 and 20 Cons. Reg't., La. Mil.
Harris, James	Captain	12 and 13 Cons. Reg't., La. Mil.
Harris, Samuel	Private	Captain Musick's Co., Mounted Riflemen, La. Militia
Harris, Thomas	Private	De Clouet's Reg't., La. Militia
Harris, Thomas	Private	16 Reg't. (Thompson's), La. Mil.
Harris, William	Private	Baker's Regiment, La. Militia
Harris, William	Private	Captain Dodge's Co., Mounted Riflemen, La. Militia
Harris, William	Private	Captain Henry's Co., Mounted Riflemen, La. Militia
Harris, William	2 Lieutenant	17, 18 and 19 Cons. Reg't., La. Militia
Harris, William B.	Private	Captain Price's Co., La. Militia
Harrison, H.	Q.M.-Sergeant	6 Reg't. (Landry's), La. Militia
Harrison, Lawrence	Private	Capt. Ashley's Co., Mounted Riflemen, La. Militia
Harrison, Lewis	Sergeant	De Clouet's Reg't., La. Militia
Harrison, William	Private	Capt. Allen's Co., Artillerists, La. Vols.
Harrison, William	Ensign	Capt. Ashley's Co., Mounted Riflemen, La. Militia
Harrison, William	Private	De Clouet's Reg't., La. Militia
Harrison, William C.	Private	17, 18 and 19 Cons. Reg't., La. Militia
Harriss, Joseph	Private	Captain Rankin's Co., Mounted Riflemen, La. Militia
Harriss, Joseph A.	Private	De Clouet's Reg't., La. Militia
Harroll, Moses	Private	12 and 13 Cons. Reg't., La. Mil.
Harry, --	Servant	Gov. Claiborne and Staff, La. Mil.
Harry, --	Servant	De Clouet's Reg't., La. Militia
Harry, --	Servant	Detachment Field and Staff Officers, 4 Brigade, La. Militia
Harry, Jacob	Private	De Clouet's Reg't., La. Militia
Hart, Hethcoat M.	Private	10 and 20 Cons. Reg't., La. Mil.
Hart, Jacob	Private	Plauche's Batt'n., La. Militia
Hart, Joseph	Private	2 Reg't. (Cavelier's), La. Militia
Hartgrove, Jesse	Private	Capt. Ashley's Co., Mounted Riflemen, La. Militia
Hartley, William	Private	19 Regiment, La. Militia
Hartman, Conrad	Private	Baker's Regiment, La. Militia
Hartmen, Jacob	Private	Baker's Regiment, La. Militia
Harvey, Blassengame W.	Private	10 and 20 Cons. Reg't., La. Mil.
Harvey, James	Private	12 and 13 Cons. Reg't., La. Mil.
Harvey, John	Corporal	10 and 20 Cons. Reg't., La. Mil.
Haslett, William	2 Lieutenant	16 Reg't. (Thompson's), La. Mil.
Hastler, Jonas	Private	La. War of 1812
Haszeur, Ls	Sen.-Musician	1 Batt'n. (Fortier's), La. Militia (Orig. under Hazeur, Ls)
Hatch, David	Captain	8 Reg't. (Meriam's), La. Militia
Hatch, David C.	Captain	8 Reg't. (Meriam's), La. Militia (Orig. under Hatch, David)
Hatch, Sylvanus	Private	10 and 20 Cons. Reg't., La. Mil.
Hatchel, William	Private	10 and 20 Cons. Reg't., La. Mil.
Hatcher, Samuel	Private	De Clouet's Reg't., La. Militia
Hatcherway, Ciruz	Private	De Clouet's Reg't., La. Militia (Orig. under Hathaway, Cyrus)
Hatchings, David	Sergeant	4 Reg't. (Morgan's), La. Militia
Hathaway, Cyrus	Private	De Clouet's Reg't., La. Militia
Hatherway, Cyrus	Private	De Clouet's Reg't., La. Militia (Orig. under Hathaway, Cyrus)
Hathorn, Robert	Private	17, 18 and 19 Cons. Reg't., La. Militia
Hathorn, William	Captain	16 Reg't. (Thompson's), La. Mil.
Hatkison, Isaac	Private	6 Reg't. (Landry's), La. Militia
Hatten, Peter D.	Private	De Clouet's Reg't., La. Militia (Orig. under Hatton, Peter D.)
Hatton, Peter D.	Private	De Clouet's Reg't., La. Militia
Haubar, --	Private	2 Batt'n. (D'Aquin's), La. Militia
Hause, James	Private	De Clouet's Reg't., La. Militia (Orig. under House, James)
Haute, F.	Private	8 Reg't. (Meriam's), La. Militia (Orig. under Haute, T.)
Haute, T.	Private	8 Reg't. (Meriam's), La. Militia
Havens, James	Private	Capt. Allen's Co., Artillerists, La. Vols.
Havens, James	Private	2 Batt'n. (Peire's), La. Vols.
Havens, Thomas	Private	Capt. Thomas' Co., La. Mil.
Hawkins, Henry	Private	10 and 20 Cons. Reg't., La. Mil.
Hawn, Peter	Private	Captain Young's Co., Mounted Riflemen, La. Militia
Hay, John	Private	De Clouet's Reg't., La. Militia
Haydel, George	2 Lieutenant	5 Reg't. (La Branche's), La. Mil. (Orig. under Haydel, In)
Haydel, In	2 Lieutenant	5 Reg't. (La Branche's), La. Mil.
Haydel, J. J.	Captain	5 Reg't. (La Branche's), La. Mil.
Haydel, Joseph	Corporal	5 Reg't. (La Branche's), La. Mil. (Orig. under Haidel, Joseph)
Haydel, Marcelin	Private	5 Reg't. (La Branche's), La. Mil.
Haydel, Ursin	Private	5 Reg't. (La Branche's), La. Mil.
Haydon, Elisha	Private	12 and 13 Cons. Reg't., La. Mil. (Orig. under Haden, Elisha)
Hayes, John	Private	Baker's Regiment, La. Militia
Hayes, Michel	Private	Baker's Regiment, La. Militia
Haynes, D.	Private	Captain Sprigg's Co., Boatmen, La. Vols.
Haynes, Joseph	Private	Capt. Callaway's Co., Cavalry, La. Militia
Hayrold, Frans	2 Lieutenant	5 Reg't. (La Branche's), La. Mil.
Hays, David	Private	Baker's Regiment, La. Militia
Hayse, James	Private	16 Reg't. (Thompson's), La. Mil.

Name	Rank	Unit
Hays, James	Corporal	17, 18 and 19 Cons. Reg't., La. Mil. (Orig. under Says, James)
Hays, John	Private	12 and 13 Cons. Reg't., La. Mil.
Hays, Nicholas	Sergeant	Captain Hughes' Co., Mounted Riflemen, La. Militia
Hays, William	Corporal	Plauche's Batt'n., La. Militia
Hays, William	Private	16 Reg't. (Thompson's), La. Mil.
Hays, William	Private	17, 18 and 19 Cons. Reg't., La. Militia
Hayse, John	Private	16 Reg't. (Thompson's), La. Mil.
Hazeur, Ls	Sen.-Musician	1 Batt'n. (Fortier's), La. Militia
Head, Anthony	Private	Capt. Van Bibber's Co., La. Mil.
Headen, Allen	Private	12 and 13 Cons. Reg't., La. Mil. (Orig. under Haden, Allen)
Headen, William	Private	17, 18 and 19 Cons. Reg't., La. Militia
Heap, John	Private	10 and 20 Cons. Reg't., La. Mil.
Heart, John	Private	17, 18 and 19 Cons. Reg't., La. Militia
Heartly, William	Private	19 Reg't., La. Vols. (Orig. under Hartley, William)
Heastley, Adam	Private	10 and 20 Cons. Reg't., La. Mil.
Heastley, Daniel	Private	10 and 20 Cons. Reg't., La. Mil.
Heastly, Adam	Private	10 and 20 Cons. Reg't., La. Mil.
Hebbrent, Chrystien	Private	De Clouet's Reg't., La. Militia
Hebert, A.	Private	8 Reg't. (Meriam's), La. Militia
Hebert, A.	Private	8 Reg't. (Meriam's), La. Militia
Hebert, Abraham	Private	8 Reg't. (Meriam's), La. Militia
Hebert, Alexander	Private	8 Reg't. (Meriam's), La. Militia
Hebert, Alexandre	Private	7 Reg't. (Le Beuf's), La. Militia
Hebert, Alexis	1 Sergeant-Sgt.	7 Reg't. (Le Beuf's), La. Militia
Hebert, Ambroise	Private	7 Reg't. (Le Beuf's), La. Militia
Hebert, Andre	Private	3 Reg't. (de la Ronde's), La. Mil.
Hebert, Auguste Jr.	Private	De Clouet's Reg't., La. Militia (Orig. under Herbert, August Jr.)
Hebert, Bon	Musician	2 Batt'n. (Peire's), La. Vols.
Hebert, Charles	Private	De Clouet's Reg't., La. Militia
Hebert, Charles	Private	De Clouet's Reg't., La. Militia
Hebert, Charles	Private	8 Reg't. (Meriam's), La. Militia
Hebert, Charles	Private	8 Reg't. (Meriam's), La. Militia
Hebert, Cromas	Private	7 Reg't. (Le Beuf's), La. Militia
Hebert, Dominique	Private	8 Reg't. (Meriam's), La. Militia
Hebert, Elie	Private	8 Reg't. (Meriam's), La. Militia
Hebert, Elie	Private	8 Reg't. (Meriam's), La. Militia
Hebert, Eloi	Corporal	8 Reg't. (Meriam's), La. Militia
Hebert, Francis	Private	De Clouet's Reg't., La. Militia
Hebert, Francis	Private	De Clouet's Reg't., La. Militia
Hebert, Francois	Private	Baker's Reg't., La. Militia
Hebert, Francois	Private	16 Reg't. (Thompson's), La. Mil.
Hebert, Gabriel	Private	8 Reg't. (Meriam's), La. Militia
Hebert, Jacques	Private	8 Reg't. (Meriam's), La. Militia
Hebert, J. Bte	Private	7 Reg't. (Le Beuf's), La. Militia (Orig. under Hebert, John B.)
Hebert, Jean Baptiste	Private	Captain Hubbard's Mounted Co., La. Militia
Hebert, Jean Bte	Private	8 Reg't. (Meriam's), La. Militia
Hebert, Jean Bte	Private	8 Reg't. (Meriam's), La. Militia
Hebert, John B.	Private	7 Reg't. (Le Beuf's), La. Militia
Hebert, Joisin	1 Lieutenant	16 Reg't. (Thompson's), La. Mil.
Hebert, Joseph	Corporal	8 Reg't. (Meriam's), La. Militia
Hebert, Joseph	Private	8 Reg't. (Meriam's), La. Militia
Hebert, Joseph	Private	16 Reg't. (Thompson's), La. Mil.
Hebert, Louis	Corporal	7 Reg't. (Le Beuf's), La. Militia
Hebert, Michel	Private	8 Reg't. (Meriam's), La. Militia
Hebert, Narcisse	Private	8 Reg't. (Meriam's), La. Militia
Hebert, Paul	Private	6 Reg't. (Landry's), La. Militia
Hebert, Paul	Private	8 Reg't. (Meriam's), La. Militia
Hebert, Paul	Private	8 Reg't. (Meriam's), La. Militia
Hebert, Paul	Private	8 Reg't. (Meriam's), La. Militia
Hebert, Pierre	Private	16 Reg't. (Thompson's), La. Mil.
Hebert, Placide	Private	De Clouet's Reg't., La. Militia
Hebert, Thimoli	Private	7 Reg't. (Le Beuf's), La. Militia
Hebert, Thomas fils	Private	8 Reg't. (Meriam's), La. Militia
Hebert, Thomas pere	Private	8 Reg't. (Meriam's), La. Militia
Hebert, V.	Private	8 Reg't. (Meriam's), La. Militia
Hebert, V.	Private	8 Reg't. (Meriam's), La. Militia
Hebert, Valerie	2 Lieutenant	8 Reg't. (Meriam's), La. Militia
Hebert, Valmond	Private	De Clouet's Reg't., La. Militia
Hebrard, Anthony	Captain	4 Reg't. (Morgan's), La. Militia
Heckle, Joseph	Private	6 Reg't. (Landry's), La. Militia
Hector, --	Servant	1 Reg't. (Dejan's), La. Militia
Hedler, Henry	Fuslier-Private	5 Reg't. (La Branche's), La. Mil.
Heidle, George	Private	16 Reg't. (Thompson's), La. Mil. (Orig. under Heydell, George)
Heifleigh, Jacob	1 Lieutenant	De Clouet's Reg't., La. Militia (Orig. under Haifleigh, Jacob)
Helen, Robert	Private	10 and 20 Cons. Reg't., La. Mil.
Helene, Louis	Sergeant	De Clouet's Reg't., La. Militia
Helene, Robert	Private	10 and 20 Cons. Reg't., La. Mil. (Orig. under Helen, Robert)
Helf, Jacques	Fusilier-Private	5 Reg't. (La Branche), La. Mil.
Hellisberg, --	Private	Capt. Chauveau's Co., Cavalry, La. Militia
Hellisburg, --	Private	Capt. Chauveau's Co., Cavalry, La. Militia (Orig. under Hellisberg, --)
Helterbran, Benjamin	Private	Captain Musick's Co., La. Mil.
Helterbrand, Benjamin	Private	Captain Musick's Co., La. Mil. (Orig. under Helterbran, Benjamin)
Helterbrand, Christian T.	Private	Captain Musick's Co., La. Mil.
Hemenes, Joachin	Private	17, 18 and 19 Cons. Reg't., La. Mil. (Orig. under Xemer, Joachim)
Hemmerson, Thomas I.	Private	Captain Beale's Co., Riflemen, La. Militia
Hempson, James	Private	De Clouet's Reg't., La. Militia (See also 44 U. S. Inf.)
Hempstead, Stephen	Private	Captain McNair's Co., Mounted Riflemen, La. Militia
Hemson, James	Private	De Clouet's Reg't., La. Militia (Orig. under Hempson, James)
Henaud, --	Private	1 Reg't. (Dejan's), La. Militia
Henaut, P.	Private	2 Reg't. (Cavelier's), La. Militia
Hencox, Moses	Private	De Clouet's Reg't., La. Militia (Orig. under Hancox, Moses)
Henderson, Charles L.	Private	4 Reg't. (Morgan's), La. Militia
Henderson, John	1 Lieutenant	Capt. Wallace's Co., Boatmen, La. Militia
Henderson, John	Private	17, 18 and 19 Cons. Reg't., La. Militia
Henderson, Joseph	Private	8 Reg't. (Meriam's), La. Militia
Henderson, Samuel	Private	Captain Hughes' Co., Mounted Riflemen, La. Militia
Henderson, Stephen	Private	1 Reg't. (Dejan's), La. Militia
Henderson, Valenin	Private	8 Reg't. (Meriam's), La. Militia
Henderson, William	2 Lieutenant	1 Reg't. (Dejan's), La. Militia
Hendisson, Vincent	Corporal	Captain Lagan's Co., La. Vols. (Orig. under Herdisson, Vincent)
Hendrickson, Richard	Private	Captain Rankin's Co., Mounted Riflemen, La. Militia
Henepel, --	Servant	4 Reg't. (Morgan's), La. Militia
Henly, Daniel	Private	10 and 20 Cons. Reg't., La. Mil. (Orig. under Heastley, Daniel)
Hennen, Alfred	Corporal	Capt. Oden's Co., Dragoons, La. Militia
Henner, Alfred	Corporal	Capt. Oden's Co., Dragoons, La. Mil. (Orig. under Hennen, Alfred)
Henning, James	Surgeon	Detachment Field and Staff Officers, 4 Brigade, La. Militia
Heno, --	Private	Plauche's Batt'n., La. Militia
Heno, I. B.	Sergeant	2 Reg't. (Cavelier's), La. Militia
Heno, J. B.	Private	Plauche's Batt'n., La. Militia
Heno, Joseph	Private	2 Batt'n. (Peire's), La. Vols.
Heno, P.	Private	1 Reg't. (Dejan's), La. Militia (Orig. under Henaud, --)
Heno, V.	Private	2 Reg't. (Cavelier's), La. Militia
Henris, Edward	Private	Capt. Alpuente's Co., La. Militia (Orig. under Harris, Edoward)
Henry, --	Servant	Gov. Claiborne and Staff, La. Mil.
Henry, --	Waiter-Servant	2 Reg't. (Cavelier's), La. Militia
Henry, --	Private	12 and 13 Cons. Reg't., La. Mil.
Henry, Andrew	Private	Captain Dodge's Co., Mounted Riflemen, La. Militia
Henry, Andrew	Captain	Captain Henry's Co., Mounted Riflemen, La. Militia
Henry, Chery	Corporal	2 Batt'n. (D'Aquin's), La. Militia
Henry, Ciery	Private	De Clouet's Reg't., La. Militia
Henry, Cotton	Private	4 Reg't. (Morgan's), La. Militia
Henry, Desire	Private	Plauche's Batt'n., La. Militia
Henry, Guillaume	Private	2 Batt'n. (D'Aquin's), La. Militia
Henry, Henry	Private	De Clouet's Reg't., La. Militia
Henry, James	Private	1 Reg't. (Dejan's), La. Militia

Name	Rank	Unit
Henry, Jean Baptiste	Private	De Clouet's Reg't., La. Militia (Orig. under Henry, John Baptiste)
Henry, John	Private	17, 18 and 19 Cons. Reg't., La. Militia
Henry, John Baptiste	Private	De Clouet's Reg't., La. Militia
Henry, Joseph	Private	1 Batt'n. (Fortier's), La. Militia
Henry, Joseph	Private	5 Reg't. (La Branche's), La. Mil.
Henry, Louis	Private	2 Batt'n. (D'Aquin's), La. Militia
Henry, N.	Private	4 Reg't. (Morgan's), La. Militia
Hensley, Willis	Private	Capt. Callaway's Co., Cavalry, La. Militia
Hensley, Willis	Private	Captain McNair's Co., Mounted Riflemen, La. Militia
Henson, Philip	Private	Capt. Ashley's Co., Mounted Riflemen, La. Militia
Heranandes, Jouachn	Private	17, 18 and 19 Cons. Reg't., La. Mil. (Orig. under Hernande, Joucharn)
Herbert, August Jr.	Private	De Clouet's Reg't., La. Militia
Herbert, Augustus	Private	De Clouet's Reg't., La. Militia (Orig. under Hubert, Augustus)
Herbert, Bte	Private	8 Reg't. (Meriam's), La. Militia
Herbert, E.	Private	8 Reg't. (Meriam's), La. Militia
Herbert, Francis	Private	De Clouet's Reg't., La. Militia (Orig. under Hebert, Francis)
Herbert, Francis	Private	De Clouet's Reg't., La. Militia (Orig. under Hebert, Francis)
Herbert, G.	Private	8 Reg't. (Meriam's), La. Militia
Herbert, John Bte	Private	De Clouet's Reg't., La. Militia
Herbert, John Louis	Private	De Clouet's Reg't., La. Militia
Herbert, Julien	Private	De Clouet's Reg't., La. Militia
Herbert, Louis	Corporal	7 Reg't. (Le Beuf's), La. Militia (Orig. under Hebert, Louis)
Herbert, Pierre S.	Private	De Clouet's Reg't., La. Militia
Herbert, Thomas Jr.	Private	De Clouet's Reg't., La. Militia
Herdisson, Vincent	Corporal	Captain Lagan's Co., La. Vols.
Hereman, Samuel	Private	De Clouet's Reg't., La. Militia (Orig. under Shereman, Samuel)
Heres, M.	Private	8 Reg't. (Meriam's), La. Militia
Heris, M.	Private	8 Reg't. (Meriam's), La. Militia (Orig. under Heres, M.)
Herman, --	Private	2 Reg't. (Cavelier's), La. Militia
Hernande, Joseph	Private	11 Reg't. (Hickey's), La. Militia
Hernande, Jouoharn	Private	17, 18 and 19 Cons. Reg't., La. Militia
Hernande, Rafael	Private	17, 18 and 19 Cons. Reg't., La. Militia
Hernandes, Anthony	Private	Capt. Thomas' Co., La. Militia
Hernandez, J. A.	Private	De Clouet's Reg't., La. Militia
Hernandez, Joseph	Private	De Clouet's Reg't., La. Militia
Hernandez, Joseph	Private	Captain Hubbard's Mounted Co., La. Militia
Hernandez, Joseph	1 Lieutenant	8 Reg't. (Meriam's), La. Militia
Hernandez, Juan	Private	Captain Hubbard's Mounted Co., La. Militia
Hernandez, Pedro	Private	6 Reg't. (Landry's), La. Militia
Hernde, Rafael	Private	17, 18 and 19 Cons. Reg't., La. Mil. (Orig. under Hernande, Rafael)
Herndon, Fleetwood	1 Lieut.-Tr.Mr.	17, 18 and 19 Cons. Reg't., La. Militia (Orig. under Horndon, F.)
Herrephel, --	Servant	4 Reg't. (Morgan's), La. Militia (Orig. under Herrepel, --)
Herrera, Jean	Private	3 Reg't. (de la Ronde's), La. Mil.
Herrin, Smyth	Private	12 and 13 Cons. Reg't., La. Mil.
Herring, Larry	Private	10 and 20 Cons. Reg't., La. Mil.
Herron, Smith	Private	12 and 13 Cons. Reg't., La. Mil. (Orig. under Herrin, Smyth)
Hesard, --	Private	2 Reg't. (Cavelier's), La. Militia
Hess, William	Corporal	Captain Sprigg's Co., Boatmen, La. Vols.
Hewlet, John	Private	1 Reg't. (Dejan's), La. Militia
Hewn, Chery	Corporal	2 Batt'n. (D'Aquin's), La. Militia (Orig. under Henry, Chery)
Hewton, Richard	Private	10 and 20 Cons. Reg't., La. Mil. (Orig. under Newton, Richard)
Heydel, Ebar	Private	Capt. Thomas' Co., La. Militia
Heydell, George	Private	16 Reg't. (Thompson's), La. Mil.
Heytas, Paulin	Private	3 Reg't. (de la Ronde's), La. Mil. (Orig. under Fleytas, Paulin)
Hibard, Jean	Private	2 Batt'n. (D'Aquin's), La. Militia
Hibber, Samuel	Private	Captain McNair's Co., Mounted Riflemen, La. Mil. (Orig. under Hibbler, Samuel)
Hibber, William	Private	Captain McNair's Co., Mounted Riflemen, La. Mil. (Orig. under Hibbler, William)
Hibbler, Samuel	Private	Captain McNair's Co., Mounted Riflemen, La. Mil.
Hibbler, William	Private	Captain McNair's Co., Mounted Riflemen, La. Militia
Hicart, Joseph	Private	1 Batt'n. (Fortier's), La. Militia
Hickman, G. B.	Private	16 Reg't. (Thompson's), La. Mil.
Hickman, William	Private	12 and 13 Cons. Reg't., La. Mil.
Hickman, William	Corporal	12 and 13 Cons. Reg't., La. Mil.
Hicks, Charles R.	Captain	De Clouet's Reg't., La. Militia
Hicks, Charles R.	Captain	1 Reg't. (Dejan's), La. Militia
Hicks, Hamlin	Private	16 Reg't. (Thompson's), La. Mil. U.S. Vols. for continuation of service on Israel Hicks
Hicks, Israel	Private	Capt. Burr's Co., Mass. Vols. (See also Co. McCobb's Reg't.)
Hicks, John	Private	19 Regiment, La. Militia
Hidalgo, F.	Private	6 Reg't. (Landry's), La. Militia
Hidalgo, Joseph	Private	6 Reg't. (Landry's), La. Militia
Hiensem, Henry	Private	5 Reg't. (La Branche's), La. Mil. (Orig. under Hiensen, Henry)
Hiensem, Tn	Private	5 Reg't. (La Branche's), La. Mil. (Orig. under Hiensen, In)
Hiensen, Henry	Private	5 Reg't. (La Branche's), La. Mil.
Hiensen, In	Private	5 Reg't. (La Branche's), La. Mil.
Hiet, Seth	Private	Captain Hughes' Co., Mounted Riflemen, La. Militia
Higgenbottom, Linsley	Private	De Clouet's Reg't., La. Militia (Orig. under Higginbothem, Lindsy)
Higgiebotham, Joseph	Private	10 and 20 Cons. Reg't., La. Mil. (Orig. under Higginbotham, Joseph)
Higginbotem, Linsley	Private	De Clouet's Reg't., La. Militia (Orig. under Higginbothem, Lindsy)
Higginbotham, Jacob	Pvt.-Sgt.	10 and 20 Cons. Reg't., La. Mil.
Higginbotham, Joseph	Private	10 and 20 Cons. Reg't., La. Mil.
Higginbotham, Linsley	Private	De Clouet's Reg't., La. Militia (Orig. under Higginbothem, Lindsy)
Higginbotham, Willis	Private	10 and 20 Cons. Reg't., La. Mil.
Higginbothem, Lindsy	Private	De Clouet's Reg't., La. Militia
Higgins, James	Private	De Clouet's Reg't., La. Militia
Higgins, John	Private	De Clouet's Reg't., La. Militia
Higgins, William	Private	De Clouet's Reg't., La. Militia
High, Mitchel	Private	Baker's Regiment, La. Militia
Highland, Nicholas	Private	12 and 13 Cons. Reg't., La. Mil.
Hilgore, James	Private	17, 18 and 19 Cons. Reg't., La. Mil. (Orig. under Kilgore, James)
Hilaire, --	Servant	De Clouet's Reg't., La. Militia
Hilaire, --	Waiter	1 Division (Villere's), La. Mil.
Hill, Daniel	Private	De Clouet's Reg't., La. Militia
Hill, George	Private	17, 18 and 19 Cons. Reg't., La. Militia
Hill, Isaac	Private	1 Reg't. (Dejan's), La. Militia
Hill, John	Private	4 Reg't. (Morgan's), La. Militia
Hill, John	2 Lieutenant	17, 18 and 19 Cons. Reg't., La. Militia
Hill, William	Private	De Clouet's Reg't., La. Militia
Hill, William	Corporal	17, 18 and 19 Cons. Reg't., La. Militia
Hillen, Nath.	Private	11 Reg't. (Hickey's), La. Militia
Hillen, Robert	Private	10 and 20 Cons. Reg't., La. Mil. (Orig. under Helen, Robert)
Hillere, --	Private-Servant	4 Brigade (Flanjae's), La. Militia
Hillo, Benitto	Private	Captain Lagan's Co., La. Vols.
Hillo, Curitto	Private	Captain Lagan's Co., La. Vols.
Hilt, Charles	Private	Captain Sprigg's Co., Boatmen, La. Vols.
Himel, Alexis	Fusilier-Private	5 Reg't. (La Branche's), La. Mil.
Himel, Bastien	Fusilier-Private	5 Reg't. (La Branche's), La. Mil.
Himel, Benjamin	Private	5 Reg't. (La Branche's), La. Mil.
Himel, Cristophe	Private	5 Reg't. (La Branche's), La. Mil.
Himel, Francois	Fusilier-Private	5 Reg't. (La Branche's), La. Mil.
Himel, Pierre	Corporal	5 Reg't. (La Branche's), La. Mil.
Himel, Zenon	Fusilier-Private	5 Reg't. (La Branche's), La. Mil.

Name	Rank	Unit
Hims, Samuel	Private	De Clouet's Reg't., La. Militia (Orig. under Sims, Samuel)
Hinch, Uriah	Private	Captain Ramsey's Co., Mounted Riflemen, La. Militia
Hinggenbottem, James	Private	De Clouet's Reg't., La. Militia (Orig. under Kenner, James)
Hingle, Eugene	Private	3 Reg't. (de la Ronde's), La. Mil.
Hingle, Jques	Private	3 Reg't. (de la Ronde's), La. Mil.
Hingle, Ursin	Private	3 Reg't. (de la Ronde's), La. Mil.
Hingues, --	Private	4 Reg't. (Morgan's), La. Militia
Hinkson, Robert	Private	Capt. Ashley's Co., Mounted Riflemen, La. Militia
Hinkson, Samuel	Private	Capt. Ashley's Co., Mounted Riflemen, La. Militia
Hisquaires, Joseph	Private	Capt. Colsson's Co., Artillery, La. Vols.
Hoa, Manuel	Private	2 Reg't. (Cavelier's), La. Militia
Hoalson, Simon	Private	17, 18 and 19 Cons. Reg't., La. Militia
Hobbs, William	Private	De Clouet's Reg't., La. Militia
Hobgood, Hugh	Private	De Clouet's Reg't., La. Militia
Hodge, John	Private	Captain Sprigg's Co., Boatmen, La. Vols.
Hodgson, William	Private	8 Reg't. (Meriam's), La. Militia
Hoff, C.	Private	4 Reg't. (Morgan's), La. Militia
Hoff, I.	Private	4 Reg't. (Morgan's), La. Militia
Hoffman, P.	Private	Plauche's Batt'n., La. Militia
Hog, Peter	Sergeant	Sergeant Hog's Detachment, La. Vols.
Hogan, James	Private	10 Regiment, La. Militia
Hoge, Alexander	Private	12 and 13 Cons. Reg't., La. Mil.
Hogon, John	Corporal	Capt. Allen's Co., Artillerists, La. Vols.
Hogue, --	Private	Plauche's Batt'n., La. Militia
Holar, Mathien	Fusilier-Private	5 Reg't. (La Branche's), La. Mil. (Orig. under Hotar, Athien)
Holden, John	Private	12 and 13 Cons. Reg't., La. Mil. (Orig. under Holdin, John)
Holden, John M.	Private	12 and 13 Cons. Reg't., La. Mil.
Holden, Joseph	Private	12 and 13 Cons. Reg't., La. Mil. (Orig. under Holding, Joseph)
Holdin, John	Private	12 and 13 Cons. Reg't., La. Mil.
Holding, Joseph	Private	12 and 13 Cons. Reg't., La. Mil.
Holding, Simeon	Private	12 and 13 Cons. Reg't., La. Mil.
Holiday, Daniel	Private	Capt. Ogden's Co., Dragoons, La. Militia
Holier, Furcy	Private	16 Reg't. (Thompson's), La. Mil. (Orig. under Hollier, Furcy)
Holier, Philip	Private	16 Reg't. (Thompson's), La. Mil. (Orig. under Hollier, Philip)
Holier, Zodia	Private	16 Reg't. (Thompson's), La. Mil.
Hollander, --	Private	Plauche's Batt'n., La. Militia
Holleman, Samuel	Private	De Clouet's Reg't., La. Militia (Orig. under Holliman, Samuel)
Hollender, --	Private	1 Reg't. (Dejan's), La. Militia
Holley, Nathaniel	Private	De Clouet's Reg't., La. Militia (Orig. under Holly, Nathaniel)
Holley, Thomas	Private	De Clouet's Reg't., La. Militia
Hollier, Clement	Private	16 Reg't. (Thompson's), La. Mil.
Hollier, Furcy	Private	16 Reg't. (Thompson's), La. Mil.
Hollier, Godfroy	Private	16 Reg't. (Thompson's), La. Mil.
Hollier, Philip	Private	16 Reg't. (Thompson's), La. Mil.
Holliman, Moody	Private	10 and 20 Cons. Reg't., La. Militia
Holliman, Samuel	Private	De Clouet's Reg't., La. Militia
Hollimon, Samuel	Private	De Clouet's Reg't., La. Militia (Orig. under Holliman, Samuel)
Holloway, James	Corporal	17, 18 and 19 Cons. Reg't., La. Militia
Holloway, John	Private	17, 18 and 19 Cons. Reg't., La. Militia
Holloway, John Jr.	Private	17, 18 and 19 Cons. Reg't., La. Mil. (Orig. under Holloway, John)
Holloway, Robert	Private	12 and 13 Cons. Reg't., La. Mil.
Holly, Nathaniel	Private	De Clouet's Reg't., La. Militia
Holly, Thomas	Private	De Clouet's Reg't., La. Militia (Orig. under Holley, Thomas)
Hollyway, John	Private	17, 18 and 19 Cons. Reg't., La. Militia (Orig. under Holloway, John)
Holmes, George	Private	Capt. Burr's Co., Mass. Vols. (See Col. McCobb's Reg't., U.S.
Holmes, Isaac	Private	17, 18 and 19 Cons. Reg't., La. Mil. (Vols. for continuation of service.)
Holms, Isaac	Private	17, 18 and 19 Cons. Reg't., La. Mil. (Orig. under Holmes, Isaac)
Holms, John	Private	De Clouet's Reg't., La. Militia
Hologneir, Ls	Private	1 Batt'n. (Fortier's), La. Militia (Orig. under Lolognier, Ls)
Holt, Benjamin	Private	17, 18 and 19 Cons. Reg't., La. Militia
Holyway, John	Private	17, 18 and 19 Cons. Reg't., La. Militia (Orig. under Holloway, John)
Hommey, F.	Sergeant	8 Reg't. (Meriam's), La. Militia
Hommey, T.	Sergeant	8 Reg't. (Meriam's), La. Militia
Hondon, --	Sergeant	1 Reg't. (Dejan's), La. Militia
Honey, John William	Lieutenant	Captain Rankins' Co., Mounted Riflemen, La. Mil. (Orig. under Hony, John William)
Honore', --	Servant	Baker's Regiment, La. Militia
Honore, --	Servant	Plauche's Batt'n., La. Militia
Honore', --	Servant	3 Reg't. (de la Ronde's), La. Mil.
Honore, Isidore	2 Lieutenant	1 Batt'n. (Fortier's), La. Militia
Honore, Pierre	Private	1 Batt'n. (Fortier's), La. Militia
Honore, Pierre	Private	1 Batt'n. (Fortier's), La. Militia
Honore, Rene	Private	1 Batt'n. (Fortier's), La. Militia
Honore, Zachrie	Private	8 Reg't. (Meriam's), La. Militia
Honori, --	Servant	Gov. Claiborne and Staff, La. Mil.
Honri, --, John	Private	Baker's Regiment, La. Militia
Hony, John William	Lieutenant	Capt. Rankin's Co., Mounted Riflemen, La. Militia
Hoock, Jacob	Private	De Clouet's Reg't., La. Militia
Hoock, Samuel	Private	De Clouet's Reg't., La. Militia
Hoofman, George	Private	Capt. Van Bibber's Co., La. Mil.
Hook, Jacob	Private	De Clouet's Reg't., La. Militia (Orig. under Hoock, Jacob)
Hook, Samuel	Private	De Clouet's Reg't., La. Militia (Orig. under Hoock, Samuel)
Hooke, Jacob	Private	De Clouet's Reg't., La. Militia (Orig. under Hoock, Jacob)
Kooke, Samuel	Private	De Clouet's Reg't., La. Militia (Orig. under Hoock, Samuel)
Hooper, Amos	Corporal	12 and 13 Cons. Reg't., La. Mil.
Hooper, Thomas	Private	Captain McNair's Co., Mounted Riflemen, La. Militia
Hooper, Thomas	Private	17, 18 and 19 Cons. Reg't., La. Militia
Hooter, John	Private	17, 18 and 19 Cons. Reg't., La. Militia
Hooter, Lewis	Private	17, 18 and 19 Cons. Reg't., La. Militia
Hooter, Michael	Private	17, 18 and 19 Cons. Reg't., La. Militia
Hoover, John	Private	10 and 20 Cons. Reg't., La. Mil.
Hopkins, James	Private	Capt. Ogden's Co., Dragoons, La. Militia
Hopkins, Jonathan	Private	10 and 20 Cons. Reg't., La. Mil.
Hopkins, Stephen A.	Brig. General	2 Brigade (Hopkins'), La. Militia
Hopson, William	Private	17, 18 and 19 Cons. Reg't., La. Militia
Horensby, Elisha	Private	12 and 13 Cons. Reg't., La. Mil.
Horndon, F.	1 Lieut. & Q.M.	17, 18 and 19 Cons. Reg't., La. Militia
Horner, John	Private	De Clouet's Reg't., La. Militia
Hornsby, Elisha	Private	12 and 13 Cons. Reg't., La. Mil. (Orig. under Horensby, Elisha)
Hornsby, James	Private	12 and 13 Cons. Reg't., La. Mil.
Horsfield, William	Private	12 and 13 Cons. Reg't., La. Mil.
Hortone, Piere	Private	Capt. Van Bibber's Co., La. Mil.
Hosfield, William	Private	12 and 13 Cons. Reg't., La. Mil. (Orig. under Horsfield, William)
Hosmer, James	Sergeant	1 Reg't. (Dejan's), La. Militia
Hossel, Alexander	Private	12 and 13 Cons. Reg't., La. Mil.
Hotar, Mathieu	Fusilier-Private	5 Reg't. (La Branche's), La. Mil.
Hotar, Simon	Fusilier-Private	5 Reg't. (La Branche's), La. Mil.
Hotard, fils	Private	5 Reg't. (La Branche's), La. Mil.
Houdershelter, John	Corporal	Captain Musick's Co., La. Mil.
Houeye, John	Corporal	1 Reg't. (Dejan's), La. Militia
Houk, George	Private	Captain Young's Co., Mounted Riflemen, La. Militia
Houk, John	Private	Captain Young's Co., Mounted Riflemen, La. Militia

Name	Rank	Unit
House, David	Private	12 and 13 Cons. Reg't., La. Mil.
House, Isaac	Private	12 and 13 Cons. Reg't., La. Mil.
House, James	Private	De Clouet's Reg't., La. Militia
House, Joseph	Private	12 and 13 Cons. Reg't., La. Mil.
House, Joseph	Private	16 Reg't. (Thompson's), La. Mil.
Houser, John G.	Private	4 Reg't. (Morgan's), La. Mil.
Houssier, Cs	1 Lieutenant	Capt. Songy's Co., Marines, La. Vols.
How, --	Corporal	3 Reg't. (de la Ronde's), La. Mil.
How, Henry	Private	17, 18 and 19 Cons. Reg't., La. Mil. (Orig. under Howe, Henry)
Howard, Elijah	Private	De Clouet's Reg't., La. Militia
Howard, John	Private	10 and 20 Cons. Reg't., La. Mil.
Howard, Thomas P.	Private	Captain McNair's Co., Mounted Riflemen, La. Militia
Howe, Henry	Private	17, 18 and 19 Cons. Reg't., La. Militia
Howell, Thomas	Trumpeter	Capt. Callaway's Co., Cavalry, La. Militia
Howell, William	Private	12 and 13 Cons. Reg't., La. Mil.
Howland, Charles A.	Private	1 Reg't. (Dejan's), La. Militia
Howlet, I.	Private	1 Reg't. (Dejan's), La. Militia (Orig. under Hewlet, John)
Howlett, Thomas P.D.	Private	De Clouet's Reg't., La. Militia
Hown, Jacob	Private	Capt. Collard's Co., La. Militia
Howye, John	Corporal	1 Reg't. (Dejan's), La. Militia (Orig. under Houeye, John)
Hozen, Daniel	Private	4 Reg't. (Morgan's), La. Mil.
Hubard, Augustus	Private	De Clouet's Reg't., La. Militia (Orig. under Hubert, Augustus)
Hubard, John	Private	2 Batt'n. (Peire's), La. Vols. (Orig. under Hubbard, John)
Hubart, Augustus	Private	De Clouet's Reg't., La. Militia (Orig. under Hubert, Augustus)
Hubart, Leonerd	Private	Captain Lagan's Co., La. Vols. (Orig. under Hubert, Leonard)
Hubbard, --	Private	Plauche's Batt'n., La. Militia
Hubbard, Augustus	Private	De Clouet's Reg't., La. Militia (Orig. under Hubert, Augustus)
Hubbard, B.	Captain	Captain Hubbard's Mounted Co., La. Militia
Hubbard, John	Private	2 Batt'n. (Peire's), La. Vols.
Hubbart, Simon M.	3rd Burser	Captain Dodge's Co., Mounted Riflemen, La. Militia
Hubbart, Simon M.	Sergeant	Captain Henry's Co., Mounted Riflemen, La. Militia
Hubbel, Habod	Sergeant	Captain Young's Co., Mounted Riflemen, La. Militia
Hubeau, Leopold	Private	8 Reg't. (Meriam's), La. Militia
Hubeau, Paul	Private	8 Reg't. (Meriam's), La. Militia
Huber, Jacob	1 Lieutenant	De Clouet's Reg't., La. Militia
Hubert, Augustus	Private	De Clouet's Reg't., La. Militia
Hubert, Cyprien	Private	1 Batt'n. (Fortier's), La. Militia
Hubert, Jacob	1 Lieutenant	De Clouet's Reg't., La. Militia (Orig. under Huber, Jacob)
Hubert, Leonard	Private	Captain Lagan's Co., La. Vols.
Hudry, Jean	Captain	Plauche's Batt'n., La. Militia
Hudson, George	Private	16 Reg't. (Thompson's), La. Mil.
Hudson, Jacob	Private	De Clouet's Reg't., La. Militia
Hudson, Luke	Private-Cpl.	De Clouet's Reg't., La. Militia
Hudson, William	Sergeant	11 Reg't. (Hickey's), La. Militia
Hudspeth, John	Private	16 Reg't. (Thompson's), La. Mil.
Huet, --	Ensign-4 Lieut.	Plauche's Batt'n., La. Militia
Huet, Abraham	Corporal	2 Batt'n. (Peire's), La. Vols.
Huet, Francisk	1 Lieutenant	2 Batt'n. (Peire's), La. Vols.
Huet, Michel	Private-Sgt.	2 Batt'n. (Peire's), La. Vols.
Huett, Francis	Private	17, 18 and 19 Cons. Reg't., La. Militia
Huffman, Robert	Private	16 Reg't. (Thompson's), La. Mil.
Huffpower, Francois	Private	16 Reg't. (Thompson's), La. Mil.
Hughes, Daniel	Private	16 Reg't. (Thompson's), La. Mil.
Hughes, Henry	Private	10 and 20 Cons. Reg't., La. Mil. (Orig. under Hughs, Henry)
Hughes, Henry	Private	12 and 13 Cons. Reg't., La. Mil.
Hughes, John	Captain	Captain Hughes' Co., Mounted Riflemen, La. Militia
Hughes, John	1 Lieut.-Qr.Mr.	6 Reg't. (Landry's), La. Militia
Hughes, Thomas	Private	10 and 20 Cons. Reg't., La. Mil.
Hughes, Thomas	Private	10 and 20 Cons. Reg't., La. Mil. (Orig. under Hughs, Thomas)
Hughes, Thomas	Private	17, 18 and 19 Cons. Reg't., La. Mil. (Orig. under Hughs, Thomas)
Hughs, Henry	Private	10 and 20 Cons. Reg't., La. Mil.
Hughs, Thomas	Private	10 and 20 Cons. Reg't., La. Mil.
Hughs, Thomas	Private	10 and 20 Cons. Reg't., La. Mil. (Orig. under Hughes, Thomas)
Hughs, Thomas	Private	17, 18 and 19 Cons. Reg't., La. Militia
Hugot, C. J.	Private	Plauche's Batt'n., La. Militia
Huguet, Joseph	Private	6 Reg't. (Landry's), La. Militia
Huit, Michel	Private-Sergeant	2 Batt'n. (Peire's), La. Vols. (Orig. under Huet, Michel)
Hulan, Jean	Sergeant	Plauche's Batt'n., La. Militia
Hulent, Jean	Private	Capt. Colsson's Co., Artillery, La. Vols.
Hulick, Abram	Private	De Clouet's Reg't., La. Militia (See Also U. S. Art'y.)
Hull, I.	Sergeant	6 Reg't. (Landry's), La. Militia (Orig. under Hull, John)
Hull, James F.	Private	Captain McNair's Co., Mounted Riflemen, La. Militia
Hull, John	Private	Plauche's Batt'n., La. Militia
Hull, John	Sergeant	6 Reg't. (Landry's), La. Militia
Hull, Thomas	Private	War of 1812 - See also 1 Batt'n. (Henry's), U.S. Vols. Ref. Card
Humbert, --	Private	Plauche's Batt'n., La. Militia
Humbert, --	Private	1 Reg't. (Dejan's), La. Militia
Humble, John	Private	De Clouet's Reg't., La. Militia
Humphrais, Jonathan	Private	10 and 20 Cons. Reg't., La. Mil. (Orig. under Humphreys, Jonathan)
Humphrais, William	Private	10 and 20 Cons. Reg't., La. Mil. (Orig. under Humphreys, William)
Humphres, Jonathan	Private	10 and 20 Cons. Reg't., La. Mil. (Orig. under Humphreys, Jonathan)
Humphress, Jacob	Private	10 and 20 Cons. Reg't., La. Mil. (Orig. under Humphreys, Jacob)
Humphreys, Jacob	Private	10 and 20 Cons. Reg't., La. Mil.
Humphreys, Jacob	Private	10 and 20 Cons. Reg't., La. Mil. (Orig. under Humphrys, Jacob)
Humphreys, J. B.	Private	Capt. Trudeau's Troop of Horse, La. Militia
Humphreys, John	Private	Capt. Allen's Co., Artillerists, La. Vols.
Humphreys, Jonathan	Private	10 and 20 Cons. Reg't., La. Mil.
Humphreys, William	Private	10 and 20 Cons. Reg't., La. Mil.
Humphry's, --	Private	Capt. Trudeau's Troop of Horse, La. Mil. (Orig. under Humphrey's, J. B.)
Hungerford, Richard	Private	Baker's Regiment, La. Militia
Hunt, Edmond D.	Private	12 and 13 Cons. Reg't., La. Mil.
Hunter, John	Private	Capt. Van Bibber's Co., La. Mil.
Hurace, Richard	Private	10 and 20 Cons. Reg't., La. Mil.
Hurau, --	Private	3 Reg't. (de la Ronde's), La. Mil.
Hurles, George	Private	Capt. Colsson's Co., Artillery, La. Vols.
Hurrey, Richard	Private	10 and 20 Cons. Reg't., La. Mil.
Hurry, Richard	Private	10 and 20 Cons. Reg't., La. Mil.
Hust, John	Private	10 and 20 Cons. Reg't., La. Mil. (Orig. under Huste, John)
Huste, John	Private	10 and 20 Cons. Reg't., La. Mil.
Huston, James	Private	10 and 20 Cons. Reg't., La. Mil.
Hutcheson, William	Private	12 and 13 Cons. Reg't., La. Mil.
Hutchings, William	Private	De Clouet's Reg't., La. Militia
Hutchins, --	Private	Plauche's Batt'n., La. Militia (Col. McCobb's Reg't., - U.S. Vols. for continuation of Service 3 as shown)
Hutchinson, Joseph	Fifer	Capt. Burr's Co., Mass. Vols. (See also Col. McCobb's Reg't., U.S. Vols. for continuation of service 3 as shown)
Hutchinson, Seth	Private	Capt. Burr's Co., Mass. Vols. (See also Col. McCobb's Reg't., U.S. Vols. for continuation of Service 3 as shown)
Hutchinson, William	Sergeant	Capt. Burr's Co., Mass. Vols. (See also Col. McCobb's Reg't., U.S. Vols. for continuation of Service 3 as shown)
Hutchison, William	Private	12 and 13 Cons. Reg't., La. Mil. (Orig. under Hutcheson, William)

Name	Rank	Unit
Hyanson, Henry	Private	De Clouet's Reg't., La. Militia
Hyanson, Jean	Private	De Clouet's Reg't., La. Militia (Orig. under Hyanson, John)
Hyanson, John	Private	De Clouet's Reg't., La. Militia
Hymel, Andre	Private	6 Reg't. (Landry's), La. Militia
Hymel, Augustin	Private	6 Reg't. (Landry's), La. Militia
Hymel, Louis	Private	6 Reg't. (Landry's), La. Militia
Hymel, Ursin	Private	6 Reg't. (Landry's), La. Militia
Iaboucle, Joseph	Private	Capt. Songy's Co., Marines, La. Vols.
Iaham, --	Private	1 Reg't. (Dejan's), La. Militia
Iaves, Samuel	Private	De Clouet's Reg't., La. Militia
Iayart, N.	Private	Capt. Songy's Co., Marines, La. Vols. (Orig. under Ibare, Jean)
Ibard, Jean	Artificer	Capt. Chaudurier's Co., Artificers, Art'y., La. Vols. (Orig. under Ibare, Jean)
Ibare, Jean	Artificer	Capt. Chaudurier's Co., Artificers, Art'y., La. Vols.
Icard, Charles	Private	2 Batt'n. (Peire's), La. Vols. See also 44 Reg't.
Ictor, James	Private	10 and 20 Cons. Reg't., La. Mil.
Ictor, John	Private	10 and 20 Cons. Reg't., La. Mil.
Ictor, William	Private	10 and 20 Cons. Reg't., La. Mil.
Ieard, Charles	Private	2 Batt'n. (Peire's), La. Vols. (Orig. under Icard, Charles)
Ignasse, Gayetau	Private	De Clouet's Reg't., La. Militia
Infante, Ramon	Private	2 Batt'n. (Peire's), La. Vols.
Infante, Rumon	Private	2 Batt'n. (Peire's), La. Vols. (Orig. under Infante, Ramon)
Infanto, Ramon	Private	2 Batt'n. (Peire's), La. Vols. (Orig. under Infanto, Ramon)
Inge, H. I.	Private	8 Reg't. (Meriam's), La. Militia
Inglehard, George	Fusilier-Private	5 Reg't. (La Branche's), La. Mil.
Inks, Joseph		Capt. Collard's Co., La. Militia
Insell, Thomas	Private	Baker's Regiment, La. Militia
Ioly, Antoine	Private	Capt. Songy's Co., Marines, La. Vols.
Iriard, --	Private	Plauche's Batt'n., La. Militia (Orig. under Iriart, --)
Iriart, --	Private	Plauche's Batt'n., La. Militia
Irvin, Henry	Private	17, 18 and 19 Cons. Reg't., La. Militia
Irvin, William H.	Private	4 Reg't. (Morgan's), La. Militia
Isaac. Negro	Servant	De Clouet's Reg't., La. Militia
Isham, --	Servant	16 Reg't. (Thompson's), La. Mil.
Isidore, --	Servant	16 Reg't. (Thompson's), La. Mil.
Isnard, --	Private	2 Reg't. (Cavelier's), La. Militia
Isnard, Jean	Private	Capt. Colsson's Co., Artillery, La. Vols.
Ives, Amasa		17, 18 and 19 Cons. Reg't., La. Militia
Ives, Samuel	Private	De Clouet's Reg't., La. Militia
Ivis, Amasa	Private	17, 18 and 19 Cons. Reg't., La. Militia
Jabion, John	Sergeant	10 Reg't., La. Militia
Jack, --	Servant	Gov. Claiborne and Staff, La. Mil.
Jack, --	Servant	De Clouet's Reg't., La. Militia
Jack, --	Servant	Plauche's Batt'n., La. Militia
Jack, --	Servant	Plauche's Batt'n., La. Militia
Jack, --	Servant	17, 18 and 19 Cons. Reg't., La. Militia
Jackler, Henry	Private	11 Reg't. (Hickey's), La. Militia
Jackman, Henry	Private	Capt. Burr's Co., Mass. Vols.- See Col. McCobb's Reg't., U.S. Vols. for continuation of service
Jackman, Richard	Private	Capt. Burr's Co., Mass. Vols.- See Col. McCobb's Reg't., U.S. Vols. for continuation of service
Jackson, Ely	Private	10 and 20 Cons. Reg't., La. Mil. (Orig. Jackson, Elza)
Jackson, Elza	Private	10 and 20 Cons. Reg't., La. Mil.
Jackson, George	Private	10 and 20 Cons. Reg't., La. Mil.
Jackson, Humphry	Private	Baker's Regiment, La. Militia
Jackson, James	Private	De Clouet's Reg't., La. Militia
Jackson, John	Private	2 Batt'n. (Peire's), La. Vols.
Jackson, Reuben	Private	10 Regiment, La. Militia
Jackson, Stephen	Private	17, 18 and 19 Cons. Reg't., La. Militia
Jackson, William B.	Private	Qr. Master, Detachment Field and Staff Officers, 4 Brigade, La. Militia
Jackson, William B.	Private	16 Reg't. (Thompson's), La. Mil.
Jacob, --	Private	4 Reg't. (Morgan's), La. Militia
Jacob, Adam	Fusilier-Private	5 Reg't. (La Branche's), La. Mil.
Jacob, Adam Father	Fusilier-Priv.	5 Reg't. (La Branche's), La. Mil.
Jacob, Adam Son	Fusilier-Private	5 Reg't. (La Branche's), La. Mil.
Jacob, Christianne	Fusilier-Private	5 Reg't. (La Branche's), La. Mil.
Jacob, Michel	Fusilier-Private	5 Reg't. (La Branche's), La. Mil.
Jacob, Pierre	Fusilier-Private	5 Reg't. (La Branche's), La. Mil.
Jacob, Ursin	Captain	5 Reg't. (La Branche's), La. Mil.
Jacobs, Henry	Private	Capt. Allen's Co., Artillerists, La. Vols.
Jacque, Charles	Private	1 Batt'n. (Fortier's), La. Militia
Jacques, --	Servant	Baker's Regiment, La. Militia
Jacques, --	Servant	De Clouet's Reg't., La. Militia
Jacques, Jr.	Private	De Clouet's Reg't., La. Militia (See also 44 U.S. Inf.)
Jacques, --	Waiter	Plauche's Batt'n., La. Militia
Jacques, --	--	1 Reg't. (Dejan's), La. Militia
Jacques, --	Servant	2 Brigade (Hopkins'), La. Militia
Jacques, Charles	Private	1 Batt'n. (Fortier's), La. Militia (Orig. under Jacque, Charles)
Jaennot, Victor	Private	De Clouet's Reg't., La. Militia (Orig. under Jeannot, Victor)
Jaffion, Hipolite	Private	17, 18 and 19 Cons. Reg't., La. Mil. (Orig. under Joffeon, Hypolite)
Jaideon, Pierre	Private	2 Batt'n. (D'Aquin's), La. Militia
Jalabert, Cadet	Corporal	2 Batt'n. (D'Aquin's), La. Militia (Orig. under Talabert, Cadet)
Jallian, Julien	Private	1 Batt'n. (Fortier's), La. Militia
Jambu, --	Surg. Mate	2 Reg't. (Cavelier's), La. Militia
James, --	Servant	General and Staff (Morgan), La. Militia
James, --	Servant	2 Batt'n. (D'Aquin's), La. Militia
James, --	Servant	4 Reg't. (Morgan's), La. Militia
James, --	--	10 and 20 Cons. Reg't., La. Mil.
James, Benjamin	Private	Captain Musick's Co., La. Mil.
James, Combalan	Private	Captain Musick's Co., Mounted Riflemen, La. Militia
James, Henri A.	Fusilier-Private	5 Reg't. (La Branche's), La. Mil.
James, James	Private	Capt. Callaway's Co., Cavalry, La. Militia
James, John G.	Private	Captain Musick's Co., La. Mil.
James, Joshua	Private	Capt. Van Bibber's Co., La. Mil.
James, Louis	Private	17, 18 and 19 Cons. Reg't., La. Militia
James, Theodore I.	Corporal	7 Reg't. (Le Beuf's), La. Militia
James, Thomas	Private	19 Regiment, La. Militia
James, Tomas	Private	12 and 13 Cons. Reg't., La. Mil.
James, William	Burser	Captain Dodge's Co., Mounted Riflemen, La. Militia
James, William	Purser	Captain Henry's Co., Mounted Riflemen, La. Militia
Jamesson, William	Private	Capt. Callaway's Co., Cavalry, La. Militia
Jamont, Pierre	Artificer	Capt. Chaudurier's Co., Artificers, Art'y., La. Vols. (Orig. under Jermont, Pierre)
Janes, Francis	Private	8 Reg't. (Meriam's), La. Militia
Jannot, Etienne	Private	1 Batt'n. (Fortier's), La. Militia (Orig. under Janot, Etienne)
Janny, Alexis	Private	16 Reg't. (Thompson's), La. Mil.
Janny, Herbert	Private	16 Reg't. (Thompson's), La. Mil.
Janny, Mami	Private	16 Reg't. (Thompson's), La. Mil.
Janot, Etienne	Private	1 Batt'n. (Fortier's), La. Militia
Janot, Gabriel	Private	1 Batt'n. (Fortier's), La. Militia
Janseme, Augustin	Private	1 Batt'n. (Fortier's), La. Militia
Jansen, David	Private	Captain Musick's Co., Mounted Riflemen, La. Militia
Janson, George	Private	1 Reg't. (Dejan's), La. Militia
Janvier, --	Servant	1 Batt'n. (Fortier's), La. Militia
Jaques, --	Servant	Plauche's Batt'n., La. Militia
Jaques, --	Waiter	2 Reg't. (Cavelier's), La. Militia
Jaquet, Francois		2 Reg't. (Cavelier's), La. Militia
Jaquith, John	Private	Capt. Burr's Co., Mass. Vols. (See Col. McCobb's Reg't., U.S. Vols. for continuation of service)
Jarboe, Stephen	Private	Captain Ramsey's Co., Mounted Riflemen, La. Militia
Jarmin, Benjamin	Surgeons Aid	2 Batt'n. (D'Aquin's), La. Militia
Jarreau, John	Private	Capt. Chauveau's Co., Cavalry, La. Militia

Name	Rank	Unit
Jarves, William	Private	10 and 20 Cons. Reg't., La. Mil. (Orig. under Jarvis, William)
Jarvis, Abraham	Private	Capt. Allen's Co., Artillerists, La. Vols.
Jarvis, James	Private	10 and 20 Cons. Reg't., La. Mil.
Jarvis, John	Private	17, 18 and 19 Cons. Reg't., La. Militia
Jarvis, William	Private	10 and 20 Cons. Reg't., La. Mil.
Jasmin, --	Servant	1 Batt'n. (Fortier's), La. Militia
Jason, --	Servant	Plauche's Batt'n., La. Militia
Jason, Gabriel	Private	1 Batt'n. (Fortier's), La. Militia
Jean, --	Servant	Baker's Regiment, La. Militia
Jean, --	Private	Plauche's Batt'n., La. Militia
Jean, --	Servant	3 Reg't. (de la Ronde's), La. Mil.
Jean, Jean	Private	2 Reg't. (Cavelier's), La. Militia
Jean, Honore	Private	1 Batt'n. (Fortier's), La. Militia
Jean, Joseph M.	Private	De Clouet's Reg't., La. Militia
Jean, Joseph Maitre	Private	2 Batt'n. (Peire's), La. Vols.
Jean, Louis	Corporal	1 Batt'n. (Fortier's), La. Militia
Jean, Louis	Servant	1 Batt'n. (Fortier's), La. Militia
Jean, Louis Maitre	Private	Plauche's Batt'n., La. Militia
Jean, Pierre	Private	La. War of 1812
Jean, S.	Private	8 Reg't. (Meriam's), La. Militia
Jeangrand, Charles	Private	De Clouet's Reg't., La. Militia
Jeangrand, Francois	Private	De Clouet's Reg't., La. Militia
Jeanne, Perre	Private	De Clouet's Reg't., La. Militia (Orig. under Tanny, Pierre Trahan)
Jeannoit, Victor	Private	De Clouet's Reg't., La. Militia (Orig. under Jeannot, Victor)
Jeannot, Victor	Private	De Clouet's Reg't., La. Militia
Jeanny, Hubert	Private	16 Reg't. (Thompson's), La. Mil. (Orig. under Janny, Herbert)
Jeansonne, Augustine	Private	16 Reg't. (Thompson's), La. Militia
Jeansonne, Baptiste	Captain	16 Reg't. (Thompson's), La. Militia
Jeantilly, Sifrois	Private	1 Batt'n. (Fortier's), La. Militia
Jeanton, Coligny	Private	2 Reg't. (Cavelier's), La. Militia
Jeanton, D.	Private	2 Reg't. (Cavelier's), La. Militia
Jeard, Gustin	Private	7 Reg't. (Le Beuf's), La. Militia
Jeay, John	Sergeant	Captain Beale's Co., Riflemen, La. Militia
Jeffre, --	Servant	De Clouet's Reg't., La. Militia
Jem, --	Servant	Plauche's Batt'n., La. Militia
Jemison, John	Private	10 and 20 Cons. Reg't., La. Mil.
Jemmison, John	Private	12 and 13 Cons. Reg't., La. Mil.
Jenkins, Abner	Private	12 and 13 Cons. Reg't., La. Mil.
Jenkins, Ephraim	Private	Captain Musick's Co., La. Mil.
Jenkins, Ephraim	Private	Captain Musick's Co., Mounted Riflemen, La. Militia
Jenkins, Peter	Private	De Clouet's Reg't., La. Militia
Jenkins, Thomas	Private	De Clouet's Reg't., La. Militia
Jenkins, William	Private	6 Reg't. (Landry's), La. Militia
Jennell, Baptist	Private	12 and 13 Cons. Reg't., La. Mil.
Jeonnot, Babtiste	Private	17, 18 and 19 Cons. Reg't., La. Militia
Jerbeau, Pierre	Sergeant	7 Reg't. (Le Beuf's), La. Militia
Jercer, --	Private	2 Batt'n. (D'Aquin's), La. Militia
Jercer, Jean Baptiste	Private	2 Batt'n. (D'Aquin's), La. Militia (Orig. under Jereer, Jean Baptiste)
Jereer, Jean Baptiste	Private	2 Batt'n. (D'Aquin's), La. Militia
Jermaine, --	Private	2 Batt'n. (D'Aquin's), La. Militia
Jermont, Peter	Artificer	Capt. Chaudurier's Co., Artificers, Art'y., La. Vols. (Orig. under Jermont, Pierre)
Jermont, Pierre	Artificer	Capt. Chaudurier's Co., Artificers, Art'y., La. Vols.
Jesse, --	Servant	General and Staff (Morgan), La. Militia
Jeter, Joseph	Private	De Clouet's Reg't., La. Militia
Jeter, Sterling	Private	De Clouet's Reg't., La. Militia
Jeune, Maurette	Artificer	Capt. Chaudurier's Co., Artificers, Art'y., La. Vols.
Jeunne, Maurette	Artificer	Capt. Chaudurier's Co., Artificers, Art'y., La. Vols. (Orig. under Jeune, Maurette)
Jim, --	Servant	Detachment Field and Staff Officers, 4 Brigade, La. Militia
Jim, --	Servant	Plauche's Batt'n., La. Militia (Orig. under Jem, --)
Jim, --	Servant	17, 18 and 19 Cons. Reg't., La. Militia
Jimmison, John	Private	10 and 20 Cons. Reg't., La. Mil. (Orig. under Jemison, John)
Jinkins, Abner	Private	12 and 13 Cons. Reg't., La. Mil. (Orig. under Jenkins, Abner)
Jinkins, Ephraim	Private	Capt. Musick's Co., La. Militia (Orig. under Jenkins, Ephraim)
Jinkins, Ephraim	Private	Capt. Musick's Co., Mounted Riflemen, La. Mil. (Orig. under Jenkins, Ephraim)
Jinkins, Thomas	Private	De Clouet's Reg't., La. Militia (Orig. under Jenkins, Thomas)
Jirard, Jean	Private	1 Batt'n. (Fortier's), La. Militia (Orig. under Girard, John)
Jnard, Jn	Private	Plauche's Batt'n., La. Militia
Job, Isaac	Private	10 and 20 Cons. Reg't., La. Mil.
Jobe, Isaac	Private	10 and 20 Cons. Reg't., La. Mil. (Orig. under Job, Isaac)
Joby, Jean Marrianere	Private	2 Batt'n. (Peire's), La. Vols. (Orig. under Jolly, Jean Mariane)
Joe, --	Servant	Capt. Chauveau's Co., Cavalry, La. Militia
Joe, --	Servant	De Clouet's Reg't., La. Militia
Joe, --	Servant-Waiter	10 and 20 Cons. Reg't., La. Mil.
Joe, --	Servant	12 and 13 Cons. Reg't., La. Mil.
Joe, --	Servant	16 Reg't. (Thompson's), La. Militia
Joe, --	Servant	16 Reg't. (Thompson's), La. Mil.
Joes, --	Private	Plauche's Batt'n., La. Militia
Joffeon, Hopolite	Private	17, 18 and 19 Cons. Reg't., La. Militia
John, --	Servant	De Clouet's Reg't., La. Militia
John, --	Servant	Detachment Field and Staff Officers, 4 Brigade, La. Militia
John, --	Servant	General and Staff (Morgan), La. Militia
John, --	Servant	General and Staff (Morgan), La. Militia
John, --	Servant	Captain Griffith's Co., Mounted Riflemen, La. Vols.
John, --	Servant	1 Reg't. (Dejan's), La. Militia
John, --	Waiter	2 Reg't. (Cavelier's), La. Militia
John, --	Servant	4 Reg't. (Morgan's), La. Militia
John, --	Servant	5 Reg't. (La Branche's), La. Mil.
John, --	Private	5 Reg't. (La Branche's), La. Mil.
John (Mulatto)	Waiter	6 Reg't. (Landry's), La. Militia
John, --	Servant	12 and 13 Cons. Reg't., La. Mil.
John, --	Servant	16 Reg't. (Thompson's), La. Mil.
John, Ezra	Private	De Clouet's Reg't., La. Militia (Orig. under Johns, Ezra)
Johns, Ezra	Private	De Clouet's Reg't., La. Militia
Johnson, --	Private	8 Reg't. (Meriam's), La. Militia
Johnson, Antony	Private	Capt. Alpuente's Co., La. Militia
Johnson, Daniel	Private	Capt. Van Bibber's Co., La. Mil.
Johnson, Daniel	Private	12 and 13 Cons. Reg't., La. Mil.
Johnson, David	Private	De Clouet's Reg't., La. Militia
Johnson, David	Private	16 Reg't. (Thompson's), La. Mil.
Johnson, Edmund	Private	16 Reg't. (Thompson's), La. Mil.
Johnson, H.	Private	Capt. Ogden's Co., Dragoons, La. Militia
Johnson, Henry	2 Lieutenant	De Clouet's Reg't., La. Militia
Johnson, Hugh	Private-Corporal	De Clouet's Reg't., La. Militia
Johnson, Hugh	Corporal	7 Reg't. (Le Beuf's), La. Militia
Johnson, I.	Corporal	8 Reg't. (Meriam's), La. Militia
Johnson, Isaac	Captain	10 Regiment, La. Militia
Johnson, James	Private	Captain Hughes' Co., Mounted Riflemen, La. Militia
Johnson, James L.	Private	Baker's Regiment, La. Militia
Johnson, John	Private	De Clouet's Reg't., La. Militia
Johnson, John	Private	Captain Sprigg's Co., Boatmen, La. Vols.
Johnson, John	Private	Capt. Van Bibber's Co., La. Mil.
Johnson, John	Private	17, 18 and 19 Cons. Reg't., La. Militia
Johnson, John G.	Private	17, 18 and 19 Cons. Reg't., La. Militia
Johnson, Jones	Sergeant	Captain Griffith's Co., Mounted Riflemen, La. Vols.
Johnson, Joseph	Private	Capt. Wallace's Co., Boatmen, La. Vols.
Johnson, Joseph	Private	17, 18 and 19 Cons. Reg't., La. Militia
Johnson, Patrick	Private	De Clouet's Reg't., La. Militia
Johnson, Robert	Private	Capt. Allen's Co., Artillerists, La. Vols.

Name	Rank	Unit
Johnson, Robert	Private	De Clouet's Reg't., La. Militia (See also 44 U.S. Inf.)
Johnson, Robert	Private	De Clouet's Reg't., La. Militia
Johnson, Robert	Private	2 Batt'n. (Peire's), La. Vols.
Johnson, William	Private	10 Regiment, La. Militia
Johnson, William	Private	16 Reg't. (Thompson's), La. Mil.
Johnson, William	Private	16 Reg't. (Thompson's), La. Mil.
Johnson, William	Private	17, 18 and 19 Cons. Reg't., La. Militia
Johnson, William B.	Private	2 Batt'n. (Peire's), La. Vols. (Orig. under Johnson, William H.)
Johnson, William H.	Private	2 Batt'n. (Peire's), La. Vols.
Johnsons, William H.	Private	2 Batt'n. (Peire's), La. Vols. (Orig. under Johnson, William H.)
Johnston, -- Jr.	Private	3 Reg't. (de la Ronde's), La. Mil.
Johnston, Hugh	Private-Corporal	De Clouet's Reg't., La. Militia (Orig. under Johnson, Hugh)
Johnston, I.	Private	4 Reg't. (Morgan's), La. Militia
Johnston, Isham	Private	10 and 20 Cons. Reg't., La. Mil.
Johnston, James	Private	1 Reg't. (Dejan's), La. Militia
Johnston, James	Private	12 and 13 Cons. Reg't., La. Mil.
Johnston, John	Private	De Clouet's Reg't., La. Militia (Orig. under Johnson, John)
Johnston, Josiah S.	Colonel	17, 18 and 19 Cons. Reg't., La. Militia
Johnston, Robert	Private	Capt. Allen's Co., Artillerists, La. Vols. (Orig. under Johnson, Robert)
Johnston, Robert	Private	De Clouet's Reg't., La. Militia (Orig. under Johnson, Robert)
Johnston, Robert	Private	10 and 20 Cons. Reg't., La. Mil.
Joice, --	Sergeant	4 Reg't. (Morgan's), La. Militia
Joice, Adam	Private	10 and 20 Cons. Reg't., La. Mil. (Orig. under Joist, Adam)
Joiner, Clark	Private	De Clouet's Reg't., La. Militia
Joiner, John	Private	12 and 13 Cons. Reg't., La. Mil.
Joiner, Nathan	Private	12 and 13 Cons. Reg't., La. Mil.
Joiny, --	Private	2 Reg't. (Cavelier's), La. Militia
Joissain, --	Private	2 Batt'n. (D'Aquin's), La. Militia
Joissin, --	Private	2 Batt'n. (D'Aquin's), La. Militia (Orig. under Joissain, --)
Joist, Adam	Private	10 and 20 Cons. Reg't., La. Mil.
Joli, --	Private	3 Reg't. (de la Ronde's), La. Mil. (Orig. under Jolly, --)
Jolibois, Philip	Private	5 Reg't. (La Branche's), La. Mil.
Jolivert, John	Private	17, 18 and 19 Cons. Reg't., La. Militia
Jolly, --	Private	3 Reg't. (de la Ronde's), La. Mil.
Jolly, Augt.	Private	1 Reg't. (Dejan's), La. Militia (Orig. under Joly, Aug.)
Jolly, Jean Mariane	Private	2 Batt'n. (Peire's), La. Vols.
Jolly, John E.	Private	1 Reg't. (Dejan's), La. Militia
Jolly, Ursen	Private	De Clouet's Reg't., La. Militia (Orig. under Joly, Ursin)
Joly, Aug.	Private	1 Reg't. (Dejan's), La. Militia
Joly, J.	Lieutenant	2 Batt'n. (D'Aquin's), La. Militia
Joly, Jean Mariane	Private	2 Batt'n. (Peire's), La. Vols. (Orig. under Jolly, Jean Mariane)
Joly, Ursin	Private	De Clouet's Reg't., La. Militia
Jonca, Christian	Private	17, 18 and 19 Cons. Reg't., La. Militia
Jones, --	Private	Plauche's Batt'n., La. Militia
Jones, Abram	Private	12 and 13 Cons. Reg't., La. Mil.
Jones, Augustus	Private	Captain Dodge's Co., Mounted Riflemen, La. Militia
Jones, Augustus	Private	Captain Henry's Co., Mounted Riflemen, La. Militia
Jones, Benjamin	Private	Capt. Callaway's Co., Mounted Riflemen, La. Militia
Jones, Blake B.	Private	De Clouet's Reg't., La. Militia
Jones, Burrell	Private	De Clouet's Reg't., La. Militia
Jones, Daniel	Private	10 and 20 Cons. Reg't., La. Mil.
Jones, Ephrim	Private	16 Reg't. (Thompson's), La. Mil.
Jones, Guilford D.	Private	10 and 20 Cons. Reg't., La. Mil.
Jones, Howel	Sergeant	16 Reg't. (Thompson's), La. Mil.
Jones, Jeremiah	Sergeant	12 and 13 Cons. Reg't., La. Mil.
Jones, Jesse R.	Pay Master	12 and 13 Cons. Reg't., La. Mil.
Jones, John	Private	4 Reg't. (Morgan's), La. Militia
Jones, John	Private	16 Reg't. (Thompson's), La. Mil.
Jones, John A.	Private	Captain Dodge's Co., Mounted Riflemen, La. Militia
Jones, John A.	Private	Captain Henry's Co., Mounted Riflemen, La. Militia
Jones, John P.	1 Lieutenant	1 Reg't. (Dejan's), La. Militia
Jones, Lettin	Private	17, 18 and 19 Cons. Reg't., La. Militia
Jones, Michael P.	Private	12 and 13 Cons. Reg't., La. Mil.
Jones, Nath	Private	11 Reg't. (Hickey's), La. Militia
Jones, Nath. T.	Private	10 and 20 Cons. Reg't., La. Mil. (Orig. under Jones, Nathan J.)
Jones, Nathan J.	Private	10 and 20 Cons. Reg't., La. Mil.
Jones, Nathan T.	Private	Capt. Thomas' Co., La. Militia
Jones, Russel	Sergeant	11 Reg't. (Hickey's), La. Militia
Jones, Thomas	Private	10 and 20 Cons. Reg't., La. Mil.
Jones, Thomas	Private	10 and 20 Cons. Reg't., La. Mil.
Jones, Wiley	Private	12 and 13 Cons. Reg't., La. Mil.
Jones, William	Private	10 and 20 Cons. Reg't., La. Mil.
Jones, William	Private	17, 18 and 19 Cons. Reg't., La. Militia
Jones, Woody	Private	12 and 13 Cons. Reg't., La. Mil.
Jonk, --	Servant	17, 18 and 19 Cons. Reg't., La. Militia
Jonsen, Daniel	Private	Captain Musick's Co., Mounted Riflemen, La. Militia (Orig. under Jansen, David)
Jonson, Robert	Private	10 and 20 Cons. Reg't., La. Mil. (Orig. under Johnston, Robert)
Jonston, Robert	Private	10 and 20 Cons. Reg't., La. Mil. (Orig. under Johnston, Robert)
Joquire, Charles	Private	17, 18 and 19 Cons. Reg't., La. Militia
Jordan, M. W.	Private	10 Regiment, La. Militia
Jordy, Joly	Private	2 Reg't. (Cavelier's), La. Militia
Josa, Ansetno Yno	Private	La. War of 1812
Joseph, --	Servant-Waiter	Captain Beale's Co., Riflemen, La. Militia
Joseph, --	--	De Clouet's Reg't., La. Militia
Joseph, --	Servant	Plauche's Batt'n., La. Militia
Joseph, --	Tembour-Drummer	2 Batt'n. (D'Aquin's), La. Militia (Orig. under Joseph, --)
Joseph, --	Tembour-Drummer	2 Batt'n. (D'Aquin's), La. Militia
Joseph, --	Waiter	2 Reg't. (Cavelier's), La. Militia
Joseph, --	Private	3 Reg't. (de la Ronde's), La. Mil.
Joseph, --	Servant	3 Reg't. (de la Ronde's), La. Mil.
Joseph, --	Waiter	3 Reg't. (de la Ronde's), La. Mil.
Joseph, Antonio	Private	8 Reg't. (Meriam's), La. Militia
Joseph, Bazille	Private	1 Batt'n. (Fortier's), La. Militia
Joseph, Fernandez	Private	2 Batt'n. (Peire's), La. Vols.
Joseph, Jean	Private	2 Batt'n. (D'Aquin's), La. Militia
Josephe, --	Private	Plauche's Batt'n., La. Militia
Josephe, --	Tembour-Drummer	2 Batt'n. (D'Aquin's), La. Militia
Josie, --	--	De Clouet's Reg't., La. Militia
Jouaney, John	Private	Capt. Chauveau's Co., Cavalry, La. Mil. (Orig. under Jouany, John)
Jouany, John	Private	Capt. Chauveau's Co., Cavalry, La. Militia
Joubert, Francois	Private	16 Reg't. (Thompson's), La. Mil.
Joubert, Joseph	Sergeant	16 Reg't. (Thompson's), La. Mil.
Joubert, P.	Private	1 Reg't. (Dejan's), La. Militia
Joublanc, --	Sergeant	Plauche's Batt'n., La. Militia (Orig. under Toublanc, --)
Lourdan, Barthelemy	Private	3 Reg't. (de la Ronde's), La. Mil.
Jourdan, Celestin	Private	1 Batt'n. (Fortier's), La. Militia
Jourdan, Daniel	Private	Plauche's Batt'n., La. Militia
Jourdan, Noel	2 Lieutenant	1 Batt'n. (Fortier's), La. Militia
Jourdan, Pierre	Private	3 Reg't. (de la Ronde's), La. Mil.
Journe', Pierre	Private	De Clouet's Reg't., La. Militia
Journesey, Joseph	Private	Capt. Songy's Co., Marines, La. Vols. (Orig. under Fournesy, Jh)
Journin, Joseph	Private	2 Batt'n. (D'Aquin's), La. Militia
Joyes, James	Private	2 Reg't. (Cavelier's), La. Militia
Joyes, Samuel	Private	2 Reg't. (Cavelier's), La. Militia (Orig. under Joyes, James)
Jsnard, --	Private	2 Reg't. (Cavelier's), La. Militia
Jsnard, Sol	Private	2 Reg't. (Cavelier's), La. Militia
Jsnard, Son	Private	2 Reg't. (Cavelier's), La. Militia
Juan, Antoin	Private	Captain Lagan's Co., La. Vols.
Juan, Pierre	Private	Captain Lagan's Co., La. Vols.
Judiffe, Erban	Private	12 and 13 Cons. Reg't., La. Mil. (Orig. under Judisse, Urban)
Judisse, Urban	Private	12 and 13 Cons. Reg't., La. Mil.
Judson, Harshibal	Private	Capt. Alpuente's Co., La. Militia

Name	Rank	Unit
Juforgue, --	Sergeant	2 Reg't. (Cavelier's), La. Militia
Juing, Raphael	Corporal	1 Batt'n. (Fortier's), La. Militia
Jule, Ane	Private	2 Reg't. (Cavelier's), La. Militia (Orig. under Jule, Anthy)
Jule, Anthony	Private	2 Reg't. (Cavelier's), La. Militia
Jules, Celestin	Corporal	De Clouet's Reg't., La. Militia
Jules, Hyacinthe	Private	De Clouet's Reg't., La. Militia
Jules, Vincent	Private	De Clouet's Reg't., La. Militia
Julien, --	Servant	Plauche's Batt'n., La. Militia
Jumonville, Coulon	Private	3 Reg't. (de la Ronde's), La. Mil.
Junior, Arieux	Sergeant	6 Reg't. (Landry's), La. Militia
Jupiter, --	Waiter	2 Reg't. (Cavelier's), La. Militia
Jupiter, --	Servant	3 Reg't. (de la Ronde's), La. Mil.
Jure', St. Loger	Private	4 Reg't. (Morgan's), La. Militia
Justice, William	Private	17, 18 and 19 Cons. Reg't., La. Militia
Kabeen, William	Private	Captain Griffith's Co., Mounted Riflemen, La. Vols.
Kaddach, James	Corporal	Capt. Callaway's Co., Mounted Riflemen, La. Militia (Orig. under Kadlock, James)
Kailler, Jne Bte	Private	6 Reg't. (Landry's), La. Militia (Orig. under Raillier, J. Bte)
Kailler, Michell	Private	6 Reg't. (Landry's), La. Militia (Orig. under Railler, Michelle)
Kailler, Nicholas	Private	6 Reg't. (Landry's), La. Militia (Orig. under Railler, Nicholas)
Kane, Edmond	Private	17, 18 and 19 Cons. Reg't., La. Militia
Kaner, Andre	Private	2 Batt'n. (Peire's), La. Vols. (Orig. under Hanner, Andre)
Kannon, James C.	Sergeant	De Clouet's Reg't., La. Militia (Orig. under Kennan, James C.)
Karns, I.	Private	Captain Sprigg's Co., Boatmen, La. Vols.
Kay, Robert	Private	4 Reg't. (Morgan's), La. Militia
Keathley, John	Private	10 and 20 Cons. Reg't., La. Mil.
Keator, A.	Sergeant	4 Reg't. (Morgan's), La. Militia
Keenting, --	Fusilier-Private	5 Reg't. (La Branche's), La. Mil.
Keer, Wm.	Private	Captain Musick's Co., La. Mil. (Orig. under Kern, William)
Keiser, John	1 Lieutenant	Capt. Thomas' Co., La. Militia
Keister, Frederick	Private	De Clouet's Reg't., La. Militia
Keith, James	Private	De Clouet's Reg't., La. Militia
Kellar, Hezek	Corporal	10 and 20 Cons. Reg't., La. Mil. (Orig. under Keller, Hezekl)
Kellar, Jacob	Private	10 and 20 Cons. Reg't., La. Mil. (Orig. under Keller, Jacob)
Kellar, Thomas	Private	10 and 20 Cons. Reg't., La. Mil. (Orig. under Keller, Thomas)
Keller, Alexander	Fusilier-Private	5 Reg't. (La Branche's), La. Mil.
Keller, Drauzin	Fusilier-Private	5 Reg't. (La Branche's), La. Mil. (Orig. under Kinelair, Drauzin)
Keller, Hezekl	Corporal	10 and 20 Cons. Reg't., La. Mil.
Keller, Jacob	Private	De Clouet's Reg't., La. Militia
Keller, Jacob	Private	10 and 20 Cons. Reg't., La. Mil.
Keller, James	Corporal	10 and 20 Cons. Reg't., La. Mil. (Orig. under Kelly, James)
Keller, John	Private	De Clouet's Reg't., La. Militia
Keller, Paul	Fusilier-Private	5 Reg't. (La Branche's), La. Mil. (Orig. under Kinelair, Paul)
Keller, Peter	Private	2 Batt'n. (Peire's), La. Vols.
Keller, Pierre	Private	De Clouet's Reg't., La. Militia (Orig. under Kelliere, Pierre)
Keller, Thomas	Private	10 and 20 Cons. Reg't., La. Mil.
Kellier, Pierre	Private	De Clouet's Reg't., La. Militia (Orig. under Kelliere, Pierre)
Kelliere, Pierre	Private	De Clouets' Reg't., La. Militia
Kelly, James	Corporal	10 and 20 Cons. Reg't., La. Mil.
Kelly, James	Private	17, 18 and 19 Cons. Reg't., La. Militia
Kelly, William	Private	10 and 20 Cons. Reg't., La. Mil.
Kelso, John	Corporal	Captain Ramsey's Co., Mounted Riflemen, La. Militia
Kelton, D. M.	Private	1 Reg't. (Dejan's), La. Militia
Kemball, Joseph	Private	17, 18 and 19 Cons. Reg't., La. Militia (Orig. under Kimball, Joseph)
Kemble, Wade	Sergeant	10 Regiment, La. Militia
Kemp, Joshua	Private	17, 18 and 19 Cons. Reg't., La. Militia
Kemp, Keleb	Private	12 and 13 Cons. Reg't., La. Mil.
Kempester, George	Private	Captain Dodge's Co., Mounted Riflemen, La. Militia
Kempester, George	Private	Captain Henry's Co., Mounted Riflemen, La. Militia
Kempster, George	Private	Captain Henry's Co., Mounted Riflemen, La. Mil. (Orig. under Kempester, George)
Kendal, Robert	Private	16 Reg't. (Thompson's), La. Mil.
Kendall, Fielding	Private	16 Reg't. (Thompson's), La. Mil.
Kendle, William	Private	16 Reg't. (Thompson's), La. Mil.
Kendrick, Benjamin	1 Lieutenant	10 Regiment, La. Militia
Kenebrue, Jordon	Corporal	10 and 20 Cons. Reg't., La. Mil. (Orig. under Kennebrew, Jordon)
Kenedy, Edison	Private	17, 18 and 19 Cons. Reg't., La. Militia
Kenerly, George H.	Private	Captain McNair's Co., Mounted Riflemen, La. Militia
Kenison, Absalom	Private	Capt. Wallace's Co., Boatmen, La. Vols.
Kenison, Hiram	Private	Capt. Wallace's Co., Boatmen, La. Vols. (Orig. under Kennison, Hiram)
Kennady, Thomas	Private	12 and 13 Cons. Reg't., La. Mil.
Kennady, William	Private	De Clouet's Reg't., La. Militia
Kennady, William Junr	Private	De Clouet's Reg't., La. Militia
Kennan, James C.	Sergeant	De Clouet's Reg't., La. Militia
Kennebrew, Jordon	Corporal	10 and 20 Cons. Reg't., La. Mil.
Kennedy, Jacques	Private	2 Batt'n. (Peire's), La. Vols.
Kennedy, Moses	Private	11 Reg't. (Hickey's), La. Militia
Kennedy, Nathan	Surgeon	12 and 13 Cons. Reg't., La. Mil.
Kennedy, Thomas		Capt. Alpuente's Co., La. Militia
Kennedy, Thomas	Private	12 and 13 Cons. Reg't., La. Mil. (Orig. under Kennady, Thomas)
Kenner, James	Private	De Clouet's Reg't., La. Militia
Kenner, Samuel	Private	10 and 20 Cons. Reg't., La. Mil.
Kennerly, George H.	Private	Captain McNair's Co., Mounted Riflemen, La. Mil. (Orig. under Kenerly, George H.
Kennerson, J.	Private	16 Reg't. (Thompson's), La. Mil. (Orig. under Kinnerson, J.)
Kennerson, Maximilian	Private	16 Reg't. (Thompson's), La. Mil. (Orig. under Kennison, Maximilian)
Kenney, Allen	Private	12 and 13 Cons. Reg't., La. Mil. (Orig. under Kinney, Allen)
Kenney, John B.	Private	De Clouet's Reg't., La. Militia (Orig. under Kinny, Jean Baptiste)
Kennidy, Jacques	Private	2 Batt'n. (Peire's), La. Vols. (Orig. under Kennedy, Jacques)
Kennison, Hiram	Private	Capt. Wallace's Co., Boatmen, La. Vols.
Kennison, Maximilian	Private	16 Reg't. (Thompson's), La. Mil.
Kennon, James C.	Sergeant	De Clouet's Reg't., La. Militia (Orig. under Kennan, James C.)
Kenny, John Bapte	Private	De Clouet's Reg't., La. Militia (Orig. under Kinny, Jean Baptiste)
Kensler, William	Private	17, 18 and 19 Cons. Reg't., La. Militia
Kent, John	1 Lieutenant	10 and 20 Cons. Reg't., La. Mil.
Ker, C.	Sergeant	1 Reg't. (Dejan's), La. Militia (Orig. under Car, C.)
Kerbey, Ephram	Private	De Clouet's Reg't., La. Militia (Orig. under Kerby, Ephraim)
Kerbs, Bazil	Private	Capt. Alpuente's Co., La. Militia
Kerbs, Joseph	Private	Capt. Alpuente's Co., La. Militia
Kerby, Ephraim	Private	De Clouet's Reg't., La. Militia
Kergoet, Allain	Private	2 Batt'n. (Peire's), La. Vols. (Orig. under Kergoit, Allain)
Kergoit, Allain	Private	2 Batt'n. (Peire's), La. Vols.
Kerkland, Edward	Private	17, 18 and 19 Cons. Reg't., La. Militia
Kerklend, Richard	Private	2 Batt'n. (Peire's), La. Vols. (Orig. under Kirkland, Richard)
Kern, William	Private	Capt. Musick's Co., La. Militia
Kerne, Andre	Fusilier-Private	5 Reg't. (La Branche's), La. Mil.
Kerne, Andre	Fusilier-Private	5 Reg't. (La Branche's), La. Mil.
Kerne, George	Private	De Clouet's Reg't., La. Militia
Kerne, In Ftr.	Fusilier-Private	5 Reg't. (La Branche's), La. Mil. (Orig. under Kerne, Jn Bte)
Kerne, Jean	Private	5 Reg't. (La Branche's), La. Mil.

Name	Rank	Unit
Kerne, Jn Bte	Fusilier-Private	5 Reg't. (La Branche's), La. Mil.
Kernes, I.	Private	Captain Sprigg's Co., Boatmen, La. Vols. (Orig. under Karns, I)
Kernion, Bedoyere	Private	2 Reg't. (Cavelier's), La. Militia
Kernion, Jaques	Private	2 Reg't. (Cavelier's), La. Militia
Kerqui, Emille	Private	2 Reg't. (Cavelier's), La. Militia
Kerr, George	Private	Captain Sprigg's Co., Boatmen, La. Vols.
Kerr, James	Private	Capt. Collard's Co., La. Militia
Kerr, John	1 Sergeant-Sgt.	10 and 20 Cons. Reg't., La. Mil.
Kerr, William	Private	De Clouet's Reg't., La. Militia
Kerre, William	Private	De Clouet's Reg't., La. Militia (Orig. under Kerr, William)
Kershaw, John W.	Private	Baker's Regiment, La. Militia
Ketes, George	Private	Capt. Collard's Co., La. Militia
Ketterland, John	Private	De Clouet's Reg't., La. Militia
Ketty, William	Private	10 and 20 Cons. Reg't., La. Mil. (Orig. under Kelly, William)
Kevez, Charles C.	Sergeant	De Clouet's Reg't., La. Militia (Orig. under Rives, Charles C.)
Key, Jobe	Private	10 and 20 Cons. Reg't., La. Mil.
Keys, Job	Private	11 Reg't. (Hickey's), La. Militia
Keys, Job	Private	10 and 20 Cons. Reg't., La. Mil. (Orig. under Key, Jobe)
Keys, John	Private-Sergeant	16 Reg't. (Thompson's), La. Mil. Louisiana War of 1812
Kick, Gregoire	Private	16 Reg't. (Thompson's), La. Mil.
Kidder, John	Private	16 Reg't. (Thompson's), La. Mil.
Kiester, Frederick	Private	De Clouet's Reg't., La. Militia (Orig. under Keister, Frederick)
Kilcrease, Charles	Private	10 and 20 Cons. Reg't., La. Mil.
Kilcrease, John	Private	10 and 20 Cons. Reg't., La. Mil.
Kilgore, James	Private	17, 18 and 19 Cons. Reg't., La. Militia
Kilgore, Jamison	Private	17, 18 and 19 Cons. Reg't., La. Militia
Killereast, Charles	Private	10 and 20 Cons. Reg't., La. Mil. (Orig. under Kilcrease, Charles)
Killeret, John	Private	10 and 20 Cons. Reg't., La. Mil. (Orig. under Kilcrease, John)
Killiam, George	Private	Capt. Alpuente's Co., La. Mil.
Killiam, George	Private	17, 18 and 19 Cons. Reg't., La. Militia
Killian, George	Private	17, 18 and 19 Cons. Reg't., La. Militia (Orig. under Killiam, George)
Kilpatrick, James	Sergeant	17, 18 and 19 Cons. Reg't., La. Militia
Kimball, Frederick	Private	10 and 20 Cons. Reg't., La. Mil.
Kimball, Joseph	Private	17, 18 and 19 Cons. Reg't., La. Militia
Kimball, Middleton	Private	17, 18 and 19 Cons. Reg't., La. Militia
Kimbel, Abraham	Private	19 Reg't., La. Vols. (Orig. under Kimble, Abraham)
Kimbel, Peter	Private	Captain Beale's Co., Riflemen, La. Militia
Kimble, Abraham	Private	19 Reg't., La. Militia
Kimble, Frederick	Private	10 and 20 Cons. Reg't., La. Mil. (Orig. under Kimball, Frederick)
Kimble, Joseph	Private	17, 18 and 19 Reg't. Cons. La. Mil. (Orig. under Kimball, Joseph)
Kimp, Calep	Private	12 and 13 Cons. Reg't., La. Mil. (Orig. under Kemp, Kaleb)
Kinchen, William	Pvt.-Sgt.-Major	12 and 13 Cons. Reg't., La. Mil. (Orig. under Kinchion, William)
Kincheon, William	Pvt.-Sgt.-Major	12 and 13 Cons. Reg't., La. Mil.
Kinchion, William	Pvt.-Sgt.-Major	12 and 13 Cons. Reg't., La. Mil.
Kind, John	Private	10 and 20 Cons. Reg't., La. Mil. (Orig. under King, John)
Kindle, Joseph	Private	17, 18 and 19 Cons. Reg't., La. Militia
Kinelair, Drauzin	Fusilier-Private	5 Reg't. (La Branche's), La. Mil.
Kinelair, George	Fusilier-Private	5 Reg't. (La Branche's), La. Mil.
Kinelair, Jacques	Fusilier-Private	5 Reg't. (La Branche's), La. Mil.
Kinelair, Jacques	Fusilier-Private	5 Reg't. (La Branche's), La. Mil.
Kinelair, Paul	Fusilier-Private	5 Reg't. (La Branche's), La. Mil.
King, Charles Y.	Private	8 Reg't. (Meriam's), La. Militia
King, David	Private	De Clouet's Reg't., La. Militia (See also 7 Inf.)
King, Edward	Major	20 Reg't., La. Militia
King, George	Private	Captain McNair's Co., Mounted Riflemen, La. Militia
King, George	Captain	16 Reg't. (Thompson's), La. Mil.
King, John	Private	10 and 20 Cons. Reg't., La. Mil.
King, John	Private	17, 18 and 19 Cons. Reg't., La. Militia
King, Stark	Private	17, 18 and 19 Cons. Reg't., La. Militia
Kingcaid, James	Servant	De Clouet's Reg't., La. Militia (Orig. under Pon, Pon)
Kinkaid, Andrew	Private-Corporal	Captain McNair's Co., Mounted Riflemen, La. Militia
Kinkaid, John	Private	Captain McNair's Co., Mounted Riflemen, La. Militia
Kinkaid, John Jr.	Private	Captain McNair's Co., Mounted Riflemen, La. Militia
Kinkaid, Samuel	1 Sgt.-Private	Captain McNair's Co., Mounted Riflemen, La. Militia
Kinkead, Andrew	Private-Corporal	Captain McNair's Co., Mounted Riflemen, La. Militia (Orig. under Kinkaid, Andrew)
Kinkead, John	Private	Captain McNair's Co., Mounted Riflemen, La. Militia (Orig. under Kinkaid, John)
Kinkead, John Jr.	Private	Captain McNair's Co., Mounted Riflemen, La. Militia (Orig. under Kinkaid, John Jr.)
Kinkead, Samuel	1 Sgt.-Private	Captain McNair's Co., Mounted Riflemen, La. Militia (Orig. under Kinkaid, Samuel)
Kinler, Drauzin	Fusilier-Private	5 Reg't. (La Branche's), La. Mil. (Orig. under Kinelair, Drauzin)
Kinler, Jacques	Fusilier-Private	5 Reg't. (La Branche's), La. Mil. (Orig. under Kinelair, Jacques)
Kinler, Paul	Fusilier-Private	5 Reg't. (La Branche's), La. Mil. (Orig. under Kinelair, Paul)
Kinley, John	Private	Captain Hughes' Co., Mounted Riflemen, La. Mil. (Orig. under Shirley, John)
Kinnerson, J.	Private	16 Reg't. (Thompson's), La. Mil.
Kinney, Allen	Private	12 and 13 Cons. Reg't., La. Mil.
Kinny, Jean Baptiste	Private	De Clouet's Reg't., La. Militia
Kirkland, Aaron	Private	19 Reg't., La. Militia
Kirkland, Archelaus	1 Lieutenant	12 and 13 Cons. Reg't., La. Mil. (Orig. under Kirkland, Archibald)
Kirkland, Archibald	1 Lieutenant	12 and 13 Cons. Reg't., La. Mil.
Kirkland, R.	Private	Captain Sprigg's Co., Boatmen, La. Vols.
Kirkland, Richd	Corporal	10 Reg't., La. Militia
Kirkland, Richard	Private	2 Batt'n. (Peire's), La. Vols.
Kirkland, Richard H.	Private	De Clouet's Reg't., La. Militia
Kirkland, Samuel	Private	Captain Griffith's Co., Mounted Riflemen, La. Vols.
Kirkland, William	Private-Corporal	Captain Griffith's Co., Mounted Riflemen, La. Vols.
Kirkland, William	Private-Corporal	Captain Griffith's Co., Mounted Riflemen, La. Vols.
Kirkland, William D.	Private	Captain Griffith's Co., Mounted Riflemen, La. Vols.
Kirklin, Richard	Private	2 Batt'n. (Peire's), La. Vols. (Orig. under Kirkland, Richard)
Kitchel, Abraham	Private	Capt. Thomas' Co., La. Militia
Kitchen, Thompson	Private	Capt. Wallace's Co., Boatmen, La. Vols.
Kleimpeter, Francis	Private	10 and 20 Cons. Reg't., La. Mil. (Orig. under Kleinpeter, Francis)
Kleinpeter, Francis	Private	10 and 20 Cons. Reg't., La. Mil.
Kleinpeter, Lewis	Private	10 and 20 Cons. Reg't., La. Mil.
Klinepeter, John B.	Corporal	Capt. Thomas' Co., La. Militia
Klinepeter, Lewis	Private	10 and 20 Cons. Reg't., La. Mil. (Orig. under Kleinpeter, Lewis)
Klumpeter, Lewis	Private	10 and 20 Cons. Reg't., La. Mil. (Orig. under Kleinpeter, Lewis)
Knab, William	Private	1 Reg't. (Dejan's), La. Militia
Knauland, Barney	Private	10 and 20 Cons. Reg't., La. Mil. (Orig. under Knowland, Barney)
Knight, George	Private	De Clouet's Reg't., La. Militia
Knight, Henry	Private	Baker's Regiment, La. Militia
Knight, Michael	Private	Baker's Regiment, La. Militia
Knight, Solomon	Private	Baker's Regiment, La. Militia
Knight, Thomas	Private	10 and 20 Cons. Reg't., La. Mil.

Name	Rank	Unit
Knight, William	Private	Baker's Regiment, La. Militia
Knight, William	Private	De Clouet's Reg't., La. Militia
Knighten, Jesse	Private	De Clouet's Reg't., La. Militia
Knighting, Josiah	Private	10 and 20 Cons. Reg't., La. Mil.
Knighton, Joshia	Private	10 and 20 Cons. Reg't., La. Mil. (Orig. under Knighting, Josiah)
Knots, Austin	Private	Capt. Collard's Co., La. Militia (Orig. under Knott, Austin)
Knott, Austin	Private	Capt. Collard's Co., La. Militia
Knowland, Barney	Private	10 and 20 Cons. Reg't., La. Mil.
Knox, A.	Private	4 Reg't. (Morgan's), La. Militia
Knox, William G.	2 Lieutenant	De Clouet's Reg't., La. Militia
Kumball, Frederick	Private	10 and 20 Cons. Reg't., La. Mil. (Orig. under Kimball, Frederick)
Kumble, Jacob	Private	17, 18 and 19 Cons. Reg't., La. Militia
Kurtana, --	Private	4 Reg't. (Morgan's), La. Militia
Kushaw, John N.	Private	Baker's Regiment, La. Militia (Orig. under Kershaw, John W.)
Kyle, James	Private	Captain McNair's Co., Mounted Riflemen, La. Militia
Labadie, --	Private	1 Reg't. (Dejan's), La. Militia
Kabadie, In.	Corporal	2 Reg't. (Cavelier's), La. Militia
Labadie, Peter	Private	2 Reg't. (Cavelier's), La. Militia
Labadie, R.	Fusilier-Private	5 Reg't. (La Branche's), La. Mil.
Labarassiere, Pierre	Private	De Clouet's Reg't., La. Militia
Labarge, William	Private	De Clouet's Reg't., La. Militia
Labarre, --	Private	Plauche's Batt'n., La. Militia
Labarre, Jn B. Volant	Private	4 Reg't. (Morgan's), La. Militia
Labarre, Lacistiere N.	Pri.-Cpl.	4 Reg't. (Morgan's), La. Militia
Labarre, Pascalis	Sergeant	4 Reg't. (Morgan's), La. Militia
La Barrure	Private	Plauche's Batt'n., La. Militia
Labassier, Antoine	Private	2 Batt'n. (Peire's), La. Vols. (Orig. under Labussiere, Antoine)
Labattu, John B.	1 Lieutenant	De Clouet's Reg't., La. Militia (Orig. under Labatut, John P.)
Labatut, John B.	Brig. General	General and Staff (Labatur), La. Militia
Labatut, John P.	1 Lieutenant	De Clouet's Reg't., La. Militia
La Bawve, Antoine	Private	De Clouet's Reg't., La. Militia
La Bauve, Francois	Private	De Clouet's Reg't., La. Militia
Labauve, Jacques	Private	8 Reg't. (Meriam's), La. Militia
Labauve, Jno Bte	Private	8 Reg't. (Meriam's), La. Militia
Labauve, Olduphe	Private	Baker's Regiment, La. Militia
La Bauve, Placide	Private	De Clouet's Reg't., La. Militia
La Bauvre, Placide	Private	16 Reg't. (Thompson's), La. Mil.
Labay, Antoine	Private	16 Reg't. (Thompson's), La. Mil.
Labbe, Baptiste	Sergeant	Capt. Le Doux's Co., Cavalry, La. Vols.
Labbe, Celesten	Corporal	Capt. Le Doux's Co., Cavalry, La. Vols.
Labee, Charles	Private	Captain Sprigg's Co., Boatmen, La. Vols.
Labelle, Joseph	Artificer	Capt. Chaudurier's Co., Artificers, Art'y., La. Vols.
Laberne, John B.	Private	Capt. Van Bibber's Co., La. Mil.
Labiche, Firmin	Private	6 Reg't. (Landry's), La. Militia
Labiche, Francis	1 Lieutenant	2 Reg't. (Cavelier's), La. Militia
LaBlanc, Andrew	2 Lieutenant	De Clouet's Reg't., La. Militia
Laboisson, J.	Private	8 Reg't. (Meriam's), La. Militia
Labord, Pierre	Private	De Clouet's Reg't., La. Militia (Orig. under Laborde, Pierre)
Laborde, --	Private	Plauche's Batt'n., La. Militia
Laborde, John B.	Corporal-Sgt.	2 Batt'n. (Peire's), La. Vols.
Laborde, Pierre	Private	De Clouet's Reg't., La. Militia
Labot, Francois	Private	1 Batt'n. (Fortier's), La. Militia
Labourrier, Jo	Private	De Clouet's Reg't., La. Militia
Labouve, Olduphe	Private	Baker's Regiment, La. Militia (Orig. under Labauve, Olduphe)
La Bouve, Placide	Private	De Clouet's Reg't., La. Militia (Orig. under LaBauve, Placide)
Labouvrier, Jo	Private	De Clouet's Reg't., La. Militia (Orig. under Labourrier, Jo)
Labove, I.	Private	8 Reg't. (Meriam's), La. Militia
Labove, Isidore	1 Lieutenant	8 Reg't. (Meriam's), La. Militia
La Branche, A.	Colonel	5 Reg't. (La Branche's), La. Mil.
La Branche, D.	Corporal-Sgt.	4 Reg't. (Morgan's), La. Militia
Labranche, Hermogene	Private	Capt. Trudeau's Troop of Horse, La. Militia
La Branche, In Bte	Fusilier-Private	5 Reg't. (La Branche's), La. Mil.
Labranche, Joseph	Private	Capt. Trudeau's Troop of Horse, La. Militia
La Branche, L.	Sergeant	4 Reg't. (Morgan's), La. Militia
Labranche, Louis	Cornet	Capt. Trudeau's Troop of Horse, La. Militia
Labranche, Octave	Private	Capt. Trudeau's Troop of Horse, La. Militia
Labranche, Similien	2 Lieutenant	Capt. Trudeau's Troop of Horse, La. Militia
Labruni, Jean	Private	2 Batt'n. (Peire's), La. Vols. (Orig. under Labruny, Jean)
Labruny, Jean	Private	2 Batt'n. (Peire's), La. Vols.
Laburni, Jean	Private	2 Batt'n. (Peire's), La. Vols. (Orig. under Laburny, Jean)
Labusiere, Antoine	Private	2 Batt'n. (Peire's), La. Vols. (Orig. under Labussiere, Antoine)
Labusierre, Antoine	Private	2 Batt'n. (Peire's), La. Vols. (Orig. under Labussiere, Antoine)
La Bussiere, Antoine	Private	2 Batt'n. (Peire's), La. Vols. (See also Regular Service)
Labussierre, Antoine	Private	2 Batt'n. (Peire's), La. Vols. (Orig. under Labussiere, Antoine)
Laby, Louis	Servant	1 Batt'n. (Fortier's), La. Militia
Lacaille, --	Private	2 Reg't. (Cavelier's), La. Militia
Lacey, Ebenezer	Private	19 Regiment, La. Militia
Lacey, Thomas	Private	10 and 20 Cons. Reg't., La. Mil.
Lachaine, --	Private	2 Batt'n. (D'Aquin's), La. Militia
Lachaise, Baptiste	Private	1 Batt'n. (Fortier's), La. Militia
Lachaise, Pierre	Private	De Clouet's Reg't., La. Militia
Lachance, Benjamin	Ensign	Capt. Callaway's Co., Mounted Riflemen, La. Militia
Lachanterie, Antoine	Private	2 Batt'n. (Peire's), La. Vols. (Orig. under Lachantrie, Antoine)
Lachantre, Antoine	Private	2 Batt'n. (Peire's), La. Vols. (Orig. under Lachantrie, Antoine)
Lachantrie, Antoine	Private	2 Batt'n. (Peire's), La. Vols.
La Chapelle, Aimable	Artificer	Capt. Chaudurier's Co., Artificers, Art'y., La. Vols.
Lachapelle, Amble	Private	4 Reg't. (Morgan's), La. Militia
La Chapelle, Hubert	Private	De Clouet's Reg't., La. Militia
Lachassem, Philip	Private	Baker's Regiment, La. Militia (Orig. under Lachausee, Philip)
Lachausee, Philip	Private	Baker's Regiment, La. Militia
Lachiapella, Celestin	Private	3 Reg't. (de la Ronde's), La. Mil.
Lacky, Andrew	Private	16 Reg't. (Thompson's), La. Mil.
Laclare, Eli	Private	De Clouet's Reg't., La. Militia (Orig. under Leclare, Elie)
Laclote, --	Private	1 Reg't. (Dejan's), La. Militia
Laclotte, --	Engineer	1 Division (Villere's), La. Mil.
Laclotte, Edouard	Private	2 Batt'n. (D'Aquin's), La. Militia
Lacomb, Charles G.	Corporal	De Clouet's Reg't., La. Militia (Orig. under Le Comb, Charles)
Lacomb, Christopher	Private	De Clouet's Reg't., La. Militia
Lacombe, Charles	Corporal	De Clouet's Reg't., La. Militia
Lacombe, Christopher	Private	De Clouet's Reg't., La. Militia (Orig. under Lacomb, Christopher)
Lacore, Lewis	Private	Captain Sprigg's Co., Boatmen, La. Vols. (Orig. under Lacore, Louis)
Lacore, Louis	Private	Captain Sprigg's Co., Boatmen, La. Vols.
Lacorte, Raimond	Private	De Clouet's Reg't., La. Militia
Lacost, Radimord	Private	De Clouet's Reg't., La. Militia (Orig. under Lacorte, Raimond)
Lacoste, --	Private	1 Reg't. (Dejan's), La. Militia
La Coste, By	Private	2 Reg't. (Cavelier's), La. Militia
Lacoste, Cadet	Private	2 Batt'n. (D'Aquin's), La. Militia
Lacoste, Joseph	Private	6 Reg't. (Landry's), La. Militia
Lacoste, Leandre	1 Sergeant-Sgt.	3 Reg't. (de la Ronde's), La. Mil.
Lacoste, Pierre	Major	1 Batt'n. (Fortier's), La. Militia
Lacoste, Francisque	Private	Capt. Songy's Co., Marines, La. Vols.
La Cour, Jr.	Private	Capt. Le Doux's Co., Cavalry, La. Vols.
La Cour, Agrieole	Private	8 Reg't. (Meriam's), La. Militia
La Cour, Anu	Private	8 Reg't. (Meriam's), La. Militia
Lacour, Brit	Private	17, 18 and 19 Cons. Reg't., La. Militia
La Cour, C.	Sergeant	Capt. Le Doux's Co., Cavalry, La. Vols.
La Cour, Charles	Private	Capt. Le Doux's Co., Cavalry, La. Vols. (Orig. under Dufour, Charles)

Name	Rank	Unit
La Cour, Luffroy	Private	Capt. Le Doux's Co., Cavalry, La. Vols.
La Cour, Sosthenes	Private	8 Reg't. (Meriam's), La. Militia
La Cour, Zenon	1 Lieutenant	Capt. Le Doux's Co., Cavalry, La. Vols.
La Croix, --	Musician	Plauche's Batt'n., La. Militia
Lacroix, --	Sergeant	2 Reg't. (Cavelier's), La. Militia
La Croix, --	Servant	2 Batt'n. (D'Aquin's), La. Militia
Lacroix, Joseph	Private	2 Reg't. (Cavelier's), La. Militia
Lacroix, Joseph	Private	8 Reg't. (Meriam's), La. Militia
Lacroix, Joseph	Private	17, 18 and 19 Cons. Reg't., La. Militia
Lacroix, Peter	Sergeant	17, 18 and 19 Cons. Reg't., La. Militia
Lacroix, Pierre	Private	8 Reg't. (Meriam's), La. Militia
Lacroix, Stephen	Private	17, 18 and 19 Cons. Reg't., La. Militia
Lacrox, Joseph	Private	8 Reg't. (Meriam's), La. Militia (Orig. under Lacroix, Joseph)
Lacrox, Pierre	Private	8 Reg't. (Meriam's), La. Militia (Orig. under Lacroix, Pierre)
Lacy, Austin	Private	12 and 13 Cons. Reg't., La. Mil.
Lacy, William	Corporal	Baker's Regiment, La. Militia
Lacy, William	Private	De Clouet's Reg't., La. Militia
La Douceur, --	Private	10 and 20 Cons. Reg't., La. Mil.
Ladue, Caesar	Private	De Clouet's Reg't., La. Militia (Orig. under Le Due, Cesar)
Lae, Brient	Private	De Clouet's Reg't., La. Militia (Orig. under Lea, Briant)
Lafargue, Fs	Sergeant	1 Reg't. (Dejan's), La. Militia
Lafargue, Hypolite	Private	2 Batt'n. (D'Aquin's), La. Militia
Lafarque, --	Sergeant	1 Reg't. (Dejan's), La. Militia (Orig. under Lafargue, --)
Lafeique, Fere	Servant	1 Reg't. (Dejan's), La. Militia
La Ferle, --	Private	4 Reg't. (Morgan's), La. Militia (Orig. under Laferte, --)
Leferranderie, --	Private	Plauche's Batt'n., La. Militia
Laferte, --	Private	4 Reg't. (Morgan's), La. Militia
Laffaw, Jean	Private	7 Reg't. (Le Beuf's), La. Militia
Laffay, B.	3 Lieutenant	Captain Lagan's Co., La. Vols. (Orig. under Lastaye, Bernard)
Laffaye, Bernard	3 Lieutenant	Captain Lagan's Co., La. Vols. (Orig. under Lastaye, Bernard)
Laffertey, Benijah	Private	Captain Ramsey's Co., Mounted Riflemen, La. Militia
Laffrance, Jeaqus	Private	Captain Lagan's Co., La. Vols. (Orig. under Lafrance, Jaque)
Lafitte, Louis	Private	Plauche's Batt'n., La. Militia
Laflaye, Bernard	3 Lieutenant	Captain Lagan's Co., La. Vols. (Orig. under Lastaye, Bernard)
Laflern, Etienne	Artificer	Capt. Chaudurier's Co., Artificers, Artillery, La. Vols. (Orig. under Lafleure, Etienne)
La Fleur, Achil	Private	5 Reg't. (La Branche's), La. Mil.
Lafleur, Ceasar	Private	16 Reg't. (Thompson's), La. Mil.
Lafleur, Dondiego	Private	16 Reg't. (Thompson's), La. Mil.
Lafleur, Etienne	Artificer	Capt. Chaudurier's Co., Artificers, Artillery, La. Vols. (Orig. under Lafleure, Etienne)
Lafleur, Francis	Private	16 Reg't. (Thompson's), La. Mil.
Lafleur, Jean	Private	16 Reg't. (Thompson's), La. Mil.
Lafleur, John Bte	Private	5 Reg't. (La Branche's), La. Mil.
Lafleur, Joseph	Private	16 Reg't. (Thompson's), La. Mil.
Lafleur, Joseph	Private	17, 18 and 19 Cons. Reg't., La. Militia
Lafleur, Olivier	Private	16 Reg't. (Thompson's), La. Mil.
Lafleur, Valerien	Private	16 Reg't. (Thompson's), La. Mil.
Lafleure, Etienne	Artificer	Capt. Chaudurier's Co., Art'y., La. Vols.
Laflour, --	--	De Clouet's Reg't., La. Militia
Lafontain, Fran	Private	2 Reg't. (Cavelier's), La. Militia (Orig. under Lafontaine, Francois)
Lafontaine, Andre	Private	2 Batt'n. (Peire's), La. Vols.
Lafontaine, Andrew	Private	De Clouet's Reg't., La. Militia
Lafontaine, Francis	Private	2 Batt'n. (Peire's), La. Vols.
Lafontaine, Francois	Private	2 Reg't. (Cavelier's), La. Militia
Lafontaine, Pierre	Private	2 Batt'n. (Peire's), La. Vols.
Laforce, Pierre	Private	16 Reg't. (Thompson's), La. Mil.
Laford, Paul	Private	17, 18 and 19 Cons. Reg't., La. Militia
Laforce, Roman	Private	16 Reg't. (Thompson's), La. Mil.
Lafortune, --	Servant	3 Reg't. (de la Ronde's), La. Mil.
Lafoucarde, --	Private	1 Reg't. (Dejan's), La. Militia (Orig. under Lafourcarde, --)
Lafountaine, Andrew	Private	De Clouet's Reg't., La. Militia (Orig. under Lafontaine, Andrew)
Lafourcarde, --	Private	1 Reg't. (Dejan's), La. Militia
Lafrance, Antoine	Private	De Clouet's Reg't., La. Militia (Orig. under Lefrance, Antoine)
La France, Francois	Private	3 Reg't. (de la Ronde's), La. Mil.
Lafrance, Francois	Private	6 Reg't. (Landry's), La. Militia
Lafrance, Fs	Private	3 Reg't. (de la Ronde's), La. Mil.
La France, Gabriel	Private	3 Reg't. (de la Ronde's), La. Mil.
Lafrance, Jaque	Private	Captain Lagan's Co., La. Vols.
Lafrance, Jn.	Private	3 Reg't. (de la Ronde's), La. Mil.
Lafrance, Jn Bte	Private	3 Reg't. (de la Ronde's), La. Mil.
Lafrance, Jques	Private	3 Reg't. (de la Ronde's), La. Mil.
La France, Sifroy	Private	3 Reg't. (de la Ronde's), La. Mil.
Lafreck, Frans	Servant	1 Reg't. (Dejan's), La. Militia (Orig. under Lafeique, Fere)
Lagan, Charles	Private	Captain Lagan's Co., La. Vols.
Lagan, Francois	Private	Captain Lagan's Co., La. Vols.
La Garde, John	Private	De Clouet's Reg't., La. Militia
Lage, John	Private	10 and 20 Cons. Reg't., La. Mil. (Orig. under Lago, John)
Lago, John	Private	10 and 20 Cons. Reg't., La. Mil.
La Grade, John	Private	De Clouet's Reg't., La. Militia (Orig. under La Garde, John)
Lagraire, Beleraire	Artificer	Capt. Chaudurier's Co., Artificers, Art'y., La. Vols. (Orig. under Lagraize, Belisaire)
Lagraise, Belisaire	Artificer	Capt. Chaudurier's Co., Artificers, Art'y., La. Vols. (Orig. under Lafraize, Belisaire)
Lagraize, Belisaire	Artificer	Capt. Chaudurier's Co., Artificers, Art'y., La. Vols.
La Grange, Auguste	Private	7 Reg't. (Le Beuf's), La. Militia
Lagrange, Bastien	Fusilier-Private	5 Reg't. (La Branche's), La. Mil.
Lagrange, George	Fusilier-Private	5 Reg't. (La Branche's), La. Mil.
Lagrange, I.	Private	4 Reg't. (Morgan's), La. Militia
LaGrange, I. P.	Private	7 Reg't. (Le Beuf's), La. Militia
Lagrange, Jacque	Private	De Clouet's Reg't., La. Militia
Lagrange, Jean	Fusilier-Private	5 Reg't. (La Branche's), La. Mil.
La Grange, Jean	Private	7 Reg't. (Le Beuf's), La. Militia
Lagrange, S.	Private	4 Reg't. (Morgan's), La. Militia (Orig. under Lagrange, I.)
Lagrare, Belisaire	Artificer	Capt. Chaudurier's Co., Artificers, Art'y., La. Vols. (Orig. under Lagraize, Belisaire)
Lagrasis, Belisaire	Artificer	Capt. Chaudurier's Co., Artificers, Art'y., La. Vols. (Orig. under Lagraize, Belisaire)
Lagrede, Blanfort	Private	2 Batt'n. (D'Aquin's), La. Militia (Orig. under Lagreze, Blanfort)
Lagreze, Blanfort	Private	2 Batt'n. (D'Aquin's), La. Militia
Lagrond, Dominique	Private	Capt. Ashley's Co., Mounted Riflemen, La. Militia
Laguin, Pierre	Private	2 Batt'n. (Peire's), La. Vols. (Orig. under Seguin, Pierre)
Lahens, --	Sergeant	Plauche's Batt'n., La. Militia
Laidlaw, --	Private	Plauche's Batt'n., La. Militia (Orig. under Laidlow, --)
Laidlow, Peter	Private	Plauche's Batt'n., La. Militia
Laignel, Simon	1 Lieutenant	4 Reg't. (Morgan's), La. Militia
Laime, Francis	Private	8 Reg't. (Meriam's), La. Militia
Lais, Theodor	Corporal	17, 18 and 19 Cons. Reg't., La. Militia
Laiseau, A. B.	Corporal	8 Reg't. (Meriam's), La. Militia
Lajaunis, Pierre	Fusilier-Private	5 Reg't. (La Branche's), La. Mil.
Lajoi, Bernard	Private	2 Batt'n. (D'Aquin's), La. Militia (Orig. under Lajoy, Bernard)
Lajoy, Bernard	Private	2 Batt'n. (D'Aquin's), La. Militia
Laland, Charles	Private	1 Batt'n. (Fortier's), La. Mil. (Orig. under Lalande, Charles)
Laland, Charles	Private	16 Reg't. (Thompson's), La. Mil.
Laland, Geon	Private	16 Reg't. (Thompson's), La. Mil.
Lalande, Bernard	Private	11 Reg't. (Hickey's), La. Militia
Lalande, Charles	Private	1 Batt'n. (Fortier's), La. Mil.
Lalande, I.	Private	6 Reg't. (Landry's), La. Militia (Orig. under Lalande, Joseph)
Lalande, Joseph	Private	6 Reg't. (Landry's), La. Militia
LaLande, Pierre	Captain	6 Reg't. (Landry's), La. Militia
Lalane, F.	Private	8 Reg't. (Meriam's), La. Militia

Name	Rank	Unit
Lalane, Jean	Private	2 Reg't. (Cavelier's), La. Militia
Lalanne, Pierre	Captain	6 Reg't. (Landry's), La. Militia (Orig. under LaLande, Pierre)
Lallande, Guillaume, fils	Private	16 Reg't. (Thompson's), La. Mil.
Lallane, fils	Private	6 Reg't. (Landry's), La. Militia
Laloire, --	Sergeant	4 Reg't. (Morgan's), La. Militia
Laloire, Claude	Captain	De Clouet's Reg't., La. Militia
Laly, John	Private	10 and 20 Cons. Reg't., La. Mil. (Orig. under Lilly, John)
Lamaniere, Paul	Private	2 Reg't. (Cavelier's), La. Militia
Lamarandier, E. fils	Private	16 Reg't. (Thompson's), La. Mil. (Orig. under Lamorandier, E. fils)
Lamasters, Evan	Private	Capt. Callaway's Co., Cavalry, La. Militia
Lamb, Thomas	Private	1 Reg't. (Dejan's), La. Militia
Lambert, --	Corporal	Plauche's Batt'n., La. Militia
Lambert, --	Private	Plauche's Batt'n., La. Militia
Lambert, Bte	Private	2 Reg't. (Cavelier's), La. Militia
Lambert, Daniel	Sergeant	5 Reg't. (La Branche's), La. Mil.
Lambert, Fulbert	Private	4 Reg't. (Morgan's), La. Militia
Lambert, James	Private	Capt. Ogden's Co., Dragoons, La. Militia
Lambert, Jeremiah	Private	Plauche's Batt'n., La. Militia
Lambert, Leon	Private	Capt. Thomas' Co., La. Militia
Lambert, Louis son	Sergeant	5 Reg't. (La Branche's), La. Mil.
Lambert, Peter	Surgeon	2 Batt'n. (Peire's), La. Vols.
Lamberton, Timothy	Private	Captain Price's Co., La. Militia
Lambie, Jos	Private	16 Reg't. (Thompson's), La. Mil. (Orig. under Lambre, Jos)
Lambre, Jos	Private	16 Reg't. (Thompson's), La. Mil.
Lambremont, Jean	Private	8 Reg't. (Meriam's), La. Militia
Lambremont, Midrel	Captain	8 Reg't. (Meriam's), La. Militia
Lambremont, Mizael	Private	8 Reg't. (Meriam's), La. Militia
Lambremont, Pre	Private	8 Reg't. (Meriam's), La. Militia
Lamie, Jean Bt	Private	8 Reg't. (Meriam's), La. Militia (Orig. under Lorrie, J. Bte)
La Moin, Joseph	Private	16 Reg't. (Thompson's), La. Mil.
Lamoine, Batea	Private	17, 18 and 19 Cons. Reg't., La. Militia
Lamolle, --	Private	2 Reg't. (Cavelier's), La. Militia
Lamontene, Alexander	Private	17, 18 and 19 Cons. Reg't., La. Mil. (Orig. under Lamontine, Alexander)
Lamontine, Alexander	Private	17, 18 and 19 Cons. Reg't., La. Militia
Lamorandier, E. fils	Private	16 Reg't. (Thompson's), La. Mil.
Lamothe, fils	Sergeant	Plauche's Batt'n., La. Militia
Lamothe, pere	Private	Plauche's Batt'n., La. Militia
Lamour, --	Private	2 Reg't. (Cavelier's), La. Militia
Lamour, Charles	Private	Captain Hubbard's Mounted Co., La. Militia
Lamoureux, Francois	2 Lieutenant	Captain Lagan's Co., La. Vols.
Lampkins, Samuel	Private	10 and 20 Cons. Reg't., La. Mil.
Lamure, --	Private	2 Reg't. (Cavelier's), La. Militia (Orig. under Lamour, --)
Lamy, Jacques	Private	2 Reg't. (Cavelier's), La. Militia
Lana, Vital	Private	1 Batt'n. (Fortier's), La. Militia
Lanaud, Arnaud	Fusilier-Private	5 Reg't. (La Branche's), La. Mil.
Lanaus, Simon	Private	6 Reg't. (Landry's), La. Militia
Lanaux, Aaine	Sergeant	Plauche's Batt'n., La. Militia
Lanaux, Chs	Private	Plauche's Batt'n., La. Militia
Lanaux, Helie	Private	6 Reg't. (Landry's), La. Militia
Lanaux, P.	Private	Plauche's Batt'n., La. Militia
Landernong, Joseph	Corporal	17, 18 and 19 Cons. Reg't., La. Militia
Landers, William	Private	Capt. Collard's Co., La. Militia
Landers, Aurora	Private	2 Batt'n. (Peire's), La. Vols. (Orig. under Landues, Aurora)
Landfou, Tho.	Private	10 Reg't., La. Militia
Landia, Francis	Private	De Clouet's Reg't., La. Militia (Orig. under Landry, Francis)
Landon, William	Private	10 and 20 Cons. Reg't., La. Mil. (Orig. under Lowdon, William)
Landrau, Jean	Private	Plauche's Batt'n., La. Militia
Landraux, Jacques	Private	2 Reg't. (Cavelier's), La. Militia (Orig. under Landreau, Jacques)
Landre, Alexandre	Private	De Clouet's Reg't., La. Militia
Landre, Alexr Ch.		Capt. Dubuclet's Troop, Hussars, La. Vols.
Landre, Eloi	Corporal	16 Reg't. (Thompson's), La. Mil.
Landre, fils	Private	De Clouet's Reg't., La. Militia (Orig. under Landry, fils)
Landre, Julian	Private	16 Reg't. (Thompson's), La. Mil.
Landre', Leander	Private	16 Reg't. (Thompson's), La. Mil.
Landreau, J.	Private	2 Reg't. (Cavelier's), La. Militia
Landreau, Jacques	Private	2 Reg't. (Cavelier's), La. Militia
Landreau, Jean	Private	Plauche's Batt'n., La. Militia (Orig. under Landrau, Jean)
Landreau, Julien	Private	17, 18 and 19 Cons. Reg't., La. Mil. (Orig. under Landreaux, Julien)
Landreaux, --	Private	4 Reg't. (Morgan's), La. Militia
Landreaux, Francois	Private	17, 18 and 19 Cons. Reg't., La. Militia
Landreaux, Julien	Private	17, 18 and 19 Cons. Reg't., La. Militia
Landreaux, Leon	Private-Sergeant	2 Batt'n. (Peire's), La. Vols.
Landres, Aurore	Private	De Clouet's Reg't., La. Militia
Landrey, Julien	2 Lieutenant	6 Reg't. (Landry's), La. Militia (Orig. under Landry, Julien)
Landri, Alex Chs.	Private	Capt. Dubuclet's Troop, Hussars, La. Vols. (Orig. under Landre, Alexr ch.)
Landry, Achilles	1 Lieutenant	8 Reg't. (Meriam's), La. Militia
Landry, Agricole	Private	De Clouet's Reg't., La. Militia
Landry, Alexander	Private	De Clouet's Reg't., La. Militia
Landry, Alexandre	Private	7 Reg't. (Le Beuf's), La. Militia
Landry, Alexre C.	Private	Capt. Dubuclet's Troop, Hussars, La. Vols. (Orig. under Landre, Alexr Ch)
Landry, Apolinaire	Private	Captain Hubbard's Mounted Co., La. Militia
Landry, Armand, A.	Private	Captain Hubbard's Mounted Co., La. Militia
Landry, Athanas	Private	De Clouet's Reg't., La. Militia
Landry, Athauase	Corporal	16 Reg't. (Thompson's), La. Mil.
Landry, August	Corporal	7 Reg't. (Le Beuf's), La. Militia
Landry, August	Private	8 Reg't. (Meriam's), La. Militia
Landry, Auguste	Private	Captain Hubbard's Mounted Co., La. Militia
Landry, Auguste	Private	6 Reg't. (Landry's), La. Militia
Landry, Auguste	Private	6 Reg't. (Landry's), La. Militia
Landry, Aurora	Private	2 Batt'n. (Peire's), La. Vols. (Orig. under Landues, Aurora)
Landry, Azani	Private	8 Reg't. (Meriam's), La. Militia
Landry, Baptiste	Private	Captain Hubbard's Mounted Co., La. Militia
Landry, Baptiste	Private	Captain Hubbard's Mounted Co., La. Militia
Landry, Belonie	Private	6 Reg't. (Landry's), La. Militia
Landry, Benjamin	Private	6 Reg't. (Landry's), La. Militia
Landry, Benjamin	Corporal	7 Reg't. (Le Beuf's), La. Militia
Landry, Bt	Private	8 Reg't. (Meriam's), La. Militia
Landry, Celestin	Private	De Clouet's Reg't., La. Militia
Landry, Cyrill	Private	De Clouet's Reg't., La. Militia
Landry, David	Private	8 Reg't. (Meriam's), La. Militia
Landry, Denis	Captain	8 Reg't. (Meriam's), La. Militia
Landry, Dennis	Private	Baker's Regiment, La. Militia (Orig. under Laudry, Dennia)
Landry, Deny	Captain	8 Reg't. (Meriam's), La. Militia (Orig. under Landry, Denis)
Landry, Desire	Private	6 Reg't. (Landry's), La. Militia
Landry, Donat	Private	6 Reg't. (Landry's), La. Militia
Landry, Donat	Private	8 Reg't. (Meriam's), La. Militia
Landry, E.	Sergeant	8 Reg't. (Meriam's), La. Militia
Landry, Edward	Corporal	6 Reg't. (Landry's), La. Militia
Landry, Edward	Sergeant	8 Reg't. (Meriam's), La. Militia
Landry, Elias	Private	6 Reg't. (Landry's), La. Militia
Landry, Eloi	Private	De Clouet's Reg't., La. Militia
Landry, Emel	Lieutenant	8 Reg't. (Meriam's), La. Militia (Orig. under Landry, M.)
Landry, Etienne	Private	Captain Hubbard's Mounted Co., La. Militia
Landry, F.	Private	8 Reg't. (Meriam's), La. Militia
Landry, Ferdinand	Captain	6 Reg't. (Landry's), La. Militia
Landry, fils	Private	De Clouet's Reg't., La. Militia
Landry, Firmin D.	Sergeant	8 Reg't. (Meriam's), La. Militia
Landry, Florentine	Private	De Clouet's Reg't., La. Militia
Landry, Francis	Private	De Clouet's Reg't., La. Militia
Landry, Hebert	Private	Baker's Regiment, La. Militia
Landry, Henry	Private	7 Reg't. (Le Beuf's), La. Militia
Landry, Henry	Private	7 Reg't. (Le Beuf's), La. Militia
Landry, Hipolite	1 Sergeant-Sgt.	8 Reg't. (Meriam's), La. Militia
Landry, Hipolite	Private	8 Reg't. (Meriam's), La. Militia

Name	Rank	Unit
Landry, I. L.	Private	8 Reg't. (Meriam's), La. Militia (Orig. under Landry, T. L.)
Landry, I. V.	Private	6 Reg't. (Landry's), La. Militia
Landry, Jean	Private	De Clouet's Reg't., La. Militia
Landry, Jean	Private	7 Reg't. (Le Beuf's), La. Militia
Landry, Jean	Private	7 Reg't. (Le Beuf's), La. Militia
Landry, Joseph	Private	De Clouet's Reg't., La. Militia
Landry, Joseph	Private	2 Batt'n. (Peire's), La. Vols.
Landry, Joseph	Private	6 Reg't. (Landry's), La. Militia
Landry, Joseph	Private	7 Reg't. (Le Beuf's), La. Militia
Landry, Joseph	Sergeant	8 Reg't. (Meriam's), La. Militia
Landry, Joseph	Private	2 Batt'n. (Peire's), La. Vols.
Landry, Joseph S.	Private	6 Reg't. (Landry's), La. Militia
Landry, Julien	2 Lieutenant	6 Reg't. (Landry's), La. Militia
Landry, Leger	Sergeant	6 Reg't. (Landry's), La. Militia
Landry, Louis	Colonel	6 Reg't. (Landry's), La. Militia
Landry, Louis	Private	8 Reg't. (Meriam's), La. Militia
Landry, M.	Lieut.-1 Lieut.	8 Reg't. (Meriam's), La. Militia
Landry, Magloire	Private	7 Reg't. (Le Beuf's), La. Militia
Landry, Mathurin	Private	8 Reg't. (Meriam's), La. Militia
Landry, Maxille	Private	Captain Hubbard's Mounted Co., La. Militia
Landry, Maximilien	Private	De Clouet's Reg't., La. Militia
Landry, N.	Private	8 Reg't. (Meriam's), La. Militia
Landry, Narcisse	Captain	6 Reg't. (Landry's), La. Militia
Landry, Nicholas	Private	6 Reg't. (Landry's), La. Militia
Landry, Pierre	Private	6 Reg't. (Landry's), La. Militia
Landry, Pierre Joseph	Captain	8 Reg't. (Meriam's), La. Militia
Landry, Pierre Paul	Private	8 Reg't. (Meriam's), La. Militia
Landry, Raphael	Private	6 Reg't. (Landry's), La. Militia
Landry, Raphael	Private	8 Reg't. (Meriam's), La. Militia
Landry, Raphiel	Private	De Clouet's Reg't., La. Militia
Landry, Rosamond	Private	De Clouet's Reg't., La. Militia
Landry, S.	Private	6 Reg't. (Landry's), La. Militia
Landry, Simon	Private	7 Reg't. (Le Beuf's), La. Militia
Landry, Simon	2 Lieutenant	8 Reg't. (Meriam's), La. Militia
Landry, T.	Private	8 Reg't. (Meriam's), La. Militia
Landry, T. L.	Private	8 Reg't. (Meriam's), La. Militia
Landry, Torissin	Private	6 Reg't. (Landry's), La. Militia
Landry, Trasimond	2 Lieutenant	7 Reg't. (Le Beuf's), La. Militia
Landry, Ursin	Private	6 Reg't. (Landry's), La. Militia
Landry, Ursin	Private	8 Reg't. (Meriam's), La. Militia
Landry, Valentine	Private	Baker's Regiment, La. Militia
Landry, Valerie	2 Lieutenant	6 Reg't. (Landry's), La. Militia
Landry, Valery	Corporal	6 Reg't. (Landry's), La. Militia
Landry, Victor	Private	De Clouet's Reg't., La. Militia
Landry, Victor	Private	6 Reg't. (Landry's), La. Militia
Landry, Xavier	Private	8 Reg't. (Meriam's), La. Militia
Landues, Aurora	Private	2 Batt'n. (Peire's), La. Vols.
Landus, Aurora	Private	2 Batt'n. (Peire's), La. Vols. (Orig. under Landues, Aurora)
Lane, Anderson	Private	12 and 13 Cons. Reg't., La. Mil.
Laneaux, Helie	Private	6 Reg't. (Landry's), La. Militia (Orig. under Lanaux, Helie)
Laneaux, Michael	Private	6 Reg't. (Landry's), La. Militia
Laneuville, A.	Adjt. & Insp. Gen.	Gov. Claiborne and Staff, La. Mil.
Lang, Stephen	Private	De Clouet's Reg't., La. Militia
Langae, --	Private	1 Reg't. (Dejan's), La. Militia
Lange, Louis P.	Private	Baker's Regiment, La. Militia
Lange, Pierre	Private	Captain Lagan's Co., La. Vols.
Langer, Louis P.	Private	Baker's Regiment, La. Militia (Orig. under Lange, Louis P.)
Langham, William	Private	De Clouet's Reg't., La. Militia
Langlais, A.	Private	8 Reg't. (Meriam's), La. Militia
Langlais, Antoine	Private	8 Reg't. (Meriam's), La. Militia
Langlais, Aye	Private	8 Reg't. (Meriam's), La. Militia
Langlais, I.	Private	6 Reg't. (Landry's), La. Militia (Orig. under Langlais, Joseph)
L'Anglais, Joseph	Private	6 Reg't. (Landry's), La. Militia (Orig. under Langlais, Joseph)
Langlena, Louis	Private	De Clouet's Reg't., La. Militia (Orig. under Langline, Louis)
Langlene, Louis	Private	De Clouet's Reg't., La. Militia (Orig. under Langline, Louis)
Langley, W. D.	Private	Captain Sprigg's Co., Boatmen, La. Vols. (Orig. under Langly, W. D.)
Langline, Jean	2 Lieutenant	16 Reg't. (Thompson's), La. Mil.
Langline, Louis	Private	De Clouet's Reg't., La. Militia
Langlois, Baptiste	Private	Capt. Le Doux's Co., Cavalry, La. Vols.
Langlois, Valerien	Private	16 Reg't. (Thompson's), La. Mil.
Langlois, Virgile	Private	1 Batt'n. (Fortier's), La. Militia
Langlois, Zenon	Private	Capt. Le Doux's Co., Cavalry, La. Vols.
Langly, W. D.	Private	Captain Sprigg's Co., Boatmen, La. Vols.
Languille, --	Private	2 Reg't. (Cavelier's), La. Militia
Lanier, Edward	Private	6 Reg't. (Landry's), La. Militia
Lanna, Vital	Private	1 Batt'n. (Fortier's), La. Militia (Orig. under Lana Vital)
Lanoix, Albert	Private	6 Reg't. (Landry's), La. Militia
Lanoix, Louis	Private	2 Batt'n. (Peire's), La. Vols.
Lanoux, Albert	Private	6 Reg't. (Landry's), La. Militia (Orig. under Lanoix, Albert)
Lansau, Phillip	Private	7 Reg't. (Le Beuf's), La. Militia
Lansford, Moses	Private	10 and 20 Cons. Reg't., La. Mil. (Orig. under Lunsford, Moses)
Lantier, Michel	Private	De Clouet's Reg't., La. Militia
Lapaule, Frederique de	Private	16 Reg't. (Thompson's), La. Mil.
Lapauze, --	Private	Capt. Chauveau's Co., Cavalry, La. Militia
Laperuse, Jean	Corporal-Private	3 Reg't. (de la Ronde's), La. Mil. (Orig. under Lapiruse, Jean)
Lapice, --	Private	Plauche's Batt'n., La. Militia
Lapicotte, I.	Corporal	Capt. Songy's Co., Marines, La. Vols.
Lapin, Baptiste	Private	6 Reg't. (Landry's), La. Militia
Lapin, John	Private	De Clouet's Reg't., La. Militia (Orig. under Lepine, John)
Lapine, John	Private	De Clouet's Reg't., La. Militia (Orig. under Lepine, John)
Lapiotte, S.	Corporal	Capt. Songy's Co., Marines, La. Vols. (Orig. under Lapicotte, I.)
Lapiruse, Jean	Corporal-Private	3 Reg't. (de la Ronde's), La. Mil.
Laplace, John	1 Sergeant	17, 18 and 19 Cons. Reg't., La. Militia
La Plante, F.	Private	8 Reg't. (Meriam's), La. Militia
Lapointe, Michel	Private	16 Reg't. (Thompson's), La. Mil.
Laporte, Edmond	Private	1 Batt'n. (Fortier's), La. Militia
Laporte, Rodenai	Private	2 Batt'n. (D'Aquin's), La. Militia
Lapuse, Pierre	Drummer	2 Batt'n. (D'Aquin's), La. Militia
Lapusse, Pierre	Drummer	2 Batt'n. (D'Aquin's), La. Militia (Orig. under Lapuse, Pierre)
Laquinte, Garcon	Private	2 Batt'n. (D'Aquin's), La. Militia
Larabas, Dominique	Private	Plauche's Batt'n., La. Militia
Lard, Isaac	Private	Captain Musick's Co., La. Mil.
Lard, Joseph	Sergeant	Capt. Musick's Co., Mounted Riflemen, La. Militia
Lard, Joseph	Sergeant	Capt. Musick's Co., La. Militia
Lareche, J. Bte	1 Lieutenant	6 Reg't. (Landry's), La. Militia (Orig. under Lariche, Jean Bte)
Laret, --	Private	4 Reg't. (Morgan's), La. Militia (Orig. under Lavet, --)
Lariche, Jean Bte	1 Lieutenant	6 Reg't. (Landry's), La. Militia
Larieu, Jean	Private	1 Batt'n. (Fortier's), La. Militia
Larieux, Emelian	Musician	1 Batt'n. (Fortier's), La. Militia
Larieux, Etienne	Musician	1 Batt'n. (Fortier's), La. Militia
Larigne, Louis	Private	2 Batt'n. (Peire's), La. Vols. (Orig. under Lavigne, Louis)
Larigue, Louis	Private	2 Batt'n. (Peire's), La. Vols. (Orig. under Lavigne, Louis)
Larmatre, Germain	Artificer	Capt. Chaudurier's Co., Artificers, Art'y., La. Vols. (Orig. under Lasmatre, Jermin)
Larnaud, John B.	Private	17, 18 and 19 Cons. Reg't., La. Mil. (Orig. under Larnaudiere, John Bapt.)
Larnaudiere, John Bapt.	Private	17, 18 and 19 Cons. Reg't., La. Militia
Larnaudiere, Philip	Private	17, 18 and 19 Cons. Reg't., La. Militia
Laroche, Peter	Private	2 Batt'n. (Peire's), La. Vols. (Orig. under Laroche, Pierre)
Laroche, Pierre	Private	2 Batt'n. (Peire's), La. Vols.
Laroze, Francois Haution	Corporal	Captain Lagan's Co., La. Vols.
Larodet, Jean	Private	Capt. Songy's Co., Marines, La. Vols.
La Rose, Pierre	Private	Capt. Songy's Co., Marines, La. Vols.
Larrabas, Dominique	Private	Plauche's Batt'n., La. Militia (Orig. under Larabas, Dominique)

Name	Rank	Unit
Larreche, Jn Bte	1 Lieutenant	6 Reg't. (Landry's), La. Militia (Orig. under Lariche, Jean Bte)
Lartigue, --	Private	4 Reg't. (Morgan's), La. Militia
Lartigue, Fs	2 Lieutenant	4 Reg't. (Morgan's), La. Militia
Lascana, Gaspart	Sergeant	17, 18 and 19 Cons. Reg't., La. Militia
Lascano, Gaspar	Sergeant	17, 18 and 19 Cons. Reg't., La. Mil. (Orig. under Lascana, Gaspar)
Lascano, Gasparda	Sergeant	17, 18 and 19 Cons. Reg't., La. Mil.
Laseigne, Andre	Private	5 Reg't. (La Branche's), La. Mil.
Laseigne, Charles	Private	5 Reg't. (La Branche's), La. Mil.
Laseigne, Piere	Corporal	5 Reg't. (La Branche's), La. Mil. (Orig. under Lasergne, Piere)
Lasergne, Piere	Corporal	5 Reg't. (La Branche's), La. Mil.
Lasmate, --	Private	2 Reg't. (Cavelier's), La. Militia
Lasmate, Jermin	Artificifer	Capt. Chaudurier's Co., Artificers, Art'y., La. Vols. (Orig. under Lasmatre, Jermin)
Lasmatre, Germain	Artificifer	Capt. Chaudurier's Co., Artificers, Art'y., La. Vols. (Orig. under Lasmatre, Jermin)
Lasmatre, Jermin	Artificifer	Capt. Chaudurier's Co., Artificers, Art'y., La. Vols.
Lasmatte, --	Private	2 Reg't. (Cavelier's), La. Militia (Orig. under Lasmate, --)
Lasour, Jacques	Private	1 Batt'n. (Fortier's), La. Militia (Orig. under Latoure, Jacques)
Lassal, --	Sergeant	2 Batt'n. (D'Aquin's), La. Militia
Lassale, --	Sergeant	2 Batt'n. (D'Aquin's), La. Militia (Orig. under Lassal, --)
Lastrance, Jeaques	Private	Captain Lagan's Co., La. Vols. (Orig. under Lafrance, Jaque)
Lastrapes, Andre	Private	16 Reg't. (Thompson's), La. Mil.
Lastrapes, Charles	Private	16 Reg't. (Thompson's), La. Mil.
Lastaye, Bernard	3 Lieutenant	Captain Lagan's Co., La. Vols.
Latchel, Joseph	Private	17, 18 and 19 Cons. Reg't., La. Militia
Latham, John	Private	17, 18 and 19 Cons. Reg't., La. Militia
Latille, E.	Sergeant	2 Reg't. (Cavelier's), La. Militia
Latille, Timecourt	Private	2 Reg't. (Cavelier's), La. Militia
Latille, Zimicont	Private	2 Reg't. (Cavelier's), La. Militia (Orig. under Latille, Timecourt)
Latiolais, Joseph	Private	Capt. Dubuclet's Troop, Hussars, La. Vols.
Latiolais, Lufra	3 Lieutenant	16 Reg't. (Thompson's), La. Mil.
Latiolie, Lefroi	3 Lieutenant	16 Reg't. (Thompson's), La. Mil. (Orig. under Latiolais, Lufra)
Latoilett, Lepoi	3 Lieutenant	16 Reg't. (Thompson's), La. Mil. (Orig. under Latiolais, Lufra)
Latour, Andre	Fusilier-Private	5 Reg't. (La Branche's), La. Mil.
Latour, Felicien	2 Lieutenant	3 Reg't. (de la Ronde's), La. Mil.
Latoure, Jacques	Private	1 Batt'n. (Fortier's), La. Militia
Latoure, Maretto	Artificer	Capt. Chaudurier's Co., Artificers, Art'y., La. Vols.
Latournel, fils	Sergeant	5 Reg't. (La Branche's), La. Mil.
Latournelle, fils	Sergeant	5 Reg't. (La Branche's), La. Mil. (Orig. under Latournels, fils)
Lattier, John Bapt.	2 Lieutenant	17, 18 and 19 Cons. Reg't., La. Militia
La-u, Francis	Private	19 Regiment, La. Militia
Laubelle, In Bte	Fusilier-Private	5 Reg't. (La Branche's), La. Mil.
Laubounier, Joseph	Private	De Clouet's Reg't., La. Militia
Laudier, --	Private	3 Reg't. (de la Ronde's), La. Mil.
Laudry, Dennis	Private	Baker's Regiment, La. Militia
Laughlin, George	Corporal	16 Reg't. (Thompson's), La. Mil.
Laughlin, Samuel	Captain	De Clouet's Reg't., La. Militia
Laughling, Samuel	Captain	De Clouet's Reg't., La. Militia (Orig. under Laughlin, Samuel)
Laughridge, Samuel	Private	12 and 13 Cons. Reg't., La. Mil.
Laulounier, Louis	Corporal	De Clouet's Reg't., La. Militia
Laumon, Bd	Private	2 Reg't. (Cavelier's), La. Militia
Laundra, Francis	Private	De Clouet's Reg't., La. Militia (Orig. under Landry, Francis)
Laundrey, Francis	Private	De Clouet's Reg't., La. Militia (Orig. under Landry, Francis)
Launtier, Michel	Private	De Clouet's Reg't., La. Militia
Laurance, John	Corporal	10 and 20 Cons. Reg't., La. Mil. (Orig. under Lawrance, John)
Laurand, Simon	Private	5 Reg't. (La Branche's), La. Mil.
Laureince, Baidle	Private	De Clouet's Reg't., La. Militia
Laurend, Jn	Private	Plauche's Batt'n., La. Militia
Laurens, Calvin	Private	Captain McNair's Co., Mounted Riflemen, La. Militia (Orig. under Lawrence, Calvin)
Laurent, --	Servant	Capt. Dubuclet's Troop, Hussars, La. Vols.
Laurent, --	Servant	4 Reg't. (Morgan's), La. Militia
Laurent, Ge	Private	Capt. Alpuente's Co., La. Mil.
Laurent, Jn	Corporal	Capt. Colsson's Co., Artillery, La. Vols.
Laurent, John	Private	4 Reg't. (Morgan's), La. Militia
Laurent, John Bte	Private	Capt. Alpuente's Co., La. Mil.
Laurent, Nicolas	Private	Capt. Alpuente's Co., La. Mil.
Laurent, Louis	Private	2 Batt'n. (D'Aquin's), La. Militia
Laurent, Pierre	Private	Plauche's Batt'n., La. Militia
Laurent, Simon	Private	16 Reg't. (Thompson's), La. Mil.
Laurent, William	Private	4 Reg't. (Morgan's), La. Militia
Laurente, --	Servant	Capt. Dubuclet's Troop, Hussars, La. Vols. (Orig. under Laurent, --)
Laurin, Fois	Private	Plauche's Batt'n., La. Militia
Lauriot, Andre	Fusilier-Private	5 Reg't. (La Branche's), La. Mil.
Lauriot, Henri	Private	5 Reg't. (La Branche's), La. Mil.
Lause, A.	Private	1 Reg't. (Dejan's), La. Mil.
Lausent, Louis	Private	2 Batt'n. (D'Aquin's), La. Militia (Orig. under Laurent, Louis)
Laussade, B.	Private	3 Reg't. (de la Ronde's), La. Mil. (Orig. under Laussade, Rd)
Laussade, Joseph	Private	3 Reg't. (de la Ronde's), La. Mil. (Orig. under Laussat, Joseph)
Laussade, Rd	Private	3 Reg't. (de la Ronde's), La. Mil.
Laussat, Joseph	Private	3 Reg't.(de la Ronde's), La. Mil.
Lausse, Benjamin	Private	6 Reg't. (Landry's), La. Militia
Lausse, Pierre	Private	6 Reg't. (Landry's), La. Militia
Lauviere, Francois	Private	Baker's Regiment, La. Militia
Lauzon, Louis	Private	Captain Lagan's Co., La. Vols.
Lauzume, Francois	Private	Captain Lagan's Co., La. Vols.
Lauzun, Francois	Private	Captain Lagan's Co., La. Vols. (Orig. under Lauzume, Francois)
Laval, Simon	Private	17, 18 and 19 Cons. Reg't., La. Militia
Lavan, Nicholas	Private	10 and 20 Cons. Reg't., La. Mil.
Lavand, Eugne	2 Lieut.	2 Reg't. (Cavelier's), La. Militia (Orig. under Laveau, Eugene)
Lavanture, --	Private	16 Reg't. (Thompson's), La. Mil.
Lavaux, Narcisse	Private	1 Batt'n. (Fortier's), La. Militia
Laveau, Eugene	2 Lieutenant	2 Reg't.(Cavelier's), La. Militia
Laveaux, Michael	Private	6 Reg't. (Landry's), La. Militia (Orig. under Laneaux, Michael)
Lavegne, Celestin	Private	Baker's Regiment, La. Militia (Orig. under Levergne, Celestin)
Lavellain, Michael	Sergeant	19 Regiment, La. Militia
Lavelline, Michl	Sergeant	19 Regiment, La. Militia (Orig. under Lavellain, Michael)
Lavenue, Joseph	Fusilier-Private	5 Reg't. (La Branche's), La. Mil.
Lavenus, Stephen	Private	17, 18 and 19 Cons. Reg't., La. Militia
Lavergne, Allain	Fusilier-Private	5 Reg't. (La Branche's), La. Mil.
Lavergne, Louis	Private	Capt. Allen's Co., Artillerists, La. Vols.
La Vergne, Louis	Private	6 Reg't. (Landry's), La. Militia
Lavergne, Louis	Private	16 Reg't. (Thompson's), La. Mil.
Lavergne, Pierre	Private	8 Reg't. (Meriam's), La. Militia
Lavergne, Urbin	Private	16 Reg't. (Thompson's), La. Mil.
Lavergne, Ursin	Private	16 Reg't. (Thompson's), La. Mil.
Lavergue, Hugues	Adj. Genl.	1 Division (Villere), La. Militia
Lavern, Nicholas	Private	10 and 20 Cons. Reg't., La. Mil. (Orig. under Lavan, Nicholas)
Laverne, Asa	Private	16 Reg't. (Thompson's), La. Mil.
Laverne, Baptist	Private	16 Reg't. (Thompson's), La. Mil.
Laverne, Dural	Private	16 Reg't. (Thompson's), La. Mil.
Laverne, Eugine	Private	16 Reg't. (Thompson's), La. Mil.
Laverne, Furel	Private	16 Reg't. (Thompson's), La. Mil. (Orig. under Laverne, Durcil)
Laverpere, -- fils	Private	17, 18 and 19 Cons. Reg't., La. Militia
Laverty, Henry	Private	Captain Beale's Co., Riflemen, La. Militia
Laverty, Kenny	Private	Captain Beale's Co., Riflemen, La. Mil. (Orig. under Laverty, Henry)

Name	Rank	Unit
Lavet, --	Private	4 Reg't. (Morgan's), La. Militia
Lavigne, Antoine	Private	6 Reg't. (Landry's), La. Militia
Lavigne, Francois	Private	2 Batt'n. (D'Aquin's), La. Militia
Lavigne, Honori	Private	Capt. Alpuente's Co., La. Mil.
Lavigne, Joseph	Private	1 Batt'n. (Fortier's), La. Militia
Lavigne, Louis	Private	2 Batt'n. (Peire's), La. Vols.
Lavigne, P.	Private	8 Reg't. (Meriam's), La. Militia
Lavigne, Pierre	Private	2 Batt'n. (D'Aquin's), La. Militia
Lavigne, Robert	Private	6 Reg't. (Landry's), La. Militia
Lavigni, Honori	Private	Capt. Alpuente's Co., La. Mil. (Orig. under Lavigne, Honori)
Lavigue, Louis	Private	2 Batt'n. (Peire's), La. Vols. (Orig. under Lavigne, Louis)
Lavillebauf, --	Private	4 Reg't. (Morgan's), La. Militia (Orig. under Lavillebeouf, --)
Lavillebeouf, --	Private	4 Reg't. (Morgan's), La. Militia
Laviolette, Jacques	Private	De Clouet's Reg't., La. Militia
Laviolette, Jean	Private	De Clouet's Reg't., La. Militia
Laviolette, Joseph	Private	Baker's Regiment, La. Militia
Lavolette, Jean	Private	De Clouet's Reg't., La. Militia (Orig. under Laviolette, Jean)
Lawdon, James	Private	10 and 20 Cons. Reg't., La. Mil. (Orig. under Lowdon, James)
Lawman, Frederick	Private	10 and 20 Cons. Reg't., La. Mil.
Lawrance, John	Corporal	10 and 20 Cons. Reg't., La. Mil.
Lawrence, Calvin	Private	Captain McNair's Co., Mounted Riflemen, La. Militia
Lawrence, Gabriel	Private	12 and 13 Cons. Reg't., La. Mil.
Lawrent, John	Private	4 Reg't. (Morgan's), La. Militia (Orig. under Laurent, John)
Lawrent, William	Private	4 Reg't. (Morgan's), La. Militia (Orig. under Laurent, William)
Lawson, Columbus	Private	Capt. Ogden's Co., Dragoons, La. Militia
Lawson, William Mc F.	Private	2 Batt'n. (Peire's), La. Vols.
Lawson, W. M. T.	Private	2 Batt'n. (Peire's), La. Vols. (Orig. under Lawson, William, Mc F)
Layman, Daniel	Private	De Clouet's Reg't., La. Militia
Layraize, B.	Artificer	Capt. Chaudurier's Co., Artificers, Art'y., La. Vols. (Orig. under Lagraize, Belisaire)
Layssard, G.	Private	4 Reg't. (Morgan's), La. Militia (Orig. under Layssard, G.
Layton, Robert	Qr. Master	1 Reg't. (Dejan's), La. Militia
Lazare, --	Lieutenant	2 Batt'n. (D'Aquin's), La. Militia (Orig. under Lazarre, --)
Lazarin, Jose	Corporal	17, 18 and 19 Cons. Reg't., La. Militia
Lazarin, Juan	Private	17, 18 and 19 Cons. Reg't., La. Militia
Lazarre, --	Lieutenant	2 Batt'n. (D'Aquin's), La. Militia
Lea, Briant	Private	De Clouet's Reg't., La. Militia
Lea, James P.	Private	12 and 13 Cons. Reg't., La. Mil.
Lea, John	Private	(See Batt'n. Henry's), U.S. Vols. La. War of 1812 - See also 1 Batt'n.
Lea, Stephen	Sergeant	12 and 13 Cons. Reg't., La. Mil. (Orig. under Lee, Stephen)
Leach, Ebenezer	Private	De Clouet's Reg't., La. Militia See also 44 Reg't., Inf.
Leach, William	Private	12 and 13 Cons. Reg't., La. Mil.
Leak, William	Private	1 Reg't. (Dejan's), La. Militia
Leake, William	Corporal-Sgt.	10 and 20 Cons. Reg't., La. Mil.
Leal, Jose	Private	17, 18 and 19 Cons. Reg't., La. Militia
Learce, Thomas	Private	De Clouet's Reg't., La. Militia
Lears, Silvester	Private	Captain Dodge's Co., Mounted Riflemen, La. Militia (Orig. under Lewis, Silvester)
Lears, Silvester	Private	Captain Henry's Co., Mounted Riflemen, La. Militia
Leaumond, Jule	Private	2 Reg't. (Cavelier's), La. Militia
Leaurant, Semon	Private	16 Reg't. (Thompson's), La. Mil. (Orig. under Laurent, Simon)
Leavens, Samuel	Captain	10 and 20 Cons. Reg't., La. Mil.
Le Bauf, Michel	Private	De Clouet's Reg't., La. Militia (Orig. under Le Bouef, M.)
Lebasque, Ferie	Corporal	Capt. Songy's Co., Marines, La. Vols.
Le Baurgeais, P.	1 Lieutenant	6 Reg't. (Landry's), La. Militia (Orig. under LeBourgeois, P.)
Le Bauve, Jacques	Private	8 Reg't. (Meriam's), La. Militia (Orig. under Labauve, Jacques)
Le Beau, Jean Baptiste	Private	3 Reg't. (de la Ronde's), La. Mil.
Lebert, P.	1 Sergeant	8 Reg't. (Meriam's), La. Militia
Le Beuf, Augustin	Private	6 Reg't. (Landry's), La. Militia
Le Beuf, Grabiel	Private	6 Reg't. (Landry's), La. Militia
Le Beuf, Michel	Private	De Clouet's Reg't., La. Militia (Orig. under Le Bouef, M.)
Leblan, Paulum	Private	10 and 20 Cons. Reg't., La. Mil. (Orig. under Withe, Paul)
Leblanc, Alexi	Private	Baker's Regiment, La. Militia
Le Blanc, Alexis	Captain	8 Reg't. (Meriam's), La. Militia (Orig. under LeBlanc, Jean Alexis)
Le Blanc, Arinable	Private	7 Reg't. (Le Beuf's), La. Militia (Could be Amiable or Annable)
Le Blanc, Andrew	2 Lieutenant	De Clouet's Reg't., La. Militia (Orig. under La Blanc, Andrew)
Le Blanc, Armoigen	Private	6 Reg't. (Landry's), La. Militia
Le Blanc, Auguste	Private	8 Reg't. (Meriam's), La. Militia
Le Blanc, B.	Private	6 Reg't. (Landry's), La. Militia
Le Blanc, B.	Corporal	6 Reg't. (Landry's), La. Militia
Le Blanc, Belonie	Private	8 Reg't. (Meriam's), La. Militia
Le Blanc, Bn	Private	6 Reg't. (Landry's), La. Militia
Le Blanc, C.	Private	6 Reg't. (Landry's), La. Militia
Le Blanc, Cesair	Private	4 Reg't. (Morgan's), La. Militia
Le Blanc, Charles	Private	7 Reg't. (Le Beuf's), La. Militia
Le Blanc, Charles	2 Lieutenant	8 Reg't. (Meriam's), La. Militia
Le Blanc, Chevallier	Private	De Clouet's Reg't., La. Militia
Le Blanc, Colin	Private	6 Reg't. (Landry's), La. Militia
Le Blanc, Corantin	Private	6 Reg't. (Landry's), La. Militia
Le Blanc, D.	Private	6 Reg't. (Landry's), La. Militia
Le Blanc, Danat	Private	6 Reg't. (Landry's), La. Militia
Le Blanc, Dermont	Corporal	6 Reg't. (Landry's), La. Militia
Le Blanc, Derneville	Private	Capt. Dubuclet's Troop, Hussars, La. Vols.
Le Blanc, Desire	Private	6 Reg't. (Landry's), La. Militia
Le Blanc, Desire	1 Lieutenant	6 Reg't. (Landry's), La. Militia
Le Blanc, Despany	Corporal	4 Reg't. (Morgan's), La. Militia (Orig. under De Blanc, Despanay)
Le Blanc, Dominique	Private	6 Reg't. (Landry's), La. Militia
Le Blanc, Dorsino	Private	Capt. Dubuclet's Troop, Hussars, La. Vols. (Orig. under DeBlanc, Dorsino)
Le Blanc, Dosia	Private	8 Reg't. (Meriam's), La. Militia
Le Blanc, Eduar	Private	6 Reg't. (Landry's), La. Militia
Le Blanc, Edward	Private	8 Reg't. (Meriam's), La. Militia
Le Blanc, Edward	Private	8 Reg't. (Meriam's), La. Militia
Le Blanc, Etienne	Private	6 Reg't. (Landry's), La. Militia
Le Blanc, Hipolite	Private	6 Reg't. (Landry's), La. Militia
Le Blanc, Hipolite	Private	8 Reg't. (Meriam's), La. Militia
Le Blanc, Hypolite	Private	6 Reg't. (Landry's), La. Militia
Le Blanc, I.	Private	6 Reg't. (Landry's), La. Militia (Orig. under Le Blanc, Joseph)
Le Blanc, J.	Private	6 Reg't. (Landry's), La. Militia
Le Blanc, Jacques	Private	6 Reg't. (Landry's), La. Militia
Leblanc, Jacques	Private	Baker's Regiment, La. Militia
Le Blanc J Bte	Private	8 Reg't. (Meriam's), La. Militia
Leblanc, Jean	Private	De Clouet's Reg't., La.
Le Blanc, Jean Alexis	Captain	8 Reg't. (Meriam's), La. Militia
Le Blanc, Jean M.	Private	7 Reg't. (Le Beuf's), La. Militia
Le Blanc, Jerome	Sergeant	8 Reg't. (Meriam's), La. Militia
Le Blanc, Jne Bte	Private	6 Reg't. (Landry's), La. Militia
Le Blanc, John	Private	6 Reg't. (Landry's), La. Militia
Le Blanc, John Bte	Private	De Clouet's Reg't., La. Militia
Le Blanc, John Bte	Private	8 Reg't. (Meriam's), La. Militia
Le Blanc, Joseph	Private	De Clouet's Reg't., La. Militia
Le Blanc, Joseph Jr.	Private	De Clouet's Reg't., La. Militia
Le Blanc, Joseph	Private	6 Reg't. (Landry's), La. Militia
Le Blanc, Joseph	Private	8 Reg't. (Meriam's), La. Militia
Le Blanc, Joseph	Private	8 Reg't. (Meriam's), La. Militia
Le Blanc, Joseph	Private	8 Reg't. (Meriam's), La. Militia
Le Blanc, Julien	Private	De Clouet's Reg't., La. Militia
Le Blanc, L.	Private	6 Reg't. (Landry's), La. Militia (Orig. under Le Blanc, S.)
Le Blanc, Laurence	Private	8 Reg't. (Meriam's), La. Militia
Le Blanc, Lewis	Servant	De Clouet's Reg't., La. Militia
Le Blanc, Louis	Private	Baker's Regiment, La. Militia
Le Blanc, Louis	Private	De Clouet's Reg't., La. Militia
Le Blanc, Lubin	Private	Captain Hubbard's Mounted Co., La. Militia
Le Blanc, M.	Corporal	6 Reg't. (Landry's), La. Militia

Name	Rank	Unit
Le Blanc, M.	Private	8 Reg't. (Meriam's), La. Militia
Le Blanc, Maxie	Private	8 Reg't. (Meriam's), La. Militia
Le Blanc, Maximilien	Private	8 Reg't. (Meriam's), La. Militia
Le Blanc, Moyes	Private	8 Reg't. (Meriam's), La. Militia
Le Blanc, N.	Private	8 Reg't. (Meriam's), La. Militia
Le Blanc, Nareisse	Corporal	8 Reg't. (Meriam's), La. Militia
Le Blanc, Octave	Col aid De Camp	Gov. Claiborne and Staff, La. Mil.
Le Blanc, Olivier	Private	6 Reg't. (Landry's), La. Militia
Le Blanc, P.	Private	6 Reg't. (Landry's), La. Militia
Le Blanc, P.	Private	8 Reg't. (Meriam's), La. Militia
Le Blanc, Paul	Corporal	6 Reg't. (Landry's), La. Militia
Le Blanc, Paul	Private	6 Reg't. (Landry's), La. Militia
Le Blanc, Paulin	Private	10 and 20 Cons. Reg't., La. Mil. (Orig. under Withe, Paul)
Le Blanc, Pierre	Private	De Clouet's Reg't., La. Militia
Le Blanc, Pierre	Private	De Clouet's Reg't., La. Militia
Le Blanc, Pierre	Private	8 Reg't.(Meriam's), La. Militia
Le Blanc, Placide	1 Sergeant-Sgt.	8 Reg't. (Meriam's), La. Militia
Le Blanc, Rosemond	Private	6 Reg't. (Landry's), La. Militia
Le Blanc, Rosemont	Private	Capt. Dubuclet's Troop, Hussars, La. Vols.
Le Blanc, S.	Private	6 Reg't. (Landry's), La. Militia
Le Blanc, Silven	Private	6 Reg't. (Landry's), La. Militia
Le Blanc, Silvester	Private	Baker's Regiment, La. Militia (Orig. under Le Blance, Silvester)
Le Blanc, Silvin	Sergeant	6 Reg't. (Landry's), La. Militia
Le Blanc, Simon	Private	7 Reg't. (Le Beuf's), La. Militia
Le Blanc, Simon	Private	8 Reg't. (Meriam's), La. Militia
Leblanc, Simonette	Private	Baker's Regiment, La. Militia
Le Blanc, St	Private	6 Reg't. (Landry's), La. Militia
Le Blanc, Stanislaus	Private	6 Reg't. (Landry's), La. Militia
Leblanc, Theophile	Private	Baker's Regiment, La. Militia
Le Blanc, Treville	Private	8 Reg't. (Meriam's), La. Militia
Le Blanc, Ursin	Private	7 Reg't. (Le Beuf's), La. Militia
Le Blanc, Ursin	Private	16 Reg't. (Thompson's), La. Mil.
Le Blanc, V.	Private	8 Reg't. (Meriam's), La. Militia
Leblanc, Valerie	Private	Captain Hubbard's Mounted Co., La. Militia
Le Blanc, Valery	Private	6 Reg't. (Landry's), La. Militia
Le Blanc, Victor	Private	8 Reg't. (Meriam's), La. Militia
Le Blanc, Zeno	Private	De Clouet's Reg't., La. Militia
Le Blance, Peer	Private	Baker's Regiment, La. Militia
Le Blance, Silvester	Private	Baker's Regiment, La. Militia
Le Blanck, Louis	Private	De Clouet's Reg't., La. Militia (Orig. under Le Blanc, Louis)
Le Boeuf, Michel	Private	De Clouet's Reg't., La. Militia (Orig. under Le Bouef, M.)
Lebon, Louis	Fusilier-Private	5 Reg't. (La Branche's), La. Mil.
Le Bouef, M.	Private	De Clouet's Reg't., La. Militia
Le Bourgeois, Dumueal	Private	6 Reg't. (Landry's), La. Militia
Le Bourgeois, Louis	Captain	6 Reg't. (Landry's), La. Militia
LeBourgeois, P.	1 Lieutenant	6 Reg't. (Landry's), La. Militia
Le Bourgeois, Pre	1 Lieutenant	6 Reg't. (Landry's), La. Militia (Orig. under LeBourgeois, P.)
Le Bourgeouis, Louis	Captain	6 Reg't. (Landry's), La. Militia (Orig. under LeBourgeois,Louis)
Le Bouvier, Placide	Private	16 Reg't. (Thompson's), La. Mil. (Orig. under La Bauvre,Placide)
Le Breton, --	Private	4 Reg't. (Morgan's), La. Militia
Le Breton, Deschapelle	Sergeant	4 Reg't. (Morgan's), La. Militia
Lebreton, Noel	Private	Capt. Chauveau's Co., Cavalry, La. Militia
Le Brie, Michael	Private	De Clouet's Reg't., La. Militia
Lecesne, In	Corporal	Capt. Songy's Co., Marines, La. Vols.
Leche, Adams	Corporal	5 Reg't. (La Branche's), La. Mil.
Leche, Jean	Sergeant	5 Reg't. (La Branche's), La. Mil.
Leck, William	Corporal-Sgt.	10 and 20 Cons. Reg't., La. Mil. (Orig. under Leake, William)
Le Clair, Eli	Private	De Clouet's Reg't., La. Militia (Orig. under Leclare, Elie)
Le Claire, A.	Private	8 Reg't. (Meriam's), La. Militia
Leclaire, Petion	Private	2 Batt'n. (D'Aquin's), La. Militia
Leclare, Elie	Private	De Clouet's Reg't., La. Militia
Leclerc, --	Private	Capt. Alpuente's Co., La. Mil.
Leclerc, Louis	Private	2 Batt'n. (D'Aquin's), La. Militia
Leclere, --	Private	Capt. Alpuente's Co., La. Mil.
La Comb, Charles	Corporal	De Clouet's Reg't., La. Militia
Lecompte, Auguste	Drummer	2 Batt'n. (D'Aquin's), La. Militia
Le Conte, Pierre	Private	6 Reg't. (Landry's), La. Militia
Lecoux, Valery	Private	Capt. Le Doux's Co., Cavalry, La. Vols.
Lecoy, Joseph	Private	Captain Price's Co., La. Militia
Le Day, Antoine	Private	De Clouet's Reg't., La. Militia
Le Day, Henry	Private	De Clouet's Reg't., La. Militia
Le Day, John Pierre	Private	De Clouet's Reg't., La. Militia
Ledeaux, Alexander	Private	De Clouet's Reg't., La. Militia
Le Doux, Jr.	Corporal	Capt. Le Doux's Co., Cavalry, La. Vols.
Ledoux, Alexander	Private	De Clouet's Reg't., La. Militia (Orig. under Ledeaux, Alexander)
Ledoux, Athanase	Private	Capt. Le Doux's Co., Cavalry, La. Vols.
Le Doux, August	Private	16 Reg't. (Thompson's), La. Mil.
Le Doux, Eugene	1 Lieutenant	16 Reg't. (Thompson's), La. Mil.
Ledoux, Jean	Private	11 Reg't. (Hickey's), La. Militia
Le Doux, Veu	Corporal	Capt. Le Doux's Co., Cavalry, La. Vols.
Le Doux, Villeneuve	Private	Capt. Le Doux's Co., Cavalry, La. Vols.
Le Doux, Zenon	Captain	Capt. Le Doux's Co., Cavalry, La. Vols.
Le Down, Joseph	Private	11 Reg't. (Hickey's), La. Militia
Le Due, Cesar	Private	De Clouet's Reg't., La. Militia
Le Duf, Jacques	Private	1 Batt'n. (Fortier's), La. Militia
Leduf, Jacques	Private	1 Batt'n. (Fortier's), La. Militia
Lee, Charles L.	Private	10 and 20 Cons. Reg't., La. Mil. (Orig. under Lee, Charles S.)
Lee, Charles S.	Private	10 and 20 Cons. Reg't., La. Mil.
Lee, George	Private	De Clouet's Reg't., La. Militia
Lee, James	Corporal	10 and 20 Cons. Reg't., La. Mil.
Lee, James	Private	16 Reg't. (Thompson's), La. Mil.
Lee, Jesse	Corporal-Private	12 and 13 Cons. Reg't., La. Mil.
Lee, John	Private	De Clouet's Reg't., La. Militia
Lee, Mark	Private	De Clouet's Reg't., La. Militia
Lee, Moses	Private	10 and 20 Cons. Reg't., La. Mil.
Lee, Stephen	Sergeant	12 and 13 Cons. Reg't., La. Mil.
Lee, Sherod	Private	10 and 20 Cons. Reg't., La. Mil.
Lee, Thomas	Sergeant	De Clouet's Reg't., La. Militia
Lee, William	Private	Captain Griffith's Co., Mounted Riflemen, La. Vols.
Lee, William	Private	17, 18 and 19 Cons. Reg't., La. Militia
Leek, Samuel	Corporal	19 Regiment, La. Militia
Lefaux, --	Private	Plauche's Batt'n., La. Militia
Lefrbre, --	Sergeant	4 Reg't. (Morgan's), La. Militia (Orig. under Lefevre, --)
Lefebre, George	Private	2 Batt'n. (Peire's), La. Vols. (Orig. under Lefevre, George)
Lefebvre, Clair	Private	Plauche's Batt'n., La. Militia
Lefebvre, Vin	Private	Plauche's Batt'n., La. Militia
Lefeire, I Bt	Private	8 Reg't. (Meriam's), La. Militia
Leferre, Etn	Private	4 Reg't. (Morgan's), La. Militia (Orig. under Lefevre, Et)
Lefert, Nicholas	Private	De Clouet's Reg't., La. Militia (Orig. under Lefort, Nicholas)
Lefevae, George	Private	2 Batt'n. (Peire's), La. Vols. (Orig. under Lefevre, George)
Lefever, Etienne	Private	2 Batt'n. (Peire's), La. Vols.
Lefevre, --	Private	Capt. Chauveau's Co., Cavalry, La. Militia
Lefevre, --	Captain	2 Batt'n. (D'Aquin's), La. Militia
Lefevre, --	Sergeant	4 Reg't. (Morgan's), La. Militia
Lefevre, Alexander	Private	Captain Price's Co., La. Militia
Lefevre, August	Private	Capt. VanBibber's Co., La. Mil.
Lefevre, Clair	Private	Plauche's Batt'n., La. Militia (Orig. under Lefebre, Clair)
Lefevre, Et.	Private	4 Reg't. (Morgan's), La. Militia
Lefevre, Etienne	Private	2 Batt'n. (Peire's), La. Vols.
Lefevre, Etienne	Private	2 Batt'n. (Cavelier's), La. Militia
Lefevre, George	Private	2 Batt'n. (Peire's), La. Vols.
Lefevre, Joseph	Private	3 Reg't. (de la Ronde's), La. Mil.
Le Fevre, Pierre	Private	2 Batt'n. (Cavelier's), La. Militia
Leflech, Francis	Private	Sergeant Hog's Detachment, La. Vols. (Orig. under Lefloch, Francois)
Lefleur, Jean	Private	16 Reg't. (Thompson's), La. Mil. (Orig. under Lefleur, Jean)
Lefleur, Marceline	Private	16 Reg't. (Thompson's), La. Mil.
Lefloch, Francois	Private	Sergeant Hog's Detachment, La. Vols.
Lefort, --	Private	2 Reg't. (Cavelier's), La. Militia
Lefort, --	Private	4 Reg't. (Morgan's), La. Militia

Name	Rank	Unit
Lefort, Nicholas	Private	De Clouet's Reg't., La. Militia
Lefort, Nicholas	Private-Corporal	2 Batt'n. (Peire's), La. Vols.
Lefrance, Antoine	Private	De Clouet's Reg't., La. Militia
Lege', Andre	Private	De Clouet's Reg't., La. Militia
Legender, Raphael	Sergeant	De Clouet's Reg't., La. Militia
Legendre, Batiste	Corporal	11 Reg't. (Hickey's), La. Militia
Legendre, Celestin	Private	De Clouet's Reg't., La. Militia
Le Gendre, John B.	Private	11 Reg't. (Hickey's), La. Militia
Legendre, Raphael	Sergeant	De Clouet's Reg't., La. Militia
Leger, Antoine	Private	Captain Lagan's Co., La. Vols.
Leger, Augustin	Private	De Clouet's Reg't., La. Militia
Leger, Augustin	Private	16 Reg't. (Thompson's), La. Mil.
Leger, Fontange	Corporal	2 Batt'n. (D'Aquin's), La. Militia
Leger, Jean	Private	16 Reg't. (Thompson's), La. Mil.
Legeune, A.	Private	8 Reg't. (Meriam's), La. Militia
Legeune, F.	Sergeant	8 Reg't. (Meriam's), La. Militia
Legeune, T.	Private	8 Reg't. (Meriam's), La. Militia
Legeune, Z.	Corporal	8 Reg't. (Meriam's), La. Militia
Legiuie, Vital	Private	De Clouet's Reg't., La. Militia (Orig. under Lejuine, Pital)
Legnio, Lewis	Private	Baker's Regiment, La. Militia (Orig. under Legniou, Louis)
Legniou, Joseph	Sergeant	Baker's Regiment, La. Militia
Legniou, Louis	Private	Baker's Regiment, La. Militia
Legre, Charles A.	Private	1 Batt'n. (Fortier's), La. Militia
Legros, --	Private	Plauche's Batt'n., La. Militia
Legros, --	Surg. Mate	5 Reg't. (La Branche's), La. Mil.
Legros, Germain	Private	2 Batt'n. (D'Aquin's), La. Militia
Leguin, Joseph	Private-Corporal	2 Batt'n. (D'Aquin's), La. Militia (Orig. under Seguin, Joseph)
Legune, A.	Private	8 Reg't. (Meriam's), La. Militia (Orig. under Legeune, A.)
Lejeune, Alexey	Corporal	7 Reg't. (Le Beuf's), La. Militia
Lejeune, Alexis	Private	7 Reg't. (Le Beuf's), La. Militia
Lejeune, Ambroise	Private	7 Reg't. (Le Beuf's), La. Militia
LeJeune, Baptiste	Private	8 Reg't. (Meriam's), La. Militia
Lejeune, Hebert	Private	16 Reg't. (Thompson's), La. Mil.
Lejeune, Jean Bte	Private	7 Reg't. (Le Beuf's), La. Militia
Lejeune, Jean Bte	Private	16 Reg't. (Thompson's), La. Mil.
Le Jeune, Mathwrin	Private	8 Reg't. (Meriam's), La. Militia
Lejeune, Osier	Private	16 Reg't. (Thompson's), La. Mil.
Lejeune, Pierre	Private	16 Reg't. (Thompson's), La. Mil.
Lejeune, Lemon	Private	7 Reg't. (Le Beuf's), La. Militia
Lejeune, Vital	Private	De Clouet's Reg't., La. Militia (Orig. under Lejuine, Pital)
Lejuine, Pital	Private	De Clouet's Reg't., La. Militia
Le Lapier, Firmin	Private	8 Reg't. (Meriam's), La. Militia
Lelerno, Lewis	Private	19 Reg't., La. Vols.(Orig. under Leturno, Louis)
Le Leu, Edward	Private	Baker's Regiment, La. Militia (Orig. under Lelu, Edward)
Le Leu, Francois	Private	Baker's Regiment, La. Militia (Orig. under Lelu, Francois)
Leleu, Louis	Private	Baker's Regiment, La. Militia
Lella, Charles	Private	2 Batt'n. (Peire's), La. Vols. (Orig. under Seller, Charles)
Le Long, Bernard	Private	11 Reg't. (Hickey's), La. Militia
Leloup, --	Private	Plauche's Batt'n., La. Militia
Lelu, Edward	Private	Baker's Regiment, La. Militia
Lelu, Francois	Private	Baker's Regiment, La. Militia
Lemaire, Moliere	Sergeant	1 Batt'n. (Fortier's), La. Militia
Lemaire, Villeneuve	Private	1 Batt'n. (Fortier's), La. Militia
Lemaire, --	Private	Plauche's Batt'n., La. Militia
Lemaitre, C.	Private	2 Reg't. (Cavelier's), La. Militia
Lemaitre, Gme	Private	2 Reg't.(Cavelier's), La. Militia
Lembert, Zadique	Private	2 Batt'n. (D'Aquin's), La. Militia
Lemelle, Alexandre	Captain	Baker's Regiment, La. Militia
Lemier, Francois	Private	De Clouet's Reg't., La. Militia (Orig. under Limieux, Francis)
Lemieur, Francois	Private	De Clouet's Reg't., La. Militia (Orig. under Limieux, Francis)
Lemieux, Francois	Private	De Clouet's Reg't., La. Militia (Orig. under Limieux, Francis)
Lemmons, William	Private	10 and 20 Cons. Reg't., La. Mil.
Lemoin, Alyes	Private	17, 18 and 19 Cons. Reg't., La. Militia
Lemoine, --	Private	Plauche's Batt'n., La. Militia
Lemonier, Y.	Surgeon	Plauche's Batt'n., La. Militia
Lemonnier, T.	Surgeon	Plauche's Batt'n., La. Militia (Orig. under Lemonier, Y.)
Lemorine, Bte	Private	17, 18 and 19 Cons. Reg't., La. Mil. (Orig. under Lamoine, Batea)
Lemos, Ferdinand	Sergeant-Major	4 Reg't. (Morgan's), La. Militia
Lenclot, Ameran	Private	8 Reg't. (Meriam's), La. Militia
Lenclot, Antoine	Private	8 Reg't. (Meriam's), La. Militia
Lenclot, Leosau	Corporal	8 Reg't. (Meriam's), La. Militia
Lendee, --	--	De Clouet's Reg't., La. Militia
Lenoir, --	Sergeant-Major	1 Reg't. (Dejan's), La. Militia
Le Noir, William	Private	Baker's Regiment, La. Militia
Lenon, Jacques	Private	2 Reg't. (Cavelier's), La. Militia
Lenzon, Louis	Private	Captain Lagan's Co., La. Vols. (Orig. under Lauzon, Louis)
Leoben, Ge	Private	1 Reg't. (Dejan's), La. Militia
Leobin, --	Private	1 Reg't. (Dejan's), La. Militia (Orig. under Leoben, Ge)
Leon, Fr.	Private	De Clouet's Reg't., La. Militia
Leon, Joseph	Private	Captain Lagan's Co., La. Vols.
Leonard, fils	Private	8 Reg't. (Meriam's), La. Militia
Leonard, A.	2 Lieutenant	8 Reg't. (Meriam's), La. Militia
Leonard, Danis	Private	10 and 20 Cons. Reg't., La. Mil.
Leonard, Dennis	Private	10 and 20 Cons. Reg't., La. Mil. (Orig. under Leonard, Danis)
Leonard, Francis	Private	2 Reg't. (Cavelier's), La. Militia
Leonard, Gilbert	Private	4 Reg't. (Morgan's), La. Militia
Leonard, Honora	Private	8 Reg't. (Meriam's), La. Militia
Leonard, Jacob	Private	4 Reg't. (Morgan's), La. Militia
Leonard, Jonas	Private	10 and 20 Cons. Reg't., La. Mil.
Leonard, Joseph	Fusilier-Private	5 Reg't. (La Branche's), La. Mil.
Leonard, William	Private	4 Reg't. (Morgan's), La. Militia
Leonardy, Aug.	Private	2 Reg't. (Cavelier's), La. Militia
Leonardy, Chevr	Private	2 Reg't. (Cavelier's), La. Militia
Lepage, Henry	Private	Captain Lagan's Co., La. Vols.
Le Page, Louis	Sergeant	3 Reg't. (de la Ronde's), La. Mil. (Orig. under Le Page, Louis)
Lepard, Leon	Private	6 Reg't. (Landry's), La. Militia
Leperge, Jenson	Private	Capt. Van Bibber's Co., La. Mil.
Lepine, --	Private	2 Batt'n. (D'Aquin's), La. Militia
Lepine, Antoine	Private	De Clouet's Reg't., La. Militia
Lepine, Antoine	Private	2 Batt'n. (Peire's), La. Vols.
Lepine, John	Private	De Clouet's Reg't., La. Militia
Lepine, Joseph	Private	De Clouet's Reg't., La. Militia
Lepine, Matthieu	Private	De Clouet's Reg't., La. Militia
Leport, Nicholas	Private-Corporal	2 Batt'n. (Peire's), La. Vols. (Orig. under Lefort, Nicholas)
Lepot, --	Sergeant	2 Reg't. (Cavelier's), La. Militia
Le Pott, Bellonnie	Private	2 Batt'n. (D'Aquin's), La. Militia (Orig. under Lepotte, Bellonnie)
Lepotte, Bellonnie	Private	2 Batt'n. (D'Aquin's), La. Militia
Lepretre, --	Private	Plauche's Batt'n., La. Militia
L'Eprine, Alexander	Private	4 Reg't. (Morgan's), La. Militia
Lerasseur, Alexander	Private	2 Reg't. (Cavelier's), La. Militia
Leret, Nicholas	Private	De Clouet's Reg't., La. Militia
Lerie, L.	Private	8 Reg't. (Meriam's), La. Militia
Lerit, Nicholas	Private	De Clouet's Reg't., La. Militia (Orig. under Lerit, Nicholas)
Leroi, Charles	Private	De Clouet's Reg't., La. Militia
Leroix, Nicolas	Private	Capt. Alpuente's Co., La. Mil.
Leroud, Pierre	Private	2 Batt'n. (Peire's), La. Vols. (Orig. under Leroux, Pierre)
Leroux, Baptiste	Private	3 Reg't. (de la Ronde's), La. Mil.
Leroux, Louis	Private	2 Reg't. (Cavelier's), La. Militia
Leroux, Louis	Private	3 Reg't. (de la Ronde's), La. Mil.
Leroux, Pierre	Private	2 Batt'n. (Peire's), La. Vols.
Le Roy, --	Private	Plauche's Batt'n., La. Militia
Le Roy, Louis	Private	2 Reg't. (Cavelier's), La. Militia
Le Roy, Nicholas	Artificer	Capt. Chaudurier's Co., Artificers, Art'y., La. Vols.
Leroy, Simon	Private	Capt. Songy's Co., Marines, La. Vols.
Lessassier, --	Private	Plauche's Batt'n., La. Militia (Orig. under Lessassier, --)
Lesassier, Alexander	Sergeant	16 Reg't. (Thompson's), La. Mil.
Le Sassier, J. B.	2 Lieutenant	2 Reg't. (Cavelier's), La. Militia
Lesassier, Julien	Private	16 Reg't. (Thompson's), La. Mil.
Lesassier, Lucius	1 Lieutenant	16 Reg't. (Thompson's), La. Mil.
Lesassier, Pierre	Corporal	16 Reg't. (Thompson's), La. Mil.
Lescal, Gabriel	Private	Captain Lagan's Co., La. Vols.
Leseay, Francois	Corporal	2 Batt'n. (D'Aquin's), La. Militia
Lesian, Poinci	Private	2 Batt'n. (D'Aquin's), La. Militia
Lesiau, Francois	Corporal	2 Batt'n. (D'Aquin's), La. Militia
Lesot, Joseph	Private	2 Batt'n. (Peire's), La. Vols. (Orig. under Lisot, Joseph)
Lesperance, --	Private	2 Reg't. (Cavelier's), La. Militia
Lesperence, --	Servant	2 Batt'n. (D'Aquin's), La. Militia

Name	Rank	Unit
Lessard, Jean Bte	Private	6 Reg't. (Landry's), La. Militia
Lessard, Lean	Private	6 Reg't. (Landry's), La. Militia (Orig. under Lepard, Leon)
Lessassier, --	Private	Plauche's Batt'n., La. Militia
Lessassier, --	Private	1 Reg't. (Dejan's), La. Militia
Lestage, Barthelemy	Private	17, 18 and 19 Cons. Reg't., La. Militia
Lestage, Francois	Private	17, 18 and 19 Cons. Reg't., La. Militia
Letaux, --	Private	Plauche's Batt'n., La. Militia (Orig. under Lefaux, --)
Leturno, Louis	Private	19 Regiment, La. Militia
Levan, James	Private	10 and 20 Cons. Reg't., La. Mil. (Orig. under Livandais, -- i no dot)
Levandais, J. L.	Private	Capt. Chauveau's Co., Cavalry, La. Mil. (Orig. under Lwandais, J. T.)
Levasserud, Siriaque	Private	Capt. Trudeau's Troop of Horse, La. Mil. (Orig. under Levassure, Siriague)
Levasseur, Victorin	Sergeant	17, 18 and 19 Cons. Reg't., La. Mil. (Orig. under Levassuer, Victorin)
Levassuer, Victorin	Sergeant	17, 18 and 19 Cons. Reg't., La. Militia
Levassure, Siriague	Private	Capt. Trudeau's Troop of Horse, La. Militia
Levaudais, Charles	Private	De Clouet's Reg't., La. Militia (Orig. under Livadides, Charles)
Leveille, --	Servant	1 Batt'n. (Fortier's), La. Militia
Levennon, Jean	Artificer	Capt. Chaudurier's Co., Artificers, Art'y., La. Vols. (Orig. under Livernon, Jean)
Leveque, Jacques	Corporal	1 Batt'n. (Fortier's), La. Militia
Leveque, Jean	Private	6 Reg't. (Landry's), La. Militia
Levarain, Charles	Musician-Fifer	2 Batt'n. (Peire's), La. Vols. (Orig. under Severain, Charles)
Levergne, Celestin	Private	Baker's Regiment, La. Militia
Levergue, Urbin	Private	16 Reg't. (Thompson's), La. Mil. (Orig. under Lavergne, Urbin)
Leverin, --	Fusilier-Private	5 Reg't. (La Branche's), La. Mil.
Leverne, Baptise	Private	16 Reg't. (Thompson's), La. Mil.
Levernon, Jean	Artificer	Capt. Chaudurier's Co., Artificers, Art'y., La. Vols. (Orig. under Livernon, Jean)
Levernus, Antoine	Private	2 Batt'n. (Peire's), La. Vols. (Orig. under Livernois, Antoine)
Levert, Francois	Private	7 Reg't. (Le Beuf's), La. Militia
Levert, Joseph	Private	7 Reg't. (Le Beuf's), La. Militia
Levier, F.	Sergeant-Private	De Clouet's Reg't., La. Militia (Orig. under Levrier, F.)
Levins, Samuel	Captain	10 and 20 Cons. Reg't., La. Mil. (Orig. under Leavins, Samuel)
Levis, L.	Private	8 Reg't. (Meriam's), La. Militia (Orig. under Lewis, L.)
Levoux, Pierre	Private	2 Batt'n. (Peire's), La. Militia
Levrier, F.	Sergeant-Private	De Clouet's Reg't., La. Militia
Levrier, Frederick	Private	2 Batt'n. (Peire's), La. Militia
Levron, Joseph	Corporal	7 Reg't. (Le Beuf's), La. Militia
Levron, Saturuin	Private	7 Reg't. (Le Beuf's), La. Militia
Levron, Vicair	Sergeant	7 Reg't. (Le Beuf's), La. Militia
Lewan, Blaise	Private	10 Regiment, La. Militia
Lewis, --	Servant	General and Staff (Labatut), La. Militia
Lewis, Benjamin	Private	Captain Wallace's Co., Boatmen, La. Vols.
Lewis, Hugh	Private	Captain Hughes' Co., Mounted Riflemen, La. Militia
Lewis, John	Servant	Gov. Claiborne and Staff, La. Mil.
Lewis, John	--	De Clouet's Reg't., La. Militia
Lewis, John	Waiter	Plauche's Batt'n., La. Militia
Lewis, John	Private	4 Reg't. (Morgan's), La. Militia
Lewis, Joseph	1 Lieutenant	Captain Beale's Co., Riflemen, La. Militia
Lewis, L.	Private	8 Reg't. (Meriam's), La. Militia
Lewis, Lindsey	Private	Captain McNair's Co., Mounted Riflemen, La. Militia
Lewis, Philip	Private	10 and 20 Cons. Reg't., La. Mil.
Lewis, Samuel	Private	Capt. Alpuente's Co., La. Mil. (Orig. under Linier, Samuel)
Lewis, Seth	Private	16 Reg't. (Thompson's), La. Mil.
Lewis, Silvester	Private	Captain Dodge's Co., Mounted Riflemen, La. Militia
Lewis, William	Private	1 Reg't. (Dejan's), La. Militia
Lewis, William	Private	10 and 20 Cons. Reg't., La. Mil.
Lewis, William	Private	12 and 13 Cons. Reg't., La. Mil.
Lewis, William	Private	17, 18 and 19 Cons. Reg't., La. Militia
Lewis, William Y.	Private	De Clouet's Reg't., La. Militia
Leynio, Joseph	Sergeant	Baker's Regiment, La. Militia (Orig. under Legnion, Joseph)
Lezer, Jean	Private	2 Reg't. (Cavelier's), La. Militia
Lhomer, Chevalier	Corporal	5 Reg't. (La Branche's), La. Mil.
Lian, Jose	Private	17, 18 and 19 Cons. Reg't., La. Militia
Liautau, A.	Corporal	Plauche's Batt'n., La. Militia
Libau, Pierre	Fusilier-Private	5 Reg't. (La Branche's), La. Mil.
Lick, William	Private	1 Reg't. (Dejan's), La. Militia (Orig. under Leak, William)
Lick, William	Corporal-Sgt.	10 and 20 Cons. Reg't., La. Mil. (Orig. under Leake, William)
Liddle, William	Private	4 Reg't. (Morgan's), La. Militia
Liles, Charles	Private	10 and 20 Cons. Reg't., La. Mil.
Liles, John	Private	19 Regiment, La. Militia
Liles, Richmond	Private	10 and 20 Cons. Reg't., La. Mil.
Lillard, Lewis	1 Lieutenant	19 Reg't., La. Vols. (Orig. under Lillard, Louis)
Lillard, Louis	1 Lieutenant	19 Reg't., La. Vols.
Lilley, Jacob	Private	10 and 20 Cons. Reg't., La. Mil. (Orig. under Lilly, Jacob)
Lilley, James	2 Lieutenant	12 and 13 Cons. Reg't., La. Mil.
Lilly, Jacob	Private	10 and 20 Cons. Reg't., La. Mil.
Lilly, John	Private	10 and 20 Cons. Reg't., La. Mil.
Limieux, Francis	Private	De Clouet's Reg't., La. Militia
Limoinnier, Y.	Surgeon	Plauche's Batt'n., La. Militia (Orig. under Lemonier, Y.)
Lindar, --	Servant	Plauche's Batt'n., La. Militia (Orig. under Lindor, --)
Linder, William	Private	10 and 20 Cons. Reg't., La. Mil.
Lindor, --	Servant	Capt. Alpuente's Co., La. Mil.
Lindor, --	Servant	General and Staff (Labatut), La. Militia
Lindor, --	Servant	Plauche's Batt'n., La. Militia
Lindor, --	Servant	1 Batt'n. (Fortier's), La. Militia
Lindor, J.	Servant	De Clouet's Reg't., La. Militia
Lindor, Pierre	Private	2 Batt'n. (D'Aquin's), La. Militia
Lindore, --	Servant	De Clouet's Reg't., La. Militia
Lindsey, Isaac	Private	12 and 13 Cons. Reg't., La. Mil.
Lineroyable, --	Servant	2 Batt'n. (D'Aquin's), La. Militia
Lingois, Louis	Private	Capt. Dubuclet's Troop, Hussars, La. Vols.
Linier, Samuel	Private	Capt. Alpuente's Co., La. Mil.
Link, Absalom	Trumpeter	Captain McNair's Co., Mounted Riflemen, La. Militia
Link, William	Sergeant	16 Reg't. (Thompson's), La. Mil.
Linn, Lewis	Private	Captain Dodge's Co., Mounted Riflemen, La. Militia
Linn, Lewis	Private	Captain Henry's Co., Mounted Riflemen, La. Militia
Linn, William	Private	Captain Henry's Co., Mounted Riflemen, La. Militia
Linsley, Isaac	Private	12 and 13 Cons. Reg't., La. Mil. (Orig. under Lindsey, Isaac)
Linzois, Louis	Private	Capt. Dubuclet's Troop, Hussars, La. Vols. (Orig. under Lingois, Louis)
Lione, Pablo	Private	17, 18 and 19 Cons. Reg't., La. Militia
Lions, Samuel	Private	16 Reg't. (Thompson's), La. Mil. (Orig. under Lyons, Samuel)
Lioteau, Ferdinand	Captain	1 Batt'n. (Fortier's), La. Militia
Lismatre, Germain	Artificer	Capt. Chaudurier's Co., Artificers, Art'y., La. Vols. (Orig. under Lasmatre, Jermin)
Lismatre, Jermin	Artificer	Capt. Chaudurier's Co., Artificers, Art'y., La. Vols. (Orig. under Lasmatre, Jermin)
Lisot, Joseph	Private	2 Batt'n. (Peire's), La. Vols.
Lissana, Raimond	Private	Plauche's Batt'n., La. Militia
Lissana, Reymond	Private	Capt. Colsson's Co., Artillery, La. Vols.
Litchley, Samuel	Private	Capt. Van Bibber's Co., La. Mil. (Orig. under Vitohly, Samuel)
Litle, John	Private	16 Reg't. (Thompson's), La. Mil.

Name	Rank	Unit
Litleton, William B.	Corporal	10 and 20 Cons. Reg't., La. Mil. (Orig. under Littleton, William B.)
Littell, Eli	Private	16 Reg't. (Thompson's), La. Mil. (Orig. under Littill, Eli)
Littiere, Jn	Corporal	1 Reg't. (Dejan's), La. Militia
Littill, Eli	Private	16 Reg't. (Thompson's), La. Mil.
Little, John	Private	16 Reg't. (Thompson's), La. Mil. (Orig. under Litle, John)
Little, Moses	Surgeon	Detachment Field and Staff Officers, 4 Brigade, La. Militia
Little, William	Private	17, 18 and 19 Cons. Reg't., La. Militia
Littlejohn, John	Sergeant-Major	12 and 13 Cons. Reg't., La. Mil.
Littleton, William B.	Corporal	10 and 20 Cons. Reg't., La. Mil.
Livadides, Charles	Private	De Clouet's Reg't., La. Militia
Livandais, J. T.	Private	Capt. Chauveau's Co., Cavalry, La. Militia
Livennon, Jean	Artificer	Capt. Chaudurier's Co., Artificers, Art'y., La. Vols. (Orig. under Livernon, Jean)
Livenon, Jean	Artificer	Capt. Chaudurier's Co., Artificers, Art'y., La. Vols. (Orig. under Livernon, Jean)
Livernoice, Antoine	Private	2 Batt'n. (Peire's), La. Vols. (Orig. under Livernois, Antoine)
Livernois, Antoine	Private	2 Batt'n. (Peire's), La. Vols.
Livernoix, Antoine	Private	2 Batt'n. (Peire's), La. Vols.
Livernon, Jean	Artificer	Capt. Chaudurier's Co., Artificers, Art'y., La. Vols.
Livernon, Jean	Corporal	De Clouet's Reg't., La. Militia
Livingston, John	Private	Capt. Ogden's Co., Dragoons, La. Militia
Lloyd, Henry	Private	Captain Griffith's Co., Mounted Riflemen, La. Vols. (Orig. under Loyd, Henry)
Lloyd, Samuel	Private	Captain Griffith's Co., Mounted Riflemen, La. Vols.
Lobdale, James	Private	10 and 20 Cons. Reg't., La. Mil.
Lobdall, James	Private	10 and 20 Cons. Reg't., La. Mil. (Orig. under Lobdale, James)
Locer, Sang	Private	17, 18 and 19 Cons. Reg't., La. Mil. (Orig. under Loura, Santiago)
Lochance, Benjamin	Ensign	Capt. Callaway's Co., Mounted Riflemen, La. Mil. (Orig. under Lachance, Benjamin)
Loche, Joseph	Private	5 Reg't. (La Branche's), La. Mil.
Locket, Wirphrey	Major	Detachment Field and Staff Officers, 4 Brigade, La. Militia
Lodenback, George	Private	5 Reg't. (La Branche's), La. Mil.
Loeimier, Augustus B.	Private	Captain Ramsey's Co., Mounted Riflemen, La. Militia (Orig. under Lorimier, Augustus B.)
Lofton, James	Private	Captain Rankin's Co., Mounted Riflemen, La. Militia
Lofton, Samuel	Private	19 Regiment, La. Militia
Logan, James	Sergeant	Baker's Regiment, La. Militia
Logate, Henry	Private	Captain Young's Co., Mounted Riflemen, La. Militia
Logue, Hugh	Private	17, 18 and 19 Cons. Reg't., La. Militia
Loid, William	Private	Captain Ramsey's Co., Mounted Riflemen, La. Militia
Loide, Braxstone	Corporal-Private	12 and 13 Cons. Reg't., La. Mil.
Loide, M. C.	Private	12 and 13 Cons. Reg't., La. Mil.
Lolognier, L.	Private	1 Batt'n. (Fortier's), La. Militia
Lomega, Francois	Sergeant-Major	Detachment Field and Staff Officers, 4 Brigade, La. Militia
Lomes, Louis	Private	2 Batt'n. (Peire's), La. Vols. (See also Pedro Redondo)
Lomo, Pancho	Private	3 Reg't. (de la Ronde's), La. Mil.
Lonadro, Jose Marie	Private	17, 18 and 19 Cons. Reg't., La. Militia
Londren, Louis Maillon	2 Lieutenant	Capt. Chaudurier's Co., Artificers, Art'y., La. Vols. (Orig. under Londrin, Louis Maillon)
Londrieux, L. Maillon	2 Lieutenant	Capt. Chaudurier's Co., Artificers, Art'y., La. Vols. (Orig. under Londrin, Louis Maillon)
Londrin, Jn Mahion	2 Lieutenant	Capt. Chaudurier's Co., Artificers, Art'y., La. Vols. (Orig. under Londrin, Louis Maillon)
Londrin, Louis Maillon	2 Lieutenant	Capt. Chaudurier's Co., Artificers, Art'y., La. Vols.
Long, Gabriel	Private	Captain McNair's Co., Mounted Riflemen, La. Militia
Long, George	Private	17, 18 and 19 Cons. Reg't., La. Militia
Long, Jacob	Private	2 Batt'n. (Peire's), La. Vols.
Long, James	Private	Capt. Callaway's Co., Mounted Riflemen, La. Militia
Long, John	Private	Captain McNair's Co., Mounted Riflemen, La. Militia
Long, Phillip P.	Private	1 Reg't. (Dejan's), La. Militia
Long, William	Corporal-Private	Captain McNair's Co., Mounted Riflemen, La. Militia
Long, William L.	Private-Sergeant	Captain McNair's Co., Mounted Riflemen, La. Militia
Longchamp, Joseph	Artificer	Capt. Chaudurier's Co., Artificers, Art'y., La. Vols. (Orig. under Longchamps, Joseph)
Longchamps, Joseph	Artificer	Capt. Chaudurier's Co., Artificers, Art'y., La. Vols.
Longcharge, Joseph	Artificer	Capt. Chaudurier's Co., Artificers, Art'y., La. Vols. (Orig. under Longchamps, Joseph)
Longinns, John T.	Private	De Clouet's Reg't., La. Militia (Orig. under Longino, John T.)
Longino, John F.	Private	De Clouet's Reg't., La. Militia (Orig. under Longino, John T.)
Longino, John T.	Private	De Clouet's Reg't., La. Militia
Longino, William	Corporal	12 and 13 Cons. Reg't., La. Mil.
Longoone, Albert	Private	7 Reg't. (Le Beuf's), La. Militia
Longpre', --	Private	1 Reg't. (Dejan's), La. Militia
Longpre, Jn	Capt.-Paymaster	2 Batt'n. (D'Aquin's), La. Militia
Longuepie, Louis	Private	8 Reg't. (Meriam's), La. Militia (Could be Longuepu)
Longuesse, Be	Private	8 Reg't. (Meriam's), La. Militia
Longuesse, F.	Private	8 Reg't. (Meriam's), La. Militia (Orig. under Longuesse, T.)
Longuesse, T.	Private	8 Reg't. (Meriam's), La. Militia
Lonquin, Antoine	Private	Captain Lagan's Co., La. Vols.
Lookin, William	Private	10 and 20 Cons. Reg't., La. Mil.
Looney, Joseph	Private	Captain Young's Co., Mounted Riflemen, La. Militia
Loongonce, Bte	Private	7 Reg't. (Le Beuf's), La. Militia
Lopdell, James	Private	10 and 20 Cons. Reg't., La. Mil. (Orig. under Lobdale, James)
Lope, Anthony	Private	10 and 20 Cons. Reg't., La. Mil.
Lope, Emanuel	Private	10 and 20 Cons. Reg't., La. Mil.
Lopez, Dionisio	Private	17, 18 and 19 Cons. Reg't., La. Militia
Lopez, Francisco	Private	2 Reg't. (Cavelier's), La. Militia
Lopez, Francois	Private	2 Batt'n. (Peire's), La. Vols.
Lopez, Jean	Private	2 Reg't. (Cavelier's), La. Militia
Lopez, John	Private	2 Reg't. (Cavelier's), La. Militia (Orig. under Lopez, Jean)
Lopes, St. Yago	Private	Capt. Songy's Co., Marines, La. Vols.
Lopez, Pierre	Private	8 Reg't. (Meriam's), La. Militia
Lopez, Prudencia	Private	17, 18 and 19 Cons. Reg't., La. Militia
Lorain, Edwin	Corporal	1 Reg't. (Dejan's), La. Militia (Orig. under Loraine, Edwin)
Loraine, Edwin	Corporal	1 Reg't. (Dejan's), La. Militia
Lorance, Gabrel	Private	12 and 13 Cons. Reg't., La. Mil.
Lord, George	Private	De Clouet's Reg't., La. Militia
Lorel, John	Private	4 Reg't. (Morgan's), La. Militia
Lorimier, Augustus B.	Private	Captain Ramsey's Co., Mounted Riflemen, La. Militia
Lorrie, J. Bte	Private	8 Reg't. (Meriam's), La. Militia
Losana, Domingo	Private	17, 18 and 19 Cons. Reg't., La. Militia
Losano, St. Yago	Private	2 Batt'n. (Peire's), La. Vols.
Lousillier, Auguste	Sergeant	16 Reg't. (Thompson's), La. Mil.
Louallier, Alexander	Corporal	16 Reg't. (Thompson's), La. Mil.
Loudon, James	Private	10 and 20 Cons. Reg't., La. Mil. (Orig. under Lowdon, James)
Loudren, L. Maillon	2 Lieutenant	Capt. Chaudurier's Co., Artificers, Art'y., La. Vols. (Orig. under Londrin, Louis Maillon)
Louga, --	Private	1 Reg't. (Dejan's), La. Militia (Orig. under Langae, --)
Loughridge, Samuel B.	Private	12 and 13 Cons. Reg't., La. Mil. (Orig. under Laughridge, Samuel)

Name	Rank	Unit
Louia, Nichol	Private	7 Reg't. (Le Beuf's), La. Militia
Louis, --	Servant	De Clouet's Reg't., La. Militia
Louis, --	Waiter-Servant	2 Reg't. (Cavelier's), La. Militia
Louis, --	Servant	2 Batt'n. (D'Aquin's), La. Militia
Louis, --	Servant	2 Brigade (Hopkins'), La. Militia
Louis, --	Servant	3 Reg't. (de la Ronde's), La. Mil.
Louis, --	Servant	4 Reg't. (Morgan's), La. Militia
Louis, Honore	Sergeant	1 Batt'n. (Fortier's), La. Militia
Louis, Hugh	Private	Captain Hughes' Co., Mounted Riflemen, La. Militia (Orig. under Lewis, Hugh)
Louis, Jean	Servant	De Clouet's Reg't., La. Militia
Louis, Jn	Servant	1 Reg't. (Dejan's), La. Militia
Louis, Jn Pre	Servant	2 Batt'n. (D'Aquin's), La. Militia
Louis, John	Private	6 Reg't. (Landry's), La. Militia
Louis, Joseph	Private	Captain Price's Co., La. Militia
Louis, Joseph	Corporal	1 Batt'n. (Fortier's), La. Militia
Louis, Pierre	Private	2 Batt'n. (D'Aquin's), La. Militia
Loupe, Franoiz	Private	2 Batt'n. (Piere's), La. Vols.
Loura, Santaigo	Private	17, 18 and 19 Cons. Reg't., La. Militia
Loustalot, Jn	Private	Plauche's Batt'n., La. Militia
Loustaonau, Bernard	2 Lieutenant	5 Reg't. (La Branche's), La. Mil. (Orig. under Loustamoux, Bernard)
Loustaumoux, Bernard	2 Lieutenant	5 Reg't. (La Branche's), La. Mil.
Loustaunoux, Bernard	2 Lieutenant	5 Reg't. (La Branche's), La. Mil. (Orig. under Loustamoux, Bernard)
Louvier, Bte	Private	6 Reg't. (Landry's), La. Militia
Louvier, Fran	Private	Baker's Regiment, La. Militia (Orig. under Lauviere, Francois)
Louvier, Fred	Private	Baker's Regiment, La. Militia (Orig. under Lovier, Frederick)
Louvier, Louis	Private	Baker's Regiment, La. Militia
Louviere, Julien	Private	De Clouet's Reg't., La. Militia
Love, William	Corporal	Capt. Allen's Co., Artillerists, La. Vols. (Orig. under Williams, William B.)
Love, William	Private	De Clouet's Reg't., La. Militia (See also Artillery)
Lovekins, William	Private	10 and 20 Cons. Reg't., La. Mil. (Orig. under Lookin, William)
Lovelace, Seneca	Private	Captain Sprigg's Co., Boatmen, La. Vols.
Loveless, Benjamin	Private	Capt. Thomas' Co., La. Militia
Loveless, Benjamin	Private	12 and 13 Cons. Reg't., La. Mil.
Lovier, Frederick	Private	Baker's Regiment, La. Militia
Loveless, Benjamin	Private	Capt. Thomas' Co., La. Militia (Orig. under Loveless, Benjamin)
Low, Jacob	Private	1 Reg't. (Dejan's), La. Militia
Lowdon, James	Private	10 and 20 Cons. Reg't., La. Mil.
Lowdon, William	Private	10 and 20 Cons. Reg't., La. Mil.
Lowe, Richard	Ensign	Capt. Collard's Co., La. Militia
Lower, Daniel	Private	De Clouet's Reg't., La. Militia
Lowest, David	Private	Capt. Collard's Co., La. Militia
Lowman, Frederick	Private	10 and 20 Cons. Reg't., La. Mil. (Orig. under Lawman, Frederick)
Lowry, John I.	Sergeant	Captain Price's Co., La. Militia
Loyd, Braxston	Corporal-Private	12 and 13 Cons. Reg't., La. Mil. (Orig. under Loide, Braxstone)
Loyd, Henry	Private	Captain Griffith's Co., Mounted Riflemen, La. Vols.
Loyd, Mack	Private	12 and 13 Cons. Reg't., La. Mil. (Orig. under Loide, M. C.)
Loyd, Samuel	Private	Captain Griffith's Co., Mounted Riflemen, La. Vols. (Orig under Lloyd, Samuel)
Lozana, Domingo	Private	17, 18 and 19 Cons. Reg't., La. Mil. (Orig. under Losona, Domingo)
Lubarge, Dennis	Private	16 Reg't. (Thompson's), La. Mil.
Luberge, Dennis	Private	16 Reg't. (Thompson's), La. Mil. (Orig. under Lubarge, Dennis)
Lucal, Jean	Private	Captain Lagan's Co., La. Vols. (Orig. under Lucas, Jean)
Lucas, --	Private	Plauche's Batt'n., La. Militia
Lucas, Charles	Sergeant	Captain Price's Co., La. Militia
Lucas, Francis	Private	2 Reg't. (Cavelier's), La. Militia
Lucas, Jean	Private	Captain Lagan's Co., La. Vols.
Lucas, Samuel	Private	Capt. Wallace's Co., Boatmen, La. Vols.
Luck, John	Private	10 and 20 Cons. Reg't., La. Mil. (Orig. under Lusk, John)
Luck, Joseph	Corporal	5 Reg't. (La Branche's), La. Mil.
Lucus, Alexander	Private	Captain McNair's Co., Mounted Riflemen, La. Militia
Luke, --	Servant	16 Reg't. (Thompson's), La. Mil.
Lum, Jesse	Private	17, 18 and 19 Cons. Reg't., La. Militia
Lum, Ralph	Private	17, 18 and 19 Cons. Reg't., La. Militia
Lumber, Pierre	Private	7 Reg't. (Le Beuf's), La. Militia
Lumes, William	Private	Capt. Collard's Co., La. Militia
Lumoex, Babtist	Private	17, 18 and 19 Cons. Reg't., La. Militia
Lumoux, Babtist	Private	17, 18 and 19 Cons. Reg't., La. Militia (Orig. under Lumoex, Babtist)
Lunsford, Moses	Private	10 and 20 Cons. Reg't., La. Mil.
Luquette, Bte	Private	6 Reg't. (Landry's), La. Militia
Luquette, J. Bte	Private	6 Reg't. (Landry's), La. Militia
Luquette, Mathias	Private	6 Reg't. (Landry's), La. Militia
Lusar, Dumas	Private	De Clouet's Reg't., La. Militia
Luscy, Paul	Fusilier-Private	5 Reg't. (La Branche's), La. Mil.
Lusk, James	1 Sergeant	7 Reg't. (Le Beuf's), La. Militia
Lusk, John	Private	10 and 20 Cons. Reg't., La. Mil.
Lussalle, Antoine	Private	Captain Lagan's Co., La. Vols.
Luto, Duconge	Private	2 Batt'n. (D'Aquin's), La. Militia
Luty, T.	Private	4 Reg't. (Morgan's), La. Militia
Lynd, John	Private	Captain Beale's Co., Riflemen, La. Militia
Lynn, Lewis	Private	Captain Dodge's Co., Mounted Riflemen, La. Mil. (Orig. under Linn, Lewis)
Lynn, William	Private	Captain Dodge's Co., Mounted Riflemen, La. Militia
Lynn, William	Private	Captain Henry's Co., Mounted Riflemen, La. Militia
Lyons, Gabriel	Private	16 Reg't. (Thompson's), La. Mil.
Lyons, Henry	Private	Baker's Regiment, La. Militia
Lyons, Samuel	Private	16 Reg't. (Thompson's), La. Mil.
Lyons, William	Private	16 Reg't. (Thompson's), La. Mil.
Macarty, Baptisse	Private	1 Batt'n. (Fortier's), La. Militia
Macarty, Barthy	Private	2 Batt'n. (D'Aquin's), La. Militia
Macarty, Barty	Col. Aid De Camp	Gov. Claiborne and Staff, La. Mil.
Macarty, Francois	Private	1 Batt'n. (Fortier's), La. Militia
Macarty, John	Private	Baker's Regiment, La. Militia (Orig. under Mc Carty, John)
Macey, --	Private	Plauche's Batt'n., La. Militia
Mach, David	Private	16 Reg't. (Thompson's), La. Mil. (Orig. under Mechee, David)
Mach, George	Private	Baker's Regiment, La. Militia (Orig. under Massh, George)
Macier, To	Private	16 Reg't. (Thompson's), La. Mil.
Mackelroy, Samuel	Private	Capt. Callaway's Co., Mounted Riflemen, La. Militia
Macken, Thomas	Private	Baker's Regiment, La. Militia
Macle, Joseph	Private	2 Batt'n. (Peire's), La. Vols.
Macli, Joseph	Private	2 Batt'n. (Peire's), La. Vols. (Orig. under Macle, Joseph)
Macoin, --	Corporal	Plauche's Batt'n., La. Militia
Macquillen, George	2 Lieutenant	4 Reg't. (Morgan's), La. Militia
Maele, Joseph	Private	2 Batt'n. (Peire's), La. Vols. (Orig. under Macle, Joseph)
Maden, John	Corporal	8 Reg't. (Meriam's), La. Militia
Maden, Joseph	Corporal	8 Reg't. (Meriam's), La. Militia (Orig. under Maden, John)
Mader, Andre,	Sergeant	5 Reg't. (La Branche's), La. Mil.
Mader, Auguste	Fusilier-Private	5 Reg't. (La Branche's), La. Mil.
Mader, Jacques	Fusilier-Private	5 Reg't. (La Branche's), La. Mil.
Mader, Michel	Fusilier-Private	5 Reg't. (La Branche's), La. Mil.
Madere, Jacques	Fusilier-Private	5 Reg't. (La Branche's), La. Mil. (Orig. under Mader, Jacques)
Madere, Michel	Fusilier-Private	5 Reg't. (La Branche's), La. Mil. (Orig. under Mader, Michel)
Madere, Nicholas	Private	5 Reg't. (La Branche's), La. Mil.
Madere, Vincent	Private	5 Reg't. (La Branche's), La. Mil.
Maele, Jh	Private	2 Reg't. (Cavelier's), La. Militia
Maerin, A.	Private	8 Reg't. (Meriam's), La. Militia
Magana, Laurent	Private	2 Batt'n. (Peire's), La. Vols.
Magano, Laurent	Private	2 Batt'n. (Peire's), La. Vols. (Orig. under Magana, Laurent)

Name	Rank	Unit
Magano, Lorenzo	Private	2 Batt'n. (Peire's), La. Vols. (Orig. under Maguna, Paurent)
Magarie, Thomas	Private	Captain Young's Co., Mounted Riflemen, La. Militia
Magawin, G.	Private	8 Reg't (Meriam's), La. Militia
Magee, Benjamin	Private	12 and 13 Cons. Reg't., La. Mil.
Magee, Evan	Private	12 and 13 Cons. Reg't., La. Mil. (Orig. under Me Gee, Evan)
Magee, Hezekiah	Private	12 and 13 Cons. Reg't., La. Mil.
Magee, Jonathan	Private	12 and 13 Cons. Reg't., La. Mil. (Orig. under McGee, Jonathan)
Magee, William	Private	12 and 13 Cons. Reg't., La. Mil.
Mageehee, Daniel	Private	12 and 13 Cons. Reg't., La. Mil. (Orig. under McGehe, Daniel)
Magehe, Daniel	Private	12 and 13 Cons. Reg't., La. Mil.
Magere, --	Private	Capt. Chauveau's Co., Cavalry, La. Militia
Maggott, Austin	Private	17, 18 and 19 Cons. Reg't., La. Militia
Magnant, Louis	Private	2 Batt'n. (D'Aquin's), La. Militia
Magnion, Hypolite	Private	7 Reg't. (Le Beuf's), La. Militia
Magnol, Ml	1 Lieutenant	2 Reg't. (Cavelier's), La. Militia
Magnon, Hypolite	Private	Captain Hubbard's Mounted Co., La. Militia
Magnon, Jean	Sergeant	2 Batt'n. (Peire's), La. Vols.
Magnon, John	Sergeant	2 Batt'n. (Peire's), La. Vols. (Orig. under Magnon, Jean)
Magnon, Pierre	Private	3 Reg't. (de la Ronde's), La. Mil.
Magnot, Mil	1 Lieutenant	2 Reg't. (Cavelier's), La. Militia (Orig. under Magnol, Ml.)
Magreder, Na John	Artificer	Capt. Chaudurier's Co., Artificers, Art'y., La. Vols. (Orig. under Magrouder, Natl John)
Magruder, Allan B.	Private	16 Reg't. (Thompson's), La. Mil.
Magrouder, Natl John	Artificer	Capt. Chaudurier's Co., Artificers, Art'y., La. Vols.
Magruder, N. G.	Artificer	Capt. Chaudurier's Co., Artificers, Art'y., La. Vols. (Orig. under Magrounder, Narl John)
Magruder, N. J.	Artificer	Capt. Chaudurier's Co., Artificers, Art'y., La. Vols. (Orig. under Magrouder, Natl John)
Mague, Laurent	Private	2 Batt'n. (Peire's), La. Vols. (Orig. under Magana, Laurent)
Magui, A.	Corporal	2 Reg't. (Cavelier's), La. Militia
Magus, A.	Corporal	2 Reg't. (Cavelier's), La. Militia (Orig. under Magui, A.)
Mahan, --	Private	Captain Hubbard's Mounted Co., La. Militia
Mahan, Jacob	Private	Capt. Ashley's Co., Mounted Riflemen, La. Militia
Mahe', --	Private	Plauche's Batt'n., La. Militia
Mahier, Anm	Private	8 Reg't. (Meriam's), La. Militia
Mahier, Me	Private	8 Reg't. (Meriam's), La. Militia
Maifredy, Fs	Private	2 Reg't. (Cavelier's), La. Militia
Maillac, Jean Baptiste	Private	2 Batt'n. (Peire's), La. Vols.
Maillae, John B.	Private	2 Batt'n. (Peire's), La. Vols. (Orig. under Maillac, Jean Baptiste)
Maillard, --	Private	4 Reg't. (Morgan's), La. Militia
Maillard, Peter	Private	2 Reg't. (Cavelier's), La. Militia
Maillaud, In	Private	Capt. Songy's Co., Marines, La. Vols.
Maille, Charles	Private	8 Reg't. (Meriam's), La. Militia
Maille, Jean (pere)	Private	8 Reg't. (Meriam's), La. Militia
Mainard, Gaspard	Private	De Clouet's Reg't., La. Militia
Mainard, Lyon	Corporal	2 Batt'n. (D'Aquin's), La. Militia
Maind, Lyon	Corporal	2 Batt'n. (D'Aquin's), La. Militia (Orig. under Mainard, Lyon)
Mains, William	Private	12 and 13 Cons. Reg't., La. Mil.
Mairot, --	Private	Plauche's Batt'n., La. Militia
Mais, Bertrand	Private	7 Reg't. (Le Beuf's), La. Militia (Orig. under Mars, Bertrand)
Maise, Joseph	Private	7 Reg't. (Le Beuf's), La. Militia
Maison, Rouge	Private	Plauche's Batt'n., La. Militia
Maitrejean, Joseph	Private	De Clouet's Reg't., La. Militia (Orig. under Matreyjean, I.)
Maitrejean, Joseph	Private	2 Batt'n. (Peire's), La. Vols.
Majanty, Jean	Private	Capt. Songy's Co., Marines, La. Vols.
Majnon, Jean	Sergeant	2 Batt'n. (Peire's), (War of 1812) (Orig. under Magnon, Jean)
Majoie, --	Corporal	2 Batt'n. (D'Aquin's), La. Militia
Major, John	Corporal	Plauche's Batt'n., La. Militia
Major, Orion	Private	De Clouet's Reg't., La. Militia
Major, Peter	Private	De Clouet's Reg't., La. Militia
Majorada, Jose'	Private	De Clouet's Reg't., La. Militia
Majorada, Jose	Private	2 Batt'n. (Peire's), La. Vols. (Orig. under Mejorada, Jose)
Malaison, I.	Private	8 Reg't. (Meriam's), La. Militia
Malarine, Gregoire	Private	2 Reg't. (Cavelier's), La. Militia
Malas, Edouard	Private	2 Batt'n. (D'Aquin's), La. Militia
Malbro, Antoine	Private	De Clouet's Reg't., La. Militia
Malbrou, Antoine	Private	De Clouet's Reg't., La. Militia (Orig. under Malbro, Antoine)
Malbrou, Nicholas	Private	De Clouet's Reg't., La. Militia
Malbrough, Francois	Private	7 Reg't. (Le Beuf's), La. Militia
Malden, John	Private	10 and 20 Cons. Reg't., La. Mil.
Maldin, John	Private	10 and 20 Cons. Reg't., La. Mil. (Orig. under Malden, John)
Maleiges, Noel	Private	De Clouet's Reg't., La. Militia
Malet, Bapteste	Private	De Clouet's Reg't., La. Militia
Malier, F.	Corporal	8 Reg't. (Meriam's), La. Militia
Malinary, --	Sergeant	1 Reg't. (Dejan's), La. Militia (Orig. under Molinary, --)
Malindro, Jose	Private	17, 18 and 19 Cons. Reg't., La. Mil. (Orig. under Lanadro, Jose Maria)
Mallay, William	Private	Capt. Wallace's Co., Boatmen, La. Vols.
Mallete, A.	Corporal	8 Reg't. (Meriam's), La. Militia
Maloy, William	Private	Capt. Wallace's Co., Boatmen, La. Vols. (Orig. under Mallay, William)
Malster, David	Private	De Clouet's Reg't., La. Militia
Maltman, Jacob	Private	De Clouet's Reg't., La. Militia (See also 44 U. S. Infy.)
Mamiotte, Cheri	Private	Capt. Alpuente's Co., La. Mil. (Orig. under Mannotte, Cherie)
Mandeville, Vincent	Private	1 Batt'n. (Fortier's), La. Militia
Mandicut, Antoine	Private	2 Batt'n. (Peire's), La. Vols. (Orig. under Mendicut, Antonio)
Mandiut, Antonio	Private	2 Batt'n. (Peire's), La. Vols. (Orig. under Mendicut, Antonio)
Mandose, Joseph	Private	Captain Sprigg's Co., Boatmen, La. Vols. (Orig. under Mandoze, Joseph)
Mandoze, Joseph	Private	Captain Sprigg's Co., Boatmen, La. Vols.
Mangeneau, Francois	Private	Bakers Regiment, La. Militia
Manya, Silvin	Sergeant	2 Batt'n. (D'Aquin's), La. Militia
Manler, David	Private	Capt. Callaway's Co., Mounted Riflemen, La. Militia
Mannan, John B.	Private	4 Reg't. (Morgan's), La. Militia (Orig. under Maunan, John B.)
Mannotte, Cherie	Private	Capt. Alpuente's Co., La. Mil.
Mansano, --	Private	Sergeant Hog's Detachment, La. Vols.
Mansau, Charles	Private	De Clouet's Reg't., La. Militia (Orig. under Manseau, Charles)
Mansau, Joseph	Private	Capt. Ashley's Co., Mounted Riflemen, La. Militia
Manseau, Charles	Private	De Clouet's Reg't., La. Militia
Mantcerat, Joseph	Private	6 Reg't. (Landry's), La. Militia
Mantel, Jean	Private	De Clouet's Reg't., La. Militia (Orig. under Montet, Jean)
Manuel, --	Private	Sergeant Hog's Detachment, La. Vols.
Manuel, --	Private	8 Reg't. (Meriam's), La. Militia
Manuel, (Negro)	Servant	17, 18 and 19 Cons. Reg't., La. Militia
Manuel, Baptiste	Private	16 Reg't. (Thompson's), La. Mil.
Manville, Phillip	Sergeant	Capt. Wallace's Co., Boatmen, La. Vols.
Manzola, Jn Je	Private	17, 18 and 19 Cons. Reg't., La. Militia
Maples, John	Private	12 and 13 Cons. Reg't., La. Mil.
Maples, Thomas	Private	De Clouet's Reg't., La. Militia
Maranda, Francis	Private	Captain Price's Co., La. Militia
Marant, --	Private	Plauche's Batt'n., La. Militia
Marbury, Leonard L.	Private	10 and 20 Cons. Reg't., La. Mil.
Marc, Francois	Private	16 Reg't. (Thompson's), La. Mil.
Marc, Lange	Private	4 Reg't. (Morgan's), La. Militia
Marcantel, Porte	Private	16 Reg't. (Thompson's), La. Mil.

Name	Rank	Unit
Marceau, Charles	Private	De Clouet's Reg't., La. Militia (Orig. under Manseau, Charles)
Marcelle, Narcisse	Corporal	6 Reg't. (Landry's), La. Militia
Marcellin, --	Private	2 Batt'n. (D'Aquin's), La. Militia
Marchand, --	Private	5 Reg't. (La Branche's), La. Mil.
Marchand, Baptiste	Private	5 Reg't. (La Branche's), La. Mil.
Marchand, E.	Private	Plauche's Batt'n., La. Militia
Marchand, Francois	Private	2 Batt'n. (Peire's), La. Vols.
Marchand, Nicholas	Private	2 Batt'n. (Peire's), La. Vols. (Orig. under Marchand, Francois)
Marchand, S.	Corporal	Plauche's Batt'n., La. Militia
Marchant, Hugue	Private	2 Batt'n. (D'Aquin's), La. Militia
Marchard, Baptiste	Fusilier-Private	5 Reg't. (La Branche's), La. Mil. (Orig. under Marchand, Baptiste)
Marcks, Frans	Private	16 Reg't. (Thompson's), La. Mil.
Marcks, J. B.	Private	16 Reg't. (Thompson's), La. Mil.
Marcostillo, --	Private	1 Batt'n. (Fortier's), La. Militia (Orig. under Marcostilo, --)
Marcostilo, --	Private	1 Batt'n. (Fortier's), La. Militia
Marcot, Augustin	Fusilier-Private	5 Reg't. (La Branche's), La. Mil.
Marcotte, Auguste	Corporal	5 Reg't. (La Branche's), La. Mil.
Marcou, --	Private	1 Reg't. (Dejan's), La. Militia
Mardis, Abner	Private	4 Reg't. (Morgan's), La. Militia
Marel, Jean Pierre	Fifer-Private	2 Batt'n. (Peire's), La. Vols. (Orig. under Marie, Jean Pierre)
Marero, Antonio	Private	2 Reg't. (de la Ronde's), La. Mil. (Orig. under Marrero, Antonio)
Marguety, Fcs	Private	Capt. Colsson's Co., Artillery, La. Vols.
Maria, Joseph	Private	2 Reg't. (Cavelier's), La. Militia
Marian, --	Private	De Clouet's Reg't., La. Militia
Marianeaux, Louis	Private	8 Reg't. (Meriam's), La. Militia
Marie, Gabriel Jean	Private	1 Batt'n. (Fortier's), La. Militia
Marie, Jn	Private	2 Batt'n. (D'Aquin's), La. Militia
Marie, Jean Pierre	Fifer-Private	2 Batt'n. (Peire's), La. Vols.
Marie, Joseph	Private	Plauche's Batt'n., La. Militia
Marie, Joseph	Private	2 Batt'n. (D'Aquin's), La. Militia
Marie, Pierre	Private	2 Reg't. (Cavelier's), La. Militia
Marigny, Celestin	Sergeant	1 Batt'n. (Fortier's), La. Militia
Marillet, --	1 Lieutenant	4 Reg't. (Morgan's), La. Militia
Marin, Joseph	Private	2 Batt'n. (D'Aquin's), La. Militia
Marin, Richard	Private	Plauche's Batt'n., La. Militia
Marine, Maturin	Private	7 Reg't. (Le Beuf's), La. Militia
Marion, --	Sergeant	8 Reg't. (Meriam's), La. Militia (Orig. under Marrion, --)
Marion, F.	Private	8 Reg't. (Meriam's), La. Militia (Orig. under Marrion, F.)
Marion, V.	Private	8 Reg't. (Meriam's), La. Militia (Orig. under Marrion, F.)
Marionneaux, Norbert	Private	8 Reg't. (Meriam's), La. Militia
Mariro, Joseph	Private	3 Reg't. (de la Ronde's), La. Mil. (Orig. under Marrero, Josef)
Marks, Andre'	Private	16 Reg't. (Thompson's), La. Mil.
Marks, Francois	Private	16 Reg't. (Thompson's), La. Mil. (Orig. under Marc, Francois)
Marks, Simon	Private	16 Reg't. (Thompson's), La. Mil.
Marks, Thomas	Private	De Clouet's Reg't., La. Militia
Marlin, --	Private	8 Reg't. (Meriam's), La. Militia (Orig. under Martin, James)
Marlow, John	Private	12 and 13 Cons. Reg't., La. Mil.
Marly, Devince	Sergeant	1 Batt'n. (Fortier's), La. Militia
Marly, Jean Baptiste	Private	1 Batt'n. (Fortier's), La. Militia
Marly, Pierre	Private	1 Batt'n. (Fortier's), La. Militia
Marmillion, Pierre	Sergeant	5 Reg't. (La Branche's), La. Mil.
Marmillon, Valsin	Fusilier-Private	5 Reg't. (La Branche's), La. Mil.
Maroot, Augustin	Corporal	17, 18 and 19 Cons. Reg't., La. Militia
Marque, --	Private	2 Batt'n. (D'Aquin's), La. Militia
Marquerie, --	2 Lieutenant	Plauche's Batt'n., La. Militia
Marques, Francis	Private	De Clouet's Reg't., La. Militia (Orig. under Marquis, Francis)
Marquete, Fois	Private	Plauche's Batt'n., La. Militia
Marquie, --	Private	2 Batt'n. (D'Aquin's), La. Militia (Orig. under Marque, --)
Marquin, --	Private	2 Batt'n. (D'Aquin's), La. Militia
Marquis, Francis	Private	De Clouet's Reg't., La. Militia
Marquis, Louis	Fusilier-Private	5 Reg't. (La Branche's), La. Mil.
Marquis, Louis fils	Private	5 Reg't. (La Branche's), La. Mil.
Marquis, Paul	Fusilier-Private	5 Reg't. (La Branche's), La. Mil.
Marrero, Antonio	2 Lieutenant	3 Reg't. (de la Ronde's), La. Mil.
Marrero, Antonio	Private	3 Reg't. (de la Ronde's), La. Mil.
Marrero, Josef	Private	3 Reg't. (de la Ronde's), La. Mil.
Marrianne, Jose	Private	16 Reg't. (Thompson's), La. Mil.
Marrion, --	Sergeant	8 Reg't. (Meriam's), La. Militia
Marrion, F.	Private	8 Reg't. (Meriam's), La. Militia
Marrion, V.	Sergeant	8 Reg't. (Meriam's), La. Militia
Marrioux, Pre Charles	Lieut-3Lieut.	2 Batt'n. (D'Aquin's), La. Militia
Marrois, Ursin	Private	6 Reg't. (Landry's), La. Militia
Marrs, M. D.	Private	Captain Sprigg's Co., Boatmen, La. Vols. (Orig. under Mars, M. D.)
Mars, Bertrand	Private	Captain Hubbard's Mounted Co., La. Militia
Mars, Bertrand	Private	7 Reg't. (Le Beuf's), La. Militia
Mars, M. D.	Private	Captain Sprigg's Co., Boatmen, La. Vols.
Marsh, Joshua	Private	10 and 20 Cons. Reg't., La. Mil.
Martain, Lewis	Private	Captain Musick's Co., La. Mil.
Marten, Coleman A.	Captain	17, 18 and 19 Cons. Reg't., La. Mil. (Orig. under Martin, Coleman A.)
Marten, Mathew	Sergeant	17, 18 and 19 Cons. Reg't., La. Mil. (Orig. under Martin, Mathew)
Martenez, Domingo	Private-Corporal	2 Batt'n. (Peire's), La. Vols. (Orig. under Martinez, Domingo)
Marter, Charles	Private	10 and 20 Cons. Reg't., La. Mil.
Marthe, Jacques	Private	3 Reg't. (de la Ronde's), La. Mil.
Marthu, Jacques	Private	3 Reg't. (de la Ronde's), La. Mil. (Orig. under Marthe, Jacques)
Martial, R. B.	Private	17, 18 and 19 Cons. Reg't., La. Militia
Martin, --	Servant	2 Batt'n. (D'Aquin's), La. Militia
Martin, A.	Private	8 Reg't. (Meriam's), La. Militia
Martin, Adam	Private	Captain Musick's Co., Mounted Riflemen, La. Militia
Martin, Andre	1 Lieutenant	De Clouet's Reg't., La. Militia
Martin, Antoine	Private	Baker's Regiment, La. Militia
Martin, Augustin	Private	2 Reg't. (Cavelier's), La. Militia
Martin, Bazile	Private	2 Batt'n. (D'Aquin's), La. Militia
Martin, Benjamin	Private	12 and 13 Cons. Reg't., La. Mil.
Martin, Bisente	Private	2 Reg't. (Cavelier's), La. Militia
Martin, Coleman A.	Captain	17, 18 and 19 Cons. Reg't., La. Militia
Martin, David	Private	Captain Musick's Co., Mounted Riflemen, La. Militia
Martin, David	Private	Captain Musick's Co., Mounted Riflemen, La. Militia
Martin, F.	1 Lieutenant	6 Reg't. (Landry's), La. Militia (Orig. under St. Martin, F.)
Martin, Francois	Private	3 Reg't. (de la Ronde's), La. Mil.
Martin, I.	Private	6 Reg't. (Landry's), La. Militia
Martin, James	Private	De Clouet's Reg't., La. Militia
Martin, James	Private	8 Reg't. (Meriam's), La. Militia
Martin, Jeremiha	Private	2 Reg't. (Cavelier's), La. Militia
Martin, Jh	Sergeant	1 Batt'n. (Fortier's), La. Militia
Martin, Joharda	Private	Captain McNair's Co., Mounted Riflemen, La. Militia
Martin, John	Private	8 Reg't. (Meriam's), La. Militia
Martin, Jques	Private	3 Reg't. (de la Ronde's), La. Mil.
Martin, Joseph	1 Lieutenant	Captain Hubbard's Mounted Co., La. Militia
Martin, Joseph	Private	Captain Lagan's Co., La. Vols.
Martin, Joseph	Private	2 Reg't. (Cavelier's), La. Militia
Martin, Levi	Sergeant	17, 18 and 19 Cons. Reg't., La. Militia
Martin, Lewis	Private	Captain Musick's Co., Mounted Riflemen, La. Militia
Martin, Louis	Private	De Clouet's Reg't., La. Militia
Martin, Louis	Private	Captain McNair's Co., Mounted Riflemen, La. Militia
Martin, Louis	Private	2 Reg't. (Cavelier's), La. Militia
Martin, Louis	Private	3 Reg't. (de la Ronde's), La. Mil.
Martin, Magloire	Fusilier-Private	5 Reg't. (La Branche's), La. Mil.
Martin, Marin	Captain	De Clouet's Reg't., La. Militia
Martin, Mathew	Sergeant	17, 18 and 19 Cons. Reg't., La. Militia
Martin, Michel	Private	7 Reg't. (Le Beuf's), La. Militia
Martin, Paul	Private	Baker's Regiment, La. Militia
Martin, Pierre	Private	Captain Lagan's Co., La. Vols.
Martin, Robert	Private	17, 18 and 19 Cons. Reg't., La. Militia

Name	Rank	Unit
Martin, Samuel	Private	De Clouet's Reg't., La. Militia
Martin, Valery	Captain	De Clouet's Reg't., La. Militia
Martin, Wyatt	Corporal-Sgt.	De Clouet's Reg't., La. Militia
Martin, Zachariah	2 Lieutenant	10 and 20 Cons. Reg't., La. Mil.
Martin, Zachariah	Private	16 Reg't. (Thompson's), La. Mil.
Martin, Zedekiah	Private	12 and 13 Cons. Reg't., La. Mil.
Martinau, Charles	Private	Capt. VanBibber's Co., La. Mil.
Martine, Antoine	Fusilier-Private	5 Reg't. (La Branche's), La. Mil.
Martineau, Charles	Private	Capt. Van Bibber's Co., La. Mil. (Orig. under Martinau, Charles)
Martines, Edmon	Corporal	2 Reg't. (Cavelier's), La. Militia
Martines, Francois	Private	De Clouet's Reg't., La. Militia
Martines, Francois	Private	Captain Hubbard's Mounted Co., La. Militia
Martines, I.	Sergeant	2 Reg't. (Cavelier's), La. Militia
Martines, J.	Private	2 Reg't. (Cavelier's), La. Militia
Martines, Joseph	Private	Captain Hubbard's Mounted Co., La. Militia
Martines, Juan	Private	Captain Hubbard's Mounted Co., La. Militia
Martines, Mignet	Private	Capt. Alpuente's Co., La. Militia
Martines, R.	Private	2 Reg't.(Cavelier's), La. Militia
Martinez, Anthony	Private	2 Batt'n. (Peire's), La. Vols.
Martinez, Domingo	Private-Cpl.	2 Batt'n. (Peire's), La. Vols. (See also 3 U.S. Inf.)
Martinez, Francois	Private	De Clouet's Reg't., La. Militia (Orig. under Martines, Francois)
Martinez, Francisco	Corporal	17, 18 and 19 Cons. Reg't., La. Militia
Martinez, Jose de Jesus	Private	17, 18 and 19 Cons. Reg't., La. Militia (Orig. under Martonez, Jose Jesus)
Martino, Jesus	Private	17, 18 and 19 Cons. Reg't., La. Militia
Martino, Pedro	Private	Captain Lagan's Co., La. Vols.
Martinos, Anto	Private	2 Batt'n. (Peire's), La. Vols. (Orig. under Martinez, Anthony)
Martonez, Jose Jesus	Private	17, 18 and 19 Cons. Reg't., La. Militia
Mary, --	Servant	17, 18 and 19 Cons. Reg't., La. Militia
Maserado, Jose	Private	De Clouet's Reg't., La. Militia (Orig. under Majorada, Jose)
Mason, John	Sergeant	Capt. Wallace's Co., Boatmen, La. Vols.
Maspero, --	Private	1 Reg't. (Dejan's), La. Militia
Mass, Bte	Private	Baker's Regiment, La. Militia
Mass, Dominique	Private	Baker's Regiment, La. Militia
Massee, Pierre	Private	De Clouet's Reg't., La. Militia
Massena, --	Private	Plauche's Batt'n., La. Militia
Masser, Siprin	Private	7 Reg't. (Le Beuf's), La. Militia (Orig. under Masset, Siprin)
Masset, Siprin	Private	7 Reg't. (Le Beuf's), La. Militia
Massey, Clement	Private	Capt. Allen's Co., Artillerists, La. Vols.
Massey, Clement	Private	2 Batt'n. (Peire's), La. Vols.
Massey, Drury	Private	De Clouet's Reg't., La. Militia
Massey, James	Private	Capt. Allen's Co., Artillerists, La. Vols.
Massey, Joshua	Private	Captain McNair's Co., Mounted Riflemen, La. Militia
Massey, William	Private	Captain McNair's Co., Mounted Riflemen, La. Militia
Massh, George	Private	Baker's Regiment, La. Militia
Massicot, Augustin	Fusilier-Private	5 Reg't. (La Branche's), La. Mil.
Massicot, Charles	Fusilier-Private	5 Reg't. (La Branche's), La. Mil.
Massie, C.	Private	Captain Sprigg's Co., Boatmen, La. Vols. (Orig. under Massy, C.)
Massiere, John B.	Sergeant	7 Reg't. (Le Beuf's), La. Militia
Massieu, John B.	Sergeant	7 Reg't. (Le Beuf's), La. Militia (Orig. under Massiere, John B.)
Massippe, Frs.	Private	17, 18 and 19 Cons. Reg't., La. Militia
Massippi, Frs.	Private	17, 18 and 19 Cons. Reg't., La. Mil. (Orig. under Massippe,Frs)
Massippi, Pierre	Corporal	17, 18 and 19 Cons. Reg't., La. Mil.
Massy, C.	Private	Captain Sprigg's Co., Boatmen, La. Vols.
Masterson, George	Private	Capt. Ashley's Co., Mounted Riflemen, La. Militia
Mate, Pierre	Private	7 Reg't. (Le Beuf's), La. Militia
Mateo, Simeon	Corporal	De Clouet's Reg't., La. Militia (Orig. under Matteo, Simeon)
Mater, Louis	Private	1 Batt'n. (Fortier's), La. Militia
Matern, Nicholas	Private	Captain Hubbards, Mounted Co., La. Militia
Matern, Nicolas	Fuslier-Private	5 Reg't. (La Branche's), La. Mil. (Orig. under Mattern, Nicolas)
Materne, Jr.	Private	7 Reg't. (Le Beuf's), La. Militia
Materre, --	Private	7 Reg't. (Le Beuf's), La. Militia (Orig. under Materne, --Jr.)
Matheas, Frederick	Private	De Clouet's Reg't., La. Militia (Orig. under Mathias, Frederick)
Mather, Jean Baptiste	Corporal	1 Batt'n. (Fortier's), La. Militia
Mathew, --	--	10 and 20 Cons. Reg't., La. Mil.
Mathews, Charles	Private	10 and 20 Cons. Reg't., La. Mil.
Mathews, George	Sergeant	10 and 20 Cons. Reg't., La. Mil.
Mathews, William	Private	De Clouet's Reg't., La. Militia
Mathias, Frederick	Private	De Clouet's Reg't., La. Militia
Mathien, Jn	Private	2 Reg't. (Cavelier's), La. Militia
Mathieu, Innocent	Private	1 Batt'n. (Fortier's), La. Militia
Mathieu, Jh	Private	2 Batt'n. (D'Aquin's), La. Militia
Mathiew, Tousin	Private	5 Reg't. (La Branche's), La. Mil.
Mathis, David	Private	Capt. Ashley's Co., Mounted Riflemen, La. Militia
Matho, Sebastien	Private	2 Batt'n. (Peire's), La. Vols. (Orig. under Matto, Sebastien)
Mathune, Paul	Private	6 Reg't. (Landry's), La. Militia
Matier, John	Private	Baker's Regiment, La. Militia
Matras, --	Corporal	2 Reg't. (Cavelier's), La. Militia
Matreyjean, I.	Private	De Clouet's Reg't., La. Militia
Matrijean, Joseph	Private	2 Batt'n. (Peire's), La. Vols. (Orig. under Maitrejean, Joseph)
Matt, Joseph	Private	16 Reg't. (Thompson's), La. Mil.
Matt. Pierre fils	Private	16 Reg't. (Thompson's), La. Mil.
Matteo, Simeon	Corporal	De Clouet's Reg't., La. Militia
Mattern, Nicolas	Fusilier-Private	5 Reg't. (Le Branche's), La. Mil.
Matthews, Charles	Private	10 and 20 Cons. Reg't., La. Mil. (Orig. under Mathews, Charles)
Matthews, David	Private	Capt. Ashley's Co., Mounted Riflemen, La. Mil. (Orig. under Mathis, David)
Matthews, George	Sergeant	10 and 20 Cons. Reg't., La. Mil. (Orig. under Mathews, George)
Matthews, William	Private	De Clouet's Reg't., La. Militia (Orig. under Mathews, William)
Matthieu, Innocent	Private	1 Batt'n. (Fortier's), La. Militia (Orig. under Mathieu, Innocent)
Mattiana, Hilaire	Private	De Clouet's Reg't., La. Militia
Mattingly, Thomas	Private	Captain McNair's Co., Mounted Riflemen, La. Militia
Matto, Bastien	Private	2 Batt'n. (Peire's), La. Vols. (Orig. under Matto,Sebastien)
Matto, Sebastien	Private	2 Batt'n. (Peire's), La. Vols.
Mattryean, Joseph	Private	2 Batt'n. (Peire's), La. Vols. (Orig. under Maitrejean, Joseph)
Matune, Michelle	Corporal	6 Reg't. (Landry's), La. Militia
Mauin, I. P.	Private	7 Reg't. (Le Beuf's), La. Militia (Orig. under Murin, I. P.)
Maullet, Antoine	Private	Capt. Callaway's Co., Cavalry, La. Militia
Maunan, John B.	Private	4 Reg't. (Morgan's), La. Militia
Maura, Balthazar	Private	2 Reg't. (Cavelier's), La. Militia
Mauraux, Manuel	Private	1 Batt'n. (Fortier's), La. Militia
Maurice, --	Musician	Plauche's Batt'n., La. Militia
Maurice, --	Private	2 Batt'n. (D'Aquin's), La. Militia (Orig. under Mauriste, --)
Maurice, Jean	Private	Captain Lagan's Co., La. Vols.
Maurin, --	Private	Plauche's Batt'n., La. Militia
Maurin, Antoine	Aid de Camp	2 Brigade (Hopkins'), La. Militia
Maurin, I. P.	Private	7 Reg't. (Le Beuf's), La. Militia
Maurin, Pierre	Private	Capt. Songy's Co., Marines, La. Vols.
Mauris, Vincent	Private	5 Reg't. (La Branche's), La. Mil. (Orig. under Morris, Vincent)
Mauriste, --	Private	2 Batt'n. (D'Aquin's), La. Militia
Maurose, --	Private	2 Batt'n. (D'Aquin's), La. Militia
Maxant, --	1 Sergeant	4 Reg't. (Morgan's), La. Militia
Maxant, Francis	Private	2 Batt'n. (Peire's), La. Vols.
Maxant, Fran	Private	16 Reg't. (Thompson's), La. Mil. (Orig. under Maxent, Francois)
Maxent, Anthony	Private	4 Reg't. (Morgan's), La. Militia

Name	Rank	Unit
Maxent, François	Private	2 Batt'n. (Peire's), La. Vols. (Orig. under Maxant, Francis)
Maxant, Francois	Private	16 Reg't. (Thompson's), La. Mil.
Maxfield, David	Drum Major	12 and 13 Cons. Reg't., La. Mil.
Maxfield, James	Private	Capt. Allen's Co., Artillerists, La. Vols.
Maxim, Jean	Private	2 Batt'n. (Peire's), La. Vols. (Orig. under Maxin, Jean)
Maxin, Jean	Private	2 Batt'n. (Peire's), La. Vols.
Maxwell, Samuel	Private	De Clouet's Reg't., La. Militia
Mayal, Miguel	Private	Captain Lagan's Co., La. Vols. (Orig. under Mayol, Miguel)
Mayars, Philip	Private	Captain Lagan's Co., La. Vols.
Mayan, Jean	Private	Capt. Songy's Co., Marines, La. Vols. (Orig. under Maillaud, In)
Maye, Alexis	Private	16 Reg't. (Thompson's), La. Mil. (Orig. under Mayer, Alexis)
Maye, Elerie	Private	8 Reg't. (Meriam's), La. Militia
Maye, Francois	Sergeant	8 Reg't. (Meriam's), La. Militia
Maye, George	Private	16 Reg't. (Thompson's), La. Mil.
Mayeny, Jean Pre	Sergeant	8 Reg't. (Meriam's), La. Militia
Mayeny, Hyplite	Sergeant	17, 18 and 19 Cons. Reg't., La. Militia
Mayeny, Joseph	Sergeant	17, 18 and 19 Cons. Reg't., La. Militia
Mayeny, Louis	Private	17, 18 and 19 Cons. Reg't., La. Militia
Mayer, Alexis	Private	16 Reg't. (Thompson's), La. Mil.
Mayer, Drauzin	Fusilier-Private	5 Reg't. (La Branche's), La. Mil.
Mayer, F.	Private	8 Reg't. (Meriam's), La. Militia (Orig. under Myer, F.)
Mayer, Jacob	Private	8 Reg't. (Meriam's), La. Militia
Mayer, Joseph	Private	4 Reg't. (Morgan's), La. Militia (Orig. under Meyer, Joseph)
Mayer, Pierre	Private	Capt. Songy's Co., Marines, La. Vols.
Mayer, Philipe	Private	Captain Lagan's Co., La. Vols. (Orig. under Mayars, Philip)
Mayere, Philip	Private	Captain Lagan's Co., La. Vols. (Orig. under Mayars, Philip)
Mayes, Francis	Private	De Clouet's Reg't., La. Militia (Orig. under Mays, Francis)
Mayfield, John	Private	12 and 13 Cons. Reg't., La. Mil.
Mayfield, Reubin	Private	De Clouet's Reg't., La. Militia
Mayhew, Thaddeus	Private	1 Reg't. (Dejan's), La. Militia
Mayol, Miguel	Private	Captain Lagan's Co., La. Vols.
Mayou, Louis	Sergeant	2 Reg't. (Cavelier's), La. Militia
Mayronne, Jr.	Private	4 Reg't. (Morgan's), La. Militia
Mayronne, D.	Private	4 Reg't. (Morgan's), La. Militia
Mayronne, Fcois son	Fus.-Private	4 Reg't. (La Branche's), La. Mil.
Mayronne, Sr.	Private	4 Reg't. (Morgan's), La. Militia
Mays, Benjamin	Sergeant	10 and 20 Cons. Reg't., La. Mil.
Mays, Francis	3 Lieutenant	De Clouet's Reg't., La. Militia
Mays, Thomas	Private	17, 18 and 19 Cons. Reg't., La. Militia
Mazanges, --	Private	3 Reg't. (de la Ronde's), La. Mil.
Mazerada, Jose	Private	De Clouet's Reg't., La. Militia (Orig. under Majorada, Jose)
Mazin, Jean Baptiste	Private	2 Reg't. (Cavelier's), La. Militia
Mazzola, Jr. Se	Private	17, 18 and 19 Cons. Reg't., La. Militia (Orig. under Manzola, Jn Je)
Mc Adams, D.	Private	4 Reg't. (Morgan's), La. Militia
Mc Adams, William	Private	Captain Sprigg's Co., Boatmen, La. Vols.
Mc Adams, William	Private	4 Reg't. (Morgan's), La. Militia
Mc Aleb, Ephrain	Lieutenant	12 and 13 Cons. Reg't., La. Mil. (Orig. under McCaleb, Ephraim)
Mc Allister, John	Private	De Clouet's Reg't., La. Militia
Mc Allister, Joseph	Private	10 and 20 Cons. Reg't., La. Mil.
Mc Arrty, Nathan	Private	Captain Young's Co., Mounted Riflemen, La. Mil. (Orig. under McCarty, Nathan)
Mc Arthur, James	Private	10 and 20 Cons. Reg't., La. Mil.
Mc Arthur, John	Private	10 and 20 Cons. Reg't., La. Mil.
Mc Arthur, Thomas	Private	10 and 20 Cons. Reg't., La. Mil.
Mc Atee, William	Private	17, 18 and 19 Cons. Reg't., La. Mil. (Orig. under Mc Atue, William)
Mc Atue, William	Private	17, 18 and 19 Cons. Reg't., La. Militia
Mc Bride, Alexander	Private	Capt. Allen's Co., Artillerists, La. Vols.
Mc Bride, Neill	Private	4 Reg't. (Morgan's), La. Militia
Mc Bride, Walter	Private	De Clouet's Reg't., La. Militia
Mc Bride, William	Private	17, 18 and 19 Cons. Reg't., La. Militia
Mc Caffery, Andrew	Drummer-Drum Major	De Clouet's Reg't., La. Militia (Orig. under McCaffrey, Andrew)
Mc Caffree, Andrew	Drummer-Drum Major	De Clouet's Reg't., La. Militia (Orig. under McCaffrey, Andrew)
Mc Caffrey, Andrew	Drummer-Drum Major	De Clouet's Reg't., La. Militia
Mc Caleb, Ephraim	Lieutenant	12 and 13 Cons. Reg't., La. Mil.
Mc Calister, James	Private	Captain Musick's Co., Mounted Riflemen, La. Mil. (Orig. under McCollester, James)
Mc Call, --	Private	Plauche's Batt'n., La. Militia
Mc Call, Jn	Private	1 Reg't. (Dejan's), La. Militia
Mc Call, Jesse	Private	Baker's Regiment, La. Militia
Mc Call, Samuel	Private	Captain Dodge's Co., Mounted Riflemen, La. Militia
Mc Call, Samuel	Private	Captain Henry's Co., Mounted Riflemen, La. Militia
Mc Callister, Joseph	Private	10 and 20 Cons. Reg't., La. Mil. (Orig. under Mc Allister, Joseph)
Mc Cantss, David B.	1 Lieutenant	10 and 20 Cons. Reg't., La. Mil. (Orig. under Mc Cants, David B)
Mc Cants, David B.	1 Lieutenant	10 and 20 Cons. Reg't., La. Mil.
Mc Carrell, Joseph	Private	19 Reg't., La. Militia
Mc Carty, A.	Private	4 Reg't. (Morgan's), La. Militia
Mc Carty, Baptiste	Private	1 Batt'n. (Fortier's), La. Militia (Orig. under Macarty, Baptisse)
Mc Carty, John	Private	Baker's Regiment, La. Militia
Mc Carty, Nathan	Private	Captain Young's Co., Mounted Riflemen, La. Militia
Mc Cauley, James	Private	De Clouet's Reg't., La. Militia
Mc Cauly, James	Private	De Clouet's Reg't., La. Militia (Orig. under McCauley, James)
Mc Causland, Robert	Brig. General	3 Brigade (Mc Causland's), La. Militia
Mc Clain, Jeremiah	Private	Captain Rankin's Co., Mounted Riflemen, La. Militia
Mc Claskey, Philip	2 Lieut.-1 Lieut.	Capt. Allen's Co., Artillerists, La. Vols. (Orig. under McLoskey, Philip)
Mc Clausen, Daniel	Private	12 and 13 Cons. Reg't., La. Mil.
Mc Clawd, Mordicay	Private	2 Batt'n. (Peire's), La. Vols. (Orig. under McLaed, Mordicay)
Mc Clellan, --	Private	Plauche's Batt'n., La. Militia (Orig. under Mc Clelland, Robert)
Mc Clelland, Robert	Private	Plauche's Batt'n., La. Militia
Mc Clendon, Alfred	Private	12 and 13 Cons. Reg't., La. Mil. (Orig. under Mc Clenen, Alfred)
Mc Clendon, Jesse	Private	12 and 13 Cons. Reg't., La. Mil. (Orig. under Mc Clennen, Jesse)
Mc Clenen, Alfred	Private	12 and 13 Cons. Reg't., La. Mil.
Mc Clenne, Jesse	Private	12 and 13 Cons. Reg't., La. Mil.
Mc Clintick, Armstrong	Private	Capt. Wallace's Co., Boatmen, La. Vols.
Mc Closkey, Philip	2 Lieut.-1 Lieut.	Capt. Allen's Co., Artillerists, La. Vols. (Orig. under McLoskey, Philip)
Mc Cloud, Mordecai	Private	De Clouet's Reg't., La. Militia
Mc Cloud, Mordecai	Private	2 Batt'n. (Peire's), La. Vols. (Orig. under McLawd, Mordicay)
Mc Clure, David	Sergeant	10 and 20 Cons. Reg't., La. Mil.
Mc Cluskey, Joseph	Private	16 Reg't. (Thompson's), La. Mil.
Mc Clusky, Lawrence	Private	17, 18 and 19 Cons. Reg't., La. Militia
Mc Collester, James	Private	Captain Musick's Co., Mounted Riflemen, La. Militia
Mc Colloe, Joseph	Corporal	De Clouet's Reg't., La. Militia
Mc Combs, Robert	Private	10 and 20 Cons. Reg't., La. Mil.
Mc Comico, John	Private	Plauche's Batt'n., La. Militia
Mc Conel, John	Lieutenant	Capt. Collard's Co., La. Militia
Mc Conly, James	Private	De Clouet's Reg't., La. Militia (Orig. under Mc Cauley, James)
Mc Connel, Charles	Private	Captain Ramsey's Co., Mounted Riflemen, La. Militia
Mc Connell, James	Private	10 and 20 Cons. Reg't., La. Mil.
Mc Connell, John	Lieutenant	Capt. Collard's Co., La. Militia (Orig. under Mc Conel, John)

Name	Rank	Unit
Mc Connico, --	Private	Plauche's Batt'n., La. Militia (Orig. under McComico, John)
Mc Coon, John	Private	12 and 13 Cons. Reg't., La. Mil.
Mc Cormac, James	Private	Capt. Rankin's Co., Mounted Riflemen, La. Militia (Orig. under McCormack, James)
Mc Cormack, James	Private	Captain Rankins, Co., Mounted Riflemen, La. Militia
Mc Cormack, William	Private	12 and 13 Cons. Reg't., La. Mil. (Orig. under Mc Cormick, William)
Mc Cormick, David	Corporal	Captain Hughes' Co, Mounted Riflemen, La. Militia
Mc Cormick, John	Corporal	Captain Hughes' Co., Mounted Riflemen, La. Militia
Mc Cormick, William	Corporal	12 and 13 Cons. Reg't., La. Mil.
Mc Cornick, David	Corporal	Captain Hughes' Co., Mounted Riflemen, La. Mil. (Orig. under David McCormick)
Mc Cornick, John	Corporal	Captain Hughes' Co., Mounted Riflemen, La. Mil. (Orig. under McCormick, John)
Mc Coy, Annania	Private	Captain Hughes' Co., Mounted Riflemen, La. Militia
Mc Coy, Joseph	Private	Capt. Collard's Co., La. Militia
Mc Coy, Thomas F.	Surgeon	12 and 13 Cons. Reg't., La. Mil.
Mc Crasson, Bernard	Private	17, 18 and 19 Cons. Reg't., La. Mil. (Orig. under Mc Crosson, Bernard)
Mc Cray, Kineth	Private	10 and 20 Cons. Reg't., La. Mil.
Mc Crosson, Bernard	Private	17, 18 and 19 Cons. Reg't., La. Militia
Mc Crummen, Kenneth	Private	17, 18 and 19 Cons. Reg't., La. Militia
Mc Cuch, John	Private	10 and 20 Cons. Reg't., La. Mil. (Orig. under McHugh, John)
Mc Cugh, Thomas	Private	10 and 20 Cons. Reg't., La. Mil.
Mc Cullen, John	Private	De Clouet's Reg't., La. Militia
Mc Cullen, Lewis	Private	De Clouet's Reg't., La. Militia
Mc Cullin, John	Private	De Clouet's Reg't., La. Militia (Orig. under Mc Cullen, John)
Mc Cullin, Lewis	Private	De Clouet's Reg't., La. Militia (Orig. under Mc Cullen, Lewis)
Mc Cullough, James	Private	Capt. Wallace's Co., Boatmen, La. Vols.
Mc Culough, James	Private	Capt. Wallace's Co., Boatmen, La. Vols. (Orig. under McCullough, James)
Mc Cune, William	Private	Captain Sprigg's Co., Boatmen, La. Vols. (Orig. under McKune, William)
Mc Curley, Moses	Corporal	17, 18 and 19 Cons. Reg't., La. Militia
Mc Cutchon, Samuel	Private	Capt. Trudeau's Troop of Horse, La. Militia
Mc Daniel, Anthony	Private	16 Reg't. (Thompson's), La. Mil.
Mc Daniel, Dennis	Private	16 Reg't. (Thompson's), La. Mil.
Mc Daniel, Ennis	Private	Captain McNair's Co., Mounted Riflemen, La. Militia
Mc Daniel, Jacob	Corporal	De Clouet's Reg't., La. Militia
Mc Daniel, John	Private	16 Reg't. (Thompson's), La. Mil.
Mc Daniel, Robert	Private	Baker's Regiment, La. Militia
Mc David, James	Private	Captain Ramsey's Co., Mounted Riflemen, La. Militia
Mc Donald, James	Private	Captain McNair's Co., Mounted Riflemen, La. Militia
Mc Donald, John	Corporal-Private	Captain McNair's Co., Mounted Riflemen, La. Militia
Mc Donald, Mans.	1 Lieutenant	11 Reg't. (Hickey's), La. Militia
Mc Donough, John	Private	Captain Beale's Co., Riflemen, La. Militia
Mc Dougald, A.	Private	8 Reg't. (Meriam's), La. Militia
Mc Down, William	Corporal	Captain Musick's Co., Mounted Riflemen, La. Militia
Mc Down, William	Corporal	Captain Musick's Co., La. Mil. (Orig. under Mc Downs, William)
Mc Downs, William	Corporal	Captain Musick's Co., Mounted Riflemen, La. Mil. (Orig. under Mc Down, William)
Mc Downs, William	Corporal	Captain Musick's Co., La. Mil.
Mc Farlan, William	Private	10 and 20 Cons. Reg't., La. Mil. (Orig. under Mc Farland, William)
Mc Farland, --	Private	Plauche's Batt'n., La. Militia
Mc Farland, T.	Private	4 Reg't. (Morgan's), La. Militia
Mc Farland, William	Private	10 and 20 Cons. Reg't., La. Mil.
Mc Farlin, William	Private	10 and 20 Cons. Reg't., La. Mil.
Mc Farling, Andrew	Private	17, 18 and 19 Cons. Reg't., La. Militia
Mc Gaham, George	Private	Captain Dodge's Co., Mounted Riflemen, La. Militia
Mc Gahan, George	Private	Captain Henry's Co., Mounted Riflemen, La. Militia
Mc Gahon, George	Private	Captain Henry's Co., Mounted Riflemen, La. Militia (Orig. under Mc Gahan, George)
Mc Garie, Thomas	Private	Captain Young's Co., Mounted Riflemen, La. Militia (Orig. under Magarie, Thos.)
Mc Gee, Benjamin	Private	12 and 13 Cons. Reg't., La. Mil. (Orig. under Magee, Benjamin)
Mc Gee, Even	Private	12 and 13 Cons. Reg't., La. Mil.
Mc Gee, Hezekiah	Private	12 and 13 Cons. Reg't., La. Mil. (Orig. under Magee, Hezekiah)
Mc Gee, Jonathan	Private	12 and 13 Cons. Reg't., La. Mil.
Mc Gee, W.	Private	1 Reg't. (Dejan's), La. Militia
Mc Gee, William	Private	12 and 13 Cons. Reg't., La. Mil. (Orig. under Magee, William)
Mc Gill, John	Private	10 and 20 Cons. Reg't., La. Mil.
Mc Gilvery, William	Private	Captain Beale's Co., Riflemen, La. Militia
Mc Glaughlin, Edward	Private	17, 18 and 19 Cons. Reg't., La. Militia
Mc Glaughlin, John	Private	Captain McNair's Co., Mounted Riflemen, La. Militia
Mc Glawd, Mordicay	Private	2 Batt'n. (Peire's), La. Vols. (Orig. under McLawd, Mordicay)
Mc Gowen, Robert	Private	1 Reg't. (Dejan's), La. Militia
Mc Grew, John	Corporal	De Clouet's Reg't., La. Militia
Mc Grew, William	Private	De Clouet's Reg't., La. Militia
Mc Henry, John	Private	De Clouet's Reg't., La. Militia
Mc Hugh, John	Private	10 and 20 Cons. Reg't., La. Mil.
Mc Hugh, Thomas	Private	10 and 20 Cons. Reg't., La. Mil. (Orig. under Mc Cugh, Thomas)
Mc Ilvain, Andrew	Private	Captain Beale's Co., Riflemen, La. Militia
Mc Ilvain, John	Corporal	Captain Beale's Co., Riflemen, La. Militia
Mc Intire, Robert	Private	17, 18 and 19 Cons. Reg't., La. Militia
Mc Intire, Samuel	Private	16 Reg't. (Thompson's), La. Mil.
Mc Intire, Stephenson	Private	Captain Sprigg's Co., Boatmen, La. Vols.
Mc Intoch, Alexander	Private	De Clouet's Reg't., La. Militia (Orig. under McIntosh, Alexander)
Mc Intosh, Abner	Private	Baker's Regiment, La. Militia
Mc Intosh, Alexander	Private	De Clouet's Reg't., La. Militia
Mc Intyre, Hugh	Private	Capt. Ashley's Co., Mounted Riflemen, La. Militia
Mc Kean, Edward	Private	12 and 13 Cons. Reg't., La. Mil.
Mc Kee, John	Private	17, 18 and 19 Cons. Reg't., La. Militia
McKeine, Edward	Private	12 and 13 Cons. Reg't., La. Mil. (Orig. under McKean, Edward)
McKenny, Daniel	Private	De Clouet's Reg't., La. Militia (Orig. under Mc Kinney, Daniel)
Mc Kenny, Elijah	Corporal	17, 18 and 19 Cons. Reg't., La. Militia
Mc Ker, John	Private	17, 18 and 19 Cons. Reg't., La. Militia (Orig. under McKee, John)
Mc Key, I.	Private	1 Reg't. (Dejan's), La. Militia
Mc Kibben, David	Sergeant	1 Reg't. (Dejan's), La. Militia
Mc Kie, James	Private	12 and 13 Cons. Reg't., La. Mil.
Mc Kim, --	Private	4 Reg't. (Morgan's), La. Militia
Mc Kiney, Daniel	Private	De Clouet's Reg't., La. Militia (Orig. under McKinney, Daniel)
Mc Kinney, Daniel	Private	De Clouet's Reg't., La. Militia
McKleroy, Samuel	Private	Capt. Ashley's Co., Mounted Riflemen, La. Militia
Mc Klewee, Stephen	Private	10 and 20 Cons. Reg't., La. Mil.
Mc Klewer, Stephen	Private	10 and 20 Cons. Reg't., La. Mil. (Orig. under Mc Klewee, Stephen)
Mc Kneily, Henry	Private	10 and 20 Cons. Reg't., La. Mil. (Orig. under McNealey, Henry)

Name	Rank	Unit
Mc Knight, John	Ensign	Captain Price's Co., La. Militia
Mc Kune, William	Private	Captain Sprigg's Co., Boatmen, La. Vols.
Mc Lain, A. W.	Private	Baker's Regiment, La. Militia
Mc Laine, A. W.	Private	Baker's Regiment, La. Militia (Orig. under Mc Lain, A. W.)
Mc Laran, John	Private	Plauche's Batt'n., La. Militia
Mc Laran, William	Private	Plauche's Batt'n., La. Militia
Mc Laughlin, James	Private	Baker's Regiment, La. Militia
Mc Laughlin, James	Private	De Clouet's Reg't., La. Militia
Mc Laughlin, James	Private	Captain Hughes' Co., Mounted Riflemen, La. Militia
Mc Laughlin, John	Private	De Clouet's Reg't., La. Militia
Mc Laughlin, John	Private	Captain McNair's Co., Mounted Riflemen, La. Mil. (Orig. under McGlaughlin, John)
Mc Laughlin, Leonard	Private	De Clouet's Reg't., La. Militia
Mc Lauren, Daniel	Private	12 and 13 Cons. Reg't., La. Mil. (Orig. under McClausen, Daniel)
Mc Lawd, Mordicay	Private	2 Batt'n. (Peire's), La. Vols.
Mc Lelland, John	Private	16 Reg't. (Thompson's), La. Mil.
Mc Lelland, John	Private	De Clouet's Reg't., La. Militia (Orig. under McCullen, John)
Mc Lellen, Lewis	Private	De Clouet's Reg't., La. Militia (Orig. under McCullen, Lewis)
Mc Loskey, Phillip	2 Lieutenant	Capt. Allen's Co., Artillerists, La. Vols.
Mc Loyd, Mordecai	Private	De Clouet's Reg't., La. Militia (Orig. under McCloud, Mordecai)
Mc Loud, Mordicai	Private	2 Batt'n. (Peire's), La. Vols. (Orig. under McLawd, Mordicay)
Mc Lowd, Mordicai	Private	2 Batt'n. (Peire's), La. Vols. (Orig. under McLawd, Mordicay)
Mc Lure, David	Sergeant	10 and 20 Cons. Reg't., La. Mil. (Orig. under McClure, David)
Mc Mahan, James	Private	De Clouet's Reg't., La. Militia
Mc Mahan, John	Private	10 and 20 Cons. Reg't., La. Mil.
Mc Mahen, John	Private	10 and 20 Cons. Reg't., La. Mil. (Orig. under Mcmahan, John)
Mc Means, Alexander	Private	Captain Rankin's Co., Mounted Riflemen, La. Militia
Mc Mullen, James	Private	De Clouet's Reg't., La. Militia
Mc Murray, Richard	Private	10 and 20 Cons. Reg't., La. Mil.
Mc Murtry, Samuel	Private	Baker's Regiment, La. Militia
Mc Naim, M.	Private	Captain Sprigg's Co., Boatmen, La. Vols.
Mc Nair, Alexander	Captain	Captain McNair's Co., Mounted Riflemen, La. Militia
Mc Nair, John	Private	Captain McNair's Co., Mounted Riflemen, La. Militia
Mc Neal, James	Private	Captain Dodge's Co., Mounted Riflemen, La. Militia
Mc Neal, James	Private	Captain Henry's Co., Mounted Riflemen, La. Militia
Mc Nealey, Henry	Private	10 and 20 Cons. Reg't., La. Mil.
Mc Nealy, Henry	Private	10 and 20 Cons. Reg't., La. Mil. (Orig. under Mc Nealey, Henry)
Mc Neely, Thomas	Private	17, 18 and 19 Cons. Reg't., La. Militia
Mc Night, John	Ensign	Captain Price's Co., La. Militia (Orig. under Mc Knight, John)
Mc Nutt, Isaac	Private	17, 18 and 19 Cons. Reg't., La. Militia
Mc Pake, Mathew	Private	Capt. Ashley's Co., Mounted Riflemen, La. Militia
Mc Pherson, A.	Private	6 Reg't. (Landry's), La. Militia
Mc Realy, John	Private	10 Regiment, La. Militia
Mc Ullen, Micajah	Private	12 and 13 Cons. Reg't., La. Mil.
Mc William, Peter	3 Lieutenant	10 and 20 Cons. Reg't., La. Mil. (Orig. under Mc Williams, Peter)
Mc William, Robert	Purser	Captain Young's Co., Mounted Riflemen, La. Militia
Mc Williams, Duke	Private	10 and 20 Cons. Reg't., La. Mil.
Mc Williams, James	Private	10 and 20 Cons. Reg't., La. Mil.
Mc Williams, Peter	3 Lieutenant	10 and 20 Cons. Reg't., La. Mil.
Meaele, Jn	Private	2 Reg't. (Cavelier's), La. Militia (Orig. under Maele, Jh)
Meagles, Miles	Private	10 and 20 Cons. Reg't., La. Mil. (Orig. under Measles, Miles)
Meance, Ed.	Q.M.-Sergeant	2 Reg't. (Cavelier's), La. Militia
Means, John	Private	10 and 20 Cons. Reg't., La. Mil.
Means, Zachariah	Private	De Clouet's Reg't., La. Militia
Measles, Miles	Private	10 and 20 Cons. Reg't., La. Mil.
Mechee, David	Private	16 Reg't. (Thompson's), La. Mil.
Medard, --	Private	7 Reg't. (Le Beuf), La. Militia
Medecing, Jean Baptisse	Private	1 Batt'n. (Fortier's), La. Militia
Medecinque, Henry	Private	1 Batt'n. (Fortier's), La. Militia
Medecinque, Jh	Private	1 Batt'n. (Fortier's), La. Militia
Medicinque, Jn	Private	1 Batt'n. (Fortier's), La. Militia (Orig. under Medecinque, Jh)
Medina, Antonio	Private	3 Reg't. (de la Ronde's), La. Mil.
Medina, I.	Private	De Clouet's Reg't., La. Militia
Medina, Joseph	Private	Capt. Alpuente's Co., La. Mil.
Medina, Laurent	Private	3 Reg't. (de la Ronde's), La. Mil.
Medino, Antonio	Private	3 Reg't. (de la Ronde's), La. Mil. (Orig. under Medina, Antonio)
Medino, Laurent	Private	3 Reg't. (de la Ronde's), La. Mil.
Medle, J.	Private	8 Reg't. (Meriam's), La. Militia (Orig. under Midle, J.)
Medsingue, Jeane B.	Private	1 Batt'n. (Fortier's), La. Militia (Orig. under Medecing, Jean Baptisse)
Meens, Samuel	Private	Captain Musick's Co., Mounted Riflemen, La. Militia
Meinard, A.	Corporal	Captain Sprigg's Co., Boatmen, La. Vols. (Orig. under Meynard, A.)
Megus, Bernard	Private	Baker's Regiment, La. Militia
Megus, Salvator	Private	Baker's Regiment, La. Militia
Meilleiun, Simon	Private	2 Batt'n. (Peire's), La. Vols. (Orig. under Meillieur, Simon)
Meilleur, --	Private	Plauche's Batt'n., La. Militia
Meilleur, Louis	Private	1 Batt'n. (Fortier's), La. Militia
Meilleur, Simon	Private	2 Batt'n. (Peire's), La. Vols. (Orig. under Meillieur, Simon)
Meillieur, Simon	Private	2 Batt'n. (Peire's), La. Vols.
Mejorada, Jose	Private	2 Batt'n. (Peire's), La. Vols.
Mejorada, Joseph	Private	2 Batt'n. (Peire's), La. Vols. (Orig. under Mejorada, Jose)
Melancoe, Merrius	Sergeant	7 Reg't. (Le Beuf's), La. Militia (Orig. under Melancon, Merrius)
Melancon, Alexander	Private	De Clouet's Reg't., La. Militia
Melancon, Alexander	Sergeant	6 Reg't. (Landry's), La. Militia
Melancon, Allain	Private	8 Reg't. (Meriam's), La. Militia
Melancon, Amelien	Private	De Clouet's Reg't., La. Militia
Melancon, Baptiste	Private	De Clouet's Reg't., La. Militia
Melancon, Charles	Private	De Clouet's Reg't., La. Militia
Melancon, Charles	Private	16 Reg't. (Thompson's), La. Mil.
Melancon, David	Private	6 Reg't. (Landry's), La. Militia
Melancon, Eugene	Private	6 Reg't. (Landry's), La. Militia
Melancon, Henry	Private	6 Reg't. (Landry's), La. Militia
Melancon, Jean	Private	De Clouet's Reg't., La. Militia
Melancon, Jerome	Private	8 Reg't. (Meriam's), La. Militia
Melancon, Joseph	Private	De Clouet's Reg't., La. Militia
Melancon, Joseph	Sergeant	6 Reg't. (Landry's), La. Militia
Melancon, Joseph	Sergeant	6 Reg't. (Landry's), La. Militia
Melancon, Joseph	Corporal	6 Reg't. (Landry's), La. Militia
Melancon, Louis	Private	6 Reg't. (Landry's), La. Militia
Melancon, Marcelin	Private	De Clouet's Reg't., La. Militia
Melancon, Merrius	Sergeant	7 Reg't. (Le Beuf's), La. Militia
Melancon, Olivier	Private	6 Reg't. (Landry's), La. Militia
Melancon, Olivier	Private	6 Reg't. (Landry's), La. Militia
Melancon, P.	Private	6 Reg't. (Landry's), La. Militia
Melancon, Paul	Sergeant	6 Reg't. (Landry's), La. Militia
Melancon, Rosemond	Private	6 Reg't. (Landry's), La. Militia
Melancon, Simon	Corporal	6 Reg't. (Landry's), La. Militia
Melancon, Zenon	Private	8 Reg't. (Meriam's), La. Militia
Melanie, Sanon	Private	1 Batt'n. (Fortier's), La. Militia
Melanson, Edward	Private	8 Reg't. (Meriam's), La. Militia
Melanson, Thomas	Private	8 Reg't. (Meriam's), La. Militia
Melenson, Anaclette	Private	De Clouet's Reg't., La. Militia
Mellason, Joseph	Private	7 Reg't. (Le Beuf's), La. Militia
Mellenson, --	Private	De Clouet's Reg't., La. Militia (Orig. under Melenson, Anaclette)
Mello, Jh	Private	1 Batt'n. (Fortier's), La. Militia (Orig. under Melo, Jh)
Mello, Pierre	Corporal	1 Batt'n. (Fortier's), La. Militia (Orig. under Melo, Pierre)
Mellon, Thomas	Private	Plauche's Batt'n., La. Militia
Mellon, Thomas	Private	1 Reg't. (Dejan's), La. Militia (See also Capt. White's Co.)
Mellse, Pierre	Private	De Clouet's Reg't., La. Militia
Melltse, Pierre	Private	De Clouet's Reg't., La. Militia (Orig. under Mellse, Pierre)

Name	Rank	Unit
Melo, Antoine	Private	2 Reg't. (Cavelier's), La. Militia
Melo, Antonio	Private	2 Batt'n. (Peire's), La. Vols.
Melo, Jh	Private	1 Batt'n. (Fortier's), La. Militia
Melo, Pierre	Corporal	1 Batt'n. (Fortier's), La. Militia
Melon, Celestin	Private	1 Batt'n. (Fortier's), La. Militia (Orig. under Milon, Celestin)
Meloncon, Jean	Private	8 Reg't. (Meriam's), La. Militia (Orig. under Maloncon, Jean)
Melong, Joseph	Private	12 and 13 Cons. Reg't., La. Mil.
Melton, William K.	Private	12 and 13 Cons. Reg't., La. Mil.
Melvin, Coleman	Private	12 and 13 Cons. Reg't., La. Mil.
Menan, Louis	Private	Captain Lagan's Co., La. Vols. (Orig. under Mesnan, Louis)
Menard, --	Private	Plauche's Batt'n., La. Militia
Menard, Andre	Private	De Clouet's Reg't., La. Militia
Menard, Gabriel Louis	Corporal	2 Batt'n. (Peire's), La. Vols.
Menard, Louis	Private	Captain Price's Co., La. Militia
Menard, Lyon	Corporal	2 Batt'n. (D'Aquin's), La. Militia (Orig. under Mainard, Lyon)
Mendez, Jean Joseph	Private	Captain Lagan's Co., La. Vols.
Mendez, Mariano	Private	2 Batt'n. (Peire's), La. Vols. (Orig. under Mendoce, Mariano)
Mendicut, Antonio	Private	2 Batt'n. (Peire's), La. Vols.
Mendoce, Mariano	Private	2 Batt'n. (Peire's), La. Vols.
Mendos, Mariane	Private	2 Batt'n. (Peire's), La. Vols. (Orig. under Mendoce, Mariano)
Mendoz, Mariane	Private	2 Batt'n. (Peire's), La. Vols. (Orig. under Mendoce, Mariano)
Mendoza, Antoine	Private	Captain Hubbard's Mounted Co., La. Militia
Mendoza, Mariano	Private	2 Batt'n. (Peire's), La. Vols. (Orig. under Mendoce, Mariano)
Mennier, Peter	Private-Sergeant	2 Batt'n. (Peire's), La. Vols. (Orig. under Monnier, Pierre)
Merceau, Francois	2 Lieutenant	De Clouet's Reg't., La. Militia
Mercer, Lewis	Private	10 Regiment, La. Militia
Mercer, Rainey	Private	12 and 13 Cons. Reg't., La. Mil.
Mercie, Pierre	Private	1 Reg't. (Dejan's), La. Militia
Mercier, --	Private	Plauche's Batt'n., La. Militia
Mercier, H.	Private	Plauche's Batt'n., La. Militia
Meriam, Nathan	Colonel	8 Reg't. (Meriam's), La. Militia
Meriot, Jean	Corporal	Capt. Chaudurier's Co., Artificers, Art'y., La. Vols.
Merle, Bte	Private	Plauche's Batt'n., La. Militia
Merles, Baptiste	Corporal	Capt. Colsson's Co., Artillery, La. Vols.
Merlin, Theodore	Private	2 Batt'n. (Peire's), La. Vols.
Merriot, John	Corporal	Capt. Chaudurier's Co., Artificers, Art'y., La. Vols. (Orig. under Meriot, Jean)
Mertin, Theodore	Private	2 Batt'n. (Peire's), La. Vols. (Orig. under Merlin, Theodore)
Mervin, Thomas M.	Private	10 and 20 Cons. Reg't., La. Mil.
Mervyn, Thomas M.	Private	10 and 20 Cons. Reg't., La. Mil. (Orig. under Mervin, Thomas M.)
Mesingle, Celestin	Private	5 Reg't. (La Branche's), La. Mil.
Mesnan, Louis	Private	Captain Lagan's Co., La. Vols.
Messenque, I. Be.	Private	7 Reg't. (Le Beuf's), La. Militia
Messier, Theophilus	Private	16 Reg't. (Thompson's), La. Mil.
Metcalf, John	Private	17, 18 and 19 Cons. Reg't., La. Militia
Metcalfe, Samuel	Private	Captain Sprigg's Co., Boatmen, La. Vols. (Orig. under Mitchell, Samuel)
Metcalfe, Thomas	Private	Captain Sprigg's Co., Boatmen, La. Vols.
Metessine, Antoine	Private	6 Reg't. (Landry's), La. Militia
Metholin, Cotman	Private	12 and 13 Cons. Reg't., La. Mil. (Orig. under Melvin, Colman)
Metz, Elias	Private	Captain McNair's Co., Mounted Riflemen, La. Militia
Metz, Jacob	Corporal	Captain McNair's Co., Mounted Riflemen, La. Militia
Metz, William	Private	Captain McNair's Co., Mounted Riflemen, La. Militia
Metzer, A.	Private	1 Reg't. (Dejan's), La. Militia
Meunier, --	Private	Plauche's Batt'n., La. Militia
Meyer, Charles	Private	Plauche's Batt'n., La. Militia
Meyer, Joseph	Private	4 Reg't. (Morgan's), La. Militia
Meyer, William	Private	Baker's Regiment, La. Militia
Meynard, A.	Corporal	Captain Sprigg's Co., Boatmen, La. Vols.
Meyon, Cola	Private	5 Reg't. (La Branche's), La. Mil.
Meys, Benjamin	Sergeant	10 and 20 Cons. Reg't., La. Mil. (Orig. under Mays, Benjamin)
Miaisse, Simon	Private	7 Reg't. (Le Beuf's), La. Militia
Michael, Thomas	Private	17, 18 and 19 Cons. Reg't., La. Militia (Orig. under Michel, Thomas)
Michamps, Eugene	Private	17, 18 and 19 Cons. Reg't., La. Militia
Michau, --	Private	Plauche's Batt'n., La. Militia
Micheau, John A.	Private	Captain Price's Co., La. Militia
Michel, --	Servant	Gov. Claiborne and Staff, La. Mil.
Michel, --	Private	Plauche's Batt'n., La. Militia
Michel, --	Servant	1 Batt'n. (Fortier's), La. Militia
Michel, --	Private	2 Reg't. (Cavelier's), La. Militia
Michel, --	Private	5 Reg't. La Branche's), La. Mil.
Michel, Albin	Private	Capt. Trudeau's Troop of Horse, La. Militia
Michel, Cadet	Private	6 Reg't. (Landry's), La. Militia (Orig. under Michelle, Cadet)
Michel, Constant	Private	Plauche's Batt'n., La. Militia
Michel, Flourentin	Private	6 Reg't. (Landry's), La. Militia (Orig. under Michelle, Flarantin)
Michel, Francois	Private	6 Reg't. (Landry's), La. Militia (Orig. under Michelle, Francois)
Michel, Joseph	Corporal	6 Reg't. (Landry's), La. Militia (Orig. under Michelle, Joseph)
Michel, Pierre	Sergeant	6 Reg't. (Landry's), La. Militia (Orig. under Michelle, Pierre)
Michel, Similien	Private	1 Batt'n. (Fortier's), La. Militia
Michel, Thomas	Private	17, 18 and 19 Cons. Reg't., La. Militia
Michell, Fils	Sergeant	6 Reg't. (Landry's), La. Militia
Michelle, --	Private	2 Reg't. (Cavelier's), La. Militia (Orig. under Michel, --)
Michelle, Cadet	Private	6 Reg't. (Landry's), La. Militia
Michelle, Eugene	Private	6 Reg't. (Landry's), La. Militia
Michelle, Flarantin	Private	6 Reg't. (Landry's), La. Militia
Michelle, Francois	Private	6 Reg't. (Landry's), La. Militia
Michelle, Joseph	Corporal	6 Reg't. (Landry's), La. Militia
Michelle, Marcellin	Private	6 Reg't. (Landry's), La. Militia
Michelle, Pierre	Sergeant	6 Reg't. (Landry's), La. Militia
Michine, Pierre	Private	2 Batt'n. (D'Aquin's), La. Militia (Orig. under Micline, Pierre)
Michne, Jn	Private	2 Batt'n. (D'Aquin's), La. Militia (Orig. under Micline, Jn)
Miclehel, --	Private	Sgt. Hog's Detachment, La. Vols. (Orig. under Mitchell, --)
Micline, Jn	Private	2 Batt'n. (D'Aquin's), La. Militia
Micline, Pierre	Private	2 Batt'n. (D'Aquin's), La. Militia
Middle, J.	Private	8 Reg't. (Meriam's), La. Militia
Midie, --	Servant	2 Batt'n. (D'Aquin's), La. Militia
Middleton, Samuel	Private	10 Regiment, La. Militia
Mignot, --	Private	Captain Hubbard's Mounted Co., La. Militia
Miguat, Joseph	Private	6 Reg't. (Landry's), La. Militia
Mijorada, Jose	Private	2 Batt'n. (Peire's), La. Vols. (Orig. under Mejorada, Jose)
Milan, Felix	Private	3 Reg't. (de la Ronde's), La. Mil.
Milancon, Amelien	Private	De Clouet's Reg't., La. Militia (Orig. under Melancon, Amelien)
Milhomme, --	Private	2 Batt'n. (D'Aquin's), La. Militia
Milhommes, Joseph	Private	7 Reg't. (Le Beuf's), La. Militia
Milhorn, Francis	Private	De Clouet's Reg't., La. Militia
Milladon, --	Private	1 Reg't. (Dejan's), La. Militia
Millan, Fcs	Private	Capt. Colsson's Co., Artillery, La. Vols.
Millar, Baptiste	Private	De Clouet's Reg't., La. Militia
Millaudon, Ls	Private	Plauche's Batt'n., La. Militia
Millelle, Pierre	Artificer	Capt. Chaudurier's Co., Artificers, Art'y., La. Vols. (Orig. under Millet, Pierre)
Miller, Aaron	Private	12 and 13 Cons. Reg't., La. Mil.
Miller, Abner	Private	12 and 13 Cons. Reg't., La. Mil.
Miller, Abraham	1 Lieutenant	Capt. Allen's Co., Artillerists, La. Vols.
Miller, Charles	Private	16 Reg't. (Thompson's), La. Mil.
Miller, Fredrick	Private	12 and 13 Cons. Reg't., La. Mil.
Miller, George	Corporal	16 Reg't. (Thompson's), La. Mil.

Name	Rank	Unit
Miller, Henry	Private	16 Reg't. (Thompson's), La. Mil.
Miller, James	Corporal	10 and 20 Cons. Reg't., La. Mil.
Miller, Jean fils	Private	16 Reg't. (Thompson's), La. Mil.
Miller, John	Private	De Clouet's Reg't., La. Militia
Miller, John	Private	Captain McNair's Co., Mounted Riflemen, La. Militia
Miller, John B.	Private	De Clouet's Reg't., La. Militia
Miller, M.	Private	4 Reg't. (Morgan's), La. Militia
Millet, Pierre	Artificer	Capt. Chaudurier's Co., Artificers, Art'y., La. Vols. (Orig. under Millet, Pierre)
Miller, Robert	Private	17, 18 and 19 Cons. Reg't., La. Militia
Miller, Samuel	Private	17, 18 and 19 Cons. Reg't., La. Militia
Miller, Stephen	Sergeant-3 Lieut.	10 and 20 Cons. Reg't., La. Mil.
Miller, W.	Private	4 Reg't. (Morgan's), La. Militia
Miller, William	Private	10 and 20 Cons. Reg't., La. Mil.
Millet, Peter	Artificer	Capt. Chaudurier's Co., Artificers, Art'y., La. Vols. (Orig. under Millet, Pierre)
Millet, Pierre	Artificer	Capt. Chaudurier's Co., Artificers, Art'y., La. Vols.
Millette, Alexis	Private	6 Reg't. (Landry's), La. Militia
Millette, J Bte	Private	6 Reg't. (Landry's), La. Militia
Millette, Noel	Private	6 Reg't. (Landry's), La. Militia
Millette, Phirman	Private	6 Reg't. (Landry's), La. Militia
Millette, Pierre	Artificer	Capt. Chaudurier's Co., Artificers, Art'y., La. Vols. (Orig. under Millet, Pierre)
Millette, Silvin	Private	6 Reg't. (Landry's), La. Militia
Millican, Francis	Private	10 and 20 Cons. Reg't., La. Mil.
Millican, John	Private	10 and 20 Cons. Reg't., La. Mil.
Millidon, --	Private	1 Reg't. (Dejan's), La. Militia (Orig. under Milladon, --)
Millingeon, --	Servant	General and Staff (Morgan), La. Militia
Millioton, --	Corporal	Plauche's Batt'n., La. Militia (Orig. under Mioton, --)
Millite, Alexis	Private	6 Reg't. (Landry's), La. Militia (Orig. under Millitte, Alexis)
Millite, J. Bte	Private	6 Reg't. (Landry's), La. Militia (Orig. under Millette, J. Bte)
Millite, Silvin	Private	6 Reg't. (Landry's), La. Militia (Orig. under Millette, Silvin)
Millitte, Alexis	Private	6 Reg't. (Landry's), La. Militia
Millome, E.	Private	8 Reg't. (Meriam's), La. Militia
Millot, Peter	Artificer	Capt. Chaudurier's Co., Artificers, Art'y., La. Vols. (Orig. under Millet, Pierre)
Mills, Josiah	Private	Captain Musick's Co., La. Mil.
Mills, Scioto	Private	De Clouet's Reg't., La. Militia
Mills, William T.	Private	Capt. Wallace's Co., Boatmen, La. Vols.
Millum, Francis	Private	De Clouet's Reg't., La. Militia
Milne, A.	Private	1 Reg't. (Dejan's), La. Militia
Milo, Antonio	Private	2 Batt'n. (Peire's), La. Vols. (Orig. under Melo, Antonio)
Milon, Celestin	Private	1 Batt'n. (Fortier's), La. Militia
Miltenberger, --	Surgeon	1 Batt'n. (Fortier's), La. Militia
Milton, William	Private	Baker's Regiment, La. Militia
Milton, William K.	Private	12 and 13 Cons. Reg't., La. Mil. (Orig. under Melton, William K)
Minard, Gabriel Louis	Corporal	2 Batt'n. (Peire's), La. Vols. (Orig. under Menard, Gabriel Louis)
Minard, Gaspard	Private	16 Reg't. (Thompson's), La. Mil.
Mindez, Jean Jph	Private	Captain Lagan's Co., La. Vols. (Orig. under Mendez, Jean Joseph)
Miner, Henry	Private	Baker's Regiment, La. Militia (Orig. under Mixer, Henry)
Miniche, Louis	Private	Plauche's Batt'n., La. Militia
Miniches, Louis	Private	Plauche's Batt'n., La. Militia (Orig. under Miniche, Louis)
Minja, Silvin	Sergeant	2 Batt'n. (D'Aquin's), La. Militia (Orig. under Manija, Silvin)
Mink, John	Private	De Clouet's Reg't., La. Militia
Minnee, Manuel	Private	16 Reg't. (Thompson's), La. Mil.
Minor, Theophilus P.	Private-Sgt.	Capt. Allen's Co., Artillerists, La. Vols.
Minor, William	Private	10 and 20 Cons. Reg't., La. Mil.
Minville, Pierre	Private	2 Batt'n. (D'Aquin's), La. Militia
Miomicio, Joseph	Private	17, 18 and 19 Cons. Reg't., La. Militia
Mioton, --	Corporal	Plauche's Batt'n., La. Militia
Miracle, Simon	Private	16 Reg't. (Thompson's), La. Mil.
Mire, Benjamin	Private	De Clouet's Reg't., La. Militia
Mire, Benjamin	1 Lieutenant	6 Reg't. (Landry's), La. Militia (Orig. under Mirre, Benjamin)
Mire, J Bte	Private	6 Reg't. (Landry's), La. Militia
Mire, Joseph fils	Private	De Clouet's Reg't., La. Militia
Mire, Placide	Private	De Clouet's Reg't., La. Militia
Mires, Jacob	Private	17, 18 and 19 Cons. Reg't., La. Militia
Mirre, Benjamin	1 Lieutenant	6 Reg't. (Landry's), La. Militia
Mirre, Benjamin	Private	6 Reg't. (Landry's), La. Militia
Mirre, Joseph	Private	6 Reg't. (Landry's), La. Militia
Mirre, Paul	Private	6 Reg't. (Landry's), La. Militia
Mirre, Pierre	Private	6 Reg't. (Landry's), La. Militia
Mirs, Jacob	Private	17, 18 and 19 Cons. Reg't., La. Mil. (Orig. under Mires, Jacob)
Missonier, Elija	Private	De Clouet's Reg't., La. Militia
Mitchel, David	Private	12 and 13 Cons. Reg't., La. Mil.
Mitchel, Hezekiah	Private	12 and 13 Cons. Reg't., La. Mil.
Mitchell, --	Private	Sgt. Hog's Detachment, La. Vols.
Mitchell, George	Sergeant	12 and 13 Cons. Reg't., La. Mil.
Mitchell, John	Private	Captain Beale's Co., Riflemen, La. Militia
Mitchell, John	Private	12 and 13 Cons. Reg't., La. Mil.
Mitchell, Samuel	Private	Captain Sprigg's Co., Boatmen, La. Vols.
Mixer, Ebenezer	Private	Baker's Regiment, La. Militia
Mixer, Henry	Private	Baker's Regiment, La. Militia
Mock, Andrew	Private	10 and 20 Cons. Reg't., La. Mil.
Modeste, Baptiste	Private	De Clouet's Reg't., La. Militia
Moillac, J. Bte	Private	2 Batt'n. (Peire's), La. Vols. (Orig. under Maillac, Jean Baptiste)
Moine, A.	Private	8 Reg't. (Meriam's), La. Militia
Moise, Joseph	Private	7 Reg't. (Le Beuf's), La. Militia (Orig. under Maise, Joseph)
Moisson, Michel	Sergeant	Capt. Colsson's Co., Artillery, La. Vols.
Molaere, Anthony	Private	De Clouet's Reg't., La. Militia (Orig. under Morlere, Anthony)
Molah, Clos	Private	Capt. Allen's Co., Artillerists, La. Vols.
Molay, Nicolas	Private	Plauche's Batt'n., La. Militia
Molere, Celestin	Private	De Clouet's Reg't., La. Militia (Orig. under Molier, Celestin)
Molero, Antonio	Private	3 Reg't. (de la Ronde's), La. Mil.
Molero, Bertolo	Sergeant	3 Reg't. (de la Ronde's), La. Mil.
Molero, Manuel	Corporal	3 Reg't. (de la Ronde's), La. Mil.
Molier, Celestin	Private	De Clouet's Reg't., La. Militia
Moliere, Anthony	Private	De Clouet's Reg't., La. Militia (Orig. under Morlere, Anthony)
Moliere, Celestin	Private	De Clouet's Reg't., La. Militia (Orig. under Molier, Celestin)
Molinary, --	Sergeant	1 Reg't. (Dejan's), La. Militia
Molinos, Pierre	Private	Capt. Songy's Co., Marines, La. Vols.
Mollay, Nicolas	Private	Plauche's Batt'n., La. Militia (Orig. under Molay, Nicolas)
Molle, Andre	Private	Captain Lagan's Co., La. Vols.
Mollen, George W.	Private	De Clouet's Reg't., La. Militia (Orig. under Mullen, George W.)
Mollens, George W.	Private	De Clouet's Reg't., La. Militia (Orig. under Mullen, George W.)
Moller, I.	2 Lieutenant	8 Reg't. (Meriam's), La. Militia (Orig. under Mollere, Joseph)
Mollere, Bte	Private	6 Reg't. (Landry's), La. Militia
Mollere, Celestin	Private	De Clouet's Reg't., La. Militia (Orig. under Molier, Celestin)
Mollere, Cyprien	Private	6 Reg't. (Landry's), La. Militia
Mollere, Francois	Captain	7 Reg't. (Le Beuf's), La. Militia
Mollere, Guillaume	Private	7 Reg't. (Le Beuf's), La. Militia
Mollere, Joseph	Private	7 Reg't. (Le Beuf's), La. Militia (Orig. under Maise, Joseph
Mollere, Joseph	2 Lieutenant	8 Reg't. (Meriam's), La. Militia
Mollere, Louis	Corporal	6 Reg't. (Landry's), La. Militia
Monbec, Barthelemy	Private	Louisiana (War of 1812)
Monbec, Julien	Private	Louisiana (War of 1812)
Monbrun, Zenon	Private	2 Reg't. (Cavelier's), La. Militia

Name	Rank	Unit
Moncant, --	Private	1 Reg't. (Dejan's), La. Militia
Monchel, Antonio	Private	2 Batt'n. (Peire's), La. Vols. (Orig. under Mouchel, Antoine)
Mondesire, Philie	Private	2 Batt'n. (D'Aquin's), La. Militia
Monet, Jos. h	Private	4 Reg't. (Morgan's), La. Militia
Money, Joseph	Private	Capt. Colsson's Co., Artillery, La. Vols.
Monferand, Julien	Private	1 Batt'n. (Fortier's), La. Militia
Monferrand, Julien	Private	1 Batt'n. (Fortier's), La. Militia (Orig. under Monferand, Julien)
Monget, Joseph	Corporal	Capt. Thomas' Co., La. Militia
Monier, Peter	Private-Sergeant	2 Batt'n. (Peire's), La. Vols. (Orig. under Monnier, Pierre)
Monier, Pierre	Private-Sergeant	2 Batt'n. (Peire's), La. Vols. (Orig. under Monnier, Pierre)
Monnier, Jacques	Private	16 Reg't. (Thompson's), La. Mil.
Monnier, Peter	Private-Sergeant	2 Batt'n. (Peire's), La. Vols. (Orig. under Monnier, Pierre)
Monnier, Pierre	Private-Sergeant	2 Batt'n. (Peire's), La. Vols.
Monren, Malcom	Private	De Clouet's Reg't., La. Militia (Orig. under Monroe, Malcom)
Monroe, John	Private	11 Reg't. (Hickey's), La. Militia
Monroe, John	Private	12 and 13 Cons. Reg't., La. Mil.
Monroe, Malcom	Private	De Clouet's Reg't., La. Militia
Monrow, Malcom	Private	De Clouet's Reg't., La. Militia (Orig. under Monroe, Malcom)
Monroy, Jean	Private	3 Reg't. (de la Ronde's), La. Mil.
Monsan, Joseph	Private	4 Reg't. (Morgan's), La. Militia
Monsignac, Louis	Private	2 Batt'n. (D'Aquin's), La. Militia
Montamat, --	Private	Plauche's Batt'n., La. Militia
Montagnac, --	Private	4 Reg't. (Morgan's), La. Militia
Montanesse, --	Private	2 Reg't. (Cavelier's), La. Militia
Montant, Lis Frans	1 Lieutenant	3 Reg't. (de la Ronde's), La. Mil.
Montas, --	Private	1 Reg't. (Dejan's), La. Militia
Montau, Francis	Private	12 and 13 Cons. Reg't., La. Mil.
Monte, Joseph	Private	7 Reg't. (Le Beuf's), La. Militia
Montegut, Auguste	Private	2 Batt'n. (D'Aquin's), La. Militia
Montengleau, Fcs	Private	Capt. Colsson's Co., Artillery, La. Vols.
Montero, Angel	Private	Captain Lagan's Co., La. Vols.
Montesquieu, --	Sergeant	1 Reg't. (Dejan's), La. Militia
Montessine, A.	Private	6 Reg't. (Landry's), La. Militia (Orig. under Metessine, Antoine)
Montet, Jean	Private	De Clouet's Reg't., La. Militia
Monteuil, Desir	Private	2 Batt'n. (D'Aquin's), La. Militia
Monteulle, --	Private	2 Batt'n. (D'Aquin's), La. Militia
Montgomery, James	Private	Captain Hughes' Co., Mounted Riflemen, La. Militia
Montgomery, John	Private	12 and 13 Cons. Reg't., La. Mil.
Montgomery, Joseph	Private	12 and 13 Cons. Reg't., La. Mil.
Montgomery, Robert	Private	Captain Beale's Co., Riflemen, La. Militia
Montgomery, W. W.	Q. Master	4 Reg't. (Morgan's), La. Militia
Montjoy, John	Sergeant	Captain Griffith's Co., Mounted Riflemen, La. Vols.
Monto, Frances	Private	12 and 13 Cons. Reg't., La. Mil. (Orig. under Montau, Francis)
Monton, Justin	Corporal	Baker's Regiment, La. Militia
Montreuil, --	Private	3 Reg't. (de la Ronde's), La. Mil.
Montreuil, Lubin	Private	1 Batt'n. (Fortier's), La. Militia
Montro, Angel	Private	Captain Lagan's Co., La. Vols. (Orig. under Montero, Angel)
Monville, Philip	Sergeant	Capt. Wallace's Co., Boatmen, La. Vols. (Orig. under Manville, Phillip)
Monzoles, Juan Jose	Private	17, 18 and 19 Cons. Reg't., La. Militia
Moor, Abram	Corporal	16 Reg't. (Thompson's), La. Mil.
Moor, William	Private	12 and 13 Cons. Reg't., La. Mil. (Orig. under Moore, William)
Moore, David	Private	Baker's Regiment, La. Militia
Moore, Elisha	Sergeant	Capt. Callaway's Co., Cavalry, La. Militia
Moore, Elisha	Private	Capt. Collard's Co., La. Militia
Moore, John	1 Lieutenant	Baker's Regiment, La. Militia
Moore, John	Sergeant	1 Reg't. (Dejan's), La. Militia
Moore, John 2"	Private	16 Reg't. (Thompson's), La. Mil.
Moore, John (Saddler)	Private	16 Reg't. (Thompson's), La. Mil.
Moore, Joseph	Private	17, 18 and 19 Cons. Reg't., La. Militia
Moore, L.	Private	Plauche's Batt'n., La. Militia
Moore, Lawrence H.	Major	12 and 13 Cons. Reg't., La. Mil.
Moore, Lewis	Sergeant	De Clouet's Reg't., La. Militia
Moore, William	Private	Capt. Allen's Co., Artillerists, La. Vols.
Moore, William	Private	12 and 13 Cons. Reg't., La. Mil.
Moore, William	Captain	16 Reg't. (Thompson's), La. Mil.
Moorehouse, R. A.	Private	4 Reg't. (Morgan's), La. Militia
Mora, Felipe	Private	17, 18 and 19 Cons. Reg't., La. Militia
Morah, E.	Private	Captain Sprigg's Co., Boatmen, La. Vols.
Morah, M.	Private	Captain Sprigg's Co., Boatmen, La. Vols.
Morales, Jean	Private	3 Reg't. (de la Ronde's), La. Mil.
Morales, Lorenzo	Corporal	3 Reg't. (de la Ronde's), La. Mil.
Morales, Michel	Private	3 Reg't. (de la Ronde's), La. Mil.
Morales, Sebastien	Private	3 Reg't. (de la Ronde's), La. Mil.
Morales, Sebastin	Private	De Clouet's Reg't., La. Militia
Moralez, Michel	Private	3 Reg't. (de la Ronde's), La. Mil.
Moran, Antoine	Private	De Clouet's Reg't., La. Militia
Morand, Jr.	Private	8 Reg't. (Meriam's), La. Militia
Morand, Pierre	Private	8 Reg't. (Meriam's), La. Militia
Morante, Joseph	Private	2 Reg't. (Cavelier's), La. Militia
Morants, --	Private	2 Reg't. (Cavelier's), La. Militia (Orig. under Morante, Joseph)
Moranty, John	Private	17, 18 and 19 Cons. Reg't., La. Militia
Morau, Moise Francois	Private-Sgt.	2 Batt'n. (Peire's), La. Vols. (Orig. under Moreau, Moise Francois)
Mordock, Alexander	Private	Capt. Collard's Co., La. Militia
More, Abraham	Corporal	16 Reg't. (Thompson's), La. Mil. (Orig. under Moor, Abram)
More, Davis	Private	De Clouet's Reg't., La. Militia
More, John	Private	16 Reg't. (Thompson's), La. Mil. (Orig. under Moore, John (Saddler))
More, John 2"	Private	16 Reg't. (Thompson's), La. Mil. (Orig. under Moore, John 2")
Moreau, --	Private	2 Reg't. (Cavelier's), La. Militia
Moreau, Alexander	Furrier-Cpl.	De Clouet's Reg't., La. Militia
Moreau, Cement	Private	Capt. Songy's Co., Marines, La. Vols.
Moreau, Clement	Private	2 Batt'n. (Peire's), La. Vols.
Moreau, Francis M.	Private-Sgt.	2 Batt'n. (Peire's), La. Vols. (Orig. under Moreau, Moise Francois)
Moreau, George	Private	1 Batt'n. (Fortier's), La. Militia (Orig. under Moro, George)
Moreau, Louis	Private	2 Batt'n. (D'Aquin's), La. Militia
Moreau, Manuel	Private	1 Batt'n. (Fortier's), La. Militia (Orig. under Mauraux, Manuel)
Moreau, Moin F.	Private-Sergeant	2 Batt'n. (Peire's), La. Vols. (Orig. under Moreau, Moise Francois)
Moreau, Moise Francois	Pri.-Sgt.	2 Batt'n. (Peire's), La. Vols.
Moreaux, Clement	Private	2 Batt'n. (Peire's), La. Vols. (Orig. under Moreau, Clement)
Morein, Louis	Private	2 Batt'n. (D'Aquin's), La. Militia
Morel, --	Private	Plauche's Batt'n., La. Militia
Morel, P.	Corporal	Plauche's Batt'n., La. Militia
Morel, Peter	Private	2 Reg't. (Cavelier's), La. Militia
Morency, Honore'	Private	16 Reg't. (Thompson's), La. Mil.
Mores, Obedah	Private	2 Batt'n. (Peire's), La. Vols. (Orig. under Moss, Obedieth)
Moret, --	Private	Plauche's Batt'n., La. Militia
Morette, Junr.	Artificer	Capt. Chaudurier's Co., Artificers, Art'y., La. Vols. (Orig. under Jeune, Maurette)
Morfield, James	Private	Capt. Allen's Co., Artillerists, La. Vols. (Orig. under Maxfield, James)
Morgan, Abel	Private	Captain Griffith's Co., Mounted Riflemen, La. Vols.
Morgan, B.	Private	8 Reg't. (Meriam's), La. Militia
Morgan, David B.	Brig. General	General and Staff (Morgan), La. Militia
Morgan, George	Private	De Clouet's Reg't., La. Militia
Morgan, G. W.	Colonel	4 Reg't. (Morgan's), La. Militia
Morgan, James	Private	Capt. Allen's Co., Artillerists, La. Vols.
Morgan, Jesse	Private	Capt. Thomas' Co., La. Militia
Morgan, John	Private	4 Reg't. (Morgan's), La. Militia

Name	Rank	Unit
Morgan, Jonathan	Private	19 Regiment, La. Militia
Morgan, Joseph	Private	10 and 20 Cons. Reg't., La. Mil.
Morgan, Laban	Private	10 and 20 Cons. Reg't., La. Mil.
Morgan, Sol	Corporal	10 Regiment, La. Militia
Morgan, Solomon	Private	Baker's Regiment, La. Militia
Morgan, Thomas	1 Sergeant	Captain Ramsey's Co., Mounted Riflemen, La. Militia
Morgan, William	Private	10 and 20 Cons. Reg't., La. Mil.
Morgan, Zacharias	Private	Capt. Thomas' Co., La. Militia
Morguecho, Tomas	Private	17, 18 and 19 Cons. Reg't., La. Mil. (Orig. under Morquecho, Tomas)
Morian, --	Private	Plauche's Batt'n., La. Militia
Morill, Jeremiah	Private	17, 18 and 19 Cons. Reg't., La. Militia
Morime, Ed	Private	4 Reg't. (Morgan's), La. Militia (Orig. under Morine, E.)
Morin, Amant	Private	2 Batt'n. (D'Aquin's), La. Militia
Morin, Baptiste	Private	Captain Price's Co., La. Militia
Morin, F.	Private	16 Reg't. (Thompson's), La. Mil.
Morin, Francois	Private	3 Reg't. (de la Ronde's), La. Mil.
Morin, Francois	Private	16 Reg't. (Thompson's), La. Mil.
Morin, In Bte	Private	Capt. Songy's Co., Marines, La. Vols.
Morin, John B.	Private	17, 18 and 19 Cons. Reg't., La. Militia
Morin, Joseph	2 Lieutenant	2 Reg't. (Cavelier's), La. Militia
Morin, Michael	Private	Captain Price's Co., La. Militia
Morine, E.	Private	4 Reg't. (Morgan's), La. Militia
Morinval, Louis Deveux	Pri.-Cpl.	2 Batt'n. (Peire's), La. Vols.
Morleire, Anthony	Private	De Clouet's Reg't., La. Militia (Orig. under Morlere, Anthony)
Morlere, Anthony	Private	De Clouet's Reg't., La. Militia
Mornet, Jeanton	Private	2 Reg't. (Cavelier's), La. Militia
Moro, Francois	Corporal	3 Reg't. (de la Ronde's), La. Mil.
Moro, George	Private	1 Batt'n. (Fortier's), La. Militia
Morquecho, Tomas	Private	17, 18 and 19 Cons. Reg't., La. Militia
Morran, Joseph B.	Private	7 Reg't. (Le Beuf's), La. Militia
Morray, James	Private	Captain Hughes' Co., Mounted Riflemen, La. Militia
Morret, Jeanton	Private	2 Reg't. (Cavelier's), La. Militia (Orig. under Mornet, Jeanton)
Morrette, Junr	Artificer	Capt. Chaudurier's Co., Artificers, Art'y., La. Vols. (Orig. under Jeune, Maurette)
Morris, Curtis	Private	Captain Hughes' Co., Mounted Riflemen, La. Militia
Morris, James	Private	4 Reg't. (Morgan's), La. Militia
Morris, John	Private	3 Reg't. (de la Ronde's), La. Mil.
Morris, John	Private	10 and 20 Cons. Reg't., La. Mil.
Morris, Shadrach	Private	10 and 20 Cons. Reg't., La. Mil.
Morris, Vincent	Private	5 Reg't. (La Branche's), La. Mil.
Morris, White	Private	12 and 13 Cons. Reg't., La. Mil.
Morris, William	Private	12 and 13 Cons. Reg't., La. Mil.
Morris, William V.	Ensign	Captain Sprigg's Co., Boatmen, La. Vols.
Morrison, Amon	Private	Capt. Thomas' Co., La. Militia
Morrison, Forgus S.	Private	Captain Ramsey's Co., Mounted Riflemen, La. Militia
Morrison, Holmes	Private	Capt. Thomas' Co., La. Militia
Morrison, James	1 Lieutenant	Captain Ramsey's Co., Mounted Riflemen, La. Militia
Morrison, James	Sergeant-Private	4 Reg't. (Morgan's), La. Militia
Morrison, Louis	Private	Capt. Ashley's Co., Mounted Riflemen, La. Militia
Morrisan, Thomas	Private	Capt. Ashley's Co., Mounted Riflemen, La. Mil. (Orig. under Morrison, Thomas)
Morrison, Thomas	Private	Capt. Ashley's Co., Mounted Riflemen, La. Militia
Morrison, W.	Private	4 Reg't. (Morgan's), La. Militia
Morrison, William	Private	De Clouet's Reg't., La. Militia
Morrord, George	Private	Captain Dodge's Co., Mounted Riflemen, La. Militia
Morrow, John	Private	12 and 13 Cons. Reg't., La. Mil.
Morse, Nathan	Private	Captain Ogden's Co., Dragoons, La. Militia
Morse, Obediah	Private	2 Batt'n. (Peire's), La. Vols. (Orig. under Moss, Obediah)
Mortin, Levi	Sergeant	17, 18 and 19 Cons. Reg't., La. Mil. (Orig. under Martin, Levi)
Morton, John	Sergeant-Private	De Clouet's Reg't., La. Militia
Morvan, Joseph B.	Private	7 Reg't. (Le Beuf's), La. Militia (Orig. under Morran, Joseph B.)
Mory, Gabrielle Jean	Private	1 Batt'n. (Fortier's), La. Militia
Moseley, John	Private	De Clouet's Reg't., La. Militia (Orig. under Mosley, John)
Mosevit, C. M.	Private-Corporal	De Clouet's Reg't., La. Militia (Orig. under Moswit, C. M.)
Mosley, John	Private	De Clouet's Reg't., La. Militia
Moss, Elisha B.	Sergeant	Captain Griffith's Co., Mounted Riflemen, La. Vols.
Moss, Henry	Private	Baker's Regiment, La. Militia
Moss, Obedieth	Private	2 Batt'n. (Peire's), La. Vols.
Moss, William	Private	12 and 13 Cons. Reg't., La. Mil.
Mossevitt, C. M.	Private-Corporal	De Clouet's Reg't., La. Militia (Orig. under Moswit, C. M.)
Mosso, N.	Private	Plauche's Batt'n., La. Militia
Moswit, C. M.	Private-Corporal	De Clouet's Reg't., La. Militia
Mouchel, Antoine	Private	2 Batt'n. (Peire's), La. Vols.
Mouchet, Antoine	Private	2 Batt'n. (Peire's), La. Vols. (Orig. under Mouchel, Antoine)
Mouchet, Francis	3 Lieutenant	Captain Hubbard's Mounted Co., La. Militia
Moulin, --	Private	4 Reg't. (Morgan's), La. Militia
Moullard, Louis	Private	6 Reg't. (Landry's), La. Militia
Mount, William	Private	1 Reg't. (Dejan's), La. Militia
Mourouse, Phillip	Private	6 Reg't. (Landry's), La. Militia
Mousson, Michel	Private	Plauche's Batt'n., La. Militia
Mouton, --	Private	Plauche's Batt'n., La. Militia
Mouton, Charles	Sergeant	De Clouet's Reg't., La. Militia
Mouton, Francois	Private	De Clouet's Reg't., La. Militia
Mouton, En	Sergeant	Capt. Songy's Co., Marines, La. Vols.
Mouton, Jean	Sergeant	Capt. Chaudurier's Co., Artificers, Art'y., La. Vols.
Mouton, John	Sergeant	Capt. Chaudurier's Co., Artificers, Art'y., La. Vols. (Orig. under Mouton, Jean)
Mouton, Sylvester	Private	De Clouet's Reg't., La. Militia
Mouton, Sylvester	Corporal	16 Reg't. (Thompson's), La. Mil.
Moxette, Junr.	Artificer	Capt. Chaudurier's Co., Artificers, Art'y., La. Vols. (Orig. under Jeune, Maurette)
Moyon, Jn Bte	2 Lieutenant	Capt. Colsson's Co., Artillery, La. Vols.
Mudd, Benjamin	2 Lieutenant	16 Reg't. (Thompson's), La. Mil.
Mudd, Benjamin S.	2 Lieutenant	16 Reg't. (Thompson's), La. Mil. (Orig. under Mudd, Benjamin)
Mugah, James	Private	Baker's Regiment, La. Militia (Orig. under Muggah, James)
Muggah, James	Private	Baker's Regiment, La. Militia
Muggah, John	Private	Plauche's Batt'n., La. Militia
Mulford, Samuel	Private	4 Reg't. (Morgan's), La. Militia
Mulholan, Henry	Private	10 and 20 Cons. Reg't., La. Mil.
Mulholan, John	Private	10 and 20 Cons. Reg't., La. Mil.
Mulkey, Philip	Private	10 and 20 Cons. Reg't., La. Mil.
Mulky, David	Private	Captain Griffith's Co., Mounted Riflemen, La. Vols.
Mulky, Joseph	Private	Captain Griffith's Co., Mounted Riflemen, La. Vols.
Mullen, George W.	Private	De Clouet's Reg't., La. Militia
Muller, Ferdinand	2 Lieutenant	16 Reg't. (Thompson's), La. Mil.
Mullin, George W.	Private	De Clouet's Reg't., La. Militia (Orig. under Mullen, George W.)
Munchel, Antoine	Private	2 Batt'n. (Peire's), La. Vols. (Orig. under Mouchel, Antoine)
Munier, John Fs	1 Sergeant-Sgt.	2 Reg't. (Cavelier's), La. Militia
Munos, Ignacio	Private	2 Batt'n. (Peire's), La. Vols. (See also 7 Reg't.)
Munroe, John	Private	12 and 13 Cons. Reg't., La. Mil. (Orig. under Monroe, John)
Munroe, Malcom	Private	De Clouet's Reg't., La. Militia (Orig. under Monroe, Malcom)
Munrow, Malcom	Private	De Clouet's Reg't., La. Militia (Orig. under Monroe, Malcom)
Muns, A.	Private	5 Reg't. (La Branche's), La. Mil.
Muns, Andre	Private	5 Reg't. (La Branche's), La. Mil.
Muns, Antoine	Private	5 Reg't. (La Branche's), La. Mil.
Muns, Christophe	Private	5 Reg't.)La Branche's), La. Mil.
Muran, Louis	Private	Captain Lagan's Co., La. Vols. (Orig. under Mesnan, Louis)

Name	Rank	Unit
Murdack, Alexander	Private	Capt. Collard's Co., La. Militia (Orig. under Mordock, Alexander)
Murphey, Daniel	Private	12 and 13 Cons. Reg't., La. Mil.
Murphey, Michael	Private	De Clouet's Reg't., La. Militia
Murphy, Daniel	Private	12 and 13 Cons. Reg't., La. Mil. (Orig. under Murphey, Daniel)
Murphy, John	Private	De Clouet's Reg't., La. Militia
Murphy, John	Private	16 Reg't. (Thompson's), La. Mil.
Murphy, Michael	Private	De Clouet's Reg't., La. Militia (Orig. under Murphey, Michael)
Murphy, Thomas	Private	16 Reg't. (Thompson's), La. Mil.
Murphy, William	Private	De Clouet's Reg't., La. Militia
Murray, N.	Private	4 Reg't. (Morgan's), La. Militia
Murray, Peter	Private	De Clouet's Reg't., La. Militia
Murray, William	1 Lieut. & Adjt.	17, 18 and 19 Cons. Reg't., La. Militia
Musick, Asa	Private	Captain McNair's Co., Mounted Riflemen, La. Militia
Musick, David	Captain	Captain Musick's Co., Mounted Riflemen, La. Militia
Musick, David	Captain	Captain Musick's Co., Mounted Riflemen, La. Militia
Musick, Eli	Private	Captain McNair's Co., Mounted Riflemen, La. Militia
Musick, Eli	Private	Captain Musick's Co., Mounted Riflemen, La. Militia
Musick, Ephraim	Private	Captain Musick's Co., Mounted Riflemen, La. Militia
Musick, James	Lieutenant	Captain Musick's Co., Mounted Riflemen, La. Militia
Musick, James	2 Lieutenant	Captain Musick's Co., La. Mil.
Musick, John	Private	Captain Musick's Co., La. Mil.
Musick, John	Private	Captain Musick's Co., La. Mil.
Musick, Lewis	Private	Captain McNair's Co., Mounted Riflemen, La. Militia
Musick, Robert	Private	Captain Musick's Co., Mounted Riflemen, La. Militia
Musick, Uel	Private	Captain Musick's Co., La. Mil.
Musick, Uel	Private	Captain Musick's Co., Mounted Riflemen, La. Militia
Musick, William	Private	Captain Musick's Co., Mounted Riflemen, La. Militia
Musino, Francisco	Private	2 Batt'n. (Peire's), La. Vols.
Musson, G.	Private	Plauche's Batt'n., La. Militia
Mustel, Pierre	Private	2 Batt'n. (Peire's), La. Vols.
Myer, A.	Private	16 Reg't. (Thompson's), La. Mil.
Myer, F.	Private	8 Reg't. (Meriam's), La. Militia
Myer, George	Private	16 Reg't. (Thompson's), La. Mil.
Myer, Michel	Private	16 Reg't. (Thompson's), La. Mil.
Myer, William	Private	Baker's Regiment, La. Militia (Orig. under Meyer, William)
Myers, Charles	Private	De Clouet's Reg't., La. Militia
Myers, David	Private	Captain Griffith's Co., Mounted Riflemen, La. Vols.
Myers, George	Private	Capt. Alpuente's Co., La. Mil.
Myrvin, Thomas M.	Private	10 and 20 Cons. Reg't., La. Mil. (Orig. under Mervin, Thomas M.)
Nachez, Pascal	Private	2 Batt'n. (Peire's), La. Vols.
Naclett, --	Private	8 Reg't. (Meriam's), La. Militia
Nadal, Michel	Private	Capt. Chauveau's Co., Cavalry, La. Militia
Nadaud, --	Corporal	Plauche's Batt'n., La. Militia
Nagall, Samuel	Private	Capt. Wallace's Co., Boatmen, La. Vols. (Orig. under Noggle, Samuel)
Nagel, --	Corporal	2 Reg't. (Cavelier's), La. Militia
Nallace, Thomas	Private	10 and 20 Cons. Reg't., La. Mil. (Orig. under Wallace, Thomas)
Nanette, Pierre	Private	De Clouet's Reg't., La. Militia
Napper, Jacob	Private	Baker's Regiment, La. Militia
Narciss, --	Servant	16 Reg't. (Thompson's), La. Mil.
Narcisse, --	Servant	De Clouet's Reg't., La. Militia
Narcisse, --	Private	8 Reg't. (Meriam's), La. Militia
Narcisse, Jacques	Private	2 Batt'n. (Peire's), La. Vols.
Narcisse, Pierre	Private	1 Batt'n. (Fortier's), La. Militia
Narsise, Pierre	Private	1 Batt'n. (Fortier's), La. Militia (Orig. under Narcisse, Pierre)
Naswonger, Joseph	Private	Captain Young's Co., Mounted Riflemen, La. Mil. (Orig. under Neiswonger, Joseph)
Natchez, Pascal	Private	2 Batt'n. (Peire's), La. Vols. (Orig. under Nachez, Pascal)
Nathal, Michel	Private	Capt. Chauveau's Co., Cavalry, La. Mil. (Orig. under Nadal, Michel)
Navar, Baptiste	2 Lieutenant	Baker's Regiment, La. Militia
Navar, Victor	Private	2 Reg't. (Cavelier's), La. Militia (Orig. under Navare, Victor)
Navare, Victor	Private	2 Reg't. (Cavelier's), La. Militia
Navarre, Baptiste	2 Lieutenant	Baker's Regiment, La. Militia (Orig. under Navar, Baptiste)
Navarre, I.	Private	4 Reg't. (Morgan's), La. Militia
Navarre, Jean	Private	7 Reg't. (Le Beuf's), La. Militia
Navarre, Pierre	Private	De Clouet's Reg't., La. Militia
Navarro, Francisco	Private	Louisiana (War of 1812)
Navarro, Jacques	Private	Captain Hubbard's Mounted Co., La. Militia
Navarro, Jean	Private	7 Reg't. (Le Beuf's), La. Militia (Orig. under Navarre, Jean)
Naverre, Pierre	Private	De Clouet's Reg't., La. Militia (Orig. under Navarre, Pierre)
Nayao, Joseph	Private	2 Batt'n. (Peire's), La. Vols.
Nazat, Antoin	Private	De Clouet's Reg't., La. Militia
Neal, Mitchel	Private	17, 18 and 19 Cons. Reg't., La. Militia
Neal, Thomas	Private	17, 18 and 19 Cons. Reg't., La. Militia
Neasom, Thomas	Captain	10 and 20 Cons. Reg't., La. Mil.
Necallestonne, I.	Private	8 Reg't. (Meriam's), La. Militia
Ned, --	Servant	De Clouet's Reg't., La. Militia
Ned, --	Servant	10 and 20 Cons. Reg't., La. Mil.
Neda, Francis	Captain	1 Reg't. (Dejan's), La. Militia
Nedas, Francisco	Captain	1 Reg't. (Dejan's), La. Militia (Orig. under Neda, Francis)
Nedas, Joseph	Captain	1 Reg't. (Dejan's), La. Militia (Orig. under Neda, Francis)
Neilson, Martin	Private	8 Reg't. (Meriam's), La. Militia
Neiswonger, Joseph	Private	Captain Young's Co., Mounted Riflemen, La. Militia
Nelson, --	Servant	General and Staff (Morgan), La. Militia
Nelson, Alexander	Private	De Clouet's Reg't., La. Militia
Nelson, Andrew	Private	10 and 20 Cons. Reg't., La. Mil.
Nelson, James	Private	10 and 20 Cons. Reg't., La. Mil.
Nelson, Jesse	Sergeant	10 and 20 Cons. Reg't., La. Mil.
Nelson, William	Private	10 and 20 Cons. Reg't., La. Mil.
Nerhveure, --	Private	8 Reg't. (Meriam's), La. Militia (Ck. for Neshveure)
Nerac, --	Private	Plauche's Batt'n., La. Militia
Nerat, Auguste	Private	Capt. Dubuclet's Troop, Hussars, La. Vols. (Orig. under Nazet, Auguste)
Nerault, --	Private	8 Reg't. (Meriam's), La. Militia (Orig. under Nereault, Jean)
Nerault, Andre	Private	16 Reg't. (Thompson's), La. Mil.
Nerault, Francois	Private	8 Reg't. (Meriam's), La. Militia
Nereault, Jean	Private	8 Reg't. (Meriam's), La. Militia
Nerret, Jean	Private	2 Batt'n. (Peire's), La. Vols. (Orig. under Verret, Jean)
Nesom, Abraham	Private	10 and 20 Cons. Reg't., La. Mil.
Nesom, Thomas	Captain	10 and 20 Cons. Reg't., La. Mil. (Orig. under Neasom, Thomas)
Nettles, Archd	2 Lieutenant	11 Reg't. (Hickey's), La. Militia
Nettles, John	Private	12 and 13 Cons. Reg't., La. Mil.
Nettles, Josiah	Private	12 and 13 Cons. Reg't., La. Mil.
Nettles, Zachariah	Private	12 and 13 Cons. Reg't., La. Mil.
Netto, Fs	Private	2 Reg't. (Cavelier's), La. Militia
Neufbourg, Philippe	Fusilier-Private	5 Reg't. (La Branche's), La. Mil.
Neuveux, Magnon	Private	2 Reg't. (Cavelier's), La. Militia (Orig. under Neveu, Magnon)
Nevault, Andre	Private	16 Reg't. (Thompson's), La. Mil. (Orig. under Nerault, Andre)
Neveu, Magnon	Private	2 Reg't. (Cavelier's), La. Militia
Newcomer, Jacob	Private	17, 18 and 19 Cons. Reg't., La. Militia
Newell, George	Private	8 Reg't. (Meriam's), La. Militia
Newell, Mark	Private	8 Reg't. (Meriam's), La. Militia
Newell, William	Private	8 Reg't. (Meriam's), La. Militia
Newman, Dickson	Private	De Clouet's Reg't., La. Militia
Newman, George	Private	2 Batt'n. (Peire;s), La. Vols. (See also MARINE)
Newman, James	Private	Baker's Regiment, La. Militia

Name	Rank	Unit
Newsom, Henry B.	Private	Captain Dodge's Co., Mounted Riflemen, La. Militia
Newson, Moses	Private	12 and 13 Cons. Reg't., La. Mil.
Newsome, Moses	Private	12 and 13 Cons. Reg't., La. Mil. (Orig. under Newsom, Moses)
Newson, Henry B.	Private	Captain Dodge's Co., Mounted Riflemen, La. Mil. (Orig. under Newsom, Henry B.)
Newson, Henry B.	Private	Captain Henry's Co., Mounted Riflemen, La. Militia
Newson, Moses	Private	12 and 13 Cons. Reg't., La. Mil. (Orig. under Newsom, Moses)
Newton, Richard	Private	10 and 20 Cons. Reg't., La. Mil.
Nezat, --fils	Private	16 Reg't. (Thompson's), La. Mil.
Nezat, Alexandre	Private	16 Reg't. (Thompson's), La. Mil.
Nezat, Antoine	Private	16 Reg't. (Thompson's), La. Mil.
Nezat, Auguste	Private	Capt. Dubuclet's Troop, Hussars, La. Vols.
Nezatte, Antoine	Private	De Clouet's Reg't., La. Militia (Orig. under Nazat, Antoin)
Nezatte, Joseph	Private	De Clouet's Reg't., La. Militia (Orig. under Nezette, Joseph)
Nezette, Joseph	Private	De Clouet's Reg't., La. Militia
Nicals, Benjamin	Private	10 and 20 Cons. Reg't., La. Mil. (Orig. under Nicholls, Benjamin)
Nicals, John	Private	10 and 20 Cons. Reg't., La. Mil.
Nicals, T.	Private	10 and 20 Cons. Reg't., La. Mil. (Orig. under Nicals, John)
Nicaud, --	Private	Plauche's Batt'n., La. Militia
Nice, --	Private	Plauche's Batt'n., La. Militia
Nice, Michelle	Artificer	Capt. Chaudurier's Co., Artificers, Art'y., La. Vols.
Nichola, --	Private	Plauche's Batt'n., La. Militia (Orig. under Nicholas, Zeno)
Nicholah, --	Private	1 Reg't. (Dejan's), La. Militia (Orig. under Nicholas, --)
Nicholas, --	Private	1 Reg't. (Dejan's), La. Militia
Nicholas, Antoine	Corporal	2 Reg't. (Cavelier's), La. Militia
Nicholas, Bastien	Private	4 Reg't. (Morgan's), La. Militia
Nicholas, Cs	Private	1 Reg't. (Dejan's), La. Militia
Nicholas, John	Private	10 Regiment, La. Militia
Nicholas, Lewis	Private	Baker's Regiment, La. Militia
Nicholas, Zeno	Private	Plauche's Batt'n., La. Militia
Nichole, Louis	2 Lieutenant	6 Reg't. (Landry's), La. Militia
Nicholes, Isam	Private	De Clouet's Reg't., La. Militia (Orig. under Nichols, Isham)
Nicholls, Benjamin	Private	10 and 20 Cons. Reg't., La. Mil.
Nicholls, Thomas	Private	Plauche's Batt'n., La. Militia
Nichols, Isham	Private	De Clouet's Reg't., La. Militia
Nichols, John	Private	De Clouet's Reg't., La. Militia
Nicholson, John	1 Sergeant-Sgt.	Captain Ogden's Co., Dragoons, La. Militia
Nicholson, Joseph	Private	Captain Ogden's Co., Dragoons, La. Militia
Nicholson, Rufus	Private	Baker's Regiment, La. Militia
Nickloss, John	Private	De Clouet's Reg't., La. Militia (Orig. under Nichols, John)
Nicklous, John	Private	De Clouet's Reg't., La. Militia (Orig. under Nichols, John)
Nickols, John	Private	De Clouet's Reg't., La. Militia (Orig. under Nichols, John)
Nicola, --	Private	1 Reg't. (Dejan's), La. Militia
Nicolas, Antne	Corporal	2 Reg't. (Cavelier's), La. Militia (Orig. under Nicholas, Antoine)
Nicolas, B.	Private	4 Reg't. (Morgan's), La. Militia (Orig. under Nicholas, Bastien)
Nicolas, Cs	Private	1 Reg't. (Dejan's), La. Militia (Orig. under Nicholas, Cs)
Nicolas, I.	Private	2 Reg't. (Cavelier's), La. Militia
Nicolas, Louis	Private	Baker's Regiment, La. Militia (Orig. under Nicholas, Lewis)
Nicolls, William	Private	12 and 13 Cons. Reg't., La. Mil.
Nicols, Ruben	Private	4 Reg't. (Morgan's), La. Militia
Nicols, William	Private	12 and 13 Cons. Reg't., La. Mil. (Orig. under Nicolls, William)
Nieball, James	Private	Capt. Callaway's Co., Mounted Riflemen, La. Militia
Nieres, Antonio	Private	3 Reg't. (de la Ronde's), La. Mil. (Orig. under Nieves, Antonio)
Nieres, Sebastien	Private	3 Reg't. (de la Ronde's), La. Mil.
Nieves, Antonio	Private	3 Reg't. (de la Ronde's), La. Mil. (Orig. under Nieves, Sebastien)
Nieves, Sebastien	Private	3 Reg't. (de la Ronde's), La. Mil.
Nimmo, Mathew	Sergeant-Private	De Clouet's Reg't., La. Militia
Ninville, Pierre	Private	2 Batt'n. (D'Aquin's), La. Mil. (Orig. under Minville, Pierre)
Nisbitt, Robert	Sergeant	Plauche's Batt'n., La. Militia
Nivet, Jacques	Private	3 Reg't. (de la Ronde's), La. Mil.
Nivette, Andre'	Private	3 Reg't. (de la Ronde's), La. Mil.
Nivette, Jean	Private	3 Reg't. (de la Ronde's), La. Mil.
Nivette, Zenon	Private	3 Reg't. (de la Ronde's), La. Mil.
Nix, William	Private	10 and 20 Cons. Reg't., La. Mil.
Nixon, John	1 Lieut. & Adjt.	1 Reg't. (Dejan's), La. Militia
Nixon, John	Private	1 Reg't. (Dejan's), La. Militia
Nixon, Judiah D.	Sergeant	De Clouet's Reg't., La. Militia
Nizate, Joseph	Private	De Clouet's Reg't., La. Militia (Orig. under Nezette, Joseph)
Noble, William	Private	Captain Sprigg's Co., Boatmen, La. Vols.
Noble, William	Private	10 and 20 Cons. Reg't., La. Mil. (Orig. under Nobles, William)
Nobles, William	Private	10 and 20 Cons. Reg't., La. Mil.
Noblett, John	Private	12 and 13 Cons. Reg't., La. Mil.
Noel, --	Waiter	1 Division (Villere's), La. Mil.
Noel, --	Domestic	4 Reg't. (Morgan's), La. Militia
Noel, --	Servant	17, 18 and 19 Cons. Reg't., La. Militia
Noeve, Dominique	Private	Plauche's Batt'n., La. Militia
Nogaies, Antoine Charpentier	Corporal	2 Batt'n. (Peire's), La. Vols. (See also 44 Regiment)
Nogais, Antoine Charps	Corporal	2 Batt'n. (Peire's), La. Vols. (Orig. under Nogaies, Antoine Charpentier)
Noggle, Samuel	Private	Capt. Wallace's Co., Boatmen, La. Vols.
Nogle, Samuel	Private	Capt. Wallace's Co., Boatmen, (Orig. under Noggle, Samuel)
Nogrit, John	Private	Capt. Chauveau's Co., Cavalry, La. Militia
Noirit, --	Private	1 Reg't. (Dejan's), La. Militia
Noiry, --	Private	1 Reg't. (Dejan's), La. Militia (Orig. under Noirit, --)
Nolan, Perry	Private	12 and 13 Cons. Reg't., La. Mil. (Orig. under Noland, Perry)
Noland, Perry	Private	12 and 13 Cons. Reg't., La. Mil.
Nold, Pierre	Fusilier-Private	5 Reg't. (La Branche's), La. Mil. (Orig. under Nolt, Pierre)
Nolen, James	Private	10 and 20 Cons. Reg't., La. Mil.
Nolt, Pierre	Fusilier-Private	5 Reg't. (La Branche's), La. Mil.
Nolte', V.	Private	Plauche's Batt'n., La. Militia
Nopes, Prudencio	Private	17, 18 and 19 Cons. Reg't., La. Militia
Nopez, Prudencio	Private	17, 18 and 19 Cons. Reg't., La. Mil. (Orig. under Nopes, Prudencio)
Norman, Charles	Private	16 Reg't. (Thompson's), La. Mil.
Norman, Francois	Private	De Clouet's Reg't., La. Militia
Norman, Francois	Sergeant	16 Reg't. (Thompson's), La. Mil.
Normand, Pierre	Private	8 Reg't. (Meriam's), La. Militia
Normond, Charles	Private	16 Reg't. (Thompson's), La. Mil. (Orig. under Norman, Charles)
Norrel, William	Private	De Clouet's Reg't., La. Militia
Norris, D. W.	Private	4 Reg't. (Morgan's), La. Militia
Norris, John	Private	8 Reg't. (Meriam's), La. Militia
Norris, P.	Private	1 Reg't. (Dejan's), La. Militia
Norrord, George	Private	Captain Henry's Co., Mounted Riflemen, La. Militia
Norrowette, Jean	Private	Captain Alpuente's Co., La. Mil.
Norse, Charles	Sergeant	Captain Sprigg's Co., Boatmen, La. Vols.
North, --	Private	1 Reg't. (Dejan's), La. Militia
Norton, Harvey	Private	11 Reg't. (Hickey's), La. Militia
Norton, I.	Private	4 Reg't. (Morgan's), La. Militia
Norton, John	Private	De Clouet's Reg't., La. Militia
Nostrom, Charles	Private	1 Reg't. (Dejan's), La. Militia
Nott, William	Private	Captain Ogden's Co., Dragoons, La. Militia
Nouchet, Gustave	Fusilier-Corporal	5 Reg't. (La Branche's), La. Mil.
Nouchet, Octave	Private	5 Reg't. (La Branche's), La. Mil.
Nougesse, --	Private	4 Reg't. (Morgan's), La. Militia
Nouvelle, Charles	Fusilier-Private	5 Reg't. (La Branche's), La. Mil.
Nowland, Barney	Private	10 and 20 Cons. Reg't., La. Mil. (Orig. under Knowland, Barney)
Noye, Narcisse	Servant	1 Batt'n. (Fortier's), La. Militia

Name	Rank	Unit
Nueman, Dickson	Private	De Clouet's Reg't., La. Militia (Orig. under Newman, Dickson)
Nugent, Isaac	Private	17, 18 and 19 Cons. Reg't., La. Militia
Nugent, John	Corporal	17, 18 and 19 Cons. Reg't., La. Militia
Nuisse, --	Private	1 Reg't. (Dejan's), La. Militia (Orig. under Nuveisse, --)
Null, Jacob	Private	Capt. Van Bibber's Co., La. Mil.
Null, William	Private	Captain Rankins' Co., Mounted Riflemen, La. Militia
Nunez, Bazeil	Corporal	3 Reg't. (de la Ronde's), La. Mil.
Nunn, John	Private	Captain Dodge's Co., Mounted Riflemen, La. Militia
Nunn, John	Private	Captain Henry's Co., Mounted Riflemen, La. Militia
Nuton, Richard	Private	10 and 20 Cons. Reg't., La. Mil. (Orig. under Newton, Richard)
Nuveisse, --	Private	1 Reg't. (Dejan's), La. Militia
Oaf, Alexander	Private	Captain McNair's Co., Mounted Riflemen, La. Militia
Oberry, James	Private	17, 18 and 19 Cons. Reg't., La. Militia
Obgiote, Palissier	Private	2 Reg't. (Cavelier's), La. Militia (Orig. under Olgiate, Patissier)
Obrian, Denis	Private	Captain Beale's Co., Riflemen, La. Militia
OBrien, Dennis	Corporal	4 Reg't. (Morgan's), La. Militia
O'Brien, James	Fusilier-Private	5 Reg't. (La Branche's), La. Mil. (Orig. under O'Brien, Jean)
O'Brien, Jean	Fusilier-Private	5 Reg't. (La Branche's), La. Mil.
O'Bryan, William	Private	2 Batt'n. (Peire's), La. Vols.
Ocman, Antoine	Fusilier-Private	5 Reg't. (La Branche's), La. Mil.
Ocman, Antoine	Fusilier-Private	5 Reg't. (La Branche's), La. Mil.
Ocman, Augustin	Fusilier-Private	5 Reg't. (La Branche's), La. Mil.
Ocman, Dominique	Fusilier-Private	5 Reg't. (La Branche's), La. Mil.
Ocman, Louis	Fusilier-Private	5 Reg't. (La Branche's), La. Mil.
Odam, Moses	Captain	10 and 20 Cons. Reg't., La. Mil.
Odaniel, James	Private	17, 18 and 19 Cons. Reg't., La. Militia
ODare, Major	Private	De Clouet's Reg't., La. Militia
Odare, Uriah	Private	12 and 13 Cons. Reg't., La. Mil. (Orig. under Odear, Uriah)
Odear, Uriah	Private	12 and 13 Cons. Reg't., La. Mil.
Odem, Richard	Private	12 and 13 Cons. Reg't., La. Mil. (Orig. under Odom, Richard)
Odenogan, Michael	Private	De Clouet's Reg't., La. Militia (Orig. under ODonegan, Michael)
Odias, Antoine	Corporal	8 Reg't. (Meriam's), La. Militia
Odier, Major	Private	De Clouet's Reg't., La. Militia (Orig. under ODare, Major)
Odom, Moses	Captain	10 and 20 Cons. Reg't., La. Mil. (Orig. under Odam, Moses)
Odom, Richard	Private	12 and 13 Cons. Reg't., La. Mil.
O Donegan, Michael	Private	De Clouet's Reg't., La. Militia
O Donell, James	Private	17, 18 and 19 Cons. Reg't., La. Mil. (Orig. under Odaniel, James)
O Donogan, Michael	Private	De Clouet's Reg't., La. Militia (Orig. under ODonegan, Michael)
Oduhigg, --	Private	4 Reg't. (Morgan's), La. Militia
Odum, Moses	Captain	10 and 20 Cons. Reg't., La. Mil. (Orig. under Odam, Moses)
Odwing, --	Private	1 Reg't. (Dejan's), La. Militia
Oeso, Jn	Private	1 Reg't. (Dejan's), La. Militia
Ofallen, Benjamin	Corporal	Captain Price's Co., La. Militia
Offre, Julien	Private	Capt. Colsson's Co., Artillery, La. Vols.
Ogden, George	Private	Captain Beale's Co., Riflemen, La. Militia
Ogden, Peter V.	Captain	Captain Ogden's Co., Dragoons, La. Militia
Ogene, Joseph	Private	De Clouet's Reg't., La. Militia (Orig. under Ugene, Joseph)
Ogle, John	Private	Captain Musick's Co., La. Mil.
Ojeda, Andri	Private	3 Reg't. (de la Ronde's), La. Mil.
Olevares, Thomas	Corporal	17, 18 and 19 Cons. Reg't., La. Militia
Olgiate, Patissier	Private	2 Reg't. (Cavelier's), La. Militia
Olibara, Jos Maria	Private	17, 18 and 19 Cons. Reg't., La. Militia
Olibares, Thomas	Corporal	17, 18 and 19 Cons. Reg't., La. Militia
Olivare, Jose Maria	Private	17, 18 and 19 Cons. Reg't., La. Militia
Olivares, Thomas	Corporal	17, 18 and 19 Cons. Reg't., La. Mil. (Orig. under Olevares, Thomas)
Oliveir, Jean	Private	7 Reg't. (Le Beuf's), La. Militia (Orig. under Olivier, Jean)
Oliver, Thomas F.	3 Lieutenant	Captain Hubbard's Mounted Co., La. Militia
Olivert, Pierre	Private	1 Batt'n. (Fortier's), La. Militia
Olivice, Charles	Brig. Major	Detachment Field and Staff Officers, 4 Brigade, La. Militia
Olivier, Delphin	Private	3 Reg't. (de la Ronde's), La. Mil.
Olivier, Esope	Private	2 Batt'n. (D'Aquin's), La. Militia
Olivier, Jean	Private	7 Reg't. (Le Beuf's), La. Militia
Olivier, Jean Baptiste	1 Lieutenant	3 Reg't. (de la Ronde's), La. Mil.
Olivier, Pierre	Corporal	Baker's Regiment, La. Militia
Olivier, Zeno	Sergeant	Baker's Regiment, La. Militia
Oneal, Arthur I.	Private	De Clouet's Regiment, La. Mil.
Oneda, Joseph	Private	Capt. Alpurnte's Co., La. Mil.
O Neil, Francis	Private	17, 18 and 19 Cons. Reg't., La. Mil. (Orig. under Oniel, Francis)
Oneil, Francis	Private	17, 18 and 19 Cons. Reg't., La. Mil.
Oporto, Joseph	Private	Sergeant Hog's Detachment, La. Vols.
Optegue, Pierre	Private	2 Batt'n. (D'Aquin's), La. Militia
Oquay, Bte	Private	7 Reg't. (Le Beuf's), La. Militia
Oramas, Jose	Private	3 Reg't. (de la Ronde's), La. Mil.
Organ, --	Private	1 Reg't. (Dejan's), La. Militia
Orick, Nicholas	Private	16 Reg't. (Thompson's), La. Mil. (Orig. under Orrick, Nicholas)
Orie, Jean Louis	Private	6 Reg't. (Landry's), La. Militia
Orie, John L.	Private	6 Reg't. (Landry's), La. Mil. (Orig. under Orie, Jean Louis)
Origore, Jean	Private	Captain Lagan's Co., La. Vols.
Orillion, Joseph	Lieutenant	8 Reg't. (Meriam's), La. Militia
Orillion, Joseph fils	Private	8 Reg't. (Meriam's), La. Militia
Orillion, Nicholas	Private	8 Reg't. (Meriam's), La. Militia
Orilliory, Joseph fils	Private	8 Reg't. (Meriam's), La. Militia (Orig. under Orillion, Joseph fils)
Oris, J. Bte	Private	6 Reg't. (Landry's), La. Militia
Oris, J. Pre	Private	6 Reg't. (Landry's), La. Militia
Ortaga, Joseph	Private	16 Reg't. (Thompson's), La. Mil. (Orig. under Ortraque, Joseph)
Orrick, Nicholas	Private	16 Reg't. (Thompson's), La. Mil.
Ortega, Pepe'	Private	16 Reg't. (Thompson's), La. Mil.
Ortega, Philip	Private	16 Reg't. (Thompson's), La. Mil.
Ortegue, Vincento	Private	Captain Lagan's Co., La. Vols.
Ortigue, Vincento	Private	Captain Lagan's Co., La. Vols. (Orig. under Ortegue, Vincento)
Ortolan, Jean	Private	16 Reg't. (Thompson's), La. Mil.
Ortraque, Joseph	Private	16 Reg't. (Thompson's), La. Mil.
Orver, Michel	Private	2 Batt'n. (D'Aquin's), La. Militia (Orig. under Erver, Michelle)
Ory, Elie	Fusilier-Private	5 Reg't. (La Branche's), La. Mil.
Ory, Jean Louis	Fusilier-Private	5 Reg't. (La Branche's), La. Mil.
Ory, Joseph	Private	5 Reg't. (La Branche's), La. Mil.
Ory, Louis	Corporal	5 Reg't. (La Branche's), La. Mil.
Ory, Nicolas	Fusilier-Private	5 Reg't. (La Branche's), La. Mil.
Ory, Nicolas	Fusilier-Private	5 Reg't. (La Branche's), La. Mil.
Ory, Pierre	Sergeant	5 Reg't. (La Branche's), La. Mil.
Osborn, John B.	Corporal	12 and 13 Cons. Reg't., La. Mil.
Oscar, --	Servant	De Clouet's Reg't., La. Militia
Oselet, Maturin	Private	Captain Hubbard's Mounted Co., La. Militia
Ostin, --	Private	Plauche's Batt'n., La. Militia
Oswell, George	Private	De Clouet's Reg't., La. Militia (Orig. under Aswell, George)
Otar, Mathieu	Fusilier-Private	5 Reg't. (La Branche's), La. Mil.
Otes, Frances	Private	10 and 20 Cons. Reg't., La. Mil. (Orig. under Otis, Francis)
Otis, Francis	Private	10 and 20 Cons. Reg't., La. Mil.
Ott, Joel	Private	12 and 13 Cons. Reg't., La. Mil.
Ott, Samuel	Private	12 and 13 Cons. Reg't., La. Mil.
Otten, Thomas	Private	10 and 20 Cons. Reg't., La. Mil. (Orig. under Otter, Thomas)
Otter, Thomas	Private	10 and 20 Cons. Reg't., La. Mil.
Ottignon, --	Private	Plauche's Batt'n., La. Militia
Ouachine, Joseph	Private	De Clouet's Reg't., La. Militia
Oubre, Andre	Private	6 Reg't. (Landry's), La. Militia

Name	Rank	Unit
Oubre, Francois	Corporal	6 Reg't. (Landry's), La. Militia
Oubre, Pierre	Private	6 Reg't. (Landry's), La. Militia
Oubre, Pierre Jr.	Private	6 Reg't. (Landry's), La. Militia
Oubres, Francois	Corporal	6 Reg't. (Landry's), La. Militia (Orig. under Oubre, Francois)
Ourbane, Andre	Private	6 Reg't. (Landry's), La. Militia
Ours, A.	Private	6 Reg't. (Landry's), La. Militia
Ours, M.	Private	6 Reg't. (Landry's), La. Militia
Overalls, William	Sergeant	Capt. Van Bibber's Co., La. Mil.
Ovide, Jean	Private	Captain Lagan's Co., La. Vols.
Owen, Samuel	Private	16 Reg't. (Thompson's), La. Mil.
Owens, James pere	Private	Captain Hubbard's Mounted Co., La. Militia
Owens, James fils	Private	Captain Hubbard's Mounted Co., La. Militia
Owens, James	Private	17, 18 and 19 Cons. Reg't., La. Militia
Owens, Robert	Private	Captain Griffith's Co., Mounted Riflemen, La. Vols.
Oyer, Charles	Private	Baker's Regiment, La. Militia
Ozenne, Edmond	Private	De Clouet's Reg't., La. Militia
Ozenne, Ursin	Private	Capt. Dubuclet's Troop, Hassars, La. Vols.
Ozor, --	Private	De Clouet's Reg't., La. Militia
Pablo, Devince	Corporal	1 Batt'n. (Fortier's), La. Militia
Paboron, William	Private	Captain Young's Co., Mounted Riflemen, La. Mil. (Orig. under Paterson, William)
Pacaud, F. Charles	Artificer	Capt. Chaudurier's Co., Artificers, Art'y., La. Vols.
Pacaud, Francis	1 Lieutenant	1 Batt'n. (Fortier's), La. Militia
Packwood, Daniel W.	Private	4 Reg't. (Morgan's), La. Militia
Packwood, H.	Corporal	1 Reg't. (Dejan's), La. Militia (See also Uniform Batt'n.)
Packwood, Henry	Private	Plauche's Batt'n., La. Militia
Paco, Fd Charles	Artificer	Capt. Chaudurier's Co., Artificers, Art'y., La. Vols. (Orig. under Pacaud, F. Charles)
Paco, Maturin	Carpenter	Capt. Chaudurier's Co., Artificers, Art'y., La. Vols.
Pacquet, Robert	Private	De Clouet's Reg't., La. Militia (Orig. under Paquet, Batiste)
Pacquetet, --	Private	2 Reg't. (Cavelier's), La. Militia (Orig. under Pacquetit, --)
Pacquetit, --	Private	2 Reg't. (Cavelier's), La. Militia
Page, Valentine	Private	Plauche's Batt'n., La. Militia
Page, Wilson	Private	12 and 13 Cons. Reg't., La. Mil.
Pageot, --	Private	Plauche's Batt'n., La. Militia
Pailleau, Pierre	Private	8 Reg't. (Meriam's), La. Militia
Paillet, Francois	Private	16 Reg't. (Thompson's), La. Mil. (Orig. under Paillette, Francois)
Paillet, Francois fils	Private	16 Reg't. (Thompson's), La. Mil.
Paillette, Francois	Corporal-Pri.	16 Reg't. (Thompson's), La. Mil.
Paillette, Francois	Private	16 Reg't. (Thompson's), La. Mil.
Painter, Alexander	Private	12 and 13 Cons. Reg't., La. Mil.
Paisant, John P.	Private	4 Reg't. (Morgan's), La. Militia
Pale, William	Private	10 and 20 Cons. Reg't., La. Mil.
Palen, James	Private	Captain Price's Co., La. Militia
Palfrey, W. H.	Private	Plauche's Batt'n., La. Militia
Palibar, Cart	Private	17, 18 and 19 Cons. Reg't., La. Mil. (Orig. under Saldibar, Caetano)
Palier, Fran	Corporal-Private	16 Reg't. (Thompson's), La. Mil. (Orig. under Paillette, Francois)
Pallerin, Alexr	Private	Capt. Dubuclet's Troop, Hussars, La. Vols. (Orig. under Pellerin, Alexr)
Palmer, Archibald	Private	10 and 20 Cons. Reg't., La. Mil.
Palmer, Charles	Private	Capt. Van Bibber's Co., La. Mil.
Palmer, Thomas	Private	1 Reg't. (Dejan's), La. Militia
Palmes, Iean	Private	Capt. Songy's Co., Marines, La. Vols.
Pamar, Romain	Private	Captain Beale's Co., Riflemen, La. Militia
Pamphlen, Robert	Private	De Clouet's Reg't., La. Militia
Panche, Bisente	Private	2 Reg't. (Cavelier's), La. Militia
Panuel, Helie	Private	6 Reg't. (Landry's), La. Militia
Panquerne, Pierre	Private	6 Reg't. (Landry's), La. Militia
Panter, Alexander	Private	12 and 13 Cons. Reg't., La. Mil. (Orig. under Painter, Alexander)
Pape, --	Private	8 Reg't. (Meriam's), La. Militia
Papet, --	Private	Plauche's Batt'n., La. Militia
Papet, --	Private	1 Reg't. (Dejan's), La. Militia
Papidai, Desideria	Private	17, 18 and 19 Cons. Reg't., La. Mil. (Orig. under Passedo, Desederia)
Papotte, --	Musician	Plauche's Batt'n., La. Militia (Orig. under Popote, --)
Pappineau, Joseph	Private	17, 18 and 19 Cons. Reg't., La. Militia
Paquet, Batiste	Private	De Clouet's Reg't., La. Militia
Parent, Baptiste	Fusilier-Sergeant	5 Reg't. (La Branche's), La. Mil.
Parent, Charles	2 Lieutenant	Capt. Chauveau's Co., Cavalry, La. Militia
Parent, J. Ls	Private	8 Reg't. (Meriam's), La. Militia
Parent, Pierre	Sergeant	1 Batt'n. (Fortier's), La. Militia
Parent, Pierre	Private	8 Reg't. (Meriam's), La. Militia
Parento, Joseph	Private	16 Reg't. (Thompson's), La. Mil.
Parina, Petorina	Private	17, 18 and 19 Cons. Reg't., La. Militia
Paris, Joseph	Private	Capt. Thomas' Co., La. Militia
Paris, William R.	Q. M. Sergeant	12 and 13 Cons. Reg't., La. Mil.
Parish, Hezekiah	Private	De Clouet's Reg't., La. Militia
Parish, Nehemiah	Private	De Clouet's Reg't., La. Militia
Parisien, Hy.	Private	Plauche's Batt'n., La. Militia
Park, Jonas	Private	Captain McNair's Co., Mounted Riflemen, La. Militia
Park, William	Private	Captain Rankin's Co., Mounted Riflemen, La. Militia
Parker, --	Private	1 Reg't. (Dejan's), La. Militia
Parker, Daniel	Private	10 and 20 Cons. Reg't., La. Mil.
Parker, Elisha	Private	12 and 13 Cons. Reg't., La. Mil.
Parker, Henry R.	Private	Capt. Allen's Co., Artillerists, La. Vols.
Parker, Isaac	Private	12 and 13 Cons. Reg't., La. Mil.
Parker, Jesse	Private	12 and 13 Cons. Reg't., La. Mil.
Parker, John	Private	De Clouet's Reg't., La. Militia
Parker, Nicholas	Private	10 and 20 Cons. Reg't., La. Mil.
Parker, Owen	Sergeant	10 and 20 Cons. Reg't., La. Mil.
Parker, Watts	Private	Captain Sprigg's Co., Boatmen, La. Vols.
Parkins, Isaac	Private	Captain Ogden's Co., Dragoons, La. Militia
Parmer, Jerrad	Private	12 and 13 Cons. Reg't., La. Mil.
Parmerley, Oliver	Private	Captain Beale's Co., Riflemen, La. Mil. (Orig. under Parmerly, Oliver)
Parmerly, Oliver	Private	Captain Beale's Co., Riflemen, La. Militia
Paroto, Francois	Fusilier-Private	5 Reg't. (La Branche's), La. Mil.
Parre, J. Ls	Private	6 Reg't. (Landry's), La. Militia
Parris, Lemon H.	Sergeant	7 Reg't. (Le Beuf's), La. Militia
Parris, Vincente	Private	De Clouet's Reg't., La. Militia (Orig. under Perrez, Vincente)
Parrish, Hezekiah	Private	De Clouet's Reg't., La. Militia (Orig. under Parish, Hezekiah)
Parrish, Nehemiah	Private	De Clouet's Reg't., La. Militia (Orig. under Parish, Nehemiah)
Parrush, Nehemiah	Private	De Clouet's Reg't., La. Militia (Orig. under Parish, Nehemiah)
Part, Etienne	Private	6 Reg't. (Landry's), La. Militia
Part, Joseph	Private	6 Reg't. (Landry's), La. Militia
Part, Joseph	Private	6 Reg't. (Landry's), La. Militia
Part, Louis	Private	De Clouet's Reg't., La. Militia
Pascal, Frederic	Private	2 Batt'n. (D'Aquin's), La. Militia
Paspartout, Andre'	Private	Capt. Songy's Co., Marines, La. Vols.
Passage, Louis	Musician	Capt. Chauveau's Co., Cavalry, La. Militia
Passalls, Archibald	Private	Capt. Allen's Co., Artillerists, La. Vols. (Orig. under Passals, Archibald)
Passals, Archibald	Private	Capt. Allen's Co., Artillerists, La. Vols.
Passaron, William	Private	De Clouet's Reg't., La. Militia (Orig. under Passarow, William)
Passarow, William	Private	De Clouet's Reg't., La. Militia
Passedo, Desederia	Private	17, 18 and 19 Cons. Reg't.
Passels, Archibald	Private	Capt. Allen's Co., Artillerists, La. Vols. (Orig. under Passals, Archibald)
Passepartour, Andre	Private	Capt. Songy's Co., Marines, La. Vols. (Orig. under Paspartout, Andre')

Name	Rank	Unit
Passepartout, André	Private	Capt. Songy's Co., Marines, La. Vols. (Orig. under Paspartour, André)
Passeron, S.	Private	De Clouet's Reg't., La. Militia (Orig. under Passarow, William)
Passrow, William	Private	De Clouet's Reg't., La. Militia (Orig. under Passarow, William)
Passia, Jn	Private	Plauche's Batt'n., La. Militia
Pate, William	Private	10 and 20 Cons. Reg't., La. Mil. (Orig. under Pale, William)
Paterson, John	Private	Captain Young's Co., Mounted Riflemen, La. Militia
Paterson, William	Private	Captain Young's Co., Mounted Riflemen, La. Militia
Patin, Ant.	Private	Capt. La Doux's Co., Cavalry, La. Vols.
Patin, H.	Cornet	Capt. La Doux's Co., Cavalry, La. Vols.
Patin, Marcel	Captain	De Clouet's Reg't., La. Militia
Patin, V.	Private	8 Reg't. (Meriam's), La. Militia
Patterson, Anguish	Private	De Clouet's Reg't., La. Militia
Patterson, Charles	Private	Captain Beale's Co., Riflemen, La. Militia
Patterson, George	Corporal	12 and 13 Cons. Reg't., La. Mil.
Patterson, John	Private	Capt. Callaway's Co., Cavalry, La. Militia
Patterson, John	Private	Captain Musick's Co., La. Mil.
Patterson, John	Private	Captain Musick's Co., Mounted Riflemen, La. Militia
Patterson, Malcom	Private	17, 18 and 19 Cons. Reg't., La. Militia
Patterson, Sanders	Private	Captain Price's Co., La. Militia
Patterson, Thomas	Captain	17, 18 and 19 Cons. Reg't., La. Militia
Patterson, William	Private	Captain Young's Co., Mounted Riflemen, La. Mil. (Orig. under Paterson, William)
Patterson, William	Private	17, 18 and 19 Cons. Reg't., La. Militia
Pattison, Thomas	Captain	17, 18 and 19 Cons. Reg't., La. Mil. (Orig. under Patterson, Thomas)
Patton, Charles	Major	2 Reg't. (Cavelier's), La. Militia
Patton, Joseph	Private	17, 18 and 19 Cons. Reg't., La. Militia
Patty, John	Private	Baker's Regiment, La. Militia
Paturel, Antoine	Private	3 Reg't. (de la Ronde's), La. Mil.
Paul, --	Servant	De Clouet's Reg't., La. Militia
Paul, --	Servant	1 Batt'n. (Fortier's), La. Militia
Paul, --	Servant	2 Batt'n. (D'Aquin's), La. Militia
Paul, Charles	Private	1 Batt'n. (Fortier's), La. Militia (Orig. under Paule, Charles)
Paul, Fernand Jean	Private	Louisiana (War of 1812)
Paul, Henry	Musician	1 Batt'n. (Fortier's), La. Militia
Paul, Isaac	Private	De Clouet's Reg't., La. Militia
Paul, Jacob	Private	17, 18 and 19 Cons. Reg't., La. Militia
Paul, John	Private	Baker's Regiment, La. Militia
Paul, Joseph	Sergeant	1 Batt'n. (Fortier's), La. Militia (Orig. under Paule, Joseph)
Paule, Charles	Private	1 Batt'n. (Fortier's), La. Militia
Paule, Joseph	Sergeant	1 Batt'n. (Fortier's), La. Militia
Paulet, Simon	Sergeant	6 Reg't. (Landry's), La. Militia
Paulit, Simon	Sergeant	6 Reg't. (Landry's), La. Militia (Orig. under Paulet, Simon)
Paulle, David	Private	6 Reg't. (Landry's), La. Militia
Paupin, --	Private	2 Batt'n. (D'Aquin's), La. Militia
Paursine, William	Private	6 Reg't. (Landry's), La. Militia
Pavi, --	Private	5 Reg't. (Morgan's), La. Militia
Paxe, --	Private	6 Reg't. (Landry's), La. Militia
Paxe, --	Private	7 Reg't. (Le Beuf's), La. Militia
Paxton, S.	Private	Plauche's Batt'n., La. Militia
Pearce, H.	Private	4 Reg't. (Morgan's), La. Militia
Pearson, Harvey	Private	12 and 13 Cons. Reg't., La. Mil.
Pearson, John	Private	De Clouet's Reg't., La. Militia
Pearson, Obadiah	Musician-Private	12 and 13 Cons. Reg't., La. Mil.
Peate, Jacob	Private	12 and 13 Cons. Reg't., La. Mil. (Orig. under Pratt, Jacob)
Pecaud, Chs	Private	1 Reg't. (Dejan's), La. Militia
Pecho, Raphael	Private	17, 18 and 19 Cons. Reg't., La. Militia
Pechon, Jean Baptiste	Private	1 Batt'n. (Fortier's), La. Militia
Peconnet, Jh	Private	2 Batt'n. (D'Aquin's), La. Militia
Pedesclaux, E.	Private	Plauche's Batt'n., La. Militia (Orig. under Pedescleaux, E.)
Pedesclaux, Hugues	Private	2 Reg't. (Cavelier's), La. Militia
Pedesclaux, P.	Private	Plauche's Batt'n., La. Militia
Pedescleaux, E.	Private	Plauche's Batt'n., La. Militia
Pedescleaux, P.	Private	Plauche's Batt'n., La. Militia (Orig. under Pedesclaux, P.)
Pedraja, Joseph	Corporal	2 Batt'n. (Peire's), La. Vols.
Pedro, Joseph	Private	2 Reg't. (Cavelier's), La. Militia
Pedros, Jose	Private	2 Batt'n. (Peire's), La. Vols.
Peeho, Raphael	Private	17, 18 and 19 Cons. Reg't., La. Mil.(Orig. under Pecho, Raphael)
Peille, Michelle, fils	Artificier	Capt. Chaudurier's Co., Artificers, Art'y., La. Vols. (Orig. under Pille, Michelle, fils)
Peille, Michelle Pater	Private	Capt. Chaudurier's Co., Artificers, Art'y., La. Vols. (Orig. under Pielle, Michello, Sr.)
Peire, Henry D.	Captain-Major	2 Batt'n. (Peire's), La. Vols.
Peiwe, Henry	Private	Baker's Regiment, La. Militia
Pela, Antoine	Private	3 Reg't. (de la Ronde's), La. Mil.
Pelado, Antonio	Private	De Clouet's Reg't., La. Militia
Pele, Michel	Private	De Clouet's Reg't., La. Militia
Pelegrain, --	Sergeant	Plauche's Batt'n., La. Militia
Pelegrin, Jean Casshitte	Private	Captain Lagan's Co., La. Vols. (Orig. under Pelegun, Jean Caseste)
Pelegrin, Mariane	Private	2 Reg't. (Cavelier's), La. Militia
Pelegun, Jean Caseste	Private	Captain Lagan's Co., La. Vols.
Pelegun, Jn Bte	Private	Captain Lagan's Co., La. Vols. (Orig. under Pelegun, Jean Caseste)
Pelerin, Delmartin	Private	2 Reg't. (Cavelier's), La. Militia
Peleteau, Louis	Private	4 Reg't. (Morgan's), La. Militia (Orig. under Pelleteau, Louis)
Pelessier, --	Private	4 Reg't. (Morgan's), La. Militia
Pelle, Michelle fils	Artificer	Capt. Chaudurier's Co., Artificers, La. Vols. (Orig. under Pille, Michello fils)
Pellegrin, Jn	1 Sergeant	Capt. Colsson's Co., Artillery, La. Vols.
Pellerin, --	Private	Plauche's Batt'n., La. Militia
Pellerin, Alexre	Private	Capt. Dubuclet's Troop, Hussars, La. Vols.
Pellerin, Edmond	Private	Capt. Dubuclet's Troop, Hussars, La. Vols.
Pellerin, Eugene	Private	Capt. Dubuclet's Troop, Hussars, La. Vols.
Pellerin, Hubert	Private	Capt. Dubuclet's Troop, Hussars, La. Vols.
Pelleteau, Louis	Private	4 Reg't. (Morgan's), La. Militia
Pellibar, Pierre	Sergeant	7 Reg't. (Le Beuf's), La. Militia (Orig. under Pellitier, Pierre)
Pellitier, Pierre	Sergeant	7 Reg't. (Le Beuf's), La. Militia
Pelltier, Francois	Private	De Clouet's Reg't., La. Militia
Pelltier, Pierre	Private	De Clouet's Reg't., La. Militia
Pelrin, Frederick	Captain	Baker's Regiment, La. Militia
Peltier, Jean	Private	Captain Hubbard's Mounted Co., La. Militia
Peltier, Pierre	Private	Louisiana (War of 1812)
Peltier, Pierre	Private	Captain Hubbard's Mounted Co., La. Militia
Penabaker, Jacob	Private	17, 18 and 19 Cons. Reg't., La. Mil. (Orig. under Pennybaker, Jacob)
Pence, William	Private	De Clouet's Reg't., La. Militia
Pendleton, James	Sergeant	12 and 13 Cons. Reg't., La. Mil.
Penington, Absalom	Private	12 and 13 Cons. Reg't., La. Mil.
Penington, Jacob	Sergeant	Capt. Callaway's Co., Mounted Riflemen, La. Militia
Penkins, Thomas	Private	De Clouet's Reg't., La. Militia (Orig. under Jenkins, Thomas)
Pennale, Simon	Private	De Clouet's Reg't., La. Militia (Orig. under Pinnale, Simon)
Penne, Fortune'	Captain	De Clouet's Reg't., La. Militia
Pennington, Absalom	Private	12 and 13 Cons. Reg't., La. Mil. (Orig. under Penington, Absalom)
Penny, William	Private	Captain Ramsey's Co., Mounted Riflemen, La. Militia
Pennybaker, Jacob	Private	17, 18 and 19 Cons. Reg't., La. Militia

Name	Rank	Unit
Peno, N.	Private	Captain Sprigg's Co., Boatmen, La. Vols.
Pepes, --	Private	2 Reg't. (Cavelier's), La. Militia
Pequele, Jean	Private	6 Reg't. (Landry's), La. Militia
Pequete, Jean	Private	6 Reg't. (Landry's), La. Militia (Orig. under Pequele, Jean)
Peralta, --	Corporal	1 Reg't. (Dejan's), La. Militia
Perault, Michel	Private	16 Reg't. (Thompson's), La. Mil.
Peraux, --	Private	3 Reg't. (de la Ronde's), La. Mil.
Peraux, Firman	Private	1 Batt'n. (Fortier's), La. Militia
Perche, Andre'	Fusilier-Private	5 Reg't. (La Branche's), La. Mil. (Orig. under Percle, Andre')
Percle, Andre'	Fusilier-Private	5 Reg't. (La Branche's), La. Mil.
Percle, Balthazard	Fusilier-Private	5 Reg't. (La Branche's), La. Mil.
Percy, Junr	Brig. Major	General and Staff (Labatut), La. Militia
Percy, Pre	Private	4 Reg't. (Morgan's), La. Militia
Perdomo, Raphael	Private	2 Batt'n. (Peire's), La. Vols.
Peref, --	Sergeant	4 Reg't. (Morgan's), La. Militia
Peres, Antoine	Private	La. (War of 1812) (See also 2 Batt'n. (Peire's), La. Vols.
Peres, Antoine	Private	2 Batt'n. (Peire's), La. Vols. (Orig. under Perez, Antoine)
Peres, Antonia	Private	2 Batt'n. (Peire's), La. Vols. (Orig. under Perez, Antonio)
Peres, Bartholome	Private	2 Batt'n. (Peire's), La. Vols. (Orig. under Rerrez, Barthelemy)
Peres, Jean	Private	3 Reg't. (de la Ronde's), La. Mil. (Orig. under Perez, Jean)
Peres, John	Private	De Clouet's Reg't., La. Militia (Orig. under Peves, John)
Peres, Joseph	Private	2 Batt'n. (Peire's), La. Vols. (Orig. under Perez, Joseph)
Perette, --	Private	7 Reg't. (Le Beuf's), La. Militia (Orig. under Bernard, Jean B.)
Perey, Joseph	Private	2 Batt'n. (Peire's), La. Vols. (Orig. under Perez, Joseph)
Perez, Antoine	Private	2 Batt'n. (Peire's), La. Vols.
Perez, Antonio	Private	2 Batt'n. (Peire's), La. Vols.
Perez, Barthelemy	Private	2 Batt'n. (Peire's), La. Vols. (Orig. under Perrez, Barthelemy)
Perez, Bartholemi	Private	La. (War of 1812) (See also 2 Batt'n. (Peire's), La. Vols.
Perez, Francis	Private	3 Reg't. (de la Ronde's), La. Mil. (Orig. under Perez, Francisco)
Perez, Francisco	Private	3 Reg't. (de la Ronde's), La. Mil.
Perez, Jean	Private	3 Reg't. (de la Ronde's), La. Mil.
Perez, Joseph	Private	2 Batt'n. (Peire's), La. Vols.
Perez, Ramon	Private	2 Reg't. (Cavelier's), La. Militia
Pericoux, George	Private	De Clouet's Reg't., La. Militia (Orig. under Peyrieux, George)
Perier, Gideon	Private	3 Reg't. (de la Ronde's), La. Mil.
Perilion, Adm	Private	5 Reg't. (La Branche's), La. Mil.
Perillon, Benjamin	Fusilier-Private	5 Reg't. (La Branche's), La. Mil.
Perillon, Jacques	Fusilier-Private	5 Reg't. (La Branche's), La. Mil.
Perillon, Louis	Fusilier-Private	5 Reg't. (La Branche's), La. Mil.
Periuex, George	Private	De Clouet's Reg't., La. Militia (Orig. under Peyrieux, George)
Perkins, Daniel	Private	12 and 13 Cons. Reg't., La. Mil.
Perkins, John	Private	Capt. Allen's Co., Artillerists, La. Vols.
Pero, Zeno	Private	De Clouet's Reg't., La. Militia
Peroe, --	Servant	10 and 20 Cons. Reg't., La. Mil.
Perois, Josephe	Private	Plauche's Batt'n., La. Militia
Peronin, Bernard	Sergeant	11 Reg't. (Hickey's), La. Militia
Perrault, Firman	Private	1 Batt'n. (Fortier's), La. Militia (Orig. under Peraux, Firman)
Perrault, I. B.	Sergeant-Major	Plauche's Batt'n., La. Militia
Perrault, I. B.	Private	Plauche's Batt'n., La. Militia
Perreau, Francis	Private	17, 18 and 19 Cons. Reg't., La. Militia
Pereaux, J. M.	Private	17, 18 and 19 Cons. Reg't., La. Militia
Perrera, A.	Private	6 Reg't. (Landry's), La. Militia
Perrera, Antoine	Private	6 Reg't. (Landry's), La. Militia
Perrera, Gravier	Private	3 Reg't. (de la Ronde's), La. Mil.
Perrera, S.	Private	6 Reg't. (Landry's), La. Militia
Perres, Vincente	Private	De Clouet's Reg't., La. Militia (Orig. under Perrez, Vindente)
Perret, Charles	Major	5 Reg't. (La Branche's), La. Mil.
Perret, Charles, son	Lieutenant	5 Reg't. (La Branche's), La. Mil.
Perret, Evariste	Fusilier-Private	5 Reg't. (La Branche's), La. Mil.
Perret, Godefroy	Corporal	5 Reg't. (La Branche's), La. Mil.
Perret, In Bte	Fusilier-Private	5 Reg't. (La Branche's), La. Mil.
Perret, Joseph	Fusilier-Private	5 Reg't. (La Branche's), La. Mil.
Perret, Justin	Adjt. & 1 Lieut.	5 Reg't. (La Branche's), La. Mil. (Orig. under Perret, T.)
Perret, Norbert	Sergeant	5 Reg't. (La Branche's), La. Mil.
Perret, Pain	Fusilier-Private	5 Reg't. (La Branche's), La. Mil. (Orig. under Perret, Pin)
Perret, Pin	Fusilier-Private	5 Reg't. (La Branche's), La. Mil.
Perret, T.	Adjt. & 1 Lieut.	5 Reg't. (La Branche's), La. Mil.
Perrette, Alphonse	Private	6 Reg't. (Landry's), La. Militia
Perrette, Drozon	Private	6 Reg't. (Landry's), La. Militia
Perrette, Ursin	Sergeant	6 Reg't. (Landry's), La. Militia
Perrez, Barthelemy	Private	2 Batt'n. (Peire's), La. Vols. (See also case of Jose Marie Campos)
Perrez, Vincente	Private	De Clouet's Reg't., La. Militia
Perrier, Charles	Corporal	Plauche's Batt'n., La. Militia
Perrieux, George	Private	De Clouet's Reg't., La. Militia (Orig. under Peyrieux, George)
Perrilact, --	1 Lieutenant	1 Reg't. (Dejan's), La. Militia (Orig. under Perrillat, Fcas)
Perrilact, --	Sergeant	1 Reg't. (Dejan's), La. Militia (Orig. under Perrillat, Cadet)
Perrillat, Cadet	Sergeant	1 Reg't. (Dejan's), La. Militia
Perrillat, Fcas	1 Lieutenant	1 Reg't. (Dejan's), La. Militia
Perrilliat, Francis	Captain	2 Reg't. (Cavelier's), La. Militia
Perrin, S.	Private	8 Reg't. (Meriam's), La. Militia
Perrington, Stephen	Private	Capt. Wallace's Co., Boatmen, La. Vols.
Perry, (Negro)	Servant-Waiter	De Clouet's Reg't., La. Militia (Orig. under Derry, (Negro))
Perry, Hardy	Private	10 and 20 Cons. Reg't., La. Mil.
Perry, J.	Private	Capt. Chauveau's Co., Cavalry, La. Militia
Perry, John	Private	1 Reg't. (Dejan's), La. Militia
Perry, Joseph	Private	Capt. Colsson's Co., Artillery, La. Vols.
Perry, Lewis	Corporal	19 Regiment, La. Vols. (Orig. under Perry, Louis)
Perry, Louis	Corporal	19 Regiment, La. Vols.
Perry, Robert	1 Lieutenant	De Clouet's Reg't., La. Militia
Persan, Julian	Private	17, 18 and 19 Cons. Reg't., La. Militia
Perseaux, Francois	Private	17, 18 and 19 Cons. Reg't., La. Mil. (Orig. under Perreau, Francis)
Person, Iean	Private	Capt. Songy's Co., Marines, La. Vols.
Person, John	Private	De Clouet's Reg't., La. Militia (Orig. under Pearson, John)
Pertue, Jean Bte	Private	6 Reg't. (Landry's), La. Militia
Peruda, Isidro	Private	17, 18 and 19 Cons. Reg't., La. Militia
Pervis, Josephe	Private	Plauche's Batt'n., La. Militia (Orig. under Perois, Joseph)
Peryman, M. S.	2 Lieutenant	Baker's Regiment, La. Militia (Orig. under Peryman, Mountford I.)
Peryman, Mountford I.	2 Lieutenant	Baker's Regiment, La. Militia
Peryrieux, George	Private	De Clouet's Reg't., La. Militia (Orig. under Peyrieux, George)
Peryrueix, George	Private	De Clouet's Reg't., La. Militia (Orig. under Peyrieux, George)
Peshoff, Leven	Private	7 Reg't. (Le Beuf's), La. Militia
Pesperes, Frd	Private	17, 18 and 19 Cons. Reg't., La. Militia (Orig. under Sesperes, Flo)
Pesson, --	Corporal	Plauche's Batt'n., La. Militia
Petavin, Jean Bte	Private	De Clouet's Reg't., La. Militia
Petenne, --	Private	7 Reg't. (Le Beuf's), La. Militia
Peter, --	Servant	Plauche's Batt'n., La. Militia
Peter, --	Servant	Capt. Songy's Co., Marines, La. Vols.
Peter, --	Waiter	1 Division (Villere's), La. Mil.
Peter, --	Waiter	2 Reg't. (Cavelier's), La. Militia
Peter, --	Servant	3 Reg't. (de la Ronde's), La. Mil.
Peter, --	Servant	5 Reg't. (La Branche's), La. Mil.
Peter, Edward	Sergeant-Private	2 Batt'n. (Peire's), La. Vols. (See also 44 Inf.)

Name	Rank	Unit
Peters, Charles	Private	1 Reg't. (Dejan's), La. Militia
Peters, John	Servant	Capt. Colsson's Co., Artillery, La. Vols.
Peterson, Hans	Private	Capt. Allen's Co., Artillerists, La. Vols.
Peterson, John	Private	Capt. Allen's Co., Artillerists, La. Vols.
Peterson, Thomas	Private	Captain Sprigg's Co., Boatmen, La. Vols.
Peti, Ml	Private	De Clouet's Reg't., La. Militia (Orig. under Pele, Michael)
Petigon, Frs	Private	Baker's Regiment, La. Militia
Petit, --	Private	4 Reg't. (Morgan's), La. Militia
Petit, Jacob	Sergeant	Capt. Ashley's Co., Mounted Riflemen, La. Militia
Petit, John Baptiste	Private	2 Reg't. (Cavelier's), La. Militia
Petit, Louis	Corporal	2 Batt'n. (D'Aquin's), La. Militia
Petit, Maurice	Private	1 Batt'n. (Fortier's), La. Militia
Petre, Antoine	Corporal	2 Reg't. (Cavelier's), La. Militia
Petre, Charles	Private	16 Reg't. (Thompson's), La. Mil.
Petre, Francois fils	Private	16 Reg't. (Thompson's), La. Mil.
Petre, John	--	De Clouet's Reg't., La. Militia
Petre, Joseph	Corporal	16 Reg't. (Thompson's), La. Mil.
Petre, Joseph	Private	16 Reg't. (Thompson's), La. Mil.
Petre, Louis	Sergeant	16 Reg't. (Thompson's), La. Mil.
Petre, Pierre	Private	16 Reg't. (Thompson's), La. Mil.
Pettegrew, Thomas	Private	2 Batt'n. (Peire's), La. Vols.
Petterin, Edmond	Private	Capt. Dubuclet's Troop, Hussars, La. Vols. (Orig. under Pellerin, Edmond)
Petterin, Eugene	Private	Capt. Dubuclet's Troop, Hussars, La. Vols. (Orig. under Pellerin, Eugene)
Pettet, John	Private	De Clouet's Reg't., La. Militia (Orig. under Pettit, John)
Pettibone, Chancey	Sergeant-Major	De Clouet's Reg't., La. Militia
Pettigrew, Thomas	Private	Capt. Allen's Co., Artillerists, La. Vols.
Pettit, James	Private	Capt. Callaway's Co., Mounted Riflemen, La. Militia
Pettit, John	Private	De Clouet's Reg't., La. Militia
Peves, John	Private	De Clouet's Reg't., La. Militia
Pew, Peter	Corporal	Capt. Collard's Co., La. Militia
Peychaud, Anatole Jr.	2 Lieut.-Capt.	2 Batt'n. (Peire's), La. Vols.
Peychaud, P.M.A.	2 Lieut.-Capt.	2 Batt'n. (Peire's), La. Vols. (Orig. under Peychaud, Anatole, Jr.)
Peye, Antoine	Private	2 Reg't. (Cavelier's), La. Militia
Peye, Joseph	Private	2 Reg't. (Cavelier's), La. Militia
Peyre, Cadet	Corporal	2 Reg't. (Cavelier's), La. Militia
Peyrieux, George	Private	De Clouet's Reg't., La. Militia
Peyroux, Peter	Captain	2 Reg't. (Cavelier's), La. Militia
Pevroux, S.	Private	Plauche's Batt'n., La. Militia
Peytavin, --	Private	4 Reg't. (Morgan's), La. Militia
Peytavin, Auguste	2 Lieutenant	Captain Hubbard's Mounted Co., La. Mil. (Orig. under Peytivan, Auguste)
Peytivan, Auguste	2 Lieutenant	Captain Hubbard's Mounted Co., La. Militia
Phares, Reuben	Private	Capt. Thomas' Co., La. Militia
Phellen, William	Private	Captain Beale's Co., Riflemen, La. Militia
Phelps, John	Private	10 and 20 Cons. Reg't., La. Mil.
Phelps, Samuel	Private	10 and 20 Cons. Reg't., La. Mil.
Phelps, Timothy	Purser	Captain Hughes' Co., Mounted Riflemen, La. Militia
Philibert, Jean	Private	2 Batt'n. (D'Aquin's), La. Militia
Philip, James	Private	Captain Ramsey's Co., Mounted Riflemen, La. Militia
Philippe, --	Servant	2 Batt'n. (D'Aquin's), La. Militia
Philips, George	Private	10 and 20 Cons. Reg't., La. Mil. (Orig. under Phipps, George)
Philips, Philip	Private	Baker's Regiment, La. Militia
Philips, Thomas	Private	17, 18 and 19 Cons. Reg't., La. Militia
Philips, William E.	Private	10 and 20 Cons. Reg't., La. Mil. (Orig. under Phillips, William E)
Phillip, James	Private	Captain Ramsey's Co., Mounted Riflemen, La. Mil. (Orig. under Philip, James)
Phillips, Alexander	2 Lieutenant	1 Reg't. (Dejan's), La. Militia
Phillips, James	Private	Captain McNair's Co., Mounted Riflemen, La. Militia
Phillips, John	Sergeant	Plauche's Batt'n., La. Militia
Phillips, Simeon	Private	Capt. Wallace's Co., Boatmen, La. Vols.
Phillips, William	Private	12 and 13 Cons. Reg't., La. Mil.
Phillips, William E.	Private	10 and 20 Cons. Reg't., La. Mil.
Philpe, Phillipe	Private	Baker's Regiment, La. Militia (Orig. under Philips, Philip)
Philps, John	Private	10 and 20 Cons. Reg't., La. Mil. (Orig. under Phelps, John)
Philps, Samuel	Private	10 and 20 Cons. Reg't., La. Mil. (Orig. under Phelps, Samuel)
Phipps, George	Private	10 and 20 Cons. Reg't., La. Mil.
Picard, Christophe	Private	Captain Lagan's Co., La. Vols.
Picard, Eloi	Private	De Clouet's Reg't., La. Militia
Picard, Jean Louis	Private	De Clouet's Reg't., La. Militia
Picau, Flechir	Private	6 Reg't. (Landry's), La. Militia (Orig. under Picou, Flechir)
Picau, Jean Bte	Private	6 Reg't. (Landry's), La. Militia (Orig. under Picou, Jean Bte)
Picena, P.	Private	Plauche's Batt'n., La. Militia (Orig. under Pissena, P.)
Piche, Raphael	Private	17, 18 and 19 Cons. Reg't., La. Mil.
Pichon, Michel	Private	2 Batt'n. (Peire's), La. Vols.
Pickett, Charles	Private	17, 18 and 19 Cons. Reg't., La. Militia
Pickett, Micage	Private	17, 18 and 19 Cons. Reg't., La. Militia
Pickens, E.	Private	Captain Sprigg's Co., Boatmen, La. Vols.
Piconnet, Jh	Private	2 Batt'n. (D'Aquin's), La. Militia (Orig. under Peconnet, Jh)
Picou, Charles	Fusilier-Private	5 Reg't. (La Branche's), La. Mil.
Picou, Ethelder	Private	6 Reg't. (Landry's), La. Militia
Picou, Flechir	Private	6 Reg't. (Landry's), La. Militia
Picou, Jean Bte	Private	6 Reg't. (Landry's), La. Militia
Picou, Louis	Fusilier-Private	5 Reg't. (La Branche's), La. Mil.
Picou, Lufroi	Private	5 Reg't. (La Branche's), La. Mil.
Picou, Nicolas	Corporal	5 Reg't. (La Branche's), La. Mil.
Picou, Norbert	Private	5 Reg't. (La Branche's), La. Mil.
Picou, Urbin	Private	2 Reg't. (Cavelier's), La. Mil.
Picou, Zenon	1 Lieutenant	6 Reg't. (Landry's), La. Mil.
Picquery, --	Private	Plauche's Batt'n., La. Militia (Orig. under Piquery, --)
Pideo, Joseph	Private	1 Reg't. (Dejan's), La. Militia
Pidoux, V.	Sergeant	Plauche's Batt'n., La. Militia
Pielle, Michelle fils	Artificer	Capt. Chaudurier's Co., Artificers, Art'y., La. Vols. (Orig. under Pille, Michello)
Pielle, Michello, Sr.	Private	Capt. Chaudurier's Co., Artificers, Art'y., La. Vols.
Piequery, --	Private	Plauche's Batt'n., La. Militia (Orig. under Piquery, --)
Pierce, --	Private	Captain Beale's Co., Riflemen, La. Militia
Pierce, Daniel L.	Private	8 Reg't. (Meriam's), La. Militia
Pierce, James	Corporal	17, 18 and 19 Cons. Reg't., La. Militia
Pierce, Joshua	Private	17, 18 and 19 Cons. Reg't., La. Militia
Pierce, Nicolon	Private	6 Reg't. (Landry's), La. Militia (Orig. under Prion, Nicola)
Pierce, Urbin	Private	6 Reg't. (Landry's), La. Militia (Orig. under Prion, Urbin)
Pierce, William	Private	17, 18 and 19 Cons. Reg't., La. Militia
Pierce, Zenon	1 Lieutenant	6 Reg't. (Landry's), La. Militia (Orig. under Picou, Zenon)
Pierche, Rosamond	Private	6 Reg't. (Landry's), La. Militia
Piere, Henry D.	Captain-Major	2 Batt'n. (Peire's), La. Vols. (Orig. under Peire, Henry D.)
Pierer, Antoine	Private	2 Batt'n. (Peire's), La. Vols. (Orig. under Perez, Antoine)
Pieriche, Rosimond	Private	6 Reg't. (Landry's), La. Militia (Orig. under Pierche, Roosamond)
Pierille, Pierre	Private	Sergeant Hog's Detachment, La. Vols.
Piernas, Louis	Private	1 Batt'n. (Fortier's), La. Militia
Pierre, --	Servant	Baker's Regiment, La. Militia
Pierre, --	Servant	De Clouet's Regiment, La. Mil.
Pierre, --	Servant	Detachment Field and Staff Officers, 4 Brigade, La. Militia

Name	Rank	Unit
Pierre, --	Servant	1 Batt'n. (Fortier's), La. Militia
Pierre, --	Servant	1 Batt'n. (Fortier's), La. Militia
Pierre, --	Private	4 Reg't. (Morgan's), La. Militia
Pierre, Baptiste	Private	1 Batt'n. (Fortier's), La. Militia
Pierre, Charles	Private	1 Batt'n. (Fortier's), La. Militia
Pierre, Edward	Sergeant-Private	2 Batt'n. (Peire's), La. Vols. (Orig. under Peter, Edward)
Pierre, Francois	Private	1 Batt'n. (Fortier's), La. Militia
Pierre, Hubert In	Private	3 Reg't. (de la Ronde's), La. Mil.
Pierre, Jean	Private	2 Batt'n. (D'Aquin's), La. Militia
Pierre, Manuel Jean	Corporal	1 Batt'n. (Fortier's), La. Militia
Pierre, Norbert	Private	1 Batt'n. (Fortier's), La. Militia
Pierre, Paul	Private	1 Batt'n. (Fortier's), La. Militia
Pierre, Pierre Jean	Private	3 Reg't. (de la Ronde's), La. Mil.
Pierre, Richard	Private	Captain Hubbard's Mounted Co., La. Militia
Pierre, Sanon	Private	1 Batt'n. (Fortier's), La. Militia
Pierre, Silvin	Private	1 Batt'n. (Fortier's), La. Militia
Pierrelle, Pierre	Private	Sergeant Hog's Detachment, La. Vols. (Orig. under Pierille, Pierre)
Pierry, Antoine	Private	Capt. Alpuente's Co., La. Mil.
Pierson, John	Private	De Clouet's Reg't., La. Militia (Orig. under Pearson, John)
Pigneging, Aime	Sergeant	Capt. Chauveau's Co., Cavalry, La. Militia (Orig. under Pigneguy, Aimi)
Pigneguy, Aimi	Sergeant	Capt. Chauveau's Co., Cavalry, La. Militia
Piguery, --	Private	4 Reg't. (Morgan's), La. Militia
Pilado, Ant.	Private	De Clouet's Reg't., La. Militia (Orig. under Pelado, Antonio)
Pile, Michel	Private	De Clouet's Reg't., La. Militia (Orig. under Pele, Michael)
Pilie, L.	2 Lieutenant	Plauche's Batt'n., La. Militia
Pille, Michello fils	Artificer	Capt. Chaudurier's Co., Artificers, Art'y., La. Vols.
Pillet, Louis P.	Corporal	17, 18 and 19 Cons. Reg't., La. Militia
Pilletier, Louis	Private	Capt. Callaway's Co., Cavalry, La. Militia
Pillie, Ist.	Private	2 Reg't. (Cavelier's), La. Militia
Pin, Charles	Private	5 Reg't. (La Branche's), La. Mil.
Pinard, --	Corporal	2 Reg't. (Cavelier's), La. Militia
Pinder, Henry	Private	Capt. Allen's Co., Artillerists, La. Vols.
Pine, Peter	Private	Captain Musick's Co., Mounted Riflemen, La. Militia
Pineau, Jean	Private	2 Batt'n. (D'Aquin's), La. Militia
Pingly, John	Fusilier-Private	5 Reg't. (La Branche's), La. Mil.
Pinnale, Simon	Private	De Clouet's Reg't., La. Militia
Pinos, E.	Corporal	6 Reg't. (Landry's), La. Militia
Pinta, I. B.	Captain	2 Reg't. (Cavelier's), La. Militia
Piper, Charles	Private	17, 18 and 19 Cons. Reg't., La. Militia
Pipes, Abraham	Private	19 Regiment, La. Militia
Pipkin, Thomas B.	Sergeant-Major	6 Reg't. (Landry's), La. Militia (See also 8 Reg't.)
Pipkin, Thomas B.	Private	8 Reg't. (Meriam's), La. Militia
Piquery, --	Private	Plauche's Batt'n., La. Militia
Pisany, Andrew	Private	De Clouet's Reg't., La. Militia
Pissena, P.	Private	Plauche's Batt'n., La. Militia
Pissette, Morice	Private	2 Reg't. (Cavelier's), La. Militia
Pition, --	Waiter	2 Reg't. (Cavelier's), La. Militia
Pitre, Guillaume	Servant	Captain Hubbard's Mounted Co., La. Militia
Pitre, I Bte	Private	7 Reg't. (Le Beuf's), La. Militia
Pitre, Jn M.	Private	7 Reg't. (Le Beuf's), La. Militia
Pitt, Thomas	Private	Captain Sprigg's Co., Boatmen, La. Vols.
Pitter, --	Domestic	4 Reg't. (Morgan's), La. Militia
Pivoto, Michael	Private	Baker's Regiment, La. Militia
Pivots, Michael	Private	Baker's Regiment, La. Militia (Orig. under Pivota, Michael)
Placar, Charles	Private	16 Reg't. (Thompson's), La. Mil.
Place, Pierre	Private	2 Batt'n. (Peire's), La. Vols.
Placentia, Baltazar	Private	Captain Hubbard's Mounted Co., La. Militia
Plaisance, John	Private	Louisiana (War of 1812)
Planchard, --	Private	Capt. Trudeau's Troop of Horse, La. Militia
Planche, Alexander	Major	17, 18 and 19 Cons. Reg't., La. Militia
Planche, Urban	1 Lieut. & Adjt.	17, 18 and 19 Cons. Reg't., La. Militia
Planchi, A.	Sergeant	4 Reg't. (Morgan's), La. Militia
Plante', Hilaire	Private	Capt. Songy's Co., Marines, La. Vols.
Plantin, Gilles	Artificer	Capt. Chaudurier's Co., Artificers, Art'y., La. Vols.
Plate, Henry	Private	1 Reg't. (Dejan's), La. Militia
Platin, Giles	Artificer	Capt. Chaudurier's Co., Artificers, Art'y., La. Vols. (Orig. under Plantin, Giles)
Plauche, Baptiste	Private	Capt. Colsson's Co., Artillery, La. Vols.
Plauche', I. B.	Major	Plauche's Batt'n., La. Militia
Plauche, Placide	Corporal	Capt. Chaudurier's Co., Artificers, Art'y., La. Vols.
Plauche', Placide	Fusilier-Private	5 Reg't. (La Branche's), La. Mil.
Ple, Pierre	Private	Capt. Hubbard's Mounted Co., La. Militia
Plicque, E. L.	1 Lieutenant	De Clouet's Reg't., La. Militia
Plicque, G. M.	Captain	4 Reg't. (Morgan's), La. Militia
Plochet, Bte	Private	Plauche's Batt'n., La. Militia
Plouse, Francois	Private	3 Reg't. (de la Ronde's), La. Mil.
Plumley, Abraham	Private	Capt. Thomas' Co., La. Militia
Plunkett, James	Private	De Clouet's Reg't., La. Militia
Plunkett, James	Private	10 and 20 Cons. Reg't., La. Mil.
Poche, Allexis	Private	6 Reg't. (Landry's), La. Militia
Poche', Andre	Private	5 Reg't. (La Branche's), La. Mil.
Poche', Benjamin	Private	6 Reg't. (Landry's), La. Militia
Poche', Francois	Private	6 Reg't. (Landry's), La. Militia
Poche, Henry	Private	6 Reg't. (Landry's), La. Militia
Poche, Jacques	Sergeant	6 Reg't. (Landry's), La. Militia
Poche, Zeno	2 Lieutenant	De Clouet's Reg't., La. Militia
Pochet, Andre	Private	5 Reg't. (La Branche's), La. Mil.
Pocte', Joseph	Sergeant	Capt. Chaudurier's Co., Artificers, Art'y., La. Vols. (Orig. under Poete, Joseph)
Pocte, Nicholas	Private	4 Reg't. (Morgan's), La. Militia
Pocti, Joseph	Sergeant	Capt. Chaudurier's Co., Artificers, Art'y., La. Vols. (Orig. under Poete, Joseph)
Pocti, Nicholas	Private	4 Reg't. (Morgan's), La. Militia (Orig. under Pocte, Nicholas)
Poete' aine, --	Private	Plauche's Batt'n., La. Militia
Poete' je, --	Private	Plauche's Batt'n., La. Militia
Poete, Joseph	Sergeant	Capt. Chaudurier's Co., Artificers, Art'y., La. Vols.
Poiche, Alexis	Private	6 Reg't. (Landry's), La. Militia (Orig. under Poche, Allexis)
Poiche, Benjamin	Private	6 Reg't. (Landry's), La. Militia (Orig. under Poche, Benjamin)
Poiche', Francois	Private	6 Reg't. (Landry's), La. Militia (Orig. under Poche', Francois)
Poiche, Henry	Private	6 Reg't. (Landry's), La. Militia (Orig. under Poche, Henry)
Pointe, --	Private	4 Reg't. (Morgan's), La. Militia
Poirier, Frs	Private	17, 18 and 19 Cons. Reg't., La. Militia
Poirier, Julien	Private	De Clouet's Reg't., La. Militia
Poirreau, Joseph	Private	6 Reg't. (Landry's), La. Militia (Orig. under Poirrier, Joseph)
Poirrier, Joseph	Private	6 Reg't. (Landry's), La. Militia
Poisson, Onesime	Private	Capt. Alpuente's Co., La. Mil.
Poissonet, Jacqe	Corporal	5 Reg't. (La Branche's), La. Mil.
Poite, je	Private	Plauche's Batt'n., La. Militia
Poiyant, Baptist	Private	Captain Price's Co., La. Militia (Orig. under Poiyaul, Baptiste)
Poiyaul, Baptiste	Private	Captain Price's Co., La. Militia
Polaskee, John	Private	De Clouet's Reg't., La. Militia (Orig. under Polaski, John)
Polaski, John	Private	De Clouet's Reg't., La. Militia
Polaskie, John	Private	De Clouet's Reg't., La. Militia (Orig. under Polaski, John)
Polek, Isaac	Private	10 and 20 Cons. Reg't., La. Mil. (Orig. under Polk, Isaac)
Poleskie, John	Private	De Clouet's Reg't., La. Militia (Orig. under Polaski, John)
Polidore, --	Servant	Plauche's Batt'n., La. Militia
Polity, Nicolas	Private	Plauche's Batt'n., La. Militia
Polk, Isaac	Private	10 and 20 Cons. Reg't., La. Mil.
Pollard, James	Private	Captain Rankin's Co., Mounted Riflemen, La. Militia

Name	Rank	Unit
Pollock, George	Private	Captain Beale's Co., Riflemen, La. Militia
Poloski, John	Private	De Clouet's Reg't., La. Militia (Orig. under Polaski, John)
Pomarelle, --	Private	2 Reg't. (Cavelier's), La. Militia
Pomerette, --	Private	4 Reg't. (Morgan's), La. Militia
Pomeretto, --	Private	4 Reg't. (Morgan's), La. Militia (Orig. under Pomerette, --)
Pomet, Garcon	Private	1 Batt'n. (Fortier's), La. Militia
Pomet, Lindor	Private	1 Batt'n. (Fortier's), La. Militia
Pomette, Lindor	Private	1 Batt'n. (Fortier's), La. Militia (Orig. under Pomet, Lindor)
Pommier, C.	Chief of the Band Chief Musician	Plauche's Batt'n., La. Militia
Pommier, Louis	Private	17, 18 and 19 Cons. Reg't., La. Militia
Pomper, --	Private	2 Batt'n. (D'Aquin's), La. Militia (Orig. under Pompere, --)
Pompere, --	Private	2 Batt'n. (D'Aquin's), La. Militia
Pompey, --	Private-Servant	4 Brigade (Flanjae's), La. Mil.
Pon Pon, --	Servant	De Clouet's Reg't., La. Militia
Ponce, Michel	Sergeant	2 Reg't. (Cavelier's), La. Militia
Ponder, Reuben	Private	10 and 20 Cons. Reg't., La. Mil.
Ponder, Thomas	Private	De Clouet's Reg't., La. Militia
Pondon, --	Sergeant	1 Reg't. (Dejan's), La. Militia (Orig. under Hondon, --)
Pondor, Thomas	Private	De Clouet's Reg't., La. Militia (Orig. under Ponder, Thomas)
Pont, Felix	Private	16 Reg't. (Thompson's), La. Militia
Pontif, Jacques	1 Sergeant-2 Lieut.	5 Reg't. (La Branche's), La. Mil.
Pontiff, Justin	Private	7 Reg't. (Le Beuf's), La. Militia
Pontiff, Pierre	Private	7 Reg't. (Le Beuf's), La. Militia
Pontio, Isidora	Private	17, 18 and 19 Cons. Reg't., La. Militia
Ponton, Joachim	Private	1 Batt'n. (Fortier's), La. Militia
Popote, --	Musician	Plauche's Batt'n., La. Militia
Populus, Bartholemy	3 Lieutenant	1 Batt'n. (Fortier's), La. Militia
Populus, Carlos	Private	1 Batt'n. (Fortier's), La. Militia
Populus, Charles	Sergeant	1 Batt'n. (Fortier's), La. Militia
Populus, Felix	Corporal	1 Batt'n. (Fortier's), La. Militia
Populus, Honore	Private	1 Batt'n. (Fortier's), La. Militia
Populus, Jean Baptiste	Corporal	1 Batt'n. (Fortier's), La. Militia
Populus, Joachim	Private	1 Batt'n. (Fortier's), La. Militia
Populus, Maurice	1 Lieutenant	1 Batt'n. (Fortier's), La. Militia
Populus, Phillipe	Private	1 Batt'n. (Fortier's), La. Militia
Populus, Vincent	Major	1 Batt'n. (Fortier's), La. Militia
Porat, John	1 Lieutenant	11 Reg't. (Hickey's), La. Militia (Orig. under Poret, John)
Porche, Augustin	Private	Capt. Le Doux's Co., Cavalry, La. Vols.
Porche, Hypolite	Private	Captain Hubbard's Mounted Co., La. Militia
Porche, Jh files	Private	Capt. Le Doux's Co., Cavalry, La. Vols.
Porche, Joachim	Corporal	Captain Hubbard's Mounted Co., La. Militia
Porche, Zeno	2 Lieutenant	De Clouet's Reg't., La. Militia (Orig. under Poche, Zeno)
Poree, Charles	Captain	1 Batt'n. (Fortier's), La. Militia
Poree, Francois	1 Lieutenant	1 Batt'n. (Fortier's), La. Militia
Poree, Joseph	2 Lieut. & Adjt.	2 Reg't. (Cavelier's), La. Militia
Poret, John	1 Lieutenant	11 Reg't. (Hickey's), La. Militia
Porier, F.	Private	17, 18 and 19 Cons. Reg't., La. Militia
Porsel, Oliver	Ensign	5 Reg't. (La Branche's), La. Mil.
Porte, aine	Private	Plauche's Batt'n., La. Militia (Orig. under Poete, aine)
Porter, B. P.	Private	Captain Beale's Co., Riflemen, La. Militia
Porter, David	Sergeant	Capt. Collard's Co., La. Militia
Porter, David	Private	12 and 13 Cons. Reg't., La. Mil.
Porter, James	2 Lieutenant	De Clouet's Reg't., La. Militia
Porter, Shadrach	Captain	Baker's Regiment, La. Militia
Porterfield, Charles	Private	10 and 20 Cons. Reg't., La. Mil.
Portia, Julian	Private	De Clouet's Reg't., La. Militia (Orig. under Poirier, Julien)
Portier, Adre	Private	6 Reg't. (Landry's), La. Militia
Portier, Anme	Private	6 Reg't. (Landry's), La. Militia
Portier, Francois	Private	6 Reg't. (Landry's), La. Militia
Portier, I. Bte	Private	5 Reg't. (La Branche's), La. Mil. (Orig. under Fortier, In Bte)
Portier, Nicolas	Sergeant	5 Reg't. (La Branche's), La. Mil.
Posey, Lloyd	Private	16 Reg't. (Thompson's), La. Mil.
Postigue, Pierre	Corporal	1 Batt'n. (Fortier's), La. Militia
Postique, Pierre	Corporal	1 Batt'n. (Fortier's), La. Militia (Orig. under Postigue, Pierre)
Pool, Benjamin	Private	19 Regiment, La. Militia
Pool, Jacob	Private	5 Reg't. (La Branche's), La. Mil.
Pool, William	Private	10 and 20 Cons. Reg't., La. Mil.
Potchia, Pierre	Private	16 Reg't. (Thompson's), La. Mil.
Potes, David	Sergeant	Capt. Collard's Co., La. Militia (Orig. under Porter, David)
Pothier, Francois	Private	2 Batt'n. (Peire's), La. Vols.
Pothiers, Francois	Private	2 Batt'n. (Peire's), La. Vols. (Orig. under Pothier, Francois)
Pothring, Alex	Sergeant	17, 18 and 19 Cons. Reg't., La. Militia
Potier, --	Private	2 Reg't. (Cavelier's), La. Militia
Potier, Alexander	Private	De Clouet's Reg't., La. Militia
Potier, Francois	Private	De Clouet's Reg't., La. Militia
Potier, Olivier	Private	7 Reg't. (Le Beuf's), La. Militia
Potier, Pierre	Private	16 Reg't. (Thompson's), La. Mil.
Potterson, August	Private	De Clouet's Reg't., La. Militia (Orig. under Patterson, Anguish)
Pottier, Pierre	Private	16 Reg't. (Thompson's), La. Mil. (Orig. under Potier, Pierre)
Pottier, S.	Private	1 Reg't. (Dejan's), La. Militia
Potts, Jonathan	Private	Captain Musick's Co., La. Mil.
Potts, Jonathan	Private	Captain Musick's Co., Mounted Riflemen, La. Militia
Puche, --	Musician	Plauche's Batt'n., La. Militia
Puga, Michel	Private	De Clouet's Reg't., La. Militia
Pounce, Francis	Private	De Clouet's Reg't., La. Militia
Poursine, William	Private	6 Reg't. (Landry's), La. Militia (Orig. under Paursine, William)
Pouson, Alexis	Sergeant	3 Reg't. (de la Ronde's), La. Mil.
Poutz, Paul	Private	1 Reg't. (Dejan's), La. Militia
Pouyesse, Louis	Sergeant	1 Batt'n. (Fortier's), La. Militia
Powell, David	Private	19 Regiment, La. Militia
Powell, James	Corporal	Captain Beale's Co., Riflemen, La. Militia
Powell, Lewis	Private	De Clouet's Reg't., La. Militia
Powers, Edward C.	Private	Capt. Thomas' Co., La. Militia
Powers, James	Private	De Clouet's Reg't., La. Militia
Powers, John	Private	11 Reg't. (Hickey's), La. Militia
Powers, John	Private	10 and 20 Cons. Reg't., La. Mil.
Powers, Luke	Private	De Clouet's Reg't., La. Militia (See Vincent Cnance and Mesor Crier)
Prabo, Pedro	Private	17, 18 and 19 Cons. Reg't., La. Militia
Prade, Sebastian	Private	1 Batt'n. (Fortier's), La. Militia
Prade, Zenon	Private	1 Batt'n. (Fortier's), La. Militia
Praderos, Pedro	Private	17, 18 and 19 Cons. Reg't., La. Militia
Pradier, Ferdinand	Private	De Clouet's Reg't., La. Militia
Prado, Martin	Private	17, 18 and 19 Cons. Reg't., La. Militia
Prado, Pedro	Private	17, 18 and 19 Cons. Reg't., La. Militia
Prado, Sebastian	Private	1 Batt'n. (Fortier's), La. Militia (Orig. under Prade, Sebastian)
Pottut, Francois	Private	2 Batt'n. (Peire's), La. Vols. (Orig. under Pothier, Francois)
Prados, Pierre	Private	1 Batt'n. (Fortier's), La. Militia
Prantinier, Francis	Private	De Clouet's Reg't., La. Militia (Orig. under Printanier, Francois)
Prather, AAron	Private	De Clouet's Reg't., La. Militia
Prather, Tilor	Private	16 Reg't. (Thompson's), La. Mil.
Prather, William	Private	De Clouet's Reg't., La. Militia
Praton, Thomas	Private	De Clouet's Reg't., La. Militia (See also 44 U. S. Inf.)
Prator, Nicholas	Private	17, 18 and 19 Cons. Reg't., La. Militia
Pratt, --	Private	5 Reg't. (La Branche's), La. Mil.
Pratt, Jacob	Private	12 and 13 Cons. Reg't., La. Mil.
Pregean, Celestin	Corporal	De Clouet's Reg't., La. Militia (Orig. under Prejean, Celestin)
Pregean, Celestin	Corporal	De Clouet's Reg't., La. Militia (Orig. under Prejean, Celestin)
Pregean, Maxl	Private	De Clouet's Reg't., La. Militia (Orig. under Prejean, Maximilian)

Name	Rank	Unit
Prejan, Valerie	Private	7 Reg't. (Le Beuf's), La. Militia
Prejean, Celestin	Corporal	De Clouet's Reg't., La. Militia
Prejean, Dominque	Private	16 Reg't. (Thompson's), La. Mil.
Prejean, Joseph	Private	De Clouet's Reg't., La. Militia
Prejean, Maximilian	Private	De Clouet's Reg't., La. Militia
Prejean, Maximillion	Private	16 Reg't. (Thompson's), La. Mil.
Prejean, Valerie	Private	7 Reg't. (Le Beuf's), La. Militia (Orig. under Prejan, Valerie)
Premont, Joseph	Private	2 Batt'n. (Peire's), La. Vols.
Presler, Joshua	Private	10 and 20 Cons. Reg't., La. Mil.
Prestler, Joshua	Private	10 and 20 Cons. Reg't., La. Mil. (Orig. under Presler, Joshus)
Preston, John	Sergeant	10 and 20 Cons. Reg't., La. Mil.
Preston, Joshua	Private	10 and 20 Cons. Reg't., La. Mil. (Orig. under Preston, Joshua)
Preval, --	Private	7 Reg't. (Le Beuf's), La. Militia
Preval, Gulien	Private	2 Reg't. (Cavelier's), La. Militia
Prevall, --	--	De Clouet's Reg't., La. Militia
Prevos, -- fils	Sergeant	3 Reg't. (de la Ronde's), La. Mil. (Orig. under Prevost, -- fils)
Prevost, --	Private	2 Batt'n. (D'Aquin's), La. Militia
Prevost, fils	Sergeant	3 Reg't. (de la Ronde's), La. Mil.
Prevost, Akin	Private	Capt. Wallace's Co., Boatmen, La. Vols.
Prevost, D.	Private	2 Reg't. (Cavelier's), La. Militia
Prevost, Francois	Private	2 Batt'n. (Peire's), La. Vols.
Prevost, Joseph	Private	De Clouet's Reg't., La. Militia
Prevost, Joseph	Private	2 Batt'n. (Peire's), La. Vols. (Orig. under Prevost, Francois)
Prevot, --	Private	2 Batt'n. (D'Aquin's), La. Militia (Orig. under Prevost, --)
Prevot, D.	Private	2 Reg't. (Cavelier's), La. Militia (Orig. under Prevost, D.)
Prevot, Honore	Private	1 Batt'n. (Fortier's), La. Militia (Orig. under Provot, Honore)
Preyce, --	Private	Capt. Chauveau's Co., Cavalry, La. Militia
Preyre, --	Private	Capt. Chauveau's Co., Cavalry, La. Mil. (Orig. under Preyce,-)
Pric, Richard O.	Private	Captain Griffith's Co., Mounted Riflemen, La. Vols.(Orig. under Prie, Richard O.)
Price, Elisha G.	Sergeant	4 Reg't. (Morgan's), La. Militia
Price, Frederick	Private	Capt. Van Bibber's Co., La. Mil.
Price, Jacob	Private	Capt. Collard's Co., La. Militia
Price, James	Private	Captain Sprigg's Co., Boatmen, La. Vols.
Price, Michael	Private	Capt. Van Bibber's Co., La. Mil.
Price, Peter	Private	Captain Musick's Co., Mounted Riflemen, La. Mil. (Orig. under Pine, Peter)
Price, Richard O.	Private	Captain Griffith's Co., Mounted Riflemen, La. Vols. (Orig. under Prie, Richard O.)
Price, Risdon H.	Captain	Captain Price's Co., La. Militia
Prichard, Drewry R.	Sergeant	Capt. Callaway's Co., Cavalry, La. Militia
Prichard, John	Private	10 and 20 Cons. Reg't., La. Mil. (Orig. under Pritchard, John)
Prickett, Josiah	Private	10 and 20 Cons. Reg't., La. Mil.
Pricur, D.	Private	Captain Beale's Co., Riflemen, La. Militia
Prie, Richard O.	Private	Captain Griffith's Co., Mounted Riflemen, La. Vols.
Priestly, William Jr.	Private	6 Reg't. (Landry's), La. Militia
Prieur, A.	Private	Plauche's Batt'n., La. Militia
Prieur, Antoine	Private	Capt. Van Bibber's Co., La. Mil.
Prieur, D.	Private	Captain Beale's Co., Riflemen, La. Mil. (Orig. under Pricur, D)
Primate, --	Private	1 Reg't. (Dejan's), La. Militia
Primus, --	Servant	12 and 13 Cons. Reg't., La. Mil.
Prince, --	--	1 Reg't. (Dejan's), La. Militia
Prince, --	Servant	3 Brigade (McCausland's), La. Militia
Prince, --	Private	3 Reg't. (de la Ronde's), La. Mil.
Prince, John	Private	16 Reg't. (Thompson's), La. Mil.
Prince, Mar	Private	Baker's Regiment, La. Militia
Printanier, Francois	Private	De Clouet's Reg't., La. Militia
Priou, Nicola	Private	6 Reg't. (Landry's), La. Militia
Priou, Urbin	Private	6 Reg't. (Landry's), La. Militia
Pristo, John	Sergeant	10 and 20 Cons. Reg't., La. Mil. (Orig. under Preston, John)
Pritchard, John	Private	10 and 20 Cons. Reg't., La. Mil.
Pritchett, Drury	Private	Captain McNair's Co., Mounted Riflemen, La. Mil. (Orig. under Pritchit, Drury)
Pritchit, Drury	Private	Captain McNair's Co., Mounted Riflemen, La. Militia
Probts, Jacob	Sergeant	Captain Young's Co., Mounted Riflemen, La. Militia
Probts, John	Private	Captain Young's Co., Mounted Riflemen, La. Militia
Prockler, Nicolas	Private	Capt. Collard's Co., La. Militia (Orig. under Procter, Nicholas)
Procter, Nicholas	Private	Capt. Collard's Co., La. Militia
Prodier, --	Private	Plauche's Batt'n., La. Militia (Orig. under Prudier, --)
Prosper, Jean	Private	8 Reg't. (Meriam's), La. Militia
Prospere, In Bt	Private	8 Reg't. (Meriam's), La. Militia
Prospere, S.	Private	8 Reg't. (Meriam's), La. Militia
Provencal, Andre	Private	3 Reg't. (de la Ronde's), La. Mil.
Provost, --	Private	3 Reg't. (de la Ronde's), La. Mil.
Provost, Celestin	Private	Baker's Regiment, La. Militia
Provost, Godfroy	2 Lieutenant	Baker's Regiment, La. Militia
Provost, Joseph	Private	De Clouet's Reg't., La. Militia (Orig. under Prevost, Joseph)
Provost, Lufroy	Sergeant	Baker's Regiment, La. Militia
Provost, Marchelin	Private	Baker's Regiment, La. Militia
Provot, Honore	Private	1 Batt'n. (Fortier's), La. Militia
Prudhomme, Michel	Private	16 Reg't. (Thompson's), La. Mil.
Prudhomme, Paul	Private	17, 18 and 19 Cons. Reg't., La. Militia
Prudier, --	Private	Plauche's Batt'n., La. Militia
Pruestly, William Jr.	Private	6 Reg't. (Landry's), La. Militia (Orig. under Priestly, William Jr.)
Pruet, Jesse	Private	12 and 13 Cons. Reg't., La. Mil.
Pruete, Robert	Private	Capt. Callaway's Co., Cavalry, La. Militia
Pruett, E.	Private	4 Reg't. (Morgan's), La. Militia
Pruett, Uriah	Private	12 and 13 Cons. Reg't., La. Mil.
Pruneaux, Augustin	Private	8 Reg't. (Meriam's), La. Militia
Pryer, --	Private	Plauche's Batt'n., La. Militia (Orig. under Pryor, James)
Pryor, --	Private	4 Reg't. (Morgan's), La. Militia
Pryor, James	Private	Plauche's Batt'n., La. Militia
Pryor, Joseph E.	1 Sergeant	Captain Sprigg's Co., Boatmen, La. Vols.
Ptumley, Abraham	Private	Capt. Thomas' Co., La. Militia (Orig. under Plumley, Abraham)
Puche, fils	Private	Plauche's Batt'n., La. Militia (Orig. under Puth, fils)
Pue, Peter	Corporal	Capt. Collard's Co., La. Militia (Orig. under Pew, Peter)
Puga, Michel	Private	De Clouet's Reg't., La. Militia (Orig. under Puga, Michel)
Puga, Miguel	Sergeant	17, 18 and 19 Cons. Reg't., La. Militia
Purcell, Lepton	Private	16 Reg't. (Thompson's), La. Mil.
Purrault, J. B.	Sergeant-Major	Plauche's Batt'n., La. Militia (Orig. under Perrault, J. B.)
Purvis, James	Private	De Clouet's Reg't., La. Militia
Putch, fils	Private	Plauche's Batt'n., La. Militia (Orig. under Puth, fils)
Puth, fils	Private	Plauche's Batt'n., La. Militia
Pyburn, Lewis	Private	Capt. Thomas' Co., La. Militia
Pyrame, --	Waiter	3 Reg't. (de la Ronde's), La. Mil.
Quarantin, Prre	Fusilier-Private	5 Reg't. (La Branche's), La. Mil.
Quatorze, Henry	Private	3 Reg't. (de la Ronde's), La. Mil.
Quatrevingt, Antoine	Fus.-Private	5 Reg't. (La Branche's), La. Mil.
Quatrevingt, Charles	Fus.-Private	5 Reg't. (La Branche's), La. Mil.
Quatrevingt, Michel	Fus.-Private	5 Reg't. (La Branche's), La. Mil.
Quene, Abraham	Corporal	17, 18 and 19 Cons. Reg't., La. Militia
Quenen, Charles	Surgeon	7 Reg't. (Le Beuf's), La. Militia
Queneu, Charles	Surgeon	6 Reg't. (Landry's), La. Militia (See also 7 Reg't.)
Querida, Joseph	Private	3 Reg't. (de la Ronde's), La. Mil.
Querre, Justin	Private	Capt. Chauveau's Co., Cavalry, La. Militia (Orig. under Quirre, Justin)
Quessart, J.	Sergeant-Major	1 Batt'n. (Fortier's), La. Militia
Quick, Daniel	Private	Capt. Callaway's Co., Cavalry, La. Militia

Name	Rank	Unit
Quillen, Leven	Private	12 and 13 Cons. Reg't., La. Mil. (Orig. under Quilling, Loving)
Quillin, Nathan	Corporal	12 and 13 Cons. Reg't., La. Mil. (Orig. under Quilling, Nathan)
Quilling, John	Private	12 and 13 Cons. Reg't., La. Mil.
Quilling, Loving	Private	12 and 13 Cons. Reg't., La. Mil.
Quilling, Nathan	Corporal	12 and 13 Cons. Reg't., La. Mil.
Quimby, Robert	Private	Capt. Wallace's Co., Boatmen, La. Vols.
Quinnelty, Dennis	Private	17, 18 and 19 Cons. Reg't., La. Mil. (Orig. under Qunelty, Denis)
Quintana, --	Private	4 Reg't. (Morgan's), La. Militia
Quirk, Thomas	Private	16 Reg't. (Thompson's), La. Mil.
Quirke, Thomas	Private	16 Reg't. (Thompson's), La. Mil. (Orig. under Quirk, Thomas)
Quirre, Justin	Private	Capt. Chauveau's Co., Cavalry, La. Militia
Quitin, --	Fusilier-Private	5 Reg't. (La Branche's), La. Mil. (Orig. under Quarantin, Prre)
Qunelty, Denis	Private	17, 18 and 19 Cons. Reg't., La. Militia
Quooge, Bernard	Private	17, 18 and 19 Cons. Reg't., La. Militia (Orig. under Quoye, Bernard)
Quoye, Bernard	Private	17, 18 and 19 Cons. Reg't., La. Militia
Rabana, Jean	Private	Capt. Alpuente's Co., La. Mil. (Orig. under Rabassa, Jean)
Rabassa, Jean	Private	Capt. Alpuente's Co., La. Mil.
Rabassa, Joseph	2 Lieutenant	Capt. Alpuente's Co., La. Mil.
Rabe, Cader	3 Lieutenant	De Clouet's Reg't., La. Militia
Rabicheau, S.	Private	8 Reg't. (Meriam's), La. Militia
Raboie, Baptiste	Private	Captain Price's Co., La. Militia
Raboin, --	Private	2 Reg't. (Cavelier's), La. Militia
Rabore, Baptist	Private	Capt. Price's Co., La. Militia (Orig. under Raboie, Baptiste)
Raby, A.	Private	Plauche's Batt'n., La. Militia
Raby, Antoine	Private	1 Batt'n. (Fortier's), La. Militia
Raby, Cader	3 Lieutenant	De Clouet's Reg't., La. Militia (Orig. under Rabe, Cader)
Raca, Louis	Drummer	De Clouet's Reg't., La. Militia
Rachal, Anthony	Private	17, 18 and 19 Cons. Reg't., La. Mil. (Orig. under Rachal, Athanas)
Rachal, Athanas	Private	17, 18 and 19 Cons. Reg't., La. Militia
Rachal, Cyprien	Private	17, 18 and 19 Cons. Reg't., La. Militia
Rachal, Hilaire	Sergeant	17, 18 and 19 Cons. Reg't., La. Militia
Rachal, John B. B.	Private	17, 18 and 19 Cons. Reg't., La. Militia
Rachal, John Joseph	Private	17, 18 and 19 Cons. Reg't., La. Militia
Rachal, Julien	Private	17, 18 and 19 Cons. Reg't., La. Militia
Rachal, Louis Julien	Private	17, 18 and 19 Cons. Reg't., La. Militia
Rachal, Octave	Private	17, 18 and 19 Cons. Reg't., La. Militia
Rachel, Ant B.	Private	17, 18 and 19 Cons. Reg't., La. Militia
Racin, Pierre	Private	7 Reg't. (Le Beuf's), La. Militia
Ragiesse, Voilleme	Private	6 Reg't. (Landry's), La. Militia
Ragusse, D que	Sergeant	3 Reg't. (de la Ronde's), La. Mil.
Rahalle, Joseph	Private	De Clouet's Reg't., La. Militia
Rahelle, Joseph	Private	De Clouet's Reg't., La. Militia (Orig. under Rahalle, Joseph)
Railler, Michelle	Private	6 Reg't. (Landry's), La. Militia
Railler, Nicholas	Private	6 Reg't. (Landry's), La. Militia
Raillier, J. Bte	Private	6 Reg't. (Landry's), La. Militia
Raimond, Honore	Private	1 Batt'n. (Fortier's), La. Militia (Orig. under Raymond, Honore)
Raimond, Jean	Private	2 Reg't. (Cavelier's), La. Militia
Raimond, John	Private	2 Reg't. (Cavelier's), La. Militia (Orig. under Raimond, Jean)
Rainay, Jean	Private	3 Reg't. (de la Ronde's), La. Mil. (Orig. under Roinay, Jean)
Rainor, Daniel	Private	12 and 13 Cons. Reg't., La. Mil.
Rajes, --	Private	De Clouet's Reg't., La. Militia
Ramage, William	Private	17, 18 and 19 Cons. Reg't., La. Militia
Ramago, John	Private	7 Reg't. (Le Beuf's), La. Militia (Orig. under Ramagos, John)
Ramagos, John	Private	7 Reg't. (Le Beuf's), La. Militia
Ramel, --	Private	2 Reg't. (Cavelier's), La. Militia
Ramerez, Louis	Private	2 Batt'n. (Peire's), La. Vols. (Orig. under Ramirez, Louis)
Ramey, John	Private	Captain Musick's Co., La. Mil.
Ramey, John	Private	Captain Musick's Co., La. Mil.
Ramillas, Louis	Private	2 Batt'n. (Peire's), La. Vols. (Orig. under Ramirez, Louis)
Ramires, Francois	Private	2 Batt'n. (Peire's), La. Vols.
Ramires, Inacio	Private	2 Batt'n. (Peire's), La. Vols.
Ramires, Louis	Private	2 Batt'n. (Peire's), La. Vols. (Orig. under Ramirez, Louis)
Ramirez, Francis	Private	De Clouet's Reg't., La. Militia
Ramirez, Inacio	Private	2 Batt'n. (Peire's), La. Vols. (Orig. under Ramires, Inacio)
Ramirez, Joseph	Private	3 Reg't. (de la Ronde's), La. Mil.
Ramirez, Louis	Private	2 Batt'n. (Peire's), La. Vols.
Ramiro, James	Private	17, 18 and 19 Cons. Reg't., La. Militia
Ramisez, Francis	Private	2 Batt'n. (Peire's), La. Vols. (Orig. under Ramires, Francois)
Ramizer, Louis	Private	2 Batt'n. (Peire's), La. Vols. (Orig. under Ramirez, Louis)
Rammond, Joseph	Private	10 and 20 Cons. Reg't., La. Mil.
Ramon, Joseph	Private	10 and 20 Cons. Reg't., La. Mil. (Orig. under Rammond, Joseph)
Ramond, Joseph	Private	1 Batt'n. (Fortier), La. Militia
Ramos, --	Corporal	4 Reg't. (Morgan's), La. Militia
Ramsay, James	Private	Captain Ramsey's Co., Mounted Riflemen, La. Mil. (Orig. under Ramsey, James)
Ramsay, William	Ensign	Captain Ramsey's Co., Mounted Riflemen, La. Mil. (Orig. under Ramsey, William)
Ramsay, Wright A.	Private	Captain Ramsey's Co., Mounted Riflemen, La. Mil. (Orig. under Ramsey, Wright A.)
Ramsey, Andrew	Captain	Captain Ramsey's Co., Mounted Riflemen, La. Mil.
Ramsey, James	Private	Captain Ramsey's Co., Mounted Riflemen, La. Mil.
Ramsey, James	Private	1 Reg't. (Dejan's), La. Militia
Ramsey, John	Private	Captain Musick's Co., La. Mil. (Orig. under Ramey, John)
Ramsey, William	Ensign	Captain Ramsey's Co., Mounted Riflemen, La. Militia
Ramsey, Wright A.	Private	Captain Ramsey's Co., Mounted Riflemen, La. Militia
Randal, Joel	Private	10 and 20 Cons. Reg't., La. Mil.
Randale, Joel	Private	10 and 20 Cons. Reg't., La. Mil. (Orig. under Randal, Joel)
Randales, Joel	Private	10 and 20 Cons. Reg't., La. Mil. (Orig. under Randal, Joel)
Randall, David A.	2 Lieutenant	De Clouet's Reg't., La. Militia
Randell, Abraham	Private	Captain Ramsey's Co., Mounted Riflemen, La. Militia
Randle, --	Servant-Waiter	10 and 20 Cons. Reg't., La. Mil.
Randolph, Isaac	Private	Baker's Regiment, La. Militia
Randolph, John Jr.	Private	Captain Beale's Co., Riflemen, La. Militia
Randolph, John	2 Lieutenant	Captain Beale's Co., Riflemen, La. Militia
Randre, --	Servant-Waiter	10 and 20 Cons. Reg't., La. Mil. (Orig. under Randle, --)
Rangal, Joseph	Private	2 Batt'n. (Peire's), La. Vols. (Orig. under Rangel, Jose)
Rangel, Jose	Private	2 Batt'n. (Peire's), La. Vols.
Rangel, Joseph	Private	2 Batt'n. (Peire's), La. Vols. (Orig. under Rangel, Jose)
Rankin, James	Captain	Captain Rankin's Co., Mounted Riflemen, La. Militia
Rannalls, Samuel I.	2 Lieutenant	Captain Sprigg's Co., Boatmen, La. Vols.
Rannells, Samuel I.	2 Lieutenant	Captain Sprigg's Co., Boatmen, La. Vols. (Orig. under Rannalls, Samuel I.)
Ranson, Norbert	Fusilier-Private	5 Reg't. (La Branche's), La. Mil.
Ranson, Zenon	Fusilier-Private	5 Reg't. (La Branche's), La. Mil.
Rantoul, Alexander	Private	4 Reg't. (Morgan's), La. Militia (Orig. under Rentoul, Alexander)

Name	Rank	Unit
Rapelje, James	Private	8 Reg't. (Meriam's), La. Militia
Raphael, fils	Private	1 Batt'n. (Fortier's), La. Militia
Raphael, Bazile	Private	2 Batt'n. (D'Aquin's), La. Militia
Raphael, Joseph	Private	Capt. Songy's Co., Marines, La. Vols.
Raphael, Joseph	Private	2 Batt'n. (Peire's), La. Vols.
Raphael, Nicholas	Private	Capt. Songy's Co., Marines, La. Vols.
Raphael, Pierre	Corporal	1 Batt'n. (Fortier's), La. Militia
Raphail, Joseph	Private	2 Batt'n. (Peire's), La. Vols. (Orig. under Raphael, Joseph)
Rapp, Pierre	Private	3 Reg't. (de la Ronde's), La. Mil.
Rappe, Henry	Artificier	Capt. Chaudurier's Co., Artificers, Art'y., La. Vols.
Raquet, Honore	Private	1 Batt'n. (Fortier's), La. Militia
Raquin, Broise	Private	7 Reg't. (Le Beuf's), La. Militia
Raquin, Pierre I.	Private	7 Reg't. (Le Beuf's), La. Militia
Rarigol, Jean	Sergeant	Captain Lagan's Co., La. Vols. (Orig. under Darigol, Jean)
Rashat, Louis D.	Private	De Clouet's Reg't., La. Militia
Rasmus, Adam	Private	6 Reg't. (Landry's), La. Militia
Raspal, Etienne	Private	Capt. Alpuente's Co., La. Mil.
Rassart, Pierre	Private	Captain Lagan's Co., La. Vols.
Ratclif, Cyrus	Private	Capt. Wallace's Co., Boatmen, La. Vols. (Orig. under Ratliff, Cyrus)
Ratcliff, Redin	Private	10 and 20 Cons. Reg't., La. Mil.
Ratiff, Jessee	Private	10 and 20 Cons. Reg't., La. Mil. (Orig. under Ratliff, Jessee)
Ratiff, Levi	Private	10 and 20 Cons. Reg't., La. Mil. (Orig. under Ratliff, Levi)
Ratiff, Richard	1 Lieutenant	10 and 20 Cons. Reg't., La. Mil. (Orig. under Ratliff, Richard)
Ratliff, Cyrus	Private	Capt. Wallace's Co., Boatmen, La. Vols.
Ratliff, Jessee	Private	10 and 20 Cons. Reg't., La. Mil.
Ratliff, Levi	Private	10 and 20 Cons. Reg't., La. Mil.
Ratliff, Richard	1 Lieutenant	10 and 20 Cons. Reg't., La. Mil.
Ratliff, Robert C.	1 Lieutenant	12 and 13 Cons. Reg't., La. Mil.
Rauano, Requinto	Private	2 Batt'n. (Peire's), La. Vols. (Orig. under Ruano, Pio V)
Raubishau, Jean	Private	7 Reg't. (Le Beuf's), La. Militia
Rauland, Raine	Corporal	2 Batt'n. (D'Aquin's), La. Militia
Rauselle, Christophe	2 Lieutenant	6 Reg't. (Landry's), La. Militia
Rausselle, Maille	Private	6 Reg't. (Landry's), La. Militia
Rausselle, Valery	Private	6 Reg't. (Landry's), La. Militia
Rausselle, Zenon	Private	6 Reg't. (Landry's), La. Militia
Raux, F. F.	Surgeons Mate	Plauche's Batt'n., La. Militia (Orig. under Raux, T. F.)
Raux, Francis	Surgeons Mate	Plauche's Batt'n., La. Militia (Orig. under Raux, T. F.)
Raux, J. F.	Surgeons Mate	Plauche's Batt'n., La. Militia (Orig. under Raux, T. F.)
Raux, T. F.	Surgeons Mate	Plauche's Batt'n., La. Militia
Ravello, Louis	Private	3 Reg't. (de la Ronde's), La. Mil. (Orig. under Ravelo, Louis)
Ravello, Manuel	Private	3 Reg't. (de la Ronde's), La. Mil. (Orig. under Ravelo, Manuel)
Ravelo, Louis	Private	3 Reg't. (de la Ronde's), La. Mil.
Ravelo, Manuel	Private	3 Reg't. (de la Ronde's), La. Mil.
Ravencamp, John	Private	10 and 20 Cons. Reg't., La. Mil.
Ravencraft, Samuel	Private	De Clouet's Reg't., La. Militia (Orig. under Ravenscraft, Samuel)
Ravenscraft, Samuel	Private	De Clouet's Reg't., La. Militia
Ravincamp, John	Private	10 and 20 Cons. Reg't., La. Mil. (Orig. under Ravencamp, John)
Ray, Fify	Private	2 Batt'n. (Cavelier's), La. Militia (Orig. under Rey, Fify)
Ray, James	Private	16 Reg't. (Thompson's), La. Mil.
Ray, Jesse Y.	Corporal	16 Reg't. (Thompson's), La. Mil.
Ray, Joseph	Private	De Clouet's Reg't., La. Militia (Orig. under Roy, Joseph)
Ray, Joseph C.	Private	De Clouet's Reg't., La. Militia
Ray, Nicholas	Sergeant	Captain Sprigg's Co., Boatmen, La. Vols. (Orig. under Wray, Nicholas)
Ray, Robert	Private	4 Reg't. (Morgan's), La. Militia (Orig. under Kay, Robert)
Ray, Turkwell	Private	De Clouet's Reg't., La. Militia
Raymond, --	Private	Plauche's Batt'n., La. Militia
Raymond, Honore	Private	1 Batt'n. (Fortier's), La. Militia
Raymond, Jean	Private	Captain Lagan's Co., La. Vols.
Raymond, L. M.	1 Lieut. & Adjt.	Plauche's Batt'n., La. Militia (Orig. under Reynaud, L. M.)
Rayner, John	Private	De Clouet's Reg't., La. Militia (See also 44 Reg't.)
Raynes, Joseph	Corporal	1 Batt'n. (Fortier's), La. Militia (Orig. under Rynes, Joseph)
Reaby, Cader	3 Lieutenant	De Clouet's Reg't., La. Militia (Orig. under Rabe, Cader)
Reach, Anthony	Private	10 and 20 Cons. Reg't., La. Mil. (Orig. under Roach, Anthony)
Reader, Robert	Private	17, 18 and 19 Cons. Reg't., La. Militia
Reader, Robert	Sergeant	17, 18 and 19 Cons. Reg't., La. Mil. (Orig. under Reeder, Robert)
Reame, Josiah	Private	10 and 20 Cons. Reg't., La. Mil.
Reames, Benjamin	Private	12 and 13 Cons. Reg't., La. Mil. (Orig. under Rheames, Benjamin)
Reames, James	Private	12 and 13 Cons. Reg't., La. Mil. (Orig. under Rheames, James)
Reames, Josiah	Private	10 and 20 Cons. Reg't., La. Mil. (Orig. under Reame, Josiah)
Reams, Jesse	Private	Captain Griffith's Co., Mounted Riflemen, La. Vols.
Reams, Josiah	Private	10 and 20 Cons. Reg't., La. Mil. (Orig. under Reame, Josiah)
Reano, Pedro	Private	2 Reg't. (Cavelier's), La. Militia
Reams, William	Private	Captain Griffith's Co., Mounted Riflemen, La. Vols.
Reau, Garcon	Private	1 Batt'n. (Fortier's), La. Militia
Reaun, Pierre	Private	3 Reg't. (de la Ronde's), La. Mil.
Reaux, Silveste	Private	1 Batt'n. (Fortier's), La. Militia
Reave, Bartlett	Private	Captain Sprigg's Co., Boatmen, La. Vols. (Orig. under Reeves, Bartlett)
Recardo, Facundo	Private	17, 18 and 19 Cons. Reg't., La. Militia
Reddin, William	Private	12 and 13 Cons. Reg't., La. Mil. (Orig. under Redding, William)
Redding, William	Private	12 and 13 Cons. Reg't., La. Mil.
Redmond, William	2 Lieutenant	Capt. Thomas' Co., La. Militia
Rednay, Jean	Private	2 Batt'n. (Peire's), La. Vols.
Redney, Jean	Private	2 Batt'n. (Peire's), La. Vols.
Redon, Jean Baptiste	Private	2 Reg't. (Cavelier's), La. Militia
Redondo, Pedro	Private	2 Batt'n. (Peire's), La. Vols. (See case of Louis Lomes)
Redouin, Jaques	Private	2 Batt'n. (D'Aquin's), La. Militia
Reece, David	Major	Detachment Field and Staff Officers, 4 Brigade, La. Militia
Reed, Anthony	Private	16 Reg't. (Thompson's), La. Mil.
Reed, Archibald	Private	17, 18 and 19 Cons. Reg't., La. Militia
Reed, James	Private	Capt. Wallace's Co., Boatmen, La. Vols.
Reed, James	Private	16 Reg't. (Thompson's), La. Mil.
Reed, John	Private	12 and 13 Cons. Reg't., La. Mil.
Reed, John	Private	17, 18 and 19 Cons. Reg't., La. Militia
Reed, Robert	Sergeant	Captain Hughes' Co., Mounted Riflemen, La. Militia
Reed, Robert S.	Private	Baker's Regiment, La. Militia
Reed, Thomas	Ensign	Captain Hughes' Co., Mounted Riflemen, La. Militia
Reed, Thomas	Private	8 Reg't. (Meriam's), La. Militia
Reed, William	Trumpter	Captain Dodge's Co., Mounted Riflemen, La. Militia
Reed, William	Trumpeter	Captain Dodge's Co., Mounted Riflemen, La. Militia
Reed, William	Private-Sgt.	Captain Hughes' Co., Mounted Riflemen, La. Militia
Reed, William	Private	16 Reg't. (Thompson's), La. Mil.
Reed, William	Private	17, 18 and 19 Cons. Reg't., La. Militia
Reeder, Robert	Sergeant	17, 18 and 19 Cons. Reg't., La. Militia
Reeder, Robert A.	Sergeant	17, 18 and 19 Cons. Reg't., La. Mil. (Orig. under Reeder, Robert)
Rees, Jonathan J.	Sergeant	De Clouet's Reg't., La. Militia
Reese, Jonathan J.	Sergeant	De Clouet's Reg't., La. Militia (Orig. under Rees, Jonathan J.)

Name	Rank	Unit
Reever, Griffin	Private	12 and 13 Cons. Reg't., La. Mil.
Reeves, Bartlett	Private	Captain Spriggs' Co., Boatmen, La. Vols.
Reeves, James D.	Private	De Clouet's Reg't., La. Militia
Reeves, Joseph	Private	1 Reg't. (Dejan's), La. Militia
Reeves, William	1 Lieutenant	Baker's Regiment, La. Militia
Reevs, I. D.	Private	De Clouet's Reg't., La. Militia (Orig. under Reeves, James D.)
Reggio, Amede	Private	3 Reg't. (de la Ronde's), La. Mil.
Reggio, Nicolas	Private	3 Reg't. (de la Ronde's), La. Mil.
Regir, --	Private	De Clouet's Reg't., La. Militia (Orig. under Rajes, --)
Reigner, Joseph	Sergeant	De Clouet's Reg't., La. Militia (Orig. under Vaignier, Joseph)
Reilhe, Antoine F.	Private	Captain McNair's Co., Mounted Riflemen, La. Militia
Reine, Alceste	Private	Capt. Trudeau's Troop of Horse, La. Militia
Reine, Etienne	Corporal	5 Reg't. (La Branche's), La. Mil.
Reine, Etienne	Private	6 Reg't. (Landry's), La. Militia
Reine, Francois	Private	6 Reg't. (Landry's), La. Militia
Reine, Marin	Corporal	Capt. Trudeau's Troop of Horse, La. Militia
Reine, Orterc	Private	6 Reg't. (Landry's), La. Militia (Could be Ortere)
Reland, --	Private	Plauche's Batt'n., La. Militia
Remie, --	Private	2 Batt'n. (D'Aquin's), La. Militia
Remy, Antoine	Private	2 Batt'n. (D'Aquin's), La. Militia
Remy, Charles	Corporal	2 Batt'n. (Peire's), La. Vols.
Renalds, James	Private	De Clouet's Reg't., La. Militia (Orig. under Reynolds, James)
Renaud, Jn.	Private	3 Reg't. (de la Ronde's), La. Mil.
Renaud, Louis	Corporal	16 Reg't. (Thompson's), La. Mil.
Rene', --	Servant	Capt. Songy's Co., Marines, La. Vols.
Rene', Alexr	Private	Baker's Regiment, La. Militia
Rene', Frs.	Private	Baker's Regiment, La. Militia
Renick, George	Private	Captain Price's Co., La. Militia
Renthrop, Frederick	Sergeant	Baker's Regiment, La. Militia
Rentoul, Alexander	Private	4 Reg't. (Morgan's), La. Militia
Rentrop, Fred	Sergeant	Baker's Regiment, La. Militia (Orig. under Renthrop, Frederick)
Rents, John	Private	Captain Griffith's Co., Mounted Riflemen, La. Vols.
Reo, Joseph	Private	16 Reg't. (Thompson's), La. Mil.
Repshaw, George	Private	12 and 13 Cons. Reg't., La. Mil.
Repshaw, John	Sergeant	12 and 13 Cons. Reg't., La. Mil.
Repsher, George	Private	La. (War of 1812) (See also 1 Batt'n.) (Henry's) U. S. Vols.
Rermeneur, In	Private	Capt. Songy's Co., Marines, La. Vols.
Resimond, Miniere	Private	1 Batt'n. (Fortier's), La. Militia (Orig. under Rosemond, Miniere)
Rester, Gideon	Private	12 and 13 Cons. Reg't., La. Mil.
Reuben, --	Servant	Detachment Field and Staff Officers, 4 Brigade, La. Militia
Reviere, Jcq.	Private	7 Reg't. (Le Beuf's), La. Militia
Rexner, George	Private	Captain Lagan's Co., La. Vols.
Rey, Antoine	Private	3 Reg't. (de la Ronde's), La. Mil.
Rey, Fify	Private	2 Reg't. (Cavelier's), La. Militia
Reyes, John Jos.	Private	La. (War of 1812) (See also 2 Batt'n. (Peire's), La. Vols.)
Reyes, Jean Joseph	Private	2 Batt'n. (Peire's), La. Vols. (Orig. under Reys, Jean Joseph)
Reynaud, --	Private	Plauche's Batt'n., La. Militia (Orig. under Reynault, --)
Reynaud, L. M.	1 Lieut. & Adjt.	Plauche's Batt'n., La. Militia
Reynault, --	Private	Plauche's Batt'n., La. Militia
Reyne, Joseph	Private	Baker's Regiment, La. Militia
Reynes, Joseph	Corporal	1 Batt'n. (Fortier's), La. Militia (Orig. under Rynes, Joseph)
Reynia, Peter	Sergeant-Major	Detachment Field and Staff Officers, 4 Brigade, La. Militia
Reynolds, James	Private	De Clouet's Reg't., La. Militia
Reynolds, Michael	Major	De Clouet's Reg't., La. Militia
Reynolds, Michael	Major	1 Reg't. (Dejan's), La. Militia
Reys, Jean Joseph	Private	2 Batt'n. (Peire's), La. Vols.
Rezamson, --	Private	Plauche's Batt'n., La. Militia
Rheams, Benjamin	Private	12 and 13 Cons. Reg't., La. Mil.
Rheams, Jacob	Private	12 and 13 Cons. Reg't., La. Mil.
Rheams, James	Private	12 and 13 Cons. Reg't., La. Mil.
Rhodas, Benjamin	Private	De Clouet's Reg't., La. Militia
Rhodos, Benjamin	Private	De Clouet's Reg't., La. Militia (Orig. under Rhodas, Benjamin)
Rhorer, David	Private	16 Reg't. (Thompson's), La. Mil. (Orig. under Rohrer, David)
Rian, William	Private	17, 18 and 19 Cons. Reg't., La. Militia
Riano, --	Private	2 Reg't. (Cavelier's), La. Militia
Ribodeaux, --	Private	1 Reg't. (Dejan's), La. Militia
Ribon, Mannuelle	Private	2 Batt'n. (D'Aquin's), La. Militia
Riboul, Appolonaire	Private	1 Batt'n. (Fortier's), La. Militia
Ricard, Agricole	Private	8 Reg't. (Meriam's), La. Militia
Ricard, Basie	Private	8 Reg't. (Meriam's), La. Militia
Ricard, Cyprian	Private	8 Reg't. (Meriam's), La. Militia
Ricard, Max	Private	8 Reg't. (Meriam's), La. Militia
Ricard, Nicholas	Private	2 Batt'n. (Peire's), La. Vols.
Ricard, Pierre	Private	8 Reg't. (Meriam's), La. Militia
Ricard, St. Lue	Private	8 Reg't. (Meriam's), La. Militia
Ricardo, Facundo	Private	17, 18 and 19 Cons. Reg't., La. Mil. (Orig. under Recardo, Facundo)
Ricardo, Nicholas	Private	2 Batt'n. (Peire's), La. Vols. (Orig. under Ricard, Nicholas)
Rice, John	Private	Baker's Regiment, La. Militia
Rice, Samuel B.	Private	Baker's Regiment, La. Militia
Rice, Thomas	Private	Captain Young's Co., Mounted Riflemen, La. Militia
Rich, John	Private	10 and 20 Cons. Reg't., La. Mil.
Richar, A.	Private	8 Reg't. (Meriam's), La. Militia (Orig. under Richard, A.)
Richard, --	Fusilier-Private	5 Reg't. (La Branche's), La. Mil.
Richard, A.	Private	Plauche's Batt'n., La. Militia
Richard, A.	Corporal	6 Reg't. (Landry's), La. Militia
Richard, A.	Private	8 Reg't. (Meriams'), La. Militia
Richard, Anaclet	Private	16 Reg't. (Thompson's), La. Mil.
Richard, Auguste	Private	De Clouet's Reg't., La. Militia
Richard, Augustus	Corporal	10 and 20 Cons. Reg't., La. Mil.
Richard, Cerile	Private	16 Reg't. (Thompson's), La. Mil.
Richard, Dominique	Private	16 Reg't. (Thompson's), La. Mil.
Richard, Etiene	Private	6 Reg't. (Landry's), La. Militia
Richard, F.	Private	De Clouet's Reg't., La. Militia
Richard, Francois	Private	16 Reg't. (Thompson's), La. Mil.
Richard, I.	Private	8 Reg't. (Meriam's), La. Militia
Richard, Jean	Sergeant	Capt. Chaudurier's Co., Artificers, Art'y., La. Vols.
Richard, John	Private	1 Batt'n. (Fortier's), La. Militia (Orig. under Girard, John)
Richard, John Bte	Private	16 Reg't. (Thompson's), La. Mil.
Richard, Joseph L.	Private	16 Reg't. (Thompson's), La. Mil.
Richard, Louis	Private	De Clouet's Reg't., La. Militia
Richard, Louis	Sergeant	6 Reg't. (Landry's), La. Militia
Richard, Louis	Sergeant	7 Reg't. (Le Beuf's), La. Militia
Richard, Louis	Private	16 Reg't. (Thompson's), La. Mil.
Richard, M.	Private	6 Reg't. (Landry's), La. Militia
Richard, Philip	Private	16 Reg't. (Thompson's), La. Mil.
Richard, Philip	Private	16 Reg't. (Thompson's), La. Mil.
Richard, Pierre	Private	6 Reg't. (Landry's), La. Militia
Richard, Pierre	Private	6 Reg't. (Landry's), La. Militia
Richard, Pierre	Private	8 Reg't. (Meriam's), La. Militia
Richard, Pierre	Private	16 Reg't. (Thompson's), La. Mil.
Richard, Pierre	Corporal	16 Reg't. (Thompson's), La. Mil.
Richard, Pierre L.	Private	16 Reg't. (Thompson's), La. Mil.
Richard, Rosimond	Private	De Clouet's Reg't., La. Militia
Richard, Simon	1 Lieutenant	8 Reg't. (Meriam's), La. Militia
Richard, Simon	Sergeant	16 Reg't. (Thompson's), La. Mil.
Richard, St. Ville	Private	6 Reg't. (Landry's), La. Militia
Richards, Dominique	Private	16 Reg't. (Thompson's), La. Mil. (Orig. under Richard, Dominique)
Richards, I.	Private	8 Reg't. (Meriam's), La. Militia (Orig. under Richard, I.)
Richards, Mathew	Private	17, 18 and 19 Cons. Reg't., La. Militia
Richards, William	Private	16 Reg't. (Thompson's), La. Mil.
Richardson, Amos	Private	Captain Griffith's Co., Mounted Riflemen, La. Vols.
Richarsson, Asa	Private	10 and 20 Cons. Reg't., La. Mil.
Richardson, Benjamin	Private	12 and 13 Cons. Reg't., La. Mil.
Richardson, Elias	Private	Captain Griffith's Co., Mounted Riflemen, La. Vols.
Richardson, Enoch	Private	Captain Griffith's Co., Mounted Riflemen, La. Vols.
Richardson, George	Private	De Clouet's Reg't., La. Militia

Name	Rank	Unit
Richardson, James	Private	10 Regiment, La. Militia
Richardson, Jesse	Private	Captain Griffith's Co., Mounted Riflemen, La. Vols.
Richardson, Jesse	Private	Captain Musick's Co., Mounted Riflemen, La. Militia
Richardson, John	Private	12 and 13 Cons. Reg't., La. Mil.
Richardson, Mathew	Private	De Clouet's Reg't, La. Militia
Richardson, Richard	Corporal	Capt. Thomas' Co., La. Militia
Richardson, Samuel	Private	12 and 13 Cons. Reg't, La. Mil.
Richardson, Silas	Private	Captain McNair's Co., Mounted Riflemen, La. Militia
Richardson, Stephen	2 Lieutenant	12 and 13 Cons. Reg't., La. Mil.
Richardson, William	Private	Baker's Regiment, La. Militia
Richardson, William	Private	12 and 13 Cons. Reg't, La. Mil.
Richarson, George	Private	De Clouet's Reg't, La. Militia (Orig. under Richardson, George)
Richarson, Mathew	Private	De Clouet's Reg't, La. Militia (Orig. under Richardson, Mathew)
Richason, Samuel	Private	12 and 13 Cons. Reg't, La. Mil. (Orig. under Richardson, Samuel)
Riches, James	Private	2 Batt'n. (Peire's), La. Vols. (Orig. under Richey, James)
Richey, James	Private	De Clouet's Reg't, La. Militia
Richey, James	Private	2 Batt'n. (Peire's), La. Vols.
Richey, William	Private	16 Reg't. (Thompson's), La. Mil. (Orig. under Richards, William)
Richou, Joseph	Private	5 Reg't. (La Branche's), La. Mil.
Richoux, Pierre	Captain	7 Reg't. (Le Beuf's), La. Militia
Rick, John	Private	10 and 20 Cons. Reg't., La. Mil. (Orig. under Rich, John)
Rickman, Abraham	Private	Captain Hughes' Co., Mounted Riflemen, La. Militia
Ricord, Pierre	Private	8 Reg't. (Meriam's), La. Militia (Orig. under Ricard, Pierre)
Ricraft, Francis	Sergeant	10 and 20 Cons. Reg't., La. Mil. (Orig. under Roycraft, Francis)
Ridenhour, Henry	Private	Capt. Van Bibber's Co., La. Mil.
Rider, Baptiste	Private	De Clouet's Reg't, La. Militia
Rider, Henry	Private	16 Reg't. (Thompson's), La. Mil.
Rider, John	Private	Captain Sprigg's Co., Boatmen, La. Vols.
Rieve, Bartley	Private	Captain Sprigg's Co., Boatmen, La. Vols. (Orig. under Reeves, Bartlett)
Riererr, Francois	Private	Capt. Chaudurier's Co., Artificers, Art'y., La. Vos. (Orig. under Rivierre, Francois)
Rieux, Honore	Corporal	De Clouet's Reg't, La. Militia
Rieux, Honore	Private	1 Batt'n. (Fortier's), La. Militia
Rieux, Jean	Private	Captain Lagan's Co., La. Vols.
Rieves, James D.	Private	De Clouet's Reg't, La. Militia
Riffel, John	Private	Capt. Collard's Co., La. Militia
Riffet, John	Private	Capt. Collard's Co., La. Militia (Orig. under Riffel, John)
Rigby, David	Private	De Clouet's Reg't, La. Militia
Riggio, Augustin	Captain	3 Reg't. (de la Ronde's), La. Mil.
Riggs, Eli	Private	Baker's Regiment, La. Militia
Riggs, Jonathan	Purser	Capt. Callaway's Co., Cavalry, La. Militia
Right, Robert	Private	De Clouet's Reg't, La. Militia (Orig. under Wright, Robert)
Rigsby, David	Private	De Clouet's Reg't, La. Militia (Orig. under Rigby, David)
Rilcrease, John	Private	10 and 20 Cons. Reg't., La. Mil. (Orig. under Kilcrease, John)
Rilles, T.	1 Lieutenant	8 Reg't. (Meriam's), La. Militia
Rilleux, Elise	2 Lieut.-1 Lieut.	5 Reg't. (La Branche's), La. Mil. (Orig. under Rillieux, Elise)
Rilleux, Francois	Captain	5 Reg't. (La Branche's), La. Mil. (Orig. under Rillieux, Francois)
Rilleux, Vincent	Corporal	Capt. Chauveau's Co., Cavalry, La. Militia
Rillieux, Elise	2 Lieut.-1 Lieut.	5 Reg't. (La Branche's), La. Mil.
Rillieux, Francois	Captain	5 Reg't. (La Branche's), La. Mil.
Rillieux, Vincent	Corporal	Capt. Chauveau's Co., Cavalry, La. Mil. (Orig. under Rilleux, Vincent)
Rills, I. Be. (J?)	Private	8 Reg't. (Meriam's), La. Militia
Rills, T.	1 Lieutenant	8 Reg't. (Meriam's), La. Militia (Orig. under Rilles, T.)
Rils, Joseph T.	1 Lieutenant	8 Reg't. (Meriam's), La. Militia (Orig. under Rilles, T.)
Rimes, Josiah	Private	10 and 20 Cons. Reg't., La. Mil. (Orig. under Reame, Josiah)
Rimira, I. Bt	Private	8 Reg't. (Meriam's), La. Militia (Morgan's,) La. Militia
Rinker, --	Private	3 Reg't. (de la Ronde's), La. Mil. (See Rinker James, General & Staff
Rinker, James	Volunteer Aid & Pri.	General & Staff (Morgan's), La. Militia
Rinter, Charles	Private	Louisiana (War of 1812)
Rinton, Alexander	Private	Baker's Regiment, La. Militia
Rio, Joseph	Private	16 Reg't. (Thompson's), La. Mil. (Orig. under Reo. Joseph)
Rios, Diego	Private	2 Batt'n. (Feire's), La. Vols.
Rios, Ignacio	Private	17, 18 and 19 Cons. Reg't., La. Mil.
Rioz, Diego	Private	2 Batt'n. (Peire's), La. Vols. (Orig. under Rios, Diego)
Ripshaw, George	Private	12 and 13 Cons. Reg't., La. Mil. (Orig. under Repshaw, George)
Riraux, E.	Corporal	La. (War of 1812) (See also 2 Batt'n. (Peire's), La. Vols.)
Riraux, E.	Corporal	2 Batt'n. (Peire's), La. Vols. (Orig. under Rivaux, Eugene)
Risener, George	Private	Captain Lagan's Co., La. Vols. (Orig. under Rixner, George)
Risley, Oliver	Sergeant-Major	10 and 20 Cons. Reg't, La. Mil.
Risquin, Jean	Private	3 Reg't. (de la Ronde's), La. Mil.
Ritchardson, James	Private	De Clouet's Reg't, La. Militia
Ritchardson, Phillip	Private	De Clouet's Reg't, La. Militia
Ritchardson, William	Private	Baker's Regiment, La. Militia (Orig. under Richardson, William)
Ritcherson, George	Private	De Clouet's Reg't, La. Militia (Orig. under Richardson, George)
Ritcherson, Mathew	Private	De Clouet's Reg't, La. Militia (Orig. under Richardson, Mathew)
Ritchew, Daniel	Private	17, 18 and 19 Cons. Reg't.; La. Mil. (Orig. under Ritchie, Daniel)
Ritchie, Daniel	Private	17, 18 and 19 Cons. Reg't., La. Militia
Riter, Antoine	Private	16 Reg't. (Thompson's), La. Mil.
Ritter, William	Private	17, 18 and 19 Cons. Reg't., La. Militia
Rinz, Diego	Private	2 Batt'n. (Peire's), La. Vols. (Orig. under Rios, Diego)
Rivarde, Archl	Private	1 Reg't. (Dejan's), La. Militia
Rivarosse, Mathurin	Private	1 Batt'n. (Fortier's), La. Militia
Rivaux, Eugene	Corporal	2 Batt'n. (Peire's), La. Vols.
Riveau, Eugene	Corporal	2 Batt'n. (Peire's), La. Vols. (Orig. under Rivaux, Eugene)
Riveaut, --	Private	Plauche's Batt'n., La. Militia (Orig. under Riveaux, --)
Riveaux, --	Private	Plauche's Batt'n., La. Militia
Riveaux, Eugene	Corporal	2 Batt'n. (Peire's), La. Vols. (Orig. under Rivaux, Eugene)
River, Antoine	Private	7 Reg't. (Le Beuf's), La. Militia
Rivera, Joseph	Private	3 Reg't. (de la Ronde's), La. Mil.
Riveras, Joseph	Private	3 Reg't. (de la Ronde's), La. Mil. (Orig. under Rivera, Joseph)
Rivero, Christoval	Private	Captain Hubbard's Mounted Co., La. Militia
Riverre, Francois	Private	Capt. Chaudurier's Co., Artificers, Art'y., La. Vols. (Orig. under Rivierre, Francois)
Rivery, Peter Achille	Captain	2 Batt'n. (Peire's), La. Vols. (Orig. under Rivery, Pierre Achille)
Rivery, Pierre Archille	Captain	2 Batt'n. (Peire's), La. Vols.
Rives, Charles C.	Sergeant	De Clouet's Reg't, La. Militia
Rivet, Joseph	Private	8 Reg't. (Meriam's), La. Militia
Rivet, Theodore	Private	8 Reg't. (Meriam's), La. Militia
Rivett, Eli	Private	8 Reg't. (Meriam's), La. Militia
Rivett, Jerome	Private	8 Reg't. (Meriam's), La. Militia
Rivett, Marcelle	Private	8 Reg't. (Meriam's), La. Militia
Rivett, Marcellin	Corporal	8 Reg't. (Meriam's), La. Militia
Rivett, Xavier	Private	8 Reg't. (Meriam's), La. Militia
Rivette, Auguste	Sergeant	8 Reg't. (Meriam's), La. Militia
Rivette, Isadon	Corporal	8 Reg't. (Meriam's), La. Militia
Rivette, Louis	Corporal	8 Reg't. (Meriam's), La. Militia
Rivette, Pierre, fils	Private	8 Reg't. (Meriam's), La. Militia

Name	Rank	Unit
Rivier, Griffin	Private	12 and 13 Cons. Reg't., La. Mil. (Orig. under Reever, Griffin)
Riviere, Francois	Private	Capt. Chaudurier's Co., Artificers, Art'y., La. Vols. (Orig. under Rivierre, Francois)
Rivierre, Francois	Private	Capt. Chaudurier's Co., Artificers, Art'y., La. Vols.
Rixner, Andre	Fusilier-Private	5 Reg't. (La Branche's), La. Mil.
Rixner, Charles	Sergeant	5 Reg't. (La Branche's), La. Mil.
Rixner, Zenon	Fusilier-Private	5 Reg't. (La Branche's), La. Mil.
Roach, Anthony	Private	10 and 20 Cons. Reg't., La. Mil.
Roach, Cleuban	Private	11 Reg't. (Hickey's), La. Militia
Roach, Faroah	Private	Capt. Thomas' Co., La. Militia
Roach, Henry	Private	De Clouet's Reg't., La. Militia (Orig. under Pettit, John)
Roach, Henry	Private	Capt. Thomas' Co., La. Militia
Roach, Pre	Captain	Plauche's Batt'n., La. Militia (Orig. under Roache, Pre)
Roark, Peter	Private	10 and 20 Cons. Reg't., La. Mil. (Orig. under Rourk, Peter)
Roboart, James	Private	De Clouet's Reg't., La. Militia
Robarts, James	Private	De Clouet's Reg't., La. Militia (Orig. under Robart, James)
Robbens, Horace	Private	10 and 20 Cons. Reg't., La. Mil. (Orig. under Robbins, Horace)
Robbin, Prospect K.	Lieutenant	Capt. Callaway's Co., Cavalry, La. Militia
Robbins, David	Private	Baker's Regiment, La. Militia
Robbins, Horace	Private	10 and 20 Cons. Reg't., La. Mil.
Robe, Jean	Private	2 Reg't. (Cavelier's), La. Militia
Robello, Jn	Private	4 Reg't. (Morgan's), La. Militia
Roben, Daniel	Private	Captain Young's Co., Mounted Riflemen, La. Militia
Roben, Francois	Private	17, 18 and 19 Cons. Reg't., La. Militia (Orig. under Robin, Francois)
Roberson, --	Private	2 Reg't. (Cavelier's), La. Militia (Orig. under Robertson, --)
Roberson, Dl	Private	2 Reg't. (Cavelier's), La. Militia
Roberson, Eli	Private	12 and 13 Cons. Reg't., La. Mil. (Orig. under Robertson, Eli)
Robert, --	Servant	De Clouet's Reg't., La. Militia
Robert, Angel	Private	2 Batt'n. (D'Aquin's), La. Militia
Robert, Antoine	Private	2 Reg't. (Cavelier's), La. Militia
Robert, Ard	Sergeant	Plauche's Batt'n., La. Militia
Robert, Charles	Private	8 Reg't. (Meriam's), La. Militia
Robert, Fifi	Private	2 Batt'n. (D'Aquin's), La. Militia
Robert, Jacques	Private	1 Batt'n. (Fortier's), La. Militia
Robert, Jean	Private	5 Reg't. (La Branche's), La. Mil.
Robert, Jean son	Private	5 Reg't. (La Branche's), La. Mil.
Robert, Peter	Private	2 Reg't. (Cavelier's), La. Militia
Robert, S.	Private	4 Reg't. (Morgan's), La. Militia
Robert, Severin	Sergeant	1 Batt'n. (Fortier's), La. Militia
Roberts, Aaron	Sergeant	Capt. Wallace's Co., Boatmen, La. Vols.
Roberts, Abner	Private	10 and 20 Cons. Reg't., La. Mil.
Roberts, Absalom	Private	10 and 20 Cons. Reg't., La. Mil.
Roberts, Andre	Private	De Clouet's Reg't., La. Militia (Orig. under Robine, Andrew)
Roberts, Bennet	Private	De Clouet's Reg't., La. Militia
Roberts, David	Private	Capt. Wallace's Co., Boatmen, La. Vols.
Roberts, Elisha	1 Lieutenant	12 and 13 Cons. Reg't., La. Mil.
Roberts, Isaac	Sergeant	De Clouet's Reg't., La. Militia
Roberts, John	Private	Capt. Allen's Co., Artillerists, La. Vols.
Roberts, John	Private	De Clouet's Reg't., La. Militia
Roberts, John	Private	19 Regiment, La. Militia
Roberts, John L.	Private	Capt. Wallace's Co., Boatmen, La. Vols.
Roberts, Paul I.	Corporal	17, 18 and 19 Cons. Reg't., La. Militia
Roberts, Reuben	Private	De Clouet's Reg't., La. Militia
Roberts, Thomas	Private	12 and 13 Cons. Reg't., La. Mil.
Roberts, William	Private	Baker's Regiment, La. Militia
Roberts, William	Private	12 and 13 Cons. Reg't., La. Mil.
Robertson, --	Private	2 Reg't. (Cavelier's), La. Militia
Robertson, Eli	Private	12 and 13 Cons. Reg't., La. Mil.
Robertson, George W.	1 Lieutenant	4 Reg't. (Morgan's), La. Militia
Robertson, Green	Private	De Clouet's Reg't., La. Militia
Robertson, John	Private	De Clouet's Reg't., La. Militia
Robertson, John	Private	10 and 20 Cons. Reg't., La. Mil.
Robertson, John	Sergeant	12 and 13 Cons. Reg't., La. Mil.
Robertson, Joseph	Private	10 and 20 Cons. Reg't., La. Mil. (Orig. under Robinson, Joseph)
Robertson, Seburn	Private	De Clouet's Reg't., La. Militia
Robertson, Wiley	Private	12 and 13 Cons. Reg't., La. Mil.
Robertson, William	Private	De Clouet's Reg't., La. Militia
Robertson, William	Private	De Clouet's Reg't., La. Militia
Robertson, William	Private	De Clouet's Reg't., La. Militia (Orig. under Robinson, William)
Robertson, William	Private	12 and 13 Cons. Reg't., La. Mil.
Robichau, John	Private	Captain Hubbard's Mounted Co., La. Militia
Robichau, Julien	2 Lieutenant	De Clouet's Reg't., La. Militia (Orig. under Robichaut, Julian)
Robichaut, Julian	2 Lieutenant	De Clouet's Reg't., La. Militia
Robichaux, Jean B.	Private	Captain Hubbard's Mounted Co., La. Militia
Robichaux, John B.	Private	7 Reg't. (Le Beuf's), La. Militia
Robichaux, Joseph	Private	7 Reg't. (Le Beuf's), La. Militia
Robichaux, Joseph	Private	7 Reg't. (Le Beuf's), La. Militia
Robicheau, Bovier	Private	8 Reg't. (Meriam's), La. Militia
Robicheau, I. Bte	Private	8 Reg't. (Meriam's), La. Militia
Robicheaux, John B.	Private	7 Reg't. (Le Beuf's), La. Militia (Orig. under Robichaux, John B)
Robigne', Iean	Private	Capt. Songy's Co., Marines, La. Vols.
Robigney, In.	Private	Capt. Singy's Co., Marines, La. Vols. (Orig. under Robigne, Iean)
Robin, Antoine	Private	16 Reg't. (Thompson's), La. Mil.
Robin, Aphe	Private	2 Reg't. (Cavelier's), La. Militia
Robin, Clement	Private	3 Reg't. (de la Ronde's), La. Mil.
Robin, Firmin	Private	3 Reg't. (de la Ronde's), La. Mil.
Robin, Francois	2 Lieutenant	16 Reg't. (Thompson's), La. Mil.
Robin, Francois	Private	17, 18 and 19 Cons. Reg't., La. Militia
Robin, Giles	Private	3 Reg't. (de la Ronde's), La. Mil.
Robin, Jean Jacques	Corporal	3 Reg't. (de la Ronde's), La. Mil.
Robin, John L.	Private	16 Reg't. (Thompson's), La. Mil.
Robin, Norbert	Private	1 Batt'n. (Fortier's), La. Militia
Robin, Sr Luc	Private	3 Reg't. (de la Ronde's), La. Mil.
Robine, Andrew	Private	De Clouet's Reg't., La. Militia
Robinet, Pierre	Private	Baker's Regiment, La. Militia
Robins, David	Private	Baker's Regiment, La. Militia (Orig. under Robbins, David)
Robins, James	Private	Capt. Wallace's Co., Boatmen, La. Vols.
Robinson, Benjamin E.	Private	De Clouet's Reg't., La. Militia
Robinson, Gabriel	Private	16 Reg't. (Thompson's), La. Mil. (Orig. under Robison, Gabriel)
Robinson, James	Private	12 and 13 Cons. Reg't., La. Mil.
Robinson, John	Private	De Clouet's Reg't., La. Militia
Robinson, John H.	Surgeon	10 and 20 Cons. Reg't., La. Mil.
Robinson, Joseph	Private	10 and 20 Cons. Reg't., La. Mil.
Robinson, M. D.	Private	17, 18 and 19 Cons. Reg't., La. Militia
Robinson, William	Private	De Clouet's Reg't., La. Militia (Orig. under Robertson, William)
Robinson, William	Private	De Clouet's Reg't., La. Militia
Robint, Zacharie	Private	6 Reg't. (Landry's), La. Militia
Robisen, Benj E.	Private	De Clouet's Reg't., La. Militia (Orig. under Robinson, Benjamin E.)
Robison, Gabriel	Private	16 Reg't. (Thompson's), La. Mil.
Roche', Ch	3 Lieutenant	Plauche's Batt'n., La. Militia
Roche, Charles	Corporal	1 Batt'n. (Fortier's), La. Militia (Orig. under Roches, Charles)
Roche, Fcs.	Private	Capt. Colsson's Co., Artillery, La. Vols.
Roche, J.	Private	2 Reg't. (Cavelier's), La. Militia
Roche, Paul	Private	Capt. Alpuente's Co., La. Mil.
Roche, Pierre	Private	2 Reg't. (Cavelier's), La. Militia
Roche, Pre	Captain	Plauche's Batt'n., La. Militia
Rochelle, --	Private	1 Reg't. (Dejan's), La. Militia
Rochelle, William	Private	Baker's Regiment, La. Militia
Roches, Charles	Corporal	1 Batt'n. (Fortier's), La. Militia
Rochon, --	Private	Baker's Regiment, La. Militia
Rochon, Bernard	Private	De Clouet's Reg't., La. Militia
Rochon, Hilaire	Private	1 Batt'n. (Fortier's), La. Militia
Rochon, Maurice	Private	Louisiana (War of 1812)
Rochor, Bernard	Private	De Clouet's Reg't., La. Militia (Orig. under Rochon, Bernard)

Name	Rank	Unit
Rocque, Jean	Private	2 Reg't. (Cavelier's), La. Militia (Orig. under Roques, Jean)
Rodal, --	Private	1 Reg't. (Dejan's), La. Militia
Rodeigue, Zenon	Private	De Clouet's Reg't., La. Militia (Orig. under Rodrigue, Zenon)
Rodenay, Pierre	Private	2 Batt'n. (D'Aquin's), La. Militia
Roderie, Matthew	Private	8 Reg't. (Meriam's), La. Militia
Roderigo, Jose	Private	De Clouet's Reg't., La. Militia
Roderigue, Joseph	Private	De Clouet's Reg't., La. Militia
Roderigue, Z.	Private	De Clouet's Reg't., La. Militia (Orig. under Rodrigue, Zenon)
Roderigues, Joseph	Private	De Clouet's Reg't., La. Militia (Orig. under Roderigo, Jose)
Roderijes, Joseph	Private	De Clouet's Reg't., La. Militia (Orig. under Roderigo, Jose)
Roderique, Joseph	Private	De Clouet's Reg't., La. Militia (Orig. under Roderigo, Jose)
Roderique, Z.	Private	De Clouet's Reg't., La. Militia (Orig. under Rodrigue, Zenon)
Rodey, James	Private	12 and 13 Cons. Reg't., La. Mil.
Rodey, John	Private	8 Reg't. (Meriam's), La. Militia
Rodgers, Atwell L.	Private	12 and 13 Cons. Reg't., La. Mil.
Rodgers, Job	Qr. Master	12 and 13 Cons. Reg't., La. Mil.
Rodrigers, Manuel	Private	4 Reg't. (Morgan's), La. Militia (Orig. under Rodriques, Manuel)
Rodrigue, Francois	Fusilier-Private	5 Reg't. (La Branche's), La. Mil.
Rodrigue, Jean Bte	Sergeant	5 Reg't. (La Branche's), La. Mil.
Rodrigue, Louis	Private	6 Reg't. (Landry's), La. Militia
Rodrigue, Pierre	Fusilier-Private	5 Reg't. (La Branche's), La. Mil. (Orig. under Rodrigues, Pierre)
Rodrigues, Francisco	Private	3 Reg't. (de la Ronde's), La. Mil.
Rodrigues, Francois	Private	3 Reg't. (de la Ronde's), La. Mil.
Rodrigues, Joseph	Private	2 Batt'n. (Peire's), La. Vols.
Rodrigues, Manuel	Private	4 Reg't. (Morgan's), La. Militia
Rodrigues, Md	Private	17, 18 and 19 Cons. Reg't., La. Militia
Rodrigues, Migl	Private	17, 18 and 19 Cons. Reg't., La. Militia
Rodrigues, Pierre	Fusilier-Private	5 Reg't. (La Branche's), La. Mil.
Rodrigues, Siprien	Private	17, 18 and 19 Cons. Reg't., La. Militia
Rodriguez, Cyprian	Private	17, 18 and 19 Cons. Reg't., La. Militia
Rodriguez, Domingo	Private	Captain Hubbard's Mounted Co., La. Militia
Rodriguez, Jose	Private	2 Batt'n. (Peire's), La. Vols. (Orig. under Rodregues, Joseph)
Rodriguez, Joseph	Private	De Clouet's Reg't., La. Militia (Orig. under Roderigo, Jose)
Rodriguez, M.	Private	6 Reg't. (Landry's), La. Militia
Rodriguez, Miguel	Private	17, 18 and 19 Cons. Reg't., La. Militia
Rodriguez, Pierre	Fusilier-Private	5 Reg't. (La Branche's), La. Mil. (Orig. under Rodrigues, Pierre)
Rodrique, Francois	Fusilier-Private	5 Reg't. (La Branche's), La. Mil. (Orig. under Rodrigue, Francois)
Rodrique, Louis	Private	6 Reg't. (Landry's), La. Militia (Orig. under Rodrigue, Louis)
Rodrique, Zenon	Private	De Clouet's Reg't., La. Militia
Rodrigues, Joseph	Private	La. (War of 1812) (See also 2 Batt'n. (Peire's), La. Vols.)
Rodriques, Joseph	Private	2 Batt'n. (Peire's), La. Vols. (Orig. under Rodrigues, Joseph)
Rodriquez, Manuel	Private	4 Reg't. (Morgan's), La. Militia (Orig. under Rodriques, Manuel)
Roe, Edward	Private	10 and 20 Cons. Reg't., La. Mil.
Roe, John	Private	10 and 20 Cons. Reg't., La. Mil.
Rochon, Narcisse	Sergeant	Baker's Regiment, La. Militia
Roger, Auguste	Private	De Clouet's Regiment, La. Mil.
Roger, Esra	Private	10 and 20 Cons. Reg't., La. Mil. (Orig. under Rogers, Esra)
Roger, Joseph	Private	Captain Lagan's Co., La. Vols.
Rogers, Atwell L.	Private	12 and 13 Cons. Reg't., La. Mil. (Orig. under Rodgers, Atwell L)
Rogers, Esra	Private	10 and 20 Cons. Reg't., La. Mil.
Rogers, James	Private	Captain Rankin's Co., Mounted Riflemen, La. Militia
Rogers, Robert	Private	16 Reg't. (Thompson's), La. Mil.
Rogers, Shadrick	Private	10 and 20 Cons. Reg't., La. Mil.
Rogers, Thimy	Captain	11 Reg't. (Hickey's), La. Mil.
Rogers, W.	Surgeon	Gov. Claiborne and Staff, La. Mil.
Rogers, William	Private	De Clouet's Reg't., La. Militia
Rogues, --	Private	Capt. Chauveau's Co., Cavalry, La. Militia
Roguigne, Jean Baptiste	Private	1 Batt'n. (Fortier's), La. Militia (Orig. under Roguignie, Jean Baptiste)
Roguignie, Jean Baptiste	Private	1 Batt'n. (Fortier's), La. Militia
Rohrer, David	Private	16 Reg't. (Thompson's), La. Mil.
Roinay, Jean	Private	3 Reg't. (de la Ronde's), La. Mil.
Rois, Solastille	Private	Capt. Dubuclet's Troop, Hussars, La. Vols. (Orig. under Roy, Solastille)
Roister, George	Private	Baker's Regiment, La. Militia
Rojert, Alexis	Private	7 Reg't. (Le Beuf's), La. Militia
Rojert, Jean Bte	Private	7 Reg't. (Le Beuf's), La. Militia
Rolah, Benhamin	Private	Baker's Regiment, La. Militia
Roland, --	Private	Plauche's Batt'n., La. Militia
Roland, Baptiste	Private	Plauche's Batt'n., La. Militia
Roland, Baptiste	Private	1 Batt'n. (Fortier's), La. Militia
Roland, George	Private	Plauche's Batt'n., La. Militia
Roland, Guillaume	Private	2 Batt'n. (D'Aquin's), La. Militia
Rolet, Felix	Private	2 Batt'n. (D'Aquin's), La. Militia
Rollain, Joshua	Private	Baker's Regiment, La. Militia (Orig. under Rollan, Jesse)
Rollan, Jesse	Private	Baker's Regiment, La. Militia
Rolland, --	Private	Plauche's Batt'n., La. Militia (Orig. under Roland, --)
Rolland, Baptiste	Private	De Clouet's Reg't., La. Militia
Rolland, Francois	Private	Captain Lagan's Co., La. Vols.
Rollins, Thomas T.	Private	10 and 20 Cons. Reg't., La. Mil.
Rolls, Amos	Private	16 Reg't. (Thompson's), La. Mil.
Romagnan, Francois	Private	1 Batt'n. (Fortier's), La. Militia
Romain, Guillaume	Corporal	De Clouet's Reg't., La. Militia
Roman, --	Musician	Plauche's Batt'n., La. Militia
Roman, Etienne	Private	6 Reg't. (Landry's), La. Militia
Roman, Francis	Private	De Clouet's Reg't., La. Militia
Roman, Onesime	Private	6 Reg't. (Landry's), La. Militia
Roman, Sosthene	Captain	6 Reg't. (Landry's), La. Militia
Roman, Victorin	Private	6 Reg't. (Landry's), La. Militia
Roman, Zenon	Private	6 Reg't. (Landry's), La. Militia
Romano, Louis	Sergeant	Captain Hubbard's Mounted Co., La. Militia
Romaro, Benard	Private	Baker's Regiment, La. Militia (Orig. under Romero, Bernard)
Romas, Thomas	Private	3 Reg't. (de la Ronde's), La. Mil.
Rome, Charles	Private	6 Reg't. (Landry's), La. Militia
Rome, Jean	Corporal	6 Reg't. (Landry's), La. Militia
Rome, Nicolas	Private	6 Reg't. (Landry's), La. Militia
Rome, Ursin	Private	6 Reg't. (Landry's), La. Militia
Romeau, --	Musician	Plauche's Batt'n., La. Militia (Orig. under Roman, --)
Romere, Francis	Private	2 Reg't. (Cavelier's), La. Militia
Romero, Bernard	Private	Baker's Regiment, La. Militia
Romero, Joseph	Private	Baker's Regiment, La. Militia
Romin, Casemire	Corporal	2 Batt'n. (D'Aquin's), La. Militia
Romine, Francis	Private	2 Reg't. (Cavelier's), La. Militia (Orig. under Romere, Francis)
Romirez, Francisco	Private	2 Batt'n. (Peire's), La. Vols. (Orig. under Ramires, Francois)
Rond, Jean Bte	Private	16 Reg't. (Thompson's), La. Mil.
Rondeau, --	Corporal	Plauche's Batt'n., La. Militia
Ronguille, Jean	Corporal	3 Reg't. (de la Ronde's), La. Mil.
Ronguille, Manuel	Sergeant	3 Reg't. (de la Ronde's), La. Mil.
Rooch, Henry	Private	Capt. Thomas' Co., La. Militia (Orig. under Roach, Henry)
Roogues, Pierre	Sergeant	2 Reg't. (Cavelier's), La. Militia (Orig. under Roques, Pierre)
Roots, George	Private	De Clouet's Reg't., La. Militia
Roque, --	Private	1 Reg't. (Dejan's), La. Militia
Roque, Elise	Private	1 Batt'n. (Fortier's), La. Militia
Roques, Jean	Private	2 Reg't. (Cavelier's), La. Militia
Roques, Pierre	Sergeant	2 Reg't. (Cavelier's), La. Militia
Rosa, Jean	Private	7 Reg't. (Le Beuf's), La. Militia
Rosan, Me	Sergeant	1 Reg't. (Dejan's), La. Militia
Rosario, Pedro	Private	Capt. Songy's Co., Marines, La. Vols.
Rose, Christian	Private	De Clouet's Reg't., La. Militia
Rose, Eloi	Corporal	De Clouet's Reg't., La. Militia
Rose, John	Private	Baker's Regiment, La. Militia
Rose, Joseph	Private	De Clouet's Reg't., La. Militia (Orig. under Rosse, Joseph)
Rose, Pierre	Private	Capt. Songy's Co., Marines, La. Vols.

Name	Rank	Unit
Rose, William P.	Private	12 and 13 Cons. Reg't., La. Mil.
Roselle, Louis	Private	4 Reg't. (Morgan's), La. Militia
Rosembuch, Guillaume	Corporal-Pvt.	2 Batt'n. (Peire's), La. Vols. (Orig. under Rosembusch, Guillaume)
Rosembuch, Joseph	Private	De Clouet's Reg't., La. Militia (Orig. under Rosenbush, William)
Rosemburch, Guillaume	Corp.-Pvt.	2 Batt'n. (Peire's), La. Vols. (Orig. under Rosembusch, Guillaume)
Rosembusch, Guillaume	Corp.-Pvt.	2 Batt'n. (Peire's), La. Vols.
Rosembush, Joseph	Private	De Clouet's Reg't., La. Militia (Orig. under Rosenbush, William)
Rosemond, Miniere	Private	1 Batt'n. (Fortier's), La. Militia
Rosemond, Vincent	Private	1 Batt'n. (Fortier's), La. Militia
Rosenbuch, Guillaume	Corp.-Pvt.	2 Batt'n. (Peire's), La. Vols. (Orig. under Rosembusch, Guillaume)
Rosenburgh, William	Corp.-Pvt.	2 Batt'n. (Peire's), La. Vols. (Orig. under Rosembusch, Guillaume)
Rosenburk, William	Corp.-Pvt.	2 Batt'n. (Peire's), La. Vols. (Orig. under Rosembusch, Guillaume)
Rosenbush, William	Private	De Clouet's Reg't., La. Militia
Roshell, Francis	Private	17, 18 and 19 Cons. Reg't., La. Militia
Rosinbush, Joseph	Private	De Clouet's Reg't., La. Militia (Orig. under Rosenbush, William)
Ross, Charles	Private	Captain Sprigg's Co., Boatmen, La. Vols.
Ross, Francis	Private	12 and 13 Cons. Reg't., La. Mil.
Ross, George T.	Major	2 Batt'n. (Peire's), La. Vols.
Ross, John Richard	Private	De Clouet's Reg't., La. Militia
Ross, Reuben	1 Lieut. & Q.Mr.	17, 18 and 19 Cons. Reg't., La. Militia
Ross, Richard	Sergeant	Capt. Allen's Co., Artillerists, La. Vols.
Ross, Samuel	Private	17, 18 and 19 Cons. Reg't., La. Militia
Ross, Stephen	Private	8 Reg't. (Meriam's), La. Militia
Ross, William	Private	Captain Beale's Co., Riflemen, La. Militia
Rossario, Pedro	Private	Capt. Songy's Co., Marines, La. Vols. (Orig. under Rosario, Pedro)
Rosse, Joseph	Private	De Clouet's Reg't., La. Militia
Rosse, Pre.	Private	Capt. Songy's Co., Marines, La. Vols. (Orig. under Rose, Pierre)
Rosseau, Iyasaint	Private	7 Reg't. (Le Beuf's), La. Militia
Rosseau, Peter	1 Lieutenant	4 Reg't. (Morgan's), La. Militia
Rosenbusch, Guillaume	Corp.-Pvt.	2 Batt'n. (Peire's), La. Vols. (Orig. under Rosembusch, Guillaume)
Rosses, Jean	Private	7 Reg't. (Le Beuf's), La. Militia (Orig. under Rosa, Jean)
Rossi, Jean	Sergeant	Captain Lagan's Co., La. Vols.
Rosson, Charles	Private	1 Batt'n. (Fortier's), La. Vols.
Roth, Eugene	Private	4 Reg't. (Morgan's), La. Militia
Roth, Godefroy	1 Sergeant-Sgt.	8 Reg't. (Meriam's), La. Militia
Roth, I Bte	Private	8 Reg't. (Meriam's), La. Militia
Roth, Philip	Private	4 Reg't. (Morgan's), La. Militia
Rotts, Francisco	Private-Corporal	2 Batt'n. (Peire's), La. Vols.
Roubelot, Louis	Fusilier-Private	5 Reg't. (La Branche's), La. Mil. (Orig. under Roublau, Louis)
Roublau, Louis	Fusilier-Private	5 Reg't. (La Branche's), La. Mil.
Roudon, E.	Private	6 Reg't. (Landry's), La. Militia
Rouesedu, -- fils	Private	3 Reg't. (de la Ronde's), La. Mil. (Orig. under Rousseau, -- fils)
Roujot, Alexandre	Private	16 Reg't. (Thompson's), La. Mil.
Roujot, Calixe	Private	16 Reg't. (Thompson's), La. Mil.
Roujot, Severin	Private	16 Reg't. (Thompson's), La. Mil.
Rouland, Rene'	Corporal	2 Batt'n. (D'Aquin's), La. Militia (Orig. under Rauland, Raine)
Roulette, Ben homme	Private	2 Batt'n. (D'Aquin's), La. Militia
Roulie, Louis	Artificer	Capt. Chaudurier's Co., Artificers, Art'y., La. Vols.
Rouly, Louis	Artificer	Capt. Chaudurier's Co., Artificers, Art'y., La. Vols. (Orig. under Roulie, Louis)
Roundtree, William	Private	Capt. Wallace's Co., Boatmen, La. Vols.
Roural, --	Private	4 Reg't. (Morgan's), La. Militia
Rourk, Peter	Private	10 and 20 Cons. Reg't., La. Mil.
Rouville, --	Corporal	3 Reg't. (de la Ronde's), La. Mil.
Rouse, Thomas	Private	10 and 20 Cons. Reg't., La. Mil.
Rouseaux, Nicolas	Private	Capt. Alpuente's Co., La. Mil. (Orig. under Rousseaux, Nicolas)
Rousel, Jean	Fusilier-Corporal	5 Reg't. (La Branche's), La. Mil. (Orig. under Roussel, Jean)
Rouselle, Zeno	Private	6 Reg't. (Landry's), La. Militia (Orig. under Raussell, Zenon)
Rouseteau, --	Private	2 Batt'n. (D'Aquin's), La. Militia
Roussau, Jean	Private	1 Batt'n. (Fortier's), La. Militia
Roussaux, Pierre	Private	1 Batt'n. (Fortier's), La. Militia
Rousseau, --	Private	Plauche's Batt'n., La. Militia
Rousseau, Charles	Private	2 Batt'n. (Peire's), La. Vols.
Rousseau, fils	Private	3 Reg't. (de la Ronde's), La. Mil.
Rousseau, In Pre	Private	4 Reg't. (Morgan's), La. Militia
Rousseau, Iyasaint	Private	7 Reg't. (Le Beuf's), La. Militia (Orig. under Rosseau, Iyasaint)
Rousseau, Jacques	Private	Captain Hubbard's Mounted Co., La. Militia
Rousseau, Jean	Corporal	Captain Hubbard's Mounted Co., La. Militia
Rousseau, Jean Jacques	Private	16 Reg't. (Thompson's), La. Mil.
Rousseau, Pierre	Private	1 Batt'n. (Fortier's), La. Militia (Orig. under Roussaux, Pierre)
Rousseaux, Charles	Private	2 Batt'n. (Peire's), La. Vols. (Orig. under Rosseau, Charles)
Rousseaux, --	Private	Plauche's Batt'n., La. Militia (Orig. under Rousseau, --)
Rousseaux, Nicolas	Private	Capt. Alpuente's Co., La. Mil.
Roussel, Archibald	Private	10 and 20 Cons. Reg't., La. Mil. (Orig. under Russell, Archibald)
Roussel, Domque	Fusilier-Corporal	5 Reg't. (La Branche's), La. Mil.
Roussel, George, fils	Fusilier-Pvt.	5 Reg't. (La Branche's), La. Mil.
Roussel, Honore	Fusilier-Pvt.	5 Reg't. (La Branche's), La. Mil.
Roussel, Jean	Fusilier-Corporal	5 Reg't. (La Branche's), La. Mil.
Roussel, Pierre	Fusilier-Private	5 Reg't. (La Branche's), La. Mil.
Roussell, Chris	2 Lieutenant	6 Reg't. (Landry's), La. Militia (Orig. under Rauselle, Christophe)
Rousselle, Christophe	2 Lieutenant	6 Reg't. (Landry's), La. Militia (Orig. under Rauselle, Christophe)
Rousselin, I.	Private	Capt. Songy's Co., Marines, La. Vols.
Rousselle, Mlle	Private	6 Reg't. (Landry's), La. Militia (Orig. under Rausselle, Maille)
Rousselle, Valery	Private	6 Reg't. (Landry's), La. Militia (Orig. under Rausselle, Valery)
Roussere, Baptiste	Corporal	De Clouet's Reg't., La. Militia
Roussere, Baptiste	Corporal	1 Batt'n. (Fortier's), La. Militia
Roussere, Manuel	Private	1 Batt'n. (Fortier's), La. Militia
Roussere, Silvaine	Private	De Clouet's Reg't., La. Militia
Rousseve, Baptiste	Corporal	1 Batt'n. (Fortier's), La. Militia (Orig. under Roussere, Baptiste)
Rousseve, Manuel	Private	1 Batt'n. (Fortier's), La. Militia (Orig. under Roussere, Manuel)
Roussi, Anthony	Private	2 Batt'n. (Peire's), La. Vols. (Orig. under Roussie, Antoine)
Roussie, Antoine	Private	2 Batt'n. (Peire's), La. Vols.
Roussue, Silvanine	Private	De Clouet's Reg't., La. Militia (Orig. under Roussere, Silvaine)
Rouval, --	Private	4 Reg't. (Morgan's), La. Militia
Rouval, --	Private	4 Reg't. (Morgan's), La. Militia (Orig. under Roural, --)
Roux, Cadet	Corporal	2 Reg't. (Cavelier's), La. Militia
Roux, Dominique	Private	Captain Hubbard's Mounted Co., La. Militia
Roux, Louis	Private	Captain Lagan's Co., La. Vols.
Rouzant, Jacques	Sergeant	1 Batt'n. (Fortier's), La. Mil.
Rouzier, Berlin	Captain	2 Batt'n. (D'Aquin's), La. Militia
Row, Andrew	Private	16 Reg't. (Thompson's), La. Mil.
Row, Edward	Private	10 and 20 Cons. Reg't., La. Mil. (Orig. under Roe, Edward)
Rowe, Andrew	Private	16 Reg't. (Thompson's), La. Mil. (Orig. under Row, Andrew)
Rowe, Jo.	Private	De Clouet's Reg't., La. Militia (See also U. S. Artillery)
Rowe, Reubin	Private	12 and 13 Cons. Reg't., La. Mil.
Rowley, Job	Private	17, 18 and 19 Cons. Reg't., La. Militia

Name	Rank	Unit
Rowley, Joel	Private	Captain McNair's Co., Mounted Riflemen, La. Militia
Rowley, John	Corporal	10 and 20 Cons. Reg't., La. Mil.
Rowser, John	Private	Captain Price's Co., La. Militia
Roy, Alexander	Private	De Clouet's Reg't., La. Militia
Roy, Alexander	Private	Capt. Van Bibber's Co., La. Mil.
Roy, Francis	Private	Capt. Van Bibber's Co., La. Mil.
Roy, Francis	Private	17, 18 and 19 Cons. Reg't., La. Militia
Roy, Jean Ba	Private	Captain Rankins' Co., Mounted Riflemen, La. Militia
Roy, John Baptiste	Private	16 Reg't. (Thompson's), La. Mil.
Roy, Joseph	Private	De Clouet's Reg't., La. Militia
Roy, Joseph	Private	19 Regiment, La. Militia
Roy, Julien	Private	Captain Price's Co., La. Militia
Roy, Lefroy	Private	16 Reg't. (Thompson's), La. Mil.
Roy, Louis	Artificer	Capt. Chaudurier's Co., Artificers, Art'y., La. Vols.
Roy, Lufroy	Private	17, 18 and 19 Cons. Reg't., La. Militia
Roy, Simeon	Private	Captain Price's Co., La. Militia (Orig. under Roy, Simon)
Roy, Simon	Private	Captain Price's Co., La. Militia
Roy, Solastille	Artificer	Capt. Dubuclet's Troop, Hussars, La. Vols.
Roy, Valery	Private	16 Reg't. (Thompson's), La. Mil.
Roya, John	Sergeant	16 Reg't. (Thompson's), La. Mil.
Roycraft, Francis	Sergeant	10 and 20 Cons. Reg't., La. Mil.
Roye, Auguste	Private	16 Reg't. (Thompson's), La. Mil.
Royer, John	Private	De Clouet's Reg't., La. Militia
Roza, Francois	Private	16 Reg't. (Thompson's), La. Mil.
Rozat, Alexandre	Private	16 Reg't. (Thompson's), La. Mil.
Rozer, Joseph	Private	Captain Lagan's Co., La. Vols. (Orig. under Roger, Joseph)
Ruand, Gio D.	Private	2 Batt'n. (Peire's), La. Vols. (Orig. under Ruano, Pio V.)
Ruano, Pio Quinto	Private	2 Batt'n. (Peire's), La. Vols. (Orig. under Ruano, Pio V.)
Ruano, Pio V.	Private	2 Batt'n. (Peire's), La. Vols.
Rucker, William	2 Lt. & Paymaster	10 Regiment, La. Mil. (Orig. under Bucker, William)
Ruddell, Abraham	Private	Captain Ramsey's Co., Mounted Riflemen, La. Militia
Ruddle, Abraham	Private	Captain Ramsey's Co., Mounted Riflemen, La. Mil. (Orig. under Ruddell, Abraham)
Ruddle, Archibald	Private	17, 18 and 19 Cons. Reg't., La. Militia
Ruddle, John	Corporal	Captain Ramsey's Co., Mounted Riflemen, La. Militia
Ruelle, John	Private	2 Batt'n. (Peire's), La. Vols.
Ruff, Daniel P.	Private	Plauche's Batt'n., La. Militia
Ruffman, Anthony	Private	De Clouet's Reg't., La. Militia
Rulong, Aaron	Corporal	16 Reg't. (Thompson's), La. Mil.
Rumage, William	Private	17, 18 and 19 Cons. Reg't., La. Militia
Rumble, Jacob	Private	17, 18 and 19 Cons. Reg't., La. Mil. (Orig. under Kumble, Jacob)
Rupsher, George	Private	12 and 13 Cons. Reg't., La. Mil. (Orig. under Repshaw, George)
Russ, Benjamin	Private	16 Reg't. (Thompson's), La. Mil.
Russ, Elias	Captain	11 Reg't. (Hickey's), La. Mil.
Russeau, Charles	Private	2 Batt'n. (Peire's), La. Vols. (Orig. under Rousseau, Charles)
Russel, Cola	Private	16 Reg't. (Thompson's), La. Mil.
Russel, Jesse D.	Private	Captain Rankins' Co., Mounted Riflemen, La. Militia
Russell, Archibald	Private	10 and 20 Cons. Reg't., La. Militia
Russell, Robert	Private	10 and 20 Cons. Reg't., La. Mil.
Russie, Anthony	Private	2 Batt'n. (Peire's), La. Vols. (Orig. under Roussie, Antoine)
Russi, Jean	Sergeant	Captain Lagan's Co., La. Vols. (Orig. under Rossi, Jean)
Russie, Antoine	Private	2 Batt'n. (Peire's), La. Vols. (Orig. under Roussie, Antoine)
Rust, Francis	Private	La. (War of 1812) See also 2 Batt'n. (Peire's), La. Vols.
Rust, Francis	Private-Corporal	2 Batt'n. (Peire's), La. Vols. (Orig. under Rotts, Francisco)
Rutledge, Samuel	Private	De Clouet's Reg't., La. Militia (Orig. under Rutledge, Samuel)
Rutledge, John	Private	10 and 20 Cons. Reg't., La. Mil.
Rutledge, Russel	Private	De Clouet's Reg't., La. Militia
Rutledge, Samuel	Private	De Clouet's Reg't., La. Militia
Rutlidge, John	Private	10 and 20 Cons. Reg't., La. Mil. (Orig. under Rutledge, John)
Rutlidge, Samuel	Private	De Clouet's Reg't., La. Militia (Orig. under Rutledge, Samuel)
Ryan, Jacob	Private	De Clouet's Reg't., La. Militia
Ryand, Jacob	Private	De Clouet's Reg't., La. Militia
Rynal, Antoine	Sergeant	Capt. Van Bibber's Co., La. Mil.
Rynes, Joseph	Corporal	1 Batt'n. (Fortier's), La. Militia
Sabadere, Joseph	Private	De Clouet's Reg't., La. Militia (Orig. under Sabadire, Joseph)
Sabadire, Joseph	Private	De Clouet's Reg't., La. Militia
Sabaque, Pierre	Private	1 Batt'n. (Fortier's), La. Militia
Sabatie, Cevaire	Private	5 Reg't. (La Branche's), La. Mil. (Orig. under Sabatier, Cevaire)
Sabatier, Cevaire	Private	5 Reg't. (La Branche's), La. Mil.
Sabbo, Pierre	Corporal	Louisiana (War of 1812)
Sabole, Pierre	Private	7 Reg't. (Le Beuf's), La. Militia
Sabaleau, Jean	Private	2 Batt'n. (Peire's), La. Vols. (Orig. under Sabouleau, Jean)
Sabouda, Joseph	Private	Capt. Songy's Co., Marines, La. Vols. (Orig. under Isaboucla, Joseph)
Sabouleau, Jean	Private	2 Batt'n. (Peire's), La. Vols.
Sackett, Reuben T.	Captain	De Clouet's Reg't., La. Militia
Sacrement, Edaine	Private	7 Reg't. (Le Beuf's), La. Militia (Orig. under Sacrement, Edaire)
Sacrement, Edaire	Private	7 Reg't. (Le Beuf's), La. Militia
Sagory, L. M.	Private	Plauche's Batt'n., La. Militia
Saimere, Urbin	Private	De Clouet's Reg't., La. Militia
Saimpe, -- Jr.	Private	4 Reg't. (Morgan's), La. Militia (Orig. under Simpe, Jr.)
Saimpe, Sr.	Private	4 Reg't. (Morgan's), La. Militia (Orig. under Simpe, Sr.)
Sainet, E.	1 Lieut. & Q. M.	Plauche's Batt'n., La. Militia
Sainte, Gime	Captain	Plauche's Batt'n., La. Militia
Saintraille, F.	Private	2 Batt'n. (D'Aquin's), La. Militia (Orig. under Staraille, F.)
Saiz, Theodore	Corporal	17, 18 and 19 Cons. Reg't., La. Militia
Salasa, Cartano	Private	17, 18 and 19 Cons. Reg't., La. Mil. (Orig. under Salazar, Cactano)
Salazar, Cactano	Private	17, 18 and 19 Cons. Reg't., La. Militia
Salazar, Caetano	Private	17, 18 and 19 Cons. Reg't., La. Militia
Saldibar, Caetano	Private	17, 18 and 19 Cons. Reg't., La. Militia
Salina, Ignacio	Private	17, 18 and 19 Cons. Reg't., La. Militia
Salombre, William	Private	Baker's Regiment, La. Militia
Salonber, Guillm	Private	Baker's Regiment, La. Militia (Orig. under Salombre, William)
Salsberry, John R.	Adjutant	12 and 13 Cons. Reg't., La. Mil. (Orig. under Salsbury, John R.)
Salsbury, John R.	Adjutant	12 and 13 Cons. Reg't., La. Mil.
Saltet, --	Private	Capt. Chauveau's Co., Cavalry, La. Militia
Salvador, --	Private	2 Reg't. (Cavelier's), La. Militia
Salvan, Jean	Private	3 Reg't. (de la Ronde's), La. Mil.
Salvan, Pierre	Private	3 Reg't. (de la Ronde's), La. Mil.
Salvant, Jean	Private	3 Reg't. (de la Ronde's), La. Mil. (Orig. under Salvan, Jean)
Salvant, Pierre	Private	3 Reg't. (de la Ronde's), La. Mil.
Sam, --	Servant	De Clouet's Reg't., La. Militia
Samson, Terence	Private	Capt. Le Doux's Co., Cavalry, La. Vols.
Sancedo, Pedro Iose	Private	17, 18 and 19 Cons. Reg't., La. Militia
Sanche, Andre	Private	2 Batt'n. (Peire's), La. Vols. (Orig. under Sanchez, Andre)
Sanche, Antonio	Private	17, 18 and 19 Cons. Reg't., La. Militia
Sanche, Damasio	Private	17, 18 and 19 Cons. Reg't., La. Militia
Sancher, Joseph Maria	Corporal	De Clouet's Reg't., La. Militia (Orig. under Sanchez, Joseph Maria)
Sanches, Andre	Private	2 Reg't. (Cavelier's), La. Militia
Sanches, Manuel	Private	17, 18 and 19 Cons. Reg't., La. Militia

Name	Rank	Unit
Sanches, Peter	Private	2 Batt'n. (Peire's), La. Vols. (Orig. under Sanchez, Pierre)
Sanches, Pierre	Private	2 Batt'n. (Peire's), La. Vols. (Orig. under Sanchez, Pierre)
Sanchez, André	Private	2 Batt'n. (Peire's), La. Vols.
Sanchez, Andrew	Private	2 Batt'n. (Peire's), La. Vols. (Orig. under Sanchez, Andre)
Sanchez, Antonio	Private	17, 18 and 19 Cons. Reg't., La. Militia (Orig. under Sanche, Antonio)
Sanchez, Cristophe	Private	3 Reg't. (de la Ronde's), La. Mil.
Sanchez, Diego	Corporal	3 Reg't. (de la Ronde's), La. Mil.
Sanchez, Domacio	Private	17, 18 and 19 Cons. Reg't., La. Mil. (Orig. under Sanchos, Domacio)
Sanchez, Francois	Private	3 Reg't. (de la Ronde's), La. Mil.
Sanchez, Jean	Private	3 Reg't. (de la Ronde's), La. Mil.
Sanchez, José Anto	Private	17, 18 and 19 Cons. Reg't., La. Militia
Sanchez, Joseph	Private	3 Reg't. (de la Ronde's), La. Mil.
Sanchez, Joseph Maria	Corporal	De Clouet's Reg't., La. Militia
Sanchez, Manuel	Private	17, 18 and 19 Cons. Reg't., La. Militia
Sanchez, Peter	Private	2 Batt'n. (Peire's), La. Vols. (Orig. under Sanchez, Pierre)
Sanchez, Pierre	Private	2 Batt'n. (Peire's), La. Vols.
Sanchez, Yqnacio	Sergeant	3 Reg't. (de la Ronde's), La. Mil.
Sancho, Damaico	Private	17, 18 and 19 Cons. Reg't., La. Mil. (Orig. under Sanche, Damasio)
Sanchos, Domacio	Private	17, 18 and 19 Cons. Reg't., La. Mil.
Sandeman, --	Private	4 Reg't. (Morgan's), La. Militia
Sanderfer, Henry	Private	17, 18 and 19 Cons. Reg't., La. Militia
Sanders, Cullen	Private	12 and 13 Cons. Reg't., La. Mil.
Sanders, J. A.	Private	1 Reg't. (Dejan's), La. Militia
Sanders, John W.	Private	16 Reg't. (Thompson's), La. Mil.
Sanderson, Thomas B.	Private	Capt. Wallace's Co., Boatmen, La. Vols.
Sandos, Isidor	Private	1 Batt'n. (Fortier's), La. Militia
Sandre, Jean	Fusilier-Private	5 Reg't. (La Branche's), La. Mil.
Sandreau, J.	Private	2 Reg't. (Cavelier's), La. Militia (Orig. under Landreaux, J.)
Sands, J. J.	Q. M.-Sergeant	4 Reg't. (Morgan's), La. Militia
Sanford, Thomas H.	Private	Capt. Ashley's Co., Mounted Riflemen, La. Militia
Sanglier, --	Private	Plauche's Batt'n., La. Militia
Sanguinett, Christian	Private	Captain Price's Co., La. Militia
Sannit, --	Lieut. & Qr. Mr.	Plauche's Batt'n., La. Militia (Orig. under Sainet, E.)
Sannon, --	Servant	1 Batt'n. (Fortier's), La. Militia
Sannon, --	Private	2 Batt'n. (D'Aquin's), La. Militia
Sanon, --	Servant	4 Reg't. (Morgan's), La. Militia
Sansan, Andrew	Private	17, 18 and 19 Cons. Reg't., La. Militia
Sansom, --	Private	1 Reg't. (Dejan's), La. Militia
Sansregret, Joseph	Private	Plauche's Batt'n., La. Militia
Sanstra, Pedro	Private	17, 18 and 19 Cons. Reg't., La. Militia
Santiago, James	Private	Capt. Thomas' Co., La. Militia
Santo, Angel	Private	17, 18 and 19 Cons. Reg't., La. Militia
Sapeda, Clement	Private	2 Batt'n. (Peire's), La. Vols. (Orig. under Sepeda, Clement)
Saphia, --	Sergeant	Plauche's Batt'n., La. Militia (Orig. under Sapia, Fois)
Sapia, Fois	Sergeant	Plauche's Batt'n., La. Militia
Sappington, Marcus	Private	Captain McNair's Co., Mounted Riflemen, La. Mil. (Orig. under Sappington, Mark)
Sappington, Mark	Private	Captain McNair's Co., Mounted Rifleman, La. Mil.
Sappington, Thomas	Private	Captain McNair's Co., Mounted Riflemen, La. Mil.
Sappington, Zephaniah	Private	Captain McNair's Co., Mounted Riflemen, La. Mil.
Saradas, Pe	Private	1 Reg't. (Dejan's), La. Militia
Saraphin, --	Sergeant	De Clouet's Reg't., La. Militia
Sarasin, Joseph	Sergeant	2 Batt'n. (D'Aquin's), La. Militia
Sarasin, Louis	Private	2 Batt'n. (D'Aquin's), La. Militia
Sarazin, Jean	Private	2 Reg't. (Cavelier's), La. Militia
Sarazin, John	Private	2 Reg't. (Cavelier's), La. Militia (Orig. under Sarazin, Jean)
Sarazin, Joseph	Sergeant	2 Batt'n. (D'Aquin's), La. Militia (Orig. under Sarasin, Joseph)
Sarbina, Jose	Private	17, 18 and 19 Cons. Reg't., La. Militia
Sardine, Manuel	Sergeant	3 Reg't. (de la Ronde's), La. Mil.
Sardine, Pierre	Private	3 Reg't. (de la Ronde's), La. Mil.
Sarestte, Baptiste	Private	1 Batt'n. (Fortier's), La. Militia (Orig. under Garcille, Baptiste)
Sarpy, Jean	Private	Capt. Trudeau's Troop of Horse, La. Militia
Sarpy, Lestant	Fusilier-Private	5 Reg't. (La Branche's), La. Mil.
Sashery, Louis	Sergeant	16 Reg't. (Thompson's), La. Mil. (Orig. under Cacherie, Louis)
Satchel, Joseph	Private	17, 18 and 19 Cons. Reg't., La. Mil. (Orig. under Latchel, Joseph)
Saterley, Elias	Private	10 and 20 Cons. Reg't., La. Mil.
Saterly, Elias	Private	10 and 20 Cons. Reg't., La. Mil. (Orig. under Saterley, Elias)
Satoon, James	Private	12 and 13 Cons. Reg't., La. Mil.
Satoon, Samuel	Private	12 and 13 Cons. Reg't., La. Mil.
Saturly, Elias	Private	10 and 20 Cons. Reg't., La. Mil. (Orig. under Saterley, Elias)
Sauche, Mcl	Private	17, 18 and 19 Cons. Reg't., La. Mil. (Orig. under Sauches, Manuel)
Saucier, Baptiste	Private	3 Reg't. (de la Ronde's), La. Mil.
Saucier, Descoleaux	Private	3 Reg't. (de la Ronde's), La. Mil.
Saucier, Julien	Private	3 Reg't. (de la Ronde's), La. Mil.
Saucier, Sefroy	Private	3 Reg't. (de la Ronde's), La. Mil.
Saudet, A.	Private	6 Reg't. (Landry's), La. Militia (Orig. under Gaudet, August)
Saudet, Valery	Private	6 Reg't. (Landry's), La. Militia (Orig. under Gaudet, Valey)
Saul, John	Private	Captain Beale's Co., Riflemen, La. Militia
Saul, William	Private	Captain Beale's Co., Riflemen, La. Militia
Saular, Lewis	Private	La. (War of 1812) See also 2 Batt'n. (Peire's), La. Vols.
Saular, Louis	Private	2 Batt'n. (Peire's), La. Vols. (Orig. under Soulard, Louis)
Sauler, Lindor	Private	De Clouet's Reg't., La. Militia (Orig. under Saulet, Lindor)
Saulet, --	Private	Capt. Trudeau's Troop of Horse, La. Militia
Saulet, B.	Private	4 Reg't. (Morgan's), La. Militia
Saulet, Lindor	Private	De Clouet's Reg't., La. Militia
Saunier, Baptiste	Private	17, 18 and 19 Cons. Reg't., La. Militia
Saustra, Pedro	Private	17, 18 and 19 Cons. Reg't., La. Mil. (Orig. under Sanstra, Pedro)
Sautelet, --	Private	1 Reg't. (Dejan's), La. Militia
Sautreau, Joseph	Private	6 Reg't. (Landry's), La. Militia (Orig. under Gautreau, Joseph)
Sautrelle, M.	Private	2 Reg't. (Cavelier's), La. Militia
Sauvage, Charles	Private	1 Batt'n. (Fortier's), La. Militia (Orig. under Sauvages, Charles)
Sauvages, Charles	Private	1 Batt'n. (Fortier's), La. Militia
Sauveur, Pierre	Private	2 Batt'n. (Peire's), La. Vols.
Sauvier, Francois	Private	De Clouet's Reg't., La. Militia
Savant, Pierre	Private	16 Reg't. (Thompson's), La. Mil.
Savarie, Bolton	Sergeant	2 Batt'n. (D'Aquin's), La. Militia
Savarin, Belton	Sergeant	2 Batt'n. (D'Aquin's), La. Militia
Savary, Joseph	Major	2 Batt'n. (D'Aquin's), La. Militia
Savary, William	Private	8 Reg't. (Meriam's), La. Militia
Savoice, Francois	Private	16 Reg't. (Thompson's), La. Mil.
Savoice, Francis fils	Private	16 Reg't. (Thompson's), La. Mil.
Savoice, John	Private	16 Reg't. (Thompson's), La. Mil.
Savoir, Cyprian	Private	Baker's Regiment, La. Militia
Savois, Hypolite	Private	De Clouet's Reg't., La. Militia
Savoix, Joseph	Private	7 Reg't. (Le Beuf's), La. Militia
Savoix, Paul	Sergeant	7 Reg't. (Le Beuf's), La. Militia
Savont, Pierre	Private	16 Reg't. (Thompson's), La. Mil. (Orig. under Savant, Pierre)
Savoy, John	Private	De Clouet's Reg't., La. Militia
Savoy, Joseph	Private	De Clouet's Reg't., La. Militia
Savoy, Joseph	Private	16 Reg't. (Thompson's), La. Mil. (Orig. under Savoye, Joseph)
Savoy, Simon	Sergeant	6 Reg't. (Landry's), La. Militia
Savoye, Joseph	Private	16 Reg't. (Thompson's), La. Mil.

Name	Rank	Unit
Savoye, Placide	Corporal	16 Reg't. (Thompson's), La. Mil.
Say, James	Private	17, 18 and 19 Cons. Reg't., La. Militia
Sayart, Nicolas	Private	Capt. Songy's Co., Marines, La. Vols. (Orig. under Sayard, Nclas)
Sayler, V.	Private	Plauche's Batt'n., La. Militia
Saylor, John	Private	4 Reg't. (Morgan's), La. Militia
Sayard, Nclas	Private	Capt. Songy's Co., Marines, La. Vols.
Says, James	Corporal	17, 18 and 19 Cons. Reg't., La. Militia
Scalin, H.	Private	8 Reg't. (Meriam's), La. Militia
Scalin, I.	Sergeant	8 Reg't. (Meriam's), La. Militia
Scamp, George	Corporal	17, 18 and 19 Cons. Reg't., La. Militia
Scapero, --	Servant	De Clouet's Reg't., La. Militia
Scarce, Thomas	Private	De Clouet's Reg't., La. Militia
Schaford, Antonia	Private	10 and 20 Cons. Reg't., La. Mil. (Orig. under Shefferd, Antoney)
Schaves, Samuel	Private	10 and 20 Cons. Reg't., La. Mil.
Schay, Thomas	Private	10 and 20 Cons. Reg't., La. Mil. (Orig. under Shay, Thomas)
Schier, William	Private	16 Reg't. (Thompson's), La. Mil. (Orig. under Schrier, William)
Schlatre, Joseph	Private	8 Reg't. (Meriam's), La. Militia
Schoff, George	Fusilier-Private	5 Reg't. (La Branche's), La. Mil.
Schrier, William	Private	16 Reg't. (Thompson's), La. Mil.
Schulz, Henry	Sergeant-Private	2 Batt'n. (Peire's), La. Vols. (Orig. under Schultz, Henry)
Schultz, Henry	Sergeant-Private	2 Batt'n. (Peire's), La. Vols. (See also 44 Regiment)
Schutz, Henry	Sergeant-Private	2 Batt'n. (Peire's), La. Vols. (Orig. under Schultz, Henry)
Scicknaid, Jacob	Private	6 Reg't. (Landry's), La. Militia
Scickaide, Adam	Corporal	6 Reg't. (Landry's), La. Militia (Orig. under Scicknaidre, Adam)
Scicknaide, Paul	Private	6 Reg't. (Landry's), La. Militia
Scicknaidre, Adam	Corporal	6 Reg't. (Landry's), La. Militia
Sciknaidre, J.	Private	6 Reg't. (Landry's), La. Militia (Orig. under Scicknaid, Jacob)
Sciknaidre, Paul	Private	6 Reg't. (Landry's), La. Militia (Orig. under Scicknaide, Paul)
Scioneau, A.	Private	6 Reg't. (Landry's), La. Militia
Scioneau, B.	Private	6 Reg't. (Landry's), La. Militia
Scioneau, Jn Bte	Private	6 Reg't. (Landry's), La. Militia
Scioneau, M.	Private	6 Reg't. (Landry's), La. Militia
Scioneau, Pre	Private	6 Reg't. (Landry's), La. Militia
Scipion, --	Private-Servant	4 Brigade (Flanjae's), La. Mil.
Scoggin, John	Private	10 and 20 Cons. Reg't., La. Mil.
Scott, Charles C.	1 Lieut. & Adjt.	17, 18 and 19 Cons. Reg't., La. Militia
Scott, Charles T.	1 Lieut. & Adjt.	17, 18 and 19 Cons. Reg't., La. Mil. (Orig. under Scott, Charles C.)
Scott, Hiram	Private	Capt. Collard's Co., La. Militia
Scott, Hugh	Private	8 Reg't. (Meriam's), La. Militia
Scott, I. S.	Sergeant	Plauche's Batt'n., La. Militia
Scott, James	Private	Captain Griffith's Co., Mounted Riflemen, La. Vols.
Scott, Jean	Private	Captain Lagan's Co., La. Vols.
Scott, Moses	Private	Captain Hughes' Co., Mounted Riflemen, La. Militia
Scott, Moses	1 Sergeant-Sgt.	Captain Price's Co., La. Militia
Scott, Robert	Private-Sergeant	Captain Griffith's Co., Mounted Riflemen, La. Vols.
Scott, Samuel	Private	10 and 20 Cons. Reg't., La. Mil.
Scott, Samuel E.	Sergeant	De Clouet's Reg't., La. Militia
Scott, Thomas	Private	Captain Griffith's Co., Mounted Riflemen, La. Vols.
Scott, Thomas W.	Captain	De Clouet's Reg't., La. Militia
Scott, William	Private	Capt. Wallace's Co., Boatmen, La. Vols.
Scott, William	Private	10 and 20 Cons. Reg't., La. Mil.
Scotte, William	Private	10 and 20 Cons. Reg't., La. Mil. (Orig. under Scott, William)
Scouffield, James	Private	Capt. Allen's Co., Artillerists, La. Vols. (Orig. under Cauffield, James)
Scouffleur, --	Corporal	Plauche's Batt'n., La. Militia
Scoufleur, --	Corporal	Plauche's Batt'n., La. Militia (Orig. under Scouffleur, --)
Scougall, Allen	Private	Capt. Allen's Co., Artillerists, La. Vols.
Scroggins, John	Private	10 and 20 Cons. Reg't., La. Mil. (Orig. under Scoggin, John)
Scoggs, William	Private	17, 18 and 19 Cons. Reg't., La. Militia
Scudder, Harley	Private	Capt. Allen's Co., Artillerists, La. Vols.
Sculfield, Samuel	Corporal	10 and 20 Cons. Reg't., La. Mil.
Seabourne, George	Private	Captain Sprigg's Co., Boatmen, La. Vols. (Orig. under Seybourne, George)
Seallears, Archy	Private	De Clouet's Reg't., La. Militia (Orig. under Seallers, Archy)
Seallers, Archy	Private	De Clouet's Reg't., La. Militia
Seatters, Archy	Private	De Clouet's Reg't., La. Militia (Orig. under Seallers, Archy)
Seckchnayter, H.	Private	5 Reg't. (La Branche's), La. Mil.
Seckchnayter, Joseph	Private	5 Reg't. (La Branche's), La. Mil.
Seckchnaytre, Hy	Private	5 Reg't. (La Branche's), La. Mil. (Orig. under Seckchnayter, Hy)
Seckchnaytre, Joseph	Private	5 Reg't. (La Branche's), La. Mil. (Orig. under Seckchnayter, Joseph)
Seeders, John	Private	10 and 20 Cons. Reg't., La. Mil.
Seegon, Jacob	Sergeant	10 and 20 Cons. Reg't., La. Mil. (Orig. under Seigar, Jacob)
Seeley, Guy	Private	Captain Price's Co., La. Militia
Seeley, William	Private	6 Reg't. (Landry's), La. Militia
Segar, Jacob	Sergeant	10 and 20 Cons. Reg't., La. Mil. (Orig. under Seigar, Jacob)
Segaur, Raphael	Private	Baker's Regiment, La. Militia
Seger, John	Private	19 Reg't., La. Militia
Seger, Joseph	Private	19 Reg't., La. Mil. (Orig. under Seger, John)
Seghars, fils	Private	2 Reg't. (Cavelier's), La. Militia
Seghars, pere	Private	2 Reg't. (Cavelier's), La. Militia
Segnoz, Battazar	Private	Baker's Regiment, La. Militia
Segond, C.	Sergeant	4 Reg't. (Morgan's), La. Militia
Segoue, I.	Private	2 Reg't. (Cavelier's), La. Militia (Orig. under Segour, I.)
Segour, Francis	Private	Baker's Regiment, La. Militia
Segour, I.	Private	2 Reg't. (Cavelier's), La. Militia
Seguin, Jacques	Musician	2 Batt'n. (Peire's), La. Vols.
Seguin, Joseph	Private-Corporal	2 Batt'n. (Peire's), La. Vols.
Seguin, Joseph	Musician	2 Batt'n. (Peire's), La. Vols. (Orig. under Seguin, Jacques)
Seguin, Pierre	Private	2 Batt'n. (Peire's), La. Vols.
Seigar, Jacob	Sergeant	10 and 20 Cons. Reg't., La. Mil.
Seigmund, John	Corporal-Sgt.	10 and 20 Cons. Reg't., La. Mil.
Seignouret, F.	Private	Plauche's Batt'n., La. Militia
Sejour, Louis	Quartermaster	2 Batt'n. (D'Aquin's), La. Militia
Sel, --	Private	Plauche's Batt'n., La. Militia
Sel, Francis	Corporal	2 Reg't. (Cavelier's), La. Militia
Sel, J. B.	Private	2 Reg't. (Cavelier's), La. Militia
Selcer, John	Private	10 and 20 Cons. Reg't., La. Mil. (Orig. under Sulcer, John)
Self, Jacob E.	Corporal	Captain Griffith's Co., Mounted Riflemen, La. Vols.
Self, Joseph	Private	12 and 13 Cons. Reg't., La. Mil.
Self, William	Private	12 and 13 Cons. Reg't., La. Mil.
Seller, Charles	Private	2 Batt'n. (Peire's), La. Vols.
Sellier, --	Private	Plauche's Batt'n., La. Militia
Selman, Louis	Private	16 Reg't. (Thompson's), La. Mil.
Selmen, Louis	Private	16 Reg't. (Thompson's), La. Mil. (Orig. under Selman, Louis)
Selvera, Enriquez	Private	17, 18 and 19 Cons. Reg't., La. Militia
Selvera, Jesus	Private	17, 18 and 19 Cons. Reg't., La. Militia
Semette, Antoine	Private	2 Reg't. (Cavelier's), La. Militia
Senecal, I.	Private	8 Reg't. (Meriam's), La. Militia
Seniker, Hubert	Private	Baker's Regiment, La. Militia
Sennet, Joseph	Private	Baker's Regiment, La. Militia
Sennette, Joseph	Private	Baker's Regiment, La. Militia (Orig. under Sennet, Joseph)
Sennott, Nicholas	Lieutenant	4 Reg't. (Morgan's), La. Militia (Orig. under Sinnott, Nicholas)
Senvir, --	Sgt.-Major-Sgt.	1 Reg't. (Dejan's), La. Militia (Orig. under Lenoir, --)
Sepeda, Clement	Private	2 Batt'n. (Peire's), La. Vols.
Sequin, Frs.	Captain	8 Reg't. (Meriam's), La. Militia

Name	Rank	Unit
Sequin, Jacques	Musician	2 Batt'n. (Peire's), La. Vols. (Orig. under Seguin, Jacques)
Sequin, Joseph	Private-Corporal	2 Batt'n. (Peire's), La. Vols. (Orig. under Seguin, Joseph)
Sequin, Pierre	Private	2 Batt'n. (Peire's), La. Vols. (Orig. under Seguin, Pierre)
Sequin, Pital	Private	De Clouet's Reg't., La. Militia (Orig. under Lejuine, Pital)
Seque, Pierre fils	Private	8 Reg't. (Meriam's), La. Militia
Serilla, --	Private	2 Reg't. (Cavelier's), La. Militia
Seringue, Ursin	Private	4 Reg't. (Morgan's), La. Militia
Sernean, Paul	Corporal	2 Batt'n. (D'Aquin's), La. Militia (Orig. under Servian, Paul)
Serpa, Antoine	2 Lieut.-Lieut.	3 Reg't. (de la Ronde's), La. Mil.
Serpa, Francois	Private	3 Reg't. (de la Ronde's), La. Mil.
Serpa, Joseph	Private	3 Reg't. (de la Ronde's), La. Mil.
Serpa, Raimond	Private	3 Reg't. (de la Ronde's), La. Mil.
Serret, A.	Private	8 Reg't. (Meriam's), La. Militia
Serret, C.	Private	8 Reg't. (Meriam's), La. Militia
Serrit, C.	Private	8 Reg't. (Meriam's), La. Militia (Orig. under Serret, C.)
Serry, Antoine	Private	Capt. Alpuente's Co., La. Mil. (Orig. under Pierry, Antoine)
Servass, T. L.	Private	1 Reg't. (Dejan's), La. Militia (Orig. under Servoss, T. L.)
Servian, Paul	Corporal	2 Batt'n. (D'Aquin's), La. Militia
Servin, Antoine	Private	Captain Lagan's Co., La. Vols.
Servoss, T. L.	Private	1 Reg't. (Dejan's), La. Militia
Sesperes, Fco	Private	17, 18 and 19 Cons. Reg't., La.
Setelly, J. Bte	Private	16 Reg't. (Thompson's), La. Mil. (Orig. under Stelly, Jean Bte)
Setelly, Michel	Private	16 Reg't. (Thompson's), La. Mil. (Orig. under Stelly, Michel)
Settoon, James	Private	12 and 13 Cons. Reg't., La. Mil. (Orig. under Satoon, James)
Settoon, Samuel	Private	12 and 13 Cons. Reg't., La. Mil. (Orig. under Satoon, Samuel)
Seummes, Estime	Private	6 Reg't. (Landry's), La. Militia
Sevan, Charles	Private	De Clouet's Reg't., La. Militia (Orig. under Sevin, Charles)
Sevan, Nicholas	Private	De Clouet's Reg't., La. Militia (Orig. under Sevin, Nicolas)
Sevare, Pierre	Private	2 Batt'n. (Peire's), La. Vols. (Orig. under Suard, Pierre)
Severain, Charles	Musician-Fife	2 Batt'n. (Peire's), La. Vols.
Severaint, Charles	Musician-Fife	2 Batt'n. (Peire's), La. Vols. (Orig. under Severain, Charles)
Severin, Charles	Musician-Fifer	2 Batt'n. (Peire's), La. Vols. (Orig. under Severain, Charles)
Severin, --	Fusilier-Private	5 Reg't. (La Branche's), La. Mil. (Orig. under Leverin, --)
Severo, John	Private	Capt. Thomas' Co., La. Militia
Severo, Joseph	Private	Capt. Thomas' Co., La. Militia
Sevin, Charles	Private	De Clouet's Reg't., La. Militia
Sevin, Guillaume	Private	Captain Hubbard's Mounted Co., La. Militia
Sevin, Nicolas	Private	De Clouet's Reg't., La. Militia
Sexnidre, Andre	Sergeant	3 Reg't. (de la Ronde's), La. Mil. (Orig. under Sexniedre, Andre)
Sexnidre, Antoine	Corporal	3 Reg't. (de la Ronde's), La. Mil. (Orig. under Sexniedre, Antoine)
Sexniedre, Andre	Sergeant	3 Reg't. (de la Ronde's), La. Mil.
Sexniedre, Antoine	Corporal	3 Reg't. (de la Ronde's), La. Mil.
Sexniedre, Ursin	Private	3 Reg't. (de la Ronde's), La. Mil.
Seybourne, George	Private	Captain Sprigg's Co., Boatmen, La. Vols.
Sgenit, Baltazar	Private	Baker's Regiment, La. Militia (Orig. under Segnoz, Baltazar)
Shaboard, William	Private	12 and 13 Cons. Reg't., La. Mil.
Shade, I.	Private	4 Reg't. (Morgan's), La. Militia
Shaford, Anthony	Private	10 and 20 Cons. Reg't., La. Mil. (Orig. under Shefferd, Antoney)
Shaner, Henry	Private	Captain Young's Co., Mounted Riflemen, La. Militia
Shannon, Charles	Private	17, 18 and 19 Cons. Reg't., La. Militia
Shannon, John	Private	16 Reg't. (Thompson's), La. Mil.
Shannon, Lindsey	Private	1 Reg't. (Dejan's), La. Mil.
Shannon, William	Private	De Clouet's Reg't., La. Militia
Sharbard, William	Private	12 and 13 Cons. Reg't., La. Mil. (Orig. under Shaboard, William)
Sharbino, Henry	Private	De Clouet's Reg't., La. Militia
Sharbino, Mitchel	Private	De Clouet's Reg't., La. Militia (Orig. under Shavino, Mitchell)
Sharp, Alvah	Private	La. (War of 1812)
Sharp, John	Private	Plauche's Batt'n., La. Militia
Sharp, Joseph	Private	11 Reg't. (Hickey's), La. Militia
Sharp, Joseph	Private	12 and 13 Cons. Reg't., La. Mil.
Sharp, William	Corporal	17, 18 and 19 Cons. Reg't., La. Militia
Sharpland, William	Private	12 and 13 Cons. Reg't., La. Mil.
Shattock, William	Private	16 Reg't. (Thompson's), La. Mil.
Shaumburg, Bartm	Col. aid de Camp	Gov. Claiborne and Staff, La. Mil.
Shaumburgh, Barthw	Col. aid de Camp	Gov. Claiborne and Staff, La. Mil. (Orig. under Shaumburg, Bartm)
Shaund, Francois	Private	10 and 20 Cons. Reg't., La. Mil. (Orig. under Shinna, Francois)
Shaver, David	Private	Baker's Regiment, La. Militia
Shaver, David	Private	10 and 20 Cons. Reg't., La. Mil.
Shaver, Shadrick	Private	10 and 20 Cons. Reg't., La. Mil. (Orig. under Chaven, Shadrach)
Shaves, Samuel	Private	10 and 20 Cons. Reg't., La. Mil. (Orig. under Schaves, Samuel)
Shavino, Henry	Private	De Clouet's Reg't., La. Militia (Orig. under Sharbino, Henry)
Shavino, Mitchell	Private	De Clouet's Reg't., La. Militia
Shaw, Daniel	Private	11 Reg't. (Hickey's), La. Mil.
Shaw, John C.	Private	De Clouet's Reg't., La. Militia
Shaw, Joseph	Private	La. (War of 1812)
Shaw, William	Corporal	Baker's Regiment, La. Militia
Shaw, Z.	Surgeon	2 Batt'n. (Peire's), La. Vols.
Shaw, Zacheus	Captain	4 Reg't. (Morgan's), La. Militia
Shay, Thomas	Private	10 and 20 Cons. Reg't., La. Mil.
Shefferd, Antoney	Private	10 and 20 Cons. Reg't., La. Mil.
Sheney, Fransway	Private	10 and 20 Cons. Reg't., La. Mil. (Orig. under Shinma, Francois)
Sheperd, --	Private	Plauche's Batt'n., La. Militia (Orig. under Shepherd, --)
Shepherd, --	Private	Plauche's Batt'n., La. Militia
Shepherd, R. D.	Private	Capt. Ogden's Co., Dragoons, La. Militia
Shereman, Samuel	Private	De Clouet's Reg't., La. Militia (See also 44 Reg't.)
Sherley, Richard	Private	Capt. Wallace's Co., Boatmen, La. Vols.
Sherwood, John	Private	Captain Dodge's Co., Mounted Riflemen, La. Militia
Sherwood, John	Private	Captain Henry's Co., Mounted Riflemen, La. Militia
Shief, --	Private	1 Reg't. (Dejan's), La. Militia (Orig. under Shiff, --)
Shields, T. C.	Corporal	1 Reg't. (Dejan's), La. Militia
Shiff, --	Private	1 Reg't. (Dejan's), La. Militia
Shine, John	Private	16 Reg't. (Thompson's), La. Mil.
Shinna, Francois	Private	10 and 20 Cons. Reg't., La. Mil.
Shiping, William	Private	Captain Sprigg's Co., Boatmen, La. Vols. (Orig. under Shipping, William)
Shipley, Thomas	Private-Sergeant	De Clouet's Reg't., La. Militia
Shipping, William	Private	Captain Sprigg's Co., Boatmen, La. Vols.
Shiras, P.	Sergeant	1 Reg't. (Dejan's), La. Militia (See also 44 La. Reg't.)
Shirley, John	Private	Captain Hughes' Co., Mounted Riflemen, La. Mil.
Shirley, Richard	Private	Capt. Wallace's Co., Boatmen, La. Vols. (Orig. under Sherley, Richard)
Shoat, David	Private	16 Reg't. (Thompson's), La. Mil.
Shomberg, --	Private	Plauche's Batt'n., La. Militia
Short, Abraham	Private	12 and 13 Cons. Reg't., La. Mil.
Short, Adam	Private	Captain Price's Co., La. Militia
Short, Davis	Private	12 and 13 Cons. Reg't., La. Mil.
Short, Odam	Private	Captain Price's Co., La. Militia (Orig. under Short, Adam)
Short, Simon	Private	De Clouet's Reg't., La. Militia
Shuff, Ely	Corporal	16 Reg't. (Thompson's), La. Mil.
Shultz, Henry	Sergeant	2 Batt'n. (Peire's), La. Vols. (Orig. under Schultz, Henry)
Sibert, Christian	Private	17, 18 and 19 Cons. Reg't., La. Militia
Sibley, Henry R.	Captain	17, 18 and 19 Cons. Reg't., La. Militia

Name	Rank	Unit
Sibley, R. H.	Captain	17, 18 and 19 Cons. Reg't., La. Militia (Orig. under Sibley, Henry R.)
Sicard, Bartheleme	Private	Captain Lagan's Co., La. Vols.
Sicard, Christophe	Private	Captain Lagan's Co., La. Vols. (Orig. under Picard, Christophe)
Sicard, Marcelin	Private	De Clouet's Reg't., La. Militia
Sicard, Rosamond	Private	De Clouet's Reg't., La. Militia
Siddick, John B.	Private	De Clouet's Reg't., La. Militia (Orig. under Sidick, John B.)
Sideck, Peter	Private	Baker's Regiment, La. Militia
Sideik, Peter	Private	Baker's Regiment, La. Militia (Orig. under Sideck, Peter)
Sides, Jacob	Private	10 and 20 Cons. Reg't., La. Mil.
Sides, John	Private	8 Reg't. (Meriam's), La. Militia
Sidick, John B.	Private	De Clouet's Reg't., La. Militia
Sidot, Pierre	1 Lieutenant	Capt. Chaudurier's Co., Artificers, Art'y., La. Vols. (Orig. under Cidot, Pierre)
Sierra, Mt.	Private	2 Reg't. (Cavelier's), La. Militia (Orig. under Sierras, Me)
Sierras, Me	Private	2 Reg't. (Cavelier's), La. Militia
Siffet, Pre	Private	Plauche's Batt'n., La. Militia (Orig. under Sifflet, Jean)
Sifflet, Jean	Private	Plauche's Batt'n., La. Militia
Sigins, Louis	Private	8 Reg't. (Meriam's), La. Militia
Sigmund, John	Corporal-Sgt.	10 and 20 Cons. Reg't., La. Mil. (Orig. under Seigmund, John)
Silliman, William	Private	10 and 20 Cons. Reg't., La. Mil.
Sillimon, William	Private	10 and 20 Cons. Reg't., La. Mil. (Orig. under Silliman, William)
Silly, Ane	Private	5 Reg't. (La Branche's), La. Militia
Silva, --	Private	4 Reg't. (Morgan's), La. Militia
Silva, Ignacio	Private	2 Batt'n. (Peire's), La. Vols. (Orig. under Sylva, Ignacio)
Silve, Alexis	Private	3 Reg't. (de la Ronde's), La. Mil.
Silve, Jean	Private	3 Reg't. (de la Ronde's), La. Mil.
Silvest, Jh.	Private	6 Reg't. (Landry's), La. Militia
Silvest, Joseph	Corporal	1 Batt'n. (Fortier's), La. Militia
Simeneau, Lubin	Private	De Clouet's Reg't., La. Militia (Orig. under Simineau, Lubin)
Simes, William	Private	12 and 13 Cons. Reg't., La. Mil. (Orig. under Simms, William)
Similien, --	Private	Plauche's Batt'n., La. Militia
Similien, --	Private	2 Batt'n. (D'Aquin's), La. Militia
Similieu, --	Private	Plauche's Batt'n., La. Militia (Orig. under Similien, --)
Simineau, Aureux	Private	De Clouet's Reg't., La. Militia (Orig. under Simoneau, Arieux)
Simineau, Lubin	Private	De Clouet's Reg't., La. Militia
Simmeau, Aurex	Private	De Clouet's Reg't., La. Militia (Orig. under Simoneau, Arieux)
Simmons, James	Private	10 and 20 Cons. Reg't., La. Mil.
Simmons, Joel	Private	12 and 13 Cons. Reg't., La. Mil.
Simmons, John	Private	12 and 13 Cons. Reg't., La. Mil.
Simmons, Robert M.	Private	12 and 13 Cons. Reg't., La. Mil.
Simmons, Silas	Private	10 and 20 Cons. Reg't., La. Mil.
Simmons, William	Private	10 and 20 Cons. Reg't., La. Mil.
Simmons, William	Private	12 and 13 Cons. Reg't., La. Mil.
Simms, Joel	Private	De Clouet's Reg't., La. Militia (Orig. under Sims, Joel)
Simms, John	Private	12 and 13 Cons. Reg't., La. Mil.
Simms, Phillip	Corporal	12 and 13 Cons. Reg't., La. Mil.
Simms, Ralph	Private	Capt. Thomas' Co., La. Militia
Simms, William	Private	12 and 13 Cons. Reg't., La. Mil.
Simon, Belony	Private	De Clouet's Reg't., La. Militia
Simon, Charles	Private	De Clouet's Reg't., La. Militia
Simon, Jean	Private	De Clouet's Reg't., La. Militia
Simon, Jean Baptiste	Private	2 Reg't. (Cavelier's), La. Militia
Simon, John B.	Private	17, 18 and 19 Cons. Reg't., La. Militia
Simon, Louis	Private	De Clouet's Reg't., La. Militia
Simon, Louis	Captain	1 Batt'n. (Fortier's), La. Militia
Simon, Louis	Private	6 Reg't. (Landry's), La. Militia
Simoneau, Arieux	Private	De Clouet's Reg't., La. Militia
Simoneau, Eugene	Private	Captain Hubbard's Mounted Co., La. Militia
Simoneau, Joseph	Sergeant	Captain Hubbard's Mounted Co., La. Militia
Simoneau, Lubin	Private	De Clouet's Reg't., La. Militia (Orig. under Simineau, Lubin)
Simoneau, Simon	Private	7 Reg't. (Le Beuf's), La. Militia
Simons, Peter	Sergeant	17, 18 and 19 Cons. Reg't., La. Militia
Simpe, Jr.	Private	4 Reg't. (Morgan's), La. Militia
Simpe, Sr.	Private	4 Reg't. (Morgan's), La. Militia
Simpson, Andrew B.	Private	10 and 20 Cons. Reg't., La. Mil.
Simpson, Frederick	Private	17, 18 and 19 Cons. Reg't., La. Militia
Simpson, George	Captain	1 Reg't. (Dejan's), La. Militia
Simpson, Henry	Private	16 Reg't. (Thompson's), La. Mil.
Simpson, James	Private	16 Reg't. (Thompson's), La. Mil.
Simpson, James	Private	17, 18 and 19 Cons. Reg't., La. Militia
Simpson, John	Private	Captain Ramsey's Co., Mounted Riflemen, La. Militia
Simpson, John	Private	16 Reg't. (Thompson's), La. Mil.
Simpson, S.	Private	1 Reg't. (Dejan's), La. Militia
Simpson, Samuel M.	Private	10 and 20 Cons. Reg't., La. Mil.
Simpson, Thomas	Sergeant-Private	Capt. Allen's Co., Artillerists, La. Vols.
Simpson, Thomas P.	Sergeant-Pvt.	10 and 20 Cons. Reg't., La. Mil.
Sims, Benjamin	Private	Captain Griffith's Co., Mounted Riflemen, La. Vols.
Sims, Joel	Private	De Clouet's Reg't., La. Militia
Sims, Samuel	Private	De Clouet's Reg't., La. Militia
Sims, William	Private	Captain Griffith's Co., Mounted Riflemen, La. Vols.
Simson, Stephen	Private	De Clouet's Reg't., La. Militia (Orig. under Stinson, Stephen)
Sinchle, John	Private	De Clouet's Reg't., La. Militia
Sinckler, John	Lieutenant	Capt. Callaway's Co., Mounted Riflemen, La. Mil. (Orig. under Sinclare, John)
Sinclair, Alexander	Private	Capt. Callaway's Co., Mounted Riflemen, La. Militia
Sinclair, John	Private	De Clouet's Reg't., La. Militia
Sinclare, John	Lieutenant	Capt. Callaway's Co., Mounted Riflemen, La. Militia
Sinclear, John	Private	De Clouet's Reg't., La. Militia (Orig. under Sinclair, John)
Sincler, John	Lieutenant	Capt. Callaway's Co., Mounted Riflemen, La. Mil. (Orig. under Sinclare, John)
Sindos, Jr.	Private	4 Reg't. (Morgan's), La. Militia
Sindos, Sr.	Private	4 Reg't. (Morgan's), La. Militia
Sinette, Antoine	Private	2 Reg't. (Cavelier's), La. Militia (Orig. under Semette, Antoine)
Singltary, Eliza	Private	10 and 20 Cons. Reg't., La. Mil. (Orig. under Singleterry, Elisha)
Singleterry, Elisha	Private	10 and 20 Cons. Reg't., La. Mil.
Singleton, Elisha	Private	10 and 20 Cons. Reg't., La. Mil. (Orig. under Singleterry, Elisha)
Singleton, George	Private	Baker's Regiment, La. Militia
Singleton, Hambrick	Private	16 Reg't. (Thompson's), La. Mil.
Singleton, John W.	Private	De Clouet's Reg't., La. Militia
Singleton, Owen	Private	Baker's Regiment, La. Militia
Singleton, Robert	2 Lieutenant	12 and 13 Cons. Reg't., La. Mil.
Singleton, T. W.	Private	De Clouet's Reg't., La. Militia (Orig. under Singleton, John W.)
Singletory, Elisha	Private	10 and 20 Cons. Reg't., La. Mil. (Orig. under Singleterry, Elisha)
Sinkle, John	Private	De Clouet's Reg't., La. Militia (Orig. under Sinchle, John)
Sinks, Jacob	Private	10 and 20 Cons. Reg't., La. Mil.
Sinnote, Nicholas	Lieutenant	4 Reg't. (Morgan's), La. Militia (Orig. under Sinnott, Nicholas)
Sinnott, Nicholas	1 Lieutenant	4 Reg't. (Morgan's), La. Militia
Sipida, Clemente	Private	La. (War of 1812) - See also 2 Batt'n. (Peire's), La. Vols.
Sipida, Clemente	Private	2 Batt'n. (Peire's), La. Vols. (Orig. under Sepeda, Clement)
Sique, Achilles	Private	8 Reg't. (Meriam's), La. Militia
Sique, Laurent	Private	8 Reg't. (Meriam's), La. Militia
Sisset, Pierre	Private	Plauche's Batt'n., La. Militia
Sittiere, T.	Corporal	1 Reg't. (Dejan's), La. Militia (Orig. under Littiere, Jn)
Sivernon, Jean	Artificer	Capt. Chaudurier's Co., Artificers, Art'y., La. Vols. (Orig. under Livernon, Jean)
Sivil, George	Private	Captain Hubbard's Mounted Co., La. Militia
Skegs, John	Private	17, 18 and 19 Cons. Reg't., La. Militia

Name	Rank	Unit
Skeilfield, Samuel	Corporal	10 and 20 Cons. Reg't., La. Mil. (Orig. under Sculfield, Samuel)
Skinner, Francis	Private	Captain Beale's Co., Riflemen, La. Militia
Skinner, Jesse	Private	10 and 20 Cons. Reg't., La. Mil.
Skinner, Reddin	Private	10 and 20 Cons. Reg't., La. Mil.
Slagle, Henry	Private	Captain Young's Co., Mounted Riflemen, La. Militia
Slater, Henry	Private	17, 18 and 19 Cons. Reg't., La. Militia
Slaysman, George	Private	Captain Sprigg's Co., Boatmen, La. Vols.
Sleysman, George	Private	Captain Sprigg's Co., Boatmen, La. Vols. (Orig. under Slaysman, George)
Sloan, Thomas	Private	La. (War of 1812) - See also 1 Batt'n. (Henry's), U. S. Vols.
Sloane, Lemuel	Private	16 Reg't. (Thompson's), La. Mil. (Orig. under Stone, Samuel)
Slokim, William	Private	12 and 13 Cons. Reg't., La. Mil.
Slokum, William	Private	12 and 13 Cons. Reg't., La. Mil. (Orig. under Slokim, William)
Slone, David	Private	16 Reg't. (Thompson's), La. Mil.
Slone, Hiram	Private	16 Reg't. (Thompson's), La. Mil.
Slone, John	Private	Captain Hughes' Co., Mounted Riflemen, La. Militia
Slone, Samuel D.	Private	Captain Hughes' Co., Mounted Riflemen, La. Militia
Slone, Thomas	Private	16 Reg't. (Thompson's), La. Mil.
Sloughl, Jacob	Private	Captain Young's Co., Mounted Riflemen, La. Mil. (Orig. under Staght, Jacob)
Slum, Elly	Private	17, 18 and 19 Cons. Reg't., La. Militia
Smelser, Michael	Quartermaster-Ensig	12 and 13 Cons. Reg't., La. Mil. (Orig. under Smelsor, Michael)
Smelsor, Michael	Quartermaster-Ensign	12 and 13 Cons. Reg't., La. Mil.
Smith, --	Private	De Clouet's Reg't., La. Militia (See also 44 Reg't. Infy.)
Smith, Abraham	Private	De Clouet's Reg't., La. Militia
Smith, A. H.	Private	Captain Beale's Co., Riflemen, La. Militia
Smith, Andrew	Private	12 and 13 Cons. Reg't., La. Mil.
Smith, Archibald	Private	Baker's Regiment, La. Militia
Smith, Bailey	Private	12 and 13 Cons. Reg't., La. Mil.
Smith, B.	Private	Captain Sprigg's Co., Boatmen, La. Vols.
Smith, Bazil	Q.M.-Sergeant	Detachment Field and Staff Officers, 4 Brigade, La. Militia
Smith, C. B.	Private	10 and 20 Cons. Reg't., La. Mil.
Smith, Charles	Private	12 and 13 Cons. Reg't., La. Mil.
Smith, Charles	Private	19 Regiment, La. Militia
Smith, Daniel	Sergeant	Capt. Thomas' Co., La. Militia
Smith, Daniel D.	Private	De Clouet's Reg't., La. Militia
Smith, D. L.	1 Sergeant-Sgt.	8 Reg't. (Meriam's), La. Militia
Smith, E. B.	Private	20 Regiment, La. Militia
Smith, Edward	Private	Captain Dodge's Co., Mounted Riflemen, La. Militia
Smith, Edward	Private	Captain Henry's Co., Mounted Riflemen, La. Militia
Smith, Elisha P.	Private	Capt. Allen's Co., Artillerists, La. Vols.
Smith, Ephraim	Private	12 and 13 Cons. Reg't., La. Mil.
Smith, Frederick	Private	De Clouet's Reg't., La. Militia
Smith, George	Private	Capt. Allen's Co., Artillerists, La. Vols.
Smith, George	Private	De Clouet's Reg't., La. Militia
Smith, George	Private	16 Reg't. (Thompson's), La. Mil.
Smith, George W.	Private	Baker's Regiment, La. Militia
Smith, Henry	Private	Captain McNair's Co., Mounted Riflemen, La. Militia
Smith, Henry	Private	2 Reg't. (Cavelier's), La. Militia
Smith, Hiram	Private	16 Reg't. (Thompson's), La. Mil.
Smith, Horace	Private	10 and 20 Cons. Reg't., La. Mil.
Smith, Horatio	Private	10 and 20 Cons. Reg't., La. Mil. (Orig. under Smith, Horace)
Smith, I. W.	Private	Captain Beale's Co., Riflemen, La. Militia
Smith, James	Private	Capt. Alpuente's Co., La. Mil.
Smith, James	Private	Sergeant Hog's Detachment, La. Vols.
Smith, James W.	Private	La. (War of 1812)
Smith, John	Corporal	Baker's Regiment, La. Militia
Smith, John	Private	Captain Sprigg's Co., Boatmen, La. Vols.
Smith, John	Sergeant	1 Reg't. (Dejan's), La. Militia
Smith, John	Private	2 Reg't. (Cavelier's), La. Militia
Smith, John	Corporal	10 and 20 Cons. Reg't., La. Mil.
Smith, John	Private	10 and 20 Cons. Reg't., La. Mil.
Smith, John	Private	12 and 13 Cons. Reg't., La. Mil.
Smith, John	Private	12 and 13 Cons. Reg't., La. Mil.
Smith, John	Corporal	16 Reg't. (Thompson's), La. Mil.
Smith, John	Corporal	17, 18 and 19 Cons. Reg't., La. Militia
Smith, John H. H.	Corporal	16 Reg't. (Thompson's), La. Mil.
Smith, Jonathan	Private	Baker's Regiment, La. Militia
Smith, Jonathan	Private	16 Reg't. (Thompson's), La. Mil.
Smith, Joseph	Private	20 Regiment, La. Militia
Smith, Joseph	Private	10 and 20 Cons. Reg't., La. Mil.
Smith, Joseph	Private	10 and 20 Cons. Reg't., La. Mil.
Smith, Joseph	Private	12 and 13 Cons. Reg't., La. Mil.
Smith, Julius	Private	Baker's Regiment, La. Militia
Smith, Labin	Private	10 and 20 Cons. Reg't., La. Mil.
Smith, Luben	Private	10 and 20 Cons. Reg't., La. Mil. (Orig. under Smith, Labin)
Smith, Marshall	Private	10 and 20 Cons. Reg't., La. Mil.
Smith, Moses	Private	De Clouet's Reg't., La. Militia
Smith, Philip	Private	16 Reg't. (Thompson's), La. Mil.
Smith, Preston	Private	10 and 20 Cons. Reg't., La. Mil.
Smith, R.	Private	Plauche's Batt'n., La. Militia
Smith, Richard	Private	1 Batt'n. (Fortier's), La. Militia
Smith, Robert	Private	Captain Dodge's Co., Mounted Riflemen, La. Militia
Smith, Robert	Private	Captain Henry's Co., Mounted Riflemen, La. Militia
Smith, Robert	Private	2 Batt'n. (Peire's), La. Vols.
Smith, Samuel	Private	10 Regiment, La. Militia
Smith, Silas	Sergeant	De Clouet's Reg't., La. Militia
Smith, Thomas	Private	Capt. Callaway's Co., Cavalry, La. Militia
Smith, Thomas	Private	12 and 13 Cons. Reg't., La. Mil.
Smith, Tobias	Private	10 and 20 Cons. Reg't., La. Mil.
Smith, Wiley	Private	17, 18 and 19 Cons. Reg't., La. Militia
Smith, William	Private	Baker's Regiment, La. Militia
Smith, William	Private	Capt. Callaway's Co., Cavalry, La. Militia
Smith, William	Corporal	Capt. Collard's Co., La. Militia
Smith, William	Private	De Clouet's Reg't., La. Militia
Smith, William	Private	De Clouet's Reg't., La. Militia
Smith, William	Corporal	4 Reg't. (Morgan's), La. Militia
Smith, William	Private	10 and 20 Cons. Reg't., La. Mil.
Smith, William	Private	12 and 13 Cons. Reg't., La. Mil.
Smith, William	Private	16 Reg't. (Thompson's), La. Mil.
Smith, William	Private	17, 18 and 19 Cons. Reg't., La. Militia
Smith, William B.	Private	Capt. Thomas' Co., La. Militia
Smith, William N.	1 Lieutenant	12 and 13 Cons. Reg't., La. Mil.
Smith, Wilmot	Corporal	4 Reg't. (Morgan's), La. Militia
Smyth, Bailey	Private	12 and 13 Cons. Reg't., La. Mil. (Orig. under Smith, Bailey)
Snead, John	Corporal	Capt. Allen's Co., Artillerists, La. Vols.
Snider, Jesse E.	Private	2 Batt'n. (Peire's), La. Vols. (Orig. under Snyder, Jesse E.)
Snider, John	Corporal	Captain Sprigg's Co., Boatmen, La. Vols.
Snipes, Dempsey	Private	Baker's Regiment, La. Militia
Snee, John	Private	2 Batt'n. (Peire's), La. Vols.
Snoddy, Andrew	Private	Captain Sprigg's Co., Boatmen, La. Vols.
Snoddy, John	Private	De Clouet's Reg't., La. Militia
Snoddy, Moses	Private	17, 18 and 19 Cons. Reg't., La. Militia
Snow, E. G.	Sergeant	Baker's Regiment, La. Militia
Snyder, Jesse E.	Private	2 Batt'n. (Peire's), La. Vols.
Soarez, Antonio	Private	2 Batt'n. (Peire's), La. Vols. (Orig. under Suarez, Anthony)
Socier, Francis	Private	17, 18 and 19 Cons. Reg't., La. Militia
Socier, Joseph	Private	16 Reg't. (Thompson's), La. Mil.
Socier, Louis	Private	17, 18 and 19 Cons. Reg't., La. Militia

Name	Rank	Unit
Sodon, John	Private	12 and 13 Cons. Reg't., La. Mil.
Soillean, Charles	Private	16 Reg't. (Thompson's), La. Mil.
Soillean, Etienne	Private	16 Reg't. (Thompson's), La. Mil.
Soillean, Henry	Private	16 Reg't. (Thompson's), La. Mil.
Soillean, Louis	Private	16 Reg't. (Thompson's), La. Mil.
Soiripe, Bte	Private	6 Reg't. (Landry's), La. Militia (Orig. under Soiresse, Bte)
Soiresse, Bte	Private	6 Reg't. (Landry's), La. Militia
Sommero, Jean	Private	6 Reg't. (Landry's), La. Militia
Somperat, Ate	Private	6 Reg't. (Landry's), La. Militia
Solesse, Joseph	Private	6 Reg't. (Landry's), La. Militia (Orig. under Sotesse, Joseph)
Solibela, Joseph	1 Lieutenant	17, 18 and 19 Cons. Reg't., La. Militia
Solibellas, Joseph M.	1 Lieutenant	17, 18 and 19 Cons. Reg't., La. Mil. (Orig. under Solibela, Joseph)
Solis, Andri	Private	17, 18 and 19 Cons. Reg't., La. Militia
Solis, Manuel	Private	3 Reg't. (de la Ronde's), La. Mil.
Sollers, Isaac	Sergeant	De Clouet's Reg't., La. Militia
Sollet, --	Private	Plauche's Batt'n., La. Militia
Sollis, Andre	Private	17, 18 and 19 Cons. Reg't., La. Mil. (Orig. under Solis, Andre)
Songy, Th	Captain	Capt. Songy's Co., Marines, La. Vols.
Soniac, Ursin	Private	4 Reg't. (Morgan's), La. Militia
Soniat, Pierre	Private	Capt. Trudeau's Troop of Horse, La. Militia
Sonier, Bte	Private	De Clouet's Reg't., La. Militia
Sonier, Louis	Private	16 Reg't. (Thompson's), La. Mil. (Orig. under Sonnier, Louis)
Sonier, Lufroy	Corporal	De Clouet's Reg't., La. Militia
Sonier, Pierre	Private	De Clouet's Reg't., La. Militia
Sonier, Placide	Private	Le Clouet's Reg't., La. Militia
Sonier, Syrile	Corporal	De Clouet's Reg't., La. Militia
Sonnier, Louis	Private	16 Reg't. (Thompson's), La. Mil.
Sonnier, Placide	Private	De Clouet's Reg't., La. Militia (Orig. under Sonier, Placide)
Sonnier, Syrile	Corporal	De Clouet's Reg't., La. Militia
Sorillia, --	Private	2 Reg't. (Cavelier's), La. Militia (Orig. under Serilla, --)
Sorita, Jos.	Private	De Clouet's Reg't., La. Militia (Orig. under Sourita, Joseph)
Sorrel, Joseph	Private	De Clouet's Reg't., La. Militia
Sorton, Henry	Private	Capt. Alpuente's Co., La. Mil.
Sotesse, Joseph	Private	6 Reg't. (Landry's), La. Militia
Sottel, --	Private	Plauche's Batt'n., La. Militia (Orig. under Sollet, --)
Souarez, Antonio	Private	2 Batt'n. (Peire's), La. Vols. (Orig. under Suarez, Anthony)
Souarez, Joseph	1 Sergeant-Sgt.	3 Reg't. (de la Ronde's), La. Mil. (Orig. under Suarez, Josef)
Soubercage, Ane	Sergeant	Plauche's Batt'n., La. Militia
Soubercase, Fs	Private	1 Reg't. (Dejan's), La. Militia
Soubercase, F.	Mily. Secretary	Gov. Claiborne and Staff, La. Mil.
Souffier, --	Private	De Clouet's Reg't., La. Militia
Soulan, Louis	Private	3 Reg't. (de la Ronde's), La. Mil.
Soular, Louis	Private	2 Batt'n. (Peire's), La. Vols. (Orig. under Soulard, Louis)
Soulard, Louis	Private	2 Batt'n. (Peire's), La. Vols.
Soulemond, Lami	Private	2 Reg't. (Cavelier's), La. Militia
Souler, Lindor	Private	De Clouet's Reg't., La. Militia (Orig. under Saulet, Lindor)
Soulit, --	Fifer	2 Batt'n. (D'Aquin's), La. Militia
Sourita, Jas.	Private	De Clouet's Reg't., La. Militia (Orig. under Sourita, Joseph)
Sourita, Joseph	Private	De Clouet's Reg't., La. Militia
Souritae, F.	Private	De Clouet's Reg't., La. Militia (Orig. under Sourita, Joseph)
Sournesey, Joseph	Private	Capt. Songy's Co., Marines, La. Vols. (Orig. under Fourney, Jn)
Souvenir, --	Servant	Plauche's Batt'n., La. Militia
Sovier, Fran	Private	De Clouet's Reg't., La. Militia (Orig. under Sanvier, Francois)
Spatt, Samuel	Private	17, 18 and 19 Cons. Reg't., La. Mil. (Orig. under Spratt, Samuel)
Spear, Edward	Private	Captain Ramsey's Co., Mounted Riflemen, La. Militia
Spears, Henry L.	Private	10 and 20 Cons. Reg't., La. Mil.
Spears, Henry Q.	Private	10 and 20 Cons. Reg't., La. Mil. (Orig. under Spears, Henry L.)
Spears, Joshua	Private	De Clouet's Reg't., La. Militia (See also U. S. Army)
Speers, Abraham	Private	12 and 13 Cons. Reg't., La. Mil.
Spell, Aaron	Private-Corporal	12 and 13 Cons. Reg't., La. Mil.
Spell, John	Private	12 and 13 Cons. Reg't., La. Mil.
Spell, Sanders	Adjutant	12 and 13 Cons. Reg't., La. Mil.
Spell, Thomas Jr.	Private	12 and 13 Cons. Reg't., La. Mil.
Spell, Thomas Sr.	Private	12 and 13 Cons. Reg't., La. Mil.
Spellers, Micajah	Private	12 and 13 Cons. Reg't., La. Mil. (Orig. under Spillars, Micajah)
Spencer, Alexander	Private	Capt. Ashley's Co., Mounted Riflemen, La. Militia
Spencer, Luther	1 Sergeant	6 Reg't. (Landry's), La. Militia
Spencer, Thomas	Sergeant	Capt. Van Bibber's Co., La. Mil.
Spencer, William	Private	Capt. Ashley's Co., Mounted Riflemen, La. Militia
Spikes, Leoman	Private	12 and 13 Cons. Reg't., La. Mil.
Spillars, John	Private	12 and 13 Cons. Reg't., La. Mil.
Spillars, Micajah	Private	12 and 13 Cons. Reg't., La. Mil.
Spiller, Blassingame	Private	De Clouet's Reg't., La. Militia
Spiller, George	Ensign	De Clouet's Reg't., La. Militia
Spiller, Jeremiah	Private	Capt. Alpuente's Co., La. Mil.
Spiller, Jeremiah	Private	4 Reg't. (Morgan's), La. Militia
Spiller, John	Private	Capt. Alpuente's Co., La. Mil.
Spillers, George	Ensign	De Clouet's Reg't., La. Militia (Orig. under Spiller, George)
Spinks, William	Private	12 and 13 Cons. Reg't., La. Mil.
Spinks, Zachariah	Private	12 and 13 Cons. Reg't., La. Mil.
Splan, Thomas	Private	10 and 20 Cons. Reg't., La. Mil.
Splan, William	Private	De Clouet's Reg't., La. Militia
Spragins, Samuel M.	Private	8 Reg't. (Meriam's), La. Militia
Spratt, Samuel	Private	17, 18 and 19 Cons. Reg't., La. Militia
Sprigg, Archibald	Sergeant	Captain Sprigg's Co., Boatmen, La. Vols.
Sprigg, Horatio	1 Lieut. & Q.M.	17, 18 and 19 Cons. Reg't., La. Militia
Sprigg, Robert	Captain	Captain Sprigg's Co., Boatmen, La. Vols.
Spruel, John	Private	10 Regiment, La. Militia
Spruel, Samuel	Private	10 and 20 Cons. Reg't., La. Mil. (Orig. under Spurvil, Samuel)
Spurvil, Samuel	Private	10 and 20 Cons. Reg't., La. Mil.
Spuvill, Samuel	Private	10 and 20 Cons. Reg't., La. Mil. (Orig. under Spurvil, Samuel)
Squire, John	Private	Captain Price's Co., La. Militia
Squires, William	Private	17, 18 and 19 Cons. Reg't., La. Militia
Squires, William P.	Private	17, 18 and 19 Cons. Reg't., La. Militia
Squires, Wilson A.	Private	17, 18 and 19 Cons. Reg't., La. Militia
Squires, Wilson R.	Private	17, 18 and 19 Cons. Reg't., La. Mil. (Orig. under Squires, Wilson A.)
Stacy, Robert	Private	8 Reg't. (Meriam's), La. Militia
Stafford, Ethelred	Private	De Clouet's Reg't., La. Militia
Stafford, Leroy	Private	17, 18 and 19 Cons. Reg't., La. Mil.
Stafford, Stephen	Sergeant	12 and 13 Cons. Reg't., La. Mil.
Stag, Henry	Private	De Clouet's Reg't., La. Militia
Staght, Jacob	Private	Captain Young's Co., Mounted Riflemen, La. Militia
Stak, I. G.	Private	2 Batt'n. (Peire's), La. Vols. (Orig. under Stat, I. G.)
Stakes, Solomon	Private	10 and 20 Cons. Reg't., La. Mil.
Stallard, Mc Clenahan	Private	De Clouet's Reg't., La. Militia
St Aman, --	Private	Plauche's Batt'n., La. Militia (Orig. under St Amand)
St Amand, --	Private	Plauche's Batt'n., La. Militia
St Amand, Bte son	Fusilier-Private	5 Reg't. (La Branche's), La. Mil.
St Amand, Fay	Private	5 Reg't. (La Branche's), La. Mil.
St Amand, Hilaire	Private	5 Reg't. (La Branche's), La. Mil.
St Amand, Joseph	Fusilier-Private	5 Reg't. (La Branche's), La. Mil.
St Amand, Onesifore	Fus.-Private	5 Reg't. (La Branche's), La. Mil.
St Amand, Sylvain	Fusilier-Private	5 Reg't. (La Branche's), La. Mil.
St Amand, Voltaire	Private	1 Batt'n. (Fortier's), La. Militia
St Amant, --	Private	Plauche's Batt'n., La. Militia (Orig. under St Amand, --)
St Amant, A.	Major	4 Reg't. (Morgan's), La. Militia
St Amant, Day	Private	5 Reg't. (La Branche's), La. Mil. (Orig. under St Amand, Day)

Name	Rank	Unit
St Amant, Hilaire	Private	5 Reg't. (La Branche's), La. Mil. (Orig. under St Amand, Hilaire)
St Amant, Ls	Private	1 Batt'n. (Fortier's), La. Militia
St Amant, M.	Sergeant	4 Reg't. (Morgan's), La. Militia
St. Amant, Ursin	Private	4 Reg't. (Morgan's), La. Militia
St Amant, Voltaire	Private	1 Batt'n. (Fortier's), La. Militia (Orig. under St Amand, Voltaire)
Stampley, George	Private	17, 18 and 19 Cons. Reg't., La. Militia
Stampley, Peter	Private	17, 18 and 19 Cons. Reg't., La. Militia
Stanley, Abner	Surg. Mate	De Clouet's Reg't., La. Militia
Stanley, Benjamin	Private	17, 18 and 19 Cons. Reg't., La. Militia
Stanley, James	Corporal	Captain Price's Co., La. Militia
Stanisclas, Victor	Private	2 Batt'n. (D'Aquin's), La. Militia
Stanislas, David	Private	3 Reg't. (de la Ronde's), La. Mil.
Stanislas, Victor	Private	2 Batt'n. (D'Aquin's), La. Militia (Orig. under Stanisclas, Victor)
Stansbury, Anson	Private	10 and 20 Cons. Reg't., La. Mil.
Stansbury, Jesse	Private	10 and 20 Cons. Reg't., La. Mil.
Stansbury, John	Private	Baker's Regiment, La. Militia
Staraille, F.	Private	2 Batt'n. (D'Aquin's), La. Militia
Stark, I. G.	Private	2 Batt'n. (Peire's), La. Vols. (Orig. under Stat, J. G.)
Stark, Jobe	Private	Capt. Collard's Co., La. Militia
Stark, John	Private	4 Reg't. (Morgan's), La. Militia
Stark, John G.	Private	2 Batt'n. (Peire's), La. Vols. (Orig. under Stat, J. G.)
Starks, William	Private	8 Reg't. (Meriam's), La. Militia
St Armand, Onesifore	Fus.-Private	5 Reg't. (La Branche's), La. Mil. (Orig. under St Amand, Onesifore)
St Armand, --	Private	Plauche's Batt'n., La. Militia (Orig. under St Amand, --)
Starnes, James	Private	12 and 13 Cons. Reg't., La. Mil.
Starnes, Samuel	Private	12 and 13 Cons. Reg't., La. Mil.
Starrard, McClanahan	Private	De Clouet's Reg't., La. Militia (Orig. under Stallard, McClenahan)
Start, John G.	Private	2 Batt'n. (Peire's), La. Vols. (Orig. under J. G.)
Stat, J. G.	Private	2 Batt'n. (Peire's), La. Vols.
Stat, John G.	Private	2 Batt'n. (Peire's), La. Vols. (Orig. under Stat, J. G.)
Statham, Barksdale	1 Sergeant	12 and 13 Cons. Reg't., La. Mil.
St Aubin, Montagne	Sergeant	2 Batt'n. (D'Aquin's), La. Militia
Staufe, Alfonse	Private	8 Reg't. (Meriam's), La. Militia
Staunton, Malikiah	Private	De Clouet's Reg't., La. Militia
Staupe, A.	Private	8 Reg't. (Meriam's), La. Militia
St Avid, J.	Private	Plauche's Batt'n., La. Militia
St Avid, S.	Private	Plauche's Batt'n., La. Militia (Orig. under St Avid, J.)
Stayre, In.	Private	5 Reg't. (La Branche's), La. Mil.
Stayre, Terence	Private	5 Reg't. (La Branche's), La. Mil.
St Clain, Ballarar	Private	Capt. Wallace's Co., Boatmen, La. Vols. (Orig. under St Clear, Battis)
St Clair, John	Private	De Clouet's Reg't., La. Militia (Orig. under Sinclair, John)
St Clare, --	Private	De Clouet's Reg't., La. Militia
St Clear, Battis	Private	Capt. Wallace's Co., Boatmen, La. Vols.
St Cyr, --	Private	Plauche's Batt'n., La. Militia (Orig. under St Cyre, --)
St Cyr, --	Sergeant	Plauche's Batt'n., La. Militia
St Cyre, --	Private	Plauche's Batt'n., La. Militia
St Denis, Charles	Private	Capt. Ashley's Co., Mounted Riflemen, La. Militia
St Dennis, Charles	Private	Capt. Ashley's Co., Mounted Riflemen, La. Militia (Orig. under St. Denis, Charles)
Stearman, Thomas	Private	Capt. Ashley's Co., Mounted Riflemen, La. Militia
Stearns, Moses	Private	10 and 20 Cons. Reg't., La. Mil.
Stebbens, K.	Private-Corporal	4 Reg't. (Morgan's), La. Militia (Orig. under Stebbins, Knolton)
Stebbins, Knolton	Private-Corporal	4 Reg't. (Morgan's), La. Militia
Steel, Andrew	Surgeon	10 Regiment, La. Militia
Steel, James	Private	Capt. Ashley's Co., Mounted Riflemen, La. Militia
Steele, John	Private	Captain McNair's Co., Mounted Riflemen, La. Militia
Steen, Elias	Corporal	16 Reg't. (Thompson's), La. Mil.
Steley, Jack	Private	16 Reg't. (Thompson's), La. Mil. (Orig. under Stelly, Jack)
Stelly, Jack	Private	16 Reg't. (Thompson's), La. Mil.
Stelly, Jean Bte	Private	16 Reg't. (Thompson's), La. Mil.
Stelly, Michel	Private	16 Reg't. (Thompson's), La. Mil.
Stely, Alexis	Private	De Clouet's Reg't., La. Militia
Stepenson, Joseph	Private	10 and 20 Cons. Reg't., La. Mil. (Orig. under Stephenson, Joseph)
Stephe, Joseph	Sergeant	7 Reg't. (Le Beuf's), La. Militia
Stephem, --	Servant	De Clouet's Reg't., La. Militia (Orig. under Steve, --)
Stephen, --	Servant-Waiter	Captain Beale's Co., Riflemen, La. Militia
Stephen, Alexr	Sergeant	De Clouet's Reg't., La. Militia (Orig. under Stephens, Alexander)
Stephen, William	Private	1 Batt'n. (Fortier's), La. Militia
Stephens, Alexander	Sergeant	De Clouet's Reg't., La. Militia
Stephens, Janson	Private	8 Reg't. (Meriam's), La. Militia
Stephens, Joseph	Private	10 and 20 Cons. Reg't., La. Mil. (Orig. under Stephenson, John)
Stephens, Joseph	Private	Captain Sprigg's Co., Boatmen, La. Vols.
Stephens, Joseph	Private	Capt. Wallace's Co., Boatmen, La. Vols.
Stephenson, John	Private	Captain McNair's Co., Mounted Riflemen, La. Militia
Stephenson, John	Private	10 and 20 Cons. Reg't., La. Mil.
Stephenson, John	Private	12 and 13 Cons. Reg't., La. Mil.
Stephenson, Joseph	Private	10 and 20 Cons. Reg't., La. Mil.
Stephenson, Marcus	Private	Captain Ramsey's Co., Mounted Riflemen, La. Militia
Stephenson, William	Private	17, 18 and 19 Cons. Reg't., La. Militia
Sterlin, --	Private	Plauche's Batt'n., La. Militia
Sterling, --	Private	10 and 20 Cons. Reg't., La. Mil.
Sterling, Lewis	Quarter Master	10 and 20 Cons. Reg't., La. Mil.
St Erman, --	Private	2 Batt'n. (D'Aquin's), La. Militia
Stern, Frederick	Private	Capt. Alpuente's Co., La. Mil. (Orig. under Sterne, Frederick)
Sterne, Frederick	Private	Capt. Alpuente's Co., La. Mil.
Sterne, Moses	Private	10 and 20 Cons. Reg't., La. Mil. (Orig. under Stearns, Moses)
Sterne, Richard	Private	Capt. Ogden's Co., Dragoons, La. Militia
Sterns, S.	Corporal	4 Reg't. (Morgan's), La. Militia
Steve, --	Servant	De Clouet's Reg't., La. Militia
Steve, Antoine	Private	7 Reg't. (Le Beuf's), La. Militia
Steve, Francois	Private	7 Reg't. (Le Beuf's), La. Militia
Stevens, George	Sergeant	16 Reg't. (Thompson's), La. Mil.
Steward, Robert	Private	10 and 20 Cons. Reg't., La. Mil. (Orig. under Stuart, Robert)
Steward, Thomas	Sergeant	Captain Sprigg's Co., Boatmen, La. Vols.
Steward, Umphrey	Private	12 and 13 Cons. Reg't., La. Mil. (Orig. under Stewart, Humphrey)
Stewart, Humphrey	Private	12 and 13 Cons. Reg't., La. Mil.
Stewart, James	Private	10 and 20 Cons. Reg't., La. Mil. (Orig. under Stuart, James)
Stewart, James	Private	12 and 13 Cons. Reg't., La. Mil.
Stewart, John	Private	Capt. Callaway's Co., Cavalry, La. Militia
Stewart, John	Private	Captain Dodge's Co., Mounted Riflemen, La. Mil. (Orig. under Stuart, John)
Stewart, Matthew	Private	12 and 13 Cons. Reg't., La. Mil.
Stewart, Robert	Private	10 and 20 Cons. Reg't., La. Mil. (Orig. under Stuart, Robert)
Stewart, Thomas	Sergeant	Captain Sprigg's Co., Boatmen, La. Vols. (Orig. under Steward, Thomas)
Stewart, William	Private	Captain Griffith's Co., Mounted Riflemen, La. Vols.
Stewart, William	1 Lieutenant	Captain Griffith's Co., Mounted Riflemen, La. Vols.
Stewart, William	Private	Captain Rankin's Co., Mounted Riflemen, La. Militia
Stewart, William	Private	10 and 20 Cons. Reg't., La. Mil. (Orig. under Stuart, William)
Stewart, Young	Private	17, 18 and 19 Cons. Reg't., La. Militia

Name	Rank	Unit
St. Germain, Martial	Private	3 Reg't. (de la Ronde's), La. Mil.
St Germain, Pierre	Private	Capt. Songy's Co., Marines, La. Vols.
Stibbins, R.	Private-Corporal	4 Reg't. (Morgan's), La. Militia (Orig. under Stebbins, Knolton)
Stibine, William	Private	1 Batt'n. (Fortier's), La. Militia (Orig. under Dtephen, William)
Sticker, John	Private	De Clouet's Reg't., La. Militia
Sticker, Laurance	Corporal-Private	12 and 13 Cons. Reg't., La. Mil.
Sticklin, John	Private	8 Reg't. (Meriam's), La. Militia (Orig. under Stiecklin, John)
Stiecklin, John	Private	8 Reg't. (Meriam's), La. Militia
Stilett, Vital	Sergeant	16 Reg't. (Thompson's), La. Mil.
Still, James	Pay Master	Detachment Field and Staff Officers, 4 Brigade, La. Militia
Stillman, William	Private	Captain Sprigg's Co., Boatmen, La. Vols. (Orig. under Stilman, William)
Stilman, William	Private	Captain Sprigg's Co., Boatmen, La. Vols.
Stine, John	Sergeant	Baker's Regiment, La. Militia
Stine, John Jr.	Private	Baker's Regiment, La. Militia
Stinson, Asher	Private	12 and 13 Cons. Reg't., La. Mil.
Stinson, Stephen	Private	De Clouet's Reg't., La. Militia (See also 44 Reg't.)
Stirling, Alex A.	Major	10 Reg't., La. Mil. (Orig. under Stirling, Alex L.)
Stirling, Alex. L.	Major	10 Reg't., La. Militia
Stirling, Lewis	Quarter Master	10 and 20 Cons. Reg't., La. Mil. (Orig. under Sterling, Lewis)
St Jean, --	1 Lieutenant	Plauche's Batt'n., La. Militia
St Jermin, F.	Private	2 Reg't. (Cavelier's), La. Militia
St Jermin, M.	Private	2 Reg't. (Cavelier's), La. Militia
St John, Louis	Private	16 Reg't. (Thompson's), La. Mil.
St Laurent, --	Sergeant-Major	2 Batt'n. (D'Aquin's), La. Militia
St Luc, --	Private	1 Batt'n. (Fortier's), La. Militia
St Marc, William	Private	1 Reg't. (Dejan's), La. Militia
St Martin, --	Captain	2 Batt'n. (D'Aquin's), La. Militia
St Martin, --	Corporal	3 Reg't. (de la Ronde's), La. Mil.
St Martin, --	Sergeant	5 Reg't. (La Branche's), La. Mil.
St Martin, F.	1 Lieutenant	6 Reg't. (Landry's), La. Militia
St Martin, Francois	1 Lieutenant	7 Reg't. (Le Beuf's), La. Militia
St Martin, Ls	Private	1 Batt'n. (Fortier's), La. Militia
Stoaks, Mitchell	Private	De Clouet's Reg't., La. Militia (Orig. under Stoots, Michael)
Stockman, George	Private	17, 18 and 19 Cons. Reg't., La. Militia
Stokes, Benjamin M.	Q. Sergeant 2 Lieutenant	De Clouet's Reg't., La. Militia
Stokes, James	Private	De Clouet's Reg't., La. Militia
Stokes, Laban	Private	10 and 20 Cons. Reg't., La. Mil.
Stoks, Laborne	Private	10 and 20 Cons. Reg't., La. Mil. (Orig. under Stokes, Laban)
Stone, John	Private	Captain Hughes' Co., Mounted Riflemen, La. Mil. (Orig. under Slone, John)
Stone, John	Private	1 Reg't. (Dejan's), La. Militia
Stone, Samuel	Private	16 Reg't. (Thompson's), La. Mil.
Stone, Samuel D.	Private	Captain Hughes' Co., Mounted Riflemen, La. Mil. (Orig. under Slone, Samuel D.)
Stoots, Michael	Private	De Clouet's Reg't., La. Militia
Stope, Jan.	Private	8 Reg't. (Meriam's), La. Militia
Stope, Philip Sen	Private	8 Reg't. (Meriam's), La. Militia
Storch, John	Private	12 and 13 Cons. Reg't., La. Mil.
Stores, William	Private	10 and 20 Cons. Reg't., La. Mil. (Orig. under Storrs, William)
Storrs, William	Private	10 and 20 Cons. Reg't., La. Mil.
Story, Benjamin	Private	Captain Beale's Co., Riflemen, La. Militia
Story, Isaac	Private	10 and 20 Cons. Reg't., La. Mil.
Story, J.	Private	Captain Sprigg's Co., Boatmen, La. Vols.
Story, Larkin	Private	10 and 20 Cons. Reg't., La. Mil.
Stotts, A.	Private	Captain Sprigg's Co., Boatmen, La. Vols.
Stout, Joseph	Private	10 and 20 Cons. Reg't., La. Mil.
Stow, Wardy	Private	19 Regiment, La. Militia
Stow, William	Private	2 Reg't. (Cavelier's), La. Militia
St Paul, Henry	Private	8 Reg't. (Meriam's), La. Militia
St Pe', --	Private	Plauche's Batt'n., La. Militia
St Pierre, Andre'	Private	4 Reg't. (Morgan's), La. Militia
St Pierre, Baptiste	Private	De Clouet's Reg't., La. Militia
St Pierre, I.	Private	4 Reg't. (Morgan's), La. Militia
St Pierre, Joseph	Private	6 Reg't. (Landry's), La. Militia
Strausberry, Jesse	Private	10 and 20 Cons. Reg't., La. Mil. (Orig. under Stansbury, Jesse)
Strauther, French H.	Private	17, 18 and 19 Cons. Reg't., La. Militia
Strawther, French A.	Private	17, 18 and 19 Cons. Reg't., La. Mil. (Orig. under Strauther, French H.)
Strenger, --	Private	Plauche's Batt'n., La. Militia (Orig. under Stringer, --)
Stringer, --	Private	Plauche's Batt'n., La. Militia
Stringer, --	Private	Plauche's Batt'n., La. Militia
Strodder, Thornton	Private	4 Reg't. (Morgan's), La. Militia (Orig. under Strother, Thornton)
Stroop, Jacob	Private	19 Reg't., La. Militia
Stropp, John	Private	Captain Rankin's Co., Mounted Riflemen, La. Militia
Stropp, Peter	Private	Captain Rankin's Co., Mounted Riflemen, La. Militia
Strother, Richard	Private	12 and 13 Cons. Reg't., La. Mil.
Strother, Thornton	Private	4 Reg't. (Morgan's), La. Militia
Strother, William	Lieutenant	Captain Hughes' Co., Mounted Riflemen, La. Militia
Strother, William	Private	12 and 13 Cons. Reg't., La. Mil.
Stroud, James	Private	De Clouet's Regiment, La. Mil.
Stroup, Samuel	Private	Captain Young's Co., Mounted Riflemen, La. Militia
Strouse, Christian	Private	Capt. Thomas' Co., La. Militia
St Sancice, --	Private	4 Reg't. (Morgan's), La. Militia
Stuard, James	Private	10 and 20 Cons. Reg't., La. Mil. (Orig. under Stuart, James)
Stuard, William	Private	Capt. Collard's Co., La. Militia
Stuart, --	Corporal	Plauche's Batt'n., La. Militia
Stuart, James	Private	10 and 20 Cons. Reg't., La. Mil.
Stuart, John	Private	Captain Dodge's Co., Mounted Riflemen, La. Militia
Stuart, John	Private	Captain Henry's Co., Mounted Riflemen, La. Militia
Stuart, Robert	Private	10 and 20 Cons. Reg't., La. Mil.
Stuart, Robert	Private	10 and 20 Cons. Reg't., La. Mil.
Stuart, Robert M.	Private	Captain Dodge's Co., Mounted Riflemen, La. Militia
Stuart, Robert M.	Private	Captain Henry's Co., Mounted Riflemen, La. Militia
Stuart, William	Private	10 and 20 Cons. Reg't., La. Mil.
St Val, --	Private	2 Batt'n. (D'Aquin's), La. Militia
St Victor, --	Private	1 Reg't. (Dejan's), La. Militia
Suard, Pierre	Private	2 Batt'n. (Peire's), La. Vols.
Suare, Pierre	Private	2 Batt'n. (Peire's), La. Vols. (Orig. under Suard, Pierre)
Suares, Anthony	Private	2 Batt'n. (Peire's), La. Vols. (Orig. under Suarez, Anthony)
Suares, Antoine	Private	De Clouet's Reg't., La. Militia (Orig. under Suarez, Antoine)
Suares, Carlos	Private	2 Batt'n. (Peire's), La. Vols. (Orig. under Suares, Charles)
Suares, Charles	Private	2 Batt'n. (Peire's), La. Vols.
Suares, D.	Private	2 Reg't. (Cavelier's), La. Militia
Suarez, Antoine	Private	De Clouet's Reg't., La. Militia
Suarez, Anthony	Private	2 Batt'n. (Peire's), La. Vols.
Suarez, Josef	1 Sergeant-Sgt.	3 Reg't. (de la Ronde's), La. Mil.
Suart, Pierre	Private	2 Batt'n. (Peire's), La. Vols. (Orig. under Suard, Pierre)
Suisse, Barthelemy	Private	Plauche's Batt'n., La. Militia
Suiter, Stephen	Private	Capt. Wallace's Co., Boatmen, La. Vols.
Suiza, Barthelemy	Private	Capt. Colsson's Co., Artillery, La. Vols.
Sulcer, John	Private	10 and 20 Cons. Reg't., La. Mil.
Sullens, Joseph	Private	Captain McNair's Co., Mounted Riflemen, La. Militia
Sullibela, Joseph	1 Lieutenant	17, 18 and 19 Cons. Reg't., La. Militia (Orig. under Solibela, Joseph)
Sullins, Nathan	Private	Captain Musick's Co., Mounted Riflemen, La. Militia
Sullivan, John C.	1 Sergeant-Sgt.	Captain McNair's Co., Mounted Riflemen, La. Militia
Summers, Alexander	Private	Captain Ramsey's Co., Mounted Riflemen, La. Militia

Name	Rank	Unit
Summer, F. H.	Private	Capt. Ogden's Co., Dragoons, La. Militia
Sullens, Nathan	Private	Captain Musick's Co., Mounted Riflemen, La. Mil. (Orig. under Sullins, Nathan)
Suros, Fx	Private	Capt. Songy's Co., Marines, La. Vols. (Orig. under Curos, Felix)
Susan, --	Servant	De Clouet's Reg't., La. Militia
Suter, John	Private	De Clouet's Reg't., La. Militia (Orig. under Sutter, John)
Suter, Peter	Private	De Clouet's Reg't., La. Militia (Orig. under Sutter, Peter)
Sutter, John	Private	De Clouet's Reg't., La. Militia
Sutter, Peter	Private	De Clouet's Reg't., La. Militia
Sutton, William	Private	Captain Sprigg's Co., Boatmen, La. Vols.
Suvin, Antoine	Private	Captain Lagan's Co., La. Vols. (Orig. under Servin, Antoine)
Swan, Andrew	Private	De Clouet's Reg't., La. Militia
Swan, James	Private	10 and 20 Cons. Reg't., La. Mil. (Orig. under Levan, James)
Swarres, Antonio	Private	De Clouet's Reg't., La. Militia (Orig. under Suarez, Antoine)
Swearingen, Thomas V.	Private	De Clouet's Reg't., La. Militia
Sweasy, Virgil	Private	17, 18 and 19 Cons. Reg't., La. Militia
Sweat, Morris	Private	10 and 20 Cons. Reg't., La. Mil.
Sweet, Morris	Private	10 and 20 Cons. Reg't., La. Mil. (Orig. under Sweat, Morris)
Sweney, James	Private	Capt. Price's Co., La. Militia
Sweney, James	Private	Capt. Wallace's Co., Boatmen, La. Vols. (Orig. under Swing, James)
Swerey, John	Private	De Clouet's Reg't., La. Militia
Swiller, Joseph	Private	4 Reg't. (Morgan's), La. Militia
Swindler, Dorsy	Sergeant	Capt. Le Doux's Co., Cavalry, La. Vols.
Swing, James	Private	Captain Sprigg's Co., Boatmen, La. Vols.
Swing, James	Private	Capt. Wallace's Co., Boatmen, La. Vols.
Sydic, Lewis	Private	17, 18 and 19 Cons. Reg't., La. Militia
Sylva, Ignacio	Private	2 Batt'n. (Peire's), La. Vols.
Sylvester, Pierre	Private	16 Reg't. (Thompson's), La. Mil. (Orig. under Sylvestre, Pierre)
Sylvestre, Joseph	Private	16 Reg't. (Thompson's), La. Mil.
Sylvestre, Pierre	Private	16 Reg't. (Thompson's), La. Mil.
Tabada, Joseph	Corporal-Private	2 Batt'n. (Peire's), La. Vols. (Orig. under Taboada, Joseph)
Tabatan, Pierre	Artificer	Capt. Chaudurier's Co., Artificers, Art'y., La. Vols. (Orig. under Tabutan, Pierre)
Tabeutean, Pierre	Artificer	Capt. Chaudurier's Co., Artificers, Art'y., La. Vols. (Orig. under Tabutan, Pierre)
Taboada, Joseph	Corporal-Private	2 Batt'n. (Peire's), La. Vols.
Taboade, Joseph	Corporal-Private	2 Batt'n. (Peire's), La. Vols. (Orig. under Taboada, Joseph)
Tabony, --	Private	4 Reg't. (Morgan's), La. Militia
Tabor, Hudson	2 Lieutenant	10 and 20 Cons. Reg't., La. Mil.
Tabor, John	Private	Captain Griffith's Co., Mounted Riflemen, La. Vols.
Tabor, John	Private	10 and 20 Cons. Reg't., La. Mil.
Tabor, William H.	Private	10 and 20 Cons. Reg't., La. Mil.
Taborda, Joseph	Corporal-Private	2 Batt'n. (Peire's), La. Vols. (Orig. under Taboada, Joseph)
Tabre, T.	Corporal	8 Reg't. (Meriam's), La. Militia
Tabutan, Pierre	Artificer	Capt. Chaudurier's Co., Artificers, Art'y., La. Vols.
Tabutean, Pierre	Artificer	Capt. Chaudurier's Co., Artificers, Art'y., La. Vols. (Orig. under Tabutan, Pierre)
Tabuteau, Pierre	Private	2 Batt'n. (D'Aquin's), La. Militia
Tacheau, P.	Private	8 Reg't. (Meriam's), La. Militia
Taham, --	Private	1 Reg't. (Dejan's), La. Militia (Orig. under Iaham, --)
Taillot, Henry	Private	2 Batt'n. (D'Aquin's), La. Militia
Tait, Charles	Private	De Clouet's Reg't., La. Militia (Orig. under Tate, Charles)
Talabert, Cadet	Corporal	2 Batt'n. (D'Aquin's), La. Militia
Talbot, John Q.	Sergeant	De Clouet's Reg't., La. Militia
Talbot, Thomas	Private	17, 18 and 19 Cons. Reg't., La. Militia
Taldevos, John I.	--	De Clouet's Reg't., La. Militia (Orig. under Uren, Friederick)
Taler, Philip	Private	17, 18 and 19 Cons. Reg't., La. Mil. (Orig. under Taylor, Philip)
Tally, John	Private	12 and 13 Cons. Reg't., La. Mil.
Tally, John	Private	16 Reg't. (Thompson's), La. Mil.
Tally, William	Private	16 Reg't. (Thompson's), La. Mil.
Talmadge, Thomas	Private	Captain Sprigg's Co., Boatmen, La. Vols.
Talmage, Thomas	Private	Captain Sprigg's Co., Boatmen, La. Vols. (Orig. under Talmadge, Thomas)
Tam, --	Servant	16 Reg't. (Thompson's), La. Mil.
Tandino, --	Private	Sergeant Hog's Detachment, La. Vols. (Orig. under Fandino, --)
Tanner, George	Private	De Clouet's Reg't., La. Militia
Tanner, John	Private	10 and 20 Cons. Reg't., La. Mil.
Tanner, Lemuel	1 Lieutenant	7 Reg't. (Le Beuf's), La. Militia
Tanner, Loderick	Private	17, 18 and 19 Cons. Reg't., La. Militia
Tanny, Pierre Trahan	Private	De Clouet's Reg't., La. Militia
Tansey, Levey	Ensign	Captain Musick's Co., La. Militia
Tansey, Levy	Cornet	Captain Musick's Co., La. Mil.
Tants, George	Private	8 Reg't. (Meriam's), La. Militia
Tany, Joseph	Private	Baker's Regiment, La. Militia (Orig. under Tarry, Joseph)
Taputaer, Peter	Artificer	Capt. Chaudurier's Co., Artificers, Art'y., La. Vols. (Orig. under Tabutan, Pierre)
Taputean, Peter	Artificer	Capt. Chaudurier's Co., Artificers, Art'y., La. Vols. (Orig. under Tabutan, Pierre)
Taputeru, Peter	Artificer	Capt. Chaudurier's Co., Artificers, Art'y., La. Vols. (Orig. under Tabutan, Pierre)
Tarabone, Joseph	Private	Capt. Colsson's Co., Artillery, La. Vols.
Taragome, --	Private	Plauche's Batt'n., La. Militia (Orig. under Taragonne, --)
Taragonne, --	Private	Plauche's Batt'n., La. Militia
Taratan, Pierre	Artificer	Capt. Chaudurier's Co., Artificers, Art'y., La. Vols. (Orig. under Tartereau, Jean)
Tarbet, William	Private	Capt. Collard's Co., La. Militia
Tardos, Etienne	Private	2 Batt'n. (D'Aquin's), La. Militia
Tarman, Isaac	Private-Sergeant	De Clouet's Reg't., La. Militia (Orig. under Turman, Isaac)
Tarry, Joseph	Private	Baker's Regiment, La. Militia
Tartarause, Jean	Artificer	Capt. Chaudurier's Co., Artificers, Art'y., La. Vols. (Orig. under Tartereau, Jean)
Tarteran, Jean	Artificer	Capt. Chaudurier's Co., Artificers, Art'y., La. Vols. (Orig. under Tartereau, Jean)
Tartereau, Jean	Artificer	Capt. Chaudurier's Co., Artificers, Art'y., La. Vols.
Tassain, Louis	Corporal	5 Reg't. (La Branche's), La. Mil.
Tassin, Pierre	Private	3 Reg't. (de la Ronde's), La. Mil.
Tate, Adam	Private	16 Reg't. (Thompson's), La. Mil. (Orig. under Terre, Adam)
Tate, Charles	Private	De Clouet's Reg't., La. Militia
Tate, Harvey	Private	12 and 13 Cons. Reg't., La. Mil.
Tate, James	Private	12 and 13 Cons. Reg't., La. Mil.
Tate, John	Private	12 and 13 Cons. Reg't., La. Mil.
Tate, Robert	Private	1 Reg't. (Dejan's), La. Militia
Taufin, Joachem	Private	De Clouet's Reg't., La. Militia
Tauges, Andre	Private	6 Reg't. (Landry's), La. Militia (Orig. under Touges, Andre)
Tauges, E. Jr.	Private	6 Reg't. (Landry's), La. Militia (Orig. under Touges, E. Jr.)
Tauges, E. Sr.	Private	6 Reg't. (Landry's), La. Militia (Orig. under Touges, E. Sr.)
Tauges, M.	Private	6 Reg't. (Landry's), La. Militia (Orig. under Touges, M.)
Taurra, Jean	Private	6 Reg't. (Landry's), La. Militia
Tause, Joseph Antoine	Private	2 Batt'n. (Peire's), La. Vols. (Orig. under Taute, Joseph Antoine)
Tauta, Joseph A.	Private	2 Batt'n. (Peire's), La. Vols. (Orig. under Taute, Joseph Antoine)

Name	Rank	Unit
Taute, Joseph Antoine	Private	2 Batt'n. (Peire's), La. Vols.
Tautin, Brunet	Private	17, 18 and 19 Cons. Reg't., La. Militia
Tavenot, Fcois	Sergeant	2 Reg't. (Cavelier's), La. Militia (Orig. under Thavenot, Francois)
Taxader, John A.	Private	17, 18 and 19 Cons. Reg't., La. Militia
Taylor, Andrew	Private	12 and 13 Cons. Reg't., La. Mil.
Taylor, Billington	Private	10 and 20 Cons. Reg't., La. Mil.
Taylor, Daniel	Private	12 and 13 Cons. Reg't., La. Mil.
Taylor, David	Private	12 and 13 Cons. Reg't., La. Mil.
Taylor, Garret	Private	Baker's Regiment, La. Militia
Taylor, James	Private	11 Reg't. (Hickey's), La. Militia
Taylor, John	Private	4 Reg't. (Morgan's), La. Militia
Taylor, John	Private	4 Reg't. (Morgan's), La. Militia
Taylor, John	Private	16 Reg't. (Thompson's), La. Mil.
Taylor, Joseph	Private	Captain Ramsey's Co., Mounted Riflemen, La. Militia
Taylor, Levi	Private	De Clouet's Reg't., La. Militia
Taylor, Lorant	Private	16 Reg't. (Thompson's), La. Mil.
Taylor, Michel	Private	16 Reg't. (Thompson's), La. Mil.
Taylor, Philip	Private	17, 18 and 19 Cons. Reg't., La. Militia
Taylor, Richard	Private	11 Reg't. (Hickey's), La. Militia
Taylor, Robert	Corporal	De Clouet's Reg't., La. Militia
Taylor, Robert	Corporal	10 and 20 Cons. Reg't., La. Mil.
Taylor, Robert	Private	16 Reg't. (Thompson's), La. Mil.
Taylor, Thomas	Private	12 and 13 Cons. Reg't., La. Mil.
Taylor, William H.	Private	De Clouet's Reg't., La. Militia
Taymer, John	Private	10 and 20 Cons. Reg't., La. Mil. (Orig. under Tanner, John)
Tayon, Francis	Private	Capt. Van Bibber's Co., La. Mil.
Taytor, Garret	Private	Baker's Regiment, La. Militia (Orig. under Taylor, Garret)
Teacle, George	Private	12 and 13 Cons. Reg't., La. Mil.
Teacle, Nathaniel	Private	12 and 13 Cons. Reg't., La. Mil.
Teacle, Richard	Private	12 and 13 Cons. Reg't., La. Mil.
Teage, Peter	Lieutenant	Capt. Van Bibber's Co., La. Mil.
Teague, Peter	Lieutenant	Capt. Van Bibber's Co., La. Mil. (Orig. under Teage, Peter)
Teal, Edward	Private	De Clouet's Reg't., La. Militia
Tear, Ignatius	Private	16 Reg't. (Thompson's), La. Mil.
Teaurrar, Jean	Private	6 Reg't. (Landry's), La. Militia (Orig. under Taurra, Jean)
Tedford, Jesse	Private	Capt. Collard's Co., La. Militia
Teekle, George	Private	12 and 13 Cons. Reg't., La. Mil. (Orig. under Teacle, George)
Teekle, Nathaniel	Private	12 and 13 Cons. Reg't., La. Mil. (Orig. under Teacle, Nathaniel)
Teekle, Richard	Private	12 and 13 Cons. Reg't., La. Mil. (Orig. under Teacle, Richard)
Telier, Louis	Private	2 Batt'n. (D'Aquin's), La. Militia (Orig. under Tellier, Louis)
Teller, John	Private	16 Reg't. (Thompson's), La. Mil.
Tellfair, M.	2 Lieutenant	De Clouet's Reg't., La. Militia
Tellier, Louis	Private	2 Batt'n. (D'Aquin's), La. Militia
Template, Auguste	Private	De Clouet's Reg't., La. Militia
Template, Charles	Private	De Clouet's Reg't., La. Militia
Temple, Florentin	Private	7 Reg't. (Le Beuf's), La. Militia
Templet, A.	Private	8 Reg't. (Meriam's), La. Militia
Templet, Baptiste	Private	Captain Hubbard's Mounted Co., La. Militia
Templet, F.	Private	8 Reg't. (Meriam's), La. Militia
Templet, Florentine	Private	Captain Hubbard's Mounted Co., La. Militia
Templet, I. M.	Corporal	8 Reg't. (Meriam's), La. Militia
Templet, Jean	Private	8 Reg't. (Meriam's), La. Militia
Tenguil, Antoine	Private	5 Reg't. (La Branche's), La. Mil.
Tenner, Miles	Private	Capt. Collard's Co., La. Militia
Tennes, Miles	Private	Capt. Collard's Co., La. Militia (Orig. under Tenner, Miles)
Tennesles, Mathew	Private	Capt. Thomas' Co., La. Militia
Tercuit, Francis	Private	De Clouet's Reg't., La. Militia (Orig. under Turcuit, Francis)
Terne, George	Private	De Clouet's Reg't., La. Militia (Orig. under Kerne, George)
Ternoir, Jean	Captain	1 Batt'n. (Fortier's), La. Militia
Terrel, John	Private	8 Reg't. (Meriam's), La. Militia
Terrell, Richmond	Private	8 Reg't. (Meriam's), La. Militia
Terrio, Joseph	Private	De Clouet's Reg't., La. Militia
Terriot, Broise	Private	7 Reg't. (Le Beuf's), La. Militia
Terriot, Charles	Private	7 Reg't. (Le Beuf's), La. Militia
Terroit, Fouville	Private	7 Reg't. (Le Beuf's), La. Militia
Terry, David	Private	12 and 13 Cons. Reg't., La. Mil.
Terry, Robert	Private	De Clouet's Reg't., La. Militia
Tessie, John	Major	2 Reg't. (Cavelier's), La. Militia
Tessier, --	Private	1 Reg't. (Dejan's), La. Militia (Orig. under Tissier, --)
Tessier, A.	Musician	Plauche's Batt'n., La. Militia
Tessier, Charles	Major	De Clouet's Reg't., La. Militia
Teste, A.	Private	Plauche's Batt'n., La. Militia
Teston, Francois	Private	La. (War of 1812)
Tette, Adam	Private	16 Reg't. (Thompson's), La. Mil.
Texader, John A.	Private	17, 18 and 19 Cons. Reg't., La. Mil. (Orig. under Taxader, John A.)
Texier, In Bte	Private	5 Reg't. (La Branche's), La. Mil.
Teysset, James	2 Lieutenant	10 and 20 Cons. Reg't., La. Mil.
Thacker, Hiram	Private	10 and 20 Cons. Reg't., La. Mil.
Thacker, James	Private	10 and 20 Cons. Reg't., La. Mil.
Thacker, William	Private	10 and 20 Cons. Reg't., La. Mil.
Thaker, William	Private	10 and 20 Cons. Reg't., La. Mil. (Orig. under Thacker, William)
Thalchill, William	Private	10 and 20 Cons. Reg't., La. Mil. (Orig. under Thraulkill, William)
Thavenot, Francois	Sergeant	2 Reg't. (Cavelier's), La. Militia
Theall, James	Sergeant	Baker's Regiment, La. Militia
Theall, John B.	1 Lieutenant	Baker's Regiment, La. Militia
Theall, Joseph	Private	Baker's Regiment, La. Militia
Theard, --	Private	Plauche's Batt'n., La. Militia
Theard, Joseph	Private	1 Batt'n. (Fortier's), La. Militia (Orig. under Hicart, Joseph)
Theare, --	Sergeant	4 Reg't. (Morgan's), La. Militia (Orig. under Thiare, --)
Thebedeau, Cyril	Private	16 Reg't. (Thompson's), La. Mil.
Thebedeau, Martin	Private	De Clouet's Reg't., La. Militia (Orig. under Thibodeaux, Martin)
Thebedeau, Sylva	Private	16 Reg't. (Thompson's), La. Mil.
Thebodau, Martin	Private	De Clouet's Reg't., La. Militia (Orig. under Thibodeaux, Martin)
Thebodeau, Baptist	Private	De Clouet's Reg't., La. Militia (Orig. under Thibodau, Baptiste)
Thebodeau, Cyril	Private	16 Reg't. (Thompson's), La. Mil. (Orig. under Thebedeau, Cyril)
Thebodeau, Cyrile	Private	16 Reg't. (Thompson's), La. Mil. (Orig. under Thibedeaux, Cyrile)
Thebodeau, Martin	Private	De Clouet's Reg't., La. Militia (Orig. under Thibodeaux, Martin)
Thebodeau, Nicholas	Private	Baker's Regiment, La. Militia (Orig. under Thibodeau, Nicholas)
Thebodeaux, Martin	Private	De Clouet's Reg't., La. Militia (Orig. under Thibodeaux, Martin)
Thebodeaux, Obin B.	Corporal	De Clouet's Reg't., La. Militia
Thebodeaux, Paul	Corporal	6 Reg't. (Landry's), La. Militia (Orig. under Thibodeaux, Paul)
Thebodeaux, Sylva	Private	16 Reg't. (Thompson's), La. Mil. (Orig. under Thebedeau, Sylva)
Thebodo, F.	Private	16 Reg't. (Thompson's), La. Mil. (Orig. under Thibedo, F.)
Thebodo, Tusant	Private	16 Reg't. (Thompson's), La. Mil.
Thebodo, Zeno	Private	16 Reg't. (Thompson's), La. Mil.
Thebodon, Narcise	Private	De Clouet's Reg't., La. Militia (Orig. under Thibodeau, Narcisse)
Thebodou, Jean	Private	De Clouet's Reg't., La. Militia (Orig. under Thibodeau, Jean)
Theboudou, Isaac	Private	De Clouet's Reg't., La. Militia
Theen, Lucien	Private	2 Batt'n. (D'Aquin's), La. Militia
Theodor, Honore	Private	1 Batt'n. (Fortier's), La. Militia
Theodore, --	Servant	Capt. Chauveau's Co., Cavalry, La. Militia
Theon, --	Private	Plauche's Batt'n., La. Militia
Theriat, Jean	Private	6 Reg't. (Landry's), La. Militia (Orig. under Theriot, Jean)
Theriant, Charles	Private	De Clouet's Reg't., La. Militia
Therio, Edouard	Corporal	Captain Hubbard's Mounted Co., La. Militia
Theriot, Ambroise	Private	Captain Hubbard's Mounted Co., La. Militia
Theriot, Celestin	Private	Captain Hubbard's Mounted Co., La. Militia
Theriot, Charles	Private	Captain Hubbard's Mounted Co., La. Militia
Theriot, Eloi	Private	6 Reg't. (Landry's), La. Militia

Name	Rank	Unit
Theriot, Francois	Private	Captain Hubbard's Mounted Co., La. Militia
Theriot, Jean	Private	6 Reg't. (Landry's), La. Militia
Theriot, Julien	Private	16 Reg't. (Thompson's), La. Mil.
Theriot, Oliver	Private	6 Reg't. (Landry's), La. Militia
Theriot, Pierre	1 Lieutenant	6 Reg't. (Landry's), La. Militia (Orig. under Theris, Pierre)
Theriot, Pre	Sergeant	8 Reg't. (Meriam's), La. Militia
Theriot, Th.	Sergeant	8 Reg't. (Meriam's), La. Militia
Theriot, Valentine	Private	6 Reg't. (Landry's), La. Militia
Theriot, Xavier	Private	8 Reg't. (Meriam's), La. Militia
Thercaut, Julien	Private	De Clouet's Reg't., La. Militia
Theris, Pierre	1 Lieutenant	6 Reg't. (Landry's), La. Militia
Therot, Th.	1 Sergeant-Sgt.	8 Reg't. (Meriam's), La. Militia (Orig. under Theriot, Th.)
Thevenet, F.	Private	Plauche's Batt'n., La. Militia (Orig. under Thevenot, Francois)
Thevenot, Francois	Private	Plauche's Batt'n., La. Militia
Thevenot, Peter Francois	Corporal	2 Batt'n. (Peire's), La. Vols.
Thevenot, Pierre Francois	Corporal	2 Batt'n. (Peire's), La. Vols. (Orig. under Thevenot, Peter Francois)
Thezand, Philipe	Sergeant	2 Reg't. (Cavelier's), La. Militia
Thiare, --	Sergeant	4 Reg't. (Morgan's), La. Militia
Thibaud, --	Corporal	2 Reg't. (Cavelier's), La. Militia
Thibaud, John	Quarter Master	1 Reg't. (Dejan's), La. Militia
Thibaud, John P.	Lieutenant	2 Batt'n. (Peire's), La. Vols. (Orig. under Thibaut, Jean Pierre)
Thibaud, Peter	Lieutenant	2 Batt'n. (Peire's), La. Vols. (Orig. under Thibaut, Jean Pierre)
Thibaudeau, Pierre Chs.	Private	8 Reg't. (Meriam's), La. Militia
Thibaut, Jean Pierre	1 Lieutenant	2 Batt'n. (Peire's), La. Vols.
Thibaut, John	Quarter Master	1 Reg't. (Dejan's), La. Militia (Orig. under Thibaud, John)
Thibaut, John Peter	Lieutenant	2 Batt'n. (Peire's), La. Vols. (Orig. under Thibaut, Jean Pierre)
Thibeaudeau, Pierre Paul	Private	Baker's Regiment, La. Militia (Orig. under Thibodeau, Pierre Paul)
Thibedeau, Pierre	Private	16 Reg't. (Thompson's), La. Mil.
Thibedeaux, Cyrile	Private	16 Reg't. (Thompson's), La. Mil.
Thibedeaux, Zeno	Private	16 Reg't. (Thompson's), La. Mil.
Thibedo, F.	Private	16 Reg't. (Thompson's), La. Mil.
Thibedo, Toussant	Private	16 Reg't. (Thompson's), La. Mil.
Thibodau, Baptiste	Private	De Clouet's Reg't., La. Militia
Thibodau, Isaac	Private	De Clouet's Reg't., La. Militia
Thibodau, Placide	Private	De Clouet's Reg't., La. Militia (Orig. under Thibodeau, Placide)
Thibodaux, Leandre	Sergeant	De Clouet's Reg't., La. Militia (Orig. under Thibodeaux, Leandre)
Thibodaux, Martin	Private	Captain Hubbard's Mounted Co., La. Militia
Thibodaux, Obin	Corporal	De Clouet's Reg't., La. Militia (Orig. under Thebodeaux, Obin B.)
Thibodeau, A.	Private	8 Reg't. (Meriam's), La. Militia
Thibodeau, Jean	Private	De Clouet's Reg't., La. Militia
Thibodeau, Joseph N.	Private	7 Reg't. (Le Beuf's), La. Militia
Thibodeau, Narcisse	Private	De Clouet's Reg't., La. Militia
Thibodeau, Nicholas	Private	Baker's Regiment, La. Militia
Thibodeau, Pierre Paul	Private	Baker's Regiment, La. Militia
Thibodeau, Placide	Private	De Clouet's Reg't., La. Militia
Thibodeaux, Charles	Private	6 Reg't. (Landry's), La. Militia
Thibodeaux, Henry S.	1 Lieutenant	De Clouet's Reg't., La. Militia
Thibodeaux, Leandre	Sergeant	De Clouet's Reg't., La. Militia
Thibodeaux, Martin	Private	De Clouet's Reg't., La. Militia
Thibodeaux, Obin	Corporal	De Clouet's Reg't., La. Militia
Thibodeaux, Paul	Corporal	6 Reg't. (Landry's), La. Militia
Thiery, Bazille	Private	1 Batt'n. (Fortier's), La. Militia
Thireaut, Charles	Private	De Clouet's Reg't., La. Militia (Orig. under Theriaut, Charles)
Thiriant, Julien	Private	De Clouet's Reg't., La. Militia (Orig. under Theriant, Julien)
Tholozan, Victor	Lieutenant	1 Reg't. (Dejan's), La. Militia
Thom, James	Private	10 and 20 Cons. Reg't., La. Mil.
Thomas, --	Servant	De Clouet's Reg't., La. Militia
Thomas, --	Servant	12 and 13 Cons. Reg't., La. Mil.
Thomas, Antoine	Private	1 Batt'n. (Fortier's), La. Militia
Thomas, Charles	Private	4 Reg't. (Morgan's), La. Militia
Thomas, Francis Speen	Private	17, 18 and 19 Cons. Reg't., La. Militia
Thomas, James	Private	1 Batt'n. (Fortier's), La. Militia
Thomas, Joe	Private	Captain Hubbard's Mounted Co., La. Militia
Thomas, John	Private	Captain Young's Co., Mounted Riflemen, La. Militia
Thomas, John L.	1 Lieut. & Adjt.	De Clouet's Reg't., La. Militia
Thomas, Joseph	Captain	Capt. Thomas' Co., La. Militia
Thomas, Joseph	Private	10 and 20 Cons. Reg't., La. Mil.
Thomas, Mathieu	Private	Plauche's Batt'n., La. Militia
Thomas, Monplaisir	Sergeant	2 Batt'n. (D'Aquin's), La. Militia
Thomas, Rouland	Private	17, 18 and 19 Cons. Reg't., La. Militia
Thomas, William	Private	16 Reg't. (Thompson's), La. Mil.
Thomas, William	Private	16 Reg't. (Thompson's), La. Mil.
Thomas, William	Private	19 Regiment, La. Militia
Thomasille, Louis	Private	17, 18 and 19 Cons. Reg't., La. Militia
Thomason, Alexander	Private	De Clouet's Reg't., La. Militia
Thomason, Jean	Sergeant	De Clouet's Reg't., La. Militia
Thomason, John	Sergeant	De Clouet's Reg't., La. Militia (Orig. under Thomason, Jean)
Thompson, George	Private	17, 18 and 19 Cons. Reg't., La. Militia
Thompson, George C.	Private	17, 18 and 19 Cons. Reg't., La. Militia
Thompson, Henry	Private	16 Reg't. (Thompson's), La. Mil.
Thompson, Israel	1 Sergeant	Capt. Alpuente's Co., La. Mil.
Thompson, James	Sergeant	Captain Ramsey's Co., Mounted Riflemen, La. Militia
Thompson, John	Private	Capt. Allen's Co., Artillerists, La. Vols.
Thompson, John	Colonel	Detachment Field and Staff Officers, 4 Brigade, La. Militia
Thompson, John	Private	16 Regiment, La. Militia
Thompson, Lemuel	Private	12 and 13 Cons. Reg't., La. Mil.
Thompson, Nathan	2 Lieutenant	Plauche's Batt'n., La. Militia
Thompson, Samuel H.	Private	Capt. Ogden's Co., Dragoons, La. Militia
Thompson, William	Private	De Clouet's Reg't., La. Militia
Thompson, William	Private	8 Reg't. (Meriam's), La. Militia
Thompson, William	Private	11 Reg't. (Hickey's), La. Militia
Thompson, William	Private	17, 18 and 19 Cons. Reg't., La. Militia
Thompsons, Israel	1 Sergeant	Capt. Alpuente's Co., La. Militia (Orig. under Thompson, Israel)
Thomson, Williams	Private	De Clouet's Reg't., La. Militia (Orig. under Thompson, William)
Thouron, Julien	2 Lieutenant	2 Reg't. (Cavelier's), La. Militia (Orig. under Touron, Julien)
Thraham, Joseph	Private	10 and 20 Cons. Reg't., La. Mil.
Thrailkill, William	Private	10 and 20 Cons. Reg't., La. Mil.
Thrilkeail, William	Private	10 and 20 Cons. Reg't., La. Mil. (Orig. under Thrailkill, William)
Thrower, Jeremiah	Private	Captain Griffith's Co., Mounted Riflemen, La. Vols.
Thuchet, Thomas	Sergeant	Plauche's Batt'n., La. Militia (Orig. under Touchet, Thomas)
Thucker, William	Private	10 and 20 Cons. Reg't., La. Mil. (Orig. under Thacker, William)
Thurston, Frederick	Private	De Clouet's Reg't., La. Militia
Tibbs, John	Private	16 Reg't. (Thompson's), La. Mil.
Ticer, Thomas	Private	10 and 20 Cons. Reg't., La. Mil.
Ticuit, Jean	Private	6 Reg't. (Landry's), La. Militia
Tiercy, --	Private	2 Batt'n. (D'Aquin's), La. Militia
Tiester, Frederick	Private	De Clouet's Reg't., La. Militia (Orig. under Keister, Frederick)
Tiller, I.	Private	8 Reg't. (Meriam's), La. Militia
Tilman, Elisha	Private	10 and 20 Cons. Reg't., La. Mil.
Tilton, Archibald	Private	Captain Sprigg's Co., Boatmen, La. Vols.
Tinque, Franque	Private	Captain Lagan's Co., La. Vols.
Tinturier, --	Corporal	4 Reg't. (Morgan's), La. Militia
Tio, Franco	Private	2 Reg't. (Cavelier's), La. Militia
Tiplon, William	Sergeant	Captain Ramsey's Co., Mounted Riflemen, La. Militia
Tippet, Stephen	Private	17, 18 and 19 Cons. Reg't., La. Militia
Tiraille, --	Private	2 Reg't. (Cavelier's), La. Militia (Orig. under Firaille, --)
Tircuit, Francois	Private	De Clouet's Reg't., La. Militia (Orig. under Turcuit, Francis)

Name	Rank	Unit
Tircuit, Jean	Private	6 Reg't. (Landry's), La. Militia (Orig. under Ticuit, Jean)
Tiserina, Jose Maria	Private	17, 18 and 19 Cons. Reg't., La. Militia
Tissier, --	Private	1 Reg't. (Dejan's), La. Militia
Tissue, Joseph	Private	De Clouet's Reg't., La. Militia
Tisue, John	Private	De Clouet's Reg't., La. Militia (Orig. under Tissue, Joseph)
Tixereno, Jose'	Private	17, 18 and 19 Cons. Reg't., La. Mil.(Orig. under Tixerino, Jose')
Tixerino, Jose'	Private	17, 18 and 19 Cons. Reg't., La. Militia
Tobin, James	Private	De Clouet's Reg't., La. Militia
Toboada, Joseph	Corporal-Private	2 Batt'n. (Peire's), La. Vols. (Orig. under Taboada, Joseph)
Toboado, Joseph	Corporal-Private	2 Batt'n. (Peire's), La. Vols. (Orig. under Taboada, Joseph)
Todd, Caswell T.	Private	De Clouet's Reg't., La. Militia
Todd, Daniel L.	Sergeant	16 Reg't. (Thompson's), La. Mil. (Orig. under Todd, David L.)
Todd, David L.	Sergeant	16 Reg't. (Thompson's), La. Mil.
Toffier, Nicolas	Private	8 Reg't. (Meriam's), La. Militia
Tolbert, John Q.	Sergeant	De Clouet's Reg't., La. Militia (Orig. under Talbot, John Q.)
Tolbert, Silas	Sergeant	17, 18 and 19 Cons. Reg't., La. Militia
Tolbot, John Q.	Sergeant	De Clouet's Reg't., La. Militia (Orig. under Talbot, John Q.)
Toledano, Christoph	Cpl.-Fourrier	Plauche's Batt'n., La. Militia
Toledano, Jerome	Private	Plauche's Batt'n., La. Militia
Toledano, Raphael	Private	Plauche's Batt'n., La. Militia
Tolimosso, Pedro	Private	17, 18 and 19 Cons. Reg't., La. Militia
Tollemotto, Pedro	Private	17, 18 and 19 Cons. Reg't., La. Mil. (Orig. under Tolimosso, Pedro)
Tolmar, Jacques	Private	8 Reg't. (Meriam's), La. Militia
Tom, --	Private-Waiter	De Clouet's Reg't., La. Militia
Tom, --	Servant	General and Staff (Morgan), La. Militia
Tom, --	Servant	Detachment Field and Staff Officers, 4 Brigade, La. Militia
Tom, --	Servant	Detachment Field and Staff Officers, 4 Brigade, La. Militia
Tom, --	Waiter	2 Reg't. (Cavelier's), La. Militia
Tom, --	Servant	16 Reg't. (Thompson's), La. Mil. (Orig. under Tam, --)
Tomay, --	Private	8 Reg't. (Meriam's), La. Militia
Tomb, William	Private	Captain Sprigg's Co., Boatmen, La. Vols.
Tomlinson, Jesse	Private	Baker's Regiment, La. Militia
Tomlinson, John	Private	10 and 20 Cons. Reg't., La. Mil.
Tommison, John	Private	10 and 20 Cons. Reg't., La. Mil. (Orig. under Tomlinson, John)
Tomplet, Jean	Private	De Clouet's Reg't., La. Militia
Tomquex, Francois	Private	16 Reg't. (Thompson's), La. Mil.
Tones, Juan	Private	17, 18 and 19 Cons. Reg't., La. Mil. (Orig. under Tores, Jn)
Tonet, F.	Private	8 Reg't. (Meriam's), La. Militia
Toney, Charles	Private	12 and 13 Cons. Reg't., La. Mil.
Toney, Drewry	Private	De Clouet's Reg't., La. Militia
Toney, William	Private	12 and 13 Cons. Reg't., La. Mil.
Tonlanant, John	Private	De Clouet's Reg't., La. Militia (Orig. under Fontino, John)
Tonnelier, A.	Private	4 Reg't. (Morgan's), La. Militia (Orig. under Connellier, A.)
Tonteno, Jn Bte	Private	6 Reg't. (Landry's), La. Militia (Orig. under Fonteno, J. Bte)
Tora, Francisco	Private	17, 18 and 19 Cons. Reg't., La. Militia
Toraille, Jean	Private	2 Batt'n. (D'Aquin's), La. Militia
Tores, Jn	Private	17, 18 and 19 Cons. Reg't., La. Militia
Torreau, Etienne	Private	Capt. Colsson's Co., Artillery, La. Vols.
Torres, Barthelemy	Private	3 Reg't. (de la Ronde's), La. Mil.
Torres, Francois	Private	3 Reg't. (de la Ronde's), La. Mil.
Torres, Francisco	Private	17, 18 and 19 Cons. Reg't., La. Militia
Torres, Juan	Private	17, 18 and 19 Cons. Reg't., La. Militia
Toublanc, --	Sergeant	Plauche's Batt'n., La. Militia
Touche, Pierre	Private	De Clouet's Reg't., La. Militia (See also 44 Reg't.)
Touchechet, Michel	Private	Baker's Regiment, La. Militia
Touchee, Francois	Private	De Clouet's Reg't., La. Militia (Orig. under Tuckett, Francois)
Touchet, Thomas	Sergeant	Plauche's Batt'n., La. Militia
Touges, Andre	Private	6 Reg't. (Landry's), La. Militia
Touges, E. Jr.	Private	6 Reg't. (Landry's), La. Militia
Touges, E. Sr.	Private	6 Reg't. (Landry's), La. Militia
Touges, M.	Private	6 Reg't. (Landry's), La. Militia
Touissant, Francois R.	Cpl.-Pvt.	2 Batt'n. (Peire's), La. Vols. (Orig. under Toussaint, Francois Remy)
Toulouse, --	Corporal	1 Reg't. (Dejan's), La. Militia
Tounoir, Martin	Private	Capt. Le Doux's Co., Cavalry, La. Vols.
Toupard, Francois	Private	3 Reg't. (de la Ronde's), La. Mil.
Toupart, Francois	Private	3 Reg't. (de la Ronde's), La. Mil. (Orig. under Toupard, Francois)
Toups, Ambroise	Private	Baker's Regiment, La. Militia
Toups, Frederick	Fusilier-Private	5 Reg't. (La Branche's), La. Mil.
Toups, Tallesfor	Private	De Clouet's Reg't., La. Militia
Tour, Ene	Private	Plauche's Batt'n., La. Militia
Tourel, A.	Private	6 Reg't. (Landry's), La. Militia
Tourla, A.	Sergeant	Plauche's Batt'n., La. Militia
Tourne, Jerome	1 Sergeant-Sgt.	Plauche's Batt'n., La. Militia
Tournoir, Ettienne	Private	Captain Lagan's Co., La. Vols.
Tournois, Ettienne	Private	Captain Lagan's Co., La. Vols. (Orig. under Tournoir, Ettienne)
Touro, I.	Private	1 Reg't. (Dejan's), La. Militia
Touron, Julien	2 Lieutenant	2 Reg't. (Cavelier's), La. Militia
Tourouille, Jh	Private	2 Reg't. (Cavelier's), La. Militia
Toussaint, fils	Private	De Clouet's Reg't., La. Militia
Toussaint, Francois Remy	Cpl.-Pvt.	2 Batt'n. (Peire's), La. Vols.
Toussant, Francis Remy	Cpl.-Pvt.	2 Batt'n. (Peire's), La. Vols. (Orig. under Toussaint, Francois Remy)
Toutant, Jacques	Captain	3 Reg't. (de la Ronde's), La. Mil.
Touzeneau, Job	Private	8 Reg't. (Meriam's), La. Militia
Townsand, Isaac	Captain	De Clouet's Reg't., La. Militia (Orig. under Townsend, Isaac)
Townsend, Isaac	Captain	De Clouet's Reg't., La. Militia
Townsend, John	Private	12 and 13 Cons. Reg't., La. Mil.
Towro, I.	Private	1 Reg't. (Dejan's), La. Militia (Orig. under Touro, I.)
Trabuc, Vincent	Surgeon	2 Reg't. (Cavelier's), La. Militia
Tradahon, George	Private	3 Reg't. (de la Ronde's), La. Mil.
Traham, V.	Private	8 Reg't. (Meriam's), La. Militia (Orig. under Trahan, V.)
Trahan, Alexander	Private	De Clouet's Reg't., La. Militia
Trahan, Baptiste	Private	De Clouet's Reg't., La. Militia
Trahan, Charles	Private	De Clouet's Reg't., La. Militia
Trahan, Denis	Private	De Clouet's Reg't., La. Militia
Trahan, Francis	Sergeant	De Clouet's Reg't., La. Militia
Trahan, Jean	Private	De Clouet's Reg't., La. Militia
Trahan, Joseph	Private	De Clouet's Reg't., La. Militia
Trahan, Joseph	Private	De Clouet's Reg't., La. Militia
Trahan, Joseph	Private	10 and 20 Cons. Reg't., La. Mil. (Orig. under Thraham, Joseph)
Trahan, Julian	Private	De Clouet's Reg't., La. Militia
Trahan, Oliver	Private	16 Reg't. (Thompson's), La. Mil.
Trahan, Paul	Private	8 Reg't. (Meriam's), La. Militia
Trahan, Pierre	Private	De Clouet's Reg't., La. Militia
Trahan, V.	Private	8 Reg't. (Meriam's), La. Militia
Traiger, Anthony	Private	De Clouet's Reg't., La. Militia (Orig. under Traigre, Anthony)
Traigre, Anthony	Private	De Clouet's Reg't., La. Militia
Traigre, John	Corporal	11 Reg't. (Hickey's), La. Militia
Traucard, John	Private	De Clouet's Reg't., La. Militia (Orig. under Trauchard, John)
Trauchard, John	Private	De Clouet's Reg't., La. Militia
Travert, Frans	Private	2 Batt'n. (D'Aquin's), La. Militia
Trebino, Paul	Corporal	1 Batt'n. (Fortier's), La. Militia
Trebino, Raimond	Private	1 Batt'n. (Fortier's), La. Militia
Tredo, Gabriel	Private	16 Reg't. (Thompson's), La. Mil.
Tregle, Jacques	Fusilier-Private	5 Reg't. (La Branche's), La. Mil.
Tregle, Leonard	Fusilier-Private	5 Reg't. (La Branche's), La. Mil. (Orig. under Tregre, Leonard)
Tregle, Theodore	Fusilier-Private	5 Reg't. (La Branche's), La. Mil.
Tregle, Urbin	Fusilier-Private	5 Reg't. (La Branche's), La. Mil.
Tregre, Andre' son	Fus.-Private	5 Reg't. (La Branche's), La. Mil.
Tregre, George	Fusilier-Private	5 Reg't. (La Branche's), La. Mil.

Name	Rank	Unit
Tregre, Jacques	Sergeant	5 Reg't. (La Branche's), La. Mil.
Tregre, Leonard	Fusilier-Private	5 Reg't. (La Branche's), La. Mil.
Tregre, Theodore, son	Fus.-Pri.	5 Reg't. (La Branche's), La. Mil.
Tregre, Urbain	Fusilier-Private	5 Reg't. (La Branche's), La. Mil.
Treme, Jr.	Musician	Plauche's Batt'n., La. Militia
Treme, Sr.	Musician	Plauche's Batt'n., La. Militia
Treme, Emile	Musician	1 Batt'n. (Fortier's), La. Militia
Treme, Felix	Musician	1 Batt'n. (Fortier's), La. Militia
Tremmel, Levi	Private	16 Reg't. (Thompson's), La. Mil.
Tremont, Joseph	Private	2 Batt'n. (Peire's), La. Vols. (Orig. under Premont, Joseph)
Tremoulet, B.	Corporal	Plauche's Batt'n., La. Militia
Tremoulet, C.	Private	Plauche's Batt'n., La. Militia
Trent, Henry	Private	10 and 20 Cons. Reg't., La. Mil.
Trent, John	Private	19 Regiment, La. Militia
Trent, William	Private	19 Regiment, La. Militia
Trepagnier, F.	Private	Plauche's Batt'n., La. Militia (Orig. under Trepanier, F.)
Trepagnier, Laurent	Private	2 Reg't. (Morgan's), La. Militia
Trepagnier, Norbert	Private	Capt. Trudeau's Troop of Horse, La. Militia
Trepanier, F.	Private	Plauche's Batt'n., La. Militia
Trepaynier, Francois	Private	Capt. Trudeau's Troop of Horse, La. Militia
Trepaynier, Pierre	Private	Capt. Trudeau's Troop of Horse, La. Militia
Trepergnier, Laurent	Private	4 Reg't. (Morgan's), La. Militia (Orig. under Trepagnier, Laurent)
Trepergnier, Pierre	Private	Capt. Trudeau's Troop of Horse, La. Mil. (Orig. under Trepaynier, Pierre)
Treperyeir, Francois	Private	Capt. Trudeau's Troop of Horse, La. Mil. (Orig. under Trepaynier, Francois)
Trevino, Antonio	Private	17, 18 and 19 Cons. Reg't., La. Militia
Tribble, James	Private	10 and 20 Cons. Reg't., La. Mil.
Tribbll, James	Private	10 and 20 Cons. Reg't., La. Mil. (Orig. under Tribble, James)
Tricon, P. I.	Private	Plauche's Batt'n., La. Militia (Orig. under Tricou, P.)
Tricou, In	Private	Plauche's Batt'n., La. Militia (Orig. under Tricou, P.)
Tricou, P.	Private	Plauche's Batt'n., La. Militia
Trimble, John	Private	Capt. Ashley's Co., Mounted Riflemen, La. Militia
Trimble, John	Private	Captain Sprigg's Co., Boatmen, La. Vols.
Trimble, Thomas	Private	Capt. Alpuente's Co., La. Mil.
Trimmell, John	Private	10 and 20 Cons. Reg't., La. Mil.
Trivrgnan, L.	Private	4 Reg't. (Morgan's), La. Militia (Orig. under Crevignan, L.)
Troes, Jose	Private	17, 18 and 19 Cons. Reg't., La. Militia
Trohile, Dominique	Private	7 Reg't. (Le Beuf's), La. Militia
Troin, William H.	Private	4 Reg't. (Morgan's), La. Militia
Trolier, N.	Private	Captain Sprigg's Co., Boatmen, La. Vols. (Orig. under Trotier, N.)
Trotier, N.	Private	Captain Sprigg's Co., Boatmen, La. Vols.
Trouard, Edward	Fusilier-Private	5 Reg't. (La Branche's), La. Mil.
Trousard, Louis	Private	Capt. Trudeau's Troop of Horse, La. Militia
Trousard, Prosper	Corporal	3 Reg't. (de la Ronde's), La. Mil.
Trouille, Andre	Private	Captain Hubbard's Mounted Co., La. Militia
Trouille, Francois	Private	Captain Hubbard's Mounted Co., La. Militia
Trouille, Santiago	Private	Captain Hubbard's Mounted Co., La. Militia
Troups, Ambroise	Private	Baker's Regiment, La. Militia (Orig. under Toups, Ambroise)
Troussale, Robert	Private	Baker's Regiment, La. Militia
Troussel, Robert	Private	Baker's Regiment, La. Militia (Orig. under Troussale, Robert)
Troxclair, Andre	Sergeant	5 Reg't. (La Branche's), La. Mil.
Troxclair, Cristophe	Fus.-Private	5 Reg't. (La Branche's), La. Mil. (Orig. under Troxelair, Christophe)
Troxclair, Firmain	Private	5 Reg't. (La Branche's), La. Mil.
Troxclair, J. B.	Fusilier-Private	5 Reg't. (La Branche's), La. Mil. (Orig. under Troxelair, Jn Bte)
Troxelair, Antoine	Fusilier-Private	5 Reg't. (La Branche's), La. Mil.
Troxelair, Christop	Fus.-Private	5 Reg't. (La Branche's), La. Mil.
Troxelair, Christophe	Fus.-Private	5 Reg't. (La Branche's), La. Mil.
Troxelair, Francois	Fus.-Private	5 Reg't. (La Branche's), La. Mil.
Troxelair, In Bte	Fus.-Private	5 Reg't. (La Branche's), La. Mil.
Troxelair, Pierre	Fus.-Private	5 Reg't. (La Branche's), La. Mil.
Troxillo, Juan	Private	8 Reg't. (Meriam's), La. Militia
Troxler, George	Private	8 Reg't. (Meriam's), La. Militia
Troxler, Jacques	Corporal	8 Reg't. (Meriam's), La. Militia
Truard, Louis	Private	Capt. Trudeau's Troop of Horse, (Orig. under Trousard, Louis)
Trudeau, A.	Private	8 Reg't. (Meriam's), La. Militia
Trudeau, Catalan	Corporal	5 Reg't. (La Branche's), La. Mil.
Trudeau, John	Private	De Clouet's Reg't., La. Militia
Trudeau, Rene	Captain	Capt. Trudeau's Troop of Horse, La. Militia
Trudeau, Valery	Private	Capt. Trudeau's Troop of Horse, La. Militia
Trudeau, Zenon	1 Sergeant-Sgt.	Capt. Trudeau's Troop of Horse, La. Militia
Trudeau, Zenon	Private	4 Reg't. (Morgan's), La. Militia
Truze, Joseph	Private	De Clouet's Reg't., La. Militia (Orig. under Fruze, Joseph)
Tubetean, Pierre	Artificer	Capt. Chaudurier's Co., Artificers, Art'y., La. Vols. (Orig. under Tabutan, Pierre)
Tuboirne, W. H.	Private	10 and 20 Cons. Reg't., La. Mil.
Tucker, Alexis	Private	Captain Henry's Co., Mounted Riflemen, La. Militia
Tucker, Allexis	Private	Captain Dodge's Co., Mounted Riflemen, La. Militia
Tucker, Henry	Private	10 and 20 Cons. Reg't., La. Mil.
Tucker, Isias	Private	Captain Dodge's Co., Mounted Riflemen, La. Militia
Tucker, Isias	Private	Captain Henry's Co., Mounted Riflemen, La. Militia
Tucker, Joseph	Private	Captain Dodge's Co., Mounted Riflemen, La. Militia
Tucker, Joseph	Private	Captain Henry's Co., Mounted Riflemen, La. Militia
Tucker, William	Private	10 and 20 Cons. Reg't., La. Mil.
Tuckett, Francois	Private	De Clouet's Reg't., La. Militia
Tuillier, Baptiste	Private	10 and 20 Cons. Reg't., La. Mil. (Orig. under Tulier, Baptiste)
Tulier, Baptiste	Private	10 and 20 Cons. Reg't., La. Mil.
Tulier, F.	Private	8 Reg't. (Meriam's), La. Militia
Tulk, John	Private	Captain Hughes Co., Mounted Riflemen, La. Mil. (Orig. under Tulle, John)
Tulle, John	Private	Captain Hughes Co., Mounted Riflemen, La. Mil.
Tullie, Jean Marie	Private	8 Reg't. (Meriam's), La. Militia
Tullier, F.	Private	8 Reg't. (Meriam's), La. Militia (Orig. under Tulier, F.)
Tuney, Drewry	Private	De Clouet's Reg't., La. Militia (Orig. under Toney, Drewry)
Turcas, Christ	Sergeant	2 Reg't. (Cavelier's), La. Militia
Turcuit, Francis	Private	De Clouet's Reg't., La. Militia
Tureaud, Theodore	Private	Capt. Trudeau's Troop of Horse, La. Militia
Turham, Frederick	Private	Capt. Wallace's Co., Boatmen, La. Vols. (Orig. under Turnham, Frederick)
Turla, A.	Sergeant	Plauche's Batt'n., La. Militia (Orig. under Tourla, A.)
Turman, Isaac	Private-Sergeant	De Clouet's Reg't., La. Militia (See also 7 Reg't. Inf.)
Turnbull, Daniel	Private	10 and 20 Cons. Reg't., La. Mil.
Turnbull, Walter	2 Lieutenant	De Clouet's Reg't., La. Militia (See also 44 U. S. Inf.)
Turner, Fielding	Private	Captain Beale's Co., Riflemen, La. Militia
Turner, Samuel	Private	De Clouet's Reg't., La. Militia
Turner, Winslow	Private	Capt. Van Bibber's Co., La. Mil.
Turner, William	Private	16 Reg't. (Thompson's), La. Mil.
Turney, George	Private	17, 18 and 19 Cons. Reg't., La. Militia
Turnham, Frederick	Private	Capt. Wallace's Co., Boatman, La. Vols.
Turpin, Jr.	Private	Plauche's Batt'n., La. Militia

Name	Rank	Unit
Turpin, Jque	Sergeant	Plauche's Batt'n., La. Militia
Turrenline, Samuel	Private	Capt. Allen's Co., Artillerists, La. Vols. (Orig. under Turrentine, Sam)
Tyler, Moses	Private	12 and 13 Cons. Reg't., La. Mil. (Orig. under Tylor, Moses)
Turrentine, Samuel	Private	Capt. Allen's Co., Artillerists, La. Vols.
Tuussaint, F. Remy	Cpl.-Private	2 Batt'n. (Peire's), La. Vols. (Orig. under Toussaint, Francois Remy)
Tylor, Moses	Private	12 and 13 Cons. Reg't., La. Mil.
Ugene, Joseph	Private	De Clouet's Reg't., La. Militia
Ulm, John	Sergeant	2 Reg't. (Cavelier's), La. Militia
Underwood, James	Sergeant	17, 18 and 19 Cons. Reg't., La. Militia
Uquain, --	Corporal	2 Reg't. (Cavelier's), La. Militia
Urick, John	Private	10 and 20 Cons. Reg't., La. Mil.
Urie, Robert	Private	Captain Hubbard's Mounted Co., La. Militia
Urquehart, David	Private	1 Reg't. (Dejan's), La. Militia
Urquhart, D.	Private	1 Reg't. (Dejan's), La. Militia (Orig. under Urquehart, David)
Urquhart, I.	Sergeant	4 Reg't. (Morgan's), La. Militia
Ursin, Andre	Private	2 Batt'n. (D'Aquin's), La. Militia
Usiau, J.	Private	8 Reg't. (Meriam's), La. Militia
Usoz, Mallurin	Private	6 Reg't. (Landry's), La. Militia (Orig. under Usoz, Maturin)
Usoz, Maturin	Private	6 Reg't. (Landry's), La. Militia
Ussery, James	Private	19 Regiment, La. Militia
Usury, James	Private	19 Regiment, La. Militia (Orig. under Ussery, James)
Utrage, William	Private	17, 18 and 19 Cons. Reg't., La. Militia
Vachar, Pierre	Private	10 and 20 Cons. Reg't., La. Mil. (Orig. under Vachard, Pierre)
Vachard, Pierre	Private	10 and 20 Cons. Reg't., La. Mil.
Vaden, Henry	Private	10 and 20 Cons. Reg't., La. Mil.
Vagneer, Joseph	Sergeant	De Clouet's Reg't., La. Militia (Orig. under Vaignier, Joseph)
Vaignier, Joseph	Sergeant	De Clouet's Reg't., La. Militia
Vaigue, E.	Private	6 Reg't. (Landry's), La. Militia
Valansuel, Joseph	Private	De Clouet's Reg't., La. Militia (Orig. under Valensuel, Joseph)
Valberou, John	Private	De Clouet's Reg't., La. Militia (Orig. under Valbrou, John)
Valberow, John	Private	De Clouet's Reg't., La. Militia (Orig. under Valbrou, John)
Valbrou, John	Private	De Clouet's Reg't., La. Militia
Valcour, --	Private	2 Reg't. (Cavelier's), La. Militia (Orig. under Valcourt, --)
Valcourt, --	Private	2 Reg't. (Cavelier's), La. Militia
Valee, Morice	Private	2 Reg't. (Cavelier's), La. Militia
Valensuel, Joseph	Private	De Clouet's Reg't., La. Militia
Valentin, --	Musician	Plauche's Batt'n., La. Militia
Valentin, James	Private	10 and 20 Cons. Reg't., La. Mil. (Orig. under Valentine, James)
Valentin, John	Private	8 Reg't. (Meriam's), La. Militia (Orig. under Valentine, John)
Valentin, Nlas	Private	4 Reg't. (Morgan's), La. Militia
Valentin, St Jacques	Private	3 Reg't. (de la Ronde's), La. Mil.
Valentin, Vincent	Corporal	10 and 20 Cons. Reg't., La. Mil. (Orig. under Valentine, Vincent)
Valentine, James	Private	10 and 20 Cons. Reg't., La. Mil.
Valentine, John	Private	De Clouet's Reg't., La. Militia
Valentine, John	Private	8 Reg't. (Meriam's), La. Militia
Valentine, Ursin	Private	1 Batt'n. (Fortier's), La. Militia
Valentine, Vincent	Corporal	10 and 20 Cons. Reg't., La. Mil.
Valere, Charles	Private	De Clouet's Reg't., La. Militia
Valere, Charles	Corporal-Sergeant	2 Batt'n. (Peire's), La. Vols. (See also 44 Inf.)
Valet, Pierre	Private	Captain Hubbard's Mounted Co., La. Militia
Valier, Charles	Corporal-Sergeant	2 Batt'n. (Peire's), La. Vols. (Orig. under Valere, Charles)
Valier, Francois	Private	La. (War of 1812)
Valiere, Antoine	Private	1 Batt'n. (Fortier's), La. Militia
Valiere, Joseph	Private	1 Batt'n. (Fortier's), La. Militia (Orig. under Valliere, Joseph)
Valiere, Ls.	Private	1 Batt'n. (Fortier's), La. Militia (Orig. under Valliere, Ls)
Valire, --	Waiter	1 Division (Villere's), La. Mil.
Valire, Chs.	Private	De Clouet's Reg't., La. Militia (Orig. under Valere, Charles)
Valle, Francis	Sergeant	Captain Henry's Co., Mounted Riflemen, La. Militia
Valle, P. R.	Private	1 Reg't. (Dejan's), La. Militia
Vallee, A.	Private	Plauche's Batt'n., La. Militia
Vallee, Francis Q.	Burser	Captain Dodge's Co., Mounted Riflemen, La. Militia
Vallee, Zenon	Fusilier-Private	5 Reg't. (La Branche's), La. Mil.
Vallentin, Urcins	Private	1 Batt'n. (Fortier's), La. Militia (Orig. under Valentine, Ursin)
Vallere, Charles	Corporal-Sergeant	2 Batt'n. (Peire's), La. Vols. (Orig. under Valere, Charles)
Valleur, Dannacien	Private	17, 18 and 19 Cons. Reg't., La. Mil. (Orig. under Vassuer, Dannacien)
Vallier, Francois Etienne	Sergeant	2 Batt'n. (Peire's), La. Vols.
Valliere, Baptiste	Corporal	1 Batt'n. (Fortier's), La. Militia
Valliere, Brunaux	Private	1 Batt'n. (Fortier's), La. Militia
Valliere, Joseph	Private	1 Batt'n. (Fortier's), La. Militia
Valliere, Louis	Private	1 Batt'n. (Fortier's), La. Militia
Valliere, Ls	Private	1 Batt'n. (Fortier's), La. Militia
Vallon, --	Private	2 Batt'n. (D'Aquin's), La. Militia
Valre, Hary	Private	12 and 13 Cons. Reg't., La. Mil. (Orig. under Villar, Henry)
Vanbebber, Isaac	Captain	Capt. Van Bibber's Co., La. Mil.
Van Bibber, Isaac	Captain	Capt. Van Bibber's Co., La. Mil. (Orig. under Vanbebber, Isaac)
Vance, Patrick	Private	De Clouet's Reg't., La. Militia
Vanderburg, Joseph	Private	Capt. Allen's Co., Artillerists, La. Vols. (Orig. under Vanderberry, Joseph)
Vanderberry, Joseph	Private	Capt. Allen's Co., Artillerists, La. Vols.
Vandozer, Isaac	Private	De Clouet's Reg't., La. Militia (Orig. under Vanduzer, Isaac)
Vanduser, Isaac	Private	De Clouet's Reg't., La. Militia (Orig. under Vanduzer, Isaac)
Vanduzer, Isaac	Private	De Clouet's Reg't., La. Militia
Vanel, --	Private	Plauche's Batt'n., La. Militia
Vanhill, Benoist	Private	16 Reg't. (Thompson's), La. Mil.
Vanhille, Benoist	Private	16 Reg't. (Thompson's), La. Mil. (Orig. under Vanhill, Benoist)
Vanier, Francs	Private	5 Reg't. (La Branche's), La. Mil.
Vanmeter, Abm W.	Private	Capt. Wallace's Co., Boatmen, La. Vols.
Vannard, John	Private	8 Reg't. (Meriam's), La. Militia
Vansong, Peter	Private	Capt. Van Bibber's Co., La. Mil.
Vaquet, Baptiste	Private	De Clouet's Reg't., La. Militia (Orig. under Paquet, Batiste)
Vara, Joseph	Private	Capt. Thomas' Co., La. Militia
Varapeur, Jn.	Private	6 Reg't. (Landry's), La. Militia (Orig. under Vavaseaur, Jn)
Vareslas, Anastasio	Private	17, 18 and 19 Cons. Reg't., La. Militia
Varnedo, Samuel	Private	12 and 13 Cons. Reg't., La. Mil.
Varner, John	Private	12 and 13 Cons. Reg't., La. Mil.
Varner, Samuel	Private	Captain Sprigg's Co., Boatmen, La. Vols.
Varshard, Peter	Private	10 and 20 Cons. Reg't., La. Mil. (Orig. under Vachard, Pierre)
Vass, Andre	Private	7 Reg't. (Le Beuf's), La. Militia
Vassal, Antoine	Private	Captain Lagan's Co., La. Vols.
Vasseal, Antoine	Private	Captain Lagan's Co., La. Vols. (Orig. under Vassal, Antoine)
Vassel, Nicolas	Corporal	Plauche's Batt'n., La. Militia
Vassuer, Dannacien	Private	17, 18 and 19 Cons. Reg't., La. Militia
Vaudry, Charles	Corporal-Sergeant	5 Reg't. (La Branche's), La. Mil.
Vaudry, Jean	Fusilier-Private	5 Reg't. (La Branche's), La. Mil.
Vaudry, Norbert	Fusilier-Private	5 Reg't. (La Branche's), La. Mil.
Vaughan, Edmund	Private	Baker's Regiment, La. Militia
Vaughan, Isaac	Private	17, 18 and 19 Cons. Reg't., La. Militia
Vaughn, Edward	Private	Baker's Regiment, La. Militia (Orig. under Vaughan, Edmund)
Vaughn, George H.	Private	Captain Griffith's Co., Mounted Riflemen, La. Vols.
Vaugie, Iean	Private	Capt. Songy's Co., Marines, La. Vols.
Vavaseaur, Jn.	Private	6 Reg't. (Landry's), La. Militia
Vavasseur, Louis	Private	2 Batt'n. (Peire's), La. Vols.

Name	Rank	Unit
Vavassieur, Louis	Private	2 Batt'n. (Peire's), La. Vols. (Orig. under Vavasseur, Louis)
Vavespart, Ambrois	Private	7 Reg't. (Le Beuf's), La. Militia
Vavespart, M.	Private	7 Reg't. (Le Beuf's), La. Militia
Vavispart, Ambroise	Private	7 Reg't. (Le Beuf's), La. Militia (Orig. under Vavespart, Ambrois)
Vavispart, M.	Private	7 Reg't. (Le Beuf's), La. Militia (Orig. under Vavespart, M.)
Vazina, Joseph	Private	16 Reg't. (Thompson's), La. Mil.
Veasey, Joshua	Private	1 Reg't. (Dejan's), La. Militia
Veator, Ennis	Private	Baker's Regiment, La. Militia
Veau, P.	Private	Plauche's Batt'n., La. Militia
Veauluisan, Fois	Private	Plauche's Batt'n., La. Militia
Vebre, Alexis	Fusilier-Private	5 Reg't. (La Branche's), La. Mil.
Vebre, Jean fils	Fusilier-Private	5 Reg't. (La Branche's), La. Mil.
Vebre, Pierre	Fusilier-Private	5 Reg't. (La Branche's), La. Mil.
Vederine, Pierre	Private	16 Reg't. (Thompson's), La. Mil.
Vedrine, Dursite	Private	16 Reg't. (Thompson's), La. Mil.
Vedrine, Florentine	Private	16 Reg't. (Thompson's), La. Mil.
Vedrine, Lapuse	Private	16 Reg't. (Thompson's), La. Mil.
Vedrine, Pierre	Private	16 Reg't. (Thompson's), La. Mil.
Vedune, Pierre	Private	16 Reg't. (Thompson's), La. Mil. (Orig. under Vederine, Pierre)
Vegia, In Bte	Private	Capt. Colsson's Co., Artillery, La. Vols.
Vegue, Jean	Private	6 Reg't. (Landry's), La. Militia
Vegue, Jn	Private	6 Reg't. (Landry's), La. Militia
Vegue, Vetaura	Private	6 Reg't. (Landry's), La. Militia
Veillon, Edward	Private	3 Reg't. (de la Ronde's), La. Mil.
Veillon, Etienne	Private	3 Reg't. (de la Ronde's), La. Mil.
Veillon, Joseph	Private	3 Reg't. (de la Ronde's), La. Mil.
Veillon, Martin	Private	Capt. Dubuclet's Troop, Hussars, La. Vols.
Veillon, Pierre	Private	3 Reg't. (de la Ronde's), La. Mil.
Veillon, Silvain	Private	3 Reg't. (de la Ronde's), La. Mil.
Veillon, St Martin	Private	Capt. Dubuclet's Troop, Hussars, La. Vols. (Orig. under Veillon, Martin)
Veillon, Valery	Private	16 Reg't. (Thompson's), La. Mil.
Veillon, Valleri	Private	Capt. Dubuclet's Troop, Hussars, La. Vols.
Vela, Miguel	Private	2 Batt'n. (Peire's), La. Vols.
Velar, Henry	Private	Capt. Thomas' Co., La. Militia
Vella, Antoine	Private	7 Reg't. (Le Beuf's), La. Militia
Velljoin, Gregoire	Private	De Clouet's Reg't., La. Militia
Velmont, --	Private	Plauche's Batt'n., La. Militia (Orig. under Vilmonr, --)
Velo, Andrew	Private	Captain Sprigg's Co., Boatmen, La. Vols. (Orig. under Vila, Andrew)
Vels, Noel	Private	5 Reg't. (La Branche's), La. Mil.
Venett, Sr.	Sergeant	6 Reg't. (Landry's), La. Militia
Venette, S.	Sergeant	6 Reg't. (Landry's), La. Militia (Orig. under Venett, Sr.)
Ventour, --	Private	4 Reg't. (Morgan's), La. Militia
Ventourind, Raymond	Musician	1 Batt'n. (Fortier's), La. Militia (Orig. under Ventourine, Raymond)
Ventourine, Raimond	Musician	1 Batt'n. (Fortier's), La. Militia
Ventura, Juan	Private	3 Reg't. (de la Ronde's), La. Mil.
Vera, Joseph	Private	12 and 13 Cons. Reg't., La. Mil. (Orig. under Verca, Joseph)
Verca, Joseph	Private	12 and 13 Cons. Reg't., La. Mil.
Verchiar, Emanuel	Private	17, 18 and 19 Cons. Reg't., La. Militia
Verdaman, Ammeziah	Private	12 and 13 Cons. Reg't., La. Mil.
Verdaman, Elijah	Private	12 and 13 Cons. Reg't., La. Mil.
Verdeel, Louis	Sergeant	2 Batt'n. (Peire's), La. Vols. (Orig. under Verdeil, Louis)
Verdeil, Louis	Sergeant	2 Batt'n. (Peire's), La. Vols.
Verdery, Francois	Private	2 Batt'n. (D'Aquin's), La. Militia
Verdine, Alexander	Private	Baker's Regiment, La. Militia
Verdine, Roma	Private	Baker's Regiment, La. Militia
Verduil, Louis	Sergeant	2 Batt'n. (Peire's), La. Vols. (Orig. under Verdeil, Louis)
Verdois, Fcs	Private	Capt. Colsson's Co., Artillery, La. Vols.
Verdois, Fois	Private	Plauche's Batt'n., La. Militia
Verette, Adalard	Private	De Clouet's Reg't., La. Militia (Orig. under Verrette, Adelard)
Verette, Marcelin	Private	De Clouet's Reg't., La. Militia (Orig. under Verrette, Marcelin)
Vernaug, John	Private	17, 18 and 19 Cons. Reg't., La. Militia
Verret, Augustin	Private-Sergeant	2 Batt'n. (Peire's), La. Vols.
Verret, Duverje	Private	3 Reg't. (de la Ronde's), La. Mil.
Verret, Jean	Private	2 Batt'n. (Peire's), La. Vols.
Verret, John	Corporal	De Clouet's Reg't., La. Militia
Verret, Marcelier	Sergeant	Captain Hubbard's Mounted Co., La. Militia
Verret, Marius	Private	Captain Hubbard's Mounted Co., La. Militia
Verrett, Godfroy	Private	De Clouet's Reg't., La. Militia
Verrette, Adelard	Private	De Clouet's Reg't., La. Militia
Verrette, Joseph	Sergeant	6 Reg't. (Landry's), La. Militia
Verrette, Marcelin	Private	De Clouet's Reg't., La. Militia
Versailles, Charles	Private	3 Reg't. (de la Ronde's), La. Mil.
Versailles, Francois	Private	3 Reg't. (de la Ronde's), La. Mil.
Versailles, Hilaire	Private	3 Reg't. (de la Ronde's), La. Mil.
Versailles, Joseph	Private	3 Reg't. (de la Ronde's), La. Mil.
Versailles, Louis	Private	3 Reg't. (de la Ronde's), La. Mil.
Verther, Emanuel	Private	17, 18 and 19 Cons. Reg't., La. Mil. (Orig. under Verchiar, Emanuel)
Verther, Joseph	Sergeant	17, 18 and 19 Cons. Reg't., La. Mil.
Verte, A. Chene	Private	8 Reg't. (Meriam's), La. Militia
Vest, Jonathan	Private	Capt. Collard's Co., La. Militia
Vexier, Fran	Private	De Clouet's Reg't., La. Militia
Vexier, Francois	Private	16 Reg't. (Thompson's), La. Mil.
Vial, Antoine	Corporal	2 Batt'n. (D'Aquin's), La. Militia
Viale, Antoine	Corporal	2 Batt'n. (D'Aquin's), La. Militia (Orig. under Vial, Antoine)
Viator, Emanuel	Private	Baker's Regiment, La. Militia
Viator, Joseph	Private	Baker's Regiment, La. Militia
Vick, Gray	Private	20 Regiment, La. Militia
Vick, Jesse	Private	10 and 20 Cons. Reg't., La. Mil.
Vick, Jordon	3 Lieutenant	10 and 20 Cons. Reg't., La. Mil.
Vick, Willis B.	Adjutant	10 and 20 Cons. Reg't., La. Mil.
Vicknar, John B.	Private	Capt. Thomas' Co., La. Militia
Vickner, Jacque	Private	5 Reg't. (La Branche's), La. Mil.
Vickner, Jean Bte	Fusilier-Private	5 Reg't. (La Branche's), La. Mil. (Orig. under Vicner, Jean Bte)
Vickner, Jn. L.	Private	5 Reg't. (La Branche's), La. Mil.
Vickner, Michel	1 Lieutenant	5 Reg't. (La Branche's), La. Mil. (Orig. under Vicner, Michel)
Vicnair, Antoine	1 Lieutenant	5 Reg't. (La Branche's), La. Mil. (Orig. under Vicner, Antoine)
Vicnair, Jean Bte	Fusilier-Private	5 Reg't. (La Branche's), La. Mil. (Orig. under Vicner, Jean Bte)
Vicnair, Nicolas	Fusilier-Private	(Orig. under Vicner, Nicolas)
Vicner, Antoine	1 Lieutenant	5 Reg't. (La Branche's), La. Mil.
Vicner, Antoine	Fusilier-Private	5 Reg't. (La Branche's), La. Mil.
Vicner, Celestin	Corporal	5 Reg't. (La Branche's), La. Mil.
Vicner, Gabriel	Fusilier-Private	5 Reg't. (La Branche's), La. Mil.
Vicner, Jean Bte	Fusilier-Private	5 Reg't. (La Branche's), La. Mil.
Vicner, Jean Louis	Corporal	5 Reg't. (La Branche's), La. Mil.
Vicner, Jean Louis	Fusilier-Private	5 Reg't. (La Branche's), La. Mil.
Vicner, Joseph	Sergeant	5 Reg't. (La Branche's), La. Mil.
Vicner, Leon	Fusilier-Private	5 Reg't. (La Branche's), La. Mil.
Vicner, Michel	1 Lieutenant	5 Reg't. (La Branche's), La. Mil.
Vicner, Nicolas	Fusilier-Private	5 Reg't. (La Branche's), La. Mil.
Vicnor, Jean Bte	Fusilier-Private	5 Reg't. (La Branche's), La. Mil. (Orig. under Vicner, Jean Bte)
Victor, --	Servant	General and Staff (Labatut), La. Militia
Victor, --	Servant	Capt. Le Doux's Co., Cavalry, La. Vols.
Victor, --	Servant	1 Reg't. (Dejan's), La. Militia
Victor, --	Private	4 Reg't. (Morgan's), La. Militia
Victor, Charles	Private	2 Batt'n. (D'Aquin's), La. Militia
Victor, Joseph	Private	16 Reg't. (Thompson's), La. Mil. (Orig. under Victore, Joseph)
Victor, Zenon	Private	De Clouet's Reg't., La. Militia
Victor, Zenon	Private	1 Batt'n. (Fortier's), La. Militia
Victore, Joseph	Private	16 Reg't. (Thompson's), La. Mil.
Victorre, --	Private	2 Batt'n. (D'Aquin's), La. Militia
Vienne, Louis	Sergeant	Capt. Alpuente's Co., La. Mil.
Vienne, Louis	Private	4 Reg't. (Morgan's), La. Militia
Vige', Charles	Private	16 Reg't. (Thompson's), La. Mil.
Vige', Pierre	Private	16 Reg't. (Thompson's), La. Mil.
Vige', Saint Luke	Private	16 Reg't. (Thompson's), La. Mil.
Vige, W.	Corporal	8 Reg't. (Meriam's), La. Militia

Name	Rank	Unit
Vigne, J. B.	Private	Capt. Le Doux's Co., Cavalry, La. Vols.
Vigneaux, --	Corporal	1 Reg't. (Dejan's), La. Militia
Vignie, I. B.	1 Lieutenant	Capt. Chauveau's Co., Cavalry, La. Militia
Vila, Andrew	Private	Captain Sprigg's Co., Boatmen, La. Vols.
Vilancan, Manuel	Private	6 Reg't. (Landry's), La. Militia (Orig. under Villaneuve, Manuel)
Vilcott, --	Private	1 Reg't. (Dejan's), La. Militia
Vileme, Joseph	Private	De Clouet's Reg't., La. Militia (Orig. under Vilime, Joseph)
Vilime, Joseph	Private	De Clouet's Reg't., La. Militia
Villabas, Evariste	Private	6 Reg't. (Landry's), La. Militia
Villaneuve, Manuel	Private	6 Reg't. (Landry's), La. Militia
Villar, Henry	Private	12 and 13 Cons. Reg't., La. Mil.
Villard, Jacques	Private	Capt. Alpuente's Co., La. Mil.
Villareal, Cayetano	Private	17, 18 and 19 Cons. Reg't., La. Militia
Villars, Duberil	Private	De Clouet's Reg't., La. Militia
Villars, Dubreuil	Private	4 Reg't. (Morgan's), La. Militia
Villars, Dutrieul	Private	De Clouet's Reg't., La. Militia (Orig. under Villars, Duberil)
Villatte, Joseph	Private	Captain Lagan's Co., La. Vols. (Orig. under Villatto, Joseph)
Villatto, Joseph	Private	Captain Lagan's Co., La. Vols.
Villefranche, C.	Private	1 Reg't. (Dejan's), La. Militia
Villere, Gabriel	Major	3 Reg't. (de la Ronde's), La. Mil.
Villere, Jacques	Major-General	1 Division (Villere's), La. Mil.
Villere, Jules	Private	3 Reg't. (de la Ronde's), La. Mil.
Villier, Charles	Private	16 Reg't. (Thompson's), La. Mil.
Villier, Damonville	Private	16 Reg't. (Thompson's), La. Mil.
Villierez, Pedro	Private	Capt. Colsson's Co., Artillery, La. Vols.
Villiers, Chevalier	Private	8 Reg't. (Meriam's), La. Militia
Vills, Alexander	Private	Baker's Regiment, La. Militia
Vills, Nazar	Private	Baker's Regiment, La. Militia
Vilmene, Pierre	Private	2 Reg't. (Cavelier's), La. Militia
Vilmine, Pierre	Private	2 Reg't. (Cavelier's), La. Militia (Orig. under Vilmene, Pierre)
Vilmont, --	Private	Plauche's Batt'n., La. Militia
Vils, Moise	Private	Baker's Regiment, La. Militia
Vils, Petit	Corporal	Baker's Regiment, La. Militia
Vilts, Petit	Corporal	Baker's Regiment, La. Militia (Orig. under Vils, Petit)
Viltz, Charles	Private	1 Batt'n. (Fortier's), La. Militia
Viltz, Philip	Private	De Clouet's Reg't., La. Militia (Orig. under Vittz, Philip)
Vince, Thomas	Private	De Clouet's Reg't., La. Militia
Vincent, Charles	Private	De Clouet's Reg't., La. Militia
Vincent, Charles	Sergeant	2 Batt'n. (Peire's), La. Vols.
Vincent, Felix	Sergeant	6 Reg't. (Landry's), La. Militia
Vincent, Joseph	Private	De Clouet's Reg't., La. Militia
Vincent, Joseph	Private	De Clouet's Reg't., La. Militia
Vincent, Joseph	Private	De Clouet's Reg't., La. Militia
Vincent, Roland	Private	2 Reg't. (Cavelier's), La. Militia
Vincent, Thomas	Private	Captain Musick's Co., La. Mil.
Vinette, I.	Private	2 Reg't. (Cavelier's), La. Militia (Orig. under Vinerre, S.)
Vinette, S.	Private	2 Reg't. (Cavelier's), La. Militia
Vinglarie, Jean	Private	6 Reg't. (Landry's), La. Militia (Orig. under Vinglavie, Jean)
Vinglavie, Jean	Private	6 Reg't. (Landry's), La. Militia
Vining, William	Private	Baker's Regiment, La. Militia
Vinot, I. M.	Private	Capt. Chauveau's Co., Cavalry, La. Militia
Vintour, Carl	Private	4 Reg't. (Morgan's), La. Militia
Vinture, Carl	Private	4 Reg't. (Morgan's), La. Militia (Orig. under Vintour, Carl)
Virgin, William	Private	Captain Ramsey's Co., Mounted Riflemen, La. Militia
Visinier, Felix	Private	Plauche's Batt'n., La. Militia
Visoro, Martin	1 Lieutenant	2 Reg't.(Cavelier's), La. Militia
Vitancourt, I.	Private	8 Reg't. (Meriam's), La. Militia
Vitohly, Samuel	Private	Capt. Van Bibber's Co., La. Mil.
Vits, Moise	Private	Baker's Regiment, La. Militia (Orig. under Vils, Moise)
Vitts, Alexander	Private	Baker's Regiment, La. Militia (Orig. under Vills, Alexander)
Vittz, Philip	Private	De Clouet's Reg't., La. Militia
Vivant, Charles	2 Lieutenant	1 Batt'n. (Fortier's), La. Militia
Vives, Hypolite	Orderly-Sergeant	Captain Hubbard's Mounted Co., La. Militia
Vizier, Henry	Private	8 Reg't. (Meriam's), La. Militia
Voary, S.	Private	Captain Sprigg's Co., Boatmen, La. Vols.
Vodre, Pierre	Private	Captain Sprigg's Co., Boatmen, La. Vols.
Vodry, Pierre	Private	Captain Sprigg's Co., Boatmen, La. Vols. (Orig. under Vodre, Pierre)
Voignier, Joseph	Private	2 Batt'n. (Peire's), La. Vols. (Orig. under Voinier, Joseph)
Voiguier, Joseph	Private	2 Batt'n. (Peire's), La. Vols. (Orig. under Voinier, Joseph)
Voinier, Joseph	Private	2 Batt'n. (Peire's), La. Vols.
Voirin, --	Private	3 Reg't. (de la Ronde's), La. Mil.
Voisin, B.	Private	Plauche's Batt'n., La. Militia
Voisin, Terence	Private	1 Batt'n. (Fortier's), La. Militia
Voisin, Th.	Captain	4 Reg't. (Morgan's), La. Militia
Voisin, Ursin	Private	4 Reg't. (Morgan's), La. Militia
Vollion, Bast	Corporal	5 Reg't. (La Branche's), La. Mil.
Voluisant, Fcs	Private	Capt. Colsson's Co., Artillery, La. Vols.
Voorhies, Cornelius	2 Lt. & Qr.Mr. Lt. & Qr.Mr.	De Clouet's Reg't., La. Militia
Vordoe, Manuel	Private	De Clouet's Reg't., La. Militia
Vorsin, Ursin	Private	4 Reg't. (Morgan's), La. Militia (Orig. under Voisin, Ursin)
Vory, S.	Private	Captain Sprigg's Co., Boatmen, La. Vols. (Orig. under Voary, S)
Voursen, Joseph	Private	12 and 13 Cons. Reg't., La. Mil. (Orig. under Vouser, Joseph)
Vouser, Joseph	Private	Capt. Thomas' Co., La. Militia
Vouser, Joseph	Private	12 and 13 Cons. Reg't., La. Mil.
Vrignaud, Joseph	Private	8 Reg't. (Meriam's), La. Militia
Vurca, Joseph	Private	12 and 13 Cons. Reg't., La. Mil. (Orig. under Verca, Joseph)
Wacsh, Nicholas	Private	17, 18 and 19 Cons. Reg't., La. Mil. (Orig. under Welch, Nicholas)
Wade, William	Private	De Clouet's Reg't., La. Militia
Wagespack, Andre son	Fus.-Private	5 Reg't. (La Branche's), La. Mil.
Wagespack, In Louis son	Private	5 Reg't. (La Branche's), La. Mil.
Wagespack, Joseph	Fus.-Private	5 Reg't. (La Branche's), La. Mil.
Waggaman, George A.	Private	Capt. Odgen's Co., Dragoons, La. Militia
Wagner, Peter K.	2 Lieutenant	4 Reg't. (Morgan's), La. Militia
Wagnespack, Andre	Private	5 Reg't. (La Branche's), La. Mil.
Wagnespack, I. Ls	Private	5 Reg't. (La Branche's), La. Mil.
Wahau, Jean	Corporal	Captain Hubbard's Mounted Co., La. Militia
Waid, William	Private	De Clouet's Reg't., La. Militia (Orig. under Wade, William)
Wailes, Levin	1 Lieutenant	16 Reg't. (Thompson's), La. Mil.
Wails, William	Private	12 and 13 Cons. Reg't., La. Mil.
Wainright, Dixon	Private	12 and 13 Cons. Reg't., La. Mil. (Orig. under Waynewright, Dixon)
Waith, F.	Private	8 Reg't. (Meriam's), La. Militia
Wake, George	Private	19 Reg't., La. Vols.(Orig. under Wiche, George)
Walch, James	Private	De Clouet's Reg't., La. Militia
Walck, William	Fusilier-Private	5 Reg't. (La Branche's), La. Mil.
Walcker, Moses	Private	De Clouet's Reg't., La. Militia (Orig. under Walker, Moses)
Wale, P.	Private	Plauche's Batt'n., La. Militia
Walker, Antoine	Private	Baker's Regiment, La. Militia
Walker, Benjamin	Private	17, 18 and 19 Cons. Reg't., La. Militia
Walker, Giles	Private	10 and 20 Cons. Reg't., La. Mil.
Walker, James	Private	2 Batt'n. (Peire's), La. Vols.
Walker, Jiles	Private	10 and 20 Cons. Reg't., La. Mil. (Orig. under Walker, Giles)
Walker, John	Private	Capt. Thomas' Co., La. Militia
Walker, John	Fusilier-Private	5 Reg't. La Branche's), La. Mil.
Walker, Moses	Private	De Clouet's Reg't., La. Militia
Walker, Samuel	Sergeant	Capt. Allen's Co., Artillerists, La. Vols.
Walker, Samuel	Private	Baker's Regiment, La. Militia
Walker, Samuel	Private	2 Batt'n. (Peire's), La. Vols.
Walker, Thomas	Private	Captain Sprigg's Co., Boatmen, La. Vols.
Walker, William	Private	Baker's Regiment, La. Militia

Name	Rank	Unit
Walker, William	Private	1 Reg't. (Dejan's), La. Militia
Walker, Zeaf	Private	16 Reg't. (Thompson's), La. Mil.
Walkman, Valentine	Private	10 and 20 Cons. Reg't., La. Mil. (Orig. under Warthman, Valentine)
Wall, Christopher	Private	10 and 20 Cons. Reg't., La. Mil.
Wallace, David C.	Captain	Capt. Wallace's Co., Boatmen, La. Vols.
Wallace, Elisha	Private	16 Reg't. (Thompson's), La. Mil. (Orig. under Wallis, Elisha)
Wallace, John D.	Private	Capt. Allen's Co., Artillerists, La. Vols.
Wallace, Thomas	Private	10 and 20 Cons. Reg't., La. Mil.
Wallace, Timothy	Private	Baker's Regiment, La. Militia
Wallace, William	Private	Captain Musick's Co., Mounted Riflemen, La. Militia
Walle, P.	Private	Plauche's Batt'n., La. Militia (Orig. under Wale, P.)
Waller, James	Private	12 and 13 Cons. Reg't., La. Mil.
Waller, Joseph	Private	4 Reg't. (Morgan's), La. Militia
Waller, M.	Private	4 Reg't. (Morgan's), La. Militia
Wallet, Louis	Private	17, 18 and 19 Cons. Reg't., La. Militia
Walley, William	Private	10 and 20 Cons. Reg't., La. Mil. (Orig. under Whatley, William)
Wallice, William	Private	Captain Musick's Co., Mounted Riflemen, La. Mil. (Orig. under Wallace, William)
Wallice, William	Fife Major	12 and 13 Cons. Reg't., La. Mil.
Wallis, Elisha	Private	16 Reg't. (Thompson's), La. Mil.
Wallis, William	Private	Captain Musick's Co., La. Mil.
Wallis, William	Private	12 and 13 Cons. Reg't., La. Mil.
Wallis, William	Fife Major	12 and 13 Cons. Reg't., La. Mil. (Orig. under Wallice, William)
Walls, Christopher	Private	10 and 20 Cons. Reg't., La. Mil. (Orig. under Wall, Christopher)
Walls, James	Private	19 Regiment, La. Militia
Walls, John	Sergeant	10 Regiment, La. Militia
Walls, John	Private	10 and 20 Cons. Reg't., La. Mil.
Walter, Jean	Private	5 Reg't. (La Branche's), La. Mil.
Walthman, Valentine	Private	10 and 20 Cons. Reg't., La. Mil. (Orig. under Warthman, Valentine)
Waltman, Jacob	Private	De Clouet's Reg't., La. Militia
Waltman, Philip	Private	Captain Griffith's Co., Mounted Riflemen, La. Mil.
Walton, George	Cornet	Captain McNair's Co., Mounted Riflemen, La. Militia
Walton, James	Private-Corporal	Captain McNair's Co., Mounted Riflemen, La. Militia
Walton, Joseph	Private	Captain McNair's Co., Mounted Riflemen, La. Militia
Walton, Michael	Sergeant	Captain McNair's Co., Mounted Riflemen, La. Militia
Wamach, Abner	Colonel	12 and 13 Cons. Reg't., La. Mil.
Wamack, Abner	Colonel	12 and 13 Cons. Reg't., La. Mil. (Orig. under Wamach, Abner)
Wamack, Abram	Private	12 and 13 Cons. Reg't., La. Mil. (Orig. under Wamuck, Abraham)
Wamack, Andrew	Private	12 and 13 Cons. Reg't., La. Mil. (Orig. under Womack, Andrew)
Wamack, John	Private	12 and 13 Cons. Reg't., La. Mil. (Orig. under Womack, John)
Wamack, Richard	Private	12 and 13 Cons. Reg't., La. Mil. (Orig. under Womack, Richard)
Wamack, Robert	Private	12 and 13 Cons. Reg't., La. Mil. (Orig. under Womack, Robert)
Wamuck, Abraham	Private	12 and 13 Cons. Reg't., La. Mil.
Wamuck, Jacob	Private	12 and 13 Cons. Reg't., La. Mil.
Ward, --	Private	1 Reg't. (Dejan's), La. Militia
Ward, Allen	Private	10 and 20 Cons. Reg't., La. Mil.
Ward, Charles	Private	De Clouet's Reg't., La. Militia (Orig. under Warde, Charles)
Ward, Francis G.	Private	2 Batt'n. (Peire's), La. Vols.
Ward, Isaac	Private	19 Regiment, La. Militia
Ward, James G.	Private	2 Batt'n. (Peire's), La. Vols.
Ward, James S.	Private	2 Batt'n. (Peire's), La. Vols. (Orig. under Ward, James G.)
Ward, John	Private	Captain McNair's Co., Mounted Riflemen, La. Militia
Ward, Robert	Private	Capt. Alpuente's Co., La. Mil.
Warde, Charles	Private	De Clouet's Reg't., La. Militia
Waren, Louis	Private	17, 18 and 19 Cons. Reg't., La. Militia
Warner, John D.	Sergeant	Capt. Thomas' Co., La. Militia
Warner, Leonard	Private	Capt. Thomas' Co., La. Militia
Warner, Thomas C.	Colonel	12 and 13 Cons. Reg't., La. Mil.
Warnis, Joseph	Private	1 Batt'n. (Fortier's), La. Militia (Orig. under Warnisse, Joseph)
Warnisse, Joseph	Private	1 Batt'n. (Fortier's), La. Militia
Warren, Robert	Private	De Clouet's Reg't., La. Militia
Warren, Samuel	Corporal	Capt. Alpuente's La. Militia
Warthman, Valintine	Private	10 and 20 Cons. Reg't., La. Mil.
Wasburn, Thomas	Private	De Clouet's Reg't., La. Militia (Orig. under Washburn, Zenas)
Wash, Robert	1 Lieutenant	Captain McNair's Co., Mounted Riflemen, La. Militia
Washbern, Zenas	Private	De Clouet's Reg't., La. Militia (Orig. under Washburn, Zenas)
Washburn, Zenas	Private	De Clouet's Reg't., La. Militia
Washburne, Zeno	Private	De Clouet's Reg't., La. Militia (Orig. under Washburn, Zenas)
Washington, --	Servant	De Clouet's Reg't., La. Militia
Washman, Zenas	Private	De Clouet's Reg't., La. Militia (Orig. under Washburn, Zenas)
Waskom, William	2 Lieutenant	De Clouet's Reg't., La. Militia
Waters, William	Sergeant	1 Reg't. (Dejan's), La. Militia
Watkins, Caleb	Private	De Clouet's Reg't., La. Militia
Watkins, William S.	Major	6 Reg't. (Landry's), La. Militia
Watmon, John	Private	11 Reg't. (Hickey's), La. Militia
Watohine, Fine	Private	De Clouet's Reg't., La. Militia (Orig. under Witchin, Fune)
Watson, Alexander	Private	La. (War of 1812), (See also 1 Batt'n. (Henry's), U. S. Vols.
Watson, John	Private	Baker's Regiment, La. Militia
Watson, Joseph A.	Private	De Clouet's Reg't., La. Militia
Watson, William	Captain	12 and 13 Cons. Reg't., La. Mil.
Watson, William Jr.	Private	12 and 13 Cons. Reg't., La. Mil.
Wattey, Elisha	Private	10 and 20 Cons. Reg't., La. Mil. (Orig. under Whatley, Elisha)
Watts, James	Private	19 Regiment, La. Vols. (Orig. under Wall, James)
Watts, John	Private	10 and 20 Cons. Reg't., La. Mil. (Orig. under Walls, John)
Waynewright, Dixon	Private	12 and 13 Cons. Reg't., La. Mil.
Weathers, William	Private	Captain Beale's Co., Riflemen, La. Militia
Weathersbee, William	Surgeon	19 Regiment, La. Vols. (Orig. under Weatherslee, William)
Weatherslee, William	Surgeon	19 Regiment, La. Vols.
Weatherton, Francis	Private	Captain Musick's Co., La. Mil.
Weatherton, John	1 Sergeant-Sgt.	Captain Musick's Co., La. Mil.
Weatherton, John	1 Sergeant-Sgt.	Captain Musick's Co., La. Mil.
Weatherton, Thomas	Private	Captain Musick's Co., La. Mil.
Weaver, Daniel	Private	17, 18 and 19 Cons. Reg't., La. Militia
Weaver, John	Private	Captain Ramsey's Co., Mounted Riflemen, La. Militia
Webb, Holland	Private	12 and 13 Cons. Reg't., La. Mil.
Webb, John	Private	10 and 20 Cons. Reg't., La. Mil.
Webb, Samuel	Private	Capt. Thomas' Co., La. Militia
Webber, Frederick	Trumpeter	Captain McNair's Co., Mounted Riflemen, La. Mil. (Orig. under Weber, Frederich)
Weber, Alexis	Private	5 Reg't. (La Branche's), La. Mil.
Weber, Antoine	Fusilier-Private	5 Reg't. (La Branche's), La. Mil. (Orig. under Webre, Antoine)
Weber, Eugene	Fusilier-Private	5 Reg't. (La Branche's), La. Mil.
Weber, Francois	2 Lieutenant	5 Reg't. (La Branche's), La. Mil.
Weber, Frederick	Trumpeter	Captain McNair's Co., Mounted Riflemen, La. Militia
Weber, In	Private	5 Reg't. (La Branche's), La. Mil.
Weber, In	Private	5 Reg't. (La Branche's), La. Mil.
Weber, John H.	Private	Capt. Ashley's Co., Mounted Riflemen, La. Militia
Weber, Lucien	1 Sergeant	5 Reg't. (La Branche's), La. Mil.
Webre, Antoine	Fusilier-Private	5 Reg't. (La Branche's), La. Mil.
Webre, Eugene	Fusilier-Private	5 Reg't. (La Branche's), La. Mil.
Webre, Francois	2 Lieutenant	5 Reg't. (La Branche's), La. Mil. (Orig. under Weber, Francois)
Webre, Pierre	Fusilier-Private	5 Reg't. (La Branche's), La. Mil.
Webster, Humphrey M.	Cpl.-Sergeant	Capt. Allen's Co., Artillerists, La. Vols.
Webster, N.	Private	4 Reg't. (Morgan's), La. Militia

Name	Rank	Unit
Weekly, Cyres	Private	16 Reg't. (Thompson's), La. Mil.
Weeks, Thomas	Private	10 and 20 Cons. Reg't., La. Mil.
Weeler, John	Private	De Clouet's Reg't., La. Militia (Orig. under Wheeler, John)
Wein, John	Private	Plauche's Batt'n., La. Militia
Weisstern, William	Private	2 Batt'n. (Peire's), La. Vols.
Welbrou, John	Private	De Clouet's Reg't., La. Militia (Orig. under Valbrou, John)
Welch, Nicholas	Private	17, 18 and 19 Cons. Reg't., La. Militia
Welch, Rob.	Private	2 Reg't. (Cavelier's), La. Militia
Wells, Benjamin	Private	12 and 13 Cons. Reg't., La. Mil.
Wells, Francis	Private	10 and 20 Cons. Reg't., La. Mil.
Wells, Henry Knox	Private	De Clouet's Reg't., La. Militia
Wells, James	Private	12 and 13 Cons. Reg't., La. Mil.
Wells, John	Private	Capt. Allen's Co., Artillerists, La. Vols. (Orig. under Wells, Robert)
Wells, John	Private	4 Reg't. (Morgan's), La. Militia
Wells, John	Private	10 and 20 Cons. Reg't., La. Mil.
Wells, Pearson	Private	12 and 13 Cons. Reg't., La. Mil.
Wells, Rice	Sergeant	12 and 13 Cons. Reg't., La. Mil.
Wells, Richard	Private	Captain Price's Co., La. Militia
Wells, Robert	Private	Capt. Allen's Co., Artillerists, La. Vols.
Wells, Rudolph B.	Private	17, 18 and 19 Cons. Reg't., La. Militia
Wells, S.	Private	4 Reg't. (Morgan's), La. Militia (Orig. under Wells, John)
Wells, Samuel	Sergeant	17, 18 and 19 Cons. Reg't., La. Militia
Wells, Solomon	Private	Captain McNair's Co., Mounted Riflemen, La. Militia
Wells, William	Private	12 and 13 Cons. Reg't., La. Mil.
Wells, William	Private	12 and 13 Cons. Reg't., La. Mil.
Wells, William F.	Private	Capt. Callaway's Co., Cavalry, La. Militia
Wells, Willis	Sergeant	17, 18 and 19 Cons. Reg't., La. Militia
Welsh, Miles	Private	16 Reg't. (Thompson's), La. Mil.
Welsh, Nicholas	Private	17, 18 and 19 Cons. Reg't., La. Militia (Orig. under Welch, Nicholas)
Wenprender, George	Sergeant	5 Reg't. (La Branche's), La. Mil. (Orig. under Wiseprender, George)
Wens, Pierre Jr.	Private	7 Reg't. (Le Beuf's), La. Militia
Wentemberker, Gg.	Private	1 Reg't. (Dejan's), La. Militia
Wenter, --	Private	5 Reg't. (La Branche's), La. Mil. (Orig. under Winter, --)
Wentzell, David	Private	10 and 20 Cons. Reg't., La. Mil.
Werthenton, John	1 Sergeant-Sgt.	Captain Musick's Co., Mounted Riflemen, La. Mil. (Orig. under Weatherton, John)
West, Berry	Private	12 and 13 Cons. Reg't., La. Mil.
West, Cato C.	1 Lieutenant	11 Reg't. (Hickey's), La. Militia
West, Crede	Private	Baker's Regiment, La. Militia
West, Edmd	2 Lieutenant	10 Regiment, La. Militia
West, Ezekial	Private	12 and 13 Cons. Reg't., La. Mil.
West, Gadi	Private	De Clouet's Reg't., La. Militia
West, James	Private	Capt. Wallace's Co., Boatmen, La. Vols.
West, James	Private	12 and 13 Cons. Reg't., La. Mil.
West, Joel	Private	16 Reg't. (Thompson's), La. Mil.
West, John	Private	10 and 20 Cons. Reg't., La. Mil.
West, John K.	Private	Captain Beale's Co., Rifleman, La. Militia
West, Levi	Private	12 and 13 Cons. Reg't., La. Mil.
West, Louis	Private	De Clouet's Reg't., La. Militia
West, William	Private	12 and 13 Cons. Reg't., La. Mil.
Western, William	Private	Capt. Allen's Co., Artillerists, La. Vols. (Orig. under Weston, William)
Weston, William	Private	Capt. Allen's Co., Artillerists, La. Vols.
Wethers, Enos	Private	17, 18 and 19 Cons. Reg't., La. Militia
Wetherton, Francis	Private	Captain Musick's Co., La. Mil. (Orig. under Weatherton, Francis)
Whaley, Thomas	Private	Capt. Ashley's Co., Mounted Riflemen, La. Militia
Whaley, William	Private	16 Reg't. (Thompson's), La. Mil.
Whalley, Elisha	Private	10 and 20 Cons. Reg't., La. Mil. (Orig. under Whatley, Elisha)
Wharry, Xerxes	Private	De Clouet's Reg't., La. Militia
Whatley, Elisha	Private	10 and 20 Cons. Reg't., La. Mil.
Whatley, William	Private	10 and 20 Cons. Reg't., La. Mil.
Wheldin, John	Private	Capt. Collard's Co., La. Militia
Wheeler, Conrad	Private	Capt. Allen's Co., Artillerists, La. Vols.
Wheeler, John	Private	De Clouet's Reg't., La. Militia
Wheeler, Zacheus	1 Sergeant-Sgt.	10 and 20 Cons. Reg't., La. Mil.
Whers, John F.	Private	1 Reg't. (Dejan's), La. Militia
Whight, John	Private	Baker's Regiment, La. Militia (Orig. under White, John)
Whitaker, Elijah	Private	De Clouet's Reg't., La. Militia
Whitaker, John	Private	Captain Griffith's Co., Mounted Riflemen, La. Vols.
Whitaker, Jesse	Private	10 and 20 Cons. Reg't., La. Mil. (Orig. under Whitaker, Joseph)
Whitaker, Joseph	Private	10 and 20 Cons. Reg't., La. Mil.
White, Amos	Private	10 and 20 Cons. Reg't., La. Mil.
White, Bledsoe	Private	12 and 13 Cons. Reg't., La. Mil.
White, Ezekiel H.	Sergeant	De Clouet's Reg't., La. Militia
White, James	Private	17, 18 and 19 Cons. Reg't., La. Militia
White, James T.	Sergeant	De Clouet's Reg't., La. Militia
White, Jesse	Private	Baker's Regiment, La. Militia
White, John	Private	Baker's Regiment, La. Militia
White, John	Private	De Clouet's Reg't., La. Militia
White, John	Private	2 Batt'n. (Peire's), La. Vols.
White, John	Sergeant	4 Reg't. (Morgan's), La. Militia
White, John	Private	10 and 20 Cons. Reg't., La. Mil.
White, John	Sergeant-Private	12 and 13 Cons. Reg't., La. Mil.
White, John	Private	17, 18 and 19 Cons. Reg't., La. Militia
White, John C.	1 Sergeant-Sgt.	10 and 20 Cons. Reg't., La. Mil.
White, Joseph	Private	10 and 20 Cons. Reg't., La. Mil.
White, Joseph	Private	10 and 20 Cons. Reg't., La. Mil.
White, Joseph	Private	17, 18 and 19 Cons. Reg't., La. Militia
White, Lee	Private	Plauche's Batt'n., La. Militia
White, Maunsel	Captain	Plauche's Batt'n., La. Militia
White, Paul	Private	10 and 20 Cons. Reg't., La. Mil. (Orig. under Withe, Paul)
White, Phillipe	Private	1 Reg't. (Dejan's), La. Militia
White, Reubin	Corporal	Baker's Regiment, La. Militia
White, Richard	Private	Plauche's Batt'n., La. Militia
White, Robert	Private	10 and 20 Cons. Reg't., La. Mil.
White, Robert	Private	12 and 13 Cons. Reg't., La. Mil.
White, William	Private	4 Reg't. (Morgan's), La. Militia
Whitemore, George	1 Lieutenant	De Clouet's Reg't., La. Militia (Orig. under Whitmore, George)
Whiten, John	Private	10 and 20 Cons. Reg't., La. Mil.
Whiterton, Daniel	Private	10 and 20 Cons. Reg't., La. Mil.
Whiteside, James	Private	Captain Musick's Co., Mounted Riflemen, La. Militia
Whitesides, James	Ensign	Capt. Callaway's Co., Cavalry, La. Militia
Whitesides, James	Private	Captain Musick's Co., La. Mil.
Whitesides, James	Private	Captain Musick's Co., Mounted Riflemen, La. Mil. (Orig. under Whiteside, James)
Whitesides, Thomas	Private	Captain McNair's Co., Mounted Riflemen, La. Militia
Whitiker, Robert	Sergeant	Baker's Regiment, La. Militia
Whitley, Paul	Private	Captain McNair's Co., Mounted Riflemen, La. Militia
Whitlock, William	Private	Baker's Regiment, La. Militia
Whitmore, George	1 Lieutenant	De Clouet's Regiment, La. Mil.
Whitmore, Jessee	Private	12 and 13 Cons. Reg't., La. Mil.
Whitney, Elijah	Private	10 and 20 Cons. Reg't., La. Mil.
Whittmore, George	1 Lieutenant	De Clouet's Reg't., La. Militia (Orig. under Whitmore, George)
Wiatt, Edward	Private	Captain Rankin's Co., Mounted Riflemen, La. Militia
Wible, Joseph fils	Private	16 Reg't. (Thompson's), La. Mil.
Wiche, George	Private	19 Regiment, La. Militia
Wick, Jesse	Private	10 and 20 Cons. Reg't., La. Mil. (Orig. under Vick, Jesse)
Wick, Jordan	3 Lieutenant	10 and 20 Cons. Reg't., La. Mil. (Orig. under Vick, Jordon)

Name	Rank	Unit
Wickerham, Aquilla	Private	Captain Rankin's Co., Mounted Riflemen, La. Militia
Wickerham, William	Corporal	Captain Rankin's Co., Mounted Riflemen, La. Militia
Wicknaire, Adam	Private	6 Reg't. (Landry's), La. Militia
Wicknaire, J. Bte	Private	6 Reg't. (Landry's), La. Militia
Wicknaire, Nicholas	Private	6 Reg't. (Landry's), La. Militia
Widney, James	Private	Plauche's Batt'n., La. Militia
Wiggin, Daniel	Private	10 and 20 Cons. Reg't., La. Mil.
Wiggins, Daniel	Private	10 and 20 Cons. Reg't., La. Mil. (Orig. under Wiggin, Daniel)
Wickoff, Manuel	Private	16 Reg't. (Thompson's), La. Mil.
Wickoff, William	Private	16 Reg't. (Thompson's), La. Mil.
Wilborn, William	Private	17, 18 and 19 Cons. Reg't., La. Militia (Orig. under Wilburne, William)
Wilburne, William	Private	17, 18 and 19 Cons. Reg't., La. Mil.
Wilconsen, Lloyd	Private	Baker's Regiment, La. Militia
Wilcoxan, Thomas	Corporal	Baker's Regiment, La. Militia
Wilcoxen, Nacy	Corporal	De Clouet's Reg't., La. Militia (Orig. under Wilcoxon, Nacy)
Wilcoxen, Thomas	Corporal	Baker's Regiment, La. Militia (Orig. under Wilcoxan, Thomas)
Wilcoxon, Nacy	Corporal	De Clouet's Reg't., La. Militia
Wilds, John B.	Private	16 Reg't. (Thompson's), La. Mil.
Wilds, J. P.	Private	16 Reg't. (Thompson's), La. Mil.
Wiles, J. P.	Private	16 Reg't. (Thompson's), La. Mil. (Orig. under Wilds, J. P.)
Wilhikar, Jon	Private	10 and 20 Cons. Reg't., La. Mil. (Orig. under Whitaker, Joseph)
Wilkey, David	Private	De Clouet's Reg't., La. Militia
Wilkie, David	Private	De Clouet's Reg't., La. Militia
Wilkins, Abraham	Private	Capt. Thomas' Co., La. Militia
Wilkins, Jesse	Private-Sgt.	De Clouet's Reg't., La. Militia
Wilkins, John	Private-Sgt.	De Clouet's Reg't., La. Militia (Orig. under Wilkins, Jesse)
Wilkins, Thomas	Private	12 and 13 Cons. Reg't., La. Mil.
Wilkinsen, Loyd	Private	Baker's Regiment, La. Militia (Orig. under Wilconsen, Lloyd)
Willard, Thomas	Private	Captain Beale's Co., Riflemen, La. Militia
Willburger, J. W.	Corporal-Sgt.	De Clouet's Reg't., La. Militia (Orig. under Wiltberger, John)
Willey, Frederick	Private	17, 18 and 19 Cons. Reg't., La. Militia
Willi, --	Servant	10 and 20 Cons. Reg't., La. Mil.
William, --	Servant-Waiter	Captain Beale's Co., Riflemen, La. Militia
William, --	Servant	General and Staff (Labatut), La. Militia
William, --	Servant	Plauche's Batt'n., La. Militia
William, --	Waiter-Servant	2 Reg't. (Cavelier's), La. Militia
William, --	Servant	2 Batt'n. (D'Aquin's), La. Militia
William, --	Servant	17, 18 and 19 Cons. Reg't., La. Militia
William, --	Servant	17, 18 and 19 Cons. Reg't., La. Militia
William, --	Servant	17, 18 and 19 Cons. Reg't., La. Militia
William, Allambe	Corporal	Capt. Collard's Co., La. Militia
William, Miciah	Private	Captain Musick's Co., La. Mil.
Williams, Absalom	Private	De Clouet's Reg't., La. Militia
Williams, Charles	Private	12 and 13 Cons. Reg't., La. Mil.
Williams, Hezekiah	Private	De Clouet's Reg't., La. Militia
Williams, I.	Private	4 Reg't. (Morgan's), La. Militia (Orig. under Williams, T.)
Williams, James	Private	Captain McNair's Co., Mounted Riflemen, La. Militia
Williams, James	Private	Capt. Ogden's Co., Dragoons, La. Militia
Williams, John	Private	10 and 20 Cons. Reg't., La. Mil.
Williams, John	Private	12 and 13 Cons. Reg't., La. Mil.
Williams, John W.	Private	12 and 13 Cons. Reg't., La. Mil.
Williams, Joseph	Corporal	De Clouet's Reg't., La. Militia
Williams, Joseph	Private	10 and 20 Cons. Reg't., La. Mil.
Williams, Membrance	1 Lieutenant	De Clouet's Reg't., La. Militia
Williams, Otha	Private	10 and 20 Cons. Reg't., La. Mil.
Williams, Samuel	Private	12 and 13 Cons. Reg't., La. Mil.
Williams, Simeon	Private	12 and 13 Cons. Reg't., La. Mil.
Williams, T.	Private	4 Reg't. (Morgan's), La. Militia
Williams, Thomas	Private	Capt. Alpuente's Co., La. Mil.
Williams, Thomas	Private	De Clouet's Reg't., La. Militia
Williams, Thomas	Private	12 and 13 Cons. Reg't., La. Mil.
Williams, William	Drummer	Captain Musick's Co., La. Mil.
Williams, William	Private	10 and 20 Cons. Reg't., La. Mil.
Williams, William	Private	12 and 13 Cons. Reg't., La. Mil.
Williams, William B.	Corporal	Capt. Allen's Co., Artillerists, La. Vols.
Williams, William S.	Sergeant	Capt. Callaway's Co., Cavalry, La. Militia
Williams, Young	Private	12 and 13 Cons. Reg't., La. Mil.
Williamson, Amos	Private	10 and 20 Cons. Reg't., La. Mil.
Williamson, Elias	Private	10 and 20 Cons. Reg't., La. Mil.
Williamson, John	Sergeant	12 and 13 Cons. Reg't., La. Mil.
Williamson, John	Private	12 and 13 Cons. Reg't., La. Mil.
Williamson, Peter	Ensign	10 and 20 Cons. Reg't., La. Mil.
Williamson, William B.	Sergeant	17, 18 and 19 Cons. Reg't., La. Militia
Willibey, William	Private	6 Reg't. (Landry's), La. Militia
Williby, William	Private	6 Reg't. (Landry's), La. Militia (Orig. under Willibey, William)
Willis, William	Lt. Colonel	10 and 20 Cons. Reg't., La. Mil.
Willoby, Alexander	Private	Capt. Ashley's Co., Mounted Riflemen, La. Militia
Wills, Jacob	Private	16 Reg't. (Thompson's), La. Mil.
Wills, Jacob	Private	16 Reg't. (Thompson's), La. Mil.
Wills, John	Private	10 and 20 Cons. Reg't., La. Mil. (Orig. under Wells, John)
Wills, John B.	Private	16 Reg't. (Thompson's), La. Mil.
Wilson, James	Private	Capt. Allen's Co., Artillerists, La. Vols. (Orig. under Wilson, James)
Willson, John	Private	Capt. Allen's Co., Artillerists, La. Vols. (Orig. under Wilson, John)
Willson, John	Private	10 and 20 Cons. Reg't., La. Mil. (Orig. under Wilson, John)
Willy, William	Private	17, 18 and 19 Cons. Reg't., La. Militia
Wilmott, W.	Private	Captain Sprigg's Co., Boatmen, La. Vols.
Wils, Bastin	Private	1 Batt'n. (Fortier's), La. Militia
Wils, Lambert	Private	1 Batt'n. (Fortier's), La. Militia
Wilson, Abner	Private	Captain Griffith's Co., Mounted Riflemen, La. Vols.
Wilson, George	Private	10 Regiment, La. Militia
Wilson, James	Private	La. (War of 1812), (See also Capt. Allen's Co., Artillerists, La. Vols.
Wilson, James	Private	Capt. Allen's Co., Artillerists, La. Vols.
Wilson, John	Private	La. (War of 1812), (See also Capt. Allen's Co., Artillerists, La. Vols.
Wilson, John	Private	Capt. Allen's Co., Artillerists, La. Vols.
Wilson, John	Private	10 and 20 Cons. Reg't., La. Mil.
Wilson, Mathias	Private	Baker's Regiment, La. Militia
Wilson, Mathias	Private	16 Reg't. (Thompson's), La. Mil.
Wilson, Oliver	Private	Baker's Regiment, La. Militia
Wilson, Samuel	Private	Captain Hughes' Co., Mounted Riflemen, La. Militia
Wilson, Thomas	Private	17, 18 and 19 Cons. Reg't., La. Militia
Wilson, William	Sergeant	De Clouet's Reg't., La. Militia
Wilson, William	Private	Captain Rankin's Co., Mounted Riflemen, La. Militia
Wilson, William	Private	12 and 13 Cons. Reg't., La. Mil.
Wiltberger, John	Corporal-Sgt.	De Clouet's Reg't., La. Militia
Wiltburger, J. W.	Corporal-Sgt.	De Clouet's Reg't., La. Militia (Orig. under Wiltberger, John)
Wiltburger, J.	Corporal-Sgt.	De Clouet's Reg't., La. Militia (Orig. under Wiltberger, John)
Wiltz, --	Corporal	1 Reg't. (Dejan's), La. Militia
Wiltz, Bastien	Private	1 Batt'n. (Fortier's), La. Militia (Orig. under Wils, Bastin)
Wiltz, Edmond	2 Lieutenant	5 Reg't. (La Branche's), La. Mil.
Wiltz, Edmond	Sergeant-Major	5 Reg't. (La Branche's), La. Mil.
Wiltz, Lambert	Private	1 Batt'n. (Fortier's), La. Militia (Orig. under Wils, Lambert)
Wiltz, L. J. L.	Corporal	4 Reg't. (Morgan's), La. Militia
Wilz, --	Corporal	1 Reg't. (Dejan's), La. Militia (Orig. under Wiltz, --)

Name	Rank	Unit
Wimburk, Samuel	Private	Capt. Wallace's Co., Boatmen, La. Vols.
Wimprender, Palsse	Fus.-Private	5 Reg't. (La Branche's), La. Mil.
Wims, John B.	Private	10 Regiment, La. Militia
Winbush, Samuel	Private	Capt. Wallace's Co., Boatmen, La. Vols. (Orig. under Wimburk, Samuel)
Wind, Jacob	Trumpeter	10 and 20 Cons. Reg't., La. Mil.
Windbush, Raford	Private	10 and 20 Cons. Reg't., La. Mil.
Winfield, John	Private	De Clouet's Reg't., La. Militia
Winfrey, Jacob	Private	16 Reg't. (Thompson's), La. Mil.
Winfrey, Philip	Private	16 Reg't. (Thompson's), La. Mil.
Winfru, William	Private	8 Reg't. (Meriam's), La. Militia
Winn, Daniel	Private	17, 18 and 19 Cons. Reg't., La. Militia
Winn, John	Private	Plauche's Batt'n., La. Militia (Orig. under Wein, John)
Winsell, David	Private	10 and ⎯ Cons. Reg't., La. Mil. (Orig. under Wentzell, David)
Winter, --	Private	5 Reg't. (La Branche's), La. Mil.
Winter, Stephen	Private	4 Reg't. (Morgan's), La. Militia
Wisbey, Patrick	Corporal	De Clouet's Reg't., La. Militia (Orig. under Wisby, Patrick)
Wisby, Patrick	Corporal	De Clouet's Reg't., La. Militia
Wisdom, Solomon	Private	10 and 20 Cons. Reg't., La. Mil.
Wisdom, William	Private	10 and 20 Cons. Reg't., La. Mil.
Wiseman, Jonathan	Private	Captain McNair's Co., Mounted Riflemen, La. Militia
Wiseprender, George	Sergeant	5 Reg't. (La Branche's), La. Mil.
Wiston, William	Private	Capt. Allen's Co., Artillerists, La. Vols. (Orig. under Weston, William)
Witchim, Fune	Private	De Clouet's Reg't., La. Militia
Withe, Paul	Private	10 and 20 Cons. Reg't., La. Mil.
Witherington, Thomas	Private	Capt. Callaway's Co., Cavalry, La. Militia
Withikar, Joseph	Private	10 and 20 Cons. Reg't., La. Mil. (Orig. under Whitaker, Joseph)
Withington, Daniel	Private	10 and 20 Cons. Reg't., La. Mil. (Orig. under Whiterton, Daniel)
Witington, Daniel	Private	10 and 20 Cons. Reg't., La. Mil. (Orig. under Whiterton, Daniel)
Wittberger, John	Corporal-Sergeant	De Clouet's Reg't., La. Militia (Orig. under Wiltberger, John)
Wittburger, I.	Corporal-Sergeant	De Clouet's Reg't., La. Militia (Orig. under Wiltberger, John)
Wolf, John	Private	1 Reg't. (Dejan's), La. Militia
Womack, Andrew	Private	12 and 13 Cons. Reg't., La. Mil.
Womack, John	Private	12 and 13 Cons. Reg't., La. Mil.
Womack, Richard	Private	12 and 13 Cons. Reg't., La. Mil.
Womack, Robert	Private	12 and 13 Cons. Reg't., La. Mil.
Wood, --	Private	3 Reg't. (de la Ronde's), La. Mil.
Wood, Abs.	Private	10 Regiment, La. Militia
Wood, Absolum	Private	10 and 20 Cons. Reg't., La. Mil.
Wood, George	Private	Captain Sprigg's Co., Boatmen, La. Vols.
Wood, John	2 Lieutenant	19 Regiment, La. Militia
Wood, Thomas	Private	Capt. Thomas' Co., La. Militia
Wood, William	Private	10 and 20 Cons. Reg't., La. Mil.
Wood, William	Captain	19 Regiment, La. Militia
Wooden, James	Private	De Clouet's Reg't., La. Militia (Orig. under Wooton, James)
Woods, John	Private	Captain Henry's Co., Mounted Riflemen, La. Militia
Woods, John	Private	12 and 13 Cons. Reg't., La. Mil.
Woods, Jonathan	Corporal	16 Reg't. (Thompson's), La. Mil.
Woods, Joseph	Private	Captain Dodge's Co., Mounted Riflemen, La. Militia
Woods, Joseph	Private	Captain Henry's Co., Mounted Riflemen, La. Mil. (Orig. under Woods, John)
Woods, Martin	Private	Capt. Collard's Co., La. Militia
Woods, William	Sergeant	16 Reg't. (Thompson's), La. Mil.
Woodward, Alusha	Private	Captain Beale's Co., Riflemen, La. Militia
Woodward, Eben	Sergeant	Captain Beale's Co., Riflemen, La. Militia
Woolf, William	Private	Capt. Van Bibber's Co., La. Mil.
Woolridge, James	Private	De Clouet's Reg't., La. Militia
Woolton, Derrickson	Private	De Clouet's Reg't., La. Militia
Woolverton, William	Private	12 and 13 Cons. Reg't., La. Mil.
Wooton, James	Private	De Clouet's Reg't., La. Militia
Wooton, Moses	1 Sergeant-Sgt.	Capt. Wallace's Co., Boatmen, La. Vols.
Wooton, William	Private	8 Reg't. (Meriam's), La. Militia
Wouaguert, Joseph	Private	7 Reg't. (Le Beuf's), La. Militia
Wouters, Jh.	Private	4 Reg't. (Morgan's), La. Militia
Wray, James	Private	Captain Beale's Co., Riflemen, La. Militia
Wray, Nicholas	Sergeant	Captain Sprigg's Co., Boatmen, La. Vols.
Wrick, John	Private	10 and 20 Cons. Reg't., La. Mil. (Orig. under Urick, John)
Wright, Adam	Corporal	Capt. Callaway's Co., Mounted Riflemen, La. Militia
Wright, Charles D.	Private	Captain Sprigg's Co., Boatmen, La. Vols.
Wright, David	Sergeant	12 and 13 Cons. Reg't., La. Mil.
Wright, John	Private	De Clouet's Reg't., La. Militia
Wright, John	Sergeant	Captain Rankin's Co., Mounted Riflemen, La. Militia
Wright, John	Private	Capt. Wallace's Co., Boatmen, La. Vols.
Wright, John	Major	12 and 13 Cons. Reg't., La. Mil.
Wright, Nathaniel	Private	Captain Price's Co., La. Militia
Wright, Robert	Private	De Clouet's Reg't., La. Militia
Wright, Sherrard	Private	De Clouet's Reg't., La. Militia
Wrinkles, David	Private	17, 18 and 19 Cons. Reg't., La. Militia
Wrinkles, John	Private	17, 18 and 19 Cons. Reg't., La. Militia
Wunprinder, Palsse	Fus.-Private	5 Reg't. (La Branche's), La. Mil. (Orig. under Wimprender, Palsse)
Wylie, Thomas	Lieutenant	Captain Young's Co., Mounted Riflemen, La. Militia
Xavier, --	Private	2 Batt'n. (D'Aquin's), La. Militia
Xemenes, Joachin	Private	17, 18 and 19 Cons. Reg't., La. Militia
Xemer, Joachin	Private	17, 18 and 19 Cons. Reg't., La. Militia
Ximenes, Joaquin	Private	17, 18 and 19 Cons. Reg't., La. Mil. (Orig. under Xemenes, Joachin)
Yakeley, Jacob	Private	17, 18 and 19 Cons. Reg't., La. Militia
Yanis, Charles	Corporal	Capt. Le Doux's Co., Cavalry, La. Vols.
Yarbor, Stephen	Private	10 and 20 Cons. Reg't., La. Mil. (Orig. under Yarboro, Stephen)
Yarboro, Stephen	Private	10 and 20 Cons. Reg't., La. Mil.
Yarboroghe, Gideon	Private-Cpl.	De Clouet's Reg't., La. Militia (Orig. under Yarburrow, Gideon)
Yarborough, Gideon	Private-Cpl.	De Clouet's Reg't., La. Militia (Orig. under Yarburrow, Gideon)
Yarborough, Lewis	Private	10 and 20 Cons. Reg't., La. Mil.
Yarborough, Stephen	Private	10 and 20 Cons. Reg't., La. Mil. (Orig. under Yarboro, Stephen)
Yarborough, William	Private	8 Reg't. (Meriam's), La. Militia
Yarbory, Richard	Private	17, 18 and 19 Cons. Reg't., La. Militia
Yarbre, Jourdain	Corporal	3 Reg't. (de la Ronde's), La. Mil.
Yarbrough, Gideon	Private-Cpl.	De Clouet's Reg't., La. Militia (Orig. under Yarburrow, Gideon)
Yarburrow, Gideon	Private-Cpl.	De Clouet's Reg't., La. Militia
Yard, Daniel	1 Lieutenant	1 Reg't. (Dejan's), La. Militia
Yardly, Joseph	Ensign	Capt. Van Bibber's Co., La. Mil. (Orig. under Yerdly, Joseph)
Yarnall, Aaron	Private	Capt. Thomas' Co., La. Militia
Yaw, Richard	Private	17, 18 and 19 Cons. Reg't., La. Militia
Yaws, Richard	Private	17, 18 and 19 Cons. Reg't., La. Mil. (Orig. under Yaw, Richard)
Ybanes, I.	Private	4 Reg't. (Morgan's), La. Mil.
Ybanes, T.	Private	4 Reg't. (Morgan's), La. Militia (Orig. under Ybanes, I.)
Ybare, Desire	Private	2 Batt'n. (D'Aquin's), La. Militia
Ybare, Jean	Artificer	Capt. Chaudurier's Co., Artificers, Art'y., La. Vols. (Orig. under Ibare, Jean)
Yeardly, Joseph	Ensign	Capt. Van Bibber's Co., La. Mil. (Orig. under Yerdly, Joseph)
Yerdly, Joseph	Ensign	Capt. Van Bibber's Co., La. Mil.
Yeyee, --	Private	2 Batt'n. (D'Aquin's), La. Militia

Name	Rank	Unit
Yiacinta, --	Servant	De Clouet's Reg't., La. Militia
Ymel, --	Private	7 Reg't. (Le Beuf's), La. Militia
Yocum, Thomas	Private	De Clouet's Reg't., La. Militia
Yong, Michiel	Private	De Clouet's Reg't., La. Militia
Yont, George	Private	Captain Young's Co., Mounted Riflemen, La. Militia
Youg, Muchiel	Private	De Clouet's Reg't., La. Militia (Orig. under Yong, Michiel)
Young, Andrew	Private	4 Reg't. (Morgan's), La. Militia
Young, Charles	Private	Capt. Thomas' Co., La. Militia
Young, Gilbert	Private	16 Reg't. (Thompson's), La. Mil.
Young, Henry	Private	17, 18 and 19 Cons. Reg't., La. Militia
Young, Jacob	Private	17, 18 and 19 Cons. Reg't., La.
Young, James	Private	Baker's Regiment, La. Militia
Young, James	1 Sergeant-Sgt.	16 Reg't. (Thompson's), La. Mil.
Young, James C.	Cornet	Captain Dodge's Co., Mounted Riflemen, La. Militia
Young, James C.	Cornet	Captain Henry's Co., Mounted Riflemen, La. Militia
Young, John Baptiste	Private	16 Reg't. (Thompson's), La. Mil.
Young, Lemuel	Private	12 and 13 Cons. Reg't., La. Mil. (Orig. under Young, Samuel)
Young, Morris	Captain	Captain Young's Co., Mounted Riflemen, La. Militia
Young, Notely	Private	16 Reg't. (Thompson's), La. Mil.
Young, Philip	Private	Captain Young' Co., Mounted Riflemen, La. Militia
Young, Richard	Private	17, 18 and 19 Cons. Reg't., La. Militia
Young, Robert	Colonel	10 Regiment, La. Militia
Young, Samuel	Private	12 and 13 Cons. Reg't., La. Mil.
Young, Wiley	Private	12 and 13 Cons. Reg't., La. Mil.
Younger, James	Private	Baker's Regiment, La. Militia
Youse, Js.	Private	4 Reg't. (Morgan's), La. Militia
Zammwald, Adam	Private	Capt. Collard's Co., La. Militia
Zammwald, John	Private	Capt. Collard's Co., La. Militia
Zamor, --	Private	2 Batt'n. (D'Aquin's), La. Militia
Zamwold, Adam	Private	Capt. Collard's Co., La. Militia (Orig. under Zammwald, Adam)
Zamwold, John	Private	Capt. Collard's Co., La. Militia (Orig. under Zammwald, John)
Zaring, Daniel	Private	16 Reg't. (Thompson's), La. Mil.
Zehender, H.	Private	De Clouet's Reg't., La. Militia (Orig. under Zender, Henry)
Zehendre, H.	Private	De Clouet's Reg't., La. Militia (Orig. under Zender, Henry)
Zeitler, --	Private	4 Reg't. (Morgan's), La. Militia
Zender, Henry	Private	De Clouet's Reg't., La. Militia
Zenon, --	Servant	4 Reg't. (Morgan's), La. Militia
Zerban, Phillip	Private	1 Reg't. (Dejan's), La. Militia
Zerben, Philip	Private	1 Reg't. (Dejan's), La. Militia (Orig. under Zerban, Phillip)
Zeringue, --	Private	3 Reg't. (de la Ronde's), La. Mil.
Zeringue, Charles	Fusilier-Private	5 Reg't. (La Branche's), La. Mil.
Zeringue, Honore	Fusilier-Private	5 Reg't. (La Branche's), La. Mil.
Zeringue, Louis	Corporal	5 Reg't. (La Branche's), La. Mil.
Zeringue, Norbert	Fusilier-Private	5 Reg't. (La Branche's), La. Mil.
Zerinque, Hubert	Private	4 Reg't. (Morgan's), La. Militia
Zerinque, I. L.	Corporal	4 Reg't. (Morgan's), La. Militia
Zerinque, Ursin	Private	4 Reg't. (Morgan's), La. Militia (Orig. under Serinque, Ursin)
Zespedes, Francisco	Private	17, 18 and 19 Cons. Reg't., La. Militia
Zezard, --	Private	7 Reg't. (Le Beuf's), La. Militia (Orig. under Cesard, --)
Zimalt, Christopher	Private	Capt. Collard's Co., La. Militia
Zimalt, John	Private	Capt. Collard's Co., La. Militia
Zimatt, Christopher	Private	Capt. Collard's Co., La. Militia (Orig. under Zimalt, Christopher)
Zimatt, John	Private	Capt. Collard's Co., La. Militia (Orig. under Zimalt, John)
Zimwalt, George	Private	Capt. Van Bibber's Co., La. Mil.
Zommult, George	Private	Capt. Van Bibber's Co., La. Mil. (Orig. under Zimwalt, George)
Zuago, Jose Maria	Private	17, 18 and 19 Cons. Reg't., La. Militia
Zuague, Jose Maria	Private	17, 18 and 19 Cons. Reg't., La. Militia (Orig. under Zuago, Jose Maria)

Final two below listed with only given name shown - surname not on cards

Name	Rank	Unit
--, James	Private	Captain Hubbard's Mounted Co., La. Militia
--, John	Corporal	2 Batt'n. (Peire's), La. Vols.

www.ingramcontent.com/pod-product-compliance
Lightning Source LLC
Chambersburg PA
CBHW080437230426
43662CB00015B/2299